MUSSOLINI
AND FASCISM:
The View from America

MUSSOLINI
AND FASCISM
The View from America

JOHN P. DIGGINS

PRINCETON UNIVERSITY PRESS
PRINCETON, NEW JERSEY

LC Card: 78-153845
ISBN 0-691-00581-8 (paperback edn.)
ISBN 0-691-04604-2 (hardcover edn.)
First Princeton Paperback Printing, 1975
This book has been composed in Linotype Caledonia
Printed in the United States of America
by Princeton University Press

TO JACY

Contents

Part Three

FASCISM AT WAR

viii

Acknowledgments

G. M. YOUNG once advised students of the past "to go on reading till you hear the people speaking. The essential matter of history is not what happened, but what people thought, and said about it." The author has read extensively in almost all the major primary and secondary materials, searching for satisfactory coverage that would do justice to the variety of American opinion. In tracking down these materials it was a pleasure to find so many individuals and libraries answering a stranger's call for help. For the assistance generously extended I am greatly thankful to the following persons and their respective institutions: Rita R. Campbell, Archivist of the Hoover Institution on War, Revolution, and Peace, Stanford, California; Elizabeth B. Drewry, Director of the Franklin D. Roosevelt Presidential Library, Hyde Park, New York; Andrea H. Durham, Curator of the Warren G. Harding Manuscripts, Ohio Historical Society, Columbus, Ohio; Gene Geisler and James Wagner of the San Francisco State College Computer Center; Phillip K. Hastings, Director of the Roper Public Opinion Research Center, Williams College, Williamstown, Massachusetts; Robert W. Hill, Keeper of Manuscripts of the New York Public Library; Carolyn E. Jakeman of the Houghton Library, Harvard University; Howard R. Marraro, Director of the Casa Italiana, Columbia University, New York; David C. Mearns, Chief of the Division of Manuscripts of the Library of Congress, Washington, D.C.; Dwight M. Miller, Director of the Herbert Hoover Presidential Library, West Branch, Iowa; Vanni B. Montana, Educational Director of the Italian-American Labor Council, Local 89 of the International Ladies Garment Workers Union, New York; Lucia Pallavicini, Assistant Director of the Istituto

ix

Italiano di Cultura, New York; E. Taylor Parks, Chief of the Division of Manuscripts of the National Archives, Washington, D.C.; Dorothy Swanson, Director of the Tamiment Institute Library, New York University; Rudolph J. Vecoli of the Immigrant Archives, University of Minnesota; Edward Weber, Curator of the Joseph A. Labadie Collection of Labor Materials, University of Michigan.

Since no traveled roads existed for me to follow, I was fortunate to have my work lightened by either correspondence or interviews with the following individuals whose generous cooperation I found encouraging as well as helpful: Luigi Antonini, Roger Baldwin, Bruce Bliven, Roberto Bollaffio, Allen Cassels, Vincent P. Carosso, Frank Demers, Norman T. di Giovanni, John Dos Passos, Theodore Draper, Max Eastman, Reverend John Tracy Ellis, William Y. Elliott, Charles B. Forcey, Lewis A. Feuer, Daria Frezza, H. Stuart Hughes, Arthur M. Johnson, Norman Kogan, William E. Leuchtenburg, Lino Molin, Max Nomad, Francis Russell, A. William Salomone, Herbert W. Schneider, M. Halsey Thomas, Richard Webster, and Enzo Tagliacozzo.

Helpful beyond measure were the following persons who were actively involved in some of the events described in this book: Max Ascoli, the learned Italian exile, who took the time when he was the publisher of the *Reporter* magazine to answer my numerous queries concerning his activities during the thirties; Luigi Barzini, Jr., the well-known Italian writer and Senator, who also found time to convey to me his reflections on Mussolini and the American press; John Nicholas Beffel, a former journalist of Wobbly sympathies, who became something of a Paul Revere of the Sacco-Vanzetti affair and who gathered together for me considerable information regarding the Italian-American Left during World War II; the late Aldino Felicani, the genial anarchist and publisher of *Controcorrente* (Boston), who made my visits to 57 Milk Street both fruitful and pleasant; Frances Keene, Gaetano Salvemini's devoted secretary, who offered many shrewd recollections on the historian's exile in America; Max Salvadori, another *fuoruscito* who became a professor of history in the United States, a learned *émigré* whose mastery of information saved me from many careless errors; George Seldes, who, as the first journalist expelled from Fascist Italy and the author of one of the first important anti-Mussolini biographies, *Sawdust Caesar* (1935), was considerate enough to allow me to examine his unpublished correspondence and several partial drafts concerning events covered in this book; the late Norman Thomas, who offered valuable advice and who, as head of the Carlo Tresca Memorial Committee files, permitted me to inspect these heretofore restricted materials; and Carmelo Zito, the vigorous publisher of the anti-Fascist *Il Corriere del Popolo* (San Francisco), who has helped me in so many ways I cannot begin to cite here his numerous kind deeds.

The author is indebted to the following scholars who read sections of the manuscript which particularly interested them: Jerald Combs, Robert D. Cross, Norman Kogan, Jay Martin, Moses Rischin, and Rudolph J. Vecoli. Of course, I alone am responsible for any remaining errors in the various chapters, many of which may be unrecognizable to earlier readers. I am also indebted to Kathy Smith for typing the manuscript and to Henry Cord Meyer for gracefully helping with the clerical expenses, and to Miriam Brokaw and Marjorie Putney of Princeton University Press, who helped prepare the text for publication. Finally, I wish to express my appreciation and gratitude to Joseph Boskin and Robert Wohl, who conscientiously supervised my original study of this subject as a dissertation; Charles F. Delzell, who was unstinting in the copious advice and encouragement he gave me every step of the way; Gerald Meaker, a good friend who knows both the art of gentle criticism and the art of style; and Gerald T. White, a meticulous scholar who first introduced me to the craft of research, a mentor to whom I shall always be deeply indebted. The book is dedicated to my wife, Jacy, whose boundless patience more than matched my endless subject and whose flashes of humor could always match my moments of labor.

Of a more tangible sort was the generous assistance provided by the following institutions to which I acknowledge utmost gratitude: the American Council of Learned Societies, the American Philosophical Society, the Mary B. Burke Foundation, San Francisco State College, and the Social Science Research Council.

Several sections of the book have appeared, in somewhat different versions, in various academic journals. I wish to thank the following publications for permission to reprint these articles in modified form: *American Historical Review, American Quarterly, The Historian, Journal of American History,* and *Journal of Contemporary History.*

I am also grateful to Harcourt Brace Jovanovich, Inc., for permission to quote from "Gerontion" by T. S. Eliot and from *Murder in the Cathedral*, copyright 1935, by T. S. Eliot; to Harper & Row, Publishers, Inc., for permission to quote from *The Autobiography of Lincoln Steffens*, copyright, 1931, by Lincoln Steffens and from *You Can't Go Home Again*, copyright, 1940, by Thomas Wolfe; to Farrar, Straus & Giroux, Inc., for permission to quote from *Christ Stopped at Eboli*, copyright 1947, 1963, by Carlo Levi; to Liveright for permission to quote from *Jefferson and/or Mussolini*, by Ezra Pound, copyright renewed 1964 by Ezra Pound; to Grove Press, Inc., for permission to quote from "The Escapist Conspiracy," in *Toward a Marxist Humanism: Essays on the Left Today*, copyright, 1968, by Leszek Kolakowski; to E. P. Dutton & Co., Inc., for permission to quote from *Naked Masks: Five Plays* by Luigi Pirandello, edited by Eric Bentley, copyright 1922, 1953, by E. P. Dutton & Co., Inc., renewal, 1950, in the names of Stefano, Fausto, and Lietta Pirandello (Dutton paperback edition, reprinted by permission of E. P. Dutton & Co., Inc.).

I would also like to thank David Levine and the *New York Review of Books* for permission to use his cartoon; and the Museum of Modern Art for permission to use "The Eternal City" by Peter Blume in the illustration section; and *Life* and the *Saturday Evening Post* for the use of pictures.

J.P.D.

Laguna Beach,
California,
1970

BENITO MUSSOLINI CAME LIKE THUNDER ON THE RIGHT. IT WAS JUST AS IF THE AUTHOR OF ALL THINGS HAD LOOKED DOWN UPON THIS LITTLE PLANET OF HIS, AND SEEING THE PHYSICAL, MENTAL, AND MORAL CONFUSION HERE, SAID TO HIMSELF, "HOW CAN I, IN A FLASH, CLEAR UP THOSE POOR HUMANS? I HAVEN'T MUCH TIME FOR SO SMALL A BALL OF MUD, BUT I MUST SOMEHOW HELP THEM TO CHANGE THEIR MINDS AND CATCH UP WITH THE CHANGES I AM MAKING." AND "I KNOW," HE SAID: "I WILL HAVE A POLITICAL THUNDERSTORM, BIG ENOUGH FOR ALL MEN TO NOTICE AND NOT TOO BIG FOR THEM TO COMPREHEND, AND THROUGH IT I WILL SHOOT A BLAZING THUNDERBOLT THAT WILL STRIKE DOWN ALL THEIR FOOLISH PRINCIPLES, BURN UP THEIR DEAD IDEAS, AND SEPARATE THE NEW LIGHT I AM CREATING FROM THE DARKNESS I HAVE MADE." AND SO HE FORMED MUSSOLINI OUT OF A RIB OF ITALY.

Lincoln Steffens,
Autobiography, 1931*

THE CURSE OF ME AND MY NATION IS THAT WE ALWAYS THINK THINGS CAN BE BETTERED BY IMMEDIATE ACTION OF SOME SORT, "ANY" SORT RATHER THAN NO SORT.

Ezra Pound to James Joyce, 1920**

AFTER SUCH KNOWLEDGE, WHAT FORGIVENESS?

T. S. Eliot, *Gerontion*, 1920***

* Reprinted by permission of Harper & Row, Publishers, Inc.
** Reprinted by permission of Liveright.
*** Reprinted by permission of Harcourt Brace Jovanovich, Inc.

Introduction

SHORTLY after the Second World War two of the more interesting "remains" of Italian Fascism turned up at St. Elizabeth's Hospital, a psychiatric institution in Washington, D.C.: a fragment of Benito Mussolini's brain tissue and Ezra Pound. Mussolini's brain would be dissected to determine if the dictator had had paresis, a paralytic condition caused by syphilis; Pound's mind would be observed to determine the mental condition of one of America's famous men of letters who had been charged with treason. St. Elizabeth's presented a somewhat macabre scene: the dictator's brilliant, self-appointed poet in residence in a mental institution and Pound's hero reduced to a package of organic matter. Whatever became of the respective investigations is uncertain. Ten years later Pound was released, and he returned to Italy. Over twenty years later Mussolini's brain fragment was also released and returned to his widow. The tissue was delivered in six test tubes in a wooden box, with the compliments of the American Ambassador in Rome.

In a way it is fitting that the next to last resting place for a portion of Il Duce's brain would be an American laboratory. A country that had once thought that Fascism might be an acceptable medicine for the sick Italian body politic could now dismiss the whole affair as nothing more than the vile degeneration of one man's mind. Having misunderstood the essence of the Fascist movement, American scientific genius could at least submit its remaining substance to the department of venereal disease.

Perhaps Hawthorne would appreciate the allegorical implications in this high-minded political postmortem. What this book embarks upon is considerably less subtle, though the subject matter may be just as elusive. For the subject is that slippery beast known as public opinion and the object that amorphous phenomenon known as Fascism. Hence the reader must try to follow the author as he gropes about in that murky area where subjective emotion and objective fact dissolve, where mass opinion becomes a hopeless mixture of illusion and reality. The playwright is all too familiar with this hazy zone of unanalyzed feelings:

> *Young Man.* But what do think, so far as you know?
> *Old Man.* Oh, my dear boy, we never know everything!
> *Young Man.* Well, in that case, what are opinions worth?
> *Old Man.* Dear me, opinions? My opinion is a view that I hold until—well—until I find out something that changes it. *
>
> Luigi Pirandello, *Each in His Own Way*
> (New York, 1923), p. 6.

A study of America's responses to and interpretations of Fascism must, it seems to me, be approached from a variety of directions. In the following narrative I have tried to explore the pervasive values underlying certain attitudes toward Fascism; undertake a rough content analysis of the dominant symbols and images of Mussolini; classify opinion according to economic, political, and religious groups; investigate the role of the press in shaping opinion; discuss the activities of certain organizations which attempted to sway the public one way or the other; and examine the views of the various administrations in Washington. More than a formal study of public opinion, what has been attempted is an examination of the historical encounter of two political cultures, cultures which in certain instances proved as dialectically attractive as they were diametrically opposed. Since my concern is primarily with the view from American shores, the encounter must be treated unilaterally. But within this limited range of vision I have attempted to encompass almost all relevant phases of American life for a period of over two decades. It is an uneven mental landscape, one in which the curbstone opinions of "gut-thinkers" are deemed as worthy of attention as the lofty reflections of intellectuals; a meandering terrain in which Italian-

---

* Reprinted by permission of E. P. Dutton & Co., Inc. (See Acknowledgments)

Americans are given more attention than their numbers warrant simply because their experience was more keenly felt. If a definition is needed, the work might best be described as an exercise in perspectives—points of view that ultimately take us to the heart of American political values and assumptions. In short, by studying this country's response to a startling phenomenon abroad we are able to enter, as it were, the American mind by the back door.

But it is a circuitous route, and one for which the construction of a proper *schema* has been something of an organizational nightmare. Essentially the problem was how to render meaningful the almost unmanageable bulk and breadth of American opinion for a period of twenty-three years. Eventually I resorted to division and classification. The work is divided into three parts. In Part One I attempted to delineate the two prevailing American images of Italy immediately prior to the advent of Fascism, to discuss the early reactions to Mussolini as a personal leader (as opposed to Fascism as an ideological curiosity), and to explain the press's role in influencing those reactions. Part Two endeavors to examine the peculiar response to Fascism on the part of various American social groups and institutions. And Part Three surveys the shifting nature of American opinion from the time of the Ethiopian War to the fall of Fascism and the rise of Christian Democracy. In these three parts, and particularly in Part Two, only by classifying opinion could some coherence be sifted from the galaxy of American attitudes. In most cases classification was relatively simple, based primarily on the particular organ of opinion under discussion, such as the *Wall Street Journal*, the *New Republic*, or *Il Progresso Italo-Americano*. In the case of individuals, however, the situation proved a bit more difficult. Readers will find many key figures reappearing in the course of the narrative: Ernest Hemingway is discussed first in his role as a journalist and later as a novelist; George Santayana as a nativist thinker and subsequently as an intellectual reactionary; Thomas Lamont as a public relations adviser and then as a Wall Street broker. Rather than elaborate the views of such individuals in isolation, it made more sense to place their remarks in the context in which they were uttered. This is not to claim, of course, that one's social or cultural role determines his ideology; it is merely to suggest that an individual's thought processes are subject to more than one mode of analysis. When Lincoln Steffens, for example, reacts ecstatically to an interview with Mussolini, his behavior might be taken as representative of a large number of journalists; when he ponders Fascism as a "scientific experiment" his musings can be legitimately regarded as reflecting the pragmatic temper of many American liberals.

Aside from organizational difficulties another problem should be mentioned at the outset—the problem of objectivity. The author makes no pretense of offering a completely objective account of America and Fascism. There are several reasons why methodological purity could not be achieved in a subject as nebulous as this one. In the first place, this book is qualitative rather than quantitative; basically it is an interpretation of the enormous sweep of American opinion rather than a history of it. Using representative figures and publications, the method was one of selection rather than of exhaustion. Only in Chapter XIII, where use is made of Gallup polls in an attempt to break down opinion into economic and religious variables, might the work pass muster as empirical research. But even the polls proved disappointing. For the questions posed in these crude opinion surveys lacked depth, and as a result the simple responses concealed more than they revealed of the rich nuances and ambiguous rationalizations which lay below the verbal surface of American opinion of foreign dictatorships. To capture the full flavor of emotions and feelings one must go beyond factual data. In this exercise the statistical method is the historian's obligation, not his salvation.

There remains a further reason why I regarded empirical objectivity as a dubious goal. Any study of America's reactions to a foreign ideology must inevitably penetrate the mainsprings of those reactions. In a word, this means coming to grips with values. Among the most subjective of all historical forces, values determine what people regard as good, right, and just. It takes no moral philosopher to see that what Americans found desirable for themselves influenced greatly their acceptance or rejection of Fascism as an alternative for the Italians. In discussing the inarticulated value assumptions in American attitudes I have not been content with mere objective description. One can, to be sure, examine values objectively. But when one sees that these very values produce opposite results—when, for instance, the

American worship of industrial efficiency led many observers to believe that Mussolini's programs would result in a greater measure of individual liberty, whereas in reality the technology fetish only served to enhance authoritarian control—I felt impelled to comment on the moral flaws that afflict America's political perceptions. Occasionally I chose to point up the ironic element in American attitudes, to show, for example, that Fascism developed into something entirely different than what many people expected. But this kind of retrospective omniscience comes cheap to students of history. More difficult was my attempt to maintain a sense of political values with the knowledge that value judgments went out with the gas lights of the last century. Since it seemed imperative to work within some reference of political ethics, readers will have no difficulty discovering that my sympathies lay with the anti-Fascists and their liberal, socialist aspirations. But whether the book succeeds in maintaining a steady ethical vigilance is another matter. It was one thing to compliment an incisive anti-Fascist critique; but to judge severely the views of many of the equally sophisticated American defenders of Mussolini and Fascism was a chore that I did not relish. Indeed, given the bleak milieu of American political life in the twenties I could, upon reading a few of the more sincere apologies for Fascism, honestly say to myself: there, but for the grace of chronology, go I. It is an awkward moral posture.

Candor also impels me to admit that I closed my book with a sense of unfinished business. Some readers may feel that several of the chapters could be expanded into full books. I readily share this feeling. Of the sins of omission the book is far from shy. There are simply many areas that need to be investigated more thoroughly, and certain subtopics clearly did not receive the attention they deserved. The black American and the Ethiopian War, for example, is a subject that needs attention apart from the Fascist issue; while diplomatic relations between Italy and the United States might be examined with more than the Fascist question in mind. The whole matter of the relations of the Italian-Americans and Mussolini also needs to be fully explored. After finishing the present work I came into possession of a complete set of L'Adunata dei Refrattari (The Call of the Refractories), the weekly organ of the Italian-American anarchists. Perusing the pages of this combative journal made me even more aware of how much remains to be done in studying the Italian-American Left. All in all, this is merely another way of saying that I could only indulge my curiosity to a limited extent over a vast surface. Barely scratched, much of it remains a virgin land for future research.

Part One

AMERICA, ITALY, AND THE
RISE OF MUSSOLINI

Abbreviations

General Abbreviations

ACWU	Amalgamated Clothing Workers Union
ACLU	American Civil Liberties Union
ACID	American Committee for Italian Democracy
AFL	American Federation of Labor
AFANA	Anti-Fascist Alliance of North America
AMG	Allied Military Government
CP	Communist Party, United States of America
FLNA	Fascist League of North America
ICPP	International Committee for Political Prisoners
ILGWU	International Ladies Garment Workers Union
IALC	Italian-American Labor Council
IAVC	Italian-American Victory Council
IWW	Industrial Workers of the World
NRA	National Recovery Administration
OSS	Office of Strategic Services
OWI	Office of War Information
PCI	Communist Party of Italy
PSI	Socialist Party of Italy
PWB	Psychological Warfare Branch
SLP	Socialist Labor Party of America

Abbreviations Used in Footnotes

CP	Calvin Coolidge Papers, Library of Congress
DS	Department of State Files, National Archives
FP	Henry P. Fletcher Papers, Library of Congress

3

FRUS	*Papers Relating to the Foreign Relations of the United States* (Washington, D.C.)
HL	Houghton Library, Harvard University
HIL	Hoover Institute Library, Stanford, California
HP	Herbert Hoover Papers, Hoover Presidential Library, West Branch, Iowa
HUAC	House Un-American Activities Committee, 75th Congress, 3rd Session, 1938
IA	Immigrant Archives, University of Minnesota
ICPP	International Committee for Political Prisoners, Files, New York Public Library
IR	Italian Records, World War II Collection of Seized Enemy Records, Group 242, National Archives
LC	Library of Congress
LD	*Literary Digest*
NYPL	New York Public Library
NYT	*New York Times*
OVP	Oswald Villard Papers, Houghton Library, Harvard University
PP	Constantine Panunzio Papers, Hoover Institute Library
PT	Ezra Pound, Transcripts of Short Wave Broadcasts from Rome, December 7, 1941—July 25, 1943, Federal Communications Commission (microfilm), Library of Congress
RCP	Richard Washburn Child Papers, Library of Congress
RP	Franklin D. Roosevelt Papers, Roosevelt Presidential Library, Hyde Park, New York
SS	Gaetano Salvemini Scrapbooks, Houghton Library, Harvard University
SEP	*Saturday Evening Post*
SP	George Seldes Papers (loaned to author)
TCR	*Tenney Committee Report*, Senate (California), 55th Session, 1943, Report of the Joint Fact-Finding Commission on Un-American Activities in California.
TMC	Tresca Memorial Committee, Files, New York Public Library
VP	Girolamo Valenti Papers, Tamiment Institute Library, New York City

1.

Arcadia and Mulberry Street: Two Italys in the American Mind on the Eve of Fascism

HOW THIS PEOPLE KEPT ANY
SPARK OF SWEETNESS AND
CHARITY AND HUMANITY ALIVE
THROUGH THE BURNINGS AND
MASSACRES OF THE MIDDLE
AGES AND THROUGH THE
WANTON WICKEDNESS OF THE
RENAISSANCE, MUST ALWAYS
BE A MATTER OF WONDER.
AND NOW, IF ONE KNOWS HOW
TO LIVE WITH THEM, THEY
ARE THE SWEETEST PEOPLE ON
EARTH. IF I EVER COME BACK,
MAY I BE BORN ITALIAN.

Charles Eliot Norton, 1871

ROMANTIC PILGRIMS AND THE CONCEPT OF ITALY

Italy is in some ways a concept as much as a country. For nineteenth-century Americans, it was a state of mind as well as a nation-state. Somewhere between the idea and the reality hovered a geographical abstraction that beguiled the imagination. "There are a good many things about this Italy which I do not understand," confessed Mark Twain in 1869. Over a century later Italy still appears a sunny enigma wrapped in the shadow of paradox: A nation steeped in history, a nation left behind by history; a culture rich in art and music, a culture poor in mass education and formal learning; a humane, ebullient, and kind people, an "inferior," indolent, and debauched people; a society ostensibly Catholic and spiritual, a social life unblushingly sensual and epicurean; a government of cool Machiavellian realism, a government of grandiose dreams and disastrous extremism; a country of genius and greatness, a country of tragedy and catastrophe.[1]

[1] Mark Twain, *Innocents Abroad* (New York, 1911), p. 325.

5

These cliché-ridden contradictions serve to remind us that we have yet to unravel the ponderous mystery of Italy which is her enduring essence. Fortunately that is not our task here; it is, rather, to examine the angles of perception in order to ascertain the American image of Italy on the eve of Fascism. The purpose of this chapter is to suggest that much of the American reaction to the rise of Fascism was preconditioned by America's impressions of Italy in the years before World War I. Only by examining in all its ambiguity the constellation of these impressions can one fully understand America's response to Mussolini and his movement.

During the nineteenth century, Americans, insofar as they thought about the subject, entertained at least two distinct images of Italy. For lack of better terms we might call these two images the "romantic" and the "nativist." The romantic picture was conceptualized by travelers and writers who looked upon Italy as a conservatory of all the cultural values of the old world: creative spontaneity, artistic sensibility, moral idealism, and worldly experience. The nativist picture, by contrast, thrust itself upon the American mind with the sudden impact of Italian immigration at the turn of the century. The former image attracted those writers who, like Henry James, longed for richer experience and deeper self-fulfillment; the latter image repelled millions of Americans who, like Woodrow Wilson, feared the contagion of such old-world vices as ignorance, poverty, and oppression. The interplay of these two images goes far toward explaining America's peculiar perspectives on Italian Fascism.[2]

From the earliest colonial times to the present age of jet-set affluence, Italy has remained for Americans one of the most visited countries in the world. Whether searching for salvation in St. Peter's basilica, for aesthetic sophistication among the Florentine *cognoscenti*, or for the "soft life" along the Via Veneto, Americans have never stopped journeying to the enchanted peninsula. Virgil hailed Italy as the "land of Saturn," and perhaps, as Luigi Barzini has observed, the Saturnian vision holds true

[2] Woodrow Wilson's derogatory references to the Italian immigrant appeared in his *A History of the American People* (5 vols., New York, 1908), v, esp. 212; for Italian-American criticism of Wilson's nativism, see *L'Italia* (Chicago), Oct. 20, 1912; for Wilson's expedient reply, during the 1912 campaign, see Arthur S. Link, *Wilson: The Road to the White House* (Princeton, 1947), Vol. 1, 385-86.

for tourists as well as poets. For Saturnalia represents a brief period when everything is permitted, the tables are turned and man's deepest desires can be realized: the old feel rejuvenated, the young defy their elders, the ignorant outwit the learned, the poor command the rich, and the shy seduce the haughty. Perhaps Jefferson was one of the few American pilgrims to keep his head when he forsook the Florentine Maria Cosway for the more earthy romance of observing Italian rice production and architecture. But others succumbed to the vibrations of the heart and the visions of imagination. James Fenimore Cooper delighted in the misty shadows of the Italian landscape and the deep purple-blue colors of the Bay of Naples; Nathaniel Hawthorne found in the arid ruins and cold museums a "remote dreamlike Arcadian charm" which he later captured in symbol and allegory in *The Marble Faun*; and William Dean Howells discovered a Whitmanesque vitality in the common people which he described in the kaleidoscopic montage, *Venetian Life*. Henry James, arriving in Rome in 1869, exclaimed: "At last—for the first time, I live! For the first time I know what the picturesque is." Thereupon James used Italy as a setting for one of his most persistent literary themes: the dialectic of American innocence and European experience. Meanwhile others used Italy as a big game reserve where the symbols of artistic taste could be collected for a price. The nineteenth-century leisure class swarmed over the peninsula like cultural scavengers, engaging in what Lewis Mumford was later to term "the pillage of the past."[3]

Most Americans who rejoiced in Italian culture also supported Italy's political causes. In the nineteenth century the political event in Italy that aroused America's intelligentsia was the *Risorgimento*. Throughout the long and arduous ordeal, the hearts of many Americans went out to the valiant Italians struggling for independence from Austria. Henry Adams praised the bold feats of General Garibaldi, Howells championed the statesman Massimo d'Azeglio, and Margaret Fuller preached the ideals of Mazzini and his republican nationalism. At one time or another, Hawthorne, Cooper, Melville, Longfellow, Tichnor, Emerson, Bryant, Lowell, and Whittier paid tribute in prose or verse to the cause of the *Risorgimento*. Yet some of the very writers who admired Italy's culture and political ideals could not sustain endur-

[3] Luigi Barzini, *The Italians* (New York, 1964), p. 14; Van Wyck Brooks, *The Dream of Arcadia* (New York, 1958), pp. 157, 237-54.

7

ing enthusiasm for Italy itself. To Henry Adams, for example, Italy seemed, upon his first visit, the ultimate attainment which left life with "no richer impressions to give." Several years later, however, Adams maintained that no law of historical progress applied to Rome. "Not even time sequences had value for it," reflected the young historian for whom the timeless land of antiquity offered no clue to the enigma of existence. For Charles Eliot Norton, on the other hand, Italy offered no guidance because it had been blighted by the industrial and political vices of America. "The railroad whistle just behind the church of the Santa Maria Novella," Norton wrote to Chauncey Wright, "sounds precisely as it sounds on the Back Bay or at the Fitchburg station,—and it and the common school are Americanizing the land to a surprising degree. Happy country! Fortunate people! Before long they may hope for their Greeleys, their Beechers, and their Fisks." Mark Twain's disenchantment was even more devastating. Commenting upon the "priest-ridden" social order, the Barnum and Bailey gimmickry of the Colosseum, and the diabolical genius of that "operatic screamer" Lucretia Borgia, he described the country as a "vast museum of magnificence and misery." The irreverent Twain was as critical of pretentious American tourists as he was of pompous Italian guides, and he exasperated both when he remarked that he could not remember who Columbus was and that Venice reminded him of an Arkansas town after a spring flood.[4]

But one reason Americans ignored Twain's advice to see Lake Tahoe instead of Lake Como was that Italy appeared an almost mythopoeic counterimage to America. Italian social customs especially offered an attractive alternative to the increasingly frantic pace of daily life in this country. American visitors observed, for example, that Italians possessed a different attitude toward time. The hours and moments of every day were savored intensely by Italians, who seemed guiltless about "wasting time." Americans soon discovered, however, that freedom from the tyranny of the clock made them uneasy. Unaccustomed to a life without the pressures of time, Americans found the prospect of a life of passive stillness and pure being disturbing. As a result many travelers

[4] *Testimonianze americane sull'Italia del Risorgimento*, ed. Elizabeth Mann Borgese (Milan, 1961); Brooks, pp. 145, 155-56; Norton's reflections are in *Discovery of Europe: The Story of American Experience in the Old World*, ed. Philip Rahv (Boston, 1947), p. 230.

hurried away from Italy ultimately reassured of the soundness of America's habitual punctuality.[5]

Perhaps Italians remained oblivious to the rush of time because of their historic consciousness. Italy, Henry James noted, is "thick with the sense of history and the taste of time." Here again one sees ambivalence. Americans, imbued with the "sovereignty of the present" (Jefferson), could hold up the mirror of Italy to search for a sense of the past. A people of restless temperament found in Italy a country which possessed a feeling for tradition and permanence. Even the riddle of Rome's decline and fall nervously fascinated many nineteenth-century Americans who looked forward to a brave new world but occasionally glanced backward to ponder the fate of other proud nations. The historian and statesman Theodore Roosevelt, for example, regarded the tragedy of Italian civilization as a case study for modern man. And yet in the end Americans found intolerable Italy's almost morbid obsession with the shadowy afterglows of antiquity. In Italy "the past is too powerful," observed Bayard Taylor. "The ancients did things by doing the business of their own day," wrote William James, "not by gaping at their grandfather's tombs—and the normal man of today will do likewise. Better fifty years of Cambridge, than a cycle of Cathay." Ultimately, the Italians' reverence for history and their tranquil resignation to the flight of time taxed the patience of Americans, with their compulsion to hard work and to "the business of their own day." Italian humanism failed to penetrate the hide of American pragmatism and puritanism.[6]

American commentary on Italian society was also characterized by ambivalence. The Italian's dedication to his family and village, his intense sense of *paese*, was viewed as a commendable effort to promote social morality and personal character. Similarly, the highly structured class system fascinated many Americans. For although nineteenth-century travelers believed in an open, fluid society, these visitors were men of wealth and leisure who experienced a lack of deference in egalitarian America. Thus as they looked upon Italy's complex social order, they rejected

[5] Paul Baker, *The Fortunate Pilgrims: Americans in Italy, 1800-1860* (Cambridge, 1964), pp. 208-11.

[6] *Ibid.*, pp. 208-12; Theodore Roosevelt to Arthur J. Balfour, March 5, 1908, *The Letters of Theodore Roosevelt*, ed. Elting E. Morrison (8 vols., Cambridge, 1951–1954), vi, 959-62.

its rigid caste barriers but respected its distinct class lines. These mixed feelings, however, betrayed more than a concern for social position. At bottom they indicated that American travelers were basically repelled by the Italians as people. Although Americans responded to their own image of the Italian national character, supposedly all festiveness and spontaneity, the people themselves presented a sorry spectacle. Backward and illiterate, incessantly noisy and incorrigibly indolent, sometimes deceitful and thievish, the masses offered a collective picture of squalor that incensed the American moral conscience. George Bancroft found the people "so corrupt, the nation so cowardly, dishonest and degenerate" that the word of an Italian was "of less weight than straw"; and Theodore Roosevelt, writing from Sorrento, exclaimed: "But the people! Praise heaven for America—even with the aldermen and the anarchists." Americans attributed the wretchedness to the dead hand of history, to Italy's ancient institutions, particularly to the Roman Catholic Church. With its empty ritual and sterile dogma, Catholicism had stunted the Italians' moral character, leaving them with a false sense of spiritual security and no sense of social responsibility. In the American mind, Romanism was the great burden of Italian history.[7]

Yet when all is said, the *idea* of Italy, if not Italy itself, continued to cast an almost magic spell over the American imagination. For within the romantic vision there resided a tension between objective fact and subjective feeling, between reality and desire. Nowhere was the ambivalence of the image revealed more eloquently than in Hawthorne's reflections upon leaving Rome:

When we have once known Rome, and left her where she lies, like a long decaying corpse, retaining a trace of the noble shape it was, but with accumulated dust and fungous growth overspreading all its more admirable features—left her in utter weariness, no doubt, of her narrow, crooked intricate streets so uncomfortably paved with little squares of lava that to tread over them is a penitential pilgrimage, so indescribably ugly, moreover, so alley-like, into which the sun never falls, and where a chill wind forces its deadly breath into our lungs— left her, tired of the sight of those immense seven-storied, yel-

[7] Baker, pp. 83, 216-20; Theodore Roosevelt to Anna Roosevelt, Jan. 30, 1887, *Letters*, I, 120.

low-washed hovels, or call them palaces, where all that is dreary in domestic life seems magnified and multiplied, and weary of climbing those staircases, which ascend from a ground floor of cookshops, cobblers' stalls, stables, and regiments of cavalry, to a middle region of princes, cardinals, and ambassadors, and an upper tier of artists, just beneath the unattainable sky—left her, worn out with shivering at the cheerless and smoking fireside by day, and feasting with our own substance the ravenous little populace of a Roman bed at night—left her, sick at heart of Italian trickery which has uprooted whatever faith in man's integrity had endured till now, and sick at stomach of sour bread, sour wine, rancid butter, and bad cookery, needlessly bestowed on evil meats—left her, disgusted with the pretense of holiness and the reality of nastiness, each equally omnipresent—left her, half lifeless from the languid atmosphere, the vital principle of which has been used up long ago, or corrupted by myriads of slaughters—left her, crushed down in spirit with the desolation of her ruin, and the hopelessness of her future—left her, in short, hating her with all our might, and adding our individual curse to the infinite anathema which her old crimes have unmistakably brought down—when we have left Rome in such a mood as this we are astonished by the discovery, by and by, that our heart strings have mysteriously attached themselves to the Eternal City and are drawing us thitherward again, as if it were more familiar, more intimately our home, than even the spot where we were born.[8]

As Hawthorne's quixotic lines suggest, there were really two Italys in the American mind. One was conceptual, the other existential; one a diffuse image of some hopeful ideal, a humanistic fantasy born of the frustration of all that seemed to be lacking in America; the other, a concrete and particular Italy discovered by direct experience, a corporeal reality of unabashed decadence and pungent confusions, a country whose people were suffocating under the dust and dirt of their tragic history. It is to this latter view—the nativist image—that we must now turn, for it was this darker outlook that came more and more to characterize the

[8] Nathaniel Hawthorne, *The Marble Faun* (Signet edn., New York, 1961), pp. 235-36.

American attitude toward Italy at the end of the nineteenth century.

AMERICAN NATIVISM AND ITALIAN IMMIGRATION

The nativist content in America's image of Italy, subtly latent in the romantic picture, emerged in full with the deluge of Italian immigrants in the late nineteenth century. One of the greatest migrations in history had taken place, as millions of eastern and southern Europeans spilled down the sluice-ways of decrepit ships seeking to find in America what had been lost in Europe. Thus, for the first time the great majority of Americans came face to face with the Italian. And it was the southern Italian and Sicilian they encountered on the streets of New York, Boston, Chicago, Philadelphia, and San Francisco. It was the Italian of swarthy complexion and unsavory mien, the unwashed creature from the *Mezzogiorno*. The startling impact of these alien *contadini* (peasants) helped bring about perhaps the first crisis of confidence in America since the Civil War.

Americans reacted to the last wave of immigration with an outburst of nativism that was as neurotic as it was narcissistic. Nativism, as John Higham has shown, consisted of three volatile ingredients: a belief in the superiority of the Anglo-Saxon heritage, a suspicion of the authoritarian tendencies of the Catholic Church, and a fear of the subversive influence of European political radicalism. The Italians were the nightmare of the American dream. Indeed, if "Rum, Romanism, and Rebellion" was the unfortunate anti-Irish shibboleth of the election of 1884, "Chianti, Catholicism, and Crime" could as easily have been the indelible stigma borne by the Italian immigrant. Inevitably a stereotyped picture of the Italian immigrant took shape: at best, an illiterate and harmless organ-grinder or musty fruit peddler; at worst, a stiletto-wielding criminal drunk on *vino* or a bomb-throwing revolutionary motivated by Marx and Malatesta. In Anglo-Saxon America, the immigrants from Naples and Sicily were clearly beyond the alchemy of the "melting-pot." "You don't call an Italian a white man?" a construction boss was asked. "No, sir," he replied, "an Italian is a Dago."[9]

[9] John Higham, *Strangers in the Land: Patterns of American Nativism* (Atheneum, paperback edn., New York, 1963), pp. 66, 194-330; Salvatore Mondello, "Italian Migration to the U.S. as Reported in American Magazines 1880-1920," *Social Science*, XXXIX (June, 1964), 131-42.

In reaction to the "new" immigration, and to the patriotic hysteria of World War I and the "Red Scare" that followed, there developed a tenuous but effective alliance among racist theoreticians, paranoic xenophobes, progressive intellectuals, trade unionists and business leaders, ethnic purists, anti-Semites and anti-Catholics, Social Darwinists and Protestant theologians, Cavalier Southerners and Brahmin Yankees; they all demanded discriminatory restriction as the last best hope of saving America for "Americans." Meanwhile the performance of Italy during the war did little to rehabilitate her image. Originally neutral, Italy joined the Allies in 1915, a move truly welcomed in America. Many students and intellectuals rushed off to serve in the Italian Red Cross. Then came Caporetto, the astounding Austro-Hungarian breakthrough that seemed to augur the complete collapse of the Italian army. Unfortunately the impression of Italians retreating in humiliation became firmly imprinted in the American mind; few Americans were aware that the Italian army regrouped and held the northern front against the combined German and Austro-Hungarian forces. It was at Versailles, however, that Italy's prestige reached its nadir. With the secret treaties of London publicized and Italy grabbing for the spoils of victory, it seemed that the Italians stood for everything narrow and Machiavellian. When the cold facts of Italy's "sacro egoismo" dissolved the mist of Wilsonian idealism, Americans could only conclude that they had been deceived by European *realpolitik*; and when Gabriele d'Annunzio seized the city of Fiume they suddenly knew the meaning of the "jackal tradition" of Italian diplomacy.[10]

Thus far I have attempted to delineate the clusters of impressions that made up the two images of Italy: the romantic view, arising from the impulses of the imagination and sustained by an almost mythical idealization of Italy and the virtues of the old world; the nativist picture, arising from the impulses of xenophobia and sustained by a dread of a motley European *canaille*

[10] See Morrell Heald, "Business Attitude Toward European Immigration, 1880-1900," *Journal of Economic History*, XIII (Summer, 1953), 291-304; Barbara Miller Solomon, "The Intellectual Background of Immigration Restriction in New England," *New England Quarterly*, xxv (March, 1952), 47-59; Rowland T. Berthoff, "Southern Attitudes Toward Immigration, 1865-1914," *Journal of Southern History*, XVII (Aug. 1951), 328-60; Charles Fenton, "Ambulance Drivers in France and Italy, 1914-1918," *American Quarterly*, III (Winter, 1951), 326-41; René Albrecht-Carrié, *Italy: From Napoleon to Mussolini* (New York, 1950), pp. 42-43, 75, 104-24.

and their old-world vices. It is against the background of these conflicting images that we should examine briefly two books on Italy written in 1922—the eve of the Fascist take-over. The works in question not only throw further light on the dynamics of the two images, but more importantly, suggest two ambiguous perspectives from which many Americans interpreted the rise of Italian Fascism.

IMMORTAL ITALY VS. BLACK MAGIC

One of the best expressions of the romantic perspective can be found in Edgar Ansel Mowrer's *Immortal Italy*. A correspondent for the *Chicago Daily News*, Mowrer wrote his book out of a genuine fondness for the Italians and an enduring enchantment with Italy itself. For Mowrer, Italy was a country that age could not wither nor could tragedy mar her remarkable resilience. More than anything else, it was Italy's amazing power of survival that emerges in the book's early chapters (where the rhetoric of resurrection is explicit). Like the "travelers to Arcadia" of the nineteenth century, Mowrer saw Italy as a land of wish-fulfillment ("Where Dreams Come True"). The grandeur of her culture and the "simplicity, frankness, melancholy, and unconquerable individualism" of her people made the country a totally new experience for the many Americans who had "grown frantic at the unrelieved ugliness" of modern life. "Notwithstanding the Italian defects," Mowrer advised, "I say that he who has known and understood Italy has added a new dimension to his experience. He has become wiser and more intimately human, less superficially optimistic but more soundly hopeful for mankind, and at the same time more charitable and tolerant of human sins."[11]

Despite his abiding respect, Mowrer did not express an idolatry of Italy and everything Italian. His comments on Italian political life, to cite one example, revealed a critical edge rarely found among the romantic pilgrims. The human virtues of the Italians, Mowrer noted, are actually political vices: their fierce individualism results in an *incivismo* (an impoverished civic consciousness), while their cynical attitude toward human frailty causes them to acquiesce to bureaucracy and corruption. In view of these traits, Mowrer could only conclude that for the Italians "democracy will always be a hair shirt."[12]

[11] Edgar Ansel Mowrer, *Immortal Italy* (New York, 1922), p. 22.
[12] *Ibid.*, p. 47.

14

Turning to contemporary political events, Mowrer devoted an extended chapter to the rise of radicalism in postwar Italy. He minced no words in describing the "arrogance" and "tyranny" of the extremist Left. After a detailed discussion of the land-hungry peasantry, the disciplined "red leagues," the industrial strikes in Turin, and the growing influence of the Third International and the "maximalist" wing of the Socialist Party, Mowrer leaves the reader with the impression that revolution was in the air. Yet, unlike so many American writers, Mowrer was careful to chart the decline of Bolshevism, spelling out in detail the enervating factionalism within the socialist movement and the general demise of revolutionary fervor in Italy in late 1921. The title of his chapter on Italian Communism suggested in five words the impotence of the radical Left: "The Revolution That Never Was."

The stillborn revolution was followed by "The Reaction That Failed." Mowrer's chapter on Fascism provided Americans with one of the few inside glimpses of the Blackshirt phenomenon in its embryonic stage. Significantly, he perceived Fascism in all its paradoxes: a syndicalist-oriented rebellion welcomed by the déclassé bourgeoisie and frightened industrialists; an impulsive, youthful revolt that called for a disciplined cult of patriotism and authority. More telling, he described the ruthless tactics of the *fascisti* and criticized officials for winking at the "barbarism" of the Blackshirts in their brutal suppression of the Left. But even more important, Mowrer had come to believe that Italy underwent a political turning point in August 1921, when the new Bonomi Ministry negotiated a pacification pact embracing the Socialist Left and Fascist Right. He even believed that Mussolini had resigned from his own movement, and he quotes Il Duce as saying on August 10: "Fascism is no longer liberation but tyranny, no longer the safeguard of the nation but the defense of private interests." "Everybody knew this," Mowrer added, "but it was comforting to have it confessed by the angry leader." Soon after, despite the lingering pockets of reactionary and revolutionary sentiment, he imagined Fascism was on the wane, a semblance of order had returned, and "Italy settled down to a condition of normal anarchy."[13]

Obviously Mowrer underestimated the Fascist threat in Italy. Perhaps because he saw the movement as devoid of any systematic program or consistent ideology he believed it would pass

[13] *Ibid.*, pp. 372-73.

from history as quickly as it had appeared. Nevertheless, what primarily concerns us is that Mowrer's early repudiation of Fascism stemmed from his sympathetic view of Italy and the Italians. Throughout his book one theme reverberates: Italy survives crisis after crisis because of the good sense of the "Italian common people." The theme is reinforced in the conclusion, where Mowrer uses the career of an Italian youth to depict the psychology of political behavior in the postwar period. After taking the reader through the depths of disenchantment experienced by the youth upon returning from the war, as well as his flirtations with both the radical Left and Right, Mowrer has his fictional character ultimately accepting the leadership of Filippo Turati and other Liberal-Socialist parliamentarians who see Italy's future in land reform, education, economic development, and a responsible "political awakening" that shuns extremist panaceas. His youth having rejected the ranting moonshine of the Left and Right, Mowrer concludes on a note of moral and political uplift. If Italy "remains true to its innate liberalism" it may even succeed Switzerland and the United States "as a refuge for the persecuted and the dissenting, a shelter for the outcasts of today who blaze the trail of to-morrow."[14]

Because of his romantic viewpoint, Mowrer could not accept a Fascist fate for Italy. With its "admirable sense of civilization, its brilliant flowering of individual genius, its wide tolerance and humanity," and its "innate liberalism," Italy would simply not tolerate a reactionary government that "is somehow unnatural and comic." There were many other observers, however, who saw Fascism as an entirely "natural" and promising future for the Italians. One of these Americans was the novelist Kenneth Roberts, whose book, *Black Magic*, reflected in naked candor the nativist response to the rise of Fascism.[15]

A popular writer of historical adventure stories and potboilers, Roberts was one of the leading American critics of unrestricted immigration. His main channel of protest was the *Saturday Evening Post*. In this repository of middle-class musings, Roberts warned again and again that the flood of Alpine, Semitic, and Mediterranean immigrants would leave the United States a "hybrid race of people as worthless and futile as the good-for-nothing mongrels of Central America and Southeastern Europe."

14 *Ibid.*, pp. 397-98.   15 *Ibid.*, pp. 396-97.

16

He was particularly concerned about Italian immigrants, especially the peasants from southern Italy. Replying to the "sentimentalists" who praised the Italians' instinct for beauty and hence their potential contribution to America, Roberts sneered: "The great mass of Italian immigrants . . . will never be anything else except stolid manual laborers. Their idea of the beautiful has always been and will always be a blue-and-pink chromo of a fat girl child standing in a field of daisies and serving as a background for a calendar issued by an enterprising macaroni firm."[16]

Roberts' defense of Fascism, which also appeared in a series in the *Saturday Evening Post* and later in his *Black Magic*, flowed logically from his bias against immigration. "Black Magic" was the marvelous brew concocted by responsible Italian statesmen who were trying to stem the tide of radical demagogy. But the Italian elixir applied to America as well, for as the subtitle indicates, America's first book on Fascism was *An Account of Its Beneficial Use in Italy, of Its Perversion in Bavaria, and of Certain Tendencies Which Might Necessitate Its Study in America.* With sarcastic delight, Roberts dedicated the book "To all Reds and Pinks. . . . To organized minorities and legislative blocs and advocates of class legislation," and to other "soft-spined" reformers who were "pandering to the worst instincts of the masses." Postwar Italy, Roberts assures the reader, was a sewer of corruption and degeneracy. In this quagmire Fascism appeared like a gust of fresh air, a tempest-like purgation of all that was defiled, leveled, fetid. Based on the invigorating instincts of nationalist idealism, Fascism "was the opposite of wild ideas, of lawlessness, of injustice, of cowardice, of treason, of crime, of class warfare, of special privilege; and it represented square-dealing, patriotism and common sense." As for Mussolini, "there has never been a word uttered against his absolute sincerity and honesty. Whatever the cause on which he embarked, he proved to be a natural-born leader and a gluttonous worker." Under Mussolini's dynamic leadership, the brave Blackshirts made short shrift of the radicals, restored the rights of property, and purged the country of self-seeking politicians who thrive on corruption endemic to mass democracy.[17]

[16] Higham, p. 273; Kenneth L. Roberts, "Guest from Italy," *SEP*, CXCIII (Aug. 21, 1920), 137. (A list of the Abbreviations Used in Footnotes is given at the beginning of Part One.)
[17] Roberts, *Black Magic* (Indianapolis, 1922), pp. 3, 29, 52, 61.

One need not continue with Roberts' list of Fascism's virtues, a trite catalogue that became depressingly familiar in many of the mass magazines of the 1920s. But what is striking in Roberts' book is that his high respect for Fascism implied a low regard for the Italians themselves. The Italy that emerges from *Black Magic* is a land teeming with illiteracy, crime, filth, and other symptoms of a deficient national character. The nativist strain of the author is unmistakable as he describes how the *fascisti* "undertook to stamp out the drug traffic, drunkenness, street-walking, crime and immorality of all sorts." Roberts even went so far as to justify the Fascist use of violence. When and if elections are held, he informed Americans, "the Black Shirts will be on hand with their pistols, knives and clubs, and see that the Italian people save themselves by giving Mussolini a working majority, whether they want it or not." An Italian dictatorship is a "national necessity," Roberts insisted, for Mussolini's strong-arm methods "are what Italy deserved and must continue to have before she can climb from the hole in which she deliberately sank herself." In short, the Italians "deserve" a dictatorship because of their "deliberate" vices. Therein lies the quintessence of the nativist response to Italian Fascism.[18]

It is tempting to conclude that the American response to Fascism falls into two distinct patterns. Those who viewed Italy through a romantic prism were, it would seem, more inclined to regard Fascism as an "unnatural" and alien force imposed upon a basically freedom-loving people; while the racial-nativists tended to approve of it as an appropriate form of authority for a politically and morally backward people. It is equally tempting to suggest that it was not so much that two Italys coexisted in the American mind as that America itself consists of two states of mind. This was, of course, the indictment George Santayana and Van Wyck Brooks leveled at the period we are studying. Brooks worked out the two concepts of "high-brow" and "low-brow," the former relating to the life of the mind of the isolated intellectuals, the latter to the catchpenny concerns of the hustling bourgeoisie. In this sense, those Americans for whom Italy had been a semi-mythical ideal might be considered of the "high-brow" cast of mind, *déracinés* looking for their intellectual place in the sun; whereas those who recoiled from Italy in nativist

[18] *Ibid.*, pp. 115, 136.

18

dismay might be regarded as "low-brow" provincials content with a homogeneous America at once pedestrian and prosperous. However useful these categories may be in analyzing America's cultural tensions around the period of World War I, they must be used with caution as a basis for explaining America's response to Fascism.

It may be true that much of the pro-Fascism of Roberts and of the *Saturday Evening Post* was based on a "low-brow" nativist mentality. But it does not necessarily follow that nativists in general supported Fascism. Indeed, some of the most extremist xenophobes, right-wing evangelists and southern Klansmen, for example, continually attacked Mussolini as an anti-Christ and Fascism as a foreign ideology. Nor does it follow that those elements in America which were antinativist, Catholics and ethnic minorities, for example, were necessarily anti-Fascist. Moreover, in regard to the "high-brows," it would be extremely difficult to assert that an intellectual admiration for Italian culture guaranteed a critical response to Fascism. Van Wyck Brooks and Santayana both identified with the "high-brow" tradition in America and, as alienated intellectuals, looked to Italy's organic culture as one source of salvation. Yet Brooks became a severe critic of Fascism and Santayana a warm admirer.

Thus it would seem that neither the "high-brow" romantic nor the "low-brow" nativist view of Italy completely encompasses America's response to Fascism. Nevertheless, what is crucial in understanding the mainsprings of America's receptivity to Fascism is the persistence of nativist sentiment in all areas of American society. Consider, for example, Santayana. Here was an eminent figure who, like Brooks, was far removed from the social and economic sources of American nativism. Yet Santayana, unlike Brooks, had a high opinion of Fascism, an opinion rooted in his utter scorn for the Italians. In 1944, in an interview with the journalist Herbert Matthews, Santayana stated: "The trouble with applying Fascism to Italy is that the people are undisciplined. They often make good Fascists, from eighteen to twenty-five, but after that they become individualists again. One can say that they are not on a high enough social level to become good Fascists." Santayana's reassessment of Fascism during World War II was echoed by other former American supporters of Mussolini who combined an idealized image of Italy with a harsh view of the Italians. Anne O'Hare McCormick, Rome cor-

19

respondent for the *New York Times*, spent almost twenty years explaining to Americans the poetic beauties of the Italian landscape as well as the political beauties of Mussolini and Fascism. When Fascism collapsed in 1943, she was less disappointed in Mussolini than in the "apathetic" Italians who let him down. Finally, there is Edgar Ansel Mowrer himself. Having rejected Fascism in 1922, Mowrer, it must be admitted, underwent a brief change of heart in 1923. Less than a year after Mussolini's advent to power, Mowrer wrote a cautious defense of Fascism as a necessary corrective to the paternalism which had "choked individual initiative" and to the "easy-going mentality" of the Italian people. To a certain extent, Mowrer's rationale was foreshadowed in his 1922 repudiation of Fascism. For in *Immortal Italy* there is the grudging concession that "The real trouble with Italy was not socialism. It must rather be an inherent weakness in the national character, content to remain unenterprising and illiterate while other nations progressed"; and in the closing sentences of his book there appeared the oblique suggestion that the future of Italy depended on the wisdom and idealism of the youth who needed "only discipline, discipline, discipline, and wise tolerance."[19]

Americans were hopelessly bewitched and bothered by Italy. While they praised Italians for their non-American virtues they bemoaned their un-American vices. Perhaps more than in any other writer this fundamental ambivalence is best seen in the attitude of Lincoln Steffens, another traveler to Italy whose lyrical admiration of Mussolini contained romantic and nativist countercurrents. Steffens viewed the Italians with a combination of condescension and affection that later characterized much of the apology for Fascism in the twenties. He often looked back upon his prewar years in Italy as the best of times because of the "happiness" of the common people and the "atmosphere of play" in the national character. Speaking of his servants, Steffens recalled: "I warned them that they might lie, politely; loaf, some; steal, the regular percentage; be careless, not overclean, and not too efficient; we'd stand for all that, and more. But if any one of them was ever or even appeared unhappy—out. They understood,

[19] Herbert Matthews, *Education of a Correspondent* (New York, 1946), pp. 468-71; *NYT*, July 26, 1943; Mowrer, "The Fascisti and Italy's Economic Recovery," *Forum*, LXIX (Feb. 1923), 1198-1206; id., *Immortal Italy*, pp. 387-88, 398.

laughed, and none was ever discharged by us." Now if Americans like Mowrer and Steffens really believed Italians were naturally "wise" and "happy," and if they found the pleasures of Italy more attractive than the pressures of America, why did they come to feel that the Italian people needed to be transformed by Fascism? The answer seems to be that many Americans were of two minds about Italy because they were of two minds about themselves. The truth is that America's dualistic image of Italy revealed both a romantic desire that Italians remain themselves and continue to offer Americans the possibility of an occasional escape to a different life style, and a more unspoken but deeper nativist desire that the American way of life prevail everywhere. Thus like the nineteenth-century American writers who hailed the *Risorgimento* only to discover that European liberalism would tear asunder Italy's classical culture, many twentieth-century writers welcomed Mussolini only to discover that Fascism would destroy the very features of Italian life that had appealed to their romantic sensibilities. Uncertain about the future, American writers looked to Italy as a model of frozen perfection that would resist the inexorable march of modernity. Uncertain about the past, many of these same writers looked to Fascism as a means of liberating Italians from the stagnation of their history. As we shall see, when Americans defended Fascism they justified it on grounds of "efficiency," "discipline," and "progress." In so doing they no longer sensed any loss for the Italy of the Arcadian dream. As cosmopolitan humanism gave way to the practical idealism of industrial progress even the romantic visions of a Mowrer yielded up more deeply embedded nativist instincts. In the end America's apologia for Fascism would betray an inevitable desire to see the Americanization of Italy.[20]

[20] Lincoln Steffens, *The Autobiography of Lincoln Steffens* (New York, 1931), II, 823; A. William Salomone, "The Nineteenth Century Discovery of Italy: An Essay in American Cultural History. Prolegomena to a Historiographical Problem," *American Historical Review*, LXXIII (June, 1968), 1359-91.

2.

Enter
Il Duce

WHEN MIRACLES CEASE, AND
  THE FAITHFUL DESERT YOU,
AND MEN SHALL ONLY DO
  THEIR BEST TO FORGET YOU,
AND LATER IS WORSE, WHEN
  MEN WILL NOT HATE YOU
ENOUGH TO DEFAME OR
  EXECRATE YOU,
BUT PONDERING THE QUALITIES
  THAT YOU LACKED
WILL ONLY TRY TO FIND
  THE HISTORICAL FACT.
WHEN MEN SHALL DECLARE
  THAT THERE WAS NO
  MYSTERY
ABOUT THIS MAN WHO PLAYED
  A CERTAIN PART IN HISTORY.

T. S. Eliot, 1935*

THE MIRROR OF THE PRESS

As he walked amidst the majestic splendor of the Palazzo Venezia in Rome, entered the huge folding doors of the Hall of the Mappamondo, and continued down the wide, arching halls filled with Madonnas, frescoes, and Byzantine chests, one question haunted biographer Emil Ludwig. For a week he had been returning every evening for his hourly conversation with Benito Mussolini. Taking his customary seat across the desk from the always composed and courteous statesman, Ludwig finally broached the question:

> Curiously enough, in the course of my travels I have found you more popular in America than anywhere else. In a hundred

* Reprinted by permission of Harcourt Brace Jovanovich, Inc. (See Acknowledgments)

22

interviews I was asked: "How do you like Mussolini?" Yet the Americans are opposed to dictatorship in any form.

"You are wrong; the Americans have a dictator," he answered promptly. "The president is almost omnipotent, his power being guaranteed by the constitution."[1]

Mussolini's reply obviously begged the question, and when Ludwig left the Palazzo that evening the riddle remained as puzzling as ever. But the German writer was not the only one troubled by the phenomenon. In the opening page of *The Public Mind* (1927) Sir Norman Angell had noted that Americans favored the "popular" Mussolini rather than "his democratic opposition." Another British writer, Harold J. Laski, put the problem in broader perspective. "The historian of the next generation," Laski told Americans in 1923, "cannot fail to be impressed by the different reception accorded to the changes of which Lenin and Mussolini have been the chief authors. Where Lenin's system has won for itself international ostracism and armed intervention, that of Mussolini has been the subject of widespread enthusiasm." To understand the extent this enthusiasm had reached in America we need only to consult that barometer of public curiosity— the *Reader's Guide to Periodical Literature*. For the period from 1925 to 1928 the *Reader's Guide* showed over one hundred articles on Mussolini compared to fifteen on Stalin. In the period from 1929 to 1932, when American interest in the Soviet Five Year Plans was at its keenest, Stalin fared better with thirty-five articles, but Mussolini still overshadowed him with forty-six.[2]

What is the explanation for the enormous publicity enjoyed by this brilliant poseur who strutted on the world stage, filling it with fury and bombast, until the melodrama ignominiously folded two decades later. Looking back, it is easy to see the hollowness of the man. Thus in his sympathetic biography of Mussolini, the late Sir Ivone Kirkpatrick begins by paraphrasing Benedetto Croce's postmortem. Mussolini was, wrote Kirkpatrick, "of limited intelligence, deficient in moral sensibility, ignorant with that fundamental ignorance which did not know and understand the elementary essence of human relationships, incapable of self-criticism or of scruple, excessively vain, lacking in taste in every

[1] Emil Ludwig, *Talks with Mussolini* (Boston, 1933), pp. 156-57.
[2] Norman Angell, *The Public Mind* (London, 1927), p. 3; Harold J. Laski, "Lenin and Mussolini," *Foreign Affairs*, II (Sept. 1923), 52-53.

word and gesture, always oscillating between arrogance and servility." Rendered by one of the greatest historians, Croce's harsh judgment may or may not offer an insightful characterization of the real Mussolini. But whatever the case, his verdict of villainy fails to do justice to the vast popularity Il Duce was able to generate abroad as well as in Italy.[3]

In the United States Mussolini's popularity was to a great extent a product of the press. Most newspapers outside New York City relied on wire services or foreign correspondents for information, and in the early years these sources were generally friendly to Mussolini and his new regime. Two areas that did enjoy direct reports were Boston, with its *Christian Science Monitor*, and Chicago, where the *Daily News* received Rome dispatches from Hiram K. Motherwell and the *Tribune* from George Seldes. In New York, because of its Italian-American population and because of its superior international news coverage, papers devoted special attention to Italy and carried articles by well-known journalists. The *New York Post* featured Percy Winner, Dorothy Thompson, and Clarance Streit. In the early twenties Winner supported Fascism but by the end of the decade he had become a severe critic. Although Thompson always held Mussolini in disdain, Streit, the *Post*'s Rome correspondent, was swayed by the "dynamism" of his style. For the *New York Tribune* Wilbur Forrest wrote a searching series of analyses, and for Walter Lippmann's *World* William Bolitho contributed hostile articles that were later published as *Italy Under Mussolini*.[4]

The most thorough coverage of Italian events could, of course, be found in the *New York Times*. The *Times*' correspondents writing on Italy included Arnaldo Cortesi, Edwin L. James, Arthur Livingston, Walter Littlefield, and Anne O'Hare McCormick. With the exception of Livingston, these journalists wrote approvingly of Fascism and its leader. Occasionally the *Times* printed critical accounts by authors and scholars like H. G. Wells and James T. Shotwell, as well as exiles like Cesare Rossi. But

[3] Sir Ivone Kirkpatrick, *Mussolini: A Study in Power* (New York, 1964), p. 11.

[4] A more extensive examination of the press can be found in John Booth Carter's "American Reactions to Italian Fascism, 1919-1933" (Ph.D. Thesis, Columbia University, 1953); and in the author's "Mussolini's Italy: The View from America" (Ph.D. Thesis, University of Southern California, 1964).

the scattered articles of the anti-Fascist "guests" were no match for the regular staff. Littlefield, for example, was one of several American reporters decorated by the Mussolini government; Cortesi, who became Rome correspondent in the early thirties, was the son of a leading journalist in Mussolini's Italy; and McCormick was a devotee who rhapsodized upon the feats of the Blackshirts and consistently defended the twists and turns of Mussolini's diplomacy, justifying the Ethiopian invasion, the Italian "volunteers" in Spain, and the Rome-Berlin Axis. Yet editorially the *Times* showed less inclination than its writers to support Fascism. Although the *Times*, like most papers, condoned Mussolini's seizure of power, by the mid-twenties the editors became disenchanted, seeing "one more parallel" after another between Fascist and Soviet totalitarianism. Nevertheless, the *New York Times'* treatment of Italy brought denunciations by anti-Fascists in the United States who were convinced that Cortesi, McCormick (and in the thirties Herbert L. Matthews and C. L. Sulzberger) and associates were championing the cause of Fascism.[5]

In addition to the daily press Americans learned of developments in Italy from popular weekly and monthly magazines. With few exceptions these magazines welcomed the *coup d'etat* and were generally uncritical of domestic Fascism while remaining skeptical of the diplomatic implications of Fascist nationalism and militarism. The only general periodicals consistently critical were those of a "high-brow" tone, like the two monthlies—the *Atlantic* and *Harper's*. Here one might find an occasional article by an apologist like Lothrop Stoddard or a *simpatizzante* like Robert Sencourt, but the great majority of the articles on Italy were by such staunch anti-Fascists as James Murphy and George Seldes, as well as by exiles like Max Ascoli and Emilio Lussu. Although H. L. Mencken lampooned the goddess of democracy in his *American Mercury*, the antidemocratic experiment in Italy found no sanction in his journal of amusing abuse. The same held true for *The New Yorker* and *Esquire*. The former satirized a Fascist "censorship that will guarantee 100 per cent moral and political purity" through the agency of Benito's "Central Pornographical Office"; while the latter ran Hemingway's caustic articles from Africa on the Fascist attempt to make Ethiopia "fit

5 *NYT*, Jan. 8, 1927; May 25, 1930; Aug. 25, Sept. 17, 1935; Nov. 15, Dec. 12, 1937; "The *New York Times* and Mussolini," *Il Mondo*, Oct. 15, 1939.

for Fiats." Moving to the "middle-brow" magazines, the weekly *Time*, which began publishing in 1925, handled Mussolini (as well as other statesmen) with a characteristically critical style that ranged from cautious curiosity to skeptical disrespect. *Time* bestowed a favorable comment now and then, but more often it displayed unflattering photos of Il Duce in a gym outfit or swimming suit. Perhaps more telling is the fact that although Mussolini appeared on eight covers of *Time* between 1923 and 1943, he never made "Man of the Year," despite the selection of Hitler once, Stalin twice, and even Haile Selassie during the Ethiopian War. By the outbreak of World War II, *Time* had been banned in Italy (along with *Esquire, The New Yorker, New Republic, Nation,* and other critical publications), apparently because of its attacks on Il Duce's daughter, Edda, as a viperine Cleopatra who wooed German statesmen and hoped to Nazify the reluctant Italian people.[6]

A number of other magazines sustained an interest in Mussolini's Italy, but within a framework of objectivity. *Forum* and *Current History* followed their customary practice of presenting the case for and against the dictatorship. In March 1927, *Survey* published "An American Looks at Fascism," a symposium in which both critics (e.g., Gaetano Salvemini and William Y. Elliott) and crusaders (e.g., Thomas W. Lamont and Giuseppe Prezzolini) aired their arguments. In a similar format the *Literary Digest* printed a special section on Italy in April 1927, and *Mentor* did the same with its November issue of that year. In 1934, however, the business monthly *Fortune* abandoned all pretense of impartiality and came out with an entire edition which reflected favorably upon the "Corporate State." This was perhaps Fascism's greatest public relations coup among America's more sophisticated publications.

But in terms of mass circulation, all of the above journals were

[6] *Time*, XXIV (July 24, 1939), 18-20. On the matter of Man of the Year, *Time* writes: "The one criterion that the editors have kept in mind over the years when making their selection is that the Man of the Year must have dominated the news of the year and left an indelible mark—for good or ill—on history. In the editor's opinion, Mussolini did not measure up to that standard during the years he was in power." (Susan Sommers [for the editors of *Time*] to the author, July 25, 1966.)

[7] For a discussion of *Fortune's* issue on the Corporate State, see Chapter VII, pp. 163-65.

excelled in their influence by the pro-Fascist *Saturday Evening Post*. Under the direction of Cyrus Curtis, this vast weekly, with subscribers numbering almost three million in 1930, effectively created a respectable image of Mussolini. Among the *Post*'s writers was Isaac F. Marcosson, who described Mussolini as a political savior who had "turned red terror into white fear" and an economic genius who had engineered a "commercial revolution"; Kenneth Roberts, who left no doubt in the reader's mind that the March on Rome was a victory of virtue over vice; Samuel G. Blythe, who characterized Il Duce as a "Latin Cromwell"; and humorist Will Rogers who, writing home after a highly publicized interview with Mussolini, declared: "Dictator form of government is the greatest form of government; that is, if you have the right Dictator."[8]

Not only did the *Post* have the above writers boost Italian Fascism but the writing of Mussolini himself was serialized in the magazine in 1928. Instrumental in negotiating the printing of Il Duce's "autobiography" in the *Post* was the American Ambassador to Italy, Richard Washburn Child. A former corporation lawyer and Harding appointee, Child became infatuated with the Italian dictator and frequently conferred with him on the state of American opinion. Child claimed he edited Mussolini's "autobiography," but it is more likely he wrote the entire book with the help of Benito's brother, Arnaldo. Mussolini later admitted this bit of ghosting in *Vita di Arnaldo*. As Ambassador and later as citizen, Child relentlessly extolled the merits of Fascism and spoke of the dictator in tones of adulation ("a Spartan genius"). His enthusiasm stemmed from his own political conservatism. "It is only fair for me when I write of Mussolini," he candidly confessed in the *Post*, "to state I believe in the least

---

[8] Isaac F. Marcosson, "After Mussolini—What," *SEP*, cxcviii (May 29, 1926), 135-43; "The Dictator Business," *SEP*, ccii (March 15, 1930), 5, 54. (In the latter article Marcosson hedged a little as he took note of Mussolini's imperialistic ambitions. Like so many apologists, however, he remains convinced that Mussolini, had he stayed out of World War II, would still be in power today and "enjoying the aid and confidence of the Free World." *Before I Forget* [New York, 1959], p. 377.) Kenneth Roberts, "Salvage of a Nation," *SEP*, cxcvi (Sept. 22, 1923), 20, 132-34; "The Ambush of Italy," *SEP*, cxcv (Feb. 24, 1923), 25, 98-102; Will Rogers, "Letters of a Self-Made Diplomat to His President," *SEP*, cxcix (July 31, 1926), 8-9, 82-84.

government . . . that I detest papa-and-mama legislation—and so does Mussolini." Acting as Mussolini's mouthpiece in America, Child's effusions approached idolatry.[9]

Taken together, the *Saturday Evening Post*'s panegyrics tell us more about the conservative bias of the authors than about Mussolini himself. It would be wrong to conclude, however, that all pro-Fascist journalists wrote from a conservative slant. Indeed a number of former muckrakers were just as complimentary toward the Italian dictatorship. In watching Lenin and Mussolini "scientifically" apply the "Russian-Italian method" to a world betrayed by Wilsonian idealism, the jaded Lincoln Steffens found a perverse consolation, and in one of his more ecstatic moments he could go so far as to claim that God had "formed Mussolini out of a rib of Italy." Similarly, Samuel S. McClure returned from Italy to debate the case for Fascism in a series of meetings with Vincenzo Nitti, son of the former Premier, and to declare that the principle of corporatism was "a great forward step and the first new ideal in government since the founding of the American Republic." Ida Tarbell, sent to Italy in 1926 to do a series for *McCall's*, also became fascinated by the experimental features of the Corporate State and wrote lavishly about the moral uplift in Mussolini's "world of work." Miss Tarbell's sojourn is noteworthy, for the State Department feared allowing this "pretty red radical" to go to Italy, believing that she would write "violent anti-Mussolini articles." But after talking to her for an hour, Under-

[9] Benito Mussolini, *My Autobiography* (New York, 1928), preface by Richard Washburn Child, p. ix; Mussolini, *Vita di Arnaldo* (Rome, 1933), pp. 124-25; Laura Fermi, *Mussolini* (Chicago, 1961), pp. 285-88.

The original manuscript of Mussolini's autobiography, deposited in the Houghton Library, Harvard University, bears the imprint of Child's characteristic halting, exclamatory prose. Another person who had a hand in the work was the then young student, Luigi Barzini, Jr. Barzini writes: ". . . as a boy I collaborated with Richard Washburn Child in 'writing' Mussolini's 'autobiography.' It was based on notes allegedly prepared by brother Arnaldo (more probably by somebody in his office). I did the translation. Child embroidered them, adding colour and purple prose pieces." (Barzini to author, April 16, 1968.)

See also Richard Washburn Child, "Making of Mussolini," *SEP*, cxcvi (June 28, 1924), 3-4, 156-58; "What Does Mussolini Mean?" *SEP*, cxcvii (July 26, 1924), 23, 87-90; "Open the Gates," *SEP*, cxcvii (July 12, 1924), 5, 55-58; "Mussolini Now," *SEP*, cc (March 24, 1928), 29, 135-38; see also Child's *A Diplomat Looks at Europe* (New York, 1925), and *The Writing on the Wall* (New York, 1929).

Secretary of State William R. Castle, convinced she would write amiable reports, informed the Ambassador in Rome: "I certainly hope that she will get the situation pretty straight because everything she writes is widely read in America and if she should write articles which see the good in the Fascist regime, it will do away with a lot of subversive talk that goes on here." Miss Tarbell did not disappoint the State Department. Upon returning she advised the Department that the new labor laws in Italy constituted an admirable social experiment.[10]

Although cosmopolitan, progressive journalists joined folksy, conservative nativists in praising Mussolini and Fascism, the chorus did not remain constant throughout the twenties and early thirties. Actually, American opinion oscillated from time to time as particular developments in Italy elicited acclaim or censure. A brief survey of these shifting attitudes will throw some light on the chronological pattern of America's reaction to Fascism.

THE FRIENDLY PERSUASION: 1922-1930

Before the March on Rome American newspapers devoted a few words to the ragged band of Blackshirts known as the *fascisti*. Most of the news derived from the wire services. Some magazines carried special articles, many of which were written by foreigners, including pro-Fascist Italians. A few publications compared the *fascisti* to American organizations, with sympathizers (e.g., the *Independent*) drawing sanguine parallels between Mussolini's men and the vigilantes of the old West, and skeptics (e.g., *Current Opinion*) seeing the proper analogue in the American Legion or the Ku Klux Klan. But until the March on Rome in October 1922, the press in general hung suspended between belief and doubt.[11]

On hearing of the Fascist take-over, however, a significant shift occurred in the press. The *Literary Digest*, which undertook one of its customary surveys, charted the pendulum of editorial opinion. A few examples suffice. The *New York Times*, on October 28, presented an editorial entitled "Violence in Italy" which

---

[10] Lincoln Steffens, *The Autobiography of Lincoln Steffens* (New York, 1931), II, 812-20; id., "Stop, Look, Listen," *Survey*, LVII (March 1, 1927), 735-37; *NYT*, Jan. 26, 1927, March 12, 1928; William Castle to Henry Fletcher, June 15, 1926, Container 13, FP; Ida Tarbell, *All in the Day's Work* (New York, 1939), pp. 380-84; Carter, p. 427.

[11] *Independent*, CV (March 12, 1921), 270; *Current Opinion*, LXXIII (Oct. 1922), 469.

depicted the Blackshirt movement as nothing less than "political terrorism." Three days later a "Fascisti in Power" editorial noted that Mussolini's coup "was a peculiar and relatively harmless type." Similarly, on October 26, the *Boston Evening Transcript* expressed fear of a "false patriotism" parading to power through "terror and intimidation"; four days later it breathed a sigh of relief, declaring that "Fascismo at the Helm" would be much more responsible than it appeared to be in its march to power. And the *New York Tribune*, which on October 27 criticized the "Ku Klux Klan of Italy," editorialized on October 31 on the "Black-Shirted Garibaldi": "The Fascisti movement is—in essentials—a reaction against degeneration through Socialistic internationalism. It is rough in its methods, but the aims which it professes are tonic. Garibaldi won freedom in a red shirt. Mussolini is fighting for normalcy and Italianism in a black one."[12]

American suspicions, then, subsided after Mussolini's bold move to power. As with the moderate section of the international press, the immediate reaction in the American papers to Mussolini's accession might be described as "una benevola aspettativa" (cautiously friendly and hopeful). Soon there emerged a common characterization of the event and the man. Typical was the treatment in *Collier's*, which began with a description of the postwar chaos in Italy followed by the drama of the Fascist march to power and concluding with a teasing personal glimpse of the disciplining strong man. Il Duce represented the triumph of law and order over anarchy and radicalism, and his assumption of government reponsibilities would, it was believed, have a sobering influence on his violent *imprudenza*. "Normalcy" was the catchword of the times, for Italy as well as for America.[13]

Despite the reiteration of this triumphant theme, many reporters admitted that the meaning and direction of Fascism remained obscure. Their uncertainty revealed itself in the questions they posed: did the March on Rome signify a simple coup d'etat, a bloodless, hence "glorious" rebellion; was it a dress rehearsal for civil war, or was it the familiar ministerial game of musical

[12] "Mussolini: Garibaldi or Caesar?" *LD*, LXXV (Nov. 18, 1922), 17-18; Carter, pp. 14-15.

[13] The reaction of the international press is briefly described in Alan Cassels, "Some Reflections on Mussolini's Cult of Public Opinion," a paper delivered before the annual meeting of the American Association of Public Opinion Research, May 1965, New London, Conn. *Collier's*, LXXII (Sept. 15, 1923), 7-8, 33.

chairs; or could it be a new kind of revolution—a revolution of the Right? However the event was interpreted, most writers shared Arthur Brisbane's conviction that Fascism sounded the awakening of a viable middle-class political life in Italy. Indeed, if there was one notion that touched the hearts of Americans it was the impression that Fascism, in the words of the *Chicago Tribune*, stood for "the most striking and successful attempt of the middle classes to meet the tide of revolutionary socialism."[14]

The leitmotiv of the American response was an intense fear of the red specter of international Communism, a fear that caused many reporters to overlook Mussolini's own radical past. Some papers drew political lessons from the episode. The *San Francisco Chronicle*, for instance, after warning its readers that Fascism was the inevitable consequence of toying with Socialism, went on to advise Mussolini to return Italy's economy to private enterprise. Given this obsession with radicalism both at home and abroad, it is not surprising that only a small minority of American papers categorized the new government as a "dictatorship" and that the *New York Times* was almost alone in asserting that the Fascists themselves were opposed to democracy. Possibly because the take-over had met so little resistance, most viewers were led to believe that the movement had the support of the Italian masses. At least one paper, the *Cleveland Plain Dealer*, was convinced that Fascism had in fact saved democracy in Italy.[15]

But Mussolini the domestic messiah could also appear as a diplomatic menace. "We like your domestic policy, Black Shirt, what we know of it," stated the *Independent*. "But we confess ourselves nervous about your foreign policy. We wait with apprehension the unfolding of that." Nervously anticipating Fascist expansion into the Mediterranean, the *Washington Post* admitted that "the mind shrinks from the consequences of such a struggle." This major reservation—the possible effect of Fascist chauvinism on the international scene—was soon confirmed during the Corfu affair in the summer of 1923. Mussolini's attempt to bombard the Greeks into submission and establish himself as the strong man of the Balkans caused an uproar in the press. Angry editors

[14] *Chicago Tribune*, Nov. 4, 1922, quoted in Carter, p. 20; Brisbane's view was printed in the *Seattle Post Intelligencer*, Oct. 31, 1922, quoted in Carter, p. 20.

[15] *San Francisco Chronicle*, Nov. 4, 1922; *Cleveland Plain Dealer*, Oct. 28, 1922, cited in Carter, p. 20.

anxiously pondered Il Duce's Caesarean ambitions. So unpleasant was the press commentary that Mussolini forbade Italian papers to discuss America's reaction to the occupation of the island. The international implications of Fascism always remained uppermost in the public mind, until finally the Abyssinian adventure caused Americans to turn against Mussolini.[16]

Until the Ethiopian War in 1935, however, Mussolini's popularity managed to survive a number of events that were either lamely criticized or deliberately overlooked by Americans. Often events in Italy occasioned sententious sermons by editors. The Acerbo electoral reform of 1923—which replaced proportional representation and thus weakened further the remnants of parliamentary government in Italy—led editors to comment on the value of representative governments; while Fascist censorship and the expulsion of newsman George Seldes provided an object lesson, readers were told, in the virtues of a free press. Yet few American papers objected to the lenient war debt settlement with Italy, and only a murmur of protest could be heard when the J. P. Morgan Company lent over one hundred million dollars to the Fascist government in 1926. The beginning of the "third phase" of the Fascist revolution—the announcement of the Corporate State in 1925—cause some perking of editorial ears. The *New York Times* endorsed corporate theory as a method of stealing thunder from the Left and of giving power to hitherto unrepresented social units. The *Times* even admitted that Mussolini's conception of power and authority "has many points in common with that of the men who inspired our own constitution —John Adams, Hamilton, and Washington. The uninformed will of 'the many' is to be 'balanced' by the experience and wisdom of 'the few.'" Yet the charm of corporatism soon wore thin. A month later, when the Fascist labor laws were announced, the *Times* issued an editorial on "Parliamentarism vs Liberty," attacking the Fascist claim that replacement of geographical for occupational representation would insure greater freedom and solidarity. As for Mussolini himself, his bellicose diplomatic utterances, such as his attack on the Locarno Pact, raised some concern in the press, but more often than not his harangues were dismissed as the innocuous braggadocio born of Italy's inferiority complex. Perhaps most revealing is the fact that the several attempts made

[16] *Independent*, CLX (Nov. 11, 1922), 255; *Washington Post*, Oct. 31, 1922; *NYT*, Nov. 29, 1923.

on Mussolini's life brought many papers to the brooding conclusion that if an assassin's bullet found the mark the nation would again revert to chaos and radicalism.[17]

The episode which caused the most revulsion in the twenties was the murder of Giacomo Matteotti (June 10, 1924), Socialist Deputy and outspoken critic of the regime. The press displayed a new-found concern for the implications of the Fascist cult of violence. *Current Opinion* believed that the *fascisti* were "outklanning" the Klan, while the *Literary Digest* reported rumors that the movement was on its last legs. Significantly, Il Duce was advised to rid his party of the ruffian and gangster elements like the *ras*—on whom most observers placed the blame—or risk being toppled. The *New York Times*, noting that "the Matteotti incident is of a kind that may kill a movement by depriving it at one stroke of its moral content," expressed hope that the surge of criticism would convince Mussolini to discard the doctrine of "salvation by force." When Mussolini made it clear he was not about to relinquish power, thereby encouraging the emergence of the anti-Fascist Aventine Opposition, the *Times* challenged the whole rationale of the regime, asserting that Fascism was simply perpetuating the very "antagonisms" it claimed to have eliminated.[18]

But Mussolini's ability to survive the Matteotti affair merely enhanced his image as a sagacious statesman. And when the dissension had subsided, and when stability was apparently restored and economic progress under way (so announced the Italian government), Il Duce commanded more respect and the picture of Italy again shone brightly. Still, several developments spoiled the view. For one thing, Mussolini's attempt to establish influence over the Italian-American population could not be tolerated by the American public, and when the Fascist League of North America was exposed in 1929, the press voiced strong disapproval and the State Department and Congress received scores of petitions demanding an investigation. Moreover, in the struggle between the Pope and Mussolini, the latter came in for considerable criticism. Although Mussolini initially drew applause for negotiating the Lateran Treaty and the Concordat of February 11,

17 *NYT*, Oct. 11, Dec. 12, 1925; Carter, pp. 378-79.
18 "Mussolini Reaps a Whirlwind," *Current Opinion*, LXXVII (Aug. 1924), 147-49; "Fascism's Fading Brilliance," *LD*, LXXXIII (Dec. 13, 1924), 21-22; *NYT*, June 18, 26, Nov. 12, Dec. 23, 1924.

1929, his subsequent clashes with the Vatican over control of Italian youth led Americans to wonder whether the Fascist educational program smacked of the same indoctrination methods as Soviet Russia's. Nor were Americans indifferent to some of the ugly incidents which occurred in Mussolini's Italy. In this connection two particular episodes of the early thirties deserve attention.[19]

MUSSOLINI WANTED FOR HIT AND RUN: THE TOSCANINI AND BUTLER AFFAIRS

In Bologna in 1931 Fascist hoodlums physically attacked the famous conductor Arturo Toscanini for refusing to play "Giovinezza," the new regime's national anthem. Shocked and angry, musicians in America immediately protested. Leopold Stokowski of the Philadelphia, Ossip Gabrilowitsch of the Detroit, and Sergei Koussevitsky (himself a victim of Russian oppression) of the Boston symphony orchestra were among the first to speak out in support of the maestro. The *New York Times* imagined that millions of Italians must be silently suffering the shame of this barbarous crime against culture. In one stroke the sinister consequences of the *fascistizzazione* of Italian culture were brought home to some Americans. Yet despite the outcry from intellectuals, the adverse publicity surrounding the Toscanini incident probably reached no further than America's small cultural enclaves. A far more arousing episode was the Smedley Butler affair.[20]

In January 1931 General Smedley Butler of the U.S. Marine Corps spoke at a private luncheon in Philadelphia. In the course of his talk he told the audience of a friend who accompanied Mussolini on an auto tour of Italy. During one of the rides, the car, traveling seventy miles an hour, struck a child, "grinding it to death under the wheels." Mussolini, according to Butler, ordered the driver not to stop, shouting "What is one life in the affairs of a State?"

The person in the car with Mussolini was Cornelius Vanderbilt. At the time Vanderbilt chose to remain silent about the in-

[19] "Mussolini's Orders to Italians Here," *LD*, LCVI (Feb. 26, 1928), 12; "Does Mussolini Rule Millions Here?" *LD*, CIII (Nov. 16, 1929), 14; Marcus Duffield, "Mussolini's American Empire," *Harper's*, CLIX (Nov. 1929), 661-72; "Fascism's Monopoly of the Child," *LD*, LCVII (Aug. 11, 1928), 28-29.
[20] *NYT*, May 31, June 4, 11, 12, 16, 1931.

cident and Butler would not divulge his name. But years later, during World War II when open season was declared on Mussolini's reputation, Vanderbilt recalled vividly the accident.

I heard a shriek and saw a group of children waving flags. I turned my head quickly. There was a shapeless little form lying on the road back of us.
"Look, Your Excellency," I shouted.
"Never look back, my friend. Always forward," he answered without turning his head, and we roared on into the night.[21]

When Butler's speech appeared in the national press, the Italian Foreign Office was enraged. The Italian Ambassador in Washington and the government in Rome demanded an explanation. Secretary of State Stimson quickly extended formal apologies. The incident did not end there, however. For Butler was ordered to appear before a courtmartial, an order that caused a storm of controversy in the Eastern press. Through newspaper editorials, letters to Congress, and various petitions and resolutions, an affronted public protested the trial. Many Americans believed that, regardless of Butler's accusation, the U.S. Government did not have to answer to Mussolini. But the *New York Times* deplored Butler's speech and approved of the action taken against him, and *Time* suggested that all Americans owed the dictator an apology. What made the event even more controversial was Butler's refusal to name the source of his information. *Time* quoted a letter from an unidentified source in Italy, printed in the anti-Fascist *Il Nuovo Mondo* (New York), which fixed the time and the place of the hit-and-run incident and named the two local police officers who, it was reported, recognized Il Duce in the car but who had since disappeared. Anti-Fascists pressed the case, attempting to gain hearings before the President and the Secretary of State. Their efforts were in vain, as were those of Senator Thomas Heflin (Dem-Ala), a leading public critic of Mussolini who demanded in Congress that Butler's charge be investigated before the trial was held. Then came the inevitable denial from Rome, with Mussolini personally cabling to the State Department that he had never taken an American on a motor trip or run over a human being—man, woman, or child.[22]

[21] *New York Post*, July 28, 1943.
[22] *NYT*, Jan. 27, 28, 29, 30, 31, 1931; *Time*, xvii (Feb. 16, 1931), 14 (Feb. 23, 1931), 4; *FRUS*, 1931, ii, 640-41.

Eventually the courtmartial of the American general was dropped. Butler, who later expressed regret for having embarrassed his government, was reinstated after a perfunctory reprimand. Although the government was less interested in establishing the truth than in maintaining amicable relations with the Mussolini regime, the entire episode cast a shadow over the dictator's heretofore almost immaculate image. A *Literary Digest* survey revealed the press to be divided. Many papers were in agreement that Butler's attacks on Mussolini and Fascism were out of order, but whether the general's accusations warranted a courtmartial was another matter. Some papers thought the trial appropriate, but others defended Butler; some decried the government's prosecution, while others even denounced the Italian dictator. In Washington newspapers the Butler case ranked first in public interest in the early spring of 1931, and these same papers reported that movie audiences applauded newsreel pictures of Butler while shouting derision at the appearance of Secretary Stimson and Mussolini on the screen. Helen Lombard, a close observer of the Washington press corps and of the social life of foreign diplomats in the capital, summed up the reaction years later: "The consensus was, that whether the report was true or not, the Fascist dictator was quite capable of such an act. Mussolini was like the woman of doubtful reputation who was accused of one more lover—it seemed academic to deny it. He was tried and convicted in the American press, not on the merits of the Butler case, but on the record of Fascismo."[23]

Miss Lombard's evaluation must be qualified. Writing her account of the affair during World War II, she, like so many others, tended to ascribe to Americans a prescient anti-Fascism that had no basis in fact. There can be no doubt that a good number of those who followed the case could believe Mussolini capable of such a deed. But whether this one "accident" was sufficient to discolor permanently Mussolini's popular image is highly doubtful. Moreover, contrary to what Miss Lombard asserted, Americans did not use the Butler issue to pass judgment "on the record of Fascismo." Rather than leading to a sustained critique of Mussolini and Fascism, the Butler affair, like so many isolated events in history, quickly passed from the public mind.

Admittedly much of the enthusiasm for Fascism had cooled by

[23] *LD,* cvii (Feb. 14, 1931), 7; *NYT,* Jan. 27, 1931; Helen Lombard, *Washington Waltz: Diplomatic People and Policies* (London, 1944), p. 207.

the end of the twenties as Americans became more aware of the unfulfilled promises of the regime. Nevertheless, in the early thirties the view of Mussolini's Italy was influenced considerably by two new factors: the world depression and the rise of the Third Reich. These sudden developments cast Mussolini in a new role as pioneering economist and peacekeeping diplomat. The spotlight may have dimmed a bit in 1933 when Franklin D. Roosevelt and Adolf Hitler moved to the center of the world stage, one with his genial verbosity, the other with his menacing tirades; but even from the sidelines Mussolini continued to play his role with superb showmanship.

MUSSOLINI: ECONOMIC AND DIPLOMATIC STATESMAN, 1930-1934

Sometime in the fall of 1929 the American people started to descend from the high promises of the American dream to the lower depths of the great depression. With faith in their economy shattered, some Americans found themselves looking to Europe for desperate alternatives. To the Left—some of the intelligentsia and the more radical labor unions—Stalin's Russia loomed as an answer to American capitalism and a program of hope for the world. But to the larger Right—the business community and the solid citizens—Mussolini's Italy appeared as a rational reproach to both the anarchy of capitalism and the tyranny of Communism. In contrast to Russia's apparent war on property, its atheism and classlessness, its subversive internationalism, and its destruction of "marriage, the home, the fireside, the family," Fascism seemed to stand for property and filial values, social mobility within a social order, and for God and country. To businessmen especially, Italy's corporatism displayed all the benefits of coherent national planning without the threat of wholesale collectivism.[24]

The Corporate State in the early thirties seemed a hive of smoking industry. While America floundered, Italy's progress in shipping, aviation, hydroelectric construction, and public works held out an attractive example of direct action and national planning. Compared to the ineptitude with which President Hoover approached the economic crisis, the Italian dictator appeared a paragon of action. Remarked *Fortune* in 1932: "In the world de-

[24] The tirade against Russia was made by Henry L. Meyers of Montana to the U.S. Senate, quoted in Peter G. Filene, *Americans and the Soviet Experiment, 1917-1933* (Cambridge, 1967), pp. 66-67.

pression, marked by governmental wandering and uncertainty, Mussolini remains direct. . . . He presents, too, the virtue of force and centralized government acting without conflict for the whole nation at once." Even liberals had become so disgusted with the decrepitude of congressional government that the anti-Fascist *Nation* could (perhaps in a fit of absentmindedness) print an article entitled "Wanted: A Mussolini."[25]

The Mussolini vogue waxed as the depression deepened. By 1933, according to the *Literary Digest*, attention in America and abroad began to look to "Italian Fascism as a Business Proposition." Meanwhile the entry of Roosevelt into the White House enabled Mussolini to pose as the gentle autocrat who was only doing for Italy what the American President was trying to do for the United States. Not only did Italian and Italian-American propagandists exploit these parallels, but liberal American economists discerned strong similarities between corporate theory and the underlying philosophy of the National Recovery Administration—not to mention Left-wing critics who were convinced that Roosevelt's middle-of-the-road approach would only result in Fascist reaction. At the same time Arnaldo Cortesi announced in the *New York Times* that in the Corporate State the Italians were creating "the greatest social experiment of modern times." To confused and anxious Americans, the only conclusion to be drawn was that Italy was weathering the depression better than other countries. As a result, admiration went out to the Italian statesman who, with the help of journalists Cortesi and McCormick, likened himself to the popular Roosevelt.[26]

While many Americans conceded that Mussolini did wonders for Italy, they remained skeptical of the ominous diplomatic implications of his regime. This unsettling matter was never completely absent from any discussion of Fascism during the twenties. Now and then a nervous chord was struck as the *Literary Digest* noted the alarm of the European press at Mussolini's explosive behavior, or as the *New York Times* detected an "increasing megalomania" in his speeches. Il Duce's intimations about revising the Versailles Treaty were equally disquieting. But it

[25] *Fortune*, v (May 1932), 37; Paul Y. Anderson, "Wanted: A Mussolini," *Nation*, cxxxv (July 6, 1932), 9-10.

[26] *LD*, cxvi (Dec. 9, 1933), 12; *NYT*, May 25, 1934. For further discussion of American opinion during the depression, see Chapter VII, pp. 162-66.

was his speech celebrating the Eighth Anniversary of the March on Rome that aroused greatest concern. Many editors viewed his jingoism as another example of the quixotic temper of the "bad boy of Europe" who was doing his utmost to exacerbate international relations. The Paris correspondent for the *New York Herald-Tribune* saw the speech as signaling an alliance with German and Austrian Fascists leading eventually to expansion eastward. Only a "generous interpretation," believed the *New York World*, could regard the anniversary address as mere propaganda to spur on the Italian masses. With much of the press critical, Cortesi of the *Times* felt compelled to assert the speech was "distinctly peaceful." Mussolini himself testified to the hostile reception of his speech when he hastened to correct it by making a radio broadcast to America on New Year's Day, 1931. Praising America's cultural achievements, he tried to reassure listeners by pledging Italy to a policy of peace and prosperity. Few Americans were impressed. One could no longer believe, the *Outlook and Independent* observed, a leader who preaches peace to foreigners while rattling sabers at home.[27]

The clatter of Italian sabers, however, sounded like a mere capriccio compared to the thunderous beat of goose steps across the Alps. More than anything else it was the rise of Hitler that helped soften the aggressive image that had grown up around Mussolini. Yet the immediate effect of Hitler on Mussolini's image was ambivalent. For although the major popular magazines initially approved of the early Nazi regime, Hitler himself was always regarded with grave suspicion. At first his appearance created the alarming impression in some circles that Der Feuhrer was Mussolini's diabolical disciple—an argument harped upon by Fascism's enemies both here and abroad. Il Duce tried to deny the damaging analogy. He reassured Italian-Americans that Italy did not depend upon Germany; told Anne O'Hare McCormick that Nazism was not an "off-shoot" of Fascism; informed American-Jewish leaders that under his regime Italian Jews enjoyed complete freedom and the respect of their countrymen; and insisted to Emil Ludwig that Italy had no "Jewish problem." It is extremely difficult to gauge the effectiveness of Mussolini's

---

[27] "Mussolini as the Menace of Europe," *LD*, LXXXIX (May 8, 1926), 19-20; *NYT*, May 29, June 1, 1927; "Mussolini Snaps His Teeth Again," *LD*, CVII (Nov. 15, 1930), 12-13; *NYT*, Jan. 2, 1931; *Outlook and Independent*, CLVIII (Jan. 14, 1931), 46.

strategy. To some Americans, the presence of a ranting, demonic dictator in Germany offered a frightening example of the excesses which Fascism could reach, as well as the possibility of a militant Fascist International. Thus although some observers were careful to distinguish between the comparatively mild and almost comical Italian dictatorship and the fanatical *Weltanschauung* of the Third Reich, the deadly parallel would not disappear. As one newsman put it, the two regimes were in many respects "political siamese twins." On the other hand, many Americans sympathetic to Mussolini's government, particularly Italian-Americans, Catholics, and conservatives, continued to point up the differences between the two dictatorships. One measure of Mussolini's success in separating himself and his regime from Hitler and Nazism may be seen in the fact that in 1933 American Jewish publishers selected him as one of the world's twelve "greatest Christian champions" of the Jews.[28]

Ultimately the growing menace of Nazism, far from discrediting Mussolini, enabled the Italian Premier to parade as the enlightened statesman who could counter Hitler's aggressive designs. In the period from 1933 to 1935 Mussolini was able to pose as the conciliator between Germany and France. During these years the most informed source of opinion, the *New York Times*, tended to dismiss lightly the old worries about Fascist militarism and came to regard Mussolini's Four-Power Pact suggestion as a sincere step to insure peace in Europe. Similarly, even the anti-Fascist *New Republic* was forced to admire Mussolini's shrewd statecraft in drawing Austria, Hungary, and Italy closer together in order to thwart the *Anschluss*. The spirit of the Stresa Front affected America as well as Europe, and when France and Italy announced an accord in the first weeks of 1935 observers everywhere outside of Germany breathed a sigh of relief. All in all, watchful Americans were confused by the contradictory machinations of Mussolini's diplomacy. He appeared an impetuous warmonger and a rational diplomat, a Nazi sympathizer and a foil

[28] *NYT*, June 5, April 16, Sept. 18, 1933, June 24, 1934; Ludwig, pp. 69-72. Those Americans willing to look could find much of the meaning of Nazism in *Mein Kampf*, with all its sadistic egoism and millenarian nationalism. By contrast, those Americans who read Mussolini's *My Autobiography* (1928) found only a clever public relations document prepared in part by the American Ambassador. For a brief discussion of America and the rise of Hitler, see Chapter XIII, pp. 314-17.

to Hitler, a blustering expansionist and a responsible arbitrator. Puzzled and anxious, most Americans hoped the positive qualities would prevail. As Gerald Johnson put it at the time of the Franco-Italian accord:

> The character of the Italian dictator manifests two sharply contrasting aspects. One aspect is that of a bombastic pseudo-Caesar who is forever reenacting the crossing of the Rubicon, without having quite made up his mind what to do after getting to the other side. The other aspect is of a man who at times seems to catch glimpses of the underlying realities of the European situation with a startling objectivity of vision rarely equaled by contemporary statesmen. Fortunately, this second aspect of Mussolini's character tends to be the dominant one at moments of imminent crisis.[29]

From this brief survey of opinion during the pre-Ethiopian period it seems clear that in spite of several embarrassing episodes Mussolini's reputation emerged almost untarnished. Yet so far we have only affirmed the observation of Ludwig and others on Mussolini's amazing popularity in America. To account for the phenomenon it is necessary, first of all, to spend some time on the very medium which enabled the dictator to command so much favorable attention: the American press.

[29] *NYT*, Aug. 23, 1933; *New Republic*, LXXVIII (March 28, 1934), 173-74; "What the Franco-Italian Accord Means," *LD*, CXIX (Jan. 12, 1935), 13; Gerald Johnson, "Will France and Italy Make Up?" *North American Review*, CCXXXIX (Jan. 1935), 52.

3.

American
Journalists and
Mussolini

THERE IS ONLY ONE THING IN
THE WORLD WORSE THAN
BEING TALKED ABOUT, AND
THAT IS NOT BEING TALKED
ABOUT.

Oscar Wilde, 1890

CENSORSHIP AND THE SELDES AFFAIR

In January 1923, the young journalist Ernest Hemingway covered the Lausanne Conference for the *Toronto Daily Star*. His first encounter with Mussolini left him distinctly unimpressed. Ushered into a room along with other journalists, Hemingway found the Premier so deeply absorbed in a book that he did not bother to look up. Curious, Hemingway "tiptoed over behind him to see what the book was he was reading with such avid interest. It was a French-English dictionary—held upside down."[1]

Unfortunately for American opinion, few reporters were as willing as Hemingway to peer behind the facade of Fascist power in order to register its lack of solidity and pretense. The American press treatment of Fascist Italy was marked by considerable obtuseness and even a shade of dishonor. A surprising number of writers succumbed to Fascist propaganda and a few actually prostituted themselves in the pay of the Italian government. There were, of course, impressive examples of critical detachment and honest courage, as with Mowrer and Percy Winner who, though vacillating, were willing to reexamine their notions about Fascism before the clichés hardened into unimpeachable dogmas. But, on the whole, the American people were poorly informed about the meaning of Italian events.

Some newsmen in Rome were compromised from the beginning. Several papers and wire services accepted the Italian gov-

[1] *Toronto Daily Star*, Jan. 27, 1923, quoted in *By-Line: Hemingway*, ed. William White (New York, 1967), p. 64.

42

ernment's offer of 5,000 words of free cable transmission per month. While it would be too much to call this a bribe, the privilege unquestionably placed correspondents in a delicate position. They could hardly doubt that its continuance bore some relation to the content of their dispatches. Thus, when George Seldes arrived in Rome he immediately had the free cable service cancelled. For this unauthorized act he was reprimanded by his boss, J. H. Hummel of the *Chicago Tribune*, who urged him to utilize the free transmission until such time as the Italian government should object to the content of the dispatches. The free cable, of course, does not explain the uncritical attitude of the American press. But the Italian government clearly expected favors in return for services rendered, and a good deal of secrecy surrounded the entire relationship. This was especially true of the Italian-American press which succumbed completely to the influence of the Mussolini regime. It was not until 1940 that the Italian Foreign Ministry ordered the cable service to *Il Progresso Italo-Americano* (New York) suspended in order to prevent the State Department from discovering the embarrassing arrangement.[2]

Of far greater influence upon American public opinion was the situation of the Italian press itself. In totalitarian Italy the press had become an instrument of the state. Accordingly, Article 1 of the Decree of February 20, 1928, provided for a Professional Roll of Journalists open only to those of "good moral and political standing." The Roll was maintained by the National Fascist Syndicate of Journalists, which in turn was controlled by the Ministry of Corporations. As a member of the syndicate, a journalist received free railway transportation and theater tickets, reductions in rent and other commodities, preferential housing in fashionable neighborhoods, tax benefits, and a host of other perquisites. The luxuries of the Syndicate could also tempt foreign correspondents since membership in the *Stampa Estera* assured international newsmen similar favors in return for good behavior. Unfortunately for some reporters, the comforts extended by the Fascist government made the mind as bland as the flesh was weak.[3]

[2] J. H. Hummel to George Seldes, April 22, 1925, SP.

[3] *Il Giornalismo italiano nel regime fascista* (Rome, 1928); Herman Finer, *Mussolini's Italy* (Universal Library edn., New York, 1965), p. 238; David Darrah, *Hail Caesar* (New York, 1936); Frank Rosengarten, *The Italian Anti-Fascist Press, 1919-1945* (Cleveland, 1968), pp. 3-30.

The issue of press control exploded with the Seldes affair. Covering Italy for the *Chicago Tribune*, George Seldes incurred the wrath of the Italian government for his stories on the Matteotti murder, which he smuggled out of the country in 1925. Italian officials were enraged when the details—especially the suspects' confessions implicating the government itself in the murder— appeared in several American dailies. Foreign Minister Dino Grandi notified the Embassy in Rome that because of Seldes' "tendenziose ed allarmistiche" dispatches he was persona non grata. Seldes himself wrote to Grandi, explaining to the statesman that "the American people are not satisfied with 'semi-official' statements" from the Italian government and that they "want to know what is going on abroad. . . . If you permit me to speak frankly, I will say that ever since the Italian censorship was announced the greatest alarm prevails in America and the greatest suspicion attaches to all news from Italy." Grandi chose not to reply to Seldes' plea for a free press.[4]

The plucky Seldes decided to circulate a petition for freedom of the press in Italy. In order to win the support of the Associated Press he wrote his publisher, Colonel Robert McCormick of the *Tribune*, informing him of both the censorship restrictions and of the role played by the Cortesi family. Salvatore Cortesi, a prominent Italian journalist and close friend of J. P. Morgan, represented the AP and Reuters in Rome, a position which made him the major news distributor for American and British correspondents alike. His son, Arnaldo, would soon become Rome correspondent for the *New York Times*. Both were avid supporters of the Fascist regime. Seldes understood from one of his associates, Beatrice Barkesville, that the Italian government had consulted the elder Cortesi ("the dean of the American press corps") before deciding whether to expel Seldes. According to Miss Barkesville, Cortesi assured Mussolini's advisors that no repercussions would arise in America as a result of the expulsion.[5]

Cortesi was correct. For McCormick, a powerful figure in American journalism and Director of the AP, chose not to interfere despite Seldes' disclosures. He instead sent to Rome another

[4] Seldes to Grandi, June 9, 1925, SP; George Seldes, "The Truth About Fascist Censorship," *Harper's*, CLV (Nov. 1927), 732-43; id., *Freedom of the Press* (New York, 1935), pp. 239-46.

[5] Barkesville to Seldes, Aug. 14, 1925; John S. Steele to Seldes, Aug. 12, 1925; Hiram Motherwell to Seldes, Aug. 13, 1925, SP.

correspondent in order to try to restore good relations. The failure of the AP to take a strong stand on the Seldes case dismayed several newsmen in Rome. Percy Winner, himself an AP correspondent, wrote to Seldes a few years later: "The important fact is that the AP backed up everything pro-Fascist of Salvatore Cortesi's to the hilt. . . . The AP in Europe crawls on its belly. The AP says as a basic maxim that the Government in power must be presumed to be right . . . AP must never run any chance of being kicked out of any important news center."[6]

Meanwhile Seldes also appealed to the American Ambassador in Rome, Henry P. Fletcher. Although Seldes believed that American newsmen in Rome regarded Fletcher as a "weak sister," the Ambassador, to his credit, earnestly defended the journalist. Called to the Embassy, Seldes informed Fletcher that the documents he possessed "proving the Duce guilty in the Matteotti murder were of both historical and front-page importance." Fletcher agreed to the value of the documents and arranged to have them sent to the United States through State Department channels. The Ambassador later tried to explain to Mussolini the desire of American journalists to be independent in their pursuit of truth and their sensitivity to censorship. He also appealed personally to Grandi to reconsider the case. Yet at no time was an official protest contemplated.[7]

In the meantime a group of anti-Fascist journalists in Rome— Winner of the AP, Barkesville of the *New York World*, Thomas Morgan of the United Press, Hiram Motherwell of the *Chicago Daily News*, and representatives of the *Philadelphia Ledger* and *Christian Science Monitor*—called upon Grandi in a final attempt to persuade him to rescind the expulsion order. With poker-faced poise, Grandi proceeded to tell his visitors that no censorship prevailed in Italy, that reporters were free to write as they pleased, and, what is more, that he had reconsidered and decided Seldes would be allowed to remain in Rome. Hearing the

[6] McCormick to Seldes, Aug. 26, 1927, SP; Winner to Seldes, Jan. 9, 1935 (quote in Seldes to author, June 27, 1966). Winner's charge was much too harsh. By no means did the AP "crawl" before the Fascist government. In fact, the Italian Ambassador in Washington suggested to Mussolini that Italy establish its own news service in order to circumvent the AP, which was proving neither cooperative nor "fair minded." De Martino to Mussolini, Feb. 3, 1926, IR 423.

[7] From an untitled manuscript on this affair, p. 5, SP; *NYT*, Dec. 5, 1926.

news, Seldes and his friends celebrated with a party in his apartment. But while the group toasted free journalism and sang ribald ditties about Grandi, there was a theatrical knock on the door. A Fascist secret service agent entered, asked for "Signor Giorgio Seldes," and announced: "You have twenty-four hours to leave the country."[8]

MUSSOLINI'S PROMOTERS—McCORMICK, HEARST, AND CHILD— AND SISSON AND THE ITALIAN PRESS SERVICE

Seldes' expulsion dramatized the curbs imposed on the foreign press in Italy. From then on, most correspondents were forced to operate within the bounds of censorship. With a really important news item a reporter might risk expulsion to get the story out of the country, either through codes, innuendoes, or some other prearranged scheme. But for the most part writers submitted to the tacit rules of the permissible; and it was this general accommodation which probably explained why news coming out of Italy was often less critical than editorials written about Fascism in the United States. It is impossible to say precisely how many journalists willingly acquiesced. The anti-Fascist historian Gaetano Salvemini observed in 1936 that "most of the foreign correspondents left in Italy today do not care a damn about what is happening to the Italian people," and that those who do not toe the line were "insulted, manhandled, or expelled." Perhaps Salvemini's judgment is a bit severe. Still, one cannot ignore the fact that a good many newsmen accepted the regimentation while allowing themselves to be wined and dined.[9]

Of all the blandishments Fascist officials could extend to visiting reporters, the most impressive was a personal interview with the Premier himself. A former journalist, Mussolini knew how to get the most *adulazione* out of a private interview, and he seldom failed to exploit to the fullest his eager audience. Hence most writers who enjoyed a private conference came away with an inflated ego and an enduring respect for the dictator. John Gunther described well the reporter's predicament:

Interviews, Mussolini knows, are the best of all possible forms of propaganda; thus he is so lavish with them. Most news-

[8] Seldes manuscript, pp. 7-8, SP.

[9] Gaetano Salvemini, "Foreign Correspondents in Italy," *New Republic*, LXXXVI (May 6, 1936), 369-70; Carter, pp. 379-80.

paper men—and their editors—cannot resist the flattery of conversation with a dictator or head of state; once they have been received by Mussolini or Hitler they feel a sense of obligation which warps their objectivity. It is very difficult for the average correspondent to write unfavorably about a busy and important man who has just donated him a friendly hour of conversation.[10]

The interview invariably sapped the reporter's objectivity and blunted the edge of his questions. The result was usually an innocuous inquiry which enabled Mussolini to retail patriotic generalities and boring clichés. "How can statesmanship and journalism best serve each other and humanity?" asked Edward Price Bell, one of a number of reporters taken in by Mussolini's punctuality and courteous attention. The cynical dictator must have been both amused and amazed by Bell's naiveté, and he replied: "By an aggressive and tireless assertion of mental and moral energy. By uttering only the truth. By fearing nothing but infidelity to the truth. By constant readiness to sacrifice themselves and their fellow men." The spectacle of a newsman allowing Mussolini to preach "fidelity to truth" while practicing censorship suggests how easy it was to fall under "the black magic" of the Fascist dictator.[11]

One reporter who fell under the spell not only of the dictator but of the country itself was Anne O'Hare McCormick. More than any other writer, she was a true Italophile and her journalism reflected the rhapsodic reactions noted earlier in connection with the American romantic image of Italy. With purple prose and wistful mood, she gave the *New York Times'* readers not so much an analysis of Fascism as a fantasy portrait of a resurrected Italy. What never failed to delight her was the national "élan" and "solidarity," as well as the general "hypnosis" of the Italians under Fascism. "You see here," she wrote a month before the outbreak of the Ethiopian War, "a remarkable manifestation—a nation moving in a kind of trance—enchanted into a conviction of invincible strength." When she interviewed Mussolini, she saw incarnated in him the ancient splendor of Rome, a revered statesman not intoxicated but mellowed by power. Neither domestic

10 John Gunther, "Mussolini," *Harper's*, CLXXII (Feb. 1936), 302.
11 Edward Price Bell, *Italy's Rebirth: Premier Mussolini Tells of Fascismo's Purpose* (reprint pamphlet, *Chicago Daily News*).

crisis nor diplomatic setback caused Miss McCormick to lose faith in the Fascist regime. For almost twenty years she carried on a political love affair with an idealized Italy and its noble leader.[12]

Though less enraptured, scores of other writers also found the Mussolini interview a moving experience. During the twenties the State Department and individual congressmen were plagued by requests from newsmen and travelers asking that an interview be arranged through the Ambassador in Rome. Occasionally the Department agreed, especially if the request came from an important figure; but more often the requests were turned down. One exasperated official exclaimed that "practically every American who goes to Italy wants an audience."[13]

The list of writers and publishers who met Mussolini reads like the directory of the "fourth estate." Walter Strong of the *Chicago Daily News*, Arthur Howe of the *Brooklyn Eagle*, William Abbott of the *Christian Science Monitor*, and William Randolph Hearst and Bradford Merrill of the Hearst chain were but a few of the journalists who took their turn waiting outside the Premier's office along with publicists like Otto Kahn, bankers like Thomas Lamont, clergymen like Cardinal O'Connell, writers like Lincoln Steffens, and politicians like Al Smith. Of all these figures, Hearst deserves special attention because of the powerful influence of his publications.

"Mussolini is a man," Hearst wrote in 1928, "I have always greatly admired, not only because of his astonishing ability, but because of his public service." Moved by his commanding presence, indefatigable vigor, and "enlightened administration," Hearst paid Mussolini a visit in 1931. The Italian Ministry of Popular Culture arranged an elaborate banquet for the occasion. The publishing titan was deeply impressed. "He is a marvelous man," Hearst later remarked in a letter to a friend. "It is astonishing how he takes care of every detail of his job." The admiration was mutual. Documents captured in Italy during World War II contain a press survey made by the Italian Ambassador in Washington during the period from 1928 to 1931. Of all the American papers, the Ambassador reported, "Il Gruppo Hearst" was "the most favorable to the regime." The Italian government has good reason to view with approval, for not only Hearst but

[12] *NYT*, Aug. 25, Sept. 17, 1935.
[13] State Department, 865.002/119, 129, quoted in Carter, p. 436.

his general manager, Colonel Frank Knox, stood literally in awe of Mussolini. In 1930 Knox tried to arrange a publicity stunt involving President Hoover and Premier Mussolini. Knox suggested to the White House press secretary that the President engage in a telephone conversation with Mussolini, the latter making his call to Washington from an airplane flying over Rome. State Department advisors were not sympathetic to the suggestion and reminded Knox that the dictator was "not even technically a Chief of State."[14]

Numerous other journalists beat the drums for the Fascist regime. When Ambassador Child resigned from his post in Rome he became an out-and-out propagandist. Possibly because the diplomat relied upon popular journalism as his sole source of livelihood, Child was quick to see the financial advantage in setting himself up as an unofficial publicity agent for Mussolini. His varied activities on behalf of the Fascist government bore all the finesse of Madison Avenue. Writing to Coolidge in 1929, he boasted to the ex-President how he "induced" Mussolini to write his "autobiography," and hinted broadly that much of the writing was his. With a shrewd instinct for a new media, Child also arranged with Will Hays of the Motion Picture Industry to do a film that would make it possible to "perpetuate a talking version of the personality of Mussolini."[15]

But Child had competition. In 1927 the Italian government organized a press service in the United States in an attempt to offset stories appearing in anti-Fascist publications. Mussolini was always keenly sensitive to shifts in American opinion. More than once he consulted with the American Ambassador on this matter, and the Italian Embassy in Washington employed a "newspaper clipping bureau" to compile all items in the American press about Italy. The press service, however, was not Mussolini's brainchild. It was suggested by Thomas W. Lamont and Martin Egan, head of the J. P. Morgan Company's press department. Negotiations

---

[14] Hearst to Watson, Nov. 28, 1928, IR 426; W. A. Swanburg, *Citizen Hearst* (Bantam edn., New York, 1965), p. 510; other papers appreciated by the Italian Embassy included the *Chicago Tribune, Philadelphia Ledger,* and *Christian Science Monitor,* IR 433; Frank Knox to George Akerson, June 5, 1930; William Castle to Akerson, July 10, 1930, Box 856, HP.

[15] Child to Coolidge, May 10, 1929, Box 111, CP; Child to Henry Fletcher, April 5, 1927, Container 13, FP. Child stressed the monetary rewards of his journalism in his various family letters, which comprise the bulk of his papers in the Library of Congress.

were carried out quietly among Lamont, Egan, Italian Finance Minister Giuseppe Volpi, Dino Grandi, and Mussolini himself. Edgar Sisson, former managing editor of *Collier's*, was hired to run the secret operation.[16]

Edgar Sisson was hardly a novice in manufacturing international news. During the First World War he had made a name for himself when he presented to the Creel Committee the notorious "Sisson Documents," which purported to show the Bolshevik Revolution as the work of the German Foreign Office and Lenin and Trotsky as "paid German agents." Sisson's familiarity with the art of inventive journalism made him an ideal candidate to head the Italian press service. With or without this knowledge, Volpi agreed to arrange a credit of $20,000 for the Ambassador in Washington—$5,000 to be used to open and equip an office, $15,000 for Sisson's salary. But shortly afterwards Sisson accepted in addition a position with a magazine. The Italian government disapproved of this moonlighting and, upon Sisson's resignation, the funds for the press service were turned over to the Italy-American Society. With Lamont as treasurer, this organization proceeded to uphold the cause of Fascism by publishing the *Italy-America Monthly*.[17]

LIPPMANN AND THE *New York World*, AND MUSSOLINI AND THE WASHINGTON PRESS CLUB

To have the support of important organs of opinion like the *Saturday Evening Post* and the Hearst publications was not enough for the thin-skinned Mussolini. One important critic he was most desirous of having in his camp was the eminent Walter Lippmann. As editor of the *New York World*, Lippmann had published articles by some of the most trenchant critics of the Fascist regime. Upset by these articles and by Lippmann's own editorials, Italian officials attempted to turn Lippmann back from what they called his "relapse into anti-Fascism." Mussolini himself sent Lippmann an autographed photo on which he complimented his "wisdom." Although the Italian Ambassador informed Mussolini that it would be difficult to get Lippmann to alter his

[16] The press service was designed to counter the "Paris falsehoods" published by anti-Fascist exiles in France. IR 423, 011884-012024; Lombard, p. 148.

[17] IR 423, 011884-012024; the "Sisson Documents" are discussed in Filene, pp. 47-48.

views, Lamont, Egan, and the Italy-American Society did all they could to win over the editor. When it was rumored in 1926 that Lippmann was to sail for Europe, Lamont wrote to Ambassador Fletcher in Rome suggesting it would be enlightening for Lippmann to establish "first hand contact with them [the Fascists] and their ideas." Lamont later told the Italian Ambassador that "Lippmann is an open-minded man, and I'm anxious to have him gain as accurate an impression as possible of present-day Italy."[18]

Lamont was convinced that if Lippmann were to travel through Italy and interview the Premier he would see the constructive side of Fascism. It is regrettable that Lippmann did not engage Mussolini in a dialogue. During the twenties Lippmann moved from a pessimistic view of political man (*Public Opinion*, 1922), to a humanistic concern for social ethics (*A Preface To Morals*, 1929), a philosophic transition that signified a reassertion of the viability of liberal rationalism. Moreover, it is difficult to imagine Lippmann, with his indifference to flamboyant personalities and his contempt for banal rhetoric, in any danger of falling under Mussolini's spell. The penetrating questions Lippmann intended to put to Mussolini (through the *World's* correspondent Edward Corsi) suggest that, contrary to Lamont's hopes, the newsman would have remained a tenacious critic of the regime.[19]

[18] Letter (author undecipherable) to Mussolini, Aug. 10, 1929, IR 432; the handwritten inscriptions on the Mussolini photo were copied for me by Frederick Schapsmeier from the Lippmann Papers, Yale University Library; Lamont to Fletcher, March 19, 1926, FP; Lamont to De Martino, Jan. 23, 1929, IR 432.

[19] Three samples of the numerous questions drawn up for Mussolini should suffice:

"1. The *New York World* is inclined to believe that Fascism is absolutely dependent on . . . Duce and that it cannot survive without his leadership. The question most frequently asked by all Americans is: 'After Mussolini, What?' Will his Excellency be so kind as to explain what, in his opinion, will happen to Italy and Fascism after he is gone?

"2. The *New York World* believes that a dictatorial form of government . . . is not [as] effective and enduring as a democratic government which governs from the bottom up. In other words government not directly responsible to the people lacks stability and permanence. Why wouldn't the Italian people be better off if they were allowed to govern themselves directly, by democratic methods?

"3. If, as the Premier and his supporters often claim, public opinion in Italy is Fascist and solidly back of the regime why is the opposition

The *New York World's* stance reflected a steadfast commitment to democratic liberalism which neither Fascist propaganda nor Mussolini's charm could crack. Nor could Il Duce worm his way into the journalism guild itself. Despite the wide support he enjoyed in daily newspapers and weekly magazines, a substantial number of writers (exactly how many is impossible to say) resented his control of the press. Italian officials were aware of the resentment within America's press establishment. In 1927, for example, the journalist Charles H. Sherrill invited Ambassador De Martino to a luncheon where he could meet influential newsmen and thereby correct the "dreadful misunderstanding so prevalent in this country" about Mussolini. Two years later a Hollywood publicity man, responding to a suggestion made by Il Duce himself, proposed the dictator's name for membership in the National Press Club in Washington. The Press Club would have provided an excellent forum for Mussolini, a former journalist himself. But a handful of anti-Fascist writers, led by Charles G. Ross and supported by Marquis Childs and Drew Pearson, succeeded in persuading the Club's governing board to reject the proposal. To the chagrin of the Italian government, Mussolini earned the odious distinction of being blackballed from the National Press Club.[20]

Thus, Mussolini enjoyed a favorable press while earning the contempt of a number of reporters. This situation is not so strange if we keep in mind that many writers who scorned Il Duce were reacting to the dictator's press regulations rather than leveling an indictment against his entire regime. In 1925 the Foreign Press Association roundly denounced Italy's censorship policies, and four years later when Ross spoke against Mussolini's membership in the Press Club he drew attention to the fate of Luigi Albertini and the *Corriere della Sera*. To say journalists were single-minded about freedom of the press is not to imply that

suppressed? Would it not be in the interest of the country to have a free expression of ideas, even if these ideas be in opposition to the progress of the Regime?"

Edward Corsi to Count Torre, n.d., IR 432, 016781-016878.

[20] Sherrill to De Martino, March 18, 1927, IR 423; Lombard, pp. 148-49; Seldes to author, June 7, 1966; Ronald T. Farrar, "Il Duce and the National Press Club: How He Almost Made It," *Journalism Quarterly*, XLIV (Autumn 1967), 556-57.

they were politically blind on other issues; it is simply to suggest that Italy's obnoxious press censorship did not necessarily cause American reporters to condemn the entire regime.[21]

"DANGEROUS STUFF": PUBLISHING *Sawdust Caesar*

But one writer who protested Mussolini's censorship and went on to condemn Fascism itself was George Seldes. Seldes' *Sawdust Caesar* bitterly depicted Fascism as an inchoate movement in search of a program and Mussolini as an opportunist in search of an image. With the possible exception of Carleton Beals' *Rome or Death: The Story of Fascism* (1923)—based upon a series of *Nation* articles on the Blackshirts' march to power—*Sawdust Caesar* was the first major exposé of Mussolini's Italy by an American journalist. Perhaps more revealing than Seldes' impressionistic narrative are the difficulties he encountered in trying to publish his book.

Shortly after Seldes was expelled from Italy he began writing his scathing biography of Mussolini; he retreated to the Vermont woods where he talked over the problem of Fascism with his neighbor Sinclair Lewis (who later used some of Seldes' information in *It Can't Happen Here*). The manuscript was completed in 1932 and Seldes started negotiating with his London literary agent, A. M. Heath & Company, Ltd. The first rejection, by a British publisher, augured ill:

> The reason was entirely one of policy. The criticisms of Mussolini are of such a personal and slashing character that the Board were of the opinion that the work might get its publisher into trouble, either on the score of libel or through the foreigners.
>
> Assuming the author's information to be correct, it is a re-

[21] *NYT*, March 15, 1925. Thomas Morgan and Percy Winner, for example, rose to Seldes' defense when he was expelled from Italy. Yet both were admirers of Mussolini and his regime. Winner in particular was one of several wavering Fascist sympathizers in the press corps. He appeared to be on close terms with Mussolini in the early years, and as late as 1929 he argued the case for Fascism in debates with exile Gaetano Salvemini. All along, however, he was capable of writing an occasional critique and by the early thirties he had become a steady critic. See his "Mussolini—A Character Study," *Current History*, xxviii (July 1928), 517-27; for the Salvemini debate, *NYT*, May 27, 1929.

53

markable piece of work, but frankly we are afraid of it, and we are therefore returning the MS to you herewith.[22]

The agent tried another publisher, but again Seldes was informed that the editors "have suddenly got cold feet over *Sawdust Caesar*. Apparently they have been talking to people at the Foreign Office who say that while there is very little chance for the F. O. stopping publication of such a book there is just the possibility. . . . A well-known publicist has read the book and advised them that he thinks it is dangerous stuff." Failing here, the agency recommended still a third publisher, who at first welcomed the manuscript and personally informed Seldes that the anticipated "libels do not amount to a row of beans as I do not think anybody will ever bring them." But the publisher also added that first he would "like to know the official attitude to this book before going ahead and I am therefore sending it quite quietly to a certain government department for their opinion." Two months later the publisher notified Seldes that he "had a chit from the authorities here saying that, at the moment, it would be unwise to publish *Sawdust Caesar*. The trouble is that our friend Musso is a bit of a king just now and I don't think that a back-stage view of him would be sympathetically received, either by the authorities or the public." Seldes was advised to sit tight on the manuscript and "fish it out at the right time," for "unless we are doomed to a terrible future under men of his breed, he must have a set back fairly soon."[23]

Seldes' manuscript fared no better in the United States. A leading American publisher, who was also a good friend of Seldes, wrote to him in December 1932:

> The first Editorial Meeting I held after my return from Europe was devoted, in large part, to *Sawdust Caesar*. You have done a brave and brilliant and fascinating piece of work, and I wish like everything that we could publish it; but after the most protracted deliberation, the final decision is a hairbreadth negative. This is partly because of the threat of bombings and stilettos, but not entirely for this reason.
>
> We carefully analyzed the sales record on most of these

[22] John Ball (of Charman & Hall, Ltd.) to A. M. Heath & Company, Ltd., May 27, 1932, SP.

[23] Patience Ross (of A. M. Heath & Company) to Seldes, Oct. 21, 1932; Arthur Barker to Seldes, Jan. 24, 1933, March 28, 1933, SP.

Mussolini books and although we recognize that yours is better than the others, we feel the sledding would be just too tough. Terribly sorry.[24]

This diffidence on the part of both British and American publishers forced Seldes to shelve his manuscript for the duration of Mussolini's éclat. The book was finally published by Harper Brothers in 1936. By then, however, the Ethiopian War had burst the bubble of Il Duce's reputation. As a naked aggressor, the celebrated dictator now made an easy target for correspondents and cartoonists who were quick to puncture with satire what they once dignified with scissors and paste.

MUSSOLINI: THE "HUMAN PSEUDO-EVENT"

That the press could tear Mussolini's image to rags after Ethiopia indicates that by and large the dictator's prestige was a phenomenon of the American press. Either consciously or unwittingly, American writers "made" Mussolini by the steady glare of publicity, and they made him simply because he made news. Il Duce was the consummate news maker. More precisely, reporters made him a "pseudo-event," to borrow Daniel Boorstin's illuminating concept. The term suggests a news event that is deliberately arranged to impress the public mind. At the least, it means "managing" the news; at the most, "milking" it for all it is worth.[25]

Mussolini, of course, was not a passive partner in the creation of his public image. Emerson, in his study of the great man in history, observed that it was "the delight of vulgar talent to dazzle and blind the beholder." No one could deny that Mussolini was a master of the "vulgar talent" of showmanship and propaganda. Indeed Mussolini displayed all the typical traits of what Barzini calls the "Cagliostro" side of the Italian character. The Italian's penchant for "polite lies" and clever flattery—too calculated to be obsequious and spontaneous enough to seem almost transparent—played beautifully into the hands of news hungry reporters and their readers. Mussolini's skillful guile, his incessant arranging for effects, his flair for self-dramatization and the proper role, in a word, his virtuosity, were more than any news-

[24] Lincoln Schuster to Seldes, Dec. 9, 1932, SP.
[25] Daniel Boorstin, *The Image: A Guide to Pseudo-Events in America* (Harper Colophon edn., New York, 1964).

man could ask for. Thus when Mussolini wrestled with a lion cub, when he stripped to the waist to harvest wheat amid bemused peasants, when he dispatched a squadron of planes to fly to Chicago, when he donned tie and tails and played his violin, when he christened ships and presided over parades celebrating the March on Rome, or when he frolicked with his children and rode his horse, he was in effect producing ready-made news for American newsmen. It is not surprising that Americans were less interested in what was important than what was contrived, less interested in Mussolini as a complex statesman than as a many-sided personality, less interested in Fascism as a system than as a spectacle. What is curious is that in this behavior the American and Italian character complemented each other superbly. Mussolini, with his typically Italian Cagliostro complex, staged the play; Americans, with their desire for the novel and adventurous, absorbed the performance. Both actor and spectator were more interested in the show than in the substance.[26]

Mussolini's theatrical instincts seldom failed him in his relations with uncritical journalists. He knew all the tricks: the news "leak," the press conference, the bulletin release, and, of course, the interview. Not only did some journalists lose all sense of critical repartee in the interview but they allowed Mussolini to use it as part of his political song and dance. The United Press, for instance, took it upon itself to forward to Herbert Hoover an "Exclusive Interview" conducted by Thomas B. Morgan. Here Il Duce lavishly praised America's "original civilization" whose strenuous work ethic had contributed to the world "mechanical and material" achievements which arose from a "magnificent . . . spiritual activity." "When I say this," the dictator emphasized, "I am thinking of William James, of Emerson, of Longfellow, Mark Twain, and the great magician of the magnetic world, Edison. It is my conviction that you will give the world an art,

[26] Barzini, esp. Chap. V. Although Barzini and Boorstin deal solely with their own cultures, the tendency of Italians and Americans to prefer the illusions of *garbo* and the shadows of "style" is striking. In the Italians' fondness for the "show" and in the Americans' hunger for the "pseudo-event" there is a common trait; and in both national characters it is the outward appearance of behavior and the symbolic value of events that matters. If Dale Carnegie's *How to Win Friends and Influence People* is America's pedestrian footnote to Baldassar Castiglione's *The Book of the Courtier* (1528), Mussolini may be described as America's first "other-directed" dictator.

a poetry and a philosophy of your own." Genuinely curious Americans, who read such a saccharine *pasticcio* to learn about Fascism, found only an echo of their own ethos.[27]

Even critical journalists who were denied a private interview tended to give Mussolini a great deal of attention. Ironically, in their preoccupation with this newsworthy commodity, critics aided Mussolini's political fortunes by perpetuating his notoriety. But whether critic or promoter, American journalists were not solely to blame for this fatuousness. The reporters who gave readers the "soft" news were no more irresponsible than the publishers who realized that the sales of anti-Fascist books would be "tough sledding." The press gives the public what it wants, and Mussolini was an irresistible "human pseudo-event" who captivated Americans simply because so much interest had been generated about him. This may seem an unsatisfactory explanation, but no amount of reasoning can explain why the public craves the adventurous—"the news behind the news." Thus, in introducing a series of articles on Mussolini by Ida Tarbell, the editor of *McCall's* could exclaim that Il Duce was "the most enigmatic of living men" and that in Italy the reader will find "the greatest story in the world today." With such a buildup, it was difficult for the American public to discriminate between a love affair with Mussolini and the collapse of Italian liberty.[28]

27 William J. Lash to Secretary Hoover, Dec. 23, 1925, Box 175, HP.
28 *McCall's*, LIV (Nov. 1926), 5.

4.

Mussolini as American Hero

WHEN CHAOS HAS PENETRATED
SO FAR INTO THE MORAL
BEING OF NATIONS THEY CAN
HARDLY BE EXPECTED TO
PRODUCE GREAT MEN. A GREAT
MAN NEED NOT BE VIRTUOUS,
NOR HIS OPINIONS RIGHT, BUT
HE MUST HAVE A FIRM MIND,
A DISTINCTIVE, LUMINOUS
CHARACTER; IF HE IS TO
DOMINATE THINGS, SOMETHING
MUST BE DOMINANT IN HIM.
WE FEEL HIM TO BE GREAT
IN THAT HE CLARIFIES AND
BRINGS TO EXPRESSION SOME-
THING WHICH WAS POTENTIAL
IN THE REST OF US, BUT WHICH
WITH OUR BURDEN OF FLESH
AND CIRCUMSTANCE WE WERE
TOO TORPID TO UTTER.

George Santayana, 1913

THE IMAGES OF MUSSOLINI

To conclude a study of the Mussolini vogue by maintaining that in America he was nothing more than a press-manufactured celebrity is only half the story. Dismissing him as the product of a news-hungry media and a public given to dramatic "pseudo-events" ignores two salient facts: that neither publicity nor propaganda can by itself create a popular "symbolic hero," and that Mussolini enjoyed the acclaim of many prominent contemporaries who were uninfluenced by the press. It would be tedious to quote here the lavish accolades heaped upon him by such astute admirers as Winston Churchill and George Bernard Shaw. Perhaps

58

it suffices to mention that Mussolini was deemed worthy of a book by Emil Ludwig, author of studies on Napoleon, Lincoln, Bismarck, Frederick the Great, Masaryk, Freud, Wagner, Goethe, Byron, Wilson, Stalin, and Franklin Roosevelt. Whatever Mussolini's reputation is today, from the time of the March on Rome to the beginning of the Ethiopian War he was an esteemed figure. Americans in particular saw in Mussolini certain enduring qualities which enabled him to qualify as a "great man" not only of his time but of the ages. Many of the images with which he was depicted in the press were of an heroic character, and the qualities projected by those images were distinctly peculiar to the American value system.[1]

Mussolini's dominant image was, of course, that of the redeemer. He and his men represented all that was healthy and redemptive in Italian life. Fascism was the righteous answer of the responsible middle class to the treachery of Communism. As such, Mussolini readily appealed to anxious Americans as a new leader who reaffirmed the old solid values and virtues: "duty," "obedience," "loyalty," and "patriotism." Reinforcing this conservative political conceptualization was the theme of spiritual savior. Il Duce was the wise and mature leader who discarded the foolish atheism of his youth and rescued his country from the malaise of materialism. Thus one writer likened his March on Rome to Christ driving the money changers out of the temple, another apologist spoke of the "monkish ascetism" of the Blackshirts, and Catholic writers sang hosannas to the convert who returned the crucifix to the classroom. Where history ended and hagiography began only the discerning could say.[2]

Mussolini's personal appeal can be explained by numerous other images. In 1926 the *Washington Post*, no great supporter of Fascism, stated the case in simple terms. "Mussolini's dictatorship evidently appeals to the Italian people. They needed a leader, and having found him they gladly confer power upon him. If he continues his policy of 'order, discipline and work,' while avoiding imperialistic adventures, Italy doubtless will find full and profitable employment within its proper field." The slogan "order, discipline and work" was repeated again and

[1] Orin Klapp, *Symbolic Leaders: Public Dramas and Public Men* (Chicago, 1964), pp. 55-56.

[2] *NYT*, Dec. 27, 1925; Roberts, "Salvage of a Nation," p. 132. For Catholic opinion see Chapter VIII, pp. 182-97.

again, not merely because it redounded to the honor of America's Protestant ethic but also because Mussolini's career symbolized these virtues. In the American mind Mussolini was nothing less than the self-made man. Benito Mussolini was "the son of a blacksmith," readers were reminded repeatedly. The Italian statesman, said Otto Kahn, was "a great man, beloved and revered in his country and much misunderstood abroad, a self-made man, if there ever was one, setting out with nothing but the force of his brain and the character and ardor of his patriotism." The drama of the success story has always had special appeal in America; Italy's Horatio Alger was no exception.[3]

Still another image was that of the "pragmatic" statesman. Il Duce was the "practical" leader who rejected the unusable democratic dogmas of the past and the unworkable moral principles of the present. Ironically it was this "realistic, pragmatic temper" that appealed to conservatives and liberals alike, to nativist reactionaries like Lothrop Stoddard and to cosmopolitan progressives like Lincoln Steffens. Indeed the conservative *Commerce and Finance* and the liberal *New Republic* could justify Fascism on the same grounds—that Mussolini gets things done and that Fascism works and works well. Seeing in modernization a source of political liberation and moral uplift, conservative businessmen and not a few liberal intellectuals admired the rationalization of Italy's economy under Fascism. Here the intellectual's critique of parliamentary government was matched by the businessman's cult of efficiency. Business editor Merle Thorpe regretfully summed up the fascination of the latter:

> I can understand why a businessman would admire Mussolini and his methods. They are essentially those of successful business. Executive actions, not conferences and talk. Mistakes, yes, but action. . . . The business executive despises the tortuous ways of government. The impression you get of him is that he is a fine type of business executive. He cuts through. No idle words. Not too few, not too many, just enough. Quietly spoken, but leaving no doubt in anyone's mind that he carried a big stick. . . . Accomplishment! Not fine-spoken theories; not plans; not speeches he is going to make. Things done! And this is your successful American executive.[4]

[3] *Washington Post*, Aug. 18, 1926; *NYT*, Nov. 16, 1923.
[4] *Nation's Business*, xv (Dec. 1927), 20-22.

In an age hungry for heroes, Mussolini was also written up as a hero of sport. Because of his daring feats and bold adventures he could gratify the vicarious need for excitement, and journalists did not hesitate to place him besides aviators like Lindbergh, actors like Barrymore, and athletes like Dempsey. Writers may have contradicted one another in describing his quixotic temperament, but one characteristic that stood out was his blinding quickness of body and mind. As John Gunther observed: "Mussolini is built like a steel spring (Stalin is a rock of granite, by comparison, and Hitler a blob of ectoplasm)." Clarance Streit summed up the essence of Il Duce in one word—"Punch." "There is punch in his eyes, the darting thrust of a rapier. There is punch in the light, springing step with which he carries his well-built body—the punch of a pugilist." Translated into politics, these qualities were reflected in Il Duce's instinct for "direct action." "Direct action is intelligible in any language," declared Anne O'Hare McCormick. "A nation that thrilled to the Vigilantes and the Rough Riders rises to Mussolini and his Black Shirt army." This activistic ideal became pervasive (despite disclaimers by anti-Fascists like Angelica Balabanoff, who wrote of his timidity and indecisiveness), and Mussolini's much publicized March on Rome, however distorted, contrasted nicely with the allegedly pusillanimous parliament he swiftly threw out.[5]

As the man of action Mussolini also became a masculine hero of both muscle and mind. Accordingly, apologists characterized him as courageous, resolute, and bold and the opposition as weak, feeble, and decadent. Ambassador Child used such phrases as "sickly liberalism" and "sentimental jelly" to contrast the Roman manliness of Mussolini with the fuzzy femininity of Giovanni Giolitti, that "nice, easy, benevolent weakling." Similarly Kenneth Roberts, while extolling the Spartan austerity of the *fascisti*, called Italian liberals "starry-eyed," "pampered," "mental perverts," a clever juxtaposition of imagery that made Mussolini seem all the more masterful. Much was also made of the dictator's mental prowess. He has "a luminous and powerful intellect [which] is his genius," exclaimed Edward Price Bell. Alice Rohe stressed his self-educated wisdom; others marveled at his multilingual abilities. Thus in 1936 John Gunther could sincerely conclude that Mussolini was "the only modern ruler who can gen-

---

[5] John Gunther, *Inside Europe* (New York, 1938), p. 194; *New York Evening Post*, Nov. 22, 1922; *NYT*, July 15, 1923.

uinely be termed an intellectual." But Mussolini was a unique intellectual. He was not a tender, "word-froth" ideologue, as one writer in the *Wall Street Journal* put it, but a tough, direct luminary who pierced the soft crust of sentiment. He was a practical thinker who, as Giovanni Gentile pointed out to Americans, scorned the "literato" (man of ideas). A masculine mind unfettered by the cobwebs of pure thought, Mussolini was, in essence, an anti-intellectual intellectual.[6]

The masculine temperament brings us to yet another image: the great lover. Perhaps one of the more curious responses to Mussolini was the manner in which so many women reporters were taken in by the swashbuckling glamor of the Italian dictator. It is, at first glance, rather ironical that women would respond to a man who had contempt (albeit political, not physical) for the female sex. As he candidly told Emil Ludwig, women must always be the underlings, lest their trivial hearts of milk unman the will to power and produce a "matriarchy." Yet the Italian maestro was shrewd enough to wear a different mask when confronting the opposite sex. In 1923, whether by coincidence or design, the International Suffrage Alliance convened in Rome. Mussolini's hypocritical support for the feminist cause did much to endear the "amazons of the press" to his regime. His appearance at the convention hall was described rapturously ("graceful, extremely quick . . . great charm and radiance") by the novelist Frances Parkinson Keyes, who was brought to tears of joy upon his entrance. When he told the convention that he would grant the vote to Italian women (within a short time he was to make Italy's franchise worthless) the audience was ecstatic. Fascist supporters made much of the rising status of women in Italy, and Italian officials made life easier for women journalists, all of which paid handsome news dividends. Women reporters, of course, generally concentrated on Mussolini's personality and physical features, and those who met him personally showed a tendency to melt under his charm. "I was entirely disarmed by his personality," said the wife of one correspondent. "Expecting to meet a cold, dispassionate, overbearing person, I was arrested by a certain wistful quality in his expression—the expression of

[6] Child, "The Making of Mussolini," pp. 3-4; Roberts, "The Ambush of Italy," pp. 67, 34-38; Bell, *Italy's Rebirth*, p. 5; Gunther, *Inside Europe*, p. 197; *Wall Street Journal*, Jan. 23, 1923; Giovanni Gentile, "The Philosophical Basis of Fascism," *Foreign Affairs*, vi (Jan. 1928), 300.

a man who is very human." The Byronic magnetism of Mussolini was as irresistible as the pageantry of the marching *fascisti*. The response of Ida Tarbell, who called Mussolini "a despot with a dimple" and described how he "kissed my hand in the gallant Italian fashion," was typical of the many female writers who were graced by a personal interview with the Blackshirt Valentino. Perhaps Alice Rohe had the last word when one of his sex scandals made the papers: "Il Duce knows how to get what he wants from women, whether it is a grand passion or a grand propaganda."[7]

Mussolini's amorous escapades titillated the generation of the 1920s, weaned, as it was, on Freud and gin. But Americans eventually got around to discussing the historic significance of the "new Italy," and when they did these discussions invariably compared Mussolini with other "great men" who shaped the course of history. Comparisons abounded. Caesar, Napoleon, Cromwell, Bismarck, and, of course, Garibaldi were but a few of the names cited. Significantly, one of the most frequent references was to Theodore Roosevelt (which recalls to mind Henry Adams' remark that Roosevelt was "pure act"). Journalists saw the similarity and were eager to emphasize it. Irving S. Cobb, for example, reported a conversation with Il Duce as follows:

> "Do you know, your excellency, what a great many Americans call you? They call you the Italian Roosevelt."
>
> By this he was obviously gratified.
>
> "For that," he said, "I am very glad and proud. Roosevelt I greatly admired." He clenched his fists. "Roosevelt had strength—had the will to do what he thought should be done. He had greatness."[8]

As the above dialogue indicates, Il Duce could readily be treated as the man of sheer will power. Benito's career, the editor of *McCall's* stated excitedly, was the spectacular story of "the strong man of Italy who has . . . bent a nation to his will." And

[7] Ludwig, pp. 170-71; *Good Housekeeping*, LXXVII (Aug. 1923), 35; *NYT*, May 15, 1923, July 27, 1928; Irene di Robilant, "The Role of Woman Under Fascism," *Survey*, LVII (March 1, 1927), 708; Tarbell, pp. 380-84; Marjorie Sheeler, "Mussolini at Close Range," *Review of Reviews*, LXVIII (Oct. 1923), 395-97; Rohe is quoted in "Mussolini, Lady Killer," *LD*, CXXIV (July 31, 1937), 37.

[8] Irving S. Cobb, "A Big Little Man," *Cosmopolitan*, LXXXII (Jan. 1927), 145-46.

the *élan vital* of Mussolini's individual will could animate the collective will of the Italians themselves. For this "new Columbus," a writer in the *Wall Street Journal* declared, transformed a "languorous Italy" into a "New World of will and work." It is not surprising that American admirers saw Mussolini as a hero of iron will, for the notion that individual success and failure is simply a matter of resolution and character is a cherished homily rooted deep in American history and in the American value system.[9]

THE AMBIGUITIES OF HERO WORSHIP

The simple description of a dictator who controlled events solely by bringing to bear the impulsive force of his will is antithetical to the whole meaning of democracy. If carried too far, such a disturbing picture would leave the impression that Mussolini was an insensitive despot who assumed infallibility and acted with total disregard for popular feelings. Could Americans respond favorably to such a chilling image? In his study of American hero worship the historian Dixon Wector gave a negative answer: "The sort of man whom Americans admire, trust, and are willing to follow . . . must be self-respecting, decent, honorable, with a sense of fair play; no Machiavelli nor Mussolini need apply." Professor Wector may have shut the door too hastily on Mussolini as a popular hero.[10]

In the first place, it is questionable that Americans admire leaders only because of genteel virtues like honesty and fair play. The unpleasant truth is, as the sociologist Orin Klapp has observed, that "Americans are not squeamish about accepting some pretty tough customers as heroes." Americans have been fascinated by unsavory creatures: Western bad men with their pornoviolent gun play; "self-made men" of the underworld like Arnold Rothstein and Al Capone; and the ruthless captain of industry, Veblen's "pecuniary personage," who stands as the symbol of the "civic virtues . . . in democratic America." Foreign dictators, too, are not beyond the pale of American esteem. In 1959, for example, the Gallup poll discovered that the American image of Khrushchev was not that of a cruel tyrant but of a hard-driving executive; few Americans, it was found, objected to his autocratic powers, while many showed a begrudging respect for the Premier as a "shrewd businessman" and a "pretty hard egg." This demo-

[9] *McCall's*, LIV (Dec. 1926), 16; *Wall Street Journal*, Jan. 23, 1923.
[10] Dixon Wector, *The Hero in America* (New York, 1941), p. 482.

cratic paganism may have reached its sublimest expression in 1964 when the *San Francisco Chronicle*, marveling at Nikita's peasant-to-Premier success story, exclaimed: "Many Americans have admitted their preference for a viable Khrushchev, and we are among them, having always believed that had fate guided his life otherwise, it might easily have led such a man to the presidency of General Motors or even of Harvard."[11]

The point is Americans as a whole are not indifferent to the dramatic appeal of foreign dictators. Americans admire the two-fisted statesman as much as the rugged individualist. Prince Ludovico Potenziani, the Governor of Rome, noted this when he remarked in 1928: "Mussolini's character and personality carry a strange fascination to Americans. . . . It is my opinion that whatever Italy might ask today of American financiers would be conceded without question, for Americans like strong people." This "strange fascination" for autocratic rulers stems from at least two sources which have little to do with Wector's faith in America's moral wisdom. First, Americans have respect for power, especially for individuals who possess and wield it deftly. Obviously the power must be used for ends that do not threaten America's interests but instead appear to advance them. Witness, for example, the widespread deification of Stalin during World War II. Moreover, to observe a foreign leader reach success through strong-armed methods is gratifying to America's nativist instincts. For his achievements can be attributed not only to his talents but to the corrupt political milieu in which he must operate, a decadent milieu which is bound to render his own behavior somewhat immoral. Even in democratic America the successful politician is not above moral suspicion. Over a century ago de Tocqueville noted that in a democracy "what is to be feared is not so much the immorality of the great as the fact that immorality may lead to greatness." As de Tocqueville observed, when judging a political leader, democratic citizens, impelled by "envy" as well as respect, are led "to impute his success mainly to some of his vices; and an odious connection is thus formed between

11 Orin Klapp, *Heroes, Villains, and Fools: The Changing American Character* (Englewood Cliffs, N.J., 1962), pp. 29, 56; Fred Palsey, *Al Capone, The Biography of a Self-Made Man* (LaSalle, Ill., 1931); Daniel Bell, "Crime as an American Way of Life," in *The End of Ideology* (Collier edn., New York, 1961), pp. 127-50; Thorstein Veblen, "The Captain of Industry," *The Portable Veblen*, ed. Max Lerner (New York, 1948), p. 394; *San Francisco Chronicle*, April 19, 1964.

the ideas of turpitude and power, unworthiness and success, utility and dishonor." If this insight be true for American democracy, how much more true must it be when Americans judge a foreign dictator? Contrary to Professor Wector's pronouncements about the democratic rewards of ethical virtues, Americans are not always outraged by the Machiavellian. Wector may have been right in stating that Americans would not be "willing to follow" Mussolini. But one can hardly infer from this reluctance that Americans did not "admire" Mussolini and "trust" him to rule the Italians well. In truth, America's admiration for Mussolini was also marked by "an odious connection" between his remarkable achievements and his repugnant methods. Watching Il Duce striving to realize what they believed were proper ends through improper means, Americans could congratulate themselves on the presumed moral superiority of their own country where such means need not be used. Americans realized that Mussolini was not a completely moral man. But they were hardly so naïve as not to sense that in Italy, even more than in America, "immorality may lead to greatness." "An Italian proverb," wrote Emerson, "declares that 'if you would succeed, you must not be too good.'"[12]

What also must be stressed is that Mussolini's American image was not as sinister as anti-Fascists later tried to make it by equating him with Hitler. True, Mussolini was often depicted in the popular press as a forceful leader of almost superhuman qualities, but this characterization was balanced by the touching portrayal of Mussolini as the "average man" responsive to human emotion and capable of warm affection. All the fuss made about his fondness for children and pets, his delight in music and sports, his common origins and sympathy for the peasants served, either intentionally or otherwise, to soften his tough image. Rather than a raw and ruthless despot, Mussolini was just a "Regular Guy," Will Rogers assured Americans; he was no different from an American senator in his boastfulness and he was merely doing for Italy what Henry Ford did for the United States. "I shall think of him as one of the most human human beings I ever saw —and one of the greatest," said Irving Cobb, who regarded the

[12] Pentenziani is quoted in *Time*, xi (June 11, 1928), 16; Alexis de Tocqueville, *Democracy in America* (Vintage edn., New York, 1943), i, 235; Ralph Waldo Emerson, *Representative Men: Nature, Addresses, and Lectures* (Cambridge, 1855), p. 218.

Premier as something of a Cincinnatus figure, a humble warrior who rescued his country but remained uncorrupted by power. So beneath his brusque willfulness Americans found a human heart. The leader of superlative abilities was also the man of general, homely impulses, a plain man of the people. Paradoxical as it may seem, the balance of all this polymorphous imagery enabled the dictator to strike the pose of a "democratic" hero, what Walter Bagehot called a common man of uncommon abilities.[13]

Finally, there was one saving touch in Mussolini and in Italian Fascism that caused them both to be taken lightly: the comical image. The impression was created by a fundamentally incongruous view of Fascism and the Italians. An easy-going people, skeptics with a capacity for humorous self-criticism; occasionally exuberant and explosive, more often melancholic and resigned; passionate individualists with a rich heritage of humanism and a realistic sense of power and the *absence* of such power—such was the material that Fascism claimed to be whipping into a totally regimented, monolithic state. Many American writers, comparing the reality with the mystique, could only chuckle. What emerged instead was something of an *opéra bouffe* conducted by a quasi-farceur whose jut-jawed posture and *sacro egoismo* only betrayed the absence of real national power. Given the irony in Mussolini's compulsion to overdramatize, he soon became the delight of cartoonists, who, with hyperbole and brushstroke, could easily transform a serious statesman into a buffoon and showman. Because of this comical image, Americans often found it difficult to take his utterances seriously, and with the fiasco of Caporetto in mind, even his aggressive speeches were often dismissed as diatribes for domestic consumption. In contrast to the Draconian militancy emanating from Hitler's Germany and Stalin's Russia, Mussolini appeared as amusing as he was amazing, the Falstaff of the *fascisti*. Even today the mention of his name can provoke laughter from those who recall his image in the press—or from those of a later generation who have viewed his balcony gyrations

[13] Rogers, "Letters," p. 82; Cobb, "A Big Little Man," p. 146. Despite Mussolini's clamorous inveighing against Western democracy, some Americans still saw him as "always a man obsessed with one idea—attaining effective democracy in Italy." See the anonymous "Mussolini the Democrat: By an American Observer," *American Review of Reviews,* LXXVII (June 1928), 600-606.

in film documentaries. "Asked to name a clumsy fool," Orin Klapp writes, "Americans think of Jerry Lewis, Jackie Gleason, Red Skelton, Stan Laurel and Oliver Hardy, Charlie Chaplin, Buster Keaton, Lou Costello; Humpty Dumpty, Gargantua, Don Quixote, Ichabod Crane, and near-sighted Mr. Magoo, Goofy (Disney), Joe Palooka; Warren G. Harding, and Benito Mussolini."[14]

One could go on discussing the many-sided and admittedly contradictory images of Mussolini in the American mind. But ultimately to comprehend his popular reception one must confront the nature of hero worship. Theorists of classical democracy tried to eliminate the role of personalized leadership in politics, yet the craving for the image of the peerless leader runs deep even in democratic society. Indeed in our own time the historian Arthur Schlesinger, Jr., could sense the hopelessness of the dilemma. Observing that the indispensable man was anathema to Locke and suspect to the Founding Fathers, and warning that the cult of the heroic leader poses a continual threat to democracy, Schlesinger nevertheless laments the passing of "the epic style of those mighty figures of our recent past who seized history with both hands." Now admiration for heroic leaders is in itself no sign of latent Fascism—even today's "New Left" rises romantically to the well-armed *caudillo*. Since the attraction to leadership mystique is characteristic of all sides of the political spectrum it would be hazardous to draw any ideological lessons from this common visceral behavior. But one lesson seems clear enough: the story of Mussolini's reception in America is a lesson in how to make a dictator democratically respectable. Perhaps Il Duce knew all along what James Fenimore Cooper came to fear—that "the true theatre of a demagogue is a democracy."[15]

"MUSSOLINIANISM": A PHENOMENON OF THE 1920s

Most Americans, then, admired not so much Fascism as "Mussolinianism," not the reactionary ideology but the cult of personality. How is this mass hero worship to be explained? One answer was offered by Oswald G. Villard, anti-Fascist editor of the *Nation*. Villard believed that Mussolini was "serving an extraordinarily useful purpose. You can measure a man's devotion to the democratic ideal by the attitude that he takes toward Mussolini.

[14] Klapp, *Heroes*, p. 70.

[15] Arthur Schlesinger, Jr., *The Politics of Hope* (Boston, 1963), pp. 23-24; James Fenimore Cooper, *The American Democrat* (New York, 1931), p. 92.

If with some knowledge of what is actually happening in Italy an American still prefers the Mussolini type of government, he is actually disloyal to our political principles." This finger of "disloyalty" pointed at Mussolini's supporters in the twenties resembles nothing so much as the finger of "treason" pointed at the Stalinist sympathizers of the thirties—which is to say that the charge tells us more about the accuser's behavior than that of the accused. Surely a more fruitful approach is to understand America's fascination with Mussolini not as conscious ideology but as a reflection of the social and cultural context of the period and the psychic needs of the American people.[16]

An age of hero worship is an age of instability. As Max Weber noted years ago, it is a period in which the traditional social order appears to be disintegrating that the phenomenon of "charismatic authority" occurs. The charismatic figure ascends to power in a time of trouble and crisis and is accepted by the masses, not on the basis of historical legitimacy, but by virtue of his "extraordinary quality," his "personal strength," and the claim to spiritual sanction bestowed on him by supporters. Deriving his authority from his spectacular display of power and ability, the rule of the charismatic leader is born of "distress" and carried forward by "enthusiasm." Now strictly speaking, most Americans did not perceive Mussolini as a classic charismatic personality. Instead of attributing his success to mysterious and "magical" powers, they believed he was merely governing Italy with good American common sense. Nevertheless, it was the "distress" of the times that created his favorable reception. Il Duce's rise to fame in America cannot be understood apart from the temper of the twenties.[17]

"The world broke in two in 1922 or thereabouts," observed Willa Cather. Although Miss Cather may not have had in mind the March on Rome, the emotional tensions she sensed go far toward explaining America's response to the event. Socially and intellectually the twenties was a decade anxious with contradiction.

[16] Oswald G. Villard, "What Cost Mussolini?" *Nation*, cxxiii (Nov. 17, 1926), 504.

[17] "The Sociology of Charismatic Authority," Chap. IX in H. H. Gerth and C. Wright Mills, eds., *From Max Weber: Essays in Sociology* (New York, 1958); see also, Klapp, "The Creation of Popular Heroes," *American Journal of Sociology*, LIV (Sept. 1948), 135-41; id., "Hero-Worship in America," *American Sociological Review*, xiv (Feb. 1949), 53-62.

It was a period of industrial progress and agrarian nostalgia, of escape from the village and the encounter with "homelessness," of tenacious nativism by patriots and adventures abroad by expatriates, of religious fundamentalism and moral revolution, of prohibition and liberation, of hero worship and idol smashing. Above all, in this dramatic period of rapid cultural change Americans hung suspended between the future and the past, rushing out to absorb the new, retreating to uphold the old. It was an untenable situation, and as society became fragmented and dislocated the traditional values began to dissolve. Although the process had actually begun much earlier, what "broke apart" in 1922 was the moral order of the world. No longer could many Americans believe in the genteel idealism of the past. Gone were the common beliefs in moral absolutism, inevitable progress, and rational man. The words "honor," "truth," and "sacred" no longer had meaning for writers like Hemingway, and for historians like Carl Becker "reason and aspiration and emotion—what we call principles, faith, ideals—[were] without their knowing it at the service of complex and subtle instinctive reactions and impulses." With the demise of traditional idealism much of the moral impulse of American progressivism collapsed as well. Americans as a whole may not have gone so far as to dispose of liberalism like "an empty whiskey flask" (Parrington), but a generation in which the best people lacked conviction about politics was hardly a generation to rebuke Mussolini, who himself was only trying to disenthrone the "goddess of liberty."[18]

Paradoxically, while some Americans could not rebuke Il Duce because he seemed to be the harbinger of a new political realism, many others welcomed him as the defender of the older idealism. To the middle class and especially to the business community, Mussolini seemed to stand for two traditional American values: rational intelligence and human willpower. Whatever Americans may have thought of Fascism as an ideology, they viewed Mussolini as an outstanding leader whose achievements were the

[18] Willa Cather is quoted in William E. Leuchtenburg, *The Perils of Prosperity* (Chicago, 1958), p. 273; Becker in Burleigh Wilkins Taylor, *Carl Becker: A Biographical Study in American Intellectual History* (Cambridge, 1961), pp. 132-33; Ernest Hemingway, *A Farewell to Arms* (Bantam edn., New York, 1949), p. 137; Vernon L. Parrington, *Main Currents in American Thought*, Vol. III: *The Beginnings of Critical Realism in America, 1860-1920* (Harbinger edn., New York, 1958), p. 412.

result of exceptional capacities of reason and will. Perhaps it is a measure of the desperate needs of Americans that they chose to see a dictator who brazenly attacked the whole rationalist tradition as a defender of reason. For at no other time was the nostalgic ideal of the rational individual under greater strain than in the twenties. The increasing regimentation of industrial life, exemplified in Frederick Taylor's efficiency treatises and realized in Henry Ford's assembly lines, seemed to be making man into a mechanomorphic mutant; while Freudian analysis and Watsonian behaviorism, each starting from different premises, appeared to reduce man to a bundle of irrational drives or a package of conditioned reflexes. At the same time the dreadful memories of World War I and the subsequent "contagiousness" of Bolshevism went far toward creating the impression that man had all but lost control of history. Amid this pervasive moral uncertainty and world insecurity, the sight of a Carlylean leader changing the course of history through sheer willpower and reason was cause for celebration. "The picture of Mussolini rallying the citizenship of Italy to the restoration of their threatened government," James Emery announced in a speech to the National Association of Manufacturers, "ought to encourage every man who believes that reason will ultimately dominate in the social and political affairs of Europe."[19]

It is true to say that Mussolini was America's answer to Communism; it is trite to say nothing more. For Il Duce was the American answer to many other things that were wrong with the modern world. Faced with frantic excitement and uncertainty, what the 1920s lacked was a genuine political hero. Toward the close of World War I there had been two towering figures: Woodrow Wilson and Vladimir Lenin, the former stirring the imagination of millions with his program of political liberation through war, the latter arousing the expectations of the masses with his program of social liberation through revolution. When both died in 1924 the world seemed to be left with pallid mediocrities who served only as ludicrous targets for Mencken's deft barbs. In America particularly the absence of "a single great leader" and of "individuals of the leader type" was noted by such disparate minds as Nicholas Murray Butler and Sigmund Freud. Thus, in 1927 the *Literary Digest*, responding to the growing

[19] *Proceedings of the 28th Annual Convention of the National Association of Manufacturers of the United States of America, 1923* (New York), p. 289.

sense of a leadership vacuum in the world, conducted an editorial survey entitled "Is There a Dearth of Great Men?" The magazine discovered that newspapers, in challenging the allegation, mentioned Mussolini more frequently than any other figure, with Lenin, Edison, Marconi, Orville Wright following in that order, and Henry Ford and George Bernard Shaw tying for sixth place.[20]

Mussolini was mentioned most frequently because, more than any other man, he seemed to give expression to certain ideals rendered precarious by the sudden changes of the twenties. It was not merely that his dynamic idealism and articulate verbosity provided an antidote to the country's materialism and Coolidge's sour and laconic style. It was also because his achievements seemed to symbolize the triumph of old virtues while at the same time evoking the adventures of a new age. Shortly after the editorial poll, for example, Charles Lindbergh made his famous trans-Atlantic solo flight. Immediately Mussolini rushed a telegram to Ambassador Fletcher congratulating America on this momentous achievement. "A Superhuman will has taken space by assault and has subjugated it," exclaimed Il Duce. "Matter once more has yielded to spirit and the prodigy is one that will live forever in the memory of men." Significantly, Mussolini's description of Lindbergh's conquest succinctly captures the American public's emotional reaction to the historic event. Symbolically, Lindbergh's flight meant to Mussolini as well as to Americans the triumph of "spirit" over "matter" through the sheer assertion of "Superhuman will." In effect, Mussolini's description was actually an exercise in self-conception which mirrored the dictator's own image in America. If Lindbergh showed that man was the master of nature, Mussolini demonstrated that man was still in control of events. The aviator disciplined an uncertain machine and the dictator an unknown movement. Mythically, Il Duce was man's answer to fatalism—a political symbol of the deep resources of will and reason for an American society weary of the rush of history.[21]

[20] *LD*, xciv (Aug. 6, 1927), 12-13; Butler's lament is quoted in the *LD* Poll; Freud's charge that America failed to produce super-ego "leader type" men is in *Civilization and Its Discontent* (New York, 1961), pp. 62-63.

[21] Mussolini to Fletcher, May 22, 1927, scrapbooks, FP; John William Ward, "The Meaning of Lindbergh's Flight," *American Quarterly*, x (Spring 1958), 3-16.

In the American popular mind Il Duce emerged as something more than a crude dictator. A complex figure, his ambiguous image appealed to the contradictory emotions of a country undergoing the stress of change: a restorer of conservative tradition, a genius of innovation and experiment; an impulsive romantic of the senses, a redeemer of religion and spiritual vision; a self-made man of almost superhuman willpower, a common man of practical idealism and homely virtue. Embracing opposite tensions, Mussolini's image combined the adventurous dash of charisma with a sober call to native folk values. If the twenties can be labeled "The Aspirin Age," he was both its stimulant and its tranquilizer.

Part Two

AMERICAN SOCIETY
AND FASCISM

5.

Italian-Americans and Mussolini's Italy

THE KINGDOM OF NAPLES HAS PERISHED, AND THE KINGDOM OF THE HOPELESSLY POOR IS NOT OF THIS WORLD. THEIR OTHER WORLD IS AMERICA. EVEN AMERICA, TO THE PEASANTS, HAS A DUAL NATURE. IT IS A LAND WHERE A MAN GOES TO WORK, WHERE HE SWEATS FOR HIS DAILY BREAD, WHERE HE LAYS ASIDE A LITTLE MONEY ONLY AT THE COST OF ENDLESS HARDSHIP AND PRIVATION, WHERE HE CAN DIE AND NO ONE WILL REMEMBER HIM. AT THE SAME TIME, AND WITH NO CONTRADICTION IN TERMS, IT IS AN EARTHLY PARADISE AND PROMISED LAND.

YES, NEW YORK, RATHER THAN ROME OR NAPLES, WOULD BE THE REAL CAPITAL OF THE PEASANTS OF LUCANIA, IF THESE MEN WITHOUT A COUNTRY COULD HAVE A CAPITAL AT ALL. AND IT IS THEIR CAPITAL, IN THE ONLY WAY IT CAN BE FOR THEM, THAT IS AS A MYTH.

Carlo Levi, *Christ Stopped at Eboli*, 1947*

* Reprinted by permission of Farrar, Straus, & Giroux, Inc. (See Acknowledgments)

WEST OF EDEN: ITALIANS IN AMERICA

Mannaggia America! (Damn America!) Whether heard in New York's Mulberry district, Boston's north end, or San Francisco's North Beach, this same thought tormented many Italian immigrants who swarmed to the United States in search of, if not streets paved with gold, something more promising than a wilderness of asphalt. No human mind is a *tabula rasa*: to forget this fact in discussing the Italian-American response is to miss the whole social meaning of that experience. Psychologically the Italian immigrant was conditioned to respond positively to Fascism even before Mussolini's regime dazzled his mind. Doubtless Fascist propaganda provided the fertilizer, but American society had planted the seed.

For one thing, during the postwar years the immigrant had to suffer through another periodic wave of "Americanization." This nativist hysteria, in part a reflection of the "Red Scare" of 1919, bore heavily on the Italians, identified, as they were, with radicalism and labor violence. On the evening of August 5, 1920, mobs in West Frankfurt, a small mining town in Illinois, stormed into the Italian district, dragged frightened occupants from their houses, clubbed and stoned them, and set their dwellings aflame. But the mental wounds were worse. The suggestion that Italians could not be assimilated into American culture hurt more than any stick or stone. In 1912, for example, the Italian paper of Chicago, *L'Italia*, advocated a "united stand" against Woodrow Wilson because the Democratic presidential nominee in his historical writings had referred to the Italians as a "cursed rabble." Although Italy's alliance with the United States during World War I brought a tenuous rapprochement between Italian-Americans and the Wilson Administration, the amity was soon shattered at the Paris Peace Conference. When Wilson stood adamantly opposed to Italy's territorial designs, disgusted Italian-Americans quickly formed a "Lega Nazione Fiume" to explain the "justice" of Vittorio Orlando's objectives and the "betrayal" of Wilsonian internationalism. Italy's cry of "multilated victory!" reverberated in the Italian communities of America. Then, following hard on the heels of the Paris debates, came a reassertion of antialien sentiment that culminated in the discriminatory immigration laws of the 1920s. The rejection of the "melting pot"

78

ideal in favor of national homogeneity caused Italians in America to bristle with indignation. But despite protests on the part of educated Italians, the ugly, stereotyped impressions persisted since they were deeply ingrained in the anxious minds of rural, native, Protestant Americans who felt threatened by the inundation of an alien *canaille*.[1]

An unwelcome stranger in a sometimes hostile land, the Italian-American looked almost desperately to his home country for personal solace and national identity. Yet even here the popular picture of pre-Fascist Italy—in part drawn from her ignominious role in the war and at Versailles—was that of an unworthy nation which spawned inferior people. Thus, after the March on Rome, when Mussolini appeared to be revitalizing Italy and restoring the grandeur of ancient Rome, Italian-Americans could not help but look on with a new sense of pride and self-respect. "But you've got to admit one thing," declared an Italian-American girl who, significantly, was herself anti-Fascist, "he enabled four million Italians in America to hold up their heads, and that is something. If you had been branded as undesirable by a quota law you would understand how much that means."[2]

Aside from compensating for the gnawing inferiority complex of Italian-Americans, Fascist Italy answered other deeply felt needs. An immigrant is a "marginal man." Confronted with the hectic pace of a strange new life, he feels the "tug of two loyalties." Emotionally he is caught between two worlds, unwilling to forsake his sentimental attachment to the old world, unable to give up the promises of the new. This theme of cultural ambivalence recurred poignantly in many Italian publications. As one paper put it, "they had merely emigrated their bodies . . . their souls remained in Italy." Massimo Salvadori, an anti-Fascist who came to the United States, recalls in his memoirs that immigrants remembered only the best aspects of the Italy they left, and Fascist propaganda easily played upon these wistful memories. Because Italians were entranced by this glowing nostalgia it was all but impossible for them to be critical of Fascist Italy.

[1] Higham, p. 264; *L'Italia* (Chicago), Oct. 20, 1912; June 27, 1920; *La Fiamma* (Chicago), Nov. 1, 1923; Antonio Stella, *Some Aspects of Italian Immigration to the United States* (New York, 1924).

[2] Quoted in Caroline Ware, ed., *The Cultural Approach to History* (New York, 1940), p. 63.

Indeed any attack leveled upon Mussolini and his government was taken as a direct slur on Italy itself.[3]

Compounding feelings of inferiority and nostalgia was the "conflict of generations," the revolt of the second generation against their immigrant heritage. The revolt was nothing less than the wholesale rejection of Old-World institutions and customs, which the young came to regard as excess baggage standing in the way of complete assimilation. As such, it was also a rejection of parental influence and authority. Mothers and fathers, greatly disturbed by this severing of the ethnic umbilical cord, tried to prevent the painful separation by inculcating in the young a strong identification with the home country. One way to assure family loyalty was to have the Italian language taught to children before they were corrupted by the bright lights and bland conformity of American life. The Italian government encouraged this practice; with the advent of Fascism, as we shall see, these language classes became centers of propaganda. Moreover, aware of the problem of filial disintegration, Fascist propaganda publications stressed "a wholesome family unit" as "the first source of a worker's moral happiness." The slogan of the leading Fascist organization in the United States was "La Religione, la Patria, e la Famiglia." In their attempt to instill national consciousness into the minds and hearts of their children, parents easily succumbed to the appeals of Fascist nationalism; while Mussolini, posing as the embodiment of the Old-World traditions of discipline and parental authority, seemed to provide a heartening answer to all those Italian-Americans clinging tenaciously to national identity as the final source of family cohesion.[4]

Pressures both external and internal, then, left Italian-Americans ripe for Fascism. A nascent inferiority complex, a nostalgic nationalism, and a fear for family solidarity and community produced a quiet but true collective anxiety. Inasmuch as Fascism

[3] Henry Carlson Smith, *Americans in the Making: The Natural History of the Assimilation of Immigrants* (New York, 1939), pp. 233-34; *La Fiamma* (Chicago), Sept. 1, 1923; Massimo Salvadori, *Resistenza ed azione: ricordi di un liberale* (Bari, 1951), pp. 162-65.

[4] Paul J. Campisi, "The Italian Family in the United States," *American Journal of Sociology*, LIII (May 1948), 443-49; Irwin L. Child, *Italian or American? The Second Generation in Conflict* (New Haven, 1943); *The Organization of Production and the Syndical Corporative System* (Italian Library of Information, New York, 1940), pamphlet; *Lega Fascista Del Nord America* (New York, 1928), pamphlet, HIL.

80

was an answer to these psychic tensions, the Italian-American reaction to it was more a socially conditioned reflex than a politically conscious response.

THE ITALIAN-AMERICAN PRESS

The Circolo Dante Alighieri of Philadelphia, meeting on the evening of November 11, 1922, begged forgiveness of its patron saint while it shifted its program to more pressing matters. Professor Michele Renzulli of Temple University had been invited to speak on the topic of Benito Mussolini and the vaguely understood movement called "fascismo." The Professor's speech was roundly applauded after the audience heard that Fascism had roots deep in Italian history, that it presaged a resurgence of Italian nationalism and repudiated the Versailles debacle, and that it meant an end to radicalism and the threat of revolution. Reassured, many of Dante's American disciples returned home that evening confident that the new Garibaldi and his colorful Blackshirts heralded the springtime of the *Risvegliamento* (great awakening). As for Renzulli, he returned to Rome where he would later write a glowing account of his "educational" activities in the United States on the eve of the Fascist revolution.[5]

Professor Renzulli's speech on Fascism, printed in Philadelphia's *La Voce della Colonia*, was read avidly by the Italian-Americans of that city. In other parts of the country a similar "introduction" to Fascism took place. But it was the Italian-American press that provided Mussolini his most important vehicle of propaganda in the United States. Most Italian language papers received their dispatches from the Stefani news agency, a pro-Fascist establishment at the time of the March on Rome which would assume enormous importance after Mussolini consolidated his power. Because the Italian press and its agencies succumbed to government control, and because Italian-American publishers on the whole did not object to such regimentation, the great majority of Italians in the United States were nursed on the pap and propaganda of the Fascist government itself.[6]

[5] Michele Renzulli, *L'Italia e il Fascismo negli Stati Uniti d'America* (Rome, 1938), HIL.

[6] The Italian press in America probably consisted of somewhere around 150 publications, with the number falling each year between 1920 and 1940 due to the decline of immigration and the process of assimilation. This figure is a rough estimate extrapolated retrospectively from a 1940 study

In December 1922, a month following the March on Rome, the *Literary Digest* polled the Italian-American press for its views on the new regime in Italy. Although a good many papers interpreted Fascism differently, most agreed that the movement had routed the Communists and had discarded the old, feeble political parties in order to pave the way for a new order characterized by peace, prosperity, and dignity. The *Popolo* of Reading (Pennsylvania), seeing Fascism as the "resurrection" of the historical ideals of Mazzini and Garibaldi, told Americans that Mussolini, despite his occasional outbursts of militarism, was not bent on imperialism but merely desired Italy to achieve parity with other nations. *L'Opinione* of Philadelphia believed that Fascism was a "moral force" which would explain to the world "the inherent respect of the Italian race for law and order and good citizenship." The Kansas City *Stampa* likened Mussolini's march to the "epoch making" French Revolution. The conservatism of the movement appealed to the *Sole* of Stockton (California), whose editor was convinced that Il Duce would restore financial stability by turning over to private enterprise the nationalized sectors of the economy. Maintaining that Fascism was based on the heroic spirit of idealism which would strike the "Latin soul" of Italians in America, the editor called upon all readers who possessed Italian bonds to "burn them upon the altar of the country" (a sacrificial holocaust for the love of Italy). In New York the self-proclaimed American voice of Fascism, *Il Carroccio*, described Mussolini's advent as a purgation of the errors, delusions, and defects of previous parliamentary governments. Finally, *Il Progresso Italo-Americano* criticized American newspapers for failing to report that the "King is Master" in Italy, not the alleged dictator Mussolini. *Il Progresso* was particularly incensed at the *New York Herald*, which had dubbed the *fascisti* the "Ku Klux Klan of Italy." The comparison is unfair, insisted *Il Progresso*, for the Klan is "narrow minded" (i.e., anti-Catholic) and not a "noble institution" like the Amer-

---

which indicated there were 129 Italian language papers. "The Foreign Language Press," *Fortune*, xxii (Nov. 1940), 90-93, 102-104; see also "A Survey of the Italian Language Press in the United States" (a mimeographed study prepared at the Institute for Advanced Study, Princeton, N.J., Sept. 1942), LC.

ican Legion, the true American counterpart to the brave Black-shirts.[7]

The obbligato of platitudes carried a few discordant notes. The *Unione* of Pueblo (Colorado), *Lavoratore Italiano* of Pittsburg (Kansas), and *La Follia di New York* had harsh words for Mussolini the "renegade and opportunist" and Fascism the "Frankenstein." By and large, these small and scattered anti-Fascist publications represented the opinion of Italian-American labor. From the beginning the views of the pro and anti-Fascist press were fixed in frozen conviction: rare was the impartial paper and rarer still a paper willing to change its views as a result of developments in Italy. In terms of circulation and financial resources the pro-Fascist press was far more important than its adversary. In New York, for example, the readership of the pro-Fascist papers outnumbered the opposition about ten to one. Newspapers sympathetic to Mussolini reflected upper-class, conservative sentiments, and they enjoyed the advertising support of large restaurants and wineries as well as manufacturers and bankers. In San Francisco the pro-Fascist *L'Italia* featured the advertisements of A. P. Giannini's Bank of America and of the Di Giorgio Fruit Corporation, both of which came close to constituting the power structure of the Italian community in California.[8]

The pro-Fascist press included such publications as *Il Popolo Italiano* (Philadelphia), *Gazzetta del Massachusetts* and *La Notizia* (Boston), *L'Italia* (Chicago), *La Stella di Pittsburgh*, *L'Araldo* (Cleveland), *La Tribuna d'America* (Detroit), *La Capitale* (Sacramento), and *Il Crociato* (Brooklyn). A good many of the pro-Mussolini papers were edited or published by the *prominenti*. *La Libera Parola* of Philadelphia, for example,

[7] "Fascist Triumph Explained by Italian Writers," *LD*, LXXV (Dec. 23, 1922), 17-18, 38-41; *LD* (Nov. 11, 1922), 20; *LD*, LXXVII (April 7, 1923), 16-17.

[8] "Fascist Triumph," pp. 17-18; Grazia Dore, "L'Avvento del fascismo attraverso la stampa italiana in America," *Rassegna di Storia e Politica*, IX (March, April, June, Sept., 1963), 31-32, 13-19, 8-16, 16-27; Alberto Cupelli, "Fedele oltre la Morte: La stampa italo-americano e Mussolini," *Il Mondo* (June 1945), pp. 31-39; "A Survey of the Italian Language Press," passim; *La Rassegna Commerciale* (La Camera di Commercio Italiana di California, San Francisco, March 1936). The *Italy-American Monthly* listed as its "commercial members" the Banca Commerciale Italiana, Di Giorgio Fruit Corporation, National City Bank of New York, Dillon, Read & Company, and the J. P. Morgan Company.

83

was headed by Anthony J. di Silvestro, a leading official in the Grand Lodge of the Sons of Italy. While most of the press enthusiastically hailed Mussolini because of what he seemed to be doing for Italy, a few papers went completely overboard on the idea of Fascism itself. One paper, Agostino de Biasi's *Il Corriere d'America* (New York), announced that it was *the* central organ of Fascist propaganda in the United States. Even more flagrant was New York's *Il Grido della Stirpe* (The Cry of the Race), which its owner, Domenico Trombetta, called the "most faithful voice of Fascism in America." Featured in this "faithful" journal were violent attacks on Jews, scurrilous satires on American democracy, and paranoiac outbursts of Anglophobia, racism, and militarism.[9]

The two most influential papers were *Il Progresso Italo-Americano* of New York and *L'Italia* of San Francisco. *Il Progresso* was owned and published by Genercso Pope, the millionaire President of the Colonial Sand & Cement Company. His daily enjoyed the largest circulation of any Italian language paper in the United States. Moreover, as an important Tammany political figure, Pope's influence carried weight in government circles, especially in the Roosevelt Administration, where, we shall see, he brought pressure to prevent Congress from revising the Neutrality Laws during the Ethiopian War. San Francisco's *L'Italia* was published by Ettore Patrizi. The leading Italian daily on the Pacific Coast, *L'Italia* also enjoyed considerable political influence, particularly during the reign of San Francisco's Mayor Angelo J. Rossi (1931-1944).

The editorial policy and financial affairs of Italian-American papers were of vital concern to Fascist officials in Italy. In more than one instance they attempted to silence anti-Fascist publications (discussed in the next chapter), and they were not reluctant to interfere in the private affairs of the pro-Fascist press. One example will suffice.

Beginning in 1928, a lengthy correspondence developed between Fascist authorities in Italy and Italian publishers in the United States. The discussion centered on the sale of *Il Progresso*, then on consignment to the Equitable Trust Company. Giacomo de Martino, Ambassador to Washington, wrote the Consul General of Italy informing him of the details and difficulties involved

[9] Trombetta is discussed in "Hitler's Helpers," *Fortune*, xxii (Nov. 1940), 86.

in the sale. Although the Italian government most likely would not consent to purchasing the paper, Martino wrote, it is imperative that ownership remain in the hands of someone absolutely faithful to Italy. It was rumored, the Ambassador noted, that "Il Gruppo Hearst" is interested in purchasing the paper, as are other rival publishers, one of whom is Luigi Barzini of *Il Corriere*. "Each of these solutions presents, in my opinion," advised Martino, "grave inconveniences and dangers. The gravest of all, that which puts the journal in the hands of Americans, even with an Italian editor, would allow the journal to slip entirely away from our influence—but also the other solutions are, in my mind, to be rejected, because they would generate hatred and rivalry among various personalities." He then related that, after long and difficult negotiations, an accord was reached whereby Barzini agreed to withdraw from the picture and Generoso Pope, with the promise of financial help from Italian-American bankers, agreed to purchase the paper. The rumor of Hearst's interest in the sale, noted Martino, drove the price up to $2,053,000.[10]

From the point of view of propaganda, it might seem that the Italian government would desire to consolidate the Italian-American press. If the various papers could be centralized the influence or control exercised by Italian officials would be all the more effective. Such was not the case. Writing to Martino, Foreign Affairs Minister Dino Grandi advised that the New York press must at all cost avoid the trend toward merger and monopoly. With the sagacity of a diplomat, Grandi reasoned as follows: as long as several journals remain in business they will have to compete with one another for favors and privileges from the government in Italy; if, on the other hand, only one paper survives, there is the danger that it "could go astray" and lose interest in maintaining good relations with the regime. "Therefore, I repeat, administrative fusion yes, union, no. . . . The papers are not only a purely business affair, but also an enterprise in ideals and politics and must be considered from such a point of view."[11]

The following month Martino informed the Foreign Secretary that Barzini now intended to sell his *Il Corriere*. Martino made it clear to Barzini that the sale of his journal to an American firm

[10] Ambassador de Martino to Consul General of Italy, Oct. 3, 1928, IR 429.
[11] Dino Grandi to de Martino, Oct. 15, 1928, IR.

would "not create a favorable impression" with the Italian government. Barzini agreed and stated, according to Martino, that he would be delighted if his paper were purchased by a person "faithful to the Royal Government." In the meantime Pope had gone to Italy in August 1929, in order to confer with authorities about the purchase of *Il Corriere*; upon his return he also talked to Ambassador Martino about "systematizing" the three major New York publications (*Il Progresso, Il Corriere, Bollettino della Sera*). Barzini, however, was vexed at the thought of Pope purchasing his paper. Writing to Mussolini himself, Barzini advised the Premier that such a sale would be unwise since Pope was an unreliable opportunist associated with Tammany Hall and the Mafia. Barzini's warnings went unanswered; Pope eventually took possession of *Il Corriere* in 1931.[12]

Thus it appears that Grandi's shrewd attempt to keep the Italian-American press under separate ownership proved unsuccessful. The failure was due to the general trend of mergers and absorptions, an inevitable consequence of the closing off of immigration in the late 1920s. But Grandi's fears were unfounded. Pope, as the dominant Italian-American publisher in the country, did not "go astray" but instead accepted the free telegraph service and other special privileges from the Italian government, remaining until 1941 a most dutiful servant of the Fascist regime.[13]

HAVE BLACKSHIRT, WILL TRAVEL

Italian-American Fascism antedated Mussolini's rise to power. Although the astounding success of Mussolini's March on Rome fired the emotions of Italians in the United States, the psychological roots of pro-Fascist sentiment originated in World War I. In the war years a sharp schism developed within the politically conscious Italians, dividing those who were swept up by patriotism and called for immediate intervention and those who re-

[12] Washington Ambassador to Minister of Foreign Affairs, Nov. 8, 1928; Luigi Barzini to Mussolini, Nov. 28, 1930, IR.

[13] Pope's relations with the Italian government are discussed further in later chapters. It is difficult to say how many other Italian-American publishers received favors from Italy. The publisher of *Il Trentino* (Hazelton, Pennsylvania) appealed directly to Mussolini for a subsidy, maintaining that while in Italy he was "a Fascist of the first hour" along with Achille Starace. Clemente to Mussolini, Oct. 8, 1929, IR 433.

mained loyal to the Socialist principle of neutralism. But the Italian-American Left could not contain the upsurge of nationalism. Arturo Giovannitti and Carlo Tresca, radical folk heroes of the Italian labor movement, tried in vain to stem the tide of this unexpected backwash of patriotism. Even former radicals were caught in the heady emotional currents. The career of Edmondo Rossoni provides a dramatic example. During the prewar years Rossoni edited the anarcho-syndicalist paper of New York, *Il Proletario*, working shoulder to shoulder with "Big Bill" Haywood, Eugene Debs, and other stalwarts in the labor struggle. At this time he demonstrated his hatred of patriotism by spitting on the flag of Italy. But when Italy entered the war in 1915, he rushed back to his homeland. By 1918 he was organizing labor unions to "fight Communism." By 1925, as Minister of Corporations under Mussolini, he was telling the workers of the world that Fascism was the ultimate expression of the syndicalist-nationalist idea.[14]

This shift from Left to Right, from radical internationalism to chauvinistic nationalism, broke the back of the Italian-American Left. But more importantly, the buoyant war patriotism, together with the postwar red scare and the nativist xenophobia, generated an impassioned nationalism among the Italian-Americans in general. And it was this nationalism that was "betrayed" at the Paris Peace Conference. As in Italy, therefore, the seeds of resentment had already been planted in the postwar years. Italian-American Fascism did not rise merely as a response to the Mussolini government. National humiliation—the vital mental germ of almost every Right-wing movement—was an experience all too familiar to Italian-Americans.

[14] Gaudens Megaro, *Mussolini in the Making* (Boston, 1936), p. 241; Edmondo Rossoni, "The Significance of Fascist Syndicalism," *International Center of Fascist Studies* (Paris, 1928), pp. 148-53; Arthur Livingston, "Italo-American Fascism," *Survey*, LVII (March 1, 1927), 738-39. In 1935 Minister Rossoni stated to Louis Fischer: "I know all about American prosperity. I was an I.W.W. I know all about it. I knew Bill Haywood. He was not a man. He was a big boy of fifty. He was a guy with an immense love of man, not a politician. He was an Italian—same temperament. We got many types here like Big Bill." (Louis Fischer, *Men and Politics: Europe between the Two World Wars* [Harper Colophon edn., New York, 1966], p. 276.) Significantly, the alleged murderer of Giacomo Matteotti, Amerigo Dumini, was also an expatriate, born and reared in St. Louis. The phenomenon of Italian-Americans returning to Fascist Italy for political reasons, however small their number, deserves close investigation.

Although Italian Fascism was based largely on the golden dream of nationalism, the movement was not without international overtones. The bold success of the Fascist march to power led many to believe that Fascism, like Bolshevism, was an ideology made for export. San Francisco's *L'Italia*, for example, reported a dispatch from Rome in 1922, claiming excitedly that an organization similar to the Blackshirts and made up of Russian exiles would soon be "introduced" in, of all places, the Soviet Union! Several American papers also reported on Fascist organizations outside of Italy and even in the United States. Beginning in 1924 rumors circulated that a "Fascist International" would be established under the auspices of the Supreme Council of the Italian Fascists. When other nations reacted nervously to such rumors, Mussolini tried to allay fears by denying publicly any intention of exporting Fascism. Yet at the same time the blaring pronouncements of avid Blackshirts—like those of Rossoni who told the workers of the world of "our revolution abroad"—could not be ignored.[15]

Did Mussolini intend to export Fascism? The historian Denis Mack Smith has maintained that such a plan was "very close to his heart" and that he intended to subsidize secretly such reactionary groups as the Belgian Rexists and the French Cagoulards. We now know, from the captured files of the Italian Ministero della Cultura Popolare, just how close this imperial dream was to his heart. Apparently two groups were determined to establish a *Fascio* in the United States: the party enthusiasts in Rome and some Italian-American *prominenti* in New York. By the same token, two groups stood opposed to the plan: career diplomats in the Italian Foreign Office and several Italian-American politicians.[16]

From the beginning enthusiasts in Rome tried to persuade Mussolini that the American soil was fertile for Fascist "seed." One report, received in 1924 by the Italian Foreign Ministry, claimed that "Fascism in America is at its most favorable juncture," and that the only obstacle standing in the way was the

[15] *L'Italia* (San Francisco), Aug. 17, 1922; "Fascist International," *Living Age*, cccxxv (May 9, 1925), 301-302; *NYT*, Jan. 27, 1924; *Nation*, cxiii (Oct. 19, 1921), 436; *ibid.*, cxxii (Feb. 3, 1926), 124-26; Rossoni, pp. 148-53.

[16] Denis Mack Smith, *Italy* (Ann Arbor, 1959), p. 446.

open reluctance of the Italian diplomats in general and the "inexplicably poor attitude" of Ambassador Gelasio Caetani in particular. At the same time many Italian-Americans stepped forward to advocate a *Fascio* in the United States. Since they had been dreaming of such an organization even before the takeover in Italy, Agostino de Biasi of *Il Carroccio*, Joseph di Silvestro of the Sons of Italy, and Umberto Menicucci, later Secretary of the New York branch of the *fascisti*, may be regarded as the forerunners of Italian-American Fascism. Taking their cue from the electrifying declarations of Gabriele D'Annunzio, they proclaimed themselves the founding fathers of American Fascism. When Mussolini seized power Silvestro hurried anxiously to Rome to present to Il Duce "the allegiance and support of three hundred thousand Italo-Americans," a move which, we shall see, caused a split in the Sons of Italy. In the meantime Menicucci contacted one of the first Fascist emissaries, Giuseppe Bottai, in order to map out plans for an organization and a program of action in the United States. But Mussolini was disturbed by what one contemporary writer called "all these applications for investiture" from Italian-Americans. Forced to move cautiously, Il Duce set up a special bureau to deal with "Fascism Abroad." To Prince Caetani, Ambassador to the United States, he entrusted the delicate task of arbitrating disputes among the various factions in the United States.[17]

Mussolini was just as puzzled by the divided counsel of his own statesmen. Ambassador Caetani, among others, believed it would be unwise to import Fascism into the United States. The critical reception of Fascism in some sections of the American press in the very early period, the rising anti-immigration sentiment, and the delicate matter of Italy's war debt to the United States all contributed to Caetani's sense of caution. There ensued, according to Allen Cassels, "a smouldering hostility" between reluctant bureaucrats like Caetani and "exuberant party zealots" like Giuseppe Bastianini, the influential party hierarch and secretary-general of the Rome *Fasci all'estero*. But the zealots, appealing to the dream so close to Il Duce's heart, won

17 Alan Cassels, "Fascism for Export: Italy and the United States in the Twenties," *American Historical Review*, LXIX (April 1964), 708; Agostino de Biasi, *La Battaglia dell'Italia negli Stati Uniti* (New York, 1927), pamphlet; Livingston, pp. 738-39.

out; and in 1924 Count Ignazio Thaon di Revel crossed the Atlantic to reorganize the disparate American factions into the Fascist League of North America (FLNA).[18]

Yet Italian-American Fascism was not so much exported as cultivated. Far in advance of Count Revel's arrival, Italian-Americans organized spontaneously their own independent Fascist groups. Immediately following Mussolini's seizure of Rome, organizations emerged in New York, Philadelphia, Cleveland, Boston, San Francisco, and several other cities. The most important of these groups was the Fascist League of North America, founded, according to one newspaper account, as early as 1921. The FLNA floundered for a year and then was "revived" in the winter of 1922 by the "authority of Premier Mussolini," according to Dino Bigongiari, Professor of Italian at Columbia University. Bigongiari, the initiator of the first FLNA, publicly announced in the spring of 1923 that an "organization will be formed in the United States to combat radicalism." Although Socialists, Communists, and Syndicalists were ineligible, Bigongiari denied the League had political objectives, insisting that "only incidentally" would its existence promote the cause of Mussolini in America. The secretary of the New York branch, Umberto Menicucci, stated there were about thirty branches throughout the country. Thus the FLNA was established well before the intervention of the Italian government.[19]

To the complete surprise of Italian-American Fascists, the plan to establish the FLNA met substantial opposition. Senator Salvatore Cotillo of the New York legislature was one of several Italian-American politicians (Fiorello La Guardia was another) who immediately declared that such an organization would be "out of place" in America. The American press was decidedly opposed to the project; the Italian language press, however, was divided. The more avid pro-Fascist papers were thrilled by the proposal. *Il Carroccio* (New York), for example, proudly announced that the "Fascisti will be called upon to repeat here in the United States among the unions the battles that Fascism has won in Italy, breaking the backbone of Bolshevism." Yet when the *New York Herald* interviewed Menicucci he flatly denied that the FLNA was being organized to "make war on

[18] Cassels, p. 709.

[19] *NYT*, March 21, 1923; "Our Black Shirts and the Reds," *LD*, LXXVII (April 7, 1923), 16-18.

radicals here." Italian consuls in various cities also denied that the League had any political significance. The innocent denials, however, did little to alter the views of the unenthusiastic majority of Italian-American newspapers. While most papers believed that the success of Fascism in Italy would mean greater respect for Italians everywhere in the eyes of the world, they opposed establishing a *Fascio* in America for fear of arousing nativist suspicion and of dividing the Italian communities. At this early stage many members of the Sons of Italy also refused to have anything to do with the movement.[20]

Faced with the general opposition of the American press and much of the Italian community, the original sponsors of FLNA held a meeting in late March 1923. Here the frustrated American *fascisti* denounced critics of the FLNA as radical "enemies of mankind." Nevertheless, the leaders realized they had to postpone the official formation of the FLNA. Ambassador Caetani, himself critical of the idea, announced to the press that no action would be taken until the matter was studied thoroughly. A few days later a number of lodges of the Sons of Italy passed resolutions opposing the League.[21]

In the fall of 1924 the FLNA was reactivated—this time at the instigation of the Italian Foreign Office. The unaggressive Prince Caetani was removed as Ambassador and replaced by Giacomo de Martino. Count di Revel now arrived in New York to take command as President of the Fascist Council and chief organizer of the American *fascisti*. Thus where the American founders failed, Italian authorities, more tactful and less blatant, quietly succeeded. Local affiliations began to spring up throughout the country numbering at least seventy branches with a dues paying membership of between 6,000 and 7,000. Although the ulterior objectives of the League were not clearly stated, most members agreed that it was established to fight "subversive influences" in America, described by one Fascist as "atheism, internationalism, free-love, communism, and class hatred." Count di Revel often likened the FLNA to the Knights of Columbus or the YMCA, maintaining its primary objective was to enlighten the American people on the "ideals of Fascism."[22]

[20] *NYT*, March 26, 1923; "Our Black Shirts," pp. 16-18; "Fascisti in the United States," *Nation*, cxvi (April 25, 1923), 502-03.

[21] *NYT*, March 25, 30, 1923.

[22] *NYT*, July 24, Sept. 17, 1924, Dec. 23, 1929; Livingston, pp. 738-40.

The framing of the League's constitution and oath was a source of contention among leaders. When finally drawn, the wording was designed to avoid all possible offense to American sentiment. The oath read:

I swear to my honor

To serve with fidelity and discipline the Fascist idea of society—based on religion, the Fatherland, and the family, and to respect the authority of the League and of the hierarchy and tradition of our race.

To love, serve, obey and exalt the United States of America and to render obedience and respect to its constitution and its laws.

To keep alive the cult with Italy as the Fatherland and eternal light of civilization and greatness.

To combat with all my might theories and ideas tending to subvert, corrupt, and disgrace religion, the Fatherland, or the family.

To do my best to improve my culture, my physique and my morals, to render me fit for the part I am to play in serving the nation in its hour of greatness.

To submit to the discipline of the hierarchy of the Fascist League of North America.[23]

As the oath indicates, Fascist authorities glossed over the problem of divided loyalty, reconciling complete "fidelity" to the "Fascist idea of society" with complete "obedience" to the Constitution of the United States. Despite the verbal gymnastics, the FLNA encountered severe criticism. Attacks leveled at the League can be reduced to two charges: that it was controlled directly by the Italian government and that its activities aimed at regimenting, either through persuasion or intimidation, Americans of Italian origin. How valid were these charges? Professor Arthur Livingston, who did a short study of the movement in 1927, maintained that the American *Fascio* had "but tenuous" connection with Mussolini. The Italian dictator, Livingston believed, had better sources than the League for inside information in America, and thus his interest in it was nothing more than fraternal. Critics, on the other hand, outlined in detail the rela-

[23] Quoted in Paul Radin, "The Italians of San Francisco: Their Adjustment and Acculturation," *Cultural Anthropology*, monograph no. 1 (mimeographed paper, July 1935), p. 35.

tionship between the FLNA and the Italian government. It seemed clear to anti-Fascists that the various League branches not only sent messages of "devotion and homage" to Mussolini but that Count di Revel himself was under "direct orders" of the Rome Bureau of Fascism Abroad. Press dispatches reveal this to be the case. On one occasion the Count went to Rome to report directly to Mussolini himself on the operations of the League. According to the *New York Times*, the Premier expressed "keen satisfaction" with Count di Revel's work in America. But even more serious was the "court of discipline" which the League instituted around 1927. The Fascist organ *Il Grido della Stirpe* brazenly announced that the purpose of the court was to provide "rigid discipline" and mete out "exemplary punishment." Even Mussolini openly declared in 1928 that a punitive tribunal was to be established within the League. Yet Count di Revel, questioned by newsmen, denied the existence of such an institution. That the existence of this tribunal of terror had been established, however, is borne out by an official publication of the FLNA, which devotes a section to "La Corte di Disciplina" and spells out in detail the types of punishments to be imposed. Thus it would seem that the charges leveled against the League were in the main valid.[24]

Criticism of the FLNA culminated in 1929 when *Harper's* published the sensational article "Mussolini's American Empire: The Fascist Invasion of the U.S." The author, Marcus Duffield, described the League as an integral instrument of International Fascism. The exposé caused some stir in Congress, where Representative Hamilton Fish and Senator William Borah had already been voicing occasional criticisms of Fascist activities. Senator Thomas Heflin succeeded in obtaining a resolution calling for a Congressional investigation. But Count di Revel moved first. In a matter of days he announced to the press that the League would be disbanded. At the time of its dissolution President di Revel reported a membership of 12,500 in some eighty branches throughout the country.[25]

The folding of the FLNA was carried out in consultation with

[24] Livingston, p. 740; Marcus Duffield, "Mussolini's American Empire," *Harper's*, CLIX (Nov. 1929), 662-66; Frank C. Hanighen, "Foreign Political Movements in the United States," *Foreign Affairs*, XVI (Oct. 1937), 11-16; *NYT*, Sept. 4, 1927, Jan. 31, 1928; *Lega Fascista del Nord America*, passim.

[25] Duffield, passim; *NYT*, Oct. 27, 1929, Dec. 23, 1929.

the State Department, whose head, Secretary Henry L. Stimson, exonerated the Fascists from the charge of subversion and ascribed the League's dissolution to a well-advised desire to avoid "adverse speculative comment and possible misunderstanding." This pleasant diplomatic rapport has led one historian to conclude that "no matter how the pill was sweetened, the League's disappearance was a serious blow to the rapid spread of Fascist ideas in the United States." This conclusion must be modified. For one thing, the message of Fascism was already well disseminated in America, as Italian-American advocates proudly pointed out. Furthermore, Fascists in America did not have to be prodded or organized by the Italian government. Whether directly controlled by the Italian government or operating independently, several organizations apart from the FLNA were more than willing to keep up the propaganda campaign. Thus, no sooner was the FLNA declared defunct than a new organization emerged as its successor, the Lictor Federation. This new movement was formed by a native Fascist, the rabid Domenico Trombetta of *Il Grido della Stirpe*. The Lictor Federation became the object of a Federal Bureau of Investigation probe in the spring of 1930. An FBI agent, under pretext, secured from Trombetta information about the Federation and a copy of its bylaws. This material, J. Edgar Hoover informed President Hoover, "clearly shows that this organization is nothing but the successor of the Fascist organization which was suppressed in 1929 in the United States by Premier Mussolini to avoid criticism to the effect that the Italian government was trying to influence the people in the United States to approve and support the Fascist ideas." Because of Trombetta's leadership, it is doubtful that the Lictor Federation enjoyed the influence of the FLNA. Still, the immediate appearance of the Federation suggests that the propagation of Fascism by Italian-Americans needed little encouragement from the Italian government.[26]

The activities of the Sons of Italy provide another example of Fascist sentiment among Italians in America. In the 1920s membership in this fraternal organization was over 300,000, with local lodges in almost all parts of the country. The issue of Fascism caused a deep rift in the "Grand Lodge" when John di Silvestro rushed to Italy in 1922 to place at the feet of Mussolini

[26] Cassels, p. 711; J. Edgar Hoover, memo, May 24, 1930, Container 1-G/856, HP.

the allegiance of the entire society. Silvestro was accused of having signed a compact with a "Lega Italiana" which placed the Sons under the complete control of the Italian government. Among those criticizing Silvestro's surreptitious move were State Senator Cotillo and Congressman La Guardia. A protracted legal battle arose over the use of the organization's name and possession of its funds. Eventually, the New York state branch, led by the minority Cotillo-La Guardia faction, bolted and formed a separate fraternity. But despite the initial dissension the Sons of Italy, now purged of all ideological laggards, became an important source of Fascist propaganda, with many of its chapters acting as unofficial organs of the Italian Ministry of Popular Culture.[27]

The Dante Alighieri Society also became a platform for propaganda as much as a center for poetry. Founded in 1890 to promote in America an awareness of Italy's great cultural heritage, the literary society succumbed to the Fascist cause in the twenties. In 1940, *Fortune* maintained that the Dante Society was a "principal tool" of Italy's propaganda ministry. Although Italian-American officials repeatedly denied that Dante's followers dared to pervert the purity of literature, a message sent to Mussolini from the Society's President, Felice Felicione, reveals the extent of the perversion. "O Duce," wrote Felicione, "Our Society, especially in these historic days, is proud of serving the Fascist revolution. It reiterates to you its pledges of unwavering loyalty, ever ready, together with the whole Italian people, to believe, to obey, to fight at your command." One could discuss countless other Italian-American organizations and their capitulation to Fascism. But it is enough to note that these organizations served Mussolini's Italy well, and that, therefore, the collapse of the FLNA did not seriously hinder the spread of Fascist ideas in America.[28]

PROPAGANDA AND TERROR

Far from changing peoples' minds, propaganda merely reinforces prior convictions. Fascist propaganda was effective on

[27] *NYT*, July 20, 1925, Sept. 26, 1926; Salvatore Benanti, *La Secessione della "Sons of Italy Grand Lodge"* (New York, 1926), NYPL.
[28] *Fortune*, XXII (Nov. 1940), 86-87. Felicione is quoted in Gaetano Salvemini, *Italian Fascist Activities in the United States* (Public Affairs pamphlet, Washington, D.C., 1940), p. 10.

Italian-Americans only because they deeply wanted to believe in Mussolini and his regime. Nonetheless, it must be admitted that the government in Italy made skillful use of every conceivable means of thought control. Mussolini himself was not unaware of the extent to which the mind could be manipulated. A showman par excellence, he was a masterful actor who could create impressions with great shrewdness. "His whole regime," Denis Mack Smith has written, "depended on a journalistic mastery of propaganda."[29]

Because the popularity of his regime depended on the refined art of propaganda, it behooves us to turn our attention to its vehicles in America. In addition to the Italian-American press, the radio was an important medium of communication. Indeed in some respects the radio was even more effective than the newspaper. Not only were immigrants repeatedly reminded that it was an Italian—Guglielmo Marconi—who had invented the "wireless," but more importantly, Italian-Americans themselves provided a captive audience. Since many Italians read no English, and since many preferred listening to the spoken word rather than struggling with the strange idioms of the Italian press in America, the regional-minded foreign language broadcast became their major source of information. Some newspaper publishers had their own programs. Ettore Patrizi of San Francisco's *L'Italia* presented a "Voce dell'Italia" hour which opened with the "Giovinezza," the Fascist anthem.[30]

Radio propaganda increased during the late 1930s when Italy was drawn into the Axis alliance. Broadcasts usually opened with the Fascist hymn and a salute to Mussolini. For the most part the listening audience consisted of the unassimilated and illiterate immigrants who revered the exploits of great men and remained deeply suspicious of any news coming from the English language media. Later some Italians tuned in to shortwave broadcasts beamed directly from Italy, which they regarded as the only "reliable" source of information before Pearl Harbor. A study of this group in Boston showed that the listeners revealed a "complex attitude, composed of militant identification

[29] Denis Mack Smith, *Italy*, p. 471.

[30] An account of Patrizi's activities can be found in Marino de Medici, "The Italian Language Press in the San Francisco Bay Area from 1930 to 1940" (Master of Journalism Thesis, University of California, Berkeley, 1963).

with Italy and resentment toward America." Exploiting the plight of the immigrant, Fascist announcers could easily play upon his hostility toward the United States.[31]

In manipulating the mass mind, physical images are often more important than the spoken word, a fact not lost sight of by Fascists who saw the propaganda possibilities of the newly established Italian motion picture industry. In New York the Italian-American could visit the Roma Cine Teatro on Broadway or the Cine Città on West 54th Street and see for themselves the wonderful happenings in the old country. Since pictures screened at these and other movie houses were made in Italy, many Italian-Americans could only conclude that the camera cannot lie. Because some movie houses were subsidized from Rome they had to register with the Secretary of State as an agency of a foreign government. Such restrictions, however, did not prevent the Italian government from shipping to the United States blatant propaganda "shorts" which praised the achievements of Fascism along with "lecture" films such as *Il Padre della Patria*. In light of the flowering of post-World War II Italian cinema it is strange that Italian propaganda films never came close to matching the brilliance of Nazi films like Leni Reifenstahl's *Triumph of the Will* or Soviet films like Sergei Eisenstein's *Ten Days That Shook the World*. Perhaps Mussolini found consolation in seeing himself appear in a Samuel Goldwyn production, although for once he was overshadowed—by Lionel Barrymore.[32]

Pamphleteering was still another means of reaching the Italian community. The plethora of leaflets and circulars that flooded Italian neighborhoods provided neat, tidy thoughts on the subject of Fascism. The Sons of Italy, the Italian Historical Society, and the Casa Italiana contributed their share of educational materials, but the most prolific source was the Italian Library of Information. Located in New York City, the Library was di-

---

[31] Jeanette Sayre Smith, "Broadcasting for Marginal Americans," *Public Opinion Quarterly*, VI (Winter 1942), 588-603; id. and Jerome Bruner, "Short-Wave Listening in an Italian Community," *ibid.* (Fall 1941), 640-56; Rudolph Arnheim and Martha Bayne, "Foreign Language Broadcasts over Local American Stations" in Paul Lasarsfeld and Frank Stanton, eds., *Radio Research* (New York, 1941), pp. 3-64; Carl J. Friedrich, "Foreign Language Radio and the War," *Common Ground*, III (Autumn 1942), 65-72.

[32] "Fascismo Says It with Movies," *Research Supplement*, Vol. V (News Research Services, Inc., April 23, 1941); for a discussion of Hollywood and Fascist Italy, see below, pp. 243-44.

rected by Ugo V. D'Annunzio, son of the flamboyant poet. The "Outline Studies" issued by the Library were designed to make it appear that Fascism held something for everybody: investment opportunities and tax concessions for business; welfare programs and full employment for labor; and for society in general new highways, hydroelectric plants, land-reclamation projects, aircraft industries, hospitals and public housing, libraries, schools, and opera houses. The more curious could read elaborate diagrams explaining the intricate "Syndical Corporate System." Intellectuals and artists could find a "new order" of culture which combined democratic inclusiveness with aristocratic tastes, while students discovered that Fascism was a youth movement from which would flow the lifeblood of Italy's future. Italian history was also treated heroically, giving free play to national greatness, both past and present. Frequently this called for some documentary face-lifting, as in Mussolini's rewriting of Italy's role in World War I; or outright forgery, as in the letter produced by the Rome government showing a panicky President Lincoln offering a commission to the great Garibaldi after the disaster of Bull Run. As history gave way to instant myths, Fascism laid claim to the entire heritage of Italy, from Imperial Rome to the glorious *Risorgimento*. Lastly, Fascism as an ideology emerged as a grand historical synthesis transcending the stale categories of traditional politics. Neither a simple dictatorship nor a cumbersome democracy, neither a capitalist order nor a socialist state, Fascism was based on the ideals of class collaboration and social justice, on the spirit of egalitarianism and the practice of elitism. It was a government of the people, by the leaders, for the nation. To the uninformed reader such slick eclecticism made Fascism seem the best of all ideological worlds.[33]

Until the late 1930s propagandists were careful not to express any anti-American sentiment. Indeed one of their favorite themes was the similarities between the institutions of the United States and those of Italy. As an organization of patriots the *fascisti* was

[33] The "Outline Studies" consisted of a series of forty large pamphlets too numerous to list here; for examples of Fascist historical revisionism, see Benito Mussolini, *Foreign Evidence on the War at the Italian Front* (Rome, n.d.), pamphlet; and "Carl Sandburg, Abraham Lincoln and Giuseppe Garibaldi," *Il Mondo* (Dec. 1941), pp. 7-8.

equated with the American Legion; the Italian youth club, the *Balilla*, likened to the Boy Scouts. Public works and welfare programs of the Corporate State had their counterpart in the New Deal, so Italian-Americans were told. Italy's expansionism in the Mediterranean was no different from American imperialism in the Caribbean. And as for Mussolini himself, his aspirations compared favorably with those of contemporary American presidents: Theodore Roosevelt, who aroused a nationalistic élan; Calvin Coolidge, who routed striking radicals; Franklin Roosevelt, who saved the country from the threat of social upheaval.

Such emotional equations enabled Italian-Americans to maintain a dual identification with both Italy and America. But propagandists were not content with sustaining the complete loyalty of older generations of immigrants; the minds of Italian-American youth had to be captured. To this end, the neighborhood schools, where Italian language instruction was conducted after regular class hours, offered an excellent opportunity to mix politics with lingustics. In Rhode Island the *Providence Journal*, investigating the Dante Alighieri School, discovered that children were being indoctrinated with Fascist ideas, that diplomas were awarded by the Marquis de Ferrante, Italian Consul in Boston, that textbooks were sent from Italy, and that the subsidy for the program itself came from Italy. In New York an Italian-American teacher rebelled at the straitjacket tactics of Fascist pedagogues. She rejected documents sent from Rome advising her "what children in Fascist schools abroad should be taught." Having done so, her classroom was visited by a consular official who proceeded to quiz her students on Mussolini and Fascism. When he discovered the pupils had not learned the Fascist catechism, the teacher was dismissed and replaced by a more politically conscious instructor sent from Italy. In California "educational agents" from Italy also worked closely with consulates and local teachers of Italian descent. Fascist textbooks were sent from Italy and distributed by the Italian consuls to every pupil to be memorized along with irregular verbs. When the California State Un-American Activities Committee investigated the schools in 1940, it found more than the verbs irregular. San Francisco's Chief of Police testified that pupils who attended the sessions in Fugazzi Hall wore the uniforms of the *Balilla*. What is more, some leading Italian-American citizens had organized a student's version of the *Fasci*

99

di Combattimento. In reality, the language classes had become a children's hour with Fascism.[34]

If parental pressures were not enough, children were also enticed with offers of a free vacation in Italy as a reward for their service to the cause. In the summer of 1929 more than a hundred youths went to Italy to attend summer camp, the trip having been arranged by the FLNA. Sporting the uniform of the *Balilla,* the pupils were directed up the ship's gangplank by local New York Fascist leaders to whom the young Blackshirts gave the official salute. Ambassador de Martino presided over the gala departure. In 1934 another pilgrimage was arranged by Piero Parini, head of Rome's Bureau of Fascism Abroad. Weighing the advantages of such ideological excursions, one newspaper in Italy editorialized: "They will return to foreign lands with an indelible impression of the new powerful generation which is rising under the emblem of Fascism. In turn these children will become *Balilla* and *Avanguardista* themselves. . . . They will find youth organizations which gather around their masters, around Fascist secretaries and consuls to cultivate their bodies and souls to the worship of their fatherland."[35]

Fascist activities were not confined to proselytizing young "bodies and souls." Control over adult Italian-Americans could also be obtained by applying economic pressure. Since many Italian businessmen in the United States were engaged in trade with Italian enterprise, they could scarcely afford to incur the displeasure of Fascist officials. Import permits would be granted only to those whose loyalty and full cooperation were unquestioned. Moreover, Italian-American merchants sponsored pro-Fascist radio programs and often they would not advertise in a newspaper which happened to disapprove of one or another of Mussolini's actions.[36]

[34] Duffield, pp. 664-68; *TCR,* "Fascist Activities," pp. 282-321. In view of the complaints that appeared in the Italian-American press there is some reason to doubt the complete effectiveness of these propaganda programs. Writers were forever admonishing Italian-Americans to study their native language, but as one paper lamented: "In America, despite all the propaganda for Italianism and the past and present glories of Italy, Italian parents appear apathetic toward their mother-country, and what is worse, they sometimes deny their nationality." *Il Corriere Italica* (Chicago), Feb. 20, 1937.

[35] Quoted in Duffield, pp. 666-67.

[36] *Ibid.,* pp. 668-71; Friedrich, p. 66.

100

Other methods of influencing and controlling the Italian community were available to Fascists. Although in his first years in power Mussolini gave his blessing to those of Italian origin who lived in America, by the end of the 1920s he was demanding that immigrants must remain Italian citizens until the "seventh generation." With similar inconsistency, he first opposed American immigration laws, then curbed Italian immigration in an attempt to build manpower at home. Thus pressure was applied on Italian residents in the United States not to take out naturalization papers. In 1927 the Commissariat of Emigration was reorganized in order to place Italians abroad under consular jurisdiction. Minister of Foreign Affairs Grandi candidly revealed the motive behind this move. "Our citizens," he stated, "especially those of the lowest classes, who are destined to live among other races are fatally and violently assimilated into them. Why should our race constitute a sort of human storehouse to feed other nations? Why should our mothers furnish soldiers for other nations?" To establish greater influence over immigrants in America, the Italian Foreign Office issued new directives to the FLNA. Members of the League were instructed to respect the laws of the land, to respect Italian representatives abroad and obey their commands, to "defend Italianism," and to be as disciplined in America as Italy "demands" Italians to be at home. Count di Revel, head of the FLNA, bluntly stated in the League's *Giovinezza* the aims of American Fascism: "To bring back to Italian citizenship all those countrymen who have been legally denationalized, and—what is worse—who, by accepting foreign ideals and foreign languages, have made themselves bastards of Italy."[37]

To arrest the bastardization of Italian-Americans, Fascist authorities had no qualms in using physical coercion. During the twenties cases were reported of American citizens of Italian descent returning to Italy for business or pleasure, only to be inducted into the Italian army. Similarly, those who spoke out against Fascism in the United States risked reprisals against their relatives in Italy. Italian officials could refuse immigration permits to their relatives or, worse still, report allegedly unlawful entries to the U.S. Immigration Service and then deal harshly with the hapless victims as they were returned to Italy. When

[37] "Mussolini's Orders to Italians Here," *LD*, xcvi (Feb. 26, 1928), 12; Grandi is quoted in *NYT*, April 1, 1927; Count di Revel in Ray Tucker, "Tools of Mussolini in America," *New Republic*, lii (Sept. 14, 1927), 89-91.

the Boston anti-Fascist Mario Chiossone was returned in 1927, he was immediately sentenced to a long prison term.[38]

The agents of intimidation were mainly the Italian consuls. Significantly, the number of consular agencies in America continued to increase during the Fascist period even though Italian immigration declined. It was the consuls who registered Italians as members of the FLNA, where they took a Fascist oath and carried an identification card with their picture and signature of the particular consular official. The consulates wielded great influence in the Italian communities. According to Interior Secretary Harold Ickes, they were also used to carry funds from Italy to the United States.[39]

In 1928 the *Nation* published an article on "Fascist Blackmail" based upon the "scores" of letters it had received from Italian workers in the industrial towns of the Northeast. The workers and their wives were warned by consular officials that unless their anti-Fascist activities ceased they would receive unpleasant news about their families back home. The *Nation* printed samples of the letters. This form of "international terrorism" brought angry protests from the historian Samuel Eliot Morison, labor leader William Green, lawyer Clarence Darrow, civil libertarian Roger Baldwin, and other members of the International Committee for Political Prisoners. The complaints eventually led to a demand for a Congressional investigation.[40]

In the House Un-American Activities Investigations, conducted in the late 1930s, further charges were leveled at Italian consul officials. One of the main witnesses at the hearings on Fascism was Girolamo Valenti, editor of the anti-Fascist *La Stampa Libera*. Valenti, who under cross examination claimed that he had been studying Fascist activities for over ten years, was ready to produce letters and affidavits from Catholic priests and Protestant ministers who were abused in one way or another for refusing to subscribe to the Fascist propaganda program. In order to support his accusation that consular officials were "secret Fas-

[38] *NYT*, July 31, 1927.

[39] *Fortune* printed photographs of these identification cards and other paraphernalia, xxii (Nov. 1940), 87; Harold Ickes, *The Secret Diary of Harold Ickes* (New York, 1953), iii, 365.

[40] "Fascist Blackmail," *Nation*, cxxvi (June 6, 1928), 629-30; *The Fascist Dictatorship* (ICPP pamphlet, New York, n.d.)

cist agents" who not only disseminated propaganda but intimidated those who opposed the will of the Italian government, Valenti presented an affidavit recording the story of a miner in Pennsylvania who had collected funds for the Spanish Loyalists. The consul in Johnstown, Pennsylvania asked him to come to his office. The miner's wife tells the story:

. . . My husband could not go. He is a miner. But I was worried. In fact, I couldn't sleep for two nights. I thought something happened to my family in Italy. So I went in his place . . . with my son-in-law, Paul Cubeta.

Consul Jannelli had no news of my family. He sent my son-in-law out of the room and began threatening to have my husband deported for collecting money for Spain. He read me a letter, which my husband had sent to the Anti-Fascist Committee in New York, along with the sum of $23, which he and Antonio Caraglio, another Nettleton miner, collected last December.

That letter must have been stolen.

The consul said: "Your man has been collecting money for Communists."

I said: "My man collected money to help poor people and orphans buy clothes."

The consul said: "Don't you know you belong to the United States and must not help people of other countries. If you help the Loyalist government, you are a Communist."

I said: "My man is not a Communist. He is a Democrat. He is a citizen of the United States."

Consul Jannelli was geting angry. His voice was growing louder. He said my husband must write a letter, saying he was sorry he had collected the money; if my husband refused, the consul said he could have him deported to Italy. He said the Labor Department gave him authority in such cases.

I said he couldn't do that. My husband is a citizen. But the consul said he could have my husband's citizenship papers taken away.

The consul was getting angrier all the time. He said the Italian Government could make trouble for my people in the old country, if we displeased Mussolini here.

"I know the place you come from in the old country," he

103

said. "The Italian Government can watch you in this country and watch your mother in the old country."[41]

Another witness at the hearings, Homer Martin, President of the United Auto Workers, testified that Fascists were interfering in local politics in Detroit and the consuls were supporting their efforts. Martin also informed the Committee that the Italian government had replaced a less militant consular agent with the notorious Giacomo Ungarelli, an aggressive blackguard who had been schooled in the methods of Fascist "coercion" in Argentina. As soon as Ungarelli arrived in Detroit he set out to seize control of economic patronage, a move which, in Martin's words, caused a "veritable reign of terror." Citizens appealed to the prosecuting attorney of Wayne County, and Larry Davidow, Chairman of the Detroit Labor Conference against Fascism, wrote directly to Roosevelt himself. When these complaints reached the State Department the charges were "so compelling" the government requested Ungarelli's recall at once.[42]

Certainly not all consular authorities behaved with the cruel arrogance of a Jannelli or an Ungarelli. Nevertheless, the potential for intimidation existed, and time and again groups like the American Civil Liberties Union had to persuade the State Department to warn consulates about summoning American citizens of Italian background for political "grilling." Although adverse publicity of this nature curbed some of the worst techniques of Fascist terrorism, it failed to halt the spread of Fascist influence. The FLNA, it is true, was disbanded, but prominent members of the League were soon to reappear in other pro-Fascist organizations. Giuseppe Previtali, for example, a leading figure in the League, became Chairman of the Italian Historical Society in 1935, an organization he used not to reclaim Italy's heritage but to acclaim Mussolini's crusade in Ethiopia. Moreover, public criticism seems to have done little to restrain Fascist groups from staging mass demonstrations, parading with Italian dignitaries, collecting funds for Mussolini's military adventures, and other brazen activities. Often these affairs resulted in clashes with anti-Fascists, some of which, as we shall see, ended in violence, blood-

[41] HUAC, II, 1181-84; Martin Dies to Valenti, June 3, 1938, VP.
[42] Davidow to Roosevelt, May 28, 1934, OF 233A, RP; HUAC, IV, 2677-79; *FRUS, 1935*, II, 543-51.

shed, and even murder. A few of the more zealous camp followers paraded in Fascist uniforms, consisting of a black sateen shirt and tie, white trousers, spiral puttees, a Lictoral emblem, and, for ready use, a *manganello,* the short whip carried by the Italian Blackshirts.[43]

The rise of the Third Reich, and particularly the advent of the Axis Alliance in 1936, produced a tenuous united front of the Right in America. The more extremist Italian-American Fascists managed to submerge their national animosities to join forces with German-American Bundists. On one occasion American Blackshirts and Silvershirts held a joint meeting at the New York Hippodrome to denounce Loyalist Spain and the Communist "menace." Perhaps the most conspicuous episode of collaboration came in the summer of 1937 in a rally at Camp Nordland, New Jersey. Here Italian war veterans clad in black uniforms marched shoulder to shoulder with Bundists. Dr. Salvatore Caridi and Fritz Kuhn, America's own "Fuehrer," delivered speeches from the same platform, to the wild applause of their fervent Storm Troopers. Doubtless the number of Italian-Americans participating in this fusion of fanatics was infinitesimal. Yet in an era when the Nazi rallies at Nuremberg thundered seismically throughout the western world, the antics of the little-league in New Jersey could not be dismissed lightly. Small wonder these boisterous demonstrations of solidarity gave substance to the suspicion that the American Fascists were part of a reactionary "International," an ideological fifth column within the gates. Perhaps writers like George Seldes, George Britt, and John Carlson (pseudonym) exaggerated the threat of a potential Fascist take-over, but in light of the surrealistic political world of the 1930s their fears are understandable.[44]

---

[43] *NYT,* Feb. 24, 1933; photographs of Italian-American Blackshirts appeared in, among other magazines, *Fortune,* xxii (Nov. 1940), 85.

[44] HUAC, i, 12-17, 69; "Fascism in America," *LD,* cxxiv (Aug. 14, 1937); *NYT,* July 19, 1937; Hanighen, pp. 11-16; George Seldes, *Facts and Fascism* (New York, 1943); George Britt, *Fifth Column in America* (New York, 1940); John Roy Carlson (pseudonym), *Under Cover* (New York, 1943); apparently the German government, unlike the Italian, had considerable reservations about its "stupid and noisy" ideological followers in America. See Joachim Remak, " 'Friends of the New Germany': The Bund and German-American Relations," *Journal of Modern History,* xxix (March 1957), 38-41.

THE PROBLEM OF ITALIAN-AMERICAN FASCISM

Although it is highly doubtful that Mussolini had anything to do with the more fanatical Italian-American activists, it is clear his government established the FLNA and made effective use of the consular agencies. In so doing, the government in Italy had two objectives in mind. First, the existence of a devoted *Fascio* in America would help stifle anti-Fascist criticism, especially the counterpropaganda campaigns of Italian exiles who fled to the United States in the late twenties. Having crushed the opposition at home, Mussolini hoped to suppress the potential pockets of opposition abroad in order to perpetuate an image of Italy as stable, prosperous, and happy. Only then would his government be in a respected position that would enable him to bargain over war debts and secure future loans. Moreover, the presence of an American *Fascio* would keep the immigrants in a thoroughly patriotic mood; and with the possibility of a future war, they would be ready to rise to the call. It is clear from Grandi's complaint about Italian mothers furnishing soldiers for America that the Fascist government looked upon the immigrant as wasted military potential. Yet here the strategy of the Fascist government proved unrealistic (for reasons that must be explained in a later chapter). During the Ethiopian War, while Italian-Americans poured forth fervent emotional support, only two small Italian-American brigades answered the call to arms. As for World War II, there was no answer but stunned silence.

How many Italian-Americans actively supported and participated in Fascist activities in the United States? Obviously the answer to this question is difficult to obtain. Aside from the problem of defining "active support," there are wide discrepancies in the numbers estimated. At the Dies hearings, witnesses testified there were about 10,000 Blackshirts plus 100,000 more who were willing to make appearances at the "public manifestations" of the 200 Fascist groups throughout the country. While the anarchist exile Armando Borghi maintained that during the Ethiopian War tens of thousands of Italian-American Blackshirts could be counted on to turn out for mass rallies (whereas anti-Fascists could attract no more than 2,000). Gaetano Salvemini believed in 1940 that 5 percent of Italian-Americans were "out and out Fascists." Congressman Martin Dies agreed with Salvemini's figure, but California State Senator Jack Tenney thought that "those truly influenced by Fascism" came closer to 10 percent. Taking four and one-half million as the approximate population of Italian-Americans in 1940, these hopelessly diverse estimates range from 10,000 Blackshirts on the one hand to somewhere between 225,000 and 450,000 all-out Fascists on the other.[45]

Even more difficult than estimating the number of Blackshirt activists is the problem of determining pro-Fascist sentiment among Italian-Americans. The Italian-American press, it should be remembered, was almost 90 percent pro-Mussolini. Not until 1941 did the press completely desert Il Duce, and then the repudiation of Fascism was a result of diplomatic developments rather than political repentance. More will be said about this in a later chapter. It is enough to point out here that even in the period immediately prior to Pearl Harbor, when Italian-Americans began to have second thoughts about Mussolini's infallibility, estimates of lingering Fascist sentiment varied considerably. These estimates, moreover, were made by anti-Fascists—who after 1940 finally obtained an audience from an American public belatedly awakened to the menace of Fascism—and thus must be accepted with caution. Carmelo Zito, editor of the anti-Fascist *Il Corriere del Popolo* (San Francisco), stated in a National Broadcasting Company interview (June 1940) that in California 75 percent of the Italian-Americans were against Fascism, 15 percent had no interest in the issue due to educational limitations, and 10 percent remained pro-Fascist despite Mussolini's alliance with Hitler and Italy's declaration of war on France and England. At the same time Salvemini maintained that 50 percent of all Italian-Americans were indifferent, 10 percent anti-Fascist, 5 percent Fascist, while the remaining 35 percent comprised a nucleus of people "with a mentality which has not yet clearly become Fascist and anti-democratic but which might crystallize at the first emergency." Count Carlo Sforza, a former Italian Foreign Minister living in the United States, Professor William Y. Elliott of Harvard, and numerous other anti-Fascists shared

[45] HUAC, I, 15-17; II, 1182; Armando Borghi, *Mezzo secolo di anarchia, 1898-1945* (Naples, 1954), pp. 339-41; Salvemini, *Fascist Activities*, p. 18; *Fortune*, XXII (Nov. 1940), 102; *Commission on Un-American Activities in California: Executive Hearing* (Sacramento, 1943), III, 1447; see also Morris Schonbach, "Native Fascism During the 1930s and 1940s: A Study of Its Roots, Its Growth and Its Decline" (Ph.D. Thesis, University of California, Los Angeles, 1958), pp. 105-18.

Salvemini's apprehensions. Sforza warned President Roosevelt and Interior Secretary Ickes that Italian-Americans were predominantly pro-Fascist, while *Fortune* magazine alarmingly claimed in 1940 that if the United States entered the war the *fascisti* would constitute "enemy soldiers within our borders."[46]

In view of the absence of any evidence of Italian-American disloyalty during the war, and in light of the rapidity with which Italian papers repudiated Mussolini and Fascism after Pearl Harbor, such fears seem unfounded. Put to the ultimate test, Italian-American Fascism proved more gesture than substance. Much of the nervousness about pro-Fascist sentiment resulted from confusing nostalgic patriotism for ideology. Too often anti-Fascists regarded the Italian-Americans' devotion to the home country as unqualified allegiance to Fascism and Mussolini, just as pro-Fascists assumed that any criticism of Mussolini and his regime bespoke a slander on Italy itself. Clearly, Italian-American reverence for Italy antedated Fascism. The millions of immigrants who were aroused by the glory of Mussolini's regime had responded in much the same way for previous Italian governments. If they applauded louder for Mussolini it was only because Fascism made national pride the answer to national humiliation. Rather than ideological true believers, Italian-Americans were sentimental fellow travelers.

That the great majority of Italian immigrants were stirred by nonideological motives by no means dismisses the problem of Italian-American Fascism. True, the sources of the phenomenon are rooted in social pressures rather than ideological convictions. But it is cold comfort to assume from this that America is a country innocent of ideology and therefore immune to the appeals of European totalitarianism. Lest we believe that American society is somehow blessed by a superior moral and political wisdom, it is necessary to recall that the great majority of "average" people in Italy and in Germany responded to Mussolini and Hitler for nonideological reasons. Economic insecurity, class stratification, status anxieties, and wounded nationalism, not the fine-spun theories of Giovanni Gentile and Alfred Rosenberg, explain the mass support of Mussolini's Italy and Hitler's Third Reich. The sad truth is that most Italians and Germans could not care less about formal political liberty, and to a certain extent

[46] De Medici, p. 158; Salvemini, *Fascist Activities*, pp. 1-2; Ickes, III, 463; *Fortune*, XXII (Nov. 1940), 108-09.

this mentality was characteristic of many Italian-Americans. Even a sympathetic observer revealed this indifference when he wrote in 1928: "The real essence of the admiration of the local Italians for Mussolini, however, is not of a political nature. The Italians of Chicago are not interested in the governmental experiments of Fascism. They do not care whether Italy has a parliamentary form of government or not. They see in Mussolini only the savior of Italy, and they admire him because of what he has been doing for the good of Italy."[47]

One can account for the attitude of Italian-Americans by rejecting ideology and stressing the chronic distresses and psychic needs of the immigrants. To be aware of these social strains is to understand the predicament of the Italian-American; but to understand all is not to forgive all. If responsibility for the misguided attitudes must be laid somewhere, the culpable ones, it seems to me, are those who knew better, and those who should have known better, especially the educated and intelligent Italian-American publishers. It was one thing for publishers to print paeans to Mussolini's Italy; it was something else to praise the idea of Fascism itself. In 1938, for example, Generoso Pope hailed the spread of "Il Corporativismo all'Estero," delightfully informing readers of *Il Progresso* that the Fascist economy was being adopted not only in Germany, France, and England but also in the United States. Similarly, Ettore Patrizi baldly declared in 1932 that "the United States does need a Mussolini. But there is only one Mussolini in this world. We should create one here." Patrizi assured readers of *L'Italia* that "there is no wrong in such a wish. . . . A Dictator is needed in the United States." By making Fascism synonymous with Italy's greatness, and by going far enough to suggest the benefits of Fascism for America, publishers like Pope and Patrizi (not to mention Trombetta and his ilk) served poorly the already bewildered Italian community.[48]

Yet the major burden of responsibility rests with American society as a whole. First of all, the nativist enmity characteristic of large sections of white, Anglo-Saxon, Protestant America nurtured in the Italians the very inferiority complexes Fascism

[47] Giovanni E. Schiavo, *The Italians of Chicago* (Chicago, 1928), p. 118; see also the same attitude described in the Public Works Administration Federal Writers Project, *The Italians of New York* (New York, 1938), p. 100.

[48] *Il Progresso*, Dec. 8, 1938; *L'Italia*, June 7, 1932.

109

so successfully played upon. In telling the Italians they were something less than "American," nativists created enclaves of emotional estrangement within the country, thereby leaving the alienated Italian-American nowhere to turn. Further, American society failed to provide meaningful political education to the masses of immigrants. The public school system notwithstanding, most immigrants never fully grasped the essential distinctions between a democracy and a dictatorship. Perhaps this was because they brought to America their weary skepticism—born of the corrupt character of Italian political life—of the whole concept of self-government; but more likely because their citizenship tests were nothing more than empty rituals and their civic "education" a ghetto-like ordeal. Finally, not just the Italian-Americans but Americans in general were caught up in the euphoric visions of a "new Italy." Surely it is unreasonable to expect Italian-Americans to have condemned what America itself praised. Most Italian immigrants were, after all, "good" Americans.

6.

The Italian-American
Anti-Fascist
Resistance

RESIST MUCH, OBEY LITTLE

Walt Whitman, 1855

THE ITALIAN-AMERICAN LEFT

America's first organized opposition to Fascism originated in
the Italian-American labor movement. Many leaders of the
Italian-American Left had received their political education
in the old country, where they had inhaled deeply the gusty
crosscurrents of anarchism, syndicalism, and socialism. In the
United States they found the radical winds of doctrine no less turbulent and dissident, ranging from Lassallean political activism
to DeLeonist revolutionary trade unionism. Italian immigrants,
who were the last to arrive in America and thus economically
at the foot of the occupational ladder, generally gravi-
tated to the Socialist Labor Party, originally an uneasy alliance
of Populist protest, Lassallean reformism, Bellamyite utopian-
ism, and Marxist vanguardism. In 1900 there were twenty Italian
branches of the SLP. The IWW syndicalists, dedicated to the
shibboleths of class warfare, "direct action," and the magic of
the well-placed bomb ("propaganda of the deed"), also attracted
scores of Italian radicals. In 1912 the Wobblies staged their most
important strike in Lawrence, Massachusetts, a dramatic *sciopero*
led by such activists as Carlo Tresca, Joseph Ettor, Giuseppe
Caruso, and Arturo Giovannitti.[1]

For almost a century America had been a refuge for Italian
radicals. In the 1850s the great Giuseppe Garibaldi worked as a
candlemaker on Staten Island. Years later the world famous
anarchist, Enrico Malatesta, toured the United States and was
shot at while visiting "the red city," Paterson, New Jersey. In

[1] Mario De Ciampis, "Note sul novimento socialista tra gli emigrati italiani negli U.S.A. (1890-1920)," *Cronache meridionali*, vi (April 1959),
255-73.

1900 the anarchist Gaetano Bresci sailed from the United States to Italy to assassinate King Humbert. After World War I another Italian-American radical, Amerigo Dumini, would cross the Atlantic to make his claim to infamy by murdering the Socialist deputy Giacomo Matteotti. All this merely indicates that some strange political creatures lurked in the ranks of the Italian-American Left. We have discussed the career of Edmondo Rossoni, the turncoat who threw off the ragged garb of the IWW and rushed to Italy to don the Blackshirt and become Mussolini's Minister of Corporations. There were others who broke on the issue of war and intervention in 1915, including Domenico Trombetta, the fanatical editor of *Il Grido della Stirpe*. But the crowning irony is that Mussolini himself had been a thunderous voice in the Italian-American Left. In his early years he wrote inflammatory articles for the IWW's *Il Proletario* (New York), blasting both the Italian monarchy and the "rapacious" American bourgeoisie. During the Lawrence strike he used his own journal, *Lotta di Classe*, to excoriate the American middle class, "the brutal people of the dollar," and to denounce the republic as a sham behind which millionaires Morgan and Rockefeller carried out the "crimes of capitalism." Curious are the twists of history— ten years later this violent Socialist would be posing as the hero of America's middle class and knocking at the vaults of Morgan's banks.[2]

The great majority of Italian-American radicals, however, held fast to the principles of neutralism and international class solidarity and had utter contempt for renegades like Rossoni and Mussolini. Thus when news of the March on Rome arrived the Italian-American resistance crystallized quickly. First came the speeches and editorials denouncing Mussolini as a pseudo-Socialist and Fascism as a "mostruosità anacronistica"; then came the rallies and street demonstrations protesting the possible spread of Fascism to America. By April 1923, the Anti-Fascist Alliance of North America (AFANA) was formed. Supported by the New York Federation of Labor, the Amalgamated Clothing Workers Union (ACWU), and the International Ladies Garment Workers Union (ILGWU), the AFANA issued a manifesto calling upon Italian-American workers to come to the aid of fellow workers in Italy. In response, the Italian Chamber of Labor pledged the

[2] Paul Ghio, *L'Anarchisme aux Etats-Unis* (Paris, 1903), esp. pp. 137-58; Megaro, pp. 201-09.

support of 150,000 members. The Alliance also attacked the Italian Embassy in Washington for trying to import Fascism into the United States, and it charged Mussolini with "crimes of high treason" and "continued violence upon the body and property of all the workers of Italy." Under the stirring leadership of the AFANA's Secretary, the fiery poet Giovannitti, the war against Fascism began with eloquent passion.[3]

The radical wing of the Italian-American press also entered the fray: the Socialist *La Parola del Popolo* (Chicago), *Il Corriere del Popolo* (San Francisco); the syndicalist *Il Proletario* (New York); the anarchist *Il Martello* (New York), *Controcorrente* (Boston), and *L'Adunata dei Refrattari* (New York); the Communist *Il Lavoratore* (Chicago) and *L'Unità del Popolo* (New York); the liberal *L'Italo-Americano* (Los Angeles) and *L'Unione* (Pueblo); the Catholic *La Voce del Popolo* (Detroit); and the ILGWU's *Giustizia*. Many of these papers had been associated with local labor organizations. But one sprang into print as a response to the threat of Fascism: *Il Nuovo Mondo*, established in New York in 1925 by Frank Bellanca. A daily with a circulation of about 30,000, *Il Nuovo Mondo* was supported by union advertisements and by a subsidy from the ILGWU. The editors declared that the paper would be to Italian workers what the *Jewish Daily Forward* was to Jewish workmen. In order to obtain news from inside Italy and circumvent censorship, they arranged for telegraph news service from a border town in northern Italy. Featured in *Il Nuovo Mondo* were Italian as well as Italian-American anti-Fascists. Two regular contributors were Vincenzo Vacirca and Arturo Labriola, both former Italian deputies in exile in the United States.[4]

To *Il Nuovo Mondo* fell the ticklish task of unifying the resistance. When the AFANA held its first congress, at Cooper Union in September 1926, the paper attempted to reconcile the faction-ridden Italian-American Left with appeals for compromise and

[3] *NYT*, March 19, April 9, 11, 1923; Minutes, Local 89, ILGWU, May 1923, IA; Nino Capraro, "Antifascismo" ("Memoria Presentata al Primo Congresso Nationale della Federazione dei Lavoratori Italiani d'America"), June 2, 1923; "Fascisti in the United States," *Nation*, cxvi (April 25, 1923), 502-03; *L'Adunata dei Refrattari*, March 17, 1923.

[4] In a series of letters the Italian Ambassador in Washington nervously reported to his Foreign Office almost every detail regarding the policies, financial straits, and tactics of *Il Nuovo Mondo*. IR, 430, 016053-016143.

tolerance. But anti-Fascist rallies had often featured a weird array of political bedfellows: conservative William Green, Socialist Norman Thomas, Communist Benjamin Gitlow, and anarchist Carlo Tresca. Not surprisingly, the mongrelized alliance proved as troublesome as it was tense. The IWW, for example, forever weary of formal political action and class cooperation, accused the "yellow" skilled craft unions of fomenting "the Fascist spirit." Mutual suspicion increased throughout the summer of 1926, despite Vacirca's plea to the Socialists to remain in the Alliance until differences could be ironed out at the congress. When the congress met for three days (September 4-6), *Il Nuovo Mondo* printed the speeches of all the delegates as well as a new AFANA manifesto, which demanded a restoration in Italy of workers' associations, cultural freedom, and civil liberty. The manifesto was signed by Tresca of *Il Martello*, Bellanca of *Il Nuovo Mondo*, Luigi Antonini of the ILGWU, Giuseppe Lupis of the "G. B. Odierna" Society, and Pietro Allegra, general secretary of the AFANA. But the manifesto could not conceal the deep divisions within the Alliance. Before the congress had ended, a number of groups seceded, led by Salvatore Ninfo of the ILGWU, Morris Feinstein of the United Hebrew Trades, and Girolamo Valenti of the ACWU. According to Ninfo, the bolt resulted from their discovery that Communists were seeking to control the Alliance by setting up "fictitious branches" in order to increase their delegate strength. The seceding groups reorganized under the auspices of the Socialists and adopted the new title, "The Anti-Fascist Federation for the Freedom of Italy." The new Secretary, John Vaccaro, welcomed "all labor, radical, and liberal groups" opposed to Communist centralism as well as Fascist totalitarianism; Eugene Debs accepted the office of Honorary Chairman. In the pages of *Il Nuovo Mondo* Vacirca pleaded with the Socialists to reconsider, but his attempts to allay suspicions between the "anarchico-communistico" elements (e.g., Tresca and Enea Sormenti) on the one hand and Socialist-Liberal (e.g., Ninfo and Valenti) on the other were in vain. Thus *Il Nuovo Mondo*'s efforts to forge a united front proved as unworkable as the international anti-Fascist "popular front" of the 1930s. Torn by dissension and bereft of funds, the paper suspended publication in 1930.[5]

[5] *Industrial Solidarity*, Oct. 14, 1925; *NYT*, Sept. 3, 4, 5, Aug. 1, 1926;

The Lantern of Boston, the first English language paper specifically devoted to the anti-Fascist struggle, met a similar fate. Published by the anarchist Aldino Felicani, *The Lantern's* editorial staff consisted of Michele Cantarella, Mary Donovan, Powers Hapgood, Catherine Huntington, Creighton Hill, Gardner Jackson, and C. W. Whitemore. *The Lantern* began publishing in 1927 immediately following the execution of Sacco and Vanzetti, whose defense had occupied this group during previous years. Perusing the yellowed pages of *The Lantern*, one finds political cartoons by artist Boardman Robinson, exposés of the "Myth of Mussolini's Efficiency" by businessman Hill, satires on George Bernard Shaw's philofascism by Professor Labriola, heartening accounts of anti-Fascist legal battles by lawyers Clarence Darrow and Arthur Garfield Hays, lyrical descriptions of the spiritual death of the city of Savona by novelist John Dos Passos, and numerous articles by European anti-Fascists like Henri Barbusse, Francesco Nitti, Count Guglielmo Salvadori, and Gaetano Salvemini. Today's reader can also find here, in an editorial published as early as March 1928, one of the first American commentaries on the relationship between Fascism and anti-Semitism. Because of these occasional prescient qualities, and because *The Lantern* appealed to a wider audience than the labor-oriented *Il Nuovo Mondo*, it is unfortunate this Boston monthly did not become a citadel around which anti-Fascists of all varieties could unite. But in 1929 *The Lantern* ceased publication when its supporters had to withdraw financial assistance. Perhaps the most that can be said is that if *The Lantern* had any impact, it was on the Italian Ministry of Foreign Affairs and on the watchful Italian Ambassador in Washington, who in his correspondence fretted and fumed over the appearance of this short-lived enemy paper.[6]

The Italian-American Left, then, could neither continue a united front nor sustain a central opposition journal. These internal difficulties, however, were by no means as insurmountable as the external situation against which the anti-Fascists struggled. Here they faced at least three serious handicaps.

Daily Worker, Sept. 5, 1926; *The New Leader*, Sept. 4, 1926; *Il Nuovo-Mondo*, Aug. 3, Sept. 9, 11, 12, 1926; Valenti to Baldwin, Jan. 6, 1933, ICPP.

[6] *The Lantern*, March-April 1928; for the Italian government's comments on *The Lantern* as well as other American publications, see IR, 433, 017249-017678.

The Burdens of Anti-Fascism

The first hindrance was the working class base upon which, ironically enough, Italian-American anti-Fascism greatly depended. As it turned out, labor support was an uncertain quantity both vertically and horizontally. Vertically, the pinnacle of labor authority in the early 1920s was the American Federation of Labor and its President, Samuel Gompers, who offered neither moral nor material support to the anti-Fascists. Not until 1924, when William Green succeeded Gompers as President, could the AFL be counted upon for even verbal support. (The views of Gompers and Green are discussed below, pp. 170-73.) Horizontally, labor was even more unreliable. Although the leadership of Italian-American labor stood unalterably opposed to Fascism, the rank-and-file Italian worker entertained ambivalent and even affectionate feelings for the "new Italy" and the charismatic Mussolini. These deep emotions surfaced particularly during the Ethiopian War when Italian labor unions, like Local 89 of the ILGWU, assailed Il Duce's aggression only to be denounced by their own workers. It is understandable why these workers would be responsive to the appeals of Fascism. As recent immigrants, Italian-American workers were more isolated from the centers of political participation and the democratic process. With little civic education and less social assimilation, they were more sensitive to the strains of economic and psychological insecurity. Add to this the Catholicism of the lower class Italian-Americans, and one can easily see why the social foundation of the anti-Fascist movement was built on sand.[7]

The emotions of the Italian-American worker were, of course, merely a reflection of the Italian community itself—the second obstacle facing the anti-Fascists. Crucial here was the ability of propagandists not only to exploit the anxieties of Italian-Americans but to identify Fascism with Italian nationalism itself. In effect, the Blackshirts had stolen the thunder of patriotism, using a rhetoric that enabled them to parade as Italy's historic heirs and the only genuine Italophiles. Significantly, the small number of anti-Fascists, who numbered "optimistically" a little less than 10 percent of a total Italian-American population of 4,600,000 in 1930, could never successfully attack Mussolini without incurring

[7] Interview with Vanni B. Montana (Educational Director of Local 89, ILGWU), Aug. 10, 1966.

116

the stigma of being "un-Italian." Patriotism had become so distasteful and reactionary to Italian-American radicals during World War I that they inadvertently allowed Mussolini's champions to adopt all its symbols. "It is undeniable," Count Carlo Sforza was to write in 1943, "that if propaganda against the Fascist swindle had meager results in the United States, it was because anti-Fascist orators did not make the masses feel that they too loved their Italian fatherland. And that they desired real glory for her with infinitely greater sincerity than the Fascist adventurers who had Italy too much on their lips to have her in their hearts. We must pay for some mistakes." In this respect the tragedy of the Italian-American opposition was not unlike that of European anti-Fascism in general. One recalls Kurt Schumacher's admonition, stated by the German Socialist after the nightmare of Nazism became an agonizing reality: "Never again will the Socialists be caught being less nationalistic than their opponents."[8]

Scarcely less burdensome was the United States government itself. Officials in Rome did not hesitate to use the power of the Executive Branch to try to crush the opposition in America. In May 1923, the Italian Embassy submitted a note to the State Department calling attention to "the notorious Italian labor agitators Carlo Tresca, Arturo Giovannitti, the Amalgamated Workers . . . and other social-communist elements in New York" who were defaming the Italian government on orders from Moscow. Forwarding in the dispatch a scurrilous, porno-political editorial by Tresca ("Down with Monarchy"), the Ambassador stated that it was "most desirable" that *Il Martello*, "which is spreading poison through all the Italian workmen in this country," be barred from the mails and its editor prosecuted. Secretary of State Charles Evans Hughes conferred with the Postmaster General, the Attorney General, and the District Attorney of New

[8] The estimate of 10 percent was arrived at after conversations with several anti-Fascists. Some of those interviewed thought this low figure "too optimistic." However, the circulation of *Il Nuovo Mondo*, approximately 30,000, was a little more than 10 percent of the combined circulation of the pro-Fascist press in New York. For insightful observations on Italian-Americans by exiles, see Armando Borghi, *Mezzo secolo di Anarchia*, pp. 333-49; and Massimo Salvadori, *Resistenza ed azione: ricordi di un liberale* (Bari, 1961), pp. 362-65; Sforza's statement is in *Il Progresso*, Oct. 17, 1943; Schumacher's in Eugen Weber, *Varieties of Fascism* (Princeton, 1964), p. 46.

117

York, the latter replying that prosecution could be initiated under sections of the penal law and that if a formal complaint were lodged he would act "promptly and vigorously." In a matter of weeks Tresca was arrested; the charge, transmitting in the mails an *Il Martello* advertisement advocating birth control literature; the sentence, a year in the federal penitentiary in Atlanta.[9]

The sentencing brought down the wrath of the liberal press. The *Nation* wondered whether the government was acting as the "agent of the Mussolini dictatorship." The *New Republic* reported that at Tresca's trial the district attorney had admitted the original complaint came from the Italian Ambassador. When Congressman La Guardia asked Secretary Hughes whether this charge were true, he received the evasive reply that "It would not be compatible with the public interest to make public complaints of this nature by foreign governments." And while the American Civil Liberties Union prepared a brief on the case, H. L. Mencken ran the same advertisement in his *American Mercury* and vainly challenged the district attorney to indict him. The government's case could hardly hold up under such criticism. Within four months Tresca was released, his sentence commuted by President Coolidge. Clearly politics rather than prophylactics explain the Tresca prosecution.[10]

The government's failure to suppress *Il Martello* did not deter the Fascist regime from continuing pressure on the State Department. The Italian Ambassador in Washington was particularly interested in silencing Vacirca, Labriola, Bellanca, and Valenti for their hostile writings in *Il Nuovo Mondo*. A series of communications eventually resulted in instructions from the government to withhold "future issues of questionable mailability," and the office of *Il Nuovo Mondo* was raided more than once by the police. Government officials, however, possibly embarrassed by their handling of the Tresca case and aware of their shaky legal position, proceeded with more caution in replying to Italian authorities. Although they continued to advise the Fascist government that no legal basis for prosecution existed,

[9] Italian Embassy to State Department, May 8, 1923, DS, 811. 918/175; *ibid.*, 811. 918/181-82.

[10] La Guardia to Hughes, Feb. 22, 1924; Hughes to La Guardia, Feb. 23, 1924, DS, 811. 918/191; *Nation*, cxvII (Aug. 29, 1923), 207; *New Republic*, xxxvII (Jan. 16, 1924), 188; *The Tresca and Karolyi Cases* (American Civil Liberties Union pamphlet, New York, 1925).

their attitude was often one of regret. "We are very sorry for this incident," wrote Assistant Attorney General Charles Tuttle to the Italian Embassy in regards to an *Il Nuovo Mondo* editorial, "sorry indeed that we cannot in any way help you to prosecute and stamp out propaganda of this kind."[11]

Handicapped by a working-class social base, an Italian community almost mesmerized by nostalgic nationalism, and a government indifferent if not reprehensive, it is remarkable that the anti-Fascists were able to carry on any kind of opposition. Yet the enemies of Mussolini waged a two-pronged assault, one designed to expose the tyranny in Italy, the other to halt the spread of Fascism to the United States.

MUSSOLINI'S ENEMIES IN AMERICA

In fighting for the cause of liberty in Italy, American anti-Fascists engaged in a variety of campaigns. First of all, they made every effort to try to prevent the deportation of Italian exiles. In the 1920s many Italian radicals sought refuge in the United States, including the anarchist Armando Borghi, the communist Enea Sormenti, and the syndicalist Arturo Labriola. In 1927 Carlo Tresca, together with Clarence Darrow and Arthur G. Hays of the ACLU, appealed to Secretary of Labor Davis to rescind the deportation orders against Sormenti. Tresca informed the government that Sormenti would be shot if forced to return to Italy. The anti-Fascist appeals, while probably having little effect on immigration authorities, did delay the decision, giving Sormenti enough time to flee to Mexico. Another effort was made in behalf of Vincenzo Vacirca, one of *Il Nuovo Mondo*'s editors. A former Italian deputy, Vacirca had entered the United States in 1925 on a six-month permit. When the term expired, the AFANA decided to make a test case of Vacirca's status, claiming that the exiled parliamentarian qualified as a political refugee who was "in danger of being executed if he is returned to Italy." At an AFANA rally Norman Thomas announced that it was common knowledge that pressure from the

[11] DS, 811. 918/216; on the harassment of *Il Nuovo Mondo*, see *Labor*, March 27, 1926; Tuttle to Royal Italian Consul, Nov. 17, 1928, IR, 430. In their complaints to the State Department Italian officials usually made no mention of Fascism or Mussolini. Anti-Fascists were charged with attacking certain Italian governmental institutions, especially the monarchy. Thus the anti-Fascist assaults were described in such a way as to threaten not the Fascist regime but the good name of Italy.

Italian Embassy led to Tresca's arrest, and that Vacirca was being held on $50,000 bail because of the intervention of "Italian agents." Whether because of or in spite of anti-Fascist efforts, the Vacirca case got lost in a labyrinth of litigation, and he too escaped a Fascist prison cell.[12]

Opposition to the deportation of Borghi was also successful, but this time with tragic results. On April 7, 1930, Borghi appeared before 1,200 anti-Fascists gathered at Cooper Union. As he was concluding his speech, a federal inspector, with either incredible naiveté or nerves of steel, strode forth in full view of the puzzled audience and, taking out a warrant, informed Borghi that he was "wanted." Borghi leaped from the stage shouting, "Stop the Police!" and disappeared out the exit. Immediately Borghi's comrades turned on the inspector and began to work him over. When a detective, who was assigned to the meeting hall, intervened, he was knocked to the floor and kicked in the ribs. But the detective, drawing his revolver, got up and headed for the exit in pursuit of Borghi. Racing out of the hall, he shot at an anti-Fascist who accidentally crossed his path; the bullet missed and fatally entered the abdomen of an innocent and unidentified bystander. Once again the elusive Borghi, who for years had been wanted by immigration authorities, slipped out of the deportation dragnet.[13]

For anti-Fascists, deportation was a gate that could swing both ways. While they opposed the expulsion of their comrades, they did not hesitate to demand the ousting of certain Italian officials in the United States. The first move made by the AFANA was a petition to President Coolidge insisting on the recall of Ambassador Gelasio Caetani on the ground that he was "encouraging the spread of Fascism" in America. But it was the more aggressive Giacomo de Martino, Caetani's successor, who was the chief target. Most active in the campaign to have Martino recalled was the veteran anti-Fascist, Dr. Carlo Fama. During the Coolidge Administration he appealed to Secretary of State Frank Kellogg and during the Hoover Administration to Secretary Henry Stimson. All along he maintained that Martino had abused the privileges of his office by proselytizing and intimidating immigrants. His appeals having fallen on deaf ears, Fama

[12] NYT, April 30, 1927; Sept. 8, 21, 1926.
[13] NYT, April 7, 1930; on Borghi's relations with the Italian-American Left, see his *Il banchetto dei Cancri* (Brooklyn, 1925).

120

led a delegation to Washington to request a personal conference with President Hoover. Again he was denied a hearing on his charges. Stimson, who also refused to receive the delegation, wrote to Fama criticizing Americans of foreign birth who quarreled among themselves over old-country politics. Absolving Martino of the charges, Stimson also declared that he would not see his office used as an acrimonious "public trumpet."[14]

While holding off against alleged deportation "plots" and trying to expose the coercive activities of Italian diplomats, anti-Fascists also watched developments in Italy closely. The one cathartic event that galvanized the Italian-American Left was the brutal murder of Socialist leader Giacomo Matteotti in June 1924. The assassination, which rocked the Fascist regime, caused an emotional earthquake throughout the "little Italys" in the United States. When word reached America, the Italian Socialists of Chicago called a rally that very evening at Hull House; in Philadelphia a mass meeting ended in a melee of flying fists when two policemen tried to stop the taking of a collection for a Matteotti memorial. In New York the Italian Chamber of Labor sponsored a protest rally in Carnegie Hall. Here Count Sforza, an eminent Italian exile, accused Mussolini of responsibility for Matteotti's death. The Communist amazon Elizabeth Curley Flynn told the audience of 25,000 that Matteotti was killed because he was about to uncover scandals in the Fascist government which would "have made the Teapot Dome scandals look sick." The Socialist writer Charles Erwin read a letter to President Coolidge demanding the resignation of Ambassador Caetani, an "avowed member of the Fascists." Jacob Panken, a Socialist municipal court justice, declared that the chant "Abasso Mussolini!" did not go far enough; it should be "Abasso capitalismo!," a familiar war cry that brought tumultuous applause from the audience. When Giovannitti called for a "state of war between the workers of the United States and the government of Fascismo in Italy," pandemonium broke loose as Carnegie Hall resounded with a crescendo of cheers.[15]

The Matteotti murder was the first of a series of events in Italy that aroused anti-Fascists in the United States. Thereafter, the

[14] *NYT*, April 9, 1923; Feb. 17, 24, March 4, 5, 29, 1931; Stimson to Hoover, March 4, 1931, Box 856, HP.

[15] *La Parola del Popolo* (Chicago), June 21, 1924; *NYT*, June 27, July 4, 1924; Sforza to Valenti, n.d., VP.

121

Italian-American opposition fought tenaciously to expose the falsehoods of Fascist propaganda. When the Italian government announced in 1932 an amnesty for all political prisoners, anti-Fascists quickly denounced the spurious gesture. To Vacirca the amnesty was a practical joke; and to the American Friends of Italian Freedom it was an "intolerable perversion of the truth." To prove their point, anti-Fascists appealed to American intellectuals to organize a committee to investigate the plight of Mussolini's opponents in Italy, and Valenti, as head of the Joint Committee for Italian Political Prisoners, asked Senator Borah to cooperate with the inquiry. These tactics, however, did not have the support of all anti-Fascists. When Roger Baldwin, chairman of the International Committee for Political Prisoners (ICPP), asked Professor Salvemini for his views on the amnesty and the proposed investigation, the historian advised that sending a committee to Italy was "foolish" since Mussolini would merely manipulate the investigation and exploit its publicity value to the hilt. Salvemini asked that his letter be kept secret. "I do not want to get into trouble with those of *Stampa Libera*," he wrote in reference to Valenti's paper. "They are not bad. They are stupid. And stupid people are more trouble." Nevertheless, exiles like Valenti and Giuseppe A. Borgese continued to work closely with the ICPP in order to bring to public light the fate of Italy's silenced opposition. In 1938, Baldwin, replying to anti-Fascist complaints that the ICPP's surveys had slighted Italy, informed Borgese that Italy was "about 9th on the list of countries in the order of political prisoners and the severity of persecution for political opinions." Interestingly enough, in 1927 Baldwin returned from a tour of Europe and listed Italy as first ("in a class by itself") in terms of political oppression. By 1938 Italy apparently had more competition.[16]

If anti-Fascists could not strike directly back at Blackshirts in Italy, they could make life unpleasant for Italian dignitaries who risked visiting the United States. On these visits an Italian-American society would usually arrange a flattering welcome attended by *prominenti* and often by uniformed *fascisti*. The receptions, however, seldom came off as smoothly as planned. For wherever Fascists paraded, noisy anti-Fascists were not far

[16] *NYT*, Nov. 11, 1932; Salvemini to Baldwin, Dec. 16, 1932; Borgese to Baldwin, March 20, 1937; Baldwin to Borgese, April 24, 1937, Feb. 15, 1938, ICPP; Baldwin, memo, n.d., Box 7, *ibid.*

behind. When the aeronautical celebrity General Umberto Nobile attempted to speak at an East Side high school in New York, more than five hundred anti-Fascists crashed the doors of the auditorium and tangled with 1,500 frustrated listeners. The police arrived, twenty-five strong, with an armored car equipped with riot guns and tear gas bombs, and drove the anti-Fascists outside the gates. Commander Francesco de Pinedo, leader of a heralded trans-Atlantic flight of Italian planes, also received a mixed welcome. In New York's City Hall Park thousands of Italian-Americans cheered and gave the Fascist salute as 200 Blackshirts stood at attention trying to ignore the hisses in the background. A scuffle occurred when an admirer carrying roses to Pinedo was halted by the police, who sniffed something less fragrant than flowers in the bouquet. (Authorities were alert to the possibility of planted bombs; later when Pinedo's plane blew up at Roosevelt Dam in Arizona, Fascists cried sabotage, even though Standard Oil officials testified that the explosion was caused by the flyers themselves, who carelessly lit cigarettes while refueling their gas tanks.) The tour of Antonio Locatelli, another celebrated Italian aviator, encountered similar harassment. A banquet in his honor given by the Philadelphia Italian Fascist Society touched off a "brick-throwing riot." In New York the following day the aviator and the Italian consul were pelted with tomatoes as they entered the Metropolitan Opera House. The performance of *Tosca* had to be stopped when anti-Fascist leaflets floated down from the balcony into Locatelli's box. At the end of the opera, radicals and *fascisti* "squared off" on 34th Street. Although quick intervention by police prevented a riot, a detective was stabbed when he grabbed a man who was about to leap on Locatelli's car. The arrested suspect was carrying an IWW card and Italian literature, which the police described as of "an incendiary Red character."[17]

These minor skirmishes with the Italian Air Force were only preliminary bouts to the all-out campaign against the visit of Foreign Minister Dino Grandi. When word was received in the fall of 1931 that Grandi was on his way to America, anti-Fascists fired off a barrage of verbal abuse. The hapless diplomat was accused of having organized the FLNA when he visited the United States in 1925, as well as pledging to Mussolini the allegiance of four million Italian-Americans. (Even Americans of

[17] *NYT*, Sept. 16, 17, 1924; Dec. 21, 1926; April 26, 1927; on the plane explosion, see *FRUS, 1927*, III, 127.

Greek ancestry joined in the attacks on Grandi for Italy's activities in the Aegean Islands.) Valenti sent a petition to President Hoover urging that Grandi not be given a reception, and the International Committee for Anti-Fascism requested a White House meeting to discuss the matter. Both requests were answered by eloquent silence. When Valenti continued to publish attacks on Grandi in his *La Stampa Libera*, his office was raided by the New York police.[18]

Meanwhile the press frowned upon the angry antics of Mussolini's enemies. Although a few papers sympathized with the anti-Fascist position, the *New York Times* expressed the tenor of editorial opinion when it remarked that Grandi, as a representative of a foreign nation, was entitled to a "warm greeting." Even some of the more moderate anti-Fascists recoiled from the excessive agitation that had been mounting in New York. Philip Bongiorno, Santo Modica, and Michele Albano, who in 1931 took over *Il Nuovo Mondo* from the more activist anti-Fascists, sent a five-page telegram to Hoover describing the demonstrators as "Communists, Anarchists, Socialists, IWWs and Parlor Radicals, who believe in no form of Government except such as reflects their extreme views and policies." The three informed Hoover that although they were not in sympathy with the government in Italy, they realized that a respectable reception for Grandi was merely a matter of protocol.[19]

So tense was the atmosphere on the day of Grandi's arrival in New York that Mayor James Walker and his police chief could not guarantee public safety. As a result, Grandi had to be whisked away privately by a Coast Guard cutter to New Jersey in order to avoid the confrontation awaiting him in Manhattan. Safely settled, the Foreign Minister enjoyed a round of hearty welcomes: a dinner at Columbia University's Casa Italiana where Nicholas Murray Butler, Marshall Field, and Ambassador de Martino were the main speakers; a White House ball, to which all the leading pro-Fascist Italian-American publishers had been invited; and a luncheon given by publisher Adolph Ochs, who complimented Grandi for supporting the same international policies as did the

[18] *NYT*, Nov. 8, 14, 26, 27, 1931.
[19] *NYT*, Nov. 16, 1931; "What Grandi's Visit Accomplished," *LD*, cxi (Nov. 28, 1931), 7; Bongiorno to Hoover, Nov. 16, 1931, Box 856, HP.

New York Times (the League of Nations and the World Court, "generous liquidation" of war debts, and disarmament).[20]

But the sweet amenities extended by the Establishment did not lessen tension. The Stimson estate, where Grandi resided, was guarded day and night by scores of security police, and the Italian Embassy seemed, in the words of the *New York World*, "like a medieval barracks. Servants act as sentries, guard the gates, peer across the strip of lawn which might be termed a modern moat. . . . The situation is fantastic. It is a sort of dance of shadows and phantoms. The entire embassy staff fears it knows not what. Gates are barred, invitations are cautiously sent out, Ambassador de Martino is in a nervous panic."[21]

Fortunately, the Grandi visit, after all the anxious preparations, was spectacularly uneventful. Perhaps the only scare was occasioned by Orlando Spartaco, a radical partisan who jumped on the running board of Grandi's car and shouted, "Down with Fascism!" Arrested, Spartaco was tried and sentenced to two years for "inciting a riot." But the urbane Grandi, a diplomat to the core, interceded in behalf of the youth; he dismissed the charges and even paid bail for his release. As for the anti-Fascists, they drew some satisfaction from the whole affair by holding a mock trial for the distinguished visitor. With Roger Baldwin as presiding judge, Tresca, as defense attorney, tried to clear Grandi of the charges of murder, arson, robbery, and "picking pockets." Tresca "defended" the Minister as a good public servant who served well the interests of J. P. Morgan, Secretary Stimson, and Premier Mussolini. But alas, "poor Dino" was found guilty and hanged in effigy in Union Square.[22]

LITTLE ITALYS AT WAR

Since Italian-American Fascism was as much an indigenous phenomenon as a product exported by Mussolini, anti-Fascists had to fight a battle on two fronts, not only against the regime in Italy but also against the philofascists and avid Blackshirts

[20] Lombard, pp. 152-56; "Program" (for Grandi's reception), Nov. 18, 1931, Box 856, *HP; NYT*, Nov. 28, 1931; "What Grandi's Visit Accomplished," p. 7.

[21] *New York World*, Nov. 17, 1931, quoted in Carter, p. 87; for Hoover's official conference with Grandi, see below, p. 269.

[22] *NYT*, Nov. 21, 22, 23, 26, 1931.

in the United States. On both fronts the odds were overwhelmingly against them; yet they made their commitment to resist, never shrinking from the long struggle even though no victory was in sight.

One arena in which the anti-Fascists engaged their enemies was the Italian language press. In several cities running feuds developed between Mussolini's friends and foes. The mutual fulminations were often as much personal as ideological, and to this day many publishers of both factions bear the vindicative grudges of twenty years of vicious ink-slinging. In San Francisco Carmelo Zito, editor of the workers' *Il Corriere del Popolo*, clashed continuously with Ettore Patrizi of *L'Italia*. In Chicago Socialist Egidio Clemente of *La Parola del Popolo* attacked Niccolo La Franco and his *L'Italia*. In Boston anarchist Aldino Felicani of *Controcorrente* exchanged verbal blows with the owners of *Gazzetta del Massachusetts*. And in New York several radical papers excoriated Generoso Pope and his powerful *Il Progresso* and Domenico Trombetta and his perverse *Il Grido della Stirpe*. The opposition also assailed such organizations as the Dante Alighieri Society, the Sons of Italy, the Casa Italiana, the Italian Historical Society, the Italian Library of Information, the Unione d'America, the Italian Chamber of Commerce, and, most importantly, the FLNA. But in reaching the larger public, they had little success and they could not ferret out the propagandists directing the various fraternal and professional associations.

Anti-Fascists fared better when openly confronting their entrenched foes. As early as 1923 a clash was narrowly averted when uniformed Fascists decided at the last minute (due to the urging of Samuel Gompers) to withdraw from the New York Memorial Day parade. But three years later the *fascisti*, now more organized and emboldened, marched in the parade clad in full regalia. The Blackshirt regiment parading up Riverside Drive featured such notables as Count di Revel of the FLNA and Professor Giuseppe Previtali of Columbia University. Although the presence of hundreds of policemen prevented a fracas, anti-Fascists on the sidewalks harassed the marching Blackshirts. Other patriotic holidays —Columbus Day festivals, the wreath-laying ceremonies on Garibaldi Day, the anniversary of the March on Rome—generated similar confrontations. Perhaps the most dramatic meeting occurred at the funeral of Rudolph Valentino. In August 1926, Americans experienced a crushing emotional event as the handsome "Sheik" lay in state in a casket covered with a cloth of gold. Almost seventy-five thousand men, women, and children crowded the streets outside the funeral parlor in the rain. Traffic on Broadway was tied up for two hours as black-shawled women fainted in the streets. Seeing propaganda possibilities in death itself, the Italian-American Blackshirts attempted to place an honor guard around Valentino's flowered bier. But anti-Fascists were on the spot and quickly challenged the odious gesture. "We hold," said an anti-Fascist spokesman, "that their presence is an insult to the memory of this great artist, who in life manifested his opposition to the anti-democratic policies of Mussolini and was for that reason outrageously treated on his last visit to Italy." When Valentino repeatedly refused to become a Fascist and when he took out citizenship papers in America, the spokesman went on to say, his films were boycotted throughout Italy by orders of Mussolini, and sentiment against him was so intense in Rome that shots were fired at the screen when his pictures were shown. Thanks to the quick work of the anti-Fascists, the incomparable star was laid to rest without ideological fanfare.[23]

The anti-Fascist struggle amounted to more than a war of words. On several occasions Mussolini's followers and their enemies would raid one another's headquarters, newspaper offices, and rallies. The bloody assaults took on the character of an urban guerrilla war in which clubs were viciously swung, stilettos brandished, bullets fired. In 1925, forty members of the FLNA crashed an anti-Fascist meeting in Newark; by the time police arrived six men had suffered knife wounds. The following year six armed men forced their way into the offices of *Il Nuovo Mondo* and *Il Martello* and smashed the printing presses. But the anti-Fascists, not easily intimidated, struck back just as fiercely. When the third anniversary of the March on Rome was celebrated at New York's Hotel Pennsylvania, Carlo Tresca and Pietro Allegra led a band of anti-Fascists in an attempt to storm the ballroom. A police cordon of almost one hundred men succeeded in holding them back. Similarly, when nine Italian delegates arrived in New York to attend, of all things, an international parliamentary conference, rioting inevitably broke out. Fortunately, the Italian Ambassador had requested elaborate protection: on hand were several steamship line detectives, ten uniformed officers, ten sergeants, twenty-five members of the bomb

[23] *NYT*, May 10, 27, 1923; June 7, 1926; Aug. 26, 1926.

squad, ten secret service agents, four special service men from the Department of State and ten from the Department of Justice, and, just for insurance, an infantry colonel, four subordinate military officers, and twenty-one fully armed soldiers. Despite all these precautions, sporadic brawls erupted and by the end of the day three persons had suffered pistol wounds.[24]

The clashes drew harsh comment from the *New York Times*. At first the paper urged the two groups not to "import their quarrels" and refrained from placing responsibility on either faction. The demonstration against the Italian delegates, however, turned the *Times* against the anti-Fascists. They are the ones who "break the peace"; hence "upon them must fall condemnation, and the police hardly could use too much severity in repressing their rioting." The proper place to settle the issue of Fascism, the *Times* urged both sides, was in Rome, not in New York.[25]

But the anti-Fascists chose, with good reason, New York City. The war they conducted on the streets of Gotham and elsewhere claimed altogether over a dozen lives. In January 1928, Mario Giletti, a twenty-one-year-old Italian anti-Fascist, was sentenced for shooting and wounding two *fascisti* in the Bronx. Another shooting occurred—this time fatal—when the Sons of Italy tried to prevent anti-Fascists from laying a wreath at the Garibaldi Memorial on Staten Island. Since it first appeared that the anti-Fascists were responsible, the victim, Salvatore Arena, was quickly eulogized as a *"bravissimo* Blackshirt of the first hour." But while arrangements were being made to have his coffin ceremoniously shipped to Italy for burial, the Arena affair took two surprising turns. First, it was soon discovered that he had been wanted by the Montreal police as a suspect in a bank robbery. At the same time, not an anti-Fascist but the blackest of Blackshirts, Domenico Trombetta, was charged by the Duce Fascist Alliance of New York with the shooting of Arena. Whether the charge was true—Trombetta was tried and acquitted—the episode revealed the rift between the older Duce Fascist Alliance and Trombetta's new Lictor Federation, a rift Valenti cited to demonstrate to Congressmen like Hamilton Fish that the "Fascist organization [FLNA] which was declared disbanded in 1928 is again functioning and fostering criminal activities."[26]

[24] *NYT*, Aug. 17, 20, Sept. 28, Oct. 11, 1925; Nov. 3, 1926.
[25] *NYT*, Aug. 18, Oct. 30, 1925.
[26] *NYT*, Jan. 5, 1928; July 5, 14, 15, 1932; *FRUS, 1932*, II, 453-54.

Of all the clashes two deserve full discussion because of the legal battles which followed: the Greco-Carillo case and the Terzani affair. On Memorial Day 1927, two Fascists were killed under the Third Avenue "El" stairs at the 183rd Street station. One, Nicholas Amoroso, was shot; the other, Joseph Carisi, was stabbed twenty-one times. Both died in an ambulance en route to the hospital. The victims were on their way, together with thirteen other Blackshirts, to downtown Manhattan to join 400 uniformed Fascists in the Fifth Avenue parade. Because of the growing public resentment against such disturbances, Count di Revel denied any political motives, terming the incident "a simple murder." Yet the twin funeral belied Revel's statement to the press. The slain Fascists were treated to all the rites of political martyrdom: a Blackshirt honor guard was posted day and night around the coffins; the press in Italy denounced the crime; Mussolini sent a lavish tribute; and the general secretary of the Italian *fascisti* announced in a cablegram to all good Italian-American Fascists: "All the ferocity of the anti-Fascists cannot do anything against the glorious march of the idea. For every Blackshirt that falls a thousand are born more brave and true."[27]

An estimated ten thousand people turned out for the funeral, crowding the streets, hanging out windows, peering over rooftops. The sidewalks were lined with flowers for two blocks—one floral display spelled the name "MUSSOLINI" in white roses. A band tried to lift the spirits of the bereaved throng by striking up both the "Star Spangled Banner" and the "Giovinezza." When one Fascist official, Giacomo Caldora, declared loudly "We are going to pay our last respects to these two Italian martyrs," a low wail murmured through the crowd. But when Caldora continued, "Do not avenge them, but hold their memory dear," a police inspector (200 officers were present) rushed to his side with the warning, "No speeches!" After the funeral the bodies were transported to Italy to be buried alongside others who lost their lives in the famous March on Rome. On burial day in Naples all business came to a halt out of respect to the fallen heroes.[28]

In searching for the killer (or killers) the district attorney indiscriminately directed raids on anti-Fascist newspaper headquarters, arresting five men who were held for lack of bail. Then on July 26, Donato Carillo and Cologero Greco, both Brooklyn

[27] *NYT*, May 31, June 1, 2, 1927.   [28] *NYT*, June 4, 5, 25, 1927.

129

tailors and members of the ACWU, were indicted as the suspected slayers. As month after month passed and the district attorney had still not set a trial date, the Greco-Carillo case became an anti-Fascist cause célèbre. A committee was formed consisting of Clarence Darrow, Arthur G. Hays, Isaac Schorr, Arthur Levy, Filippo Greco (brother of the accused), and the International Labor Defense. Appealing to all anti-Fascist factions and civil libertarians, the committee raised $20,000. The famous criminal lawyer, Darrow, took the case because he "detested Mussolini and everything he stands for," and because he had seen in the Sacco-Vanzetti affair how "prejudice and passion" could result in a questionable verdict. Unlike Italian-American anti-Fascists, however, Darrow did not believe that the killing was necessarily a "frame-up" staged by Mussolini's henchmen, and he conceded that an anti-Fascist was probably responsible. What infuriated Darrow was the arbitrary arrest of Greco and Carillo merely because they were prominent anti-Fascists, an arrest made all the more repugnant by an ambitious district attorney willing to lend himself to the whole proceeding.[29]

In the courtroom, Greco told his story in a calm voice, sometimes speaking in English, sometimes in his native Sicilian tongue (translated by an interpreter), while his grief-stricken mother hovered in the background. The case dragged on for weeks. Then an unexpected break for the defense occurred when one of the Fascist witnesses, Giacomo Caldora, President of the Duce Fascist Alliance of New York, turned on the FLNA. He not only called the FLNA a "bunch of criminals," but he testified that Count di Revel and Carlo Vinti of the FLNA had offered him $2,500 to swear falsely that the accused were the assassins. Moreover, Caldora swore that Alexander Rocco, a Fascist organizer and witness for the state, had "given a job" to a Blackshirt to place a bomb in Tresca's office. These surprising developments led the defense to ask the jury not only for a verdict of not guilty but for a recommendation to investigate what Darrow now came to believe might indeed be a Fascist "frame-up." In his final plea, Darrow stressed the political insensitivity of American officials who allowed Blackshirts, "with flags bearing the death mark of

[29] *NYT*, Nov. 12, 1927; Feb. 20, 1928; Robert Morss Lovett, *All Our Years* (New York, 1928), pp. 191-92; Clarence Darrow, *The Story of My Life* (New York, 1934), pp. 312-13.

those who have placed in power one who does not believe in liberty," to march in the Decoration Day parade. The jury, reminded earlier by the judge that political implications were immaterial, returned a verdict of not guilty. Apparently the state's witnesses, some of whom were Fascists and at least one of whom chose not to deny under oath the bribery charge, cracked under the strain of Darrow's imposing presence and deft probes. Robert Morss Lovett, chairman of the defense committee, later recalled: "I never saw Darrow in better form than when he cross-examined a hostile witness. He would lead the victim to the brink of the precipice, where one question more would topple him into the abyss of perjury, and then turn away as if discouraged. Four hands would shoot up in the jury box, and in spite of the judge's deprecation of such activity the fatal question would emerge and the shattered witness would retire in confusion. Greco and Carillo did not follow Sacco and Vanzetti."[30]

The Terzani affair ranks with the Greco-Carillo trial in the annals of Italian-American resistance. On July 14, 1933, Arthur J. Smith, Commander of the Khaki Shirts of America, addressed a rally of his followers in Queens, New York. The Khaki Shirts were more impatient than the Italian-American Blackshirts. "General" Smith, wearing riding breeches, a four-starred riding coat, and a plumed hat, planned a Mussolini-inspired March on Washington for Columbus Day. The march on the capital, to be made by several million men behind a rolling fortress of tanks, aimed to topple Congress in the same manner that the *fascisti* swept out Italy's parliament. But several Italian-American students and workers, convinced that one Duce was already one too many, showed up at the July rally in Queens. When they denounced Mussolini and heckled Smith from the floor they were pounced upon and beaten with clubs and swagger sticks. The riot quickly spread throughout the hall and, amid flashing knives and flying furniture, the outnumbered anti-Fascists were thrown down the stairs. But several Khaki Shirts had cornered a twenty-two-year-old student

[30] *NYT*, Dec. 20, 23, 24, 1927; Lovett, pp. 191-92; Arthur Garfield Hayes, "A Second Sacco-Vanzetti Tragedy Averted," *The Lantern* (Jan. 1928), 5-6; Clarence Darrow, "The New York Fascist Frame-Up," *ibid.* (Feb. 1928), 13-14; Aldo Garosci, *Storia dei fuorusciti* (Bari, 1953), pp. 269-70; Charles Yale Harrison, *Next, Please! The Story of Greco and Carillo* (International Labor Defense, pamphlet, New York, 1927).

named Antony Fierro. Taking charge, "General" Smith smashed the bleeding head of the young anti-Fascist again and again with his leaded riding crop. Suddenly a shot rang out, and Fierro slumped to the floor, mortally wounded.[31]

Fierro was the first martyr among Mussolini's enemies in America. Yet strangely enough, it was an anti-Fascist, Athos Terzani, who was arrested as the suspected killer. When the police arrived Terzani had identified the real killer, one Frank Moffer, and even showed them where Moffer had hidden the gun (in the piano). But Smith, with shrewd presence of mind, somehow managed to convince the district attorney, Charles Colden, that Terzani was about to shoot him when a Khaki Shirt grabbed the gun, thereby causing the bullet to strike Fierro. Upon hearing this version, Colden ordered Terzani's arrest and released Moffer without bothering to take his fingerprints or those on the gun.[32]

Once again the opposition had to move fast. Tresca and Norman Thomas organized a Terzani Defense Committee that represented all anti-Fascist elements: Roger Baldwin of the ACLU, Herbert Mahler of the IWW, and Lawrence Emery of the Communist-oriented International Labor Defense. Interviewing scores of witnesses in New York and in Philadelphia, where Smith's headquarters were located, the committee discovered several repentant Khaki Shirts who were willing to testify in Terzani's behalf. One witness, Samuel Wein, was brought by Norman Thomas to the home of Rabbi Louis I. Newman where, on the Jewish holiday Rosh Hashana, he broke down and confessed that he had originally sworn falsely to the grand jury because Smith had threatened to kill him as "an example to all Jews." When it appeared that the district attorney had no intention of following up this new lead, the committee requested Governor Herbert Lehman and the New York State Bar Association to remove Colden from the case. The threat apparently forced Colden to prosecute. In April 1934, trials were held in which Terzani was acquitted; Moffer, who confessed to shooting Fierro, was sentenced to a term of from five to ten years for

[31] John Herling and Morris Shapiro, *The Terzani Case* (pamphlet, New York, 1934); *NYT*, July 15, 1933.

[32] *NYT*, April 14, 28, 1934; John Nicholas Beffel to the author, Sept. 16, 1965. (Mr. Beffel, to whom I am grateful for the materials he has made available regarding the case, was in charge of publicity for the Terzani Defense Committee.)

first degree manslaughter; and Smith, who still pleaded innocent, was given a term of from three to six years for perjury.[33]

While the Terzani case was being conducted in New York, Hitler was staging his Reichstag fire trials in Berlin. Fortunately the opposition in the United States fared well in court. Unfortunately, a few extremists took the battle to the streets, where bombing as an instrument of terror was used by both sides. In December 1931, three mailmen were killed and four injured when bombs exploded in the post office at Easton, Pennsylvania. Since the packages carrying the bombs were addressed to an owner of a pro-Fascist Italian newspaper, anti-Fascists were held responsible. Yet when the *New Republic* echoed the charge, Tresca and the pacifist A. J. Muste, who was chairman of the Committee for International Anti-Fascist Protest, wrote an angry reply. Admitting that the bombing was a "dreadful crime," they noted that the bomb squad inspector refused to conclude that anti-Fascists were involved and that such terrorism was characteristic of the "agent-provocateur" acts of the European *fascisti*.[34]

Although anti-Fascists continued to denounce the use of violence, and although Dr. Fama asked for a government investigation (which was rumored under way), the bombings continued. In 1933, the home of John di Silvestro, pro-Fascist head of the Sons of Italy, was destroyed by a bomb. The explosion killed his wife and injured four of his children and several neighbors. Silvestro and police authorities agreed that the crime was the work of anti-Fascists, and the Sons of Italy offered a reward for an arrest and conviction. Mussolini sent a message of sympathy and later granted Silvestro's sons, who were enrolled in the Fascist party, an audience in Rome.[35]

Doubtless most of these barbaric acts were the work of a few anti-Fascist extremists. Admittedly among the opposition there were a few millenarian anarchists and Wobblies who naively believed that a timely act of isolated terror was sufficient to bring down the whole social order. It would be a mistake, however, to claim that Italian-American anti-Fascists in general had anything to do with the deliberate bombings. Acutely aware that

[33] *NYT*, April 14, 28, 1934.
[34] Carlo Tresca and A. J. Muste, letters to the *New Republic*, LXIX (Jan. 27, 1932), 297-98; *NYT*, Dec. 31, 1931, Jan. 2, 1932; "Murder in the Mails," *LD*, CXII (Jan. 16, 1932), 4-5.
[35] *NYT*, Jan. 28, 29, 30, 31, Aug. 31, 1933.

their entire strategy depended on winning over the minds of Italian-Americans and Americans alike, the anti-Fascists had nothing to gain and everything to lose by condoning such bloody acts of terror. It would also be a mistake to conclude that violence was a tactic used only by the anti-Fascists. In truth, it was a weapon employed by extremists in both factions. No one was more aware of this than Carlo Tresca, whose remarkable career deserves special attention.

CARLO TRESCA AND OTHER ANTI-FASCISTS

The prime target of the Fascists themselves was the ubiquitous and elusive Tresca. Attempts upon his life were so numerous they have become almost legendary. In championing the cause of labor and anti-Fascism he was arrested thirty-six times, "had his throat cut by a hired assassin, been bombed, been kidnapped by the Fascisti, been shot at four times . . . been marked for death by the agents of Mussolini, and snatched from death's jaws by the magic power of the Black Hand"—so wrote Max Eastman in 1934. Fleeing Italy in 1904 because of his attacks on the Crown and Church, Tresca brought to America the European anarchist's sense of social justice, love of adventure, and talent for agitation. Tall, with thin-rimmed glasses, a shock of disheveled hair and a gray beard grown to conceal the gaping scar down his cheek and throat, often wearing the broad-brimmed black hat of the Italian anarchists, Tresca seemed a cross between Leon Trotsky and Wyatt Earp. He excited the imagination of liberal intellectuals and Italian-American radicals alike. "Big, bearded, boastful, life-loving," was Eugene Lyons' description, while Susanne La Follette remembers him as "a most impressive looking man" with "the kindest blue eyes twinkling through his glasses." Warm and affectionate toward his friends, he was without a trace of the embittered fanaticism one tends to associate, whether correctly or not, with anarchists. His passions were baiting priests, lampooning Fascists, gulping spaghetti, quaffing wine, and changing mistresses. In the 1920s he became the common-law husband of Elizabeth Gurley Flynn, a slim, dark-haired, blue-eyed "East Side Joan of Arc" who combined beauty with radicalism.[36]

[36] Max Eastman, "Profile: Troublemaker," *The New Yorker*, x (Sept. 15, 1934), 31; Francis Russell, "The Last of the Anarchists," *Modern Age*, VIII (Winter 1963-64), 63.

Although his life was surrounded with violence (and ended in a violent death), Tresca did not equate real power with infantile gunplay. Once, when threats were made on his life by the *fascisti*, he decided to buy a revolver. But the very day he bought the gun he shot himself in the toe while trying to stuff it into his pants pocket. His ebullience and winning humor could affect friend and foe alike. He always got along well with the police; even the District Attorney of New York (who publicly denounced him as an enemy of law and order) would drink at his table. Reporters also delighted in his uncanny charm. On several occasions the "terrible" Tresca made front-page news. In 1924, after he had been released from Atlanta prison on the birth-control charge, he stopped off at Washington for a tourist's look at the capital. At the gates of the White House he found himself surrounded by children. When the attendant beckoned the children to come inside, they insisted on taking the affable stranger along by the hand. The tour was climaxed by a hand shake with President Coolidge. The incongruous sight of the "dangerous" and "wild" anarchist shaking hands with the somber and stern Coolidge was played up in the press the following day: "TRESCA AT WHITE HOUSE. CRIMINAL ANARCHIST RELEASED FROM ATLANTA MAKES PEACE WITH PRESIDENT."[37]

Tresca was neither a callous *apparatchik* nor a doctrinaire ideologue. Indeed the pattern of his career is testimony to his unfailing integrity. In his first years in the United States he considered himself a Socialist, which in those days (circa 1904-1906) was a loose enough category to include anarchist and syndicalist tendencies. In a coal-mining town near Pittsburgh he edited *La Plebe* (The Common Man), the journal of the Italian Socialist Federation. When the IWW was formed in 1905, Tresca was attracted to the Wobbly dreams of workers' syndicates and "direct action." Along with Haywood, Giovannitti, and Ettor, he roused the strikers at Lawrence, Massachusetts, and at Paterson, New Jersey. Later Tresca moved to New York and became editor of the anarchist *L'Avvenire* (The Future). Like the rest of the anarcho-syndicalists and Socialists, he opposed World War I, and like his comrades, he was hounded by superpatriots and government officials during the war and in the hysterical "Red Scare" that followed. When *L'Avvenire* was suppressed by the postal authorities, Tresca started in the early twenties his own

[37] Russell, pp. 72-73.

paper, *Il Martello* (The Hammer), which he was to publish and edit the rest of his life. When Sacco and Vanzetti were arrested in 1920, it was Tresca who rescued the case from obscurity by his early organizational and publicity work. After Mussolini came to power, Tresca devoted almost all of his energy to the anti-Fascist struggle, maintaining close contact with Italian-American labor unions. Although he was an antagonist of the AFL and of Luigi Antonini and the ILGWU, his vague anarchism was broad enough to tolerate differences. By the end of the 1930s he would give critical support even to certain programs of the New Deal. In the depression Tresca would also be fighting Communists on the Left as well as Fascists on the Right. But wherever he found enemies, he never lost sight of his life-long goal of social justice and complete human freedom. "Individual liberty," John Dos Passos said of Tresca, "was his daily passion."[38]

Rebels like Tresca are all too rare in history. A freedom fighter who possessed all the virtues of political engagement without the vices of ideological commitment, he commanded the enduring admiration of American intellectuals of all stripes. While Oswald Villard likened him to the militant abolitionist William Lloyd Garrison, Sidney Hook saw him as "a kind of Renaissance figure" whose "sunny enthusiasms" for ideas, people, and freedom flowed from an "enormous appetite for life." Max Eastman, the ex-Trotskyite who had known Tresca since the days of the Lawrence strike in 1912, believed that if Carlo had learned English he could have become "the biggest man in the history of American labor." Nevertheless, Eastman in 1934 maintained that, after the death of Debs, Tresca was "the most universally esteemed and respected man in the revolutionary movement." Americans admired Tresca not only for his romantic rebelliousness but for his profound mind as well. Dos Passos has remarked that his "comments on men and politics were the shrewdest I heard anywhere," and Edmund Wilson observed that Tresca "would calculate political probabilities with a logic of trenchant intellect and an insight of intimate experience which made him one of the most profitable of all commentators to consult."[39]

[38] Carlo Tresca, "Autobiography," TMC; Dos Passos' statement is in *Who Killed Carlo Tresca?* (TMC, pamphlet, New York, 1945), p. 5.

[39] The statements of Villard, Hook, and Wilson are in *Omaggio alla Memoria Imperitura di Carlo Tresca* (New York, Il Martello, 1943), pp. 43, 44, 46; Eastman, pp. 31-32; Dos Passos to author, April 21, 1966.

Tresca possessed a beautiful combination of mind and nerve. So endowed, he could write and direct his ribald play (*L'Attentato a Mussolini*), as well as plan and direct guerrilla tactics against the Blackshirts in the back alleys of New York City. His scurrilous barbs against Il Duce and the Monarchy were so unsparing that it is no surprise the *fascisti* tried several times to eliminate him. On one occasion the attempt was bungled ludicrously when the car carrying the bomb blew up outside his office, killing three passengers—two later identified as FLNA members. Tresca informed the police that earlier in the evening he had received a phone call: "You people tried to kill Mussolini," the voice warned, referring to an assassination attempt in Rome. "We are going to get our revenge tonight." As the biting *bête noire* of the Blackshirts, Tresca was fond of boasting that he had so frightened the Fascists they stopped holding open meetings in New York. Norman Thomas also declared that "Carlo Tresca blocked the rise of blackshirted Fascists who terrorized the streets of Italian-American districts. This was a great and too little appreciated service to American democracy." In reality, neither Tresca nor any anti-Fascist was able to check the infiltration of Blackshirts, for the opposition was operating at a distinct psychological disadvantage. Still, Tresca's courage, while offering moral inspiration to Fascism's enemies, was an omnipresent physical fact that Blackshirts could ignore only at their peril. What Tresca contributed to the resistance was an unswerving integrity and purity of purpose that could not be menaced by anyone. "One felt," Sidney Hook writes, "that a lost cause always had a chance, that it was never a dead cause, if Carlo was part of it." Because of the tenacious Tresca, the cause of Italian-American anti-Fascism was neither lost nor dead.[40]

Although Tresca was unquestionably the folk hero of the resistance, there were numerous other anti-Fascists who cannot be ignored. Dr. Carlo Fama is one. An Italian of American birth, the eminent physician was always present at rallies, arousing the audience with his speeches, drafting resolutions, and petitioning prominent politicians. Fama fought incessantly to have Ambassador Martino recalled, and although he never succeeded, the extent to which he frustrated the *fascisti* may be indicated by the fact that he often had to have a police guard day and night

[40] *NYT*, Sept. 12, 13, 1926; *Il Nuovo Mondo*, Sept. 12, 13, 1926; the Thomas and Hook statements are in *Omaggio*, pp. 44, 46.

because of threats on his life. Trombetta was so incensed he wrote a slanderous tract in a desperate attempt to malign the doctor's reputation in the Italian community.[41]

Another notable who may be admired for the enemies he made was Girolamo Valenti. Unlike Fama, Valenti had close connections with the Italian labor movement and at one time or another he edited or published several papers, including *Il Nuovo Mondo*. When the latter folded in 1929, Valenti started his own *La Stampa Libera* in New York. Valenti had the muckraker's instinct for the timely exposé, and he kept congressmen constantly informed of the activities of Fascist organizers. At the Dies hearings, Valenti, with his copious briefcase of documents and affidavits, was one of the chief witnesses against the Fascists.

A similar role was performed on the West Coast by Carmelo Zito. Educated as a lawyer in Calabria, Zito came to the United States in 1924 and immediately participated in publishing the new *Il Vetro* (The Window), an anti-Fascist weekly that preceded the daily *Il Nuovo Mondo*. In the early thirties Zito went to San Francisco and assumed editorship of *Il Corriere del Popolo*. Under the direction of the energetic and peppery Zito, *Il Corriere del Popolo* became the leading anti-Fascist paper in the West. Like Valenti, Vito also kept careful records of Fascist activities in the Bay Area, records that came in handy when he was called to Sacrámento in 1943 to testify before the "Un-American" Investigating Committee of the California Senate.

Equally prominent in the anti-Fascist groups were Italian-American labor leaders. The suave and dapper Luigi Antonini—who sported, as a symbol of oppression, the black butterfly tie worn by protégés of the anarchist Errico Maletesta—commanded the loyalty of thousands of Italian men and women who worked in the needle trades. As head of Local 89 of the ILGWU, Antonini never hesitated to remind workers (many of whom were indifferent to the menace of Fascism) of the urgency of the cause. His assistant, the husky and affable Vanni B. Montana, also played an active role as head of the Italian Chamber of Labor's educational division. Among other labor leaders were Joseph Salerno and Frank Bellanca of the ACWU and Salvatore Ninfo and August Bellanca of the ILGWU.

In addition to the leadership of organized labor, the resistance

[41] Domenico Trombetta, *Pervertimento L'Antifascismo di Carlo Fama* (pamphlet, New York, n.d.), HIL.

was spurred by the unorganized Italian-American Left. Here the spectrum ranged from the gentle anarchist Aldino Felicani, a Gandhi-like figure with saintly eyes and large expressive hands who won the hearts of all factions; to the violently aggressive Enea Sormenti, whose irrepressible instinct to bolshevize the resistance from within alienated all save the Communists. There was, too, the Chicago Socialist, Egidio Clemente, whose influential *La Parola del Popolo* reached the conscience of social democrats in Europe as well as in America. Finally, there was Arturo Giovannitti. A towering figure with a full beard and tightly drawn face, the "poet of the proletariat" offered a magnificent sight on either soapbox or podium. Giovannitti was a self-made bard who, unlike Tresca and others, could speak elegant English; and his verse, blending a democratic humanism with environmental realism, articulated the human condition of the Italian-American masses. Among anti-Fascists, he had the stature of an Italian Lincoln.

FUORUSCITI IN AMERICA

In their twenty-three-year struggle the Italian-American anti-Fascists were not completely alone. One great source of encouragement was the arrival in the United States of Italian political exiles (*fuorusciti*). In the 1920s Professor Giuseppe Bertelli, Vincenzo Vacirca, and Arturo Labriola came to New York and took part in publishing several opposition papers; and in 1934 the venerable Italian labor leader Giuseppe Modigliani toured the country lecturing to Italian-American workers. The *fuorusciti* represented a broad political spectrum. There was, at one end, Armando Borghi, the world-famous anarchist who lived in the United States from 1926 until the end of the war, somehow managing to evade the immigration authorities by the skin of his teeth. A distinguished looking figure with spiked mustache and trimmed Vandyke, Borghi wrote the scathing *Mussolini: Red and Black* (1938) and contributed regularly to *L'Adunata dei Refrattari*, a New York anarchist weekly published by Nick di Domenico. There was also, perhaps at the other end of the spectrum, Count Carlo Sforza, the esteemed Italian statesman who combined aristocratic sensibilities with democratic sympathies. Although Sforza spent most of his prewar exile years in Belgium and France, from time to time he visited this country to speak at anti-Fascist rallies. After the outbreak of World War

139

II he took up residence in the United States and became one of the chief spokesmen for the *fuorusciti* in America.

In the late 1930s the United States became one of the major sanctuaries for Italian refugees. Some, like Leonardo Olschki, Enzo Tagliacozzo, Giorgio De Santillana, and Bruno Zevi, fled directly from Italy after the Italian anti-Semitic decrees of 1938. Others arrived in the last wave after the fall of France in 1940: liberals like Sforza, Alberto Tarchiani, Aldo Garosci, Alberto Cianca, Randolfo Pacciardi, Nicola Chiaromonte; Christian Democrats like Luigi Sturzo; and Communists like Ambrogio Donini and Giuseppe Berti. More will be said in a later chapter regarding the role of these exiles. What is important to note here is that the *fuorusciti* who arrived in successive waves in the 1930s gave respectability to the resistance in America. Such exiles as conductor Toscanini and physicist Enrico Fermi represented the cream of Italian culture. Many others had access to America's academic circles. In order to find positions for the *fuorusciti* in American universities, Italian-American anti-Fascists and liberal intellectuals often worked together. Max Ascoli, who would later publish the *Reporter* magazine, came to the United States in 1932 on a Rockefeller Foundation fellowship. A young law instructor at the University of Rome, Ascoli visited several American universities and was befriended by such scholars as Felix Frankfurter, Learned Hand, Charles Merriam, and Paul Douglas. After publishing "Fascism in the Making" in the *Atlantic Monthly* in 1933, he deliberately burned all bridges back to Rome. That fall he joined the Graduate Faculty of the New School for Social Research, originally established as a haven for German scholars and called the "University in Exile." When his fellowship expired, the influence of Frankfurter and Hand was sufficient to secure him a permanent position at the New School, the only non-German on the Graduate Faculty. With Giuseppe Borgese at Chicago, Ascoli at the New School, and other exiles like Lionello Venturi at Johns Hopkins, the *fuorusciti* made up a nucleus of scholars whose influence carried weight in the intellectual community.[42]

The most influential of all was Gaetano Salvemini. An historian of international distinction, Salvemini's politics represented a

[42] Charles F. Delzell, *Mussolini's Enemies: The Italian Anti-Fascist Resistance* (Princeton, 1961), pp. 198-201; interview with Carmelo Zito, June 3, 1966; Ascoli to the author, June 24, 1966.

fusion of nineteenth-century *Risorgimento* liberalism and twentieth-century democratic socialism. He opposed Fascism from the very beginning, even to the point of being challenged by Mussolini to a duel. In 1925 Salvemini, together with the legal scholar Piero Calamandrei, published the underground periodical *Non Mollare!* (Don't Give In!). As a result the historian was arrested, but while awaiting trial he escaped to France. In 1927 he visited the United States on a speaking tour, and in 1933 he returned to accept the Lauro De Bosis Chair of History at Harvard University.[43]

With his thin-rimmed glasses, pointed goatee, and his worried, bald head, Salvemini had the physical features of a "bespectacled" Lenin. He led a rather lonely life in America, living in a small book-cluttered apartment in Cambridge and behaving, in the eyes of Italian-American radicals, like a typically improvident professor with one suit of clothes. Yet he was warmly admired by some colleagues and students, for Salvemini was a scholar who could move as easily in the quiet world of academe as in the turbulent world of politics. Profound and prolific, he made significant contributions to scholarship (*Historian and Scientist*, 1939), and he was willing to stoop to conquer with polemics (*Under the Axe of Fascism*, 1936). In 1927 he wrote *The Fascist Dictatorship in Italy*, twenty copies of which were smuggled into Italy with a fake cover and title page (" 'The Life of Tim Healy,' by Liam O'Flaherty"). His inside knowledge of developments in Italy, his fingertip statistics on Italy's economy, and his perceptive comprehension of the social basis of Mussolini's support made him one of the most trenchant critics of Fascism in the United States.[44]

In one respect Salvemini was to Mussolini what Trotsky was to Stalin—he knew too much. Not surprisingly, Italian authorities tried their utmost to silence the outspoken exile. Having failed in the 1920s to persuade the State Department to refuse him a visa, they accused him—after a bomb explosion in 1934 in Rome's St. Peter's Square—of conspiring against Mussolini's life. Con-

---

[43] Delzell, pp. 30-32.

[44] Interview with Frances Keene (Salvemini's former secretary), Aug. 10, 1966; Norman Kogan, "Salvemini in America," *Il Mondo* (Rome), Oct. 8, 1957, pp. 9-10; Gaetano Salvemini, *The Fascist Dictatorship in Italy* (London, 1928), the manuscript copy with fake cover and title is deposited in the Treasure Room Book Collection, Harvard University.

vinced that the accusation was designed to prevent his reappointment at Harvard, Salvemini contacted attorneys in an attempt to bring a libel suit against the Associated Press and *Il Progresso*, both of which relayed the scandalous story concocted by the Fascist government. He also prepared his own defense in a brief entitled "Saint Peter, Mussolini and Salvemini: The Story of a Plot," and he cabled the dictator to let him know that he welcomed the opportunity for extradition, challenging him to "lay down the evidence before an American court." But Mussolini did not see fit to accept the challenge, and Salvemini, on the advice of his lawyers, dropped the libel suit. Viewing the affair, the *New York Times* supported Salvemini and praised American colleges for offering refuge to exiles of his political dedication.[45]

If Salvemini was able to elicit the sympathy of the *New York Times*, he was unable, as were all the anti-Fascists, to impress the Italian communities in America. To the very end he remained deeply grieved because he had not reached the immigrant masses. Although he wrote prodigiously for organs like *Controcorrente* and *Il Mondo*, these publications were read only by a small group of radicals and liberals who were already anti-Fascist. With sadness, Salvemini eventually came to believe that 98 percent of Italian-Americans "know nothing about politics and do not want to know about it."[46]

Yet Salvemini was one of the few *fuorusciti* who not only had great influence among American liberal intellectuals, but equally important, had some contact with Italian-American anti-Fascists. For the most part, the *fuorusciti* and the Italian-American radicals found themselves separated by old-country social distinctions and educational barriers. Where exiles like Sforza and Ascoli were cultured *signori*, American radicals like Antonini and Montana were rugged labor *combattenti*; and where the *fuorusciti* regarded the resistance with single-minded passion, Italian-American leaders could not afford to lose sight of the struggle in America against management and capital. The difference between the *fuorusciti* and Italian-American anti-Fascists

[45] Regarding the visa, the State Department did not side with Salvemini, but simply had no ground to deny him admission. Fletcher to Castle, July 27, 1926, Container 13, FP. Salvemini collected nine slim volumes of correspondence and news clippings on Mussolini's conspiracy "plot." See SS; see also *NYT*, March 6, 7 (editorial), 21, 1934.

[46] Quoted in Kogan, p. 9.

was the social difference between two generations of Italians: the latter, a peasant-proletariat multitude driven out of Italy at the turn of the century by the squeeze of economic necessity; the former, a bourgeois and aristocratic intelligentsia swept out in the 1920s by the scourge of totalitarianism. But Salvemini, possibly because of his own peasant background, was able to bridge the gap and occasionally establish a dialogue between the two groups. While most of the *fuorusciti*, then, gained entrée to the genteel front parlors of academe, Salvemini was one of the few who also had access to the musty back rooms of the Wobblies and needle workers.

The intellectual respectability which *fuorusciti* like Salvemini and Sforza brought to the resistance was matched by the personal strength of radical partisans in America. True, when considered as a whole, Italian-American anti-Fascists never constituted a coherent political force because of their mulish factionalism. Considered individually, however, each anti-Fascist had something to offer: Antonini lent his organizational talents and Zito his journalistic zest; Valenti possessed a sleuthing instinct for the incriminating document; Tresca had a true flair for the *flagrante bello*; Felicani had a saving human warmth and Giovannitti a touch of the poet. If their combined efforts failed to awaken the Italian-American community and America itself to the realities of Fascism, it is only because too many Americans failed to see that Mussolini's worst American enemies were among America's best friends.

7.

Business and Labor

FASCISM SEEMS TO ME RATHER (IN THE FORM IN WHICH IT HAS SUCCEEDED UP TO DATE) TO REPRESENT THE NAPOLEONIC IDEA. THE LATTER, IN CONTRAST TO THE IDEA OF MONARCHY, IS A FAIRLY CONVENTIONAL MODERN IDEA; IT IS THE DOCTRINE OF SUCCESS. THE FEELING TOWARDS A DICTATOR IS QUITE OTHER THAN THAT TOWARDS A KING; IT IS MERELY THE CONSUMMATION OF THE FEELING WHICH THE NEWSPAPERS TEACH US TO HAVE TOWARDS MR. HENRY FORD OR ANY OTHER BIG BUSINESS MAN.

T. S. Eliot, 1929

"NORMALCY" IN ITALY

On March 18, 1923, Benito Mussolini, flanked by a platoon of Blackshirts, entered the Fine Arts Building amid, according to the *New York Times*, "flourishes of trumpets and all the pomp and solemnity to which Rome so well lends itself." His stately appearance was greeted by the earnest cheers of the 1,000 businessmen who gathered in Rome for the Second Congress of the International Chamber of Commerce. For the American delegation—numbering 200 and the largest present—Il Duce had special words of welcome. The large American audience indicated the abiding interest of American businessmen in European affairs, and the holding of the Congress in Rome only

144

months after the ascendancy of Fascism "offers to the world the best proof that the Italian nation is rapidly regaining normalcy in its political and economic life." Turning to all the delegates, the Italian maestro showed he could play a pretty tune. He spoke of the staying power of the free market and ridiculed the Socialist illusion that capitalism was on its last legs. Mouthing still stranger words, the ex-Socialist denounced "state control" and "paternalism" and praised the proven wisdom of individual "initiative."[1]

Seated prominently at the speakers' table were many distinguished American men of business, including Julius Barnes, President of the U.S. Chamber of Commerce; Lewis Pierson, Board Chairman of the Irving National Bank of New York and representative at the Congress of the American Bankers Association; Alba B. Johnson, President of the Railway Business Association; and Willis Booth, Vice President of the Guaranty Trust Company, who days later would be elected President of the International Chamber of Commerce. Returning home, the delegates upheld the case for Fascism in the language of conventional wisdom. Barnes referred to "the beginning of a new era in Italy"; Booth lauded Mussolini for bringing Italy "out of the slough of despair into the bright realm of promise." Another delegate, James Emery, the venerated counsel of the National Association of Manufacturers, described to a NAM convention "the spectacle of a radical Socialist, and extreme leader, not only converted by the lightning stroke of intelligence and falling from his error like Saul of Tarsus from his horse, but leading through the streets of a reunited country a great body of citizens" who saved the nation from "the blighting hand of radical socialism." Pierson, speaking to the Merchants Association of New York, in a speech punctuated with applause at the mention of Mussolini, hailed the new Premier for restoring "the ideals of individualism," pledging the country to a program based on the "inviolable rights of property and contract," and insisting that progress can only come through "thrift and hard work."[2]

Pious phrases of this sort soon became the stock and trade of

[1] NYT, March 19, 1923.

[2] Barnes, Booth, and Pierson are quoted in "Why Mussolini Charms the American Businessman," LD, LXXVII (June 9, 1923), 72-74; Emery in Proceedings of the 28th Annual Convention of the National Association of Manufacturers of America, 1923 (New York), p. 289.

the businessman's apology for Fascism. Yet business did not champion the "convert" from the very beginning. Before the March on Rome the business press appeared jittery. In describing Mussolini's bid for power, the *Wall Street Journal* worried about the lawlessness of the *fascisti*, the *Journal of Commerce* feared their "bombastic nationalism," and *Barron's* looked askance at the labor support they enjoyed. Once Mussolini was in power, however, business suspicions subsided within a year, and as the conservative image of the regime unfolded, American approval seemed fully confirmed. Businessmen congratulated the Premier for establishing law and order, reviving the economy, negotiating the war debt questions, restoring efficient (i.e., "private") management to various industries, ending strikes and disciplining labor, espousing patriotism and the doctrine of hard work, and, above all, stabilizing the lira. Visiting businessmen came away from Italy with lavish praise for municipal reforms as well as hydroelectric and reclamation projects, while the launching of passenger liners like the *Rex* and the *Conte di Savoia* and the trans-Atlantic flights of Francesco De Pinedo and Italo Balbo caught the eye of growth-minded industrialists in the United States. Thus conviction as well as courtesy led E.H.H. Simmons, President of the New York Stock Exchange, to tell the bankers of Italy that Il Duce's marvelous achievements and the Blackshirts' victory over Communism ("that evil disease from the Orient") had captured the businessman's imagination.[3]

"QUIET PREACHERS": BUSINESSMEN AND FASCISM, THOMAS LAMONT AND THE MORGAN LOAN

With few exceptions, the dominant voices of business responded to Fascism with hearty enthusiasm. Favorable editorials could be read in publications such as *Barron's, Journal of Commerce and Commercial Bulletin, Commerce and Finance, Nation's Business* (the official organ of the U.S. Chamber of Commerce), and the reputable *Wall Street Journal*. Aside from the

---

[3] Dante L. Posella, "The American Business Press and the Rise of Fascism in Italy, 1919-1926" (M.A. Thesis, Columbia University, 1949), pp. 14-17; *Aviation*, XXII (April 4, 1927), 662-69; *Fortune*, V (May 1932), 37; T. F. Reynolds, "Milan as Seen by an American Business Man," *Review of Reviews*, LXXIV (Sept. 1926), 282-84; E.H.H. Simmons, *Italy and America* (Address before the General Bankers Confederation of Italy, Milan, 1930), pamphlet.

press, the list of outspoken business admirers reads like a Wall Street "Who's Who." Otto Kahn, the cultural impresario and representative of Kuhn, Loeb and Company, the investing house, made speeches throughout the country lauding the leadership of Il Duce and of the "courageous, wise, and skillful financial statesmanship" of Economic Minister De Stefani. Ivy Lee, the public relations genius, interviewed the Premier in 1923 and reported to newsmen Mussolini's encouraging ideas on balanced budgets, stable government, and American investment opportunities. Judge Elbert H. Gary, Chairman of the United States Steel Corporation, exclaimed that "the entire world needs strong, honest men," and that America "can learn something by the movement which has taken place in Italy." Julius Barnes, one of the most vocal commentators on Fascism, used pen and podium to promote goodwill for Italy. "Mussolini is without question a great man," Barnes told the Executive Council of the American Bankers Association. "Today he is the one real living force, not only in Italy, but in all Europe, and the conversion of that man with his strength and his following to the principle of the so-called capitalistic system that we believe in is the most extraordinary encouragement to us who want to see and hear sound and sane economics put into play."[4]

Of all American business leaders, the one who most vigorously patronized the cause of Fascism was Thomas W. Lamont. Head of the powerful J. P. Morgan banking network, Lamont served as something of a business consultant for the government of Fascist Italy. In 1925, after a visit to Italy, he wrote Henry Fletcher, the American Ambassador in Rome. "I am grateful to you for giving me so many excellent pointers as to the Italian political situation. I feel that it is much sounder than most Americans appreciate, and you have turned me into something like a missionary for a little quiet preaching on my return to New York." For years Lamont did "missionary" work for Fascism, only it was solvency rather than salvation that interested him.[5]

[4] *Barron's*, II (Nov. 13, 1922), 4; *Journal of Commerce and Commercial Bulletin*, Nov. 9, 1922; *Commerce and Finance*, CXV (Nov. 11, 1922), 2083; Basil Miles, "Italy's Black Shirts and Business," *Nation's Business*, XI (Feb. 1923), 22-23; Julius Barnes, "The World of Business," *ibid.* (May 1923), p. 53; *NYT*, April 28, 1923; "Needed, A Mussolini," *Wall Street Journal*, Jan. 15, 1923; Otto Kahn, *Of Many Things* (New York, 1926), pp. 388-418; Lee and Gary are quoted in Carter, pp. 114, 116.

[5] Thomas Lamont to Henry Fletcher, April 17, 1925, Container 12, FP.

Lamont's appraisal was as mundane as a cost analysis. He extolled Italy's economic "progress" under Mussolini, claiming that a "modus vivendi" had been worked out between capital and labor, industry returned to private enterprise, the national debt reduced, inflation curbed. He admitted he was moved by the entrepreneurial "romance" of underdeveloped Italy, but even more appealing to the banker's sensibilities was the matter of inflation, an "evil which the Italian government, as contrasted with certain other governments that might be named, set itself resolutely and successfully to curb." On several occasions Lamont publicly debated William Y. Elliott and Gaetano Salvemini, the latter trying vainly to explain to American businessmen that the Italian economy was propped up by foreign loans and false statistics, and that any economic developments currently taking place were well under way in the pre-Fascist Giolitti Government. One debate, before the Foreign Policy Association in New York, led to an exchange of letters between Lamont and Oswald Villard, editor of the *Nation* and long-time friend of the banker. Villard asked Lamont for an explanation of his pro-Fascist argument as publicized in the press. Lamont, noting that the *New York Times* gave an "inaccurate" and "misleading" account of the affair, stated he was praising not Fascism and Mussolini but solely the country's economic improvements. He also advised Villard to make a trip to Italy and speak to government officials as well as members of the opposition. The following month, when Villard asked Lamont to write a rejoinder to a critical exposé by James Murphy in the *Nation*, the financier offered to submit his private estimate of the article but was reluctant "to jump into the arena in the role of defending anything and everything that the Government may have done." Lamont preferred "quiet preaching."[6]

Though not the most voluble business spokesman for the Italian government, Lamont was clearly the most valuable. For it was he who translated verbal apologetics into hard cash, securing for Mussolini a $100,000,000 loan in 1926. The significance of this loan must be understood against the background of Italo-American economic relations in general. Just before the outbreak

[6] Lamont, "Italy's Economic and Social Progress Since 1922," *Survey*, LVII (March 1, 1927), 723-25, 55; Gaetano Salvemini, *Memorie di un fuoruscito* (Milan, 1960), pp. 59-62; "Twelve Years of Fascist Finance," *Foreign Affairs*, XIII (April 1935), 473-82; Lamont to Villard, Feb. 6, 1926, March 4, 1926, OVP.

of World War I the United States had been Italy's third largest source of imports. During the war America surpassed Germany and England and became the chief exporter to Italy; Italy in turn became America's sixth best customer. Between 1920 and 1922, however, exports to Italy declined from $371,762,274 to $150,894,442. The decline, in part due to the general postwar slump, also reflected America's misgivings about Italy's labor unrest, fiscal and import irregularities, and, according to *Nation's Business*, her government's "socialistic tendencies . . . repelling foreign capital." On the eve of Fascism, American investors remained, the *Wall Street Journal* aptly advised, "diffident."[7]

After Mussolini came to power diffidence turned to deference as the new Italian government appeared to open up fresh commercial possibilities. Early in 1923, Judge Gary returned from a conference with Mussolini and told reporters he was "very favorably impressed" about the prospects of American economic activity under the new regime, while Otto Kahn felt "certain that American capital invested in Italy will find safety, encouragement, opportunity, and reward." At first there was speculation about investment in Italian railroads. The inability of Finance Minister De Stefani to return the railroads to private enterprise, however, scotched that proposition. Thereafter public utilities became the focus of attention, especially hydroelectric energy. Italy was "magnificently endowed with water-power resources," advised *The Financial World*. Accordingly, one of the first important American investments was a $20,000,000 loan for the Italian Power Company, the oversubscription of which indicated, in the opinion of the *Wall Street Journal*, the investors' appreciation of "proven enterprise abroad in stable countries and under strong American auspices." By 1929 investments in utilities amounted to $66,500,000. In addition, there were numerous American companies with concerns in Italy, including Otis Elevator, Worthington Pump and Machinery, Westinghouse Airbrake, Allied Machinery, National Cash Register, and a Ford assembly plant. All these companies, reported a publicist, were "sharing in the business revival under the thoroughly levelheaded Premier Mussolini."[8]

Aside from utilities Italy offered attractive opportunities for

[7] Posella, p. 10; A. C. Bedford, "Italy's Skies Grow Brighter," *Nation's Business*, ix (April 1921), 25; *Wall Street Journal*, April 3, 1923.

[8] The statements and statistics are from Posella, pp. 63-67.

the oil industry. But here one of the first episodes of American economic activity in Italy ended under the shadow of scandal and the stain of greased palms. A year after Mussolini came to power the Sinclair Exploration Company began negotiating with the Italian government for the privilege of seeking deposits and obtaining rights to drill oil-bearing lands. For its initial investment in research and exploration, the American company was to receive exclusive rights to exploit for fifty years mineral oils and natural gas vaults in Sicily and Emilia. In return, the Italian government would receive a percentage of the company's profits and preferred treatment in the purchase of oil. Throughout the negotiations the Sinclair Company had the complete cooperation of the American Chargé d'Affaires in Rome, M. F. Gunther.[9]

The transaction proceeded smoothly until it was publicly announced in Rome in May 1924. The announcement set off a fierce debate in Parliament (which until 1925 was capable of potential resistance) where not only the opposition but even the "legalist" faction of the Fascists attacked Finance Minister Alberto De Stefani for allegedly giving away the country's resources. Although Mussolini leaped to the defense of his Minister and squashed the debate by dismissing the deputy who led the attack, two events doomed the American-Italian petroleum project. First, the Matteotti affair, which occurred weeks after the announcement of the contract, was quickly linked to the transaction. Immediately the State Department instructed the Embassy in Rome to "investigate and report on" the rumor that Matteotti was abducted in order to prevent revelations of an oil scandal involving the Sinclair concession. Second, shortly before the Matteotti murder the Teapot Dome story broke, a scandal that shocked the United States and damaged Sinclair's reputation. Mussolini, with "a body between his feet," and Sinclair, facing charges of conspiracy and bribery, were hardly in a position to consummate an international oil deal. Thus the Sinclair Company and the Italian government agreed by "mutual consent" to can-

[9] The Chargé in Rome acted on his own initiative. In fact, when Secretary of State Charles Evans Hughes heard of Gunther's participation in the transaction the latter was quickly reprimanded. See Louis De Santi, "U.S. Relations with Italy Under Mussolini, 1922-1942" (Ph.D. Thesis, Columbia University, 1951), p. 78. After Hughes left office, however, the State Department and the Embassy in Rome facilitated American business activity in Italy. See below, pp. 153, 155-56, 267-68.

cel the contract, which, according to the Italian Foreign Ministry, "has failed to materialize on account of circumstances
completely independent from the good will of both parties
concerned."[10]

To anti-Fascists, such shabby transactions merely proved that
American oil was the lubricant of reaction—recall Elizabeth Curley Flynn's charge that Matteotti was about to reveal dealings
in the Mussolini regime that would "have made the Teapot Dome
scandals look sick." In reality, American oil money pumped into
Italy, when compared to that invested elsewhere in the world,
amounted to very little. For example, Standard of New Jersey's
annual net income from Italy was considerably higher in the
pre-Fascist period, declining from $1,150,000 in 1922 to $591,000
in 1923 and to $329,000 in 1924; and although the figures rose to
$639,000 in 1925 and to $931,000 in 1926, they dropped to a *loss*
of $336,000 in 1927. Indeed for Standard and other large Ameri-
can companies the most exciting area for oil exploration in the
1920s was not reactionary Italy but radical Russia.[11]

Nevertheless, American money did find the road to Rome. In
the summer of 1925 Wall Street was rife with rumors of an impending loan from the J. P. Morgan Company. Lamont, representing the Morgan firm, tried to squelch the rumor by claiming
he was in Italy for his "health." Yet discerning observers knew
that something other than a water cure was afoot. "Mr. Lamont
went to Italy for 'nothing more than a vacation,'" *Time* remarked
when Lamont made another trip months later; "but banker's 'va-
cations' have come to possess a special and technical significance
—something akin to the sudden 'illness' of diplomats." The State
Department also knew the score. On December 18, 1925, Ambassador Fletcher recorded in his diary: "Mussolini, whom I like
and admire very much, made a characteristic speech yesterday. . . . He promised to make Rome the greatest city in the
world and he probably will, if he gets the fifty million dollar loan
he wants to raise in the U.S. for this purpose." Similarly, President
Coolidge was pleased with the prospect of a loan, informing the

[10] *NYT*, May 17, 1924; Department to Embassy, June 19, 1924, 865.
6363 Si 6/13; Dr. Vestch to Secretary of State, Jan. 20, 1925, 865. 6363 Si
6/16, cited in De Santi, pp. 76-77.

[11] See Table 17, p. 504 in George Sweet Gibb and Evelyn H. Knowlton,
The Resurgent Years: History of Standard Oil Company, New Jersey (New
York, 1956); for American oil activity in Russia, see *ibid.*, pp. 335-58.

press that it represented a "hopeful sign" that Italy was progressing to the point where she could consider paying her debts; and Secretary of State Frank Kellogg made it clear to Italian authorities that he could do nothing for the Morgan loan unless the Italian government took "suitable steps" toward settling its debt to the United States.[12]

Here we must pause for a moment to discuss the matter of Italian war debts. Italy emerged from the war owing the United States nearly two billion dollars. American money, extended to the Allies during the war for the military effort and after the armistice for reconstruction purposes, was made available on the assumption that it would be repaid over a period of years at 5 percent interest. Mussolini, probably aware that the State Department would not approve of private loans to countries in default, reassured America that the Fascists, unlike the Bolsheviks, would honor their debts. But Ambassador Martino also insisted that Italy should be assessed according to her low "capacity to pay" since Italy was "not as rich a country as France." The State Department was unmoved by such arguments and informed the Italian Embassy, in the plainest language possible, that "once the debt is funded it will be far easier to get money in America." Lured by the prospect of a loan, and prodded by the fact that in 1925 the lira had taken a sudden fall in value, Mussolini sent a mission to America headed by the new Finance Minister, Count Giuseppe Volpi.[13]

The mission brought to the United States numerous documents to prove that Italy, because of her impoverished soil, dense population, and limited wealth, ought to be assessed according to her low ability to pay. In view of the Italian government's simultaneous attempt to secure loans from American bankers, this pauper's oath was a bit much. "I laughingly pointed out to Count Volpi," Ambassador Fletcher reported, "that this can be overdone, especially if Italy intends to borrow money on good terms immediately after her debt is funded." Nevertheless, the U.S. Debt Commission released in January 1926 the final figure for the Italian payment: $2,407,677,500, to be paid over a period

[12] *Time*, VIII (Nov. 22, 1926), 17; Fletcher Diary, Dec. 18, 1925, FP; *NYT*, June 3, 1925; Department to Embassy, May 29, 1925, 800. 51W89 Italy 29a, cited in De Santi, pp. 86-87.

[13] Department Official to Italian Embassy Official, Aug. 13, 1925, 800. 51W89 Italy 41, cited in De Santi, p. 89.

of sixty-two years, with immediate annual payments of $5,000,000 for the next five years. Although the sum represented no reduction in the principal, the interest was reduced to the strikingly low rate of 0.4 percent (compared to a 3.3 percent rate for England and 1.6 percent for France). For whatever the reason, Italy received better terms than any European nation save Greece.[14]

Within a week after the Debt Commission released its figures for Italy, Lamont announced the Morgan loan of $100,000,000. The timing of these two developments sparked an uproar in Congress. House Speaker Henry Rainey and Senator Thomas Reed led the attack on both the debt terms and the loan. Convinced that the Morgan Company had obtained inordinate rates, Reed demanded to know how Italy could pay such an interest and at the same time request lenient debt terms on the grounds of her low capacity to pay. Congressman La Guardia also lashed out at the New York bankers who "reaped a harvest" on the loan to Italy. As opposition mounted in Congress—discussed in a later chapter—the Administration quietly but effectively rounded up support. Treasury Secretary Andrew Mellon informed the President that failure of the settlement in Congress would have grave consequences for the economy. "The Italian government has borrowed in the American market the $100,000,000 that it needed for Government purposes. The closing of the American money market would simply mean that Italian industries and municipalities would go to the London market." Commerce Secretary Herbert Hoover advised financier Bernard Baruch that the opposition was based "solely on prejudices against the situation in Italy." Noting that the United States could not expect any better terms from "some subsequent Italian government," Hoover asked Baruch if he "could get this information over to some of the people who are opposing it without a full understanding of where it leads." Backstairs pressures of this sort, together with party discipline, were sufficient to obtain approval of the debt terms in late April 1926.[15]

In general the business community supported both the debt settlement and the loan. *The Commercial and Financial Chroni-*

[14] Embassy to Department, Aug. 13, 1925, 800. 51W89 Italy 85, cited in De Santi, p. 94; *ibid.*, pp. 95-96.

[15] *NYT*, Jan. 7, 9, 16, Feb. 11, 1926; Mellon to Coolidge, Feb. 10, 1926, Box 133, CP; Hoover to Baruch, Feb. 13, 1926, Box 375, HP.

cle reported that the debt fund was "favorably received in local banking circles." *The Financial Chronicle* defended Italy's ability to pay argument, and the *Wall Street Journal*, noting that investors' comment was "universally commendatory," maintained that "in Italy we are cultivating a good customer, which is well worth any interest sacrificed on the future of debt payments." The business press reacted strongly to Congressional opposition. *Barron's* agreed with Secretary Mellon that the settlement was the best bargain possible, and *Bradstreet's* supported Coolidge's argument that approval of the terms was vital to America's own economy, while the *Wall Street Journal* indignantly remarked that there was "something disgustingly un-American about kicking a country when it was down." As for the Morgan loan, most papers approved, with *Barron's* believing that its rapid over-subscription indicated the extent of confidence investors placed in Italy's progress. Yet the *Journal of Commerce*, one of the few anti-Fascist business publications, rejected all such arguments and insisted that the debt terms and the loan enabled Mussolini to consolidate his power and thus represented a victory for Fascism.[16]

No doubt the settlement and the loan demonstrated Mussolini's statecraft at its best. What the transaction demonstrated regarding Wall Street's relationship to Fascism is less clear when we consider America's economic involvement in Italy in comparison to the rest of the world. One could easily conclude from the transactions of 1925-1926, as well as from the earlier Sinclair venture, that American capital was eager to exploit Blackshirt Italy. Such an impression was implicit in La Guardia's accusation that the Morgan interests took advantage of Italy and extracted an exorbitant rate of 9 percent on the loan. Replying to the charge, Lamont informed the *New York Times* that the agreed rate was 4.5 percent. Actually, the rate was 7 percent, as indicated by the Morgan Company's own records submitted in 1931 to the Senate Hearings on America's foreign investments. This figure, although considerably higher than Lamont was willing to admit during the negotiations, was about par for most American loans abroad during the 1920s. Moreover, an examination of all the foreign bonds and securities extended during the 1920s indicates that Italy was sixth in total volume received from

[16] Posella, pp. 57-62.

America, ranking behind Canada, England, France, Germany, and Argentina, and just a little ahead of Cuba. The Morgan Company, National City Bank of New York, Lee & Higginson, Dillon & Reed, Kuhn & Loeb, and other major firms all had investments in Italy that might be described as sizable but not spectacular, and the rates they received on loans to European countries ranged from 6 to 8 percent. In terms of hard facts, then, there was nothing unusual about America's economic relations with Fascist Italy.[17]

The hard fact, however, is the fetish of the statistician, not the historian. In a study which deals with opinion the matter of perception is as important as the margin of profit. If by the end of the 1920s Italy did not pan out as a Mediterranean bonanza, it was not for want of high expectations on Wall Street. In 1923 the business press spoke almost in a single voice about the "remarkable recovery" and "splendid progress" Italy was making, advancing "full steam ahead with Mussolini's hand on the throttle." By 1925, when the debt terms were negotiated, business betrayed some doubt about the sustained success of the Fascist program; even while praising Mussolini's material achievements financiers insisted that Italy's economy may come to a grinding halt if it failed to receive a lenient settlement and further loans. Nevertheless, the Morgan loan encouraged other investors and American activity in Italy picked up after 1925 when the debt was settled and the lira stabilized. More important, the business community could work hand in hand with the Administration and State Department in order to facilitate economic ties with Italy. Coolidge, Hoover, and Mellon maneuvered behind the scenes to obtain easy terms for Italy, and the American Ambassador in Rome—who, as we shall see, was specifically chosen because of his awareness of business needs and his "commercial vision"—availed his office to Wall Street prospectors looking for investments up and down the Italian peninsula. No sooner had the debt terms been released than one investor, William Strong, wired Ambassador Fletcher that he was on his way to Rome to throw out a "feeler" to the Bank of Italy. Strong asked Fletcher

[17] Lamont, letter to the NYT, Jan. 16, 1926; 72nd Cong., 1st Sess., "Sale of Foreign Bonds or Securities in the United States," Hearings before the Committee on Finance, U.S. Senate, Washington, 1932; regarding loans to Italy, see also the Table in Fletcher to Secretary of State, April 30, 1927, Container 12, FP.

if he could "whisper" to Volpi that he was arriving (ostensibly to visit his mother) to pursue "exploration and inquiry." Eliciting the cooperation of the Embassy, the investor cautioned the Ambassador to be discreet: "It would not make a good impression for me to appear traveling around Europe with a basket of gold on my back." In the early 1920s Italy *appeared* to be, even though it did not prove to be, a highly attractive market for America's "baskets of gold."[18]

THE BUSINESSMAN'S APOLOGY

The admiration of American businessmen for Italian Fascism was a proud and open affair that caught the attention of many writers in the twenties. In response the opinion-minded *Literary Digest* conducted two surveys on the phenomenon, first in 1923 in "Why Mussolini Charms the American Businessman," and then in 1926 in "Why Our Bankers Like Mussolini." The infatuation seriously worried anti-Fascists like Clarence Darrow, but others merely ridiculed it with satire. Chiding the businessman's panegyrics, the *New York Post* commented that Americans "will be surprised to learn that Mussolini is the one who struck the rocks of Italy and made hydroelectric energy to flow, a development which is at least a half century old." At times the businessman's naiveté "comes perilously near to assuming that Mussolini not only created order and discipline in Italy, but before that created the Apennine and the blue Italian skies and the outlook from Sorrento over the Bay of Naples."[19]

Although they may have ignored sarcastic liberal editorials, American bankers, industrialists, and investors could not as easily ignore the dictatorial nature of Mussolini's government. No sooner had the Chamber of Commerce delegates settled in Rome than Mussolini made his infamous "Corpse of Freedom" address in which he spoke of marching over the decomposed body of liberty. Yet few businessmen seem to have suffered any qualms about Il Duce's unconcealed authoritarianism. Their apology ranged from democratic idealism to political cynicism. One

[18] Posella, p. 41; Shepherd Clough, *Economic History of Modern Italy* (New York and London, 1964), p. 228; Strong to Fletcher, Jan. 20, 1926, Container 12, FP.

[19] Quoted in the first survey, *LD*, LXXVII (June 9, 1923), 72-74; for the second survey see *LD*, LXXXVII (Feb. 13, 1926), 11-12; for Darrow's remarks, *NYT*, Feb. 20, 1928.

rationale, voiced by a number of business leaders and particularly by Henry Morgenthau and the *Wall Street Journal*, held that the dictatorship was merely a "receivership" for a bankrupt government. Once the country's financial affairs were tidied up some form of republican government would re-emerge. Thus Fascism merely represented a stage of political reorganization that would be terminated as soon as possible. Other businessmen were simply convinced that no contradiction existed, that loyalty to American democratic principles by no means precluded admiration for Il Duce. "It is entirely possible," Otto Kahn argued, "for a man to cherish freedom, to adhere to progressive political and social tendencies and liberal conceptions, as I do, and to look upon Fascism, or anything resembling it, as utterly unthinkable and intolerable in the United States, as, of course, I do— and yet admire Mussolini." Still a few others believed that dictatorship itself offered many worthwhile attractions. Julius A. Basche, described by *World Tomorrow* as "a leading spokesman for Wall Street," presented the argument with complete candor: "Mussolini is a man every country needs. Autocracy is the only solution to the world's problems; that is, if we could only be sure that every autocrat would be a good autocrat."[20]

These adulations are distressing but hardly surprising. During the 1920s business thought was shot through with an elitist distrust of the common man, an unchallenged belief in the businessman's superior worth and leadership, and an obsession with the cult of efficiency and beneficence and "progressive" character of the traditional capitalist system. Given these values, it was natural that Mussolini would emerge as the political personification of business genius. The following poem, which appeared in the *Wall Street Journal*, captures the *Geist* at its euphoric best:

> On formula and etiquette
> He seems a trifle shy;
> But when it comes to 'got and get,'
> He's some two-fisted guy!
>
> On constitutional technique
> And precedents he's lame,
> On grace and glamour rather weak—
> Such lacks don't cramp his game!

[20] *LD*, LXXXVIII (Feb. 13, 1926), 11-12; *Outlook*, CXIV (Feb. 1927), 237; Kahn, pp. 388-89; *World Tomorrow*, IX (Dec. 1926), 242.

Instead they're assets for his job,
　　Rough, rude, plain word and act,—
To mould a nation through a mob,
　　To make a dream a fact!

Red nonsense had its mischief proved;
　　His black-shirts curbed and quelled,
Perhaps in ways not graced or grooved,—
　　How the reins be held?

A blacksmith's son to purple Rome
　　A brusque command he brought;
Italia, cleansed and rescued home—
　　But more than her he's taught!

Word-froth and demagogues and drones
　　Banned; sweat and service praised;
Desks manned when A.M. intones,—
　　Languorous Italy dazed!

History maybe holds a chance
　　Of more for blacksmith's son,—
If he, 'twixt Germany and France,
　　Sees justice kindly done.

Whate'er that outcome, write his name
　　That history may not shirk,—
A new Columbus with his fame
　　New world of will and work![21]

Almost all the values of America's business culture are reflected in this homage: elitism, efficiency, salvation by work, anti-intellectualism and anti-statism, practical idealism and the rhapsody of "plain word and act." Mussolini may not have been flattered by being made into a bourgeois hero, but American businessmen projected their own values in order to make him stand for the triumph of industrial vision over the "word-froth" politician. "I stepped into a large room," wrote Merle Thorpe after an interview, "and there, at the farther end, rising behind a mammoth desk, was a clean-shaven, stockily built, well-groomed man, with an expression of friendly welcome on his face. He might have been any successful American business executive." So conceived, some businessmen saw him as a technical genius, others as an

[21] *Wall Street Journal*, Jan. 23, 1923.

organizational wizard. One called him "The Greatest Advertising Man of All Time," another a "Master Sales Manager." "It is the business instinct of the man that has been most surprising," Isaac Marcosson remarked. "I told him he would get a great welcome in the United States." Endowed with the proper "instinct," it was logical that Mussolini be named Honorary President of the Third International Congress of Scientific Management, which met in Rome in 1927. Indeed, in an age when advertiser Bruce Barton could ingenuously remake the genteel Jesus into a hard-headed, aggressive capitalist in sack-cloth (*The Man Nobody Knows*, 1924), surely the "business executive" in Blackshirt and white spats deserved no less a metamorphosis.[22]

BUSINESS CRITICISM OF FASCISM

Although occasionally many businessmen were moved to eulogistic rapture, the business community as a whole was not without its critics. Some business writers had always tempered their praise with a remark either about the dangers of Fascist militarism, the possibility of a state-controlled economy, or, after the Matteotti murder, the regime's instability and terror. Around 1925 an occasional article appeared that was more skeptical than commendable. For example, one observer saw the dictatorship, despite its economic progress, as a political *cul de sac*; another acutely perceived that Mussolini would rather "flatter the patriotic vanities of his people than . . . seek internally and externally more deeply permanent advantages." Moreover, although the majority of business journals continued to ignore or play down such signs, three periodicals became notable critics of Fascism after 1925. The *Commercial and Financial Chronicle* found it could no longer countenance the permanent demise of representative government in Italy; the *Journal of Commerce* decided, after much equivocation, that the price of economic growth was not worth the sacrifice of liberty; and *Forbes* came out against the whole concept of dictatorship, both Right and Left. Yet even these publications vitiated their criticisms with kind words for

[22] *Nation's Business*, XV (Dec. 1927), 20-22; Christopher James, *Advertising and Selling*, XIII (May 1929), 36; Robert R. Undergraff, *Magazine of Business*, LV (June 1929), 71; Isaac F. Marcosson, "After Mussolini, What?" p. 138; W. H. Leffingwell, "Watch Italy Industrially," *Magazine of Business*, LIII (Feb. 1928), 163-65; for the climate of opinion see James W. Prothro, *Dollar Decade: Business Ideas in the 1920's* (Baton Rouge,, 1954).

Mussolini's role in rescuing Italy from radicalism. Fascism had still to be fully repudiated.[23]

Interestingly enough, the announcement of the Corporate State idea in 1926 drew no emphatic criticism from American business spokesmen. Perhaps the concept proved too amorphous for systematic analysis. In theory, the corporate system called for government-controlled syndicates of labor and capital, all supposedly working for the common good through the autocratic guidance of the Ministry of Corporations. In reality, the system was designed to bind labor and give capital an upper hand, if not a free one. In practice, corporatism turned out to be haphazard humbuggery. Most curious businessmen did not know what to make out of the hybrid theory, nor did many Fascists for that matter. The notion of "class collaboration" seemed harmless enough, but could not the corporative system, which was based on the unifying power of the State, be wielded against capital as well as labor? The answer was far from clear. Chester S. Braithwaite expressed doubts when, comparing volunteer American associations with compulsory Fascist syndicates, he spoke vaguely of the "fatally contradictory" tendencies in the Italian economy. But it took a French economist to see the real contradictions of corporatism for the genuine American capitalist. "Under the Fascist regime," said Yves-Guyot, "there would be no place for a Henry Ford. Having his own ideas, he would be suspect; and his profit seeking would be considered as embezzlements perpetrated against the Corporate State." It may well be that business theorists in America were unprepared to repudiate corporatism because their own attitude toward the State was profoundly ambivalent. In rhetoric Jeffersonian, in reality Hamiltonian, business spokesmen could find no great menace in a government that promoted economic growth, respected property rights, channeled vital entrepreneurial energy, and accepted the inevitability of consolidation. Like many Italian industrialists, American businessmen failed to see that corporatism was a two-edged sword that could cut both ways. Thus the announcement of the theory in 1926 aroused at most only a sense of cautious curiosity.[24]

[23] *American Bankers Association Journal*, XVIII (Dec. 1925), 397-99; John Calder, "Autocracy Holds Italy's Industry," *Iron Age*, CXVIII (Oct. 7, 1926), 998-1000, quoted in Carter, pp. 140-42; Posella, pp. 98-101.

[24] Chester S. Braithwaite, "Mussolini's Challenge to Industrial Democracy," *Magazine of Wall Street*, XL (May 7, 1927), 12-13; Yves-Guyot,

But the following year Mussolini made one of the first propaganda *gaucheries* of his career; he defied any country to produce as much "material progress" as Italy had achieved under Fascism. American business spokesmen immediately rose to the challenge. Writing in *Nation's Business*, Julius Barnes, a former admirer of Mussolini, rejoined with capitalism's complete catechism of virtues. The free play of economic forces, argued Barnes, is not only more productive but more liberal. An unregimented economy may blunder, but it is "better to blunder now and then so long as the blunder be made by free people, working freely together, than to escape that blunder by the edict of government." Mussolini's codes violated the "whole conception of the opportunities and responsibilities of modern business." Although Il Duce "recognizes that the driving power of individual initiative must in some way be enlisted to conduct business enterprise" unfettered by the "stifling atmosphere of state bureaucracy," his conception of government "is itself the arbiter and director of private enterprise." Conceding that the Italian dictator had done much in the "intangible sphere of human emotions" and in restoring "social order and public safety," Barnes believed that Italy's "benevolent despotism" could never compensate for the loss of "free discussion" of economic policy.[25]

Generally the American press supported Barnes' "Answer to Mussolini's Challenge," although a few papers doubted whether American critics of Fascism had anything constructive to offer. Nevertheless, it was a tactless and rash gesture on the part of Il Duce who, by laying claim to Italy's superior "material progress," in effect questioned the American businessman's very *raison d'être*. As such the challenge could not go unanswered. Yet Barnes' rebuttal did not signify a marked defection of business opinion. Although the original enthusiasm for Fascism had waned with the passage of time, and although the appearance of corporatism aroused a murmur of skepticism, the coming of the depression cast a new light on Italy, and once again the view from Wall Street shifted appreciably.[26]

"Réponse Americaine au Défi de Mussolini," *Journal des Economistes*, Series 6, Vol. 88 (Oct. 1927), 1-21.

25 *NYT*, Sept. 1, 1927; Julius Barnes, "An Answer to Mussolini's Challenge," *Nation's Business*, xv (Sept. 1927), 15-17.

26 "American Democracy versus Fascism," *LD*, xcv (Oct. 15, 1927), 16.

DEPRESSION, THE NEW DEAL, AND THE CORPORATE STATE

Until the New Deal began to take shape in the mid-thirties, America was in the doldrums with no fresh winds of doctrine in sight. The business community especially found itself ideologically bankrupt. The sacrosanct ideas which had sustained its faith—free enterprise, self-help, property rights—now seemed stale and pernicious. Gripped by apprehension, business leaders lost their celebrated instinct for adventure and innovation and sank into a state of helpless indecision. Yet amid this seeming paralysis of will, Italy was one country that appeared not only to withstand the strains of depression but to maintain a sense of historical direction. As the unencumbered Mussolini *ordered* employers to keep up production and wages, directed public works projects and reclaimed waste marshlands, and in general controlled the economy with iron-willed determination, Italy emerged as an island of action in a world of stagnation. One writer in *Barron's* exclaimed that Mussolini had only to "wave his hand" in order to vitalize Italy's economy.[27]

Obviously, not every American observer agreed. Samuel Lubell found Mussolini's "Strong-Arm Economics" less efficient than traditional *laissez-faire*, while the young historian Shepard B. Clough pointed out to readers of the *Harvard Business Review* that Italy's productivity had been achieved only by considerable sacrifice on the part of workers and consumers. Yet the desperate need of the moment was not detached analysis but direct action. The relatively liberal *Business Week*, which in 1931 preferred "collective intelligence" to the "recklessness" of the "New Era," and which in 1933 would defend Roosevelt's bold use of executive power, stated loud and clear a dictum for the depression: "to plan or not to plan is no longer the question. The real question is, who is to do it." As *Business Week* noted, however, the very word "planning" had become identified with the "Soviet menace." What was needed, then, was some alternative experiment that avoided the dangers of coercion from the top down and chaos from the bottom up. To some contrite businessmen, riddled with doubt about the anarchy of capitalism and fearful of the collectivism of Communism, the Italian economy seemed

[27] *Barron's*, XIV (April 30, 1934), 12.

the essence of human rationality. *Fortune*'s special 1934 issue on Italy's Corporate State best illustrates this attiude.[28]

The well-illustrated edition featured such topics as the Roman Church, Naples, youth and sport, the colonial empire, the Florentine arts, and the Italian nobility. But Italy's economic accomplishments received the biggest spread. Believing movements similar to Fascism had "all but conquered half of Europe and Asia," *Fortune* wondered whether universal Fascism would achieve in a few decades what Christianity achieved in ten centuries. The reader was warned to "beware of glib generalities" about Fascism and to recognize in it the rebirth of such "ancient virtues" as "Discipline, Duty, Courage, Glory, and Sacrifice." In a section on "Fascist Finance," *Fortune* rejected the charge that Italy was on the brink of disaster. Italy's statistics were not "fakes," and even though the current budget and debt were "staggering," the tax rate was not as "alarming" as in other "collectivist" countries. The increased trade balance, the gold standardized lira, and the absence of "revolutionary carelessness" among Mussolini's finance ministers all led to one conclusion: "In financial words—Italy's credit is good." Yet the sophisticated *Fortune* did express doubts that the Italian economy had helped uplift the masses. The living standards had improved but slightly, the editors conceded. Increased wages had been cancelled by higher prices, income by taxes. Hence so far Fascism had paid dividends to the people more in "the coinage of patriotic excitement" than in the hard cash of consumer comfort.

But the real worm in the apple was the Italian "State." The chapter on the Corporate State carried the significant subheading: "Which is not yet the be-all but is certainly the end of all of the Fascist conception of Statehood. It binds all Italian labor. Does it also bind capital?" The question clearly troubled American businessmen, with their uneasy ambivalence toward state power. Although *Fortune* noted that capital was safer since corporatism had "tamed" class disturbances, it was also aware that Mussolini would not hesitate to curb capital, especially in the

---

[28] Samuel Lubell "Strong-Arm Economics," *North American Review*, CCXXXVIII (Oct. 1934), 346-52; Shepard B. Clough, "The Evaluation of Fascist Economic Practice and Theory," *Harvard Business Review*, x (April 1932), 302-310; *Business Week* (July 9, 1930), 40; *ibid.* (Dec. 10, 1930), 40; *ibid.* (June 24, 1931), 44; *ibid.* (June 17, 1933), 32.

163

event of war. Whether Il Duce would move in this direction, only time would tell.

Meanwhile this one caveat did not prevent *Fortune* from explaining the benefits that could be derived from a corporate economy. Indeed the most significant feature of the special issue was the parallels drawn between corporatism and the direction of America's economy. Not a little interested in the relationship between government and business, the editors saw corporatism functioning somewhat along the lines of the U.S. Chamber of Commerce under Secretary Hoover. As *Fortune* explained it, the Corporate State could promote business expansion by setting standards and formulating production codes, by permitting special freight rates and by using the government to foster international trade. *Fortune* did not use the phrase "trade association," but clearly it had Hoover's neo-mercantile philosophy in mind. In fact the only difference between the American and the Italian systems was that the former had to be conducted covertly.

Although Mr. Hoover and Mussolini held similar ideas on the value of Private Initiative, the great difference in their point of view upon the relationship between the State and Industry is that Mussolini could only regard the relationship as a highly honorable marriage, whereas Mr. Hoover looked upon it—or was politically forced to look upon it—as an illicit liaison. The American businessman under Mr. Hoover had, when he needed succor, to sneak through the servant's quarters; the Italian businessman went in and goes in, proud and unashamed, through the front door.[29]

Just as analogies could be seen in Hoover's trade associations and Italian corporatism, so could they be discerned in Roosevelt's and Mussolini's depression policies. "The Corporate State is to Mussolini what the New Deal is to Roosevelt," declared *Fortune*. The economist Calvin B. Hoover, speaking before the American Economic Association in 1934, noted that Roosevelt's philosophy of government-business cooperation followed the pattern of Italian Fascism and German National Socialism, with the crucial difference that in the United States free political institutions were being preserved. William Welk, a scholar who had been studying the Fascist economy, believed that the New Deal's NRA

[29] *Fortune*, x (July 1934), 137-38.

codes read like the regulations of Italian labor and business syndicates, even though the latter contained more comprehensive social justice programs. To Charles Wright, an engineer who returned from operating mines in Italy, the essence of the Italian system was the establishment of "industrial self-government under Federal supervision." While most enthusiasts seemed certain that corporatism could not be transplanted to America, they were confident that America could learn from the Italian experiment. "Italy shows us," stated Welk, "that this central authority can itself be a direct emanation of the existing national syndical structure—a freely chosen elite which, inspired by new ideals of social right and social justice, is ready and able to limit, through its dependent organizations, the freedom of the one in the interests of the many."[30]

When world interest began to focus on the anti-depression programs of America, the Italian Fascist propagandists seized the opportunity to demonstrate the superiority of the corporate system. Giuseppe Bottai advised Americans that the universal "associative tendency" in human nature led inexorably to the planned economy, whether in the American method of industrial cooperation (in which, Bottai patronizingly noted, labor was left out) or in the more inclusive Italian method of class cooperation. In an address at the University of Virginia, Benjamin de Ritis explained the Fascist economy in a fine-spun blend of Keynesian rhetoric and syndicalist slogans. And Mussolini himself, reviewing Roosevelt's *Looking Forward*, was pleased to describe the American President as "boldly interventionist." Not until 1935 did liberals like Gilbert Montague take the trouble to deny the similarities between corporatism and the NRA.[31]

That parallels could be seen between the Corporate State and the New Deal goes far toward explaining the businessman's belated rejection of Fascism. While Fascism appeared in the 1920s

[30] *Ibid.*, p. 57; *NYT*, Dec. 27, 1934; William G. Welk, "Fascist Economic Policy and the NRA," *Foreign Affairs*, xii (Oct. 1933), 98-109; Charles Wright, "Capital and Labor under Fascism in Italy," American Academy of Political and Social Science, *Annals*, clxxiv (July 1934), 166-72.

[31] Giuseppe Bottai, "Corporate State and NRA," *Foreign Affairs*, xiii (July 1935), 612-24; Benjamin de Ritis, "Aims and Policies of the Fascist Regime in Italy," *International Conciliation*, no. 306 (New York, 1935); Gilbert Montague, "Is NRA Fascistic?" American Academy of Political and Social Science, *Annals*, clxxx (July 1935), 149-61; on Mussolini's evaluation of Roosevelt, see below, pp. 281-82.

to be a bulwark against radicalism, business could shower it with accolades. While it appeared, as it did during the depression and early New Deal, as a concerted effort to rationalize the economy through a wholesome marriage of government and industry, business could still look on with equanimity, if not envious enthusiasm. But once it became clear that the New Deal meant a regulatory state rather than self-government by corporate wealth, business reacted against Roosevelt and Mussolini with equal vehemence. An economy controlled from Washington rather than from Wall Street caused men of money to suspect the very centralized power they had previously admired. Where formerly reference to Italy and Mussolini was something of a compliment, it now became a matter of denigration. Editorial comment about the New Deal increasingly made reference to Mussolini's Italy, Hitler's Germany, and Stalin's Russia. Fascism was likened to Communism, corporatism to collectivism, and the New Deal to both. Distinctions were blurred in a fog of fulmination. *Fortune*, which had paid homage to the Corporate State in its special issue, would come to find Fascism a sacrilegious affront to the "American Dream" of individual liberty. *Forbes, Nation's Business, Business Week*, and *Barron's* rivaled one another in denouncing "State Socialism" in Italy. When the Corporate State took a more active form in 1936, and when Mussolini began to utter radical slogans and inveigh against the bourgeoisie and industrial capitalism, the lesson was complete. With the ghost of Adam Smith twinging their collective conscience, businessmen now saw Mussolini as a menace to the "American System." The "convert" to capitalism had fallen once again to Socialism; the apostate had failed his apologists.[32]

CONCLUSION: "MINOR PROBLEMS" AND BUSINESS VALUES

Up to 1935 business opinion of Fascism might be characterized as falling roughly into five chronological patterns: at first, before

[32] E.g., "Big Business and Government," *Fortune*, xviii (Dec. 1938), 55-56; B. C. Forbes, "Americanism or Rooseveltism," *Forbes*. xxxvii (Nov. 1, 1936), 1; James Harvey Rogers, "If Not the American System—What?" *Nation's Business* (April 1938), 23-24; "Mussolini's State Socialism," *Business Week*, viii (March 8, 1936), 36; "Control and Democracy," *Barron's*, xiv (Jan. 1, 1934), 12; see also *The American Economic System Compared with Collectivism and Dictatorship* (Chamber of Commerce of the United States, Washington, D.C., 1936), pamphlet.

166

the March on Rome, a mood of uncertainty marked by suspicion of Fascist violence and lawlessness; after the take-over, a shift from cautious optimism to outright enthusiasm as the regime showed its anti-radical colors; with the announcement of corporatism in 1926, mild skepticism about the potential of state intervention; during the early depression years, a brief but positive reassessment of Italy's centralized economy; after 1934, a clamorous repudiation of the whole Fascist experiment.

Although business ultimately repudiated Fascism as a threat to freedom, the repudiation must be regarded as both expedient and spurious; expedient because it was part and parcel of the swelling anti-New Deal feeling; spurious because it defined freedom in the narrowest sense of the term. There were, to be sure, some notable business writers who became critical, but even many of their criticisms were so equivocal as to amount to nothing more than mild reservations. Indeed at times it seemed that the skeptics were not so much speaking ill of Fascism as praising it with faint damns.

But ultimately business support for Fascism must be understood as part of the philosophy of the "New Economic Era," the euphoric businessman's creed of the 1920s. The "New Era's" boundless faith in material progress, scientific management, and "economic democracy" affected not only Babbitts and Rotarians but liberals and reformers as well. So pervasive was the mystique of "welfare capitalism" that businessmen easily adopted the rhetoric of reform and posed as the new progressives. Thus when Thomas Lamont spoke before the Foreign Policy Association he could—after outlining the remarkable economic strides of Mussolini's government—conclude with the frank question: "At this gathering today we all count ourselves liberals, I suppose. Are we sure that we are liberal enough to be willing for the Italian people to have the sort of government they apparently want?" It was irrelevant to ask Lamont, as did the *Nation*, whether he would be willing to extend his generous "liberal" tolerance to the Russian people and their government. Business sympathy for Fascism was simply not a question of political principle. Lamont's justification for loans to Fascist Italy, for example, almost echoed Henry Ford's rationale for investing in the Soviet Union. Where the financier told his friend Oswald Villard that American money will hasten the happiness and freedom of the Italians, the industrialist informed *Nation's Business* that "Russia is beginning to

167

build. It makes little difference what theory is back of the real work, for in the long run facts will control." Assuming that experience would triumph over ideology, that in the end industrial progress would lead to political freedom and even to spiritual well-being, American businessmen could advocate recognition of the Soviet Union as easily as they could advance loans to Fascist Italy, and Thomas Lamont felt no contradiction in championing both causes.[33]

Business behavior, then, was determined by the curious self-deception of interests and ideals. Convinced of the inevitability of some form of corporate capitalism, business spokesmen somehow believed—or at least professed to believe—that they could help liberalize totalitarian regimes by subverting their theories with the economic facts of American life. American businessmen may have been sincere in believing that the exportation of America's industrial philosophy would help Italy politically as well as economically. But the American doctrines of "Taylorism" and "Fordism"—technological rationality, optimality of output, and economic growthmanship—were the very doctrines Italian Fascists used to smooth over the old tensions of class confrontation and social division and to promote the hegemony of a unified, authoritarian, corporatist state. Perhaps the American businessman refused to see that there was no place in Mussolini's *produttivismo* for political and personal freedom because his own creed relegated such principles to the bottom of the scale. With his values rooted deep in the American past—in the Protestant ethic, in the philosophies of Social Darwinism and Algerism, and in two centuries of Lockean individualism nurtured by abundance in a society free of the dead weight of feudalism—the American businessman was brought up to believe that economic freedom was the sole basis for political democracy. Hence when confronted with Fascism, the businessman's central concern was not the suppression of civil liberties, the muzzling of the press, or the dissolution of parliament. The question business asked was

[33] Paul Glad, "Progressives and the Business Culture of the 1920's," *Journal of American History*, LIII (June 1966), 75-89; "Remarks of T. W. Lamont at Foreign Policy Association Luncheon" (Jan. 23, 1926), MS in the OVP; the *Nation*'s rebuttal of Lamont is mentioned in "Why Our Bankers Like Mussolini," p. 12; Lamont to Villard, Aug. 10, 1931, OVP; for an illuminating discussion of Ford's attitude toward the Soviet Union, as well as the business community in general, see Filene, pp. 119-29, passim.

whether Fascism was compatible with private enterprise—whether capitalists could have their corporatism and eat their profits too. We can get the full flavor of this rationale from a 1926 *Journal of Commerce* editorial on "Admiring Mussolini." Written as a warning to the countless businessmen impressed by Italy's state support of private industry, the *Journal* reminded them that intervention can be used not only to assist industry but to promote the prosperity of all social classes. Would American business, the editorial asked, accept such a proposition? Moreover, how costly would be the "heavy burden" of taxes needed to finance Italy's militaristic ambitions? "It may be very agreeable superficially," concluded the *Journal of Commerce*, "to admire the success of Mussolini in suppressing socialism, trade unionism, and various other isms disliked by 'conservative' observers. But it is quite essential to remember the actual cost of their achievements, even disregarding such minor problems as constitutionalism and individual rights and liberties." The conscience of the "New Era" was all too willing to "disregard" such precious "minor problems."[34]

SAMUEL GOMPERS: FASCISM AS RECONCILIATION

American labor was far from united on the issue of Fascism in the early years. In part the dissidence reflected the motley social composition of the labor movement itself. Unions of predominantly immigrant workers took a firm stand against Fascism from the very beginning. Spearheading the opposition was the ILGWU and the ACWU, whose membership consisted not only of Italian but of Russian, Polish, Jewish, Lithuanian, Czech, and a host of other uprooted East Europeans. Despite the veritable babel of tongues, the garment unions possessed a sense of solidarity and their members tended to regard the struggle as a continuation of the class wars of the old world. Among the more native workers, however, Europe's class struggles always seemed remote and alien, a chronic disease of a continent sick with social strife. Compared to the ethnic groups, American workers had slight interest in the plight of the European proletariat and, unlike the recent immigrants, saw no connection between the fate

[34] *Journal of Commerce*, July 28, 1926; Charles S. Maier, "Between Taylorism and Technology: European Ideologies and the Vision of Industrial Productivity in the 1920's," *Journal of Contemporary History*, v (1970), 22-61.

of Italian workers and the future of the labor movement in the United States. Indeed, if a connection could be discerned, it only seemed to reaffirm America's philosophy of conservative craft unionism. Nowhere was this nativist perspective better revealed than in Samuel Gompers' response to the rise of Fascism.[35]

Shortly after World War I Gompers visited Italy and gave several lectures to workers' meetings in an attempt to clarify his controversial philosophy of organized labor. Not surprisingly, Gompers' talks on craft unionism sounded to many listeners about as superfluous as a Horatio Alger *storiella*. Thus Gompers returned to America more convinced than ever of the idle dreams of European radicalism. When the Blackshirts came to power Egisto Rossi, an Italian union official who had met Gompers in Naples, wrote the AFL leader a reassuring letter describing Fascism's benefits for the Italian workers. The labor organizations springing up under Fascism, Rossi claimed, "are much more in accordance with the spirit of American labor unions than were the old ones, most of which have become political organizations affiliated with Moscow, and the leaders of which were out-and-out Communists caring not a snap of their fingers for the welfare and prosperity of the country to which they belong." Spelling out in detail Italy's new programs such as the eight-hour day, health care, and old-age insurance, Rossi was certain that Fascism would win the sympathy of the AFL president. For Gompers also believed that "the true interests of working men are not served by radicals who speculate on the ignorance of the masses to further their own selfish political ambition," and his philosophy was likewise committed to "the steady uplifting through better social legislation and more just working conditions of the mental and moral atmosphere surrounding labor, whose welfare can never be realized except by making it concurrent with that of the majority of citizens of the whole country."[36]

Rossi's anticipation of Gompers' response could not have been

[35] Frank Bellanca, "A Black Page of Italian History," *American Labor Monthly*, I (June 1923), 37-40; *Report of Proceedings of the Seventeenth Convention of the International Ladies Garment Workers Union* (Boston, May 5-17, 1924), pp. 320-21; *Report of the General Executive Board of the Amalgamated Clothing Workers of America to the Sixth Biennial Convention* (Philadelphia, New York, May 12-17, 1924), p. 32.

[36] The full text of Rossi's letter has been reprinted in Ronald Radosh, "Corporatism, Liberal and Fascist as Seen by Samuel Gompers," *Studies on the Left*, III (Summer 1963), 69-70.

170

more correct. Shortly after receiving the letter Gompers wrote his own "Analysis of Fascism" in the *American Federationist*, the AFL's official monthly. He was prompted to expound his views by an unsuccessful AFL convention resolution condemning Mussolini and by the appearance of Odon Por's *Fascism*, issued by the Labour Publishing Company of London. Accepting the imminence of a Communist take-over and the decadence of Italy's parliamentary government, Gompers welcomed Fascism as a movement "capable of decisive action on a national scale" and as a system that was "rapidly reconstructing a nation of collaborating units of usefulness." In place of the old industrial unions, prostrate from the pacifist malaise of World War I and the subsequent Bolshevik hysteria, Gompers saw the new "vocational parliaments" as a step in the right direction. Like the syndicalists, Gompers favored reorganizing industrial society to give producers a fuller measure of sovereignty. The new "industrial franchise" was therefore an improvement over the "innocuous" political franchise. Unlike the syndicalists, however, Gompers seemed insensitive to the fact that reorganization would be dictated from above. Indeed on the question of dictatorship Gompers appeared deeply confused. In one instance he claimed that Fascism would not result in an all-embracing "super state" and that Mussolini's much quoted statement about burying the "more or less decomposed body of the Goddess of Liberty" had been torn from context. On the other hand, he wondered whether democracy could ever evolve from dictatorship, remarking candidly that the "historic tendency of autocracy is always to perpetuate and enlarge its existing powers." Yet Gompers was greatly impressed with Mussolini himself: "However repugnant may be the idea of dictatorship and the man on horseback, American trade unionists will at least find it possible to have some sympathy with the policies of a man whose dominating purpose is to get something done; to do rather than theorize; to build a working, producing civilization instead of a disorganized, theorizing aggregation of conflicting groups." Ultimately Gompers was moved more by Fascism's "functional democracy" than by Mussolini's dictatorship, and although he was aware that American labor could take only a negative view of autocracy, he nonetheless urged a "wide reading" of Por's book. "Certainly," Gompers concluded, "the promise of the industrial democracy in Italy, pledged in declarations and phrases which might easily enough have been

171

taken from the mouths of American trade unionists, makes the book one of tremendous and exciting interest."[37]

In essence, Gompers' apology reflected his undying abhorrence of European ideology. Convinced that the shibboleths of class war were so much hot air, Gompers always believed that American labor should instruct European workers to "return to sound principles" of class cooperation and "pure and simple" business unionism, thereby sharing with management the administration of the capitalist system. Because he wanted to integrate the worker into the industrial order, because he believed that representation should be based on functional economic units, and because he accepted a corporate society based on national cohesion and social harmony, Gompers saw Fascism as a model of class reconciliation that vindicated his own trade union philosophy.[38]

WILLIAM GREEN AND LABOR OPPOSITION

One can only speculate how long Gompers' inverted syndicalism—or what the "New Left" of the 1960s would call "corporate liberalism"—would have sustained his support of Fascism. In any event, with Gompers' death in 1924 the AFL, under the new President William Green, moved into the anti-Fascist camp along with the rest of organized labor. Under new leadership, the *American Federationist* turned away from much of Gompers' righteous parochialism, and the more international-minded Green spoke of the dangers of Fascism in Britain, France, and Germany as well as in Italy. What particularly concerned Green, however, was the Fascist attempt to infiltrate the American labor movement. Informed of the Fascist activities among immigrants, especially the Italian miners of Pennsylvania and the needle workers of New York, Green addressed a letter to approximately five million organized wage earners, warning them of the "menacing" efforts of American Blackshirts, the violent methods of Mussolini, and the reactionary nature of Fascist "unions" in Italy. Probably because Green coupled his attack on Fascism with a blast at Communism as well, his letter received warm support from the press. The following year, the AFL convention of 1926 reversed its previous stand (taken at the 1923 convention) and adopted

[37] Samuel Gompers, "An Analysis of Fascism," *American Federationist*, xxx (Nov. 1923), 927-33.

[38] E.g., Gompers, "Labor in Europe and America—Idle Words vs. Practical Works," *American Federationist*, xxx (June 1923), 461-67.

a resolution condemning Fascism. At the same time Matthew Woll, the conservative AFL Vice President, told the respectable National Civic Federation that labor could not go along with the businessman's tolerance of Mussolini, while Green informed the radical AFANA convention of 1926 that the AFL "will stand with you and work with you until we have succeeded in driving Fascism from the face of the earth."[39]

AFL affiliates and rival unions gradually joined the campaign as typesetters, electrical workers and operators, locomotive engineers, barbers, bookbinders, moulders, machinists, and the American Federation of Teachers began attacking Mussolini in their respective publications. Although primarily an urban phenomenon of garment workers' locals, anti-Fascism had the support of a few miners' unions with Italian members and anarcho-syndicalist leanings. It also enjoyed the solid support of two agrarian groups: the Farmer-Labor Party of the twenties and the Farmers Holiday Association of the thirties. In 1923 farmer-laborites sent W. H. Green as a delegate to the Peasants International Conference in Moscow. Speaking in the former Czar's ornate palace before peasant leaders from all over the world, Green called upon American farmers and proletarians to unite against Fascism. At New York anti-Fascist rallies a farmer-labor spokesman often made an appearance, and in Congress the small band of midwestern farmer-labor representatives could be counted upon to present the case against Mussolini whenever the subject came up for debate. During the depression Milo Reno, leader of the militant Farmers Holiday Association, lectured to the desperate growers on the dangers of Fascism, "the brutal dictatorship of the big exploiters"; while Richard Bosch, a dirt farmer who divided his time between raising corn and reading Salvemini and

---

[39] E.g., "Fascism and the Workers," *American Federationist*, xxxiii (Feb. 1926), 219-20; *NYT*, Jan. 30, Sept. 6, 1926; the text of Green's letter was reprinted in the Salvemini and Elliott pamphlet, *The Fascist Dictatorship*, pp. 80-83; as to the AFL resolutions, the 1923 convention failed to pass an ILGWU motion denouncing all manifestations of Fascism, and adopted instead a mild and vague statement opposing the "imposition of tyranny" in America; in 1926 and 1927 the resolutions, although expressing sympathy for the Italian masses and emphatically condemning Fascism, still expressed greater concern about Blackshirt activities in America. *Report of the Proceedings of the 43rd Annual Convention of the AFL* (Washington, D.C.), pp. 66, 175, 178; *ibid.*, *46th Annual Convention*, pp. 106, 154, 262; *ibid.*, *47th Annual Convention*, pp. 168-69, 374-76.

Konrad Heiden, declared: "We should learn from Fascist Italy and Germany that farmers should seek their political and economic allies with labor and progressive middle-class groups rather than with industry and finance." The cornbelt rebels almost instinctively identified Fascism with eastern capital, the traditional *bête noire* of midwestern radicalism. Using the rhetoric of populism, Henry Wallace would later define an "American Fascist as one who in the case of conflict puts money and power ahead of human beings. . . ." The demons of William Jennings Bryan had returned in black shirts.[40]

Labor's response was more hostile than that of any other social group because Italian Fascism was perceived as a direct threat and not simply as a distant red scare in reverse. Farmer-labor leaders could hardly look on impassively as they read about the destruction of Italian agricultural co-ops by the *Squadre*, while radical union officials, seeing Il Duce emerge as the darling of Wall Street, could only regard him as the most brutal strikebreaker of all times. The behavior of American businessmen seemed to confirm the Amalgamated's warning that the "enemies of labor everywhere have greeted the Fascisti as saviors of Society." Labor leaders feared that if Il Duce's method were adopted in America, as some businessmen brazenly advocated, the union movement would be finished. Thus in 1926, when Mussolini lengthened the working day from eight to nine hours and many American papers applauded the "prosperity by edict" technique, American labor officials denounced the "castor oil and club" legislation. This total suspicion of Mussolini's every move also led union leaders to react skeptically to the Fascist Labor Charter, an obscurantist document contained in the Corporate State proclamation of 1927. Although some of the more syndicalist unions commended the new plans for occupational representation, they quickly saw the hook within the bait. "Organization around occupation with freedom of expression, a freedom of voice and vote," stated the *Garment Worker*, "might be an experiment worth thinking about. But dictatorship takes all meaning from it." William Green summed up his reaction in three

[40] Carter, pp. 169-72; *NYT*, April 7, Oct. 13, 1923; Richard Bosch, *The Farmer and the Fascist Dictatorship* (Farm Holiday News, Des Moines, Iowa, n.d.), pamphlet; Henry A. Wallace, "Fascism: The American Brand," *NYT*, April 19, 1944, reprinted in *Man and the State: Modern Political Ideas*, ed. William Ebenstein (New York, 1947), p. 316.

words: "autocracy gone mad." The method of this madness seemed evident three years later when the Italian government ordered another wage cut, "the third since Mussolini started saving Italy" quipped the *Locomotive Engineers' Journal*.[41]

Although it offered the only major organized opposition to Mussolini in the twenties, the American labor movement—encompassing footloose Wobblies as well as hand-tied brown-collar workers—was hardly a model of anti-Fascist solidarity. Like the Italian-American Left, American labor suffered internal dissension, but the dissension within labor was less a matter of ideological conviction than social position. Whereas the AFL represented middle-class aspirants, most of whom accepted Gompers' conservative nationalism, the ILGWU and the Amalgamated represented unskilled workers still steeped in socialist internationalism. Thus, while the AFL's denunciation of Fascism reflected a basic concern for the legal rights of labor, that of the garment workers evoked an international war against capitalism. Significantly, when the AFL attacked Fascism it almost invariably assailed Communism as well. The folly of this method of attack reached its most futile expression in the "Law of Causality" enunciated by C. L. Rosemund, President of the International Federation of Technical Engineers. In essence, Rosemund declared in the *American Federationist*, "Fascism is the effect caused by Communism." No doubt there was a germ of truth in this assertion, but its reiteration frustrated the non-Communist labor position and conjured up the old bugbear that had been used to justify the March on Rome in the first place. Even more seriously, to argue that without the threat of Communism there would be no Fascism implied that the resistance to Fascism could only begin with the destruction of Communism. AFL spokesmen like Rosemund were bewitched by the "Law of Causality," a reasonable historical premise that could lead to the most unreasonable political conclusions—even to the conclusion that America, by tolerating Mussolini's proclaimed war on Communism, was temporarily fighting Fascism with Fascism.[42]

41 *Advance*, vii (May 11, 1923), 4; "Prosperity by Edict," *LD*, xc (July 17, 1926), 9-11; *NYT*, April 23, 1927; William Green, "The Fascist Labor Charter," *Current History*, xxvi (June 1927), 445-47; *Garment Worker*, xxvi (June 1927), 5; *Locomotive Engineers' Journal*, lxv (Jan. 1931), 38, quoted in Carter, p. 168.

42 C. L. Rosemund, "Threat of Fascism?" *American Federationist*, xlii (Oct. 1935), 1292-93.

If the issue of Communism divided labor's hierarchy, the issue of religion divided the workers themselves. When directly confronted with the Fascist question, the ranks of labor broke on the rock of St. Peter. This was especially true in the thirties when lower-class Catholic workers sided with Franco during the Spanish Civil War, and when Catholics of all classes registered an emphatic preference for Fascism over Communism in several opinion polls. It is difficult to get at the thoughts of the inarticulate working masses, but in light of the pro-Fascist sympathies among Catholics it would be sheer sentimentality to speak of the American working force—comprised in large part of various Catholic immigrant groups—as a disciplined industrial army dedicated to the overthrow of Mussolini. As far as American anti-Fascism was concerned, the myth of the proletariat fell prey to the "opiate of the people."[43]

"Tygers of Wrath": Labor's Interpretation of Fascism

Whatever may have been the attitude of the rank and file worker, we may get some idea of the views of union officials and writers by examining the major ideas in the labor press. Drastically reduced, labor's commentary boils down to five recurring themes. First of all, there was never any doubt in labor's mind that Fascism was a capitalist conspiracy pure and simple. The *coup d'état* had been "engineered" by Italian bankers and industrialists who took Mussolini to their bosom in order to stem the onrush of Socialism. And in this foul play of filthy lucre American business was directly involved. "Mussolini Using American Dollars to Aid Militarism" was a typical headline workers read week after week. That "Mussolini Loads the Fascist Club with American Gold" became an obsessive notion after the Italian debt was settled and the Morgan loan negotiated. Secondly, the suspicions of labor went beyond Wall Street to the alleged power structure which supposedly did its bidding. This was not only true of the White House and the State Department, which labor attacked for praising Mussolini, but of the American press itself. Whether owing to the press's capitalist sympathies or to

---

[43] Allen Guttmann, *Wound in the Heart: America and the Spanish Civil War* (New York, 1962), pp. 65-66; for further elaboration on the views of Catholic workers, see id., "An Indictment of American Policy" in *American Neutrality and the Spanish Civil War*, ed. id. (Boston, 1963), pp. 94-96; for public opinion polls, see below, pp. 333-40.

Fascism's censorship policies, labor was certain that newspapers engaged in a conspiracy of silence regarding Mussolini's atrocities. Workers were warned that news coverage of Italy was deliberately misrepresented and were advised to read labor's own correspondents in Rome, who remained anonymous to escape the secret police. Otherwise the only reliable papers, labor cautioned, were the *New York World* and, occasionally, the *Baltimore Sun*.[44]

As for Mussolini himself, labor viewed him as a creature of capitalism, a renegade opportunist who changed ideologies like a chameleon changing colors, and a murderous "thug" whose whole regime was based on "political racketeering" and "international gangsterism." The vilifications inevitably focused on a single image: Il Duce as puppet. "He isn't a monarch," stated the Socialist Charles E. Russell, "he is a megaphone. Business interests pull strings and Il Duce barks despotic orders." Capitalism, declared another writer, "jerked out the puppet Mussolini and blinded the populace with the glare of so-called dictatorship and power." From these caricatures Mussolini emerged as a make-believe image in a capitalist Punch and Judy show. As *Advance* put it: "In a world of myths, Mussolini is the master myth. The alchemists of the middle ages who claimed the power to mint gold out of nothing were pikers compared with this Cagliostro of the 20th century." Similarly, Fascism was depicted as a delusion and a facade. Italy's heralded revolutionary ideology was nothing more than sound and fury, a veneer of verbiage spewed forth by conniving capitalists lurking in the shadows or "hiding under the cloak of national patriotism." Always the meaning of Fascism was to be found "behind," "beneath," or "beyond" the blare of propaganda and the glare of publicity. "The true master of the forces," wrote Charles Erwin, "though not conspicuous in the play, big capital of the cities and of the land, cared little about the words Fascism used: masters always concern themselves with substance rather than with form." The metaphysics of ideology, the power of ideas and symbols, the emotional appeal of nationalist idealism was only a deceptive veil that must be unmasked. The reality was capitalism, nothing more, nothing less.[45]

[44] *Labor*, VII (March 27, 1926), 3-4, (July 31, 1926), 1; *Advance*, x (April 16, 1926), 9, x (April 30, 1926), 11, (July 6, 1926), 5; *Justice*, v (April 6, 1927), 6.

[45] *Advance*, VII (Sept. 7, 1923), 4, XI (April 7, 1926), 9 (April 23, 1926),

Regarding Mussolini as a spineless pawn clinging to the silk sleeve of a phantom government, labor readily concluded that Fascism had no future. Of all the themes that reappeared the prediction of Fascism's downfall was one that labor writers took special satisfaction in announcing time and again. The moral of the Matteotti murder, William Green prophesied, demonstrates that tyranny "always" ends in defeat. Two years later, after Mussolini shrewdly survived the crisis, Green remained adamant, declaring that the "pendulum of reaction and autocracy . . . will eventually swing back and democracy and freedom will be substituted for autocracy and enslavement." Convinced of its complete decadence, labor was certain Fascism could not survive the slightest of economic or political strains. Moreover, it was pressures from within that would bring down the regime. Exactly what these pressures were did not have to be spelled out, so certain was labor that Fascism harbored the seeds of self-destruction. "For two years, week after week, in these columns," announced *Advance* in 1926, "we have been telling the truth about the Dictator's rule gathered from unimpeachable sources and have deduced from the information gathered that his rule was doomed to come to an end in a mighty crash and that this end would come from forces on the inside and not the outside. The same forces of physical violence and corruption on which the Italian dictatorship has been built are destined to pull it to pieces."[46]

Perhaps it would be unfair to suggest that labor rightly condemned Fascism but for the wrong reasons. Yet balancing passion with perspective, one cannot avoid the conclusion that labor's anti-Fascism conveyed more wrath than wisdom. Labor conceded nothing to Fascism; not even Rossoni's paternalistic workers' syndicates, which synthesized guild socialism with corporatism and which did, after all, win some support from the Italian masses. Nor did labor acknowledge the nationalistic and religious appeals of Fascism to the patriotic and Catholic Italians. Instead,

---

11, (June 25, 1926), 9; *American Labor Monthly*, I (Oct. 1923), 89-91; Russell's article, "Mussolini—Megaphone," appeared in the *International Moulders Journal*, XLIV (April 1928), 216-17, quoted in Carter, p. 181; Charles Erwin, "Ten Years of Fascism in Italy," *Advance*, XVIII (Oct. 1932), 4-5.

[46] *American Federationist*, XXXII (April 1925), 250; Green, "Fascist Labor Charter," pp. 446-47; *Advance*, XI (Nov. 12, 1926), 7.

in the face of Mussolini's popularity both in Italy and abroad, labor dismissed all such noneconomic explanations as mere window dressing. Labor's facile reductionism had serious consequences. By viewing Fascism strictly in economic terms, labor ignored the psychological aspects of the phenomenon. By interpreting the movement as a capitalist conspiracy, it scarcely considered Fascism's broad appeal to the workers as well as to the *petite bourgeoisie.* By regarding the regime as doomed decadence, it blinded itself to some of the genuinely dynamic and revolutionary features of Fascism. The practical upshot was that labor seriously underestimated the staying power of Fascism and the political prowess of Mussolini. Thus the annual March on Rome celebrations staged by Il Duce continued to dramatize to other Americans the weakness of the anti-Fascist argument expounded by both labor and the Italian-American opposition.

One need only contrast the attitudes described above with those of Italian exiles in order to fully appreciate the unfounded optimism of American labor. Both Salvemini and Sforza, for example, attempted to explain to Americans—and especially to labor and the Italian-American Left—that Fascism enjoyed diverse support and thus should not be dismissed as sheer capitalist reaction. Salvemini especially warned that it was "schoolboy romanticism" to believe that a counterrevolution would occur from within. The few anti-Fascists remaining in Italy, noted Salvemini, were powerless and disorganized. As to other groups, it was doubtful whether the clergy, the peasantry, or the military would rise against the regime, no matter how deep their disaffection. Nor was it hopeful to think that dissension among the leaders would topple the government, for Mussolini cunningly played subordinates off against one another in order to nip in the bud any possible opposition. And most importantly, Salvemini continued, it was vain to believe that the dictatorship would break down with the first economic crisis, since Italians historically have been resigned to bearing hardship in silence.

How then was Fascism to be overthrown? Salvemini's answer to this question, written in 1927, displayed amazing prescience of what would occur sixteen years later. The answer was foreign war. Mussolini, Salvemini observed, had been cultivating in Italy a mood of "frenzied exaltation," a "strange mixture of megalomania and persecution mania" which he would eventually exploit to embark on a diplomatic adventure in order to deflect

179

domestic unrest. When this occurred, Salvemini advised, on the basis of the experience of Allied policy toward the German people at the conclusion of World War I, foreign countries will be in a position to appeal to the emotionally spent Italians to rise against the dictator and his henchmen. In light of subsequent events, Salvemini's realistic assessment of Fascism's strengths and weaknesses proved far more accurate than the wishful fantasy of labor and the Italian-American opposition. True, their hearts were in the right places, but in the twenties American anti-Fascists were whistling in the dark with their extravagant expectations of Mussolini's imminent collapse. In the end it would take a world war to bring down Fascism, and the decision to enter that war was made by Mussolini and Mussolini alone, not by vague sinister forces pulling the strings of a mechanical "puppet."[47]

By the early thirties, however, many discerning labor officials discarded all talk about Fascism's inevitable doom. In the Great Depression, after all, Mussolini survived the most severe of crises, and with the rise of Hitler the whole issue of Fascism became more desperate than ever. In 1934 the AFL invited Walter Citrine, General Secretary of the British Trade Union Congress, to address its San Francisco convention on the subject. Meanwhile unions began publishing a variety of pamphlets in order to educate the workers to the dangers of Fascism and to steer them away from the growing Right-wing movements in America. At the same time, Italian-American union officials redoubled their efforts to assist the Italian underground. In 1934, the ILGWU raised $50,780 for an anti-Fascist fund, and at a rally it started a drive for another $250,000 for the "liberation of the workers of Europe." In light of these activities and attitudes it could be said that labor's sober reassessment of Fascism compares favora-

[47] Salvemini also insisted it was crucial that Mussolini go down with his regime. For his "dramatic instinct and theatrical inventiveness" had so captivated the people that if he were to vanish beforehand Italy's democratic future would be greatly endangered. There would always remain a "number of old ladies and retired generals" who would maintain that Fascism with Mussolini was "invincible" and call for another man on horseback. Thus the defeat of Fascism must be dramatized in the personal collapse of its leader. If not, the "collective failure of the dictatorship would teach little or nothing because it would not be a personal failure of the dictator. Fascism would be robbed of its value as an experiment." "Mussolini, the Pope and the King," *Century*, cxiv (May 1927), 6-16.

bly not only to the bland admiration of the general public but to the blind arrogance of American Communists, who welcomed Hitler as the gravedigger of capitalism's "final crisis." Labor and the Italian-American Left, having fought Fascism for a whole decade, could no longer regard Fascism as the death spasm of capitalism. Thus despite their earlier misconceptions of Italian Fascism, labor leaders and Italian-American radicals were better prepared than most Americans to see the menace of Nazism. Indeed Charles E. Ervin presaged the spirit of the Popular Front when he offered American workers the following advice:

> In these ten years everything has changed about Fascism except two things: Its anti-labor nature and its leader. Fascism has lost every vestige of its old glamor but the lesson is: If a system of government is permitted to entrench itself and to establish the conditions of its perpetuation the probabilities are that it will develop tenacity almost beyond the power of any opposition to break. Reaction must not be allowed to settle in the saddle. It must be fought at all times, on all fronts, by all means.[48]

These words were written in 1932. Not until 1935 did Stalin realize the wisdom of such advice. Many Americans took even longer. But for labor and the Italian-American opposition the lesson of 1922 had not been lost. Perhaps "The Tygers of wrath are wiser than the horses of instruction."

[48] *Advance*, xx (Nov. 1934), 10; *NYT*, Oct. 10, 14, Nov. 5, 11, 1934; Erwin, "Ten Years of Fascism in Italy," pp. 4-5.

8.

Church Windows

MUSSOLINI— ". . . A MAN
WHOM PROVIDENCE HAS CAUSED
US TO MEET."

Pope Pius XI, 1929

"IF GOD MADE US IN HIS IMAGE,
WE CERTAINLY RETURNED THE
COMPLIMENT."

Voltaire, 1788(?)

CATHOLICS AND MUSSOLINI'S ITALY

"If anyone ventures today to suggest that the Vatican in any sense supported the Fascist regime," wrote Giorgio La Piana and Gaetano Salvemini in 1943, "every Catholic voice in America is raised in formidable protest." The charge levelled by the two Harvard historians reflected the bitterness of many exiles whose anti-Fascism appeared vindicated during the war but whose anti-Catholicism remained as vindictive as ever. In their eyes it was not only the Vatican that bestowed its blessings upon Mussolini but American Catholicism itself. Angrily reflecting upon this unholy alliance, the anti-Fascist *Il Mondo* (New York) issued the following indictment in 1941:

> If any one should assume the task of gathering together between two covers all the utterances of American cardinals and bishops concerning Mussolini, all the sermons, all the articles and essays of Catholic priests and monks, all the effusions of the Jesuits of *America* and the minor organs of Catholic action in this country, from the beginning of Fascism to the death of Pius XI, we should have the most impressive and astounding anthology of Fascist glorification made in any country outside Italy.[1]

[1] Gaetano Salvemini and Giorgio La Piana, *What to do with Italy* (New

182

Although it fails to do justice to the complexity of Catholic opinion, there is considerable truth to this overwrought charge. At first glance it does appear that the American clergy had indeed composed a political choir in behalf of Fascism. In the early twenties ecclesiastical dignitaries like Archbishop O'Connell of Boston and Archbishop Hayes of New York returned from Italy singing praises of the great "transformation" under Fascism and applauding the restoration of the crucifix in the classroom. After a personal audience with the dictator Bishop Bernard Mahoney told Mussolini how eager he had been to meet the leader "whom the Holy Father calls a man of Providence," and he informed Il Duce that many Americans likened his values to those of George Washington, who also believed in religion as the bedrock of morality. Another priest, the Reverend Joseph Hickey, referred to the Italian Premier as a "superman who has solved order out of chaos." Prelates did not have to travel to Italy to fall under the spell of Fascism's superficial splendor. Even the articulate Monsignor Fulton J. Sheen, one of the most learned Catholic thinkers in America, could glance across the Atlantic and see in the vaguely understood Blackshirt movement the possibility of a spiritual "resurrection."[2]

But the most notorious display of idolatry came from Father Charles E. Coughlin, the pro-Fascist "radio priest" of Detroit. Coughlin, who in the early depression years enjoyed a Sunday evening audience of ten million listeners, originally championed the idea of the Corporate State. By 1936 even corporatism seemed too timid a compromise with the forces of evil. Instead of the collaboration of capital and labor, he demanded a complete purge of all money lenders. Yet when Mussolini was criticized in 1938 for adopting the German pogrom, Coughlin leaped to his defense. He appealed personally to Il Duce, asking the dictator to write for his weekly, *Social Justice*, an article "in which you can clarify your attitude toward the Jews, toward the national question and toward any other point that you wish to make clear for the American readers. *SOCIAL JUSTICE* magazine has a million

York 1943), p. 80; E. Ruperto, "Italian Fascism in America," *Il Mondo*, Feb. 1941, p. 11.

[2] *NYT*, Feb. 29, 1924; Feb. 7, Oct. 3, 1926; July 8, 1932; Fulton J. Sheen, "Conqueror of Death," *Commonweal*, XIII (Feb. 18, 1931), 432-34.

readers and will be happy not only to publicize your article but to support it editorially."[3]

The clerical blessings of Father Coughlin were matched by the lay genuflections of Catholic writers. James J. Walsh ("M.D., Ph.D., Sc.D., Litt.D., etc.") dedicated his *What Civilization Owes to Italy* (1930) to Il Duce; John Gibbons announced the dedication in the title itself—*Old Italy and New Mussoliniland* (1933). Catholic politicians like Al Smith and James Curley also contributed to the litany of platitudes. Such benedictions from clerical and lay Catholics created the impression of a dark, reactionary church in America. In the thirties when the hierarchy publicly supported Franco and remained relatively silent in the face of Nazi aggression, and when the Catholic Ambassador to England, Joseph P. Kennedy, sided with Franco and advocated appeasing Nazi Germany, the impression seemed confirmed.[4]

Despite the apprehensions of Italian exiles and American anti-Fascists, however, the Catholic chorus was neither a monolith nor a monotone. Italian-American clerics may, as Salvemini charged, have preached the virtues of Fascism to their immigrant parishioners, although one might ask whether this behavior was due to their Catholicism or to their Italophilism. In any case, it is unfortunate that Salvemini was not aware of the role of Monsignor Joseph Giarrocchi, editor of the Catholic *La Voce del Popolo* (Detroit), a valiant anti-Fascist paper that exposed the propaganda activities of Italian consular officials in the United States. Indeed Catholic anti-Fascism was not unknown in America. For every Father Mahoney there was a Father James Cox, a priest who went to Italy in 1932 to study Fascism and returned to expose the complete denigration of spiritual and personal freedom under Mussolini; for every Father Coughlin there was a Father Francis Duffy, the famous World War I chaplain who admonished Americans for admiring a dictator who "robbed" the Italian people of their civil liberties; and for every Catholic statesman like Joseph Kennedy there was his son, the young John

[3] *Social Justice*, April 3, 1936; Father Coughlin to Mussolini, Sept. 6, 1938, IR 419.

[4] Guttman, pp. 66, 117; for the ambassadorial career of Joseph P. Kennedy, see William W. Kaufmann, "Two American Ambassadors: Bullitt and Kennedy," in *The Diplomats: 1919-1939*, eds. Gordon Craig and Felix Gilbert (Princeton, 1953), II, 649-81.

184

Fitzgerald Kennedy who supported the Spanish Republic and advocated collective security against Fascist aggression.[5]

All this merely suggests how hazardous it is to speak of a coherent Catholic view of Fascism. American Catholics did tend to be pro-Fascist, as we shall see in a subsequent chapter where the opinion polls of the late thirties are analyzed. But when we examine the mainstream of Catholic thought in the twenties we find several crosscurrents of opinion. These currents flowed through the pages of the three major Catholic periodicals: *America, Commonweal,* and *Catholic World.* In contrast to *The Tablet,* the Brooklyn diocesan paper that spiced its pro-Fascism with doses of racism, and the *Catholic Worker,* the voice of the small and isolated anti-Fascist Catholic Left, these three national journals reflected the general climate of Catholic philosophy and political opinion. Significantly each interpreted Fascism in a different light.

The Jesuit *America* looked favorably upon the rise of Fascism. Before the March on Rome it printed some mild criticism of the extremism and lawlessness displayed by a few Blackshirts. Shortly afterwards reservations disappeared as the *fascisti* came to be seen as true patriots in the war against Bolshevism. Whether the *fascisti* were true Catholics was another matter. For the image of a movement supposedly based upon the revival of sacred values like Church and family hardly squared with the background of its leader, a former Socialist who wrote the viciously anticlerical *The Cardinal's Mistress.* Nevertheless, for Jesuit writers the real interests of the Papacy seemed more important than the hazy images of Fascism. Thus the relationship of Fascism to the Vatican was *America's* political touchstone. Although the relationship was obscure in the early days, Mussolini eventually began to court the Church with the cunning of a thirteenth-century monarch and the psychology of a twentieth-century demagogue—granting political appointments to Catholics, in-

[5] "Father Cox Has a Closeup View of Mussolini," *Christian Century,* XLIX (July 27, 1932), 925-26. Father Duffy is mentioned, along with several other anti-Fascist Catholics, in John Hearley's *Pope or Mussolini* (New York, 1929), a rare book which attempted to explain to American Catholics the anti-democratic nature of Italian Fascism. Some of Father Giarrocchi's activities are recorded in the Valenti Papers. John F. Kennedy's attitudes toward the Spanish Civil War are briefly noted in Guttmann, p. 29.

troducing compulsory religious instruction in the schools, and denouncing pagan Communism as the nation's number one enemy. As the Mussolini regime appeared more amenable to the Vatican, *America*'s editorials, often influenced by the Pope's statements on Fascism, were filled with admiration and gratitude.[6]

Convinced that Fascism's opposition came from the radical Left, *America* believed that Italy, "now more than ever," must be "purged of all dangerous agitators." But *America* also realized that some opposition had developed even among Italian Catholics, especially the Catholic *Popolare* party. Thus the editors watched closely the position of the *Popolare* leader, Don Luigi Sturzo. Yet when the Sicilian priest repudiated the Fascist government and went into exile in 1924, *America* supported that faction of the *Popolare* party that remained loyal to Mussolini's regime. *America* also approved of Mussolini's banning the Italian Freemasons, dismissing them as "secret societies" and thus a "danger to the State." Either indifferent or shamed into silence, *America* passed over atrocities like the Matteotti murder without comment. Throughout the twenties the editorials stressed the material accomplishments of Fascism as well as its restoration of spiritual idealism and suppression of sectarianism. In the thirties neither the Ethiopian War nor the Italian anti-Semitic decrees caused *America* to reconsider its position on Il Duce's Italy.[7]

Less parochial were the views of *Commonweal*, a relatively liberal weekly published by lay Catholics. *Commonweal* maintained a more discerning and flexible view of Fascism. Unlike the Jesuit organ, *Commonweal* printed articles both for and against the dictatorship. Yet editorially it tended to favor the regime. Although from time to time *Commonweal* objected to Il Duce's reckless harangues and Fascism's aggressive chauvinism, the editors concluded in 1931 that Mussolini posed no threat to world peace and that there was "a complete absence of military bombast" in Italy. *Commonweal* also approved of the dissolution

[6] Daniel A. Binchy, *Church and State in Fascist Italy* (London, 1941), pp. 100-66; *America*, xxviii (Nov. 11, 1922), 74-75; (Dec. 2, 1922), 147; Thomas O'Hagen, "Who Are the Fascisti?" *ibid.*, pp. 150-51.

[7] *Ibid.*, xlvi (March 10, 1923), 482; xxxii (Feb. 7, 1925), 338; xxxiii (Aug. 1, 1925), 366; for *America*'s attitudes in the late thirties, see below, pp. 300, 329.

of Italian Masonry and defended Mussolini when he was attacked by Senator Thomas Reed and by Julius Barnes. According to *Commonweal*, Barnes failed to recognize those conditions in Italy which made Fascism adoptable and workable. No one desires to introduce "Mussolini methods" into the United States, *Commonweal* insisted, but we should "concede frankly" the value of these methods when applied to Italy. *Commonweal's* basic rationale was best expressed in this 1927 editorial statement: "The fact remains that these methods accomplished a great deal after a regime of corrupted democracy accomplished nothing." Yet it was not simply Mussolini's splendid use of autocratic methods that impressed *Commonweal*; it was the Fascist movement itself, a movement based on "'the idea of a thorough-going opposition to what is termed liberalism and is the final cataclysmic result of the far-flung nineteenth-century attempt to push back the forces of human nature by using the art of persuasion." Contemptuous of the liberal rationalism of the nineteenth century, *Commonweal* looked approvingly on the "substance of Fascismo" and suggested that possibly "the idea will survive" even its charismatic leader.[8]

Far less susceptible to Fascism's radiant halo was the *Catholic World*. Here the inimitable editor, Father James Gillis, offered a weekly column notable for its powerful convictions and scrupulous analyses. Although he featured writers both pro and con, Gillis himself attempted to understand the movement before pronouncing judgment. In the very early years he expressed tempered optimism. He accepted the widespread notion that Mussolini had saved Italy from bolshevism, and he found "encouraging and gratifying" Italy's war on irreligion and the outlawing of Freemasonry. On the other hand, Father Gillis admitted that Mussolini did not save Italy for democracy's sake, and he was disturbed by the dictator's scorn for the idea of liberty and by his "high-handed and occasionally violent" techniques. Nevertheless, the Fascist "virtues" of discipline, hierarchy, and order appealed to his Catholic political values, and thus Father Gillis pondered the possibility of Mussolini building a government on these virtues without violating basic liberties. If the Premier

[8] *Commonweal*, v (Nov. 17, 1926), 33-34; xiii (Jan. 21, 1931), 311; vi (Sept. 21, 1927), 457; ii (Oct. 21, 1925), 580; vi (Sept. 21, 1927), 457; v (Nov. 10, 1926), 4.

could achieve this goal, announced the *Catholic World*, he could well be the "greatest statesman since Justinian."[9]

By 1925 Father Gillis could no longer entertain the hope that liberty and justice would eventually emerge from the Italian experiment. The means Mussolini employed, Gillis reasoned, could never justify his ends, for the "customs of civilized government" had been lost in the process. The *Catholic World* grew more caustic as years passed. Always suspicious of Fascism's militarism, Gillis went on to describe Mussolini as a dangerous jingoist whose idols were Napoleon and Caesar. To the typical Catholic remark that Il Duce had "restored the crucifix," Gillis replied that such a statement was "obnoxious" and the move itself an empty gesture. He rejected scores of articles praising Mussolini, a policy which incurred the wrath of many readers. Yet the monthly remained firm in its opposition, a lonely temple of Catholic anti-Fascism in America.[10]

The *Catholic World* also found itself alone in its skeptical reaction to the 1929 announcement of the Concordat and Lateran Treaty between the Vatican and the Fascist regime. Many enthusiastic Catholics interpreted these agreements as the long sought reconciliation between Church and State in Italy. It did seem, after all, that Mussolini had succeeded in remaking a divisive and inert Italy ("The Home of the Church and of the Pope") into a cohesive and dynamic nation of which Catholics everywhere could be proud. Thus it was only fitting that the editor of *America*, Wilfrid Parsons, should write a pamphlet praising Il Duce for the historic rapprochement. The editors of *Commonweal*, although more concerned with the plight of non-Catholics and the problem of spiritual freedom in Italy, also expressed gratitude for the settlement. One of the most significant defenses of the Concordat to appear in *Commonweal* was written by the historian Carlton J. H. Hayes. The Columbia University professor believed that Mussolini and his movement were "the expression of a great and widespread will of the people" and that the Concordat consummated Italy's historic dream of unification. But the American press had interpreted the Concordat to mean that Catholic canon law would replace civil law in

[9] *Catholic World*, cxvi (March 1923), 842; cxvii (April-June, 1923), 120, 261-62, 406-07.

[10] *Ibid.*, cxxi (June 1925), 408-09; cxxii (March 1926), 838.

Italy. Attempting to correct the misconception, Hayes argued that Catholic law affected only education, marriage, and ecclesiastical appointments, that the settlement would tame the "madly ultra-nationalistic" character of Fascism, and that, rather than making the Church dependent on Fascist rule, it would give the Vatican a sphere of sovereignty no government would dare violate.[11]

In March 1929 the Vatican-Fascist accord was debated before a Foreign Policy Association luncheon. Count Sforza and Charles Marshall (the latter a legal critic of the Church and an antagonist of Al Smith) delivered the major indictments against the settlement; Father John A. Ryan, a staunch liberal Catholic and vociferous anti-Fascist, offered the defense. That an anti-Fascist like Father Ryan supported the Concordat indicates that Catholics could regard it as an ecclesiastical rather than an ideological affair. Still, the Concordat placed the anti-Fascist Catholics in a delicate predicament. Did the settlement mean that the Vatican had reconciled itself to Mussolini and Fascism? The answer, insisted Father Gillis in 1930, was definitely no. Referring to the Pope's remark in 1927 that Fascism posited the State as "an end to itself and citizens mere means to that end," Father Gillis concluded that the Church could never be committed to Fascism. The following year he asserted that the Pope was "at the moment the only conspicuous and powerful protagonist" of freedom in Italy. Yet *Catholic World* was hard-pressed to define "freedom" in the context of a Concordat which sanctioned a state religion and seemed to give tacit consent to autocracy. Father Gillis could only express the hope that anti-Fascists would rally around the Pope. Such expectations became more credible after Mussolini

11 Wilfrid Parsons, *The Pope and Italy* (America Press, 1929). Elsewhere Parsons pointed out proudly, as evidence of the elimination of "anti-religious forces," that the Pope no longer had to protest "the laxness of the government in dealing with Protestant anti-Catholic propaganda in Italy." If Mussolini does not abrogate the Concordat, Parsons stated, this will enable Pius XI "to see that the Catholic idea prevails in Italy and everywhere." "The Church in Contemporary Italy," *Catholic Historical Review*, xviii (April 1932), 17-18. See also Paul Bernardini, "The Lateran Concordat," *ibid.*, xvi (April 1930), 19-27; Moorehouse F. X. Miller, S.J., "The Meaning of the Roman Settlement," *Thought*, iv (June 1929), 5-19; *Commonweal*, ix (March 27, 1929), 582; Carlton J. H. Hayes, "Italy and the Vatican Agree," *ibid.*, ix (April 3, 1929), 619-22.

began to move against Catholic lay organizations like *Azione Cattolica*. The Vatican responded with the Encyclical "Non abbiamo bisogno" (We have no need), an important document which marked the first open disenchantment between Pius XI and the regime. Fascist encroachment on Papal sovereignty confirmed the stand of the *Catholic World*, and even *Commonweal* now came to believe that the Church-State tangle could never be resolved under the Mussolini government. But *America* maintained that Fascist attacks were the work of "the atheists, the socialists, and all the left wingers," thus condemning not Fascism but merely its "excesses."[12]

The "excesses" of Fascism, however, were never excessive enough to cause most American Catholics to repudiate completely Mussolini's anti-democratic experiment. In the late twenties and early thirties when middle and southern Europe produced various Rightist movements, Catholic writers preferred these authoritarian alternatives to the nineteenth-century liberalism of the Protestant West and the twentieth-century Bolshevism of the Godless East. Even when Catholic periodicals began having second thoughts in the late thirties some tended to equate Right-wing and Left-wing totalitarianism, conjuring up the convenient beast, "Soviet Fascism." All along, however, Mussolini escaped almost unscathed. Indeed when Hitler first came to power many Catholics viewed him as a mere student of Mussolini. As a respectable school for dictators, Mussolini's Italy, *America* explained, could provide a model that would mitigate the viciousness of Nazism. When the pupil proved a disappointment and started spouting racist doctrines, many Catholics could only agree with one writer who said of Hitler: "He now stands half way between Mussolini and the elemental madness of Communist Russia. For the sake of Germany I can only hope he will lean more in the direction of Italy." Despite German Nazism, Italian Fascism still appeared an act of political grace.[13]

[12] *The Vatican-Italian Accord* (Foreign Policy Association, New York, 1929), pamphlet; *Catholic World*, cxxx (Feb. 1930), 612-13; cxxxiii (Aug. 1931), 611; e.g., Carmen Haider, "The Vatican and Italian Fascism," *ibid.*, cxxxvii (July 1933), 395-402; "Caesar Challenges Peter," *Commonweal*, xiv (June 10, 1931), 141-43; John Wiltbye, "Fascism and the State," *America*, xlv (July 18, 1931), 353-54.

[13] Quoted in F. K. Wentz, "American Catholic Periodicals React to Nazism," *Church History*, xxxi (Dec. 1962), 400-20.

190

THE CATHOLIC APOLOGY: NATURAL LAW IN LIMBO

When considered in light of its own theological premises, the Catholic apology for Fascism offers a study in historical amnesia. In the late thirties and early forties, as we shall see in the concluding chapter, Catholics maintained that the ideological movements of Fascism, Communism, and Nazism arose from a historical relativism and philosophical nihilism that denied objective value, moral certainty, and natural law. According to Catholic thought, man's freedom is supposedly rooted in his essential spiritual nature and in a conscious awareness of the majestic force of God's natural law. By contrast, modern political thought, secularized by pragmatism and positivism, lacks a firm faith in a transcendent moral order. Devoid of such faith, it is without the ethical gyroscope that gives meaning to human freedom, the divine moral ballast that provides the inner resistance to totalitarianism. Given this argument, one might expect Catholic thinkers to have been better prepared than most Americans to resist the appeals of Fascism. Yet Catholics as a whole failed to reject Italian Fascism, and the reasons for this failure are perhaps best understood by examining the Catholic case for Mussolini.

The apology revolved roughly around four lines of argument. The first, a worldly blend of *realpolitik* and rationalization, asserted that the Church in Italy had to come to terms with Fascism as the only possible friendly and stable government. The Pope is merely making the best of the situation, and the Church must enhance its influence regardless of political circumstances if it is to save souls. On this basis "there can be no question between what is right and what is wrong," advised the convert L.J.S. Wood. A frequent contributor to Catholic periodicals, Wood informed readers that there was no "need to probe curiously into his [Mussolini's] soul." Wood bluntly preached accommodation. "He certainly is a Catholic. It would be going too far to infer from what he has said and done . . . that he has now suddenly become a fervent, practicing Catholic." But even if Mussolini is a spurious Catholic and political manipulator, "it would surely be the wiser policy, for political opportunists as well as for Catholic claimants to rigorism, instead of looking the gift horse in the mouth, to accept without cavil what is given, to refrain from opposition and complaint, at least until there is cause for

191

such." Until the thirties Mussolini gave Catholics no cause to question the argument that politics comes before piety.[14]

A second argument arose from the anti-democratic bias of many Catholic thinkers themselves. Catholicism had long been disturbed by the rise of mass democracy, the ascendancy of natural man, and the growth of industrial capitalism. During the twenties not a few Catholic thinkers contemplated the passing of democratic government and the return to some form of authoritarian order and economic discipline. Hilaire Belloc and G. K. Chesterton eloquently articulated the case against democracy in Catholic journals, and their ideas were often cited by Americans who defended Mussolini. But Mussolini's apologists did not have to import their authoritarian arguments from Englishmen like Belloc and Chesterton. American Catholic thinkers, too, nurtured a native scorn for democratic liberalism that was as contemptuous as it was complete. Such writers as T. S. Eliot, Paul Elmer More, Gorham Munsom, and Ross J. Hoffmann all dismissed liberalism as a nineteenth-century illusion, a figment of freedom collapsing before the centrifugal forces of twentieth-century economic chaos, political venality, and spiritual alienation. Rejecting the idea of democracy, Catholic intellectuals (both Roman and Anglican) opted for a Christian culture based on some form of distributive justice, integral humanism, and authoritarian order. One Catholic writer believed that liberalism's bankruptcy would be succeeded by Fascism's principle of *gerarchia* (hierarchy); another was sure that autocracy was "inevitable"—the only question was whether it would be of the "Russian or Italian type." The Catholic critique of democracy left liberal Catholics almost defenseless. Thus when the pro-Fascist polemicist Harvey Wickham attacked the few liberal Catholics by ridiculing their belief in the "mystic doctrine of the equality of souls," and at the same time praised Mussolini for puncturing the "hollow phrases of liberalism," *Commonweal* scarcely raised an editorial eyebrow.[15]

[14] L.J.S. Wood, "Mussolini and the Roman Question," *Catholic World*, cxix (April 1924), 64-75; for other arguments for Fascism by Wood, see *Commonweal*, i (Nov. 19, 1924), 42-43; iii (March 31, 1926), 369-70; iv (June 16, 1926), 149-50; vi (May 18-25, 1927), 38-39, 67-68.

[15] G. K. Chesterton, "The Fascist Method," *Catholic World*, cxxxii (Nov. 1930), 216-17; William Orton, "Is Democracy Breaking Down?" *Commonweal*, vii (Nov. 9, 1927), 660-62; Stanley James, "Democracy in the New

Catholic skepticism about democracy was rooted in a theology of human nature and political order. Catholic thinkers traditionally rejected the liberal version of a secular state as mistakenly based on the principle of popular sovereignty rather than the "moral authority" of the Church. As late as 1943, in the midst of the Second World War, Bishop Sheen declared: "We are not fighting to preserve the liberal concept of freedom." The genuine "Christian idea" of freedom, he argued, was founded on the spiritual principle of duties as well as rights, and on the social ideal of community as well as the popular notion of individualism. Sheen also rejected the liberal principle of contractual government based on individual representation in favor of the functional grouping of classes based on the "services they render to the nation." These organicist tendencies in Catholic thought led some writers to see elements of compatibility between Fascism and Catholic doctrine. While no American Catholic went so far as to claim that Fascism was the ultimate expression of political Catholicism, the embodiment of St. Thomas Aquinas' *Communitas Perfecta*, as did the Englishman James Strachey Barnes, few found Mussolini's Italy ideologically repugnant.[16]

If doubts about democracy could lead to a favorable judgment on Fascism, so could a narrow view of the Italian national character. Many who favored Fascism, Catholics and non-Catholics alike, asserted that it was not an alien ideology but a peculiar Italian movement that grew naturally from the historic traditions of the Italian people. Wilfrid Parsons, editor of *America*, claimed that the word "Fascism" was not merely a "party tag" but synonymous with the term "Italian" itself, and thus signified both the "Italian system of government" and the "Italian mentality." This justification based on the mystique of national character is singled out here not because it was an argument characteristic of Catholics

---

Age," *Catholic World*, cxxxvii (Aug. 1933), 513-18; Harvey Wickham, "The Facts of Fascism," *Commonweal*, v (Dec. 29, 1926), 204-06; id., "The Renaissance of Machiavelli," *ibid.*, vi (Sept. 21, 1927), 565-66.

16 John A. Ryan and Moorehouse F. X Miller, S.J., *The State and the Church* (New York, 1922); Fulton J. Sheen, *Philosophies at War* (New York, 1943), pp. 112-13, 175; see also Sheen's *Freedom Under God* (Milwaukee, 1940); Carmen Haider, "The Meaning of Economic Planning," *Thought*, viii (June 1933), 107-17; John Strachey Barnes, *The Universal Aspects of Fascism* (London, 1927), pp. 97-130, esp. p. 99.

alone, but rather because it is essentially "un-Catholic" reasoning. By claiming that distinct ethnic traits provide the basis for a type of government, Catholic thinkers were inadvertently denying the universality of their Catholicism, ignoring what Jacques Maritain has called "a common human creed, the creed of freedom" that transcends nationality. As Father Gillis declared, after having observed prelates in both Italy and the United States give their blessing to Mussolini's venture into Ethiopia, "If our Catholic ethics is colored by nationalism, can it still be Catholic?" Most Catholic thinkers in America were apprehensive about Italian nationalism, but those who argued in terms of national character were only one step from the quagmire of relativism.[17]

Commonweal took this step. In 1927 the lay magazine concluded that the Mussolini government ought to be "judged pragmatically—that is, on the basis of actual results." Although the journal dismissed Fascist ideology as "essentially critical and negative," the regime itself deserved "almost universal commendation" for having pulled a "nation out of chaos" and given it "order and prosperity." By insisting that the fruits of Fascism sanctioned its methods, *Commonweal* employed a logic that made Catholic reasoning indistinguishable from its erstwhile foe, liberal pragmatism. The confusion is compounded when we observe the reactions of Walter Lippmann to Sturzo's anti-Mussolini book, *Italy and Fascism* (1927), and of Dino Bigongiari to Prezzolini's paean, *Il Fascismo* (1927). Lippmann, one of the outstanding pragmatic social philosophers in America, accepted Sturzo's anti-Fascist analysis and, more importantly, saw the principle of the absolute state, the Italian *totalitario*, as a violation of Catholic political theory. Liberal Catholics, he warned *Commonweal*'s readers, must heed the dicta of Thomas Aquinas and Lord Acton which assert a natural law superior to the state, for the principle of the limited state offered "the only conception of politics which is consistent with a free and civilized life." Ironically it was Bigongiari, a Catholic professor at Columbia University and a leading proponent of scholastic philosophy, who elaborated a defense of Fascism that ignored the whole meaning of Catholic political theory. Fascism was not "Mussolinianism," Bigongiari insisted, but rather a "genuine" and inevitable culmination of Italian history, an irresistible idealism which revived religious

[17] Parsons, "The Church in Contemporary Italy," p. 9; James Gillis, "The Ambition of Mussolini," *Catholic World*, cxLII (Oct. 1935), 1-9.

awareness and allowed the individual to realize his freedom and spirituality through the ethical and organic state. The editorials of *Commonweal* and the writings of a scholastic like Bigongiari might lead one to conclude that, in respect to Fascism, some Catholic thinkers out-pragmatized the pragmatists. And if Catholic political thought is pragmatic, is it Catholic?[18]

One eminent cleric who had an answer to the dilemma was Monsignor John A. Ryan. A Professor at Catholic University and, as head of Catholic Social Action, a leader in the progressive reform movement, Ryan waged a relentless assault upon Mussolini's dictatorship and upon the Catholic defense of Fascism. His numerous writings and speeches derived from his unwavering commitment to liberal democracy and to Pope Leo XIII's ideals of social justice. Offering the most complete counterargument to the Catholic apology, he challenged the widespread notion that Fascism represented the will of the great majority, that it was best suited for the Italian people ("a cruel libel"), that the suppression of Freemasonry was justified, and that the Corporate State's labor laws were in accord with the encyclical *Rerum Novarum*. Even more significantly, he exploded the two basic ideological justifications of Mussolini's American disciples: that Fascist theory evolved from philosophical foundations and that it could be reconciled with the teachings of the Church. Fascist theory, Father Ryan stated, was "narrowly empirical" and "eclectic," improvised immorally and used expediently. As to the alleged affinity between Fascism and Catholicism: "Fascism contradicts the Catholic doctrine on the authority, function, and purpose of the state, on the natural rights of the individual, and on the means which the state may use; it rejects the principle of political democracy; and it promotes a spirit of excessive nationalism which is not conducive to international peace. In other words, the Fascist theory is a pragmatic combination of absolutism, Machiavellianism, Toryism, and chauvinism." Clearly more than any other clerical thinker in the twenties, Father Ryan was the theological thorn in the flesh of complacent Catholic apologists.[19]

[18] *Commonweal*, v (Jan. 5, 1927), 231; Walter Lippmann, "Autocracy Versus Catholicism," *ibid.*, v (April 13, 1927), 627; Dino Bigongiari, "Mussolini: Servant of Italy," *ibid.*, p. 628.

[19] John A. Ryan, "Fascism in Practice," *Commonweal*, v (Nov. 24, 1926), 73-76; id., "The Doctrine of Fascism," *ibid.*, v (Nov. 17, 1926), 42-44.

Although the political theory of liberal Catholicism offered the philosophical basis for anti-Fascism, the record indicates that in America it remained a theory sorely in need of practice. Of those who spoke out on the issue of Fascism, only Fathers Ryan and Gillis sustained a steady democratic critique, attacking both the opportunism and the much-heralded pragmatic character of Fascist ideology as well as its Hegelian ethos of the all-embracing State. Most other articulate Catholic spokesmen merely aped the public in praising the orderly and efficient dictatorship of Il Duce, thereby becoming what Father Gillis was later to call a "shameful specimen of clerical fallibility." More often than not their views of Fascism expressed slight concern for Catholic social theory, and their rhetoric often revealed a relativism they themselves were fond of associating with the "poison" of liberal pragmatism.[20]

Most Catholic thinkers responded to Fascism not as a challenging ideological phenomenon but as a historical movement whose usefulness should be measured in light of the interests of the Church; not as a novel "theory" to be examined theologically but as an inevitable "reality" to be considered politically. Nowhere was this secularized approach better illustrated than in a pamphlet written by John La Farge, a distinguished Jesuit who later became editor of *America*. In order to clarify the Catholic position on Mussolini's dictatorship, Father La Farge tried to explain the fundamental difference between Fascism and Communism in terms of the causal role of ideas in history. Fascism, he maintained, is in "proverbial contrast with Marxianism, where the deed grows largely out of the revolutionary theory." Unlike Marxism, Fascist "reality," if not its theory, "accepts globally the historic greatness of Italy, and accepts religion as an essential feature of that historic greatness." Even though Fascist theory—chauvinistic nationalism, militant irrationalism, the cult of the state—contradicts Church dogma, in practice Fascism has been forced to subdue its ideology and recognize "historic reality, and the Church is part of that historic reality." As a result the Pope "has expressed the hope and expectation that the Fascist deeds would be better than the Fascist theory," a hope, Father La Farge pointed out, that has been "somewhat realized" in the Italian government's "respectful" attitude toward religion

[20] James M. Gillis, "Catholicism and Fascism," *Catholic World*, CLVII (June 1943), 225-34.

196

and in the "humane and often strikingly just provisions" of Fascist labor laws.[21]

From this study of apology and amnesia one would have to conclude that the great majority of Catholics, cleric and lay, were no better prepared to evaluate philosophically the meaning of totalitarianism than were most other Americans. The Catholics' response to Fascism reveals precious little evidence that a sense of the supernatural offers the best resistance to the cunning appeals of totalitarianism. Indeed the supreme irony is that in judging Fascism not on the basis of its philosophical foundations but on its actual practice, Catholic thinkers were behaving more pragmatically than liberal pragmatists. Where some pragmatic liberals, as we shall see, engaged in a brief flirtation with the Italian phenomenon as a fresh and exciting social theory, Catholics chose to ignore the theory and praise instead the practical consequences of Fascism. By using mundane deeds rather than moral doctrine as the focus of their judgment, Catholic thinkers lost sight of natural law and committed their own *trahison des clercs*.

PROTESTANTS AND JEWS

Whereas Catholics were deeply concerned about Fascism because of the presence of the Holy Father in Rome, Protestants had only a peripheral interest. Significantly, Mussolini's coup did not generate among non-Catholics the bitter hostility toward clerical reaction caused by Franco's coup fourteen years later. George Seldes' *The Catholic Crisis* was conceived in the blood-drenched battlefields of Spain in 1936, not in the placid March on Rome in 1922. The earlier Protestant response to Italian Fascism comprised a mild mixture of cautious sympathy and gentle criticism. At least two possible explanations for this tolerance may be suggested.

First of all, in the early years Protestant publications saw in Mussolini's former anti-clericalism a hopeful sign of what was in store for non-Catholics in Italy—an impression strengthened when the Italian government permitted non-Catholic schools to provide their own religious instruction. Even the Concordat, sur-

[21] La Farge also argued that a "Christian society" can be "authoritarian" and "nondemocratic," provided the state "gives full recognition to the God-given dignity and destiny of the human person." *Fascism in Government and in Society* (The America Press, New York, 1938), pamphlet, pp. 3-5.

prisingly enough, did not arouse immediate Protestant suspicions. The *Christian Century* believed that the Italian government would counter any threat to Protestant liberties posed by the established Roman church. More optimistically, the *Missionary Review* was convinced that "God has intervened to save the 'little flock' from being scattered. . . . Protestantism in Italy has always been regarded as an intrusion and was simply 'tolerated' in law and persecuted in practice. Premier Mussolini has now admitted it into the State and we thank God for this religious liberty." Secondly, the new regime's crusade against "vile" books, its sanitary reforms, and its ascetic idealism made Italy a showcase for moral rearmament which contrasted with America's backsliding worldliness in the tawdry twenties. This was especially true for Protestant nativists who took seriously the Fascist pieties of industry and responsibility. Dr. Edward S. Young, of the Bedford Park Presbyterian Church in Brooklyn, heralded Mussolini as a prudent taskmaster, the first Italian who made his indolent people do honest work. As the Reverend W.H.P. Paunce declared in one of his sermons: "But he has so transformed the soul of his country that . . . [he] has driven out of the Italian city every mere pleasure-seeker, every man who put himself above his country. And by putting all that pleasure-loving people under the strictest discipline of the modern world he has restored to Italy joy, confidence, and immortal hope."[22]

The spiritual and economic ideals of Fascism may have provided sermons of uplift for American pulpits, but nativist homilies themselves were not sufficient to assure complete support from the Protestant establishment. The comments of the inter-denominational *Christian Century* indicate that the Protestant response to Fascism was not all sweetness and light. In the beginning *Christian Century* reiterated the standard American argument that Mussolini's positive achievements justified his unconstitutional methods. But during the mid-twenties the prestigious weekly wavered between sympathy and opposition. The editors often criticized Americans who idolized Il Duce, and they found it hard to admit that democratic institutions were as "dead" as Mussolini claimed. Moreover, they were aware of the implications of the dictator's undying militarism, his "savage

[22] *Missionary Review*, xlvii (Sept. 1924), 750; lii (Aug. 1929), 622, 643, quoted in Carter, pp. 230-31; *Christian Century*, xlviii (March 18, 1931), 364; *NYT*, Sept. 13, 1926, Aug. 20, 1928.

intent of shattering the peace of the world." At the same time, however, *Christian Century* continued to concede that Fascism was "a system of government with a reasoned philosophy, a passionate patriotism, an extraordinary capacity for commanding devotion of a mystical quality, and a record of practical results"; and in 1929 readers were advised that the "hope of democracy will revive when it learns how to do the things that need to be done as efficiently as autocracy does them." Thus by the end of the twenties *Christian Century's* attitude toward Fascism, though occasionally critical, was as irresolute as ever. Then in 1931, when the Fascist regime began to tangle with the Vatican, the journal finally took a firm stand as it joined Catholics in support of the Papacy. Ironically this shift represented a sudden political awaking. Whereas during the Concordat *Christian Century* believed that the Fascist government would intercede to protect Protestant liberties against the Roman church, by 1931 it could only conclude that "year by year it becomes clearer that the alleged gain of freedom for the papacy has in reality placed it more than ever under the thumb of the Fascist dictatorship." Many Protestant spokesmen shared this conviction. The popular Congregationalist Dr. S. Parker Cadman told a conclave of pastors in Cleveland that in clerical circles throughout the world the Holy See had the "warm sympathy" of numerous non-Catholics. "The Roman Catholic Church," Cadman stated, "has taken bigger men than Mussolini and eaten them for breakfast."[23]

On the issue of Fascism the Protestant community was either indifferent or ambivalent; and where ambivalent the most recurring sentiment might be described as one of critical support, especially for the patriotism and practical idealism of the regime. But Protestant tolerance could not be sustained in the face of Mussolini's clash with the Vatican, a clash that many regarded as a threat to religious liberty everywhere. Moreover, comments occasionally printed in the press from individual ministers indicate that no Protestant consensus existed. True, Mussolini en-

[23] W. E. Garrison, "Today in Italy," *Christian Century*, XLI (March 6, 1924), 303-04; XLIV (June 23, 1927), 708; XLVI (April 11, 1929), 476, (July 31, 1929), 957, (Dec. 11, 1929), 1534; XLVIII (May 6, 1931), 597, (June 10, 1931), 763, (July 15, 1931), 916, (Sept. 16, 1931), 1133. For another balanced but critical evaluation, see "Fascism," *The Social Service Bulletin* (The Methodist Federation for Social Service, New York, April 1, 1933); Cadman was quoted in *Time*, XVII (June 15, 1931), 23.

joyed the admiration of several nativist churchmen, but he also suffered the censure of officials such as Dr. W. Russell Bowie, Rector of the Grace Episcopal Church in New York; Dr. Fred B. Smith of the World Alliance for International Friendship through the Church; and Dr. Bertrand Tipple, former head of the Methodist Church in Rome. True, the *Wall Street Journal* gave a full page to Dr. Ernest W. Stires' eulogy of Mussolini before the Foreign Policy Association, but Salvemini could print in his anti-Fascist pamphlets the eloquent admonitions of the noted Unitarian John Haynes Holmes. Stires' description of Fascism as a "great constructive and patriotic movement of a nation reborn," and Holmes' call to resist "Fascist despotism, to expose its injustice and horror, to labor for its overthrow [as] a first duty in the cause of liberty," suggest the breadth of the Protestant spectrum.[24]

The Protestant spectrum was also strained by diverse emotions. For although certain ranking churchmen betrayed a touch of nativist elitism in supporting Fascism, many of the more fundamentalist preachers were haunted by the specter of Catholicism. In the Midwest especially, various evangelists warned their followers that Mussolini may be the prophesied "man of sin" bent on reviving decadent Romanism. The Reverend W. D. Herrstorm claimed that Mussolini's "background of occult could easily prepare him to be in league with the fallen spirits who are directed by Satan," a fear that led C. S. Tubby to ask the question that was on the lips of every evangelist: was Mussolini an anti-Christ? Of all the fundamentalists the one who was both fascinated as well as repelled by Mussolini was the ultra-Right wing Kansas minister, Gerald B. Winrod. In 1928 Winrod wrote the weird pamphlet, *Mussolini and the Second Coming of Christ*. Noting that "the eyes of the world are upon" Il Duce, the anti-Catholic Winrod was forced to acknowledge Mussolini's shrewd instinct for power and Fascism's wise repudiation of the "equalitarian tradition." With the rise of Nazism, however, Winrod found a more genuine, purified hero in *Der Fuehrer*. Thus in 1933 he warned that the prophet Daniel had predicted the coming of a southern European anti-Christ to whom all Jews would turn.

[24] *NYT*, March 15, 1926, Sept. 17, 1926, May 9, 1927; *Christian Century*, XLIII (April 1, 1926), 429; *Wall Street Journal*, Dec. 19, 1923; *NYT*, Dec. 2, 1923; Holmes is quoted in Salvemini's pamphlet, *The Fascist Dictatorship* (New York, 1926), p. 74.

Even Hitler, Winrod advised his rapt listeners, disliked Mussolini because the latter was "pro-Semitic." Such preachings merely indicate that extreme nativist Protestantism could find Italian Fascism politically enlightened but spiritually depraved.[25]

But several of the more moderate Protestant denominations also harbored suspicions of the Catholic Church in Italy. In 1926 officials of the Southern Baptist Convention, the Methodist Episcopal Church, and the Foreign Missions Abroad sent a resolution to Secretary of State Kellogg protesting a rumor that the League of Nations was arranging the transfer of Italian property to the Vatican. "We wish to stress our judgment," the statement read, "that we believe the mass of Italian people do not understand the strength of Protestantism within the United States, nor are they in a position to understand how serious the reaction from such legislation would become." As nothing came of this particular rumor, the "serious reaction" of American Protestants failed to materialize. But among American non-Catholics apprehensions regarding the Papacy die hard. Hence when Mussolini outlawed Freemasonry in Italy various Masonic lodges in the United States denounced the legislation, and *New Age*, official organ of the Supreme Council of the Scottish Rite, claimed that the Catholic Church and the Fascist government had collaborated to harass Italian Masons. In 1926 John H. Cowles, Grand Commander of the Supreme Council, sent a resolution to every member of Congress asking that they reject the Italian debt settlement on grounds of the anti-Masonic persecution. Secretary Kellogg informed Ambassador Fletcher that one of the major obstacles to the debt ratification was "the religious opposition," which included some Baptist groups as well as the Masons and the violently anti-Catholic Klan.[26]

Opposition to Mussolini on the part of southern Baptists and midwestern evangelists reflects the enlightenment of reaction.

[25] Nicholas Pirolo, *Babylon: Political and Ecclesiastical Showing Characteristics of Anti-Christ and False Prophet Considering Mussolini and the Pope* (Milwaukee, 1937); W. D. Herrstorm, *Mussolini and Fascism* (Wichita, 1937), pamphlet, and *The Revived Roman Empire* (Grand Rapids, 1939), pamphlet; C. S. Tubby, *Mussolini the Marvel-Man: Superman or Satan?* (Springfield, 1929), pamphlet; Gerald B. Winrod, *Mussolini and the Second Coming of Christ* (Wichita, 1928), pamphlet, and *Mussolini's Place in Prophecy* (Wichita, 1933), pamphlet.

[26] *New Age*, xxxiii (May 1925), 281, cited in Carter, p. 243; Kellogg to Fletcher, Feb. 5, 1926. Container 12, FP.

Born in bigotry, their anti-Fascism amounted to little more than an anti-Catholic reflex. But what seems ironic is that whereas the Protestant Right castigated Mussolini, the moderate Left proved susceptible to Fascism's twin-mystique of piety and patriotism. To be sure, American Protestantism provided no "amen corner" for the propagation of Fascism, but the failure of *Christian Century* to repudiate unconditionally its doctrines does suggest something about the shame and the glory of Liberal Protestantism.

In the Jewish community opposition to Fascism sprang mainly from trade unions, especially those like the ILGWU and the ACWU where Socialist slogans with Yiddish accents could be heard above the babel of tongues and the roar of looms. Yet though the Jewish Left—perhaps best represented by Abraham Cahan's *Daily Forward* and Herman Bernstein's *Jewish Tribune* —was unquestionably opposed to Fascism, the opposition should be regarded more a matter of ideology than theology. Not the Mosaic law but the laws of Marx explain the anti-Fascism of Jewish labor leaders like David Dubinsky, Morris Feinstein, and Sidney Hillman. However that may be, aside from Jewish radicals and intellectuals, what is significant is that during the twenties the synagogues remained relatively silent on the Fascist question. Although Rabbis like Stephen S. Wise and Louis I. Newman actively opposed Blackshirt activities in the United States, Jewish officialdom itself showed scant interest in the Italian phenomenon. Obviously this inattention can be explained by the fact that Italian Fascism appeared to be completely free of anti-Semitism. Thus when Hitler came to power Mussolini appeared in Jewish eyes as a sane counterforce to Nazism's Aryan madness. *B'nai B'rith Magazine*, surveying European Fascist movements in 1934, reassured its readers that no anti-Semitism existed within the borders of Italy. It will be remembered that Mussolini repeatedly denied to Americans that Italy had a "Jewish problem." Il Duce's whitewash was a masterstroke of public relations. For in the fall of 1933, editors of forty-three American Jewish publications took a poll to select twelve Christians who "have most vigorously supported Jewish political and civil rights and who have been the most outstanding in their opposition to anti-Semitism." Mussolini was one of the twelve selected because, the press reported, "he took pains to demonstrate that Italian Fascism does not tolerate racial or religious persecution." Mussolini may not have tolerated much else, but, despite his struggle with the Vatican, he appeared to American Jews a most welcomed defender of the faith.[27]

American attitudes toward Fascism were shaped in no small part by religion, an important factor in the Protestant and Jewish communities, a decisive one in the Catholic. In a subsequent chapter dealing with the late thirties we shall be able to examine opinion polls and analyze with precision the religious breakdown of Fascist sentiment. At this point it is enough to state that during the twenties neither Protestantism nor Judaism proved to be a spiritual sentinel against the vogue of Italian Fascism, while Catholicism demonstrated that an elastic apologia could accommodate both religiosity and reaction.

[27] E.g., Bernard Postal, "Colored Shirts on Parade," *B'nai B'rith Magazine*, XLVIII (April 1934), 228-31; *NYT*, Sept. 18, 1933. The author has not studied thoroughly Jewish opinion, an exercise that would require close examination of the Yiddish press. My generalizations derive from the scarcity of articles on Fascism in various Jewish publications in English and the lack of any commentary by the Rabbinical hierarchy in the daily press. As to anti-Semitism, American Jews were deceived by its apparent absence in Italy. Although not a central ingredient, anti-Semitism was potential in Italian Fascism. For further discussion, see below, pp. 302, 319-21, 333n.

9.

Three Faces for Fascism: The American Right, Left, and Center

CIRCUMSTANCES MAY ARISE WHEN WE ESTEEM OURSELVES FORTUNATE IF WE GET THE EQUIVALENT OF MUSSOLINI; HE MAY BE NEEDED TO SAVE US FROM THE AMERICAN EQUIVALENT OF A LENIN.

Irving Babbitt, 1924

BY UNMASKING CAPITALIST DEMOCRACY, AND BY SHOWING IT UP IN ITS TRUE COLORS AS A HEARTLESS DICTATORSHIP, THE NEW RULERS OF ITALY WILL DO A GREAT SERVICE BY DISILLUSIONING THE CONFUSED MASSES OF THE ITALIAN PROLETARIAT. THEY WILL MAKE THEM SEE AND UNDERSTAND THEIR CLASS INTERESTS AS THEY NEVER COULD UNDER THE PSEUDO-DEMOCRACY OF THE ERA JUST PASSED. THE FASCISTI COUP IS A LONG STEP TOWARDS THE ULTIMATE REVOLUTION.

William Z. Foster, 1922

WHATEVER THE DANGERS OF FASCISM, IT HAS AT ANY RATE SUBSTITUTED MOVEMENT FOR STAGNATION, PURPOSIVE BEHAVIOR FOR DRIFTING, AND VISIONS OF GREAT FUTURE FOR COLLECTIVE PETTINESS AND DISCOURAGEMENT.

Herbert Croly, 1927

FASCISM was the political wonder of the twentieth century. Whereas the Bolshevik Revolution appeared to Americans as the culmination of nineteenth-century revolutionary radicalism, the March on Rome seemed shrouded in a thick ideological fog. Significantly, no American thinker clearly anticipated the rise of European Fascism. Looking back, one can find vague premonitions in Brooks Adams' martial elitism and Herbert Croly's corporate nationalism, in Thorstein Veblen's and Randolph Bourne's descriptions of imperial Germany and its "cosmic heroisms"; and above all, in Jack London's *The Iron Heel*, which depicted the revolutionary immaturity of the masses and their liquidation by a master "oligarchy." In an age of democratic faith, however, such rare skepticism was, as Bourne put it, "the most intolerable of all insults." Moreover, as it emerged, Italy's strange revolution from the Right wrapped itself in a tissue of synthetic ideologies, a deliberate exercise in obscurantism enabling Mussolini to exploit the ambiguity of his movement and present to Americans a many-sided image. Yet between the image and the reality lies a stark body of doctrine which, when stripped of its trappings, represented nothing less than a negation of America's basic political ideas and values: the irrationality and inequality of man, the organic and elitist nature of the state, the glorification of power and violence, the cult of the super-personality who stands above the law. Curiously, few Americans perceived Fascism in light of this direct ideological challenge. The reason many failed to do so can perhaps best be understood by examining America's diverse political spectrum.[1]

THE RIGHT: FASCISM AS LESSON

At one end of the spectrum stood two inchoate groups which, because of their deep-seated fear of all that was modern and progressive, might be regarded as part of the American Right: the native fundamentalists and the intellectual reactionaries. Among the various manifestations of fundamentalism none was more militant than the patriotism of the American Legion. Officially organized in 1919 in response to the patriotic upsurge of

[1] Randolph Bourne, *War and the Intellectuals*, ed. Carl Resek (New York, 1964), pp. 3-14. Years later many writers would agree with Trotsky that "Jack London already foresaw and described the fascist regime as the inevitable result of the defeat of the proletarian revolution." Quoted in Joan London, *Jack London and His Times* (New York, 1939), p. 313.

the war and the backwash of the red scare, the Legion was an answer to the divisive doctrines of internationalism and class conflict. Not surprisingly, the Legion quickly found a European counterpart in the Italian war veterans who provided the shock troops for the Fascist march to power. Deeply stirred, the National Commander, Alvin Owsley, invited Mussolini to attend the San Francisco Legionnaire convention in 1923. Il Duce cordially declined, but Owsley, unrebuffed, proudly declared:

"If ever needed, the American Legion stands ready to protect our country's institutions and ideals as the Fascisti dealt with the destructionists who menaced Italy."

"By taking over the government?" he was asked.

"Exactly that," he replied. "The American Legion is fighting every element that threatens our democratic government—soviets, anarchists, I.W.W., revolutionary socialists and every other 'red.' . . . Do not forget that the Fascisti are to Italy what the American Legion is to the United States."[2]

Despite Owsley's boasts, the *American Legion Monthly* carried a regular column by Frederick Palmer, who occasionally lectured to Mussolini about abolishing suffrage and exporting Fascism to the United States. Palmer's remarks embarrassed a group of Legionnaires visiting Rome in 1929. Confronted by angry Italian war veterans, the new Legion Commander, Paul McNutt, maintained that Palmer's comments were entirely personal and assured Italian officials that the Legion bore no ill will toward their government. Satisfied with the explanation, officials invited the Legionnaires to Mussolini's palace where the Premier welcomed them "with marked cordiality and friendliness." A few years later Mussolini received the ultimate American compliment when Colonel William Eastwood of Dallas pinned a Legion button on his lapel, making him an honorary member. In turn, portly Il Duce posed for a photograph wearing a Texan's hat.[3]

Unlike the American Legion, the Ku Klux Klan greatly resented being compared to the *Fascisti*. Even though in 1923 an ex-Klans-

[2] Quoted in Norman Hapgood, *Professional Patriots* (New York, 1928), pp. 61-62.

[3] Frederick Palmer, "A Personal View," *American Legion Monthly*, i (Oct. 1926), 88; *ibid.*, iv (March 1928), 63-64; *NYT*, Aug. 24, 1929; Eastwood's gesture caused some consternation at the Legion's national headquarters; see *NYT*, July 4, 7, 10, Oct. 5, 1933.

man, Edgar I. Fuller, started to form an American *Fascio* in order
to fight radicalism, and even though as late as 1930 an organization arose in Georgia which called itself "The American Fascisti
Association and Order of Black Shirts" and published the *Black
Shirt*, most Klansmen never deigned to acknowledge any respect
for Mussolini and Fascism. The Klan instead sent flowers to a
New Jersey policeman who was suspended for removing a Fascist
flag from a car leading a parade of Italian-American Blackshirts;
and the "Krusaders," a northern branch of the KKK, denounced
Mussolini along with the Reverend S. Parker Cadman ("chief of
the Jesuits"), Governor Al Smith, and the Boy Scouts of America.
Obviously the Klan's hostility derived from a rural, Protestant
bias against all that was urban, Catholic and "foreign," namely
the Italian-Americans. Thus the fundamentalist South was in no
position to applaud the achievements of Mussolini, whose possible
success in remaking Italy into a first-class nation of morally disciplined citizens could undermine the argument against unrestricted immigration. Ironically, however, while southern nativists
had no great interest in seeing Fascism succeed, other nativists had no desire to see it fail. Not only would the demise of
Il Duce revive the alleged threat of bolshevism, but, more
importantly, it would mean the failure of the first anti-democratic
political experiment in the twentieth century. In this respect
America's racial-nativists had a stake in Fascism, and their attack
on democracy and defense of authoritarianism found its most
mordant spokesman in Lothrop Stoddard. Convinced that democracy was unworkable for most peoples of the world, Stoddard
made a strong case for Fascism in prestigious *Harper's*. The
strength of the *fascisti*, claimed Stoddard, lies in the shrewd
"realism" with which they cry, "Down with our idols! Down with
Democracy! Down with Equality!" Fascism creates new idols,
Stoddard conceded with condescension, but only to keep the
people in "a Roman mood." Because Mussolini punctured the
hollow doctrines of republicanism and equality, Fascism had
"a distinct tonic value," for even if it is an over-dramatic protest,
"it is at least a healthy, virile protest against the sentimentality
and phrase worship of our age."[4]

[4] *NYT*, June 18, 1923; Aug. 25, Nov. 14, 15, 1927; *San Francisco Chronicle*, March 21, 1923; Edwin Tribble, "Black Shirts in Georgia," *New Republic*, LXIV (Oct. 8, 1930), 204-06; Lothrop Stoddard, "Realism: The True
Challenge of Fascism," *Harper's*, CLV (Oct. 1927), 578-83.

Moving from the narrow fundamentalism and harsh racism of the far Right to the wholesome sobriety of Main Street, one encounters another source of conservative pro-Fascism in the twenties. Nativists like Stoddard may have exploited Fascism to demonstrate to tough-minded Americans the delusions of democracy, but much of Mussolini's appeal to the more tender-minded Babbitts and Rotarians sprang from the anxieties of middle-class Americans toward social radicalism. Ambassador Child and Kenneth Roberts never allowed the *Saturday Evening Post* readers to forget that Fascism was a lesson not only to Italians but to the "pampered" American progressives and their parasitical welfare programs. Events in Italy, Roberts warned in 1923, show that a "nation doesn't have to endure demagoguery." Apprehensive about the fate of economic liberty, the solid citizens who cheered on the pro-Fascism of the *Saturday Evening Post* exposed the nervous tic of bourgeois America.[5]

Had these same Americans read Albert J. Nock's *The Freeman* they would have discovered how a true proponent of economic freedom evaluated Fascism. Nock's short-lived but provocative monthly provided perhaps the only intelligent and consistent critique of Fascism from the American Right. Unlike so many champions of "American individualism," Nock was one of the few to see that Fascism posed a threat to free enterprise as great as that of Communism. Watching the Fascists maneuver to change Italy's electoral system, he observed that replacing majoritarian for plurality representation would only return the country to the authoritarianism of the Bourbon age. "The Fascisti are right, of course, when they say that democracy will not work in a great centralized State," declared one of the last sincere Jeffersonians in America; "but does it follow of necessity that democracy must be sacrificed, in order that the State may survive? There is an alternative possibility which promises something better than a return to the tyranny of the past." In another instance, when Judge Elbert Gary was quoted as having asked "whether we don't think we need a man like Mussolini" in America, Nock concluded that businessmen secretly lusted after a powerful state in order to crush organized labor. "In Italy today political government fulfills its natural coercive function more frankly and directly than under the old fashioned parliamentary

[5] Kenneth Roberts, "The Salvation of a Nation," passim.

208

forms; and to Americans of a certain type the system may seem well worthy of emulation."[6]

Unfortunately other spokesmen for the intellectual Right lacked Nock's anarcho-conservative suspicion of the centralized state. Partly as a result of this political insensibility, Fascism could command the admiration of at least one representative from each of the three expressions of cultural conservatism in the twenties: Southern Agrarianism, New Humanism, and Aristocratic Naturalism. Stark Young, drama critic for the *New Republic* and contributor to the famous manifesto *I'll Take My Stand*, elaborated a defense of Fascism that sprouted from the pastoral bias of a southern intellectual. Enamored of the historic glory of Italian civilization, the presumed simplicity of the land-rooted people and the mystical power of their Catholicism, Young believed that Fascism offered a natural political order that would save the Italians from "the greedy and vulgar scrimmage of the modern world" and preserve the beauty of backwardness. The New Humanist scholar Irving Babbitt also saw Fascism as the politics of preservation. Distrusting man's natural impulses, Babbitt called for a return to classical standards, humanistic discipline, and moral character. In *Democracy and Leadership* (1924), an unqualified assault on the cult of the common man, Babbitt sought to substitute the "doctrine of the right man for the doctrine of the rights of man." One leader who represented the "right man" was Benito Mussolini, whose puritanical will, Babbitt cryptically warned, "may be needed to save us from the American equivalent of a Lenin."[7]

If it is difficult to imagine Babbitt, with the humanist ethic of the "inner check," swayed by a Fascism that preached as its highest value the emotional power of pure action, it is equally difficult to explain George Santayana's respect for the Mussolini government. Whereas Fascism was based on "its will to power, its will to be, its attitude in the face of the fact of violence and of its own courage," Santayana's naturalism demanded restraining man's irrational impulses; whereas Fascists conceived life as a struggle against the material world, Santayana adhered to a quietistic philosophy of the inner life of mind; whereas Fascism

[6] *The Freeman*, VII (Aug. 22, 1923), 557-58; (April 18, 1923), 122.

[7] Stark Young, "Notes on Fascism in Italy Today," *New Republic*, LXVII (July 22, 29, Aug. 5, 1931), 258-60, 281-83, 312-14; Irving Babbitt, *Democracy and Leadership* (Boston, 1924), pp. 246, 313.

preached a politics of rigorous strife and ultimate spiritual transcendence, Santayana made light of reformers who tried to legislate "progress" instead of resigning themselves to the inescapable tragedies of the human condition; and whereas Fascist theorists believed essence could be realized in the will to action, Santayana believed essence could be found, if at all, only in ideal forms of beauty and in spiritual contemplation. Yet despite these differences, America's most brilliant, conservative philosopher was attracted to Mussolini's Italy, an attraction that is perhaps best explained by his rejection of American civilization. Convinced that America was divided into two states of mind, Santayana saw in Fascism a higher organic Italian culture that appealed to his atheistic catholicism and his Mediterranean anti-puritanism. Thus in addition to his unconcealed contempt for Italians as a people, Santayana's support of Fascism also reflected a life-long disenchantment with a stunted, bifurcated American culture frantic with motion and bereft of direction. Taking up residence in Italy, he came to see in the Fascist principle of *gerarchia* an approximation of his own belief in a Platonic timocracy based on order, inequality, and aristocracy. After World War II Santayana neither tried to deny nor rationalize his attachment to the Fascist idea, and, as his letter to Corliss Lamont reveals, his convictions remained unshakened despite Mussolini's ignominious exit.

Of course I was never a Fascist in the sense of belonging to that Italian party, or to any nationalistic or religious *party*. But considered, as it is for a naturalist, a product of the generative order of society, a nationalist or religious *institution* will probably have its good sides, and be better perhaps than the alternative that presents itself at some moment in some place. That is what I thought and still think, Mussolini's dictatorship was for Italy in its home government. Compared with the disorderly socialism that preceded or the impotent party chaos that has followed it. If you had lived through it from the beginning to end, as I have, you would admit this. But Mussolini personally was a bad man and Italy a half-baked political unit; and the *militant* foreign policy adopted by Fascism was ruinous in its artificiality and folly. But internally, Italy was until the foreign militancy and mad alliances were adopted, a stronger, happier, and more united country than it is or had ever been.

210

Dictatorships are surgical operations, but some diseases require them, only the surgeon must be an expert, not an adventurer.[8]

In the thirties the intellectual Right in America made the conservatism of Young, Babbitt, and Santayana a matter of politics as well as culture. Faced with the rising prestige of Soviet Communism, the Fascist alternative seemed all the more urgent to a reactionary intelligentsia that scorned Marxist egalitarianism as much as American liberalism. This theme was driven home in the *American Review*, a journal notable for the perversity of its brilliance. Founded by one of Babbitt's disciples, Seward Collins, the *American Review* offered its small circle of readers the programs of the "Revolutionary Conservatives": the New Humanism of Babbitt and More, the Southern Agrarianism of Young and Alan Tate, the Distributism of G. K. Chesterton and Hillaire Belloc, and the Neo-Thomism of Christopher Dawson and Father D'Arcy. Among the journal's political heroes were Mussolini, Eamon De Valera, Jozef Pilsudski, Hitler, and Franco. Unlike the futuristic fantasies of some of the European Fascist movements, however, the *American Review* declared war on the whole world of modernity and progress. In its pages one heard the distant wail of guildists, medievalists, royalists, and other isolated social critics who called for a return to a past age. A. J. Penty, the British disciple of Ruskin and Morris, saw in Italian corporatism an enlightened return to the "Regulative Guild State." Harold Goad conceived Fascism as an historic folk ideal, an organic government not "by" but "of" and "for" the people. And Ross J. S. Hoffmann, a New York University professor who placed himself on the "Catholic Right" and who believed Fascism represented a timely revival of the autonomous state, was certain that "Mussolini is a man of tradition with whom Aristotle or St. Thomas or Machiavelli might without too great difficulty feel at ease."[9]

---

[8] Benito Mussolini, "The Doctrine of Fascism," in *Communism, Fascism and Democracy*, ed. Carl Cohen (New York, 1962), p. 361; George Santayana, "Apologia Pro Mente Sua," in *The Philosophy of George Santayana*, ed. Paul A. Schilpp (Chicago, 1940), pp. 497-605; *The Letters of George Santayana*, ed. Daniel Cory (New York, 1955), p. 405.

[9] *American Review*, I (April 1933), 137, 80-93; vII (Oct. 1936), 481-506; IX (Sept. 1937), 321-28; see also Albert E. Stone, "Seward Collins and

During the thirties many American reactionaries believed Fascism inevitable. For the Right-wing intelligentsia had always found democracy undesirable, and the depression seemed to prove that it was also unworkable. The most articulate analysis of this argument could be found in Lawrence Dennis' *The Coming of American Fascism.* Defining Fascism as "a revolutionary formula for the frustrated elite" in a period of capitalist crisis, Dennis saw in the growing desperation of the middle class a popular base for reaction in America. Although he never explicitly acknowledged indebtedness to European Fascism, his study of power resembled that of many Italian ideologues. With Giovanni Gentile and Alfredo Rocco, Dennis asserted that democracy was only a form of government, the actual substance being a ruling class which relied on force and deceit. And like his Italian counterparts, he desired to purge society of both Communism and capitalism and subordinate class divisions to a ruling elite. Impressed by the myth-making power of slogans and symbols, inspired by the dynamics of political power, Dennis also felt quite at ease with Mussolini.[10]

Other American reactionaries felt exhilarated. The Naziphile George Sylvester Viereck, who would be tried for treason during World War II, classified Mussolini among the greatest political leaders of the modern age. William Dudley Pelley's Silver Shirts, Arthur J. Smith's Khaki Shirts, and Gerald L. K. Smith's "Iron and Cross" also looked to Mussolini and Hitler as models of political salvation. Yet it would be a mistake to conclude that all these elements comprised a unified pro-Fascist front. Dennis strove to forge a master elite, but America's gutter Fascists offered only the demimonde of the demented. Nor did any of these elements share the views of the cultural conservatives. Whereas Dennis' pro-Fascism was based on respect for the realities of power, that of the Humanists and Agrarians derived from an idealist contempt for the crass industrialism and vulgarity of American life. Opposed to the chaos of liberal pluralism and the

---

the *American Review*: Experiment in Pro-Fascism, 1933-1937," *American Quarterly*, XII (Spring 1960), 3-19.

[10] Lawrence Dennis, "Portrait of American Fascism," *American Mercury*, XXXVI (Dec. 1935), 404-13; "Fascism for America," American Academy of Political and Social Sciences, *Annals*, CLXXX (July 1935), 62-73; *The Coming of American Fascism* (New York, 1936).

cruelty of Communist perfectionism, the *American Review* stood for decorum and deference, virtue and discipline. Thus unlike the power-minded Right, which saw Mussolini as the mastermind of anti-democratic formulas, and unlike the pedestrian Right, which saw in Fascism the promise of America's industrial virtues, the haughty intellectual Right saw in Mussolini's cohesive regime a remedy for America's amorphous culture and its atomistic individualism. The readers of the *Saturday Evening Post* had nothing in common with the deracinated intelligentsia of the *American Review*. Yet it is a measure of Fascism's diffuse image that Mussolini could be the answer to the anxieties of both the bourgeois citizen and the alienated intellectual.[11]

The Left: Fascism as the Unlearned Lesson

Mussolini may have been a man for all seasons to the American Right; to the American Left he seemed a man of no great historical importance. One of the curious features of the Left's response to the rise of Fascism is that there was no response. Reading the tattered, precious pages of the various factional journals, one is hardly aware the Blackshirts are in power. Indeed the Left-wing press reacted to the take-over of Rome almost with a yawn. Shortly after the event the *Weekly People*, official organ of the Socialist Labor Party (SLP), reprinted from the *New Republic* Giuseppe Prezzolini's "The Fascisti and the Class Struggle." Prezzolini, who later became an avid champion of Fascism while teaching at Columbia, gave a sanguine account of the movement, insisting that the *fascisti* had wisely stolen the syndicalist program and adapted it to Italian institutions and national character. Socialism will march forward under the Blackshirts, wrote Prezzolini, for "pressure from the proletariat is just as great whether it be manifested under the Fascist tri-color or under the flag of Socialism and Communism." Complimenting Prezzolini's factual information, the *Weekly People* dismissed Fascism as basically an anarchist movement of "the slum elements" who lacked the discipline and consciousness of organized labor.[12]

The *Daily Worker*, the voice of the American Communist Party (CP), appeared equally placid. The *Daily Worker* did not

[11] George Sylvester Viereck, *Glimpses of the Great* (London, 1930).
[12] *Weekly People*, Nov. 18, 1922.

213

appear on newstands until 1924, too late to register an immediate reaction to the Fascist take-over. Yet the Communist daily carried no thorough analysis of the phenomenon. From time to time it dutifully reported Italian-American anti-Fascist rallies and it participated in the martyrization of Matteotti, but for the most part the *Daily Worker* was busy fighting "La Folletteism" and advocating such Sisyphean causes as recognizing Soviet Russia and impeaching Calvin Coolidge. Nor did Earl Browder feel compelled to comment on Fascism in the *Workers Monthly*. Although the *Workers Monthly* and its successor, *The Communist*, paid considerable attention to Germany, Poland, France, Britain, Yugoslavia, and, of course, rapturous Russia, in the twenties not a single article was devoted to Mussolini's Italy. As for the independent Left, one finds the same inattention. Max Eastman's *The Liberator*, which had on its editorial staff Arturo Giovannitti, featured only one short article on "Fascismo," while V. F. Calverton's literary *Modern Quarterly* appeared oblivious to the subject. For example, in one essay, "Revolt and Reaction in Contemporary European Literature," Calverton failed to cite either pro-Fascist (e.g., Pirandello) or anti-Fascist (e.g., Silone) Italian writers.[13]

Not until the economic crash of 1929 did the American Left give much thought to Fascism. As the depression gripped the world, Left-wing publications began to discover an ideological problem that actually existed for almost a decade. Mike Gold's *New Masses* now invited exiles like Vincenzo Vacirca and European Marxists like John Strachey to explain to Americans the significance of this strange movement that seemed to be sweeping Europe. The *New Masses* also featured Calverton's blasts at the "Literary Fascism" of the New Humanists as well as the slashing cartoons of William Gropper and Hugh Gellant which depicted Mussolini as the worst of political perverts. As editor, Gold attacked what he regarded as the saccharine pro-Fascism of American liberals, maintaining that Lincoln Steffens' admiration for "Scarface Mussolini" was characteristic of his "Jesus philosophy" of simply loving everybody. Gold also took on Ezra Pound, who had written from Rapallo telling the *New Masses* group they did not know enough about Italy to criticize the regime:

[13] *The Modern Quarterly*, v (Nov. 1928), 31-52.

Ezra, I assure you that we KNOW. We know too well; we have read, analyzed, thought and sweated these ten years, reflecting on this thing. It may be a new discovery to you; to us it has become as familiar as Herbert Hoover's "cooperative state." In fact, it is the same thing: Big Business in the throne, Labor in the ditch.

When a cheese goes putrid, it becomes limburger, and some people like it, smell and all. When the capitalist state starts to decay, it goes fascist. . . .

I am sorry you think otherwise. I am sorry, Ezra Pound, when an honest man like yourself falls for a cheap lie like this one.[14]

That Fascism stunk in the nostrils of the *New Masses* may have been true after 1930. For the radicals of the twenties the whiff from Italy carried no foul ideological odor. One reason why radicals did not "sweat" about Fascism was they were too busy pointing the finger of blame. *The Liberator* claimed that Italy's "yellow Socialist Party" sold out to the *fascisti* "in a common lineup against bolshevism," and at the time of the Matteotti murder the *Daily Worker* accused Socialists of being the "cowardly accomplices" of Mussolini. While the CP cried socialist betrayal, the SLP blamed the collapse of the Italian Left on its undisciplined "Social Democracy" which had carelessly embraced "the loosest bourgeois reform ideas to the wildest of anarchist notions." Amid this gnashing of ideological teeth, the Fascist "cheese" went undigested.[15]

It was, moreover, only a short step from the accusation of collaboration to the theory of "social fascism." Announced in Moscow in 1928, the doctrine of social fascism, officially called the "third period" of Comintern policy, amounted to a declaration of war not only on Fascism or capitalism but on Socialist and liberal parties everywhere. The term was taken up with gusto by the CP and heaped upon all "enemies" on the Right, from Franklin Roosevelt to Norman Thomas. In branding the stigma of "social fascism," Communists were only making clear their traditional scorn for democratic liberalism. In 1930 Calverton maintained that "what remains of democracy today in Europe

[14] *New Masses*, VI (June 1931), 5-6; *ibid.*, V (Oct. 1930), 3-5.
[15] *The Liberator*, V (Dec. 1922), 9; *Daily Worker*, Aug. 18, 1924; *Weekly People*, March 31, 1923.

—or in America—is scarcely more than an empty fiction"; and when Hitler strode to power three years later Ludwig Lore hailed the failure of the opposition to Nazism as evidence of the chimera of constitutional government. Communists welcomed Fascism because it was the ultimate demonstration of the grotesque "contradictions of capitalism." Fascism actually foreshadowed Communism because, as Marx "predicted," capitalists would now, with the naked instrument of the totalitarian state, desperately intensify their exploitation of the proletariat and hold down its purchasing power, thereby bringing on the final workers' revolution. Fascism, in short, was an ideological victory for Communism.[16]

All this eschatalogical excitement heightened as the Weimar Republic fell in 1933. In the case of Italian Fascism eleven years earlier, however, the situation was quite different. First of all, despite belated claims about Marx's "predictions," no Left-wing thinker in America anticipated the rise of Fascism in Europe. On October 14, 1922, two weeks before the March on Rome, the *Weekly People* admonished the Italian Socialist Giuseppe E. Modigliani for his faltering hope in revolution, declaring that the revolution "is coming, has to come and will come." When Mussolini came instead, the Left saw no great cause for reflection. *The Liberator* remained unperturbed by events in Italy and described Fascism as "Extra-Legal Patriotism," while the *Weekly People* invincibly announced that the "Fascisti dictatorship cannot escape the operation of economic law." Compared to the apocalyptic mood with which the Left welcomed Nazism, the few scattered comments generated by the appearance of Fascism read like musings recollected in tranquillity.[17]

The American Left gave little thought to Fascism because, as we shall see shortly, the Soviet Union had not singled it out as *the* enemy. Moreover, the Marxist faith in the inevitable triumph of the proletariat was not to be shaken by cloudy events taking

[16] A. B. Magil, "Toward Social-Fascism—The 'Rejuvenation of the Socialist Party,'" *The Communist*, II (April 1930), 309-20; Abelard Stone, "Roosevelt Moves Toward Fascism," *The Modern Monthly*, VII (June 1933), 261-65; Ludwig Lore, "The Death of Social Democracy," *ibid.*, VII (Dec. 1933), 381-87; "Democracy versus Dictatorship," (editorial), *The Modern Quarterly*, V (Spring 1930), 397-406.

[17] *Weekly People*, Oct. 14, 1922, March 31, 1923; *The Liberator*, VI (June 1923), 5.

216

place in a peripheral area of Europe. Thus the *Daily Worker* could cheerily pronounce that Mussolini's regime "built to keep the iron heel of the capitalist on the neck of labor will be smashed by the iron fist of the Italian working class." In this rhetorical exercise Communist metaphors of might were matched by Socialist sermons of strength. The *Weekly People*, although more chastened by the shattering of the Italian labor movement, virtually echoed William Z. Foster in the *Labor Herald* when it spoke of Fascism as a valuable educational experience:

> If the lessons of the past teach the Italian workers to build up alongside of their political movement a sound, revolutionary industrial organization, an organization such as we in this country are striving for, a De Leonist organization if you please, then, in the days to come, Fascism may, in retrospect, be looked upon as a blessing in the guise of a setback. Who knows? Strange things, much stranger than fiction, are happening in this world of ours.[18]

Smiling optimism of this sort merely indicates that the American Left, like much of the European, seriously misjudged Fascism. The misreading of events in Italy may be due to the unfortunate fact that in the twenties few outstanding European Marxists gave serious thought to the subject.[19] With Communist

[18] *Daily Worker*, Sept. 17, 1924; *The Labor Herald*, Dec. 22, 1922; *Weekly People*, May 5, 1923.

[19] Aside from Italians, the only important European radicals to devote attention to Fascism in the twenties were Leon Trotsky and Karl Radek. In 1924 Trotsky stated that Fascism was merely an emergency instrument of the bourgeiosie for use in extreme situations and that it would soon be replaced by Menshevism. Radek, on the other hand, argued as early as 1923 that Fascism was not an Italian but an international problem, that it should not be confused with the familiar agrarian-feudal reactions taking place in Horthy's Hungary and other parts of eastern Europe, and that it was a movement of broad popular support from the nationalistic masses and *déclassé* bourgeoisie. Glumly viewing the Fascist victory as the greatest setback to world revolution since the War, Radek presaged the doctrine of the "Popular Front" by urging Communists not to try to fight Fascism alone but instead try to win over the petite bourgeoisie in the coming struggle. "Fascism is middle-class Socialism, and we cannot persuade the middle classes to abandon it until we can prove to them that it only makes their condition worse." Radek's address on "Communism and Fascism" appeared in the German Communist, *Die Rote Fahne* on July 29, 1923, and was reprinted in *Living Age*, cccxviii (Sept. 29, 1923), 585-87; for Trotsky's views, see Walter Laquer, *Russia and Germany: A Century of Conflict*

theoreticians in Europe ignoring Italy, American radicals remained in the dark about Fascism. When the American Left turned its attention to Fascism in the thirties it was too late. By now much of the Left, with the exception of the Lovestone Opposition and a few independent Marxist Socialists, had subordinated itself to the Comintern and thereby accepted the Soviet definition of Fascism as capitalism's final hour. This interpretation, while psychologically satisfying to all who continued to believe in the proletarian millennium, proved sadly deficient in comprehending what was taking place in Italy, not to mention Germany. Extracting the economic substance, the Marxist view stripped Fascism of its essential Italian context. In America it was only the Italian exiles who were in a position to interpret Fascism in its fullest complexity. Vincenzo Vacirca, writing in the *American Socialist Quarterly*, and G. Cannatta in *The Liberator*, were among the few to see Fascism in terms broader than economic. Vacirca, for example, while professing a "Marxian Interpretation," pointed out that much of the psychology of Fascism sprang from postwar national humiliation, that the large industrialists and landowners were smarting under Mussolini, that the "spiritual contagion" must be "taken into account in examining social phenomenon," and that an important factor, especially in Germany, was "the military caste—a social group which is above any economic classes and forms a world by itself." The standard Marxist interpretation, Vacirca informed his American comrades, failed to consider the peculiar institutions of Italy.[20]

Interpreting Fascism in the categories of class conflict also failed to account for the many elements that rallied to Mussolini: the idealistic nationalists, the adventurous youths, the religious-minded peasants and workers, and the amorphous middle class, composed of salaried bureaucrats, petty merchants, diverse white-

---

(Boston, 1965), pp. 218-20. At the annual world congresses the Communist International paid some attention to Italian Fascism. For an analysis of the Comintern's shifting positions, see John S. Cammett, "Communist Theories of Fascism, 1930-1935," *Science and Society*, xxxi (Spring 1967), 149-63.

[20] See, first, the Thesis of the Thirteenth Plenum of the Executive Committee of the Comintern, and then Earl Browder's report to the Eighteenth Plenary Meeting of the CPUSA's Central Committee, in "Fascism, the Danger of War and the Tasks of the Parties," *The Communist*, xiii (Feb. 1934), 131-77; Vincenzo Vacirca, "The Essence of Fascism," *The American Socialist Quarterly*, ii (Spring 1933), 40-47.

collar professionals, and what Antonio Gramsci called the "new agrarian bourgeoisie." Nor could Fascism be dismissed as mere "reaction." Not only did the charge ignore the progressive features of Fascism—for example, its "futurismo" cultural motif and the syndicalist programs of Rossoni and Bottai[21]—but more importantly, it created the impression of Fascism as a static defense of the old order when in reality the movement's all-pervasive *Geist* was its dynamism.[22] Lastly, because the Left saw Fascism as the conspiracy of monopoly capital it jumped to the conclusion that it was an evanescent phenomenon which would soon crumble along with world capitalism. With unwarranted optimism, the Left therefore pronounced the death of Fascism. As late as 1930, when Mussolini had consolidated power and driven out all overt opposition, Mike Gold gave Fascism one more year. The autopsy was, to say the least, premature; indeed it was fatally wrong. For the Left—and especially the Communist Left during the early thirties—indulged in a cataclysmic fantasy that caused it to welcome in America as well as in Europe the rise of the Right as a reaction to the growing strength of the proletariat, a desperate reaction that heralded the imminence of revolution itself. To gaze gleefully on the rise of the Right as a signal of the approaching revolution only indicates that the American Left had learned nothing from the lesson of 1922.[23]

The American Left was condemned to repeat the past because for the most part it aped Moscow's indifference to Italian Fas-

[21] Although the Left grudgingly conceded that Fascism won some support from labor it tended to dismiss these workers under the convenient rubric of *lumpenproletariat*. The suggestion that the Italian working class possessed "capitalist tendencies" and was genuinely attracted to the labor programs of Rossoni was anathema. *New Masses*, IV (Feb. 1929), 77. Unlike American Marxists, Gramsci realized that Fascism drew support not merely from industrial capitalists but from a middle class so heterogenous that the regime was forced to promote a bourgeois "organic culture." John Cammett, *Antonio Gramsci and the Rise of Italian Communism* (Stanford, 1967), pp. 178-80.

[22] One Fascist official explained: "The genuine fascism has a divine repugnance for being crystallized into a State. . . . The Fascist State is, more than a State, a dynamo." Another stated: "We Fascists must never abandon the dynamism which is one of our most marked characteristics; to remain in the static position which has recently been reached was for us the negation of the fascist idea." Quoted in Adrian Lyttelton, "Fascism in Italy: The Second Wave," *Journal of Contemporary History*, I (1966), 77.

[23] *New Masses*, V (April 1930), 4; *Daily Worker*, Feb. 18, 1930.

cism. The reasons for this regrettable *sangfroid* were both ideological and diplomatic. In view of orthodox Marxism, the rise of Fascism in agrarian, backward Italy did not upset the timetable of world revolution. Russia's backwardness notwithstanding, the Bolsheviks were more interested in the industrialized countries of western Europe. Thus the fall of the Weimar Republic in the thirties was of crucial concern to the Soviets, for in Germany, unlike in Italy, the collapse took place in the most highly developed country in Europe and in a period of severe capitalist crisis. Diplomatically, too, the Soviets were keenly interested in the political fate of Germany upon which, again in contrast to Italy, hung the future of Russia. No wonder, then, that Grigori Zinoviev, making a speech in Moscow at the time of the March on Rome, could take the whole affair lightly. In historical perspective, Zinoviev said, the Blackshirts will be looked back upon as something of a comedy. Just as Moscow refused to heed the warnings of Palmiro Togliatti and Antonio Gramsci,[24] so too did the American CP ignore the advice of exiles like Vacirca and Salvemini. As a result, Communists were as grossly unprepared to oppose Hitler in the thirties as they were to understand Mussolini in the twenties. Marx's aphorism must be reversed: events repeat themselves, first as "farce," then as "tragedy."[25]

The Center: Fascism as Constructive Experiment and as Repressive Tyranny

When Max Lerner interviewed Governor Philip La Follette in 1938 he noticed that "his sitting room is cluttered with photo-

[24] Gramsci and Togliatti, who realized that Fascism was historically novel and geographically widespread, warned Moscow against viewing it merely as an ephemeral form of reactionary terrorism. Russia may have been impervious to these warnings because at the time it was enjoying good political and economic relations with Italy. Hence when Mussolini recognized the Soviet Union in 1924 the *Daily Worker* gratefully printed a cartoon with the caption: "A Reminder for Secretary of State Hughes" (*Daily Worker*, Jan. 18, 1924). The rapport between the two countries may also explain why Moscow was reluctant to sponsor openly an Italian anti-Fascist resistance (Laqueur, p. 203). Moreover, both American and European Communists could derive satisfaction from seeing Fascist idealogues in Italy attack the United States as an "imperialist" power. (See, for example, Jay Lovestone, "America Facing Europe," *The Communist*, vi [March 1927], 11.)

[25] Zinoviev's views are briefly discussed in Laqueur, p. 201.

graphs of the great ones of the earth. There is one of Justice Brandeis and one of Mussolini. That *in parvo* is Phil." For the son of one of America's greatest progressives to pay homage to a bold Fascist dictator as well as a brilliant liberal jurist is strange indeed. Whatever it suggests about La Follette's political illusions, the juxtaposition of Brandeis and Mussolini indicates that the liberal mind in America was not immune to Fascism's curious appeals.[26]

Of the many splendid images which Mussolini enjoyed in America none received greater attention from intellectuals than his pose as the pragmatic statesman. Robert Penn Warren, who completed his fictional study of American demagoguery and Fascism while in Rome during the thirties, recalled that behind the reaction in Mussolini's Italy and in Huey Long's Louisiana lay the long shadow of the "scholarly and benign figure of William James." Unfortunately, the notion that the brilliant pioneer of pragmatic thought influenced Fascism was widely entertained in the twenties. Like most popular notions, there is a grain of truth here; America's only native philosophy did find a following among Italian intellectuals at the turn of the century. In 1903 Giovanni Papini, Giuseppe Prezzolini, and other philosophers established the journal *Leonardo* in an attempt to move beyond the pale negations of positivism. Observing these developments, James himself came to believe that "Italian pragmatism is the most radical to be found anywhere"; and to the philosopher F.C.S. Schiller he exclaimed: "Papini is a jewel! To think of that little Dago putting himself ahead of every one of us (even of you, with his *Uomo-Dio*) at a single stride." Yet what James believed to be "a very serious philosophical movement" in Italy turned out to be a transitory interlude. By the end of the first decade of the new century idealist philosophers like Benedetto Croce and Giovanni Gentile rejected pragmatism as a method without a meaning. Ultimately Italy's humanism proved stronger than American empiricism, leading Prezzolini to Crocean idealism and Papini to Catholicism.[27]

[26] Max Lerner, *Ideas for the Ice Age* (New York, 1941), p. 218.

[27] Robert Penn Warren, *All the King's Men* (New York, 1953), vi, and "All the King's Men: Matrix of Experience," *Yale Review*, LIII (Winter 1964), 161-67; Giovanni Gullace, "The Pragmatist Movement in Italy," *Journal of the History of Ideas*, XXIII (Jan.-March 1962), 91-105.

Still, the propaganda potential of this Italian-American cultural tie could not be ignored by those seeking democratic respectability to give an aura of doctrinal legitimacy to the Fascist government. Hence, whenever Mussolini spoke to Americans about his intellectual development he frequently cited James as one of his principal mentors. The influence of James—on Mussolini at least —was more apparent than real. When Horace Kallen, a disciple of James, questioned the Premier about the American philosopher, Mussolini could make only vague references to titles of books. Kallen came away from the interview rightly convinced that the dictator was more interested in James' reputation than in his ideas.[28]

Nevertheless, the pragmatic posture of the Italian statesman elicited enthusiastic acclaim from a number of American students of politics who regarded Mussolini as something of a Jamesian philosopher-king. Professor William K. Stewart of Dartmouth College, for example, became convinced, after studying Fascism's philosophical origins, that the Italian Premier operated as a wise improviser in "a world with the lid off," as James had termed the world of flux and change. The Italian "Battle of the Grain" program, said Stewart, was the clearest example of James' "Moral Equivalent of War" principle, an "equivalent discipline" for the energetic Fascist state. Phillip Marshall Brown, professor of international law at Princeton University, maintained that, unlike Marxism and other "preconceived" *a priori* theories, Fascism had its basis in "experience," and "its philosophy is pragmatism; its sole guiding principle is that working principles are to be discovered in actual practice." Some scholars saw Fascism as the natural reintegrating response to the centrifugal effects of democratic pluralism; others admired Mussolini for repudiating the sterile ideas of the past and formulating a "scientific" philosophy suitable to the contingencies of an irrational world. In his provocative *Harper's* article, Lothrop Stoddard advised Americans that the tough-mindedness of Fascist thought presented "the great intellectual challenge of the age," which laid bare the rigid determinism of Marxism and the shallow formalism of democracy, permitting both experimentation with "hard-headed practicality" and manipulation of myths (such as nationalism) to give free

[28] Horace Kallen, "Fascism: For the Italians," *New Republic*, XLIX (Jan. 12, 1927), 211; and "Mussolini, William James, and the Rationalists," *Social Frontier*, IV (May 1938), 253-56.

play to the moving power of beliefs discovered by James and Georges Sorel.[29]

Mass democracy, the pragmatic defense of Fascism suggested, was questionable; universal democracy was unworkable. It is perhaps not surprising that a conservative nativist like Stoddard would reach such a conclusion. That a small but highly significant number of liberals reached the same conclusion represented a reorientation of the progressive's democratic convictions, a reorientation that was part of a larger intellectual malaise characteristic of the postwar period. The failure of Wilsonianism and the demise of progressivism led to a cold re-examination of the uneasy assumptions of liberal thought regarding the rationality and goodness of man, the certainty of moral values and political standards, and the inevitability of human progress and world democracy. During the twenties progressives like Walter Weyl and Harold Stearns believed the idea of democracy moribund, Walter Lippmann questioned the wisdom of majoritarianism, and John Chamberlain abandoned the whole democratic dream. Those on the far Left, armed with the Marxist critique of bourgeois democracy, declared that the bankruptcy of liberalism left them with, in the words of Max Eastman, "this inexorable alternative—Lenin or Mussolini." Attacked from both Left and Right, progressives found themselves without a vigorous intellectual defense. Faith in democracy had been eroded by the rude facts of history, and the philosophical rationale of the "vital center"— pragmatism—now offered liberals little more than methodology and a set of preferences based on faith in human intelligence. While Communists and Fascists tried to rush into this ideological vacuum, both claiming the infallibility of science, Croce attempted to reassure Americans that liberalism was still a vital force and that Fascism was merely "transitory and provisory."[30]

[29] William K. Stewart, "The Mentors of Mussolini," *American Political Science Review*, xxii (Nov. 1928), 843-69; Phillip Marshall Brown, "The Utility of Fascism," *Current History*, xxxiv (May 1931), 161-64; W. B. Munro, "The Pendulum of Politics," *Harper's*, cliv (May 1927), 718-25; Corrado Gini, "The Scientific Basis of Fascism," *Political Science Quarterly*, xlii (June 1927), 99-115; Stoddard, "Realism: The True Challenge of Fascism," pp. 578-83.

[30] Walter Weyl, *Tired Radicals* (New York, 1920); Harold Stearns, *Liberalism in America* (New York, 1919); Walter Lippmann, *Public Opinion* (New York, 1922); John Chamberlain, *Farewell to Reform* (New York, 1932); Max Eastman, "Political Liberty" in *Freedom in the Modern World*,

Few Americans could share Croce's faith in the inevitable triumph of liberty. For the generation of the twenties, Mussolini appeared to many as the harbinger of a new political movement, one that rejected the tired dogmas of democracy and the paralyzing principles of liberalism. Nowhere is this point of view better illustrated than in the reaction of Lincoln Steffens to the advent of Fascism.

A leading fighter for democratic reform in the progressive era, Steffens came to regard Mussolini as one of the few men who emerged from the war enlightened by realism rather than betrayed by idealism. Interviewing Mussolini at the Lausanne Conference, Steffens was stunned when the statesman turned on him and "shot that searching question into me." Had not the innocent American liberals learned anything in the war, Il Duce contemptuously asked. "God's question to man, that!" Steffens reflected, pondering the plight of liberals who refused to learn from experience ("the conscience of history") and remained bound by the "dead logic" of their own preconceptions. Legalism, constitutions, and parliaments were only sham institutions controlled by "petty persons with petty purposes." Mussolini, like Albert Einstein, succeeded because he challenged ancient axioms. The leaders of the Bolsheviks and the Fascists were men of action whose "Russian-Italian method" forced Steffens to ask himself: "Is not the whole moral basis of liberalism and [democratic] political action unscientific?" Is not liberty a psychological matter, "a measure of our sense of security," a state of mind that can be realized only when new economic arrangements abolish fear? Although Steffens confessed he had no clear answer to his own question, he remained fascinated by the empirical technique of Fascism and believed that Mussolini's charismatic dictatorship of the Right could lead to a new realistic path to the goals of the Left.[31]

While other former muckraker liberals such as S. S. McClure and Ida Tarbell saw in Mussolini the strenuous idealism of Theodore Roosevelt, serious scholars were more interested in the

---

ed. Horace Kallen (New York, 1928), pp. 159-82; Morton White, *Social Thought in America: The Revolt Against Formalism* (New York, 1957), Chap. xii; Benedetto Croce, "Has Liberalism a Future?" *New Republic*, xlii (April 29, 1925), 256-58.

[31] *The Autobiography of Lincoln Steffens* (2 vols., New York, 1931), ii, 812-20, and "Stop, Look, Listen," *Survey*, lvii (March 1, 1927), 735-37.

224

experimental features of the Corporate State. During the twenties traditional economic ideas and institutions were subjected to a searching reevaluation, and, significantly enough, the announcement of the theory of corporatism came at a time when American intellectuals themselves were groping toward a positive reconstruction of society. Whether this reconstruction would lead to controlled currency, economic institutionalism, or scientific management, the answer, liberals were convinced, could be found neither in economic individualism nor in Marxist Socialism. The historic bourgeois liberal state appeared too factional and artificial and only masked the real sources of economic power. Under our capitalist democracy, Oswald Garrison Villard stated in 1925, power continued to "elude the people." This was also the case in the Socialist state where, as events in Russia demonstrated, repressive political power simply replaced oppressive economic power. Searching for a new experiment that would avoid acquisitive individualism and socialist regimentation, a number of pragmatic liberals recalled their prewar discussion of the virtues of Graham Wallas' and G.D.H. Cole's syndicalism and guild socialism. When the theory of corporatism was first proclaimed in 1926 it appeared that the Italian system integrated the best of these British ideas into its plans for a workers' confederation, achieving a more genuine representation than that offered by any contemporary government. It is no coincidence that in the years from 1926 to 1928 Italian Fascism commanded greater attention from American intellectuals. A system based upon the guiding influence of a paternal state, a system that brought to the surface the subterranean struggles of classes and interest groups and harmonized these forces in official institutions, struck a positive note in the minds of those political thinkers tired of the old formulas and fictions of progressivism. The philosopher Herbert W. Schneider's study of Italy in 1928 and the historian Charles Beard's response to this study best reflected this attitude.[32]

Schneider had been sent to Italy by Charles E. Merriam of the National Social Science Research Council in order to investigate more closely the unprecedented political system. Concerned pri-

[32] Oswald Garrison Villard, "Facing Our World," Nation, cxxi (Sept. 2, 1925), 248; the liberals' desire to reconstruct society on the basis of some principle that would unify institutions and classes found persuasive expression in T. V. Smith's popular work, The Democratic Way of Life (New York, 1927).

marily with the theory underlying corporatism and with the syndicalist aspirations of Edmondo Rossoni, Schneider was greatly impressed by this new "institutional synthesis" which allowed Italy to coordinate private interests in the service of higher "national interests," thereby realizing a "conscious, intelligent ordering of society." Acknowledging the illegal and violent activities of the rank-and-file Blackshirt, he believed that by the late twenties much of the militancy and unruliness of Fascism had been tamed from above. Because the American social theorist regarded the Lockean concept of a contractual, atomistic government as unreal and impractical, and because he maintained, like Calhoun a century earlier and the Guild Socialists before World War I, that only economic interests and not individual citizens could be truly represented in any government, he dismissed the Fascist struggle with parliament as "a mere stage play" and congratulated the regime for penetrating the ineffective fictions of formal democracy. Liberalism having served its historic purpose of undermining the *ancien régime*, the "real democracy" of the twentieth century must be based on an honest recognition of "economic associations," the only institutions capable of organizing diverse energies into a higher bond of community. Italy, in essence, was realizing the Durkheimian dream of social solidarity.[33]

When Schneider returned from Italy in 1928 Beard enthusiastically questioned him about his research. Like the philosopher, the historian seemed undisturbed by the anti-democratic nature of Fascism. The "fathers of the American Republic, notably Hamilton, Madison, and John Adams," he noted, "were as voluminous and vehement [in opposing democracy] as any Fascist could desire." Untroubled by the excessive nationalism of the Fascists, he likened Mussolini's nervous energy to the "American gospel of action, action, action," preached and practiced by Theodore Roosevelt. But instead of focusing on these activistic aspects, Beard suggested that Americans turn their attention to the "original feature of Fascism," to the philosophy of corporatism with its elaborate schemes for council functions and occupational representation. It was through this instrument that Italy alone

[33] Herbert W. Schneider, *Making the Fascist State* (New York, 1928); *Italy Incorporated* (Italian Historical Society, pamphlet no. 3, New York, 1928); "Italy's New Syndicalist Constitution," *Political Science Quarterly*, XLII (June 1927), 161-202.

had "brought about by force of the State the most compact and unified organization of capitalists and laborers into two camps which the world has ever seen." Although Beard admitted that capital enjoyed advantages over labor in Italy, and although he regarded Mussolini as an impetuous adventurer who might resort to war rather than face up to domestic problems, he believed that through "patience and technical competence" Italy could modernize itself by relying on the practical wisdom of corporatism and class collaboration. Viewing Italy as something akin to a political laboratory, he called upon American liberals to take a broader look at the regime.

> This is far from the frozen dictatorship of the Russian Tsardom; it is more like the American check and balance system; and it may work out in a new democratic direction. . . . Beyond question, an amazing experiment is being made here, an experiment in reconciling individualism and socialism, politics and technology. It would be a mistake to allow feelings aroused by contemplating the harsh deeds and extravagant assertions that have accomplished the Fascist process (as all other immense historical changes) to obscure the potentialities and the lessons of the adventure—no, not adventure, but destiny riding without any saddle and bridle across the historic peninsula that bridges the world of antiquity and our modern world.[34]

Schneider and Beard found Fascist corporatism an enlightened economic theory, the former because it appeared a coherent system of national planning that transcended classes and class interests, the latter because it recalled a modern Madisonian expression of the equilibrium of contending social forces. Other liberals looked favorably on Fascism for different reasons. One of the few American liberals who had firsthand experience in Italy was Horace Kallen, a student of James and a professor of social philosophy. After traveling throughout Europe in 1926 he returned to address American intellectuals on the myths and realities of the "new" Italy. Kallen's defense of the regime appeared in the *New Republic*, where he admitted that the ruthless militarism and the "paranoid magniloquence" contained in Fascism made it a movement liberals would find difficult to accept. But these repelling aspects, the philosopher cautioned, should not

[34] Interview with Schneider, Aug. 25, 1964; Charles Beard, "Making the Fascist State" (review), *New Republic*, LVII (Jan. 23, 1929), 277-78.

shroud the substantial accomplishments in economic, educational, and administrative reform. Living in Italy, he advised, made one realize there could be "intolerence of liberalism also." Fascism, a theory that, in contrast to Socialism, stressed "human differences" and reinvigorated the spirit of nationalism and of the *Risorgimento,* was the proper philosophy for the peculiar history, needs, and psychology of the Italian people. Liberals should therefore suspend judgment until the full-grown tree of the new theory bore the fruit of social justice or the seeds of oppressive reaction. "In this respect," concluded Kallen, "the Fascist revolution is not unlike the Communist revolution. Each is the application by *force majeure* of an ideology to a condition. Each should have the freest opportunity once it has made a start, of demonstrating whether it be an exploitation of men by a special interest or a fruitful endeavor after the good life."[35]

Kallen's plea for patience won the backing of the *New Republic.* In an editorial the liberal journal provided a supporting preface to Kallen's arguments by elaborating further on the need to give Fascism a sympathetic hearing. In view of the bleak record of Italy's parliamentary government from 1871 to 1921, advised the editorial, it was a "great mistake" to judge harshly and narrowly the recent regime. One could not measure the political actions of another country by one's own standards and values. Fascism had given the Italians a sense of unity and direction, a national self-consciousness that awakened the country's potential. The militarism of the Fascists should not alarm us, for their boastfulness was nothing more than a "virile and somewhat pathetic attempt to compensate for the absence of such power." Seen in the light not only of the "weary centuries" of Italy's past but of the general instability of contemporary European governments, the promising Fascist venture, however costly it may have proved, could not be any worse than sinking back into the "stagnation" and "cheap corruption" of traditional parliamentary politics.[36]

The apologetics of the *New Republic* revealed the ambivalence of pragmatic liberalism as well as the ambiguous appeal of Fascism itself. Although the liberals' support of the movement was, as we shall see, brief and confined to a small minority, their support reflected the tenets of pragmatic philosophy, tenets that

[35] Kallen, "Fascism: For the Italians," pp. 212-13.

[36] "An Apology for Fascism," *New Republic,* XLIX (Jan. 12, 1927), 207-09.

provided both the strengths and weaknesses in this rich vein of American social thought. For Fascism appealed, first of all, to the pragmatic ethos of experimentation. It held out a new possibility for integrating man with his technological environment. If the system called for sacrificing temporarily certain liberties, through collective effort and organized intelligence the Italians could learn from this educational experience. And just as each individual must learn from experience, the Italians themselves could best judge the results of the regime. Exactly how the people would render this judgment, with their political parties destroyed and civil liberties crushed, the *New Republic* did not say. The fruits of Fascism, liberals were told, could and must be submitted to "measurement." The Fascists attempted to promote "national cohesion and national welfare," and the "conscience of the Italian people will insist on appraising the result. Thus, willy-nilly, Fascism is an experiment. . . . If the Italian people are capable of political self-education, they will preserve that part of the program which is useful to them and discard that which is not."[37]

Fascism also appealed to liberals because of its presumed non-doctrinaire openness. The Italian philosopher Papini was fond of saying that pragmatism was a method of doing without a philosophy. It might also be said that to some American liberals Fascism was a method of doing without an ideology. Beard, for example, was pleased to find Fascism flexible and unencumbered by any "consistent scheme." Unlike Socialism, Fascism recognized that the road to reform was relative. When the political scholar Robert MacIver asked the *New Republic* how it could profess to be an "exponent of liberal principles" and at the same time support a dictatorship, and why suppression was so necessary in Italy if Fascism meant, as the *New Republic* claimed, "mastery and self-control," the journal replied that the traditional "formulas" of liberalism were inadequate to appraise developments either in Italy or in Russia. Comparing the deep-rooted particularism of the Italian peninsula to the sectionalism that brought on the American Civil War, the *New Republic* argued that just as the North had had to resort to force and bloodshed to save the Union and end slavery so too did the Fascists have to use similar methods to end the strife and disunity that plagued postwar Italy. Moreover, because of the "collective irresponsibility" of the

[37] "Liberalism vs. Fascism," *ibid.*, L (March 2, 1927), 35.

Italian Left, which failed to rally to the defense of the state as had the French parliamentarians in the Dreyfus affair, the old statesmen surrendered by default their right to lead the nation. Thus, although the *New Republic* did not approve of the suppression of liberty in Italy, it found itself unable to pass judgment since it had not (as MacIver claimed) set itself up as an "exponent" of such vacuous and abstract categories as "liberal principles." "Liberalism, as we understand it," reminded the editorial, "is an activity. It is an effort to emancipate human life by means of the discovery and the realization of truth. But truth emerges as a function of individual and corporate life, and it needs for its vindication the subordination of principles to method." So conceived, liberalism shared with Fascism a common scorn for definite systems and fixed theories. Fascism, like liberalism, appeared to be a continuously creative effort that found its affirmation in the subordination of ends to means. In its attempt to strike a balance between the dogmas of capitalism and Socialism, moreover, Fascism avoided doctrinal myopia. Rejecting the fetishes of both the Left and Right, it presented an admirable alternative to an ironclad ideology on the one hand and a tenaciously shallow sentimentalism on the other. This sailing without an ideological ballast was politically dangerous, the *New Republic* admitted, but it was also intellectually adventurous.[38]

As an exciting adventure, however, Fascism offered more than a repudiation of ideology and a case study of scientific politics and social engineering. The editor of the *New Republic* had long insisted that reform must be more than a matter of empirical method. If liberalism were to have any deeper personal meaning, Herbert Croly insisted in 1922, it must transcend technology and achieve a spiritual reconstruction of society. Five years later, when Croly was coming to grips with Fascism, the *New Republic* was defining liberalism in terms of "self-knowledge" and "self-liberation." More than social justice, liberalism should work toward a religious regeneration that could not be realized through the traditional efforts of reformers, "who attempt to redeem human nature without asking human beings to participate in their own redemption." The Fascist counterpart of the "Socratic Liberalism" of the *New Republic* was the élan of Italian nationalism,

[38] Beard, "Making the Fascist State," p. 277; Robert MacIver, letter to the editor, *New Republic*, L (March 2, 1927), 47; "Liberalism vs. Fascism," p. 36.

which Croly believed would enable the Italians to master themselves through a renewal of moral vision. "Alien critics should beware," liberals were thus warned, "of outlawing a political experiment which aroused in a whole nation an increased moral energy and dignified its activities by subordinating them to a deeply felt common purpose." The *New Republic* could not help but admire an original philosophy that broke through the husk to reach the human heart, that claimed to present a new political "science" freed of false emotions yet emotional enough to mold a nation of people, that displayed to the world a hopeful example of rational class reconciliation and high national purpose.[39]

Fascism's appeal to liberals, then, was found in its experimental nature, anti-dogmatic temper, and moral élan. Their friendly interest, most pronounced in the years from 1926 to 1928, may be best described as a positive but cautious curiosity, one riddled with doubt about the use of violence and the "moonshine" pretensions of Fascist aspirations. As the decade drew to a close, the freshness of Fascism waned and the *New Republic* grew wary of the Italian government, commenting critically on the increasing "archaic imperialism" of Mussolini, his "perilous" attempt at autarchy, and his sustained suppression of liberty. Ultimately, however, it was not only the unfulfilled promises of the regime but the death of Croly in 1929, the impact of the depression shortly afterward, and the arrival of Italian *fuorusciti* that brought a complete repudiation of Fascism. Croly's death meant the passing from the *New Republic* of his brand of liberalism, and as his successor, Bruce Bliven, recalls, liberals were later to learn about Italy from Giuseppe Borgese, Max Ascoli, Count Sforza, and other exiles who began to arrive in the United States in increasing numbers in the thirties. The depression, in addition, caused a profound shift in liberal thinking about both capitalism

[39] "Reconstruction of Religion," *New Republic*, xxxi (June 21, 1922), 100-02; "Realistic Liberalism," *ibid.*, liii (Nov. 23, 1927), 5-7; "Socratic Liberalism," *ibid.* (Dec. 28, 1927), 155-57; "Apology for Fascism," pp. 208-09. There can be no question that the editorials on Fascism were the work of Herbert Croly alone. Bruce Bliven, who succeeded Croly as editor in 1929, writes: "These editorials were, I am sure, all the work of Herbert Croly. . . . While he was editor of the paper, he would always listen to arguments by other members of the staff in opposition to his own views . . . but when he felt something strongly, he insisted on expressing it as the editorial view." (Bliven to author, March 10, 1965.)

and corporatism. Under the spell of Marxist prophecy, some pragmatic liberals tended to reinterpret Fascism as the decadent response of a historically condemned system. The belated repudiation of Fascism was, therefore, also a rejection of the middle-of-the-road policy of managed capitalism that seemed so attractive in the 1920s. As intellectuals moved to the Left, even Roosevelt's New Deal, which emerged as a hopeless muddle of chaotic experiments, seemed to many radical critics an insidious form of creeping corporatism. Liberals as well as radicals now traveled to Russia and admired the Soviet Five-Year Plans. The courtship with corporatism had ended; the romance with collectivism had begun.[40]

By focusing on the *New Republic*'s flirtation with Fascism in 1927 one can easily overemphasize the extent of Fascist sympathies among American liberals. In fairness, it must be noted that while Stark Young shared Croly's pro-Fascism (albeit for entirely different reasons), other members of the *New Republic*'s editorial board refrained from commenting on the subject.[41] Moreover, many *New Republic* articles blasted Fascism's suppression of free speech, Il Duce's cult of personality ("Fascism—c'est moi"), and the regime's imperialism and "obstreperous, jingoistic glorification of war." Still, one cannot ignore the fact that several outstanding liberals harbored Fascist sympathies, a fact that has been overlooked by historians. In his study of the intellectual sources of the New Deal, Arthur Schlesinger, Jr., stated, in reference to the "ideology of social regeneration" and "national planning," that "this native progressvism opposed fascism and communism as brutal and false." While this statement is doubtless true for the 1930s when the rise of Hitler gave Fascism a demonic image, it overlooks the different tendencies of liberalism in the 1920's, inner tendencies that explain why some liberals were

[40] "Apology for Fascism" pp. 207-08; *New Republic*, LI (June 6, 1927), 56; LII (Aug. 24, 1927), 82; LIII (Nov. 23, 1927), 2; LIV (April 11, 1928), 232. Kallen's support of Fascism was short lived (see "Arts Under a Dictatorship," *Saturday Review of Literature*, v [Dec. 29, 1928], 549-51), as was Beard's (see "Democracy Holds Its Ground," *Harper's*, CLVII [Nov. 1928], 680-91); Bliven to author, March 10, 1965; Lewis S. Feuer, "Travelers to the Soviet Union: The Formation of a Component of New Deal Ideology," *American Quarterly*, XIV (Summer 1962), 119-42.

[41] The other editors were Bruce Bliven, Alvin Johnson, Robert Littell, Robert Morss Lovett, and George Soule.

taken in by Italian Fascism and why others, the great majority, were not.[42]

In this connection the contrasting reactions of the *New Republic* and of the *Nation* must be considered as reflections of contrasting liberal temperaments. The *New Republic* represented the twentieth-century pragmatic strain of progressivism, the *Nation* the nineteenth-century liberal strain. The difference between these two liberal currents was, among other things, the difference between a relativistic approach to reform on the one hand and a traditional faith in the standard democratic road to social justice on the other, the difference beween the empiricism of social engineering and the humanitarianism of "good hope." Thus it was the *Nation* that attacked with ringing moral certitudes the Americans who doubted the wisdom of mass rule and glorified the efficacy of the Corporate State. There can be no sacrifice of democracy to efficiency, Villard warned the *New York Herald Tribune*, one of the many American papers that had warm praise for Mussolini. "The broader the base of government, the surer its results. Democracy works poorly enough, but there is no substitute for it." The *Nation*'s surviving democratic idealism clearly rendered it better prepared to answer the rise of totalitarianism. But equally important was the *Nation*'s attitude toward nationalism. Whereas the *Nation* had been, even during the war years, vigorously anti-nationalist, the *New Republic* had looked to nationalism as the driving reform stimulus. In the twenties Croly's faith in nationalism, although chastened by the war, was as unyielding as Villard's faith in formal democracy. The *New Republic* could therefore maintain that "the only way for the Italians to cultivate the sense of unity and common responsibility which is indispensable to self-government is to allow the Fascist doctrine to vaccinate them with a powerful patriotic virus." To the *Nation* this sort of reasoning smacked of reaction, for odious nationalism and shallow patriotism Villard saw as the enemies of liberalism everywhere. The American counterpart of the Fascists, said the *Nation*, was the Ku Klux Klan. In the name of order, efficiency, and patriotism, Mussolini and Miklós von

[42] Peter Brooklyn, "Mussolini vs. Fascism," *New Republic*, XLIX (Dec. 8, 1926), 65-67; Robert C. Binkley, "Free Speech in Fascist Italy," *ibid.*, LXI (Feb. 5, 1930), 291-93; Pasquino Ianchi, "Mussolini in Sheep's Clothing," *ibid.*, LXX (Feb. 24, 1932), 36-38; Arthur Schlesinger, Jr., "Sources of the New Deal," in *Paths of American Thought*, eds. id. and Morton White (Boston, 1962), p. 381.

Horthy, Hitler and Erich Ludendorff, Attorney General A. M. Palmer and the Klan had all attempted to crush democracy by a program of flag-waving fanaticism. Aside from the pragmatic "methodolatry" of the *New Republic* and the liberal idealism of the *Nation*, these differing attitudes toward nationalism also explain why the former regarded lightly Mussolini's militarism, saw psychological utility in Fascist slogans, and admired the cohesive features of corporate theory, while the latter took seriously Mussolini's menacing gestures, looked upon Fascist slogans as cruel lies, and perceived corporatism as mere window dressing that cloaked the interests of unregenerate capitalists.[43]

Croly's lifelong dream of a "new Nationalism," first envisioned in 1912, contained disturbing overtones of authoritarian corporatism. This passionate quest played no small part in Croly's seeing Fascism (as did Croce before 1925) as a temporary stage through which Italy must pass in order to reach a higher level of political consciousness. Partly as a result, the *New Republic* remained more susceptible to a social movement that called for individual sacrifice and national discipline, hardheaded elitism and egalitarian enthusiasm. Although the *New Republic* objected to Mussolini's arbitrary acts, and although its anti-Fascist contributors outnumbered the defenders of Il Duce, it was the *Nation* that attacked Italian reaction from the very beginning. The blistering editorials by Villard and the scathing articles by Carleton Beals, Louis Adamic, James Murphy, and Marcus Duffield all pointed to one conclusion: Mussolini and Fascism meant imperialism and war. When Matteotti was murdered, the *Nation* printed the "Filippelli Memorial," a document smuggled out of Italy that implicated high officials of the Fascist government, including Mussolini, in the death of the Socialist deputy. No moral condemnation of the murder appeared in the *New Republic*.[44]

The *Nation*, of course, was not the only source of liberal opposition in the twenties. As we saw earlier, the ACLU, the trade

[43] Oswald Garrison Villard, "Mussolini and the Klan," *Nation*, cxix (July 2, 1924), 5; "Apology for Fascism," p. 208.

[44] "Who Killed Matteotti?" *Nation*, cxx (April 8, 1925), 392-95. Regarding the charge that Croly's early social philosophy presaged a form of paternalistic totalitarian nationalism, see Arthur A. Ekirch, Jr., *The Decline of American Liberalism* (Atheneum paperback ed., New York, 1967), p. 188; see also a critique of this charge in Charles B. Forcey, *Crossroads of Liberalism: Croly, Weyl, Lippmann and the Progressive Era* (New York, 1961), pp. 36-41.

unions, and the academic community all contributed to the anti-Fascist cause. But of greater significance is the fact that even among the majority of pragmatic liberals Fascism found no audience. Hence the favorable views of Beard, Steffens, Kallen, Schneider, and Croly must be balanced against the attitudes of Carl Becker, Morris Ernst, Oliver Wendell Holmes, Jr., Thorstein Veblen, James Harvey Robinson, and John Dewey, all of whom saw nothing promising in Mussolini's great adventure.

The case of Dewey deserves attention. During the twenties he traveled throughout Europe and the Far East, recording many of his impressions in the *New Republic*. In his numerous articles and multivolume work, *Character and Events*, he presented incisive studies of the political cultures of Russia, China, Turkey, and other developing nations. Italy, however, was ignored. It is possible that Dewey avoided visiting Italy because of the tragic death of his beloved son, Morris Dewey, in Milan in 1895. But a more plausible explanation of his silence on Fascism may be found in his close relationship with Carlo Tresca and in his unfailing commitment to the principles of the open society.[45] Tresca collaborated with Dewey in championing many causes, including the Sacco and Vanzetti case and the "counter-trial" of Leon Trotsky. From his deep personal friendship with the Italian-American anti-Fascist, Dewey could have formed only the most negative view of the reaction in Italy. Fascism's blatant attack on democratic values and its exalted irrationalism, moreover, would have been repugnant to Dewey's firm belief in democratic means and his faith in freedom and human intelligence. In one rare instance where Dewey did mention Fascism in the twenties he criticized "the disciples of Lenin and Mussolini [who] vie with the captains of capitalist society in endeavoring to bring about a formation of dispositions and ideas which will conduce to a preconceived goal." To the American educator, Italy's intellectual regimentation and academic thought control, which attempted to instill "a mental picture of some

[45] James T. Farrell recalls that "Dewey became a good friend of Carlo Tresca. There was a funny incident with Tresca. Carlo gave a party one night at his home in Brooklyn. And you know John; he would take a drink, but he wouldn't get drunk or anything like that. Carlo had one of his boys go up to Dewey and say, 'Professor, Carlo he say you getta drunk as you want; I taka care of you.' And John started smiling and said, 'I'm being taken care of.' But he liked Carlo very much." *Dialogue on John Dewey,* ed. Corliss Lamont (New York, 1959), pp. 74-75.

desired end," only flew in the face of its own claims to pragmatic openness and spontaneity. Committed to the "sound principle of interdependence of means and end," to the conviction that practice validates theory, Dewey remained skeptical of the theoretical tinsel of the Fascist program.[46]

Other liberals like Eduard C. Lindeman and Morris Cohen also had doubts about the ideological claims of Mussolini's Italy. Rather than as a pragmatic experiment, they saw Fascism as a dogmatic state worship that would soon ossify into a "doctrinaire finality." From a different angle of vision, Walter Lippmann, who earlier in his career had called for a dynamic, pragmatic interpretation of politics, tempered his relativism with a touch of Catholic moral theology in the twenties so that when he surveyed Italy in 1927 he rebuked Fascism for violating the antistatist principles of Thomas Aquinas and Lord Acton. Finally, many liberals dismissed Fascism as sheer sophistry, perceiving, as they did, a cynical and crude will to power behind its dialectical verbiage. "They proclaim that Fascism is pragmatic, empirical, eclectic," stated one writer after studying Mussolini's speeches. "The pragmatism of the Fascio consists in hitting first, inventing a justification afterwards, and pointing with pride to the efficacy of *ex post facto* wisdom. Empiricism, in Fascist parlance, is Greek for inconsistency."[47]

Despite the widespread opposition among progressives in this country, the fact that Fascism received a "pragmatic sanction" from some American liberals stirred attacks from intellectuals both in Europe and in America. In *La Trahison des Clercs* (1927), Julien Benda indicted James and his followers for focusing on the particular and the practical at the cost of the universal and the spiritual, and for surrendering to an empirical obsession that lost sight of transcendental values and led to authoritarian op-

[46] I am indebted to M. Halsey Thomas, Dewey's bibliographer, for informing me of the death of Dewey's son (Thomas to author, Feb. 23, 1965); see Dewey's letter to Tresca in *Omaggio alla Memoria Imperitura di Carlo Tresca* (New York, 1943), p. 48; John Dewey, *The Public and Its Problems* (New York, 1927), p. 200; id., "Means and End," *New International*, IV (Aug. 1938), 232-33.

[47] Eduard C. Lindeman, "A New Challenge to the Spirit of 1776," *Survey*, LVII (March 1, 1927), 679-82; Morris Cohen, "Dictatorship on Trial," *Current History*, XXXIV (Aug. 1931), xii-xv; Lippmann, "Autocracy versus Catholicism," pp. 627-28; *Eugene S. Bagger*, "The Playboy of the Southern World," *New Republic*, XLI (Dec. 3, 1924), 49-50.

portunism. The burden of taking up the anti-pragmatic assault in the United States was assumed by William Y. Elliott, professor of government at Harvard University. Elliott's criticism of pragmatism sprang less from humanism than from a reverence for normative legalism. In briefest terms, it was Elliott's conviction that Sorel's philosophy of violence stemmed from James' insight into the myth as motive force, that Dewey's stress on "organic" functionalism came too close to Léon Duguit's philosophy of social "solidarism," and that both these syndicalist ideas resulted in anti-democratic reaction. "Instrumentalism is the same development away from the radical empiricism of James's doctrines which Fascism represents in relation to syndicalism." In short, Dewey's collectivism and Sorel's activism, however democratically conceived at the outset, carried the seeds of authoritarianism, for both theories gave way to the contingencies of reality and followed a "pragmatic progress toward the negation of [their] premises." Lacking an ethical gyroscope, pluralistic pragmatism provided no inner check to prevent the corruption of power and the tyranny of the state. The culminating creature of this fleeting moral order was Mussolini, the "prophet of political pragmatism."[48]

[48] Julien Benda, *The Betrayal of the Intellectuals*, trans. Richard Aldington (Boston, 1964), pp. 98-99; William Y. Elliott, *The Pragmatic Revolt in Politics: Syndicalism, Fascism, and the Constitutional State* (New York, 1928), p. 324; id., "Mussolini: Prophet of the Pragmatic Era in Politics," *Political Science Quarterly*, XLI (June 1926), 161-92. Although Elliott was unaware of the liberal defense of Fascism in this country by the writers discussed above, he saw the potential for such a defense in the social philosophy of Laski, who during the twenties was interpreting Duguit's "solidarism" to American pragmatists. (Elliott to author, Feb. 15, 1965.) Liberals of the pragmatic school received Elliott's book with understandable resentment. Kallen, who never regarded Mussolini as a pragmatist but whose own pragmatic disposition, ironically enough, made him briefly susceptible to certain features of Fascist thought, later made the distinction between liberal and authoritarian rationalism—the former being rooted in pluralism and tolerance, the latter in an intransigent cult of the state. He also attacked Elliott for lumping together a smattering of similarities in syndicalism, Fascism, and Bolshevism to claim that they all came from pragmatism. "The same kind of thinking could assimilate the philosophy of the Declaration of Independence to the political notions of Thomas Aquinas and identify a horsechestnut with a chestnut horse." (Kallen, "Mussolini, William James, and the Rationalists," p. 256; see also Schneider's critical review of the Elliott book, *New Republic*, LVII [Nov. 21, 1928], 23.)

However tenuous may have been Elliott's thesis connecting Fascism to pragmatism, as a staunch liberal dedicated to the traditional forms of democracy, Elliott was, among American political thinkers, the most active critic of Mussolini's Italy. In his debates, lectures, and writings he continually warned political commentators that Fascism represented a dangerous departure from historic liberalism, and he chided the press for tolerating Mussolini's methods while condemning those of Stalin. Elliott also helped organize the International Committee for Political Prisoners in order to aid Italian anti-Fascists and to awaken an uncritical American public.[49]

That the only thorough American critique of Fascist philosophy should come from an anti-pragmatic liberal suggests the theoretical weakness of the pragmatic Left in the twenties. More than one historian, generally with Hitler and Stalin in mind, has commented upon the inability of liberals to answer the rise of dictatorships because of their debilitating relativism. But in fairness to the pragmatic liberals, their reaction to Mussolini must be measured against the response of American society as a whole, and in this light they emerge rather well. In contrast to the favorable opinion of the mass public, which continued until the Ethiopian crisis, the liberals' support lasted no more than a few years and was confined to the small minority discussed above. We would do well to bear in mind that Fascism, because of its novelty, eclecticism, and ambiguity, drew admiration from conservatives as well as from liberals, from Christian disciples of natural law, from humanist advocates of ordered hierarchy, and from nervous defenders of private property. In the end it was, after all, not Dewey and Kallen but Santayana and Pound who found their spiritual home in Italy.[50]

[49] William Y. Elliott and Gaetano Salvemini, *The Fascist Dictatorship* (New York, 1928), pamphlet.

[50] Eric F. Goldman, *Rendezvous with Destiny: A History of Modern American Reform* (New York, 1960), pp. 157-58, 240-42, 290-97; Arthur M. Schlesinger, Jr., *The Vital Center: The Politics of Freedom* (Boston, 1962), pp. 39-43; Daniel Aaron, *Men of Good Hope: A Story of American Progressives* (New York, 1951), p. 301; David Noble, *The Paradox of Progressive Thought* (Minneapolis, 1958), pp. 247-48. Although the above historians have rightly criticized pragmatic liberals for failing to meet the challenge of totalitarianism, the charge should not be restricted to this group. Indeed it was the old-fashioned, moralistic liberal Oswald Villard who, though best prepared to perceive the menace of Fascism in the twen-

Indeed, rather than pointing up the ethical pitfalls of pragmatic relativism, the liberals' flirtation with Fascism reveals that they were not pragmatic enough. To be sure, Fascism won some liberal approval in this country because, as the first example of a society that was economically mixed and technically managed, it symbolized an untried challenge, a historical innovation that opened up new possibilities for purposeful planning. But the relationship between planning and performance raised a central contradiction in the pragmatic estimate of the Fascist system. Although several liberals endorsed Fascism because it signified the triumph of practice over theory, it was the theoretical appeals of corporatism that essentially interested them. Thus the precise benefits of "class cooperation," the party control over labor syndicates, the connection between foreign loans and industrial growth, and other such crucial concerns all went uninvestigated. Nor was the testimony of exiles like Salvemini consulted. Too caught up in the official proclamations of the Fascist government, liberals failed to see if the system was really working. This failure is most obvious in Schneider's studies. As a colleague of Dewey, who gave him "encouragement, advice, and criticism" with his book, Schneider wrote a highly complimentary study of Fascism on the ground that it was realistic and "functional." Yet he refused to address himself to the "deeds" and "practical value" of the government, regarding his point of view as an author as something akin to that of Plato toward the republic, an indulging in "an adventure of the philosophic imagination." In refusing to ascertain Fascism's "fortunes in the world of practice," Schneider was committing the most unpardonable of pragmatic sins: he was assuming the role of, to use Dewey's own phrase, the "otiose observer."[51]

By concentrating on words rather than on deeds, by separating theory from practice, the pro-Mussolini liberals were simply not acting as good pragmatists. This chapter in intellectual history thus reveals less about the inherent flaws of pragmatic philosophy than about the human limitations of pragmatic thinkers. As such, the episode may still serve as a cautionary history for modern American liberalism.

---

ties, was least prepared to fight it in the thirties. See Michael Wreszin, *Oswald Garrison Villard: Pacifist at War* (Bloomington, 1965).

[51] Schneider, *Italy Incorporated*, pp. 3-4.

10.

Politics and Culture

THE CHALLENGE OF MUSSOLINI TO AMERICA IS SIMPLY:

DO THE DRIVING IDEAS OF JEFFERSON, QUINCY ADAMS, VAN BUREN, OR WHOEVER ELSE THERE IS IN THE CREDITABLE PAGES OF OUR HISTORY, FUNCTION ACTUALLY IN THE AMERICA OF THIS DECADE TO THE EXTENT THAT THEY FUNCTION IN ITALY UNDER THE DUCE?

THE WRITER'S OPINION IS THAT THEY DON'T, AND THAT NOTHING BUT VIGOROUS REALIGNMENT WILL MAKE THEM, AND THAT IF, OR WHEN, THEY ARE MADE SO TO FUNCTION, MUSSOLINI WILL HAVE ACTED AS STIMULUS, WILL HAVE ENTERED INTO AMERICAN HISTORY, AS LENIN HAS ENTERED INTO WORLD HISTORY.

Ezra Pound, *Jefferson and/or Mussolini*, 1935*

THE MAESTRO AND HIS ARTISTS

"Politics in a work of literature is like a pistol-shot in the middle of a concert, something loud and vulgar, and yet a thing to which it is not possible to refuse one's attention." Stendhal's remark applies especially to Fascism, the first modern political movement to blare the noise of ideology into concert halls, art galleries,

* Reprinted by permission of Liveright. (See Acknowledgments)

and literary salons. Unable to resist the "loud and vulgar," the author has addressed this chapter to the faint but occasionally important repercussions of Italian Fascism upon American cultural, literary, and academic life.[1]

Mussolini seemed the appropriate statesman to preside over the flowering of Italy's "new" Renaissance. He was, after all, not only a powerful writer but an "accomplished" violinist whose talents drew praise from the professional journal *Étude* and from Fritz Kreisler in *Literary Digest*, and whose politics won the early support of Italy's two greatest musicians, Giacomo Puccini and Arturo Toscanini. (Toscanini had been a Fascist candidate for political office in 1919; he did not break openly with the regime until 1931.) Moreover, as Italian culture was mobilized to add luster to Mussolini's melodrama, the writings of D'Annunzio, Pirandello, Deledda, Panzini, and Papini seemed to indicate Fascism and culture were entirely compatible. In a special *Survey* issue on Fascism, Americans read about the awakening of Italy's literary imagination by writers who either revived classical formalism or experimented with new techniques. The sensuous D'Annunzio and the continent Papini emerged as the guiding lights of a new intellectual movement based upon restless idealism and artistic vision. According to H. G. Wells, the publication of Papini's *Life of Christ* created a "sensation in America." And Arnaldo Fratelli, as though he were answering the naturalistic despair of Joseph Wood Krutch's *The Modern Temper*, informed Americans that "modern intellectualism, with its doubts, criticisms, negations and uncertain affirmations, appeared overwhelmed, drowned in the luminous certainty of Faith, in the 'Storia di Cristo' of Giovanni Papini."[2]

In depicting Fascism as the affirmation of "Faith" Italian propagandists could, curiously enough, cite the testimony of the era's two greatest playwrights and greatest infidels, George Bernard Shaw and Luigi Pirandello. Convinced that the "democratic idealism of the nineteenth century is as dead as a doornail," Shaw shared Lincoln Steffens' view of Mussolini as the only Socialist to come to power and meet a political payroll, a

---

[1] Quoted in Irving Howe, *Politics and the Novel* (Cleveland, 1957), p. 15.

[2] "Mussolini and His Violin," *Étude*, XLV (Oct. 1927), 772; *LD*, XIC (May 30, 1931), 17; cited in Carter, pp. 314-15; Mario Labroca, "Musical Life in Italy," *Survey*, LVII (March 1, 1927), 716-17; Arnaldo Fratelli, "Figures of Literary Italy," *ibid.*, pp. 712-14; "Italian Literature Today," *LD*, XCIII (April 23, 1927), 35-38.

241

cynical view that led Salvemini to write a political satire on "The Taming of the Shaw." Pirandello also supported Fascism while winning popular acclaim in the United States as a renowned dramatist. Indeed the pro-Fascist theater critic Silvio D'Amico told Americans that Pirandello had been influenced by Eugene O'Neill; and after the war when Arthur Miller's *Death of a Salesman* opened in Rome Italians spoke of *pirandellismo.* All this, of course, is highly dubious—O'Neill could never accept Pirandello's faith in the protection of private illusions and Willy Loman is hardly the protagonist for Pirandello's theory that the public image is more important than the private self. More significantly, American playwrights were highly critical of Pirandello's politics.[3] About the only thing that impressed Americans was Italy's subsidy of the dramatic arts, but even here doubts were voiced concerning the intrusion of politics into the theater. Nor did Mussolini's own play, based on the last days of Napoleon, help matters. When it flopped in London Rebecca West wondered whether his political advisers were as spineless as his literary editors were sycophantic.[4]

Nevertheless, the Italian government's sponsorship of the arts and Mussolini's professed interest in the Carnegie Institute exhibition seemed to point up the creative energy of the new regime. Hence a few American architects commended Il Duce's city renewal projects, several artists had him pose for a portrait, and even the famous sculptor Jo Davidson did a dramatic bust of the Premier. But here too the question of politics and culture often arose. While the *American Magazine of Arts* allowed Homer Saint-Gaudens to claim that Mussolini tolerated the freest artistic expression, in the *Saturday Review of Literature* and in the *Literary Digest* Americans read philosopher Horace Kallen's and

[3] When Pirandello arrived in the United States in 1935 several American playwrights, among them Clifford Odets and John Howard Lawson, visited his suite in the Waldorf-Astoria. The Americans tried to get him to disavow Fascism and repudiate Mussolini's expected invasion of Ethiopia. But Pirandello pleaded for a divorce of art from politics, and the conference broke up in rancor (*NYT*, July 24, 1935).

[4] Gaetano Salvemini, *G. B. Shaw e il fascismo* (Parma, 1955); "G.B.S. As Mussolini's Champion," *LD*, xcv (Nov. 26, 1927), 14-15; "Pirandello and the Italian Stage Crisis," *LD*, xciii (April 23, 1927), 36-38; Silvio D'Amico, "The Theatre," *Survey*, lvii (March 1, 1927), 714-15; Eduard Storer, "New Trends in the Theatre," *Forum*, lxxiii (March 1925), 379-86; LD, cxiv (July 23, 1932), 14; Eric Bentley, "Appendix ii," in *Naked Masks: Five Plays by Luigi Pirandello* (New York, 1952), pp. 377-81.

art critic Elsie McCormick's accounts of the regimentation of cultural life in Fascist Italy. Italian propagandists, it is true, made much of Marinetti's *Futurismo e Fascismo*, and in the postwar period Futurism gained an audience in America, especially among the *Broom* writers who translated Marinetti's "Revolution of the Word" into literary cubism and expressionism. But a few keen observers like Kallen perceived that Futurism, with its aesthetic defense of violent action and pagan pleasure, could hardly be reconciled to Fascism's statist bureaucracy and political clericalism. Even more ironically, whereas Futurists exalted the industrial dynamo and the sublime thrill of speed, many American intellectuals had taken flight from the fetish of machine culture. Thus Harold Loeb, the editor of *Broom*, was stunned when in Rome he found the Futurists in "praise of skyscrapers in the cities of fountains, of jazz in the home of opera, of advertisement in the country where Dante had done a superlative job on hell— all in vociferous broken English."[5]

While Mussolini commanded little respect among America's *avante-garde* artists, he fared considerably better in other media, especially in the Hollywood film industry. Il Duce granted fullest assistance to the production of American films in Italy, and studio directors repaid him in footage. It will be recalled Ambassador Child planned to do a screen biography of Mussolini. Will Hays, the "czar" of the motion picture industry, petitioned the State Department about a similar project. Whatever became of these proposals is unclear, but Movietone released a film on Mussolini and in 1931 Columbia Studios produced *Mussolini Speaks*, based on his Tenth Anniversary speech on Fascism delivered in Naples. No doubt a few filmmakers were impressed with the political super-star: Producer Walter Wanger hung Il Duce's picture in his office until the outbreak of the Ethiopian War. Mussolini also opened his door to American film stars. The swashbuckler Francis X. Bushman, who dined with the Premier, recalled he "was all romance and sex. He loved the ladies and wanted to learn how to say, in English 'You are very beautiful. You will have dinner with me?'" Perhaps his greatest coup came in 1924 when

[5] *NYT*, Jan. 20, 1929; Cipriano E. Oppo, "Italian Art of Today," *Survey*, LVII (March 1, 1927), 718-22; *American Magazine of Arts*, XVIII (Dec. 1927), 629-48, cited in Carter, pp. 347-48; Kallen, "Arts Under a Dictatorship," pp. 549-51; *LD*, CIX (June 13, 1931), 19; Harold Loeb, *The Way It Was* (New York, 1959), p. 67; see also the recent evaluation by Katharine Kuh, "Art Under Mussolini," *Saturday Review of Literature*, L (June 24, 1967), 42-43.

he personally appeared along with Lionel Barrymore and Barbara LaMarr in *The Eternal City.* "His deportment on the screen," quipped the young film reviewer Robert Sherwood, "lends weight to the theory that this is just where he belongs."[6]

In the meantime American movies played to enthusiastic audiences in Italy, with Shirley Temple and Mickey Mouse ("Topolino") the popular idols. The Italian government, which in the twenties depended a great deal on the importation of American films, used the screen to good advantage. Hollywood's pervasive sex and gangsterism provided canned propaganda which Fascists used to contrast the austere ideals of Italy with a debauched America. The film *Mary of Scotland*, which depicted British royalty as a family of fiends, was displayed in Italy as an anti-Anglo-Saxon tract. In the late thirties, however, Italy began to restrict American films. The discrimination against American movies reflected the strained relations between Italy and the United States after the Ethiopian War. The mixed welcome which Vittorio Mussolini received on his visit to Hollywood in 1937 only exacerbated the situation. The young Mussolini had journeyed to California to organize with producer Hal Roach a joint Italy-American film company. But Vittorio's arrival was met by angry demonstrators (many of whom remembered his sadistic delight in bombing African natives), and in Hollywood especially Jewish and non-Jewish cinema figures criticized Roach's business venture with Fascist officialdom. At the same time the elder Mussolini saw his screen image subjected to the mocking caricatures of Charlie Chaplin's *The Dictator* and Orson Welles' *Julius Caesar.* As far as Hollywood was concerned, for Mussolini the show was over.[7]

AMERICAN WRITERS, FASCISM, AND THE ITALIAN LITERATI

"It was possible for young writers, myself included," wrote

[6] *NYT*, Jan. 19, 1926; Carter, pp. 396-97; *Newsweek*, I (March 18, 1933), 29; Bushman was later quoted in a eulogy in *Newsweek*, LXVIII (Sept. 5, 1966), 23; Sherwood is quoted in John Mason Brown, *The Worlds of Robert E. Sherwood: Mirror to His Time* (New York, 1965), p. 188; Wanger's picture of Mussolini is mentioned in Murray Kempton, *Part of Our Time* (New York, 1955), p. 195.

[7] "Mussolini's Roach," *Time*, xxx (Oct. 11, 1937), 24; *NYT*, Sept. 16, 23, 27, Oct. 12, 1937; *Los Angeles Times*, Sept. 26, 27, 28, 1937. On American films in Italy, see "Doom Over Hollywood," an unpublished address by Constantine Panunzio in the Panunzio papers.

Malcolm Cowley of the nineteen-twenties, "to disregard the Ruhr, *fascismo*, reparations, the New Economic Policy, the birth of prosperity, as they bedazzled themselves with the future of their arts." In the twenties, unfortunately, many major writers did withdraw from the world of politics to cultivate a detached aesthetic sensibility. Yet the rise of Fascism was not entirely without repercussions in American literary life. However limited Mussolini's impact on American writers, in light of George Orwell's observation that "the relationship between Fascism and the literary intelligentsia badly needs investigation," the problem at least deserves a brief discussion.[8]

In Europe D'Annunzio's ecstatic espousal of the Italian Blackshirts and William Butler Yeats' flirtation with the Irish Blueshirts offers an appalling sideshow, a political blank verse all the more disturbing when the poets claim to be "the unacknowledged legislators of the world." In America, too, the response of some of the greatest contemporary poets to Fascism suggests a flawed political vision. Wallace Stevens is a case in point. Admitting in 1935 that "I am pro-Mussolini, personally," Stevens was one of the very few American writers to side with Il Duce during the Abyssinian crisis. "The Italians," Stevens wrote to a friend, "have as much right to take Ethiopia from the coons as the coons had to take it from the boa-constrictors."[9] Stevens did not expound on the subject, but the few remarks he made at the time of the Ethiopian War indicate he saw Fascism as "a transitional phase" of a state which hopefully would, like his poetry, wrest order from chaos and thereby lessen the "disillusionment" and "misery" in the modern world.[10]

Less reticent but no less oblique was T. S. Eliot's response to

[8] Malcolm Cowley, *Exile's Return: A Literary Odyssey of the 1920s* (Viking edn., New York, 1951), p. 175; George Orwell, *Dickens, Dali and Others* (New York, 1946), p. 169.

[9] But in a subsequent letter to Lane Latimer, Stevens tempered his remark while still retaining faith in Mussolini. "While it is true that I have spoken sympathetically of Mussolini, all my sympathies are the other way: with the coons and the boa-constrictors. However, ought I, as a matter of reason, to have sympathized with the Indians as against the Colonists in this country? A man would have to be very thick-skinned not to be conscious of the pathos of Ethiopia or China, or one of these days, if we are not careful, of this country. But that Mussolini is right, practically, has certainly a great deal to be said for it." *Letters of Wallace Stevens*, ed. Holly Stevens (New York, 1966), p. 295.

[10] *Ibid.*, pp. 289-90, 295.

Fascism. In discussing the politics of the American poet it is necessary to mention Eliot, not because he completely embraced reaction, as critics later charged, but rather because he loved democracy less than he hated Fascism. Eliot's revulsion at the sordidness and sterility of modern life resulted in a pilgrim's progress that began with humanism and ended in Anglo-Catholicism. During the odyssey he stopped in 1927 to ponder the meaning of events in Italy. Since Eliot had rejected liberalism's atomized "hollow men" as well as Marxism's soulless proletarians, it is surprising Fascism's cultural elitism and professed spiritualism had little appeal to the author of *The Waste Land*. But Eliot's abiding "supernaturalism" had no place for Fascism which was, like Communism, an "elaborate facade," a futile and naturalistic attempt to lift the spiritual burden off the shoulder of mankind.[11] Eliot had little patience with British writers like James S. Barnes who claimed that Fascism and Catholicism were compatible. Instead he saw Fascism as a "false emotion" that tried to impose itself on the authentic emotions of religion. Compared to the clamorous nonsense of Italian Fascism, the *Action Française*, with Charles Maurras' doctrine of "basic emotion," seemed a far more plausible political creed to Eliot, who wondered why the Vatican condemned the *Action Française* and not the Blackshirts. The most that can be said, then, is that in the twenties Eliot was seeking an authoritarian alternative to democratic liberalism, and although he saw possibilities in the *Action Française* (and later in Jacques Maritain's *Humanisme intégral*), he saw in Mussolini's Italy only a playland of paganism.[12]

Inevitably any discussion of poets and Fascism brings us to Ezra Pound, *l'enfant terrible* of modern American literature. Like Eliot, Pound found America mendacious, but unlike Eliot, he took seriously Fascism as a politics of the spirit. What Pound liked about the Italian phenomenon was its "lack of mental coherence." He candidly admitted that "any thorough judgment of Mussolini will be . . . an act of faith, it will depend on what you

[11] Twelve years later Eliot would maintain that the "fundamental objection to fascist doctrine, the one which we conceal from ourselves because it might condemn ourselves as well, is that it is pagan." "The Idea of a Christian Society" (1939) in *T. S. Eliot: Christianity and Culture* (New York, 1949), p. 15.

[12] T. S. Eliot, "The Literature of Fascism," *Criterion*, vii (Dec. 1928), 280-90.

believe the man means, what you believe he wants to accomplish." So willed, Pound saw in Mussolini the reincarnation of Jeffersonian agrarianism and Jacksonian anti-capitalism. Hence Il Duce represented an invigorating answer to bourgeois materialism and Marxist determinism, both of which denied the poet's creative consciousness a revolutionary role. Thus the author of the famous *Cantos*, who looked upon all recent history as a vast "usurocratic conspiracy," could find only in Italy a leader brave enough to expel the moneylenders and establish a program of "social credit." Attracted by these ill-founded visions, Pound cut himself off from his native America, a "half savage country" in a "botched civilization," and became a permanent expatriate in Italy. During World War II he conducted garbled short-wave broadcasts in behalf of the Fascist government.[13]

Turning from poets to playwrights one finds little reference to Fascism in the American theater during the twenties. Robert Sherwood's play *The Road to Rome* (1927) offered an unveiled assault on militarism in general, and Elmer Rice, in *See Naples and Die* (1928), managed a few jabs at the pretensions of Mussolini's "new Italy." Not until the thirties did the stage become a medium for anti-Fascism in works like Archibald MacLeish's *Panic* (1935), Maxwell Anderson's *Knickerbocker Holiday* (1938), Elmer Rice's *American Landscape* (1939), and Dorothy Thompson's and Fritz Kortner's *Another Sun* (1940). In exposing the German-American Bund, anti-Semitism, and the totalitarian state, American dramatists naturally showed more concern about the rising Hitler than the fading Mussolini. Significantly the first popular play of this nature to reach the Broadway stage, Clare Booth Luce's *Margin for Error* (1939), was written by an authoress who, while opposed to Hitler, was not known to have criticized Mussolini. Nevertheless, Il Duce was not completely spared: in Richard Rohman's *Tell My Story* (1939) American theater-goers saw a dramatization of the murder of Giacomo Matteotti.

Among American novelists Henry Miller was the only literary aesthete taken in by the crude cult of personality. Whereas most pro-Fascist intellectuals found much to admire in the social doc-

[13] Ezra Pound, *Jefferson and/or Mussolini* (London, 1935); *Money Pamphlets: An Introduction to the Economic Nature of the United States; America, Roosevelt and the Causes of the Present War; Selected Radio Speeches*, trans. Carmine Amore (London, 1950).

trines of Fascism but had doubts about the quixotic Il Duce, Miller felt just the opposite. For Miller the Italian dictator was one leader whose brusque but honest style broke through the cant and false sentiment that surrounded fawning democratic governments. In a world of venal politicians and sycophantic statesmen, his rule stood out as an example of tenacious purpose and bold power. Writing to Lawrence Durrell in 1937, Miller advised: "The man who sticks to his guns has the world at his feet. That's why I prefer Mussolini a thousand times, much as I despise his program, to the whole British Empire. Mussolini's politics is real-politik. That's something in a world of cagey bastards, of pussy footers and stinking hypocrites."[14]

In the twenties the few American novelists who traveled through Italy and saw Fascism firsthand generally rendered a harsh verdict. Louis Bromfield's "total impression was one of impending disaster." Sinclair Lewis, writing his father from Italy in 1923, described the *fascisti* as "a kind of Ku Klux Klan, but more efficient," and Mussolini as "a flabby hard-jawed, mad-eyed fanatic." Scott Fitzgerald, beaten and jailed in Rome after taking a swing at a policeman in an argument over a taxi fare, dismissed Italy as "a dead land" and warned "whoever is deceived by the pseudo activity under Mussolini is deceived by the spasmodic last jerk of a corpse." But it was Ernest Hemingway who proved to be America's greatest literary foil to Fascism's martial mystique. *A Farewell to Arms* (1929), revealing Italy at its most ignominious moment (Caporetto) and excoriating war-time patriotism, was antithetical to the whole warrior spirit of the Blackshirts. It was only fitting that Hemingway, who spent his life wrestling with the moral problem of courage and violence, saw through the veneer of virility surrounding Mussolini and his followers. The novelist summed up his initial reaction in January 1923:

Mussolini is the biggest bluff in Europe. . . . Take one of his photographs and study it. You will see the feebleness of his mouth, which obliges him to cast that famous Mussolinian frown which every Fascist in Italy imitates. . . . Study his gift for developing small ideas into great words. Study his inclination to dueling. Truly courageous people do not have to duel,

[14] Lawrence Durrell and Henry Miller, *A Private Correspondence* (New York, 1963), pp. 107-08.

and many cowards must duel in order to give the impression that they themselves possess courage. And then look at his black shirt and white spats. There is something that doesn't go together, also from the point of view of histrionics, in a man who wears white spats with a black shirt.[15]

As the above remarks indicate, most American novelists offered little more than visceral polemics, passing barbs which, in Hemingway's case, could descend almost to the level of pornoracism.[16] Perhaps had they made Rome rather than Paris their place of exile, they might have come to see in Fascism a symptom of the moral sickness and social disintegration of modern life, as did Alberto Moravia and Thomas Mann. Not until the thirties did American writers take up this theme of universal political decay. Robert Penn Warren, who wrote the original dramatic version of *All the King's Men* (1946) in Perugia and in Rome with "the boot heels of Mussolini's legionnaires clanging on the stones," saw that the same moral degeneracy and "fetid slums" which produced the "inspired idiot" in Italy "made possible the rise of 'Huey.'" Sinclair Lewis sounded a similar alarm in *It Can't Happen Here* (1935), a tour de force on native reaction in which Lewis drew his information on Fascism from his Vermont neighbor, journalist George Seldes. With keener insight, Nathaniel West in *A Cool Million* (1934) showed how a savage combination of resentment and idealism could result in a populistic dictatorship, while Edward Dahlberg, in *Those Who Perish* (1934), pondered darkly the meaning of Nazism for America upon his return from Germany. Ultimately, of course, it was the Spanish Civil War that brought the overwhelming majority of literary intellectuals into an unequivocal anti-Fascist front. Yet faced with Franco's reactionary coup, the lessons of Mussolini's movement were not lost: "Three years of residence in Italy was more

---

[15] Bromfield is quoted in *Time*, VIII (Nov. 22, 1926), 17; Lewis in Mark Schorer, *Sinclair Lewis: An American Life* (New York, 1961), p. 386; Fitzgerald in Andrew Turnbull, *Scott Fitzgerald* (New York, 1962), p. 148; Hemingway in Aldo Garosci, *Gli intellettuali e la guerra di Spagna* (Turin, 1959), p. 352; see also Hemingway's cryptic short story, "Italy, 1927," *New Republic*, L (May 18, 1927), 350-53, which later appeared in various anthologies as "Che ti dice la patria."

[16] In a crude prose-poem Hemingway described the size of the breasts of Ambassador Child's wife and then commented: "Mussolini has nigger eyes and a bodyguard and has his picture taken reading a book upside down." *The Little Review*, IX (Spring 1923), 20.

than enough to convince me that Fascism is an unmixed evil," stated Leonard Bacon in *Writers Take Sides*, a poll on the war in Spain conducted by the League of American Writers.[17] William Carlos Williams believed that "without Mussolini there could not be Franco," for the Italian dictator showed the way to all who would thwart democratic liberalism and social justice. American writers were also appalled at what Fascsim had done to the Italian people. "At first, when you go to Italy you hardly notice it," Hamilton Basso recalled. "But slowly, little by little, it sinks into your awareness. . . . It is some dark blight on the human spirit. It is a cold black shadow on the land." Similarly, American intellectuals deplored the death of culture in Mussolini's Italy. Hemingway, Cowley, Kenneth Burke, Martha Gelhorn, Newton Arvin, Albert Rhys Williams, Walter Duranty, Donald Ogden Stewart, Muriel Draper, and Archibald MacLeish were among those who attended the American Writers Conference in 1937 and heard Francis Winwar, the poet and Italian literature specialist, announce that every book coming out of Italy is "approved" and "therefore dull."[18]

With Fascist literary life dead from the neck up, the publication of Ignazio Silone's *Fontamara* (1934) was the most exciting Italian-American cultural event of the thirties. This moving account of the plight of the *contadini* under Fascism so deeply affected American writers that Stark Young felt impelled to offer a rejoinder. Young, criticizing what he regarded as a provincial reaction to Fascism, maintained that Americans were oblivious to the Italians' "austere dignity" and "passionate sense of tradition" which made Fascist ideology entirely compatible with their character and history. Young's earlier defense of Fascism in the *New Republic* in 1931 had gone unchallenged; but his 1937 criticism of Silone was answered by Josephine Herbst, among others. Young's philo-Fascism, Herbst maintained, "heaved" no differ-

[17] Of the 418 writers who responded to this poll, 98 percent favored the Loyalist government and opposed Franco, 1.75 percent were neutral (e.g., Robinson Jeffers), and one quarter of one percent were for Franco (actually only one writer, Gertrude Atherton). *Writers Take Sides* (The League of American Writers, New York, 1938).

[18] Robert Penn Warren, *All the King's Men* (New York, 1953), vi, and "All the King's Men: Matrix of Experience," *Yale Review*, LIII (Winter 1964), 161-67; *Writers Take Sides*, pp. 3, 64-65; Hamilton Basso, "Italian Notebook, 1938," *New Republic*, xcv (June 15, 1938), 147-49; *NYT*, June 5, 6, 1937.

ently than the romantic sighs of other southern intellectuals who defended stoop labor as a matter of the soul rather than the soil. Thus "Mr. Borgese and Mr. Silone, although born, bred and suffering Italians, would do well to consider that poverty is negligible when watered with grace, and that ignorance if suffused with dignity is not only tragic. The moral seems to be that poverty and dignity is grace and that all writers going to Spain, Germany, South America and points east and west should take cotton for their ears and study the art of the country in the last five centuries before writing their pieces." The defense of Silone on the part of Herbst and others suggests that after *Fontamara* no socially conscious writer could remain indifferent to Italian Fascism. As Alfred Kazin has recently recalled in his memoirs, *Fontamara's* political leitmotiv translated the nineteenth-century Russian intelligentsia's cry *"What must we do?"* into an agonizingly personal *"What must I do?"* As a "summons to action through love," the novel "expressed the necessity of some urgent, personal act of solidarity. In light of *Fontamara*, oppression, misery and injustice took on a luminous quality and became guarantees of response, the ground of human values."[19]

As American writers responded to the literature of the Italian resistance, so did Italian intellectuals become interested in American literature as an expression of their "inner emigration" and as a protest against totalitarianism. Fascist authorities deliberately published John Steinbeck's *Grapes of Wrath*, assuming its depressing agrarian scenes would demonstrate the virtues of the Corporate State to Italian intellectuals. But the strategy backfired; instead, Italians came to admire a country which allowed authors like Steinbeck and Lillian Smith to write such caustic social criticism. Enduring the insults of Fascism's cultural autarchy, essayists like Mario Praz, Emilio Cecchi, and Carlo Linati translated and introduced to their countrymen the works of Melville, Poe, O'Neill, Eliot, Wilder, and Whitman. Hemingway's works in particular influenced several Italian novelists—indeed

[19] See, first, Mario Michele, "Fontamara Revisited," *New Republic*, XCI (May 26, 1937), 69-71; for Young's comments, *ibid.*, XCIII (Jan. 12, 1938), 283-84; for Herbst, letter to editor, *ibid.*, XCIV (Feb. 9, 1938), 20-21; Alfred Kazin, *Starting Out in the Thirties* (New York, 1965), p. 25; Silone also wrote a special preface for Italian-Americans in a subsequent edition of *Fontamara* to be published by the anti-Fascist press in the United States. Silone to Valenti, June 25, 1936, VP.

Praz has called Elio Vittorini's *Uomini e no* "the Italian counterpart of *For Whom the Bell Tolls*." By the end of the thirties, when American works became difficult to obtain because of a censorship crackdown, Italian writers published their own underground anthology, *Americana*, which was soon confiscated by authorities. In responding to literary fugitives like Melville and Whitman, Italian writers still remained appalled by the violence and vulgarity of contemporary American life. Cecchi's *America amara* ("Bitter America" [1938]) presented a desperately crass country on the edge of anxiety. Yet many Italians also sensed, as did Whitman a century earlier, some strange connection between the coarseness of America's vitality and the sinews of her political idealism. "The barbarities which are seen by Linati, Praz and Cecchi," wrote Agostino Lombardo, ". . . [are seen] as a positive factor, as new blood to be transfused into the sick and bloodless body of Italian literature. The more so in that this 'barbarous America,' this land of 'nature,' is also a land of liberty, of the democracy scorned by fascism; the progressive America of Roosevelt and of the New Deal." An American literature that could embrace the humanitarian social realism of a Steinbeck as well as the Christian ethical idealism of a Wilder represented for many Italian writers that "luminous quality" of political value which Kazin perceived in *Fontamara*.[20]

AMERICAN EDUCATORS AND FASCISM

In 1928 *School and Society* reprinted the following statement:

Education is daily more appreciated by the masses and has become a social necessity. I have always exacted and obtained discipline by very simple means—by stimulating emulation and interest in the work on hand, and by unobtrusively studying each boy's character and special inclinations. Discipline ob-

[20] Massimo Salvadori, *Resistenza ed azione*, pp. 158-59; Mario Praz, "Hemingway in Italy," *Partisan Review*, xv (Oct. 1948), 1092. Praz's estimate, however, must be tempered by that of novelist Vasco Pratolini: "The reading of Hemingway is like a childhood disease. Whoever has not gone through it remains a child. Hemingway was, for a number of writers of my generation, our Stendhal. Then we began to see that there was a little D'Annunzio in him. Then came the parting of ways." Quoted in Donald Heiney, *America in Modern Italian Literature* (New Brunswick, 1964), p. 81; "Italian Criticism of American Literature: An Anthology," ed. Agostino Lombardo, *The Sewanee Review*, LXVIII (Summer 1960), 364.

tained by methods of coercion is no real discipline. It checks boyish individuality in the bud and gives rise to latent sentiments of revolt. Until school and home go hand-in-hand in the work of education, true discipline is destined to remain a pious and utterly hopeless Utopian wish.

How can you expect a boy to bring a clean copybook to school when he has probably been doing his lesson in a cowshed? Practice has taught me to throw many ideals to the winds, and that is why I get along very well with my boys.[21]

This pedagogic manifesto could have been written by a gentle American Mr. Chips. Actually it comes from a 1901 report made to the Mayor of Gualteri by a nineteen-year-old teacher named Benito Mussolini. Il Duce as "School Master" was merely one more image in the maestro's repertoire. But in this pose Mussolini was overshadowed, for it was the educational reforms of Giovanni Gentile that commanded attention in America. The *New York Times* described the "round, humorous professor" as "the originator of the ideas back of the new doctrines swaying Italy— he puts group interests above individual liberty"; and one contemporary student of Gentile's educational philosophy doubted "there is a more influential teacher in the intellectual world today."[22]

The Gentile reforms were embodied in the Education Act of 1923. A neo-idealist philosopher who believed in knowledge as a means to self-consciousness, the Fascist Minister of Education tried to humanize the learning process by bringing the schools into closer relation to life, by stressing a vital, creative relationship between teacher and pupil, by ridding the classroom of rote examinations, and by decentralizing the entire bureaucratic system. American teachers and administrators readily applauded. One educator told his American colleagues of the "devotion and intensity of purpose" of the teachers he met in Italy and of the "energetic and cooperative spirit" he witnessed in the secondary classrooms. In *School and Society* Fredericka Blankner described Italy's "new educational ideal" as a revolt against "theoristic naturalism and positivism" and as a new emphasis "on the con-

[21] "Mussolini as a School Master," *School and Society*, xxviii (July 28, 1928), 102.

[22] *NYT*, Sept. 26, 1926; Merritt M. Thompson, *The Educational Philosophy of Giovanni Gentile* (Los Angeles, 1934), p. 2.

crete, and on attention to the application rather than to the abstract principle." At the Progressive Education Conference in 1926 there was talk of an "extraordinary educational renaissance" taking place in Italy; and delegates to the 1929 convention of the National Education Association heard Maria Castellani explain with lavish superlatives "What Mussolini Has Done for Italy." Even athletic coaches could read in the *Journal of Health and Physical Education* a University of Illinois professor covetously describe the toughening of Italian youth under the new regime.[23]

What of course is obvious when one finds American educators using such terms as "cooperative spirit" and "practical application" is the educational philosophy of John Dewey and the classroom methodology of Maria Montessori. That learning is a creative, collective exercise related to varying individual abilities and social needs was a principle seemingly shared by American and Italian educators alike, and the connection between the "Chicago School" and "la tecnica Montessori" was noted in both the *Literary Digest* and in Croce's *La Critica*. Unfortunately, few writers were aware that Dewey had no use for Fascism and that even Miss Montessori had to flee to India when the Blackshirts harassed her schools.[24]

Although education periodicals carried an occasional critical article, more often American teachers and administrators gave gold stars to Gentile and his pupils. What is remarkable is the failure of educators, as educators, to pay attention to the total picture of Italian society under Fascism. Not only did they fail to question the compatibility of a creative curriculum under a regimented dictatorship, but they appeared unaware that Gentile's reforms were soon perverted by party hacks more interested

[23] E. A. Miller, "Il Fascismo, Italian Education, and the Church," *School Review*, XXXVIII (Sept. 1930), 510-24; Fredericka Blankner, "Education in Italy," School and Society, XXXII (July 5, 1930), 21; *Progressive Education*, III (July-Sept. 1926), 254; Maria Castellani, "What Mussolini Has Done for Modern Italy," *National Educational Association*, LXVII (1929), 88-96; Seward C. Staley, "Physical Education in Fascist Italy," *Journal of Health and Physical Education*, I (April 1930), 3-7. See also A. E. Meyer, "Education in Modern Italy," *School and Society*, XXII (July 25, 1925), 96-99; and Emma Menna, "The Gentile Reforms in Italian Education," *Educational Administration and Supervision*, XXII (1936), 551-55.

[24] "Italy's Education Upheavel," *LD*, XCIII (April 23, 1927), 65-67; Guido De Ruggiero, "Note sulla più recente filosofia europea e americana: John Dewey," *La Critica*, XXIV (Sept. 1931), 341-57.

in posting the slogan "Mussolini Is Always Right!" in front of every classroom. In the twenties Fascism as institutionalized thought control did not seem to disturb those very Americans supposedly dedicated to the life of the mind.

Much less susceptible to the glitter of *Gentilismo* were the groves of academe. Higher education in America, always sensitive to the dangers of state control and the erosion of academic freedom, remained on the whole critical of Fascism in all phases of Italian life. Columbia University, however, was an exception. Columbia's pro-Fascism emanated largely from its Italian Department which, under the chairmanship of Giuseppe Prezzolini, functioned as something of an overseas branch of Italy's Ministry of Culture and Propaganda. Others in the department included Peter Riccio, Dino Bigongiari, and Howard Marraro. Riccio had written a dissertation, "On the Threshold of Fascism," which offered the thesis that Prezzolini and his *La Voce* group comprised the intellectual vanguard of Fascism. Bigongiari, who, it will be remembered, was instrumental in organizing the FLNA, furthered the cause of Fascism by translating the works of Gentile, Rocco, and other theoreticians. Marraro also wrote numerous articles and books in praise of Italian education, one of which was introduced by Nicholas Murray Butler.[25]

In Columbia University's Casa Italiana, Fascism found a veritable home in America. The Casa was constructed through the collaborative efforts of various American friends of Italy (e.g., Otto Kahn), Italian-American businessmen, the Italian government, and Mussolini himself, who shipped over exquisite baroque furniture. Completed in 1926, the Casa was first directed by Bigongiari and later by Prezzolini. The Casa featured its own publication *Italy-American Monthly*, which was used together with seminars, forums, and guest lecturers to make it a schoolhouse for budding Fascist ideologues. In the fall of 1934 the *Nation* publicized the Casa's activities in "Fascism at Columbia University." Addressing the first of a series of articles to President Butler, the *Nation* demanded to know how academic freedom could exist in either the Casa or the Italian Department

[25] Peter Riccio, *On the Threshold of Fascism* (New York, 1929), cited in Carter, pp. 263-64; Howard R. Marraro, "Education in Italy Under Mussolini," *Current History*, xxiii (Feb. 1926), 705-09; id., "The New Education in Italy," *ibid.*, xxxvii (Feb. 1933), 571-76; id., *Nationalism in Italian Education* (New York, 1927).

where no anti-Fascists were allowed to speak or teach. Arthur Livingston, the one anti-Fascist in the Italian Department, the *Nation* pointed out, had been transferred to the French Department. The editorial also accused Bigongiari of deliberately hiring pro-Fascist instructors and using graduate students of Italian descent to make political speaking tours through Italian-American neighborhoods.

Responding immediately, Butler maintained that the *Nation's* charge was "utter nonsense" since the Casa was "without political purpose or significance." It was Butler's contention that a number of anti-Fascists had been asked to speak at the Casa, specifically Sforza and Croce, the latter when he planned to visit Columbia while addressing a convention of the American Historical Association. Butler also maintained that the notable anti-Fascist Max Ascoli was extended "prolonged hospitality" at the Casa. In its rejoinder, the *Nation* pointed out that Ascoli stayed at the Casa for a few weeks in 1931, before Prezzolini took charge, and that Livingston was not switched for "budgetary reasons," as Butler claimed, but rather because "a leading Fascist" would not contribute funds to the Casa unless the anti-Fascist teacher were removed. While the debate raged the Graduate Club in Italian Studies and the History Graduate Club stepped into the controversy, informing the *Nation* that many of its charges were false since speakers such as Salvemini were to be invited to the Casa. When put to the test, however, Prezzolini refused to approve the invitation to Salvemini, thereby forcing the dismayed students to withdraw from the Casa and renew their invitation as an independent organization.[26]

[26] The case did not end here, however. A few months after Salvemini was invited he received a letter from the Graduate Club in Italian informing him that the invitation had been withdrawn once again. Students let him know that the Italian Department had re-established its influence over the graduate clubs. *Nation*, cxl (April 3, 1935), 377-78, 388. After World War II, Salvemini and Prezzolini thrashed out this episode in their respective memoirs. See Salvemini, *Memorie di un fuoruscito* (Milan, 1960), and Prezzolini, *L'Italiano inutile* (Milan, 1953), esp. pp. 241-90, 363-88.

The running debate is in *Nation*, cxxxix (Nov. 7-21, 1934), 523-24, 550-52, 565, 590; cxl (Jan. 30-April 3, 1935), 129-30, 377-78, 388; cxli (Nov. 27, 1935), 610; on the organization of the Casa Italiana, see also *Il Mondo* (May 15, 1941), pp. 5-7; (July 15, 1941), pp. 11-13; for an interesting private letter about Prezzolini's politics, written in 1934 by Bruno Roselli to Oswald Villard with the request that it not be printed in the *Nation*, see *Il Mondo* (Feb. 15, 1941), pp. 11-13.

There can be little doubt that President Butler acted with intemperate haste. Instead of appointing an independent committee to investigate, he rushed to the side of the Italian Department, defending on the basis of academic freedom a teacher who himself was unwilling to tolerate the principles of free discourse. In fairness to Butler it should be mentioned that when Carlo Sforza spoke at the Casa two years later—the only anti-Fascist to do so—it was because the President overruled Prezzolini. By the end of the thirties Butler played an important role in introducing anti-Fascists to the Roosevelt administration.[27]

Butler's own views on Fascism became a subject of considerable acrimony and misunderstanding. Although anti-Fascists tended to regard him as the reactionary major domo of Morningside Heights, Butler was actually disturbed about the demise of democracy and the rise of dictatorships, Right as well as Left. True, Butler found much to admire in Fascist Italy, and in turn Mussolini sent him an autographed photo expressing gratitude to the President for his "most valuable contribution" in promoting understanding between the two countries. On several occasions, moreover, he spoke favorably of Fascism in Italy, seemingly convinced that it was the best form of government for that country and represented the popular will. On the other hand, Butler also believed that Fascism was a dangerous doctrine, far more dangerous than Communism. Unlike Communism, which had "failed" as an experiment, the threat of Fascism lay in its very success. "There can be no question," Butler informed an audience at the University of Virginia, "if we are to accept the philosophy of pragmatism—which I hasten to say I do not—if we are to say with Pope: 'for forms of government let fools contest, whate'er is best administered is best,' then we must accept the demonstration that Fascism is a form of government at the very first order of excellence." In fine, Butler worried lest Fascism's "manifest achievements" attract a following in America; and although he commended the Italian government he could neither worship Mussolini nor accept the logical conclusion of Fascist political theory—the doctrine of the absolute state.[28]

What other college presidents thought of Fascism is difficult to say. Frederick B. Robinson, President of City College of New York, created a campus uproar when he insisted that the student

[27] Interview with Howard Marraro, July 9, 1965.
[28] *NYT*, Sept. 28, 1924, April 14, 1927, May 2, 28, 1931.

body receive a delegation of Fascist students from Italy. John Grier Hibben, President of Princeton University, allowed his name to be used to promote the FLNA, then resigned as an honorary member when the anti-Fascist Dr. Fama informed him of the nature of the organization. On the other hand David Starr Jordan, President Emeritus of Stanford University, was willing to write a statement for Salvemini's and Elliott's pamphlet, *The Fascist Dictatorship*, and James B. Conant of Harvard stood by Salvemini when he was harassed by the Boston Italian-American establishment and when the Rome government charged him with an attempt to assassinate Mussolini. More active were William Neilson of Smith College, who joined Borgese, Van Wyck Brooks, Dorothy Canfield Fisher, Felix Frankfurter, Lewis Mumford, and Salvemini in starting the anti-Fascist *News from Italy*, and Alvin Johnson of the New School for Social Research, who made fellowships available to refugee Italian scholars.[29]

In addition to giving aid and comfort to Mussolini's intellectual enemies various American campuses provided forums in which the Fascist question could be openly debated. The result of one such conference in 1931 was the publication of *Bolshevism, Fascism, and Capitalism,* a symposium in which the prominent Italian-American pro-Fascist Luigi Villari tried to explain away the suppression of academic freedom in Italy to an audience that remained skeptical if not hostile. The American academic community also contributed to a growing scholarship on Mussolini's Italy. Ugo D'Annunzio, who, together with Villari, ran the Italian Library of Information, boasted in a private letter that "through our influence" the Corporate State had become the "subject à la mode" of thousands of college theses throughout the country. Columbia University, where Schneider published *Making the Fascist State* (1928) and where he collaborated with his colleague Shepard Clough in publishing *Making Fascists* (1929), gives some substance to D'Annunzio's claim. Other books bearing the Columbia imprimatur were Carmen Haider's *Capital and Labor Under Fascism* (1930), G. Lowell Field, *The Syndical*

[29] *LD*, xcIV (Aug. 6, 1927), 12; Jordan is quoted in *The Fascist Dictatorship*; on Italian refugee scholars, see *NYT*, Dec. 28, 1938; on the affair at City College of New York, see Hal Draper, "The Student Movement in the Thirties," in *As We Saw the Thirties*, ed. Rita James Simon (Urbana, 1969), p. 183.

and Corporate Institutions of Fascism (1938), and William Welk's *Fascist Economic Policy* (1938). These works made an attempt at objectivity, which cannot be said for Count Antonio Cippico's *Italy: The Central Problem of the Mediterranean* (1926), an unadulterated tract published by Yale University Press.

But far more significant, because more numerous and influential, were the scholarly works by anti-Fascists. Aside from Salvemini's prolific studies, the critical scholarship included Columbia historian Michael Florinsky's *Fascism and National Socialism* (1936), Duke economist Calvin Hoover's *Dictators and Democracies* (1938), Yale sociologist Jerome Davis' *Contemporary Social Movements* (1930); and, more illuminating, Columbia agronomist Carl Schmidt's *The Corporate State in Action* (1939), a sophisticated Marxist interpretation; University of Chicago political scientist Herman Finer's *Mussolini's Italy* (1935), a thorough study that has become a minor classic in American scholarship on Fascism; and Queens College historian Gaudens Megaro's *Mussolini in the Making* (1938), a meticulously researched exposé of Il Duce's early career which was translated into Italian immediately following World War II. In 1934 *Fascism at Work* was smuggled out of Germany and published in London under the pseudonym "William Elwin." The author, William Ebenstein, would soon flee Hitler's Germany and become a professor of government at Princeton University where he published his valuable *Fascist Italy* (1939). By the late thirties these hostile studies came to be accepted in academic circles as valid treatments of a topic no longer academic. In 1939, for example, the *Saturday Review of Literature* was asked by readers to recommend reliable books on "national trends and policies in Italy." The literary weekly recommended the works of Salvemini, Florinsky, and Finer as well as Seldes' *Sawdust Caesar.*[30]

Like other American institutions, higher education had its share of philofascists. Clark P. Bissett, a law professor at the University of Washington who likened Mussolini to Whitman ("I celebrate myself"), printed his own personal tribute which was peddled at fifty cents a pamphlet. William Lyon Phelps, the eminent Yale English professor who enjoyed an audience with Mussolini, believed that one of Il Duce's profoundest reforms,

[30] Ugo D'Annunzio to Ruth Ricci, Nov. 24, 1939, IR, 435; *Saturday Review of Literature,* XVI (Jan. 12, 1939), 20.

which gave him "an imperishable place in history," was his decree increasing school hours for young Italians. But aside from these occasional unscholarly bits of adulation, the academic community as a whole opposed Fascism. Even Columbia University, where Schneider, Clough, and Carlton J. H. Hayes wrote sympathetically on Fascism, had on its faculty such outspoken anti-Fascists as economists Underhill Moore and Carl Schmidt, law professor Lindsay Rogers, and historian Michael Florinsky. Well before the rise of Hitler, moreover, a sizable number of American scholars had declared themselves opposed to Fascism, including Edward M. East, A. L. Holcombe, Samuel Eliot Morison, and William Y. Elliott of Harvard; Robert Morss Lovett of Chicago; Morris Cohen of City College of New York; Edward A. Ross and Frederick A. Ogg of Wisconsin; Oscar Jaszi of Oberlin; and Father John A. Ryan of Catholic University. The conscience of democratic liberalism was perhaps best reflected in the views of James T. Shotwell and Eduard C. Lindeman. Shotwell, a Columbia history professor, participated in the 1928 *Current History* symposium, "Is Democracy a Failure?" which featured written contributions by Kaiser Wilhelm II and Benito Mussolini. Here Shotwell answered Mussolini's attack on western liberalism with a foreboding critique of Italy's closed society. Lindeman, a New School social psychologist, prepared the 1927 *Survey* issue on "An American Looks at Fascism." Aware that property-minded Americans were imbued with efficiency and "narrowed nationalism," Lindeman warned that Fascism could "easily be made compatible with large sectors of American thought and practice." Thus unlike Bolshevism, Fascism "constitutes the first realistic challenge to the spirit of freedom and democracy which emerged from our Revolution in 1776."[31]

The scholars mentioned above, together with the *fuorusciti* discussed earlier and such Italian-American professors as Constantine Panunzio of the University of California at Los Angeles, George La Piana of Harvard, and Rudolph Altrochi of Berkeley,

[31] *Saturday Review of Literature*, xvi (Jan. 1939), 20. Clark P. Bisset, *Mussolini and Fascismo* (Seattle, 1925, pamphlet, cited in Carter, p. 285; William Lyon Phelps, "Mussolini and the New Spirit in Italy," *Delineator*, cxxi (Oct. 1932), 4; statements by scholars mentioned above were printed in Salvemini's pamphlet, *The Fascist Dictatorship*; James T. Shotwell, "The Historian's Answer to the Autocrats," *Current History*, xxvii (May 1928), 196-202; Eduard C. Lindeman, "A New Challenge to the Spirit of 1776," *Survey*, lvii (March 1, 1927), 679-82.

made the universities one of the few anti-Fascist ramparts in America. Uppermost in the minds of American educators was, of course, the suppression of academic freedom in Italy. When Italy imposed the "Professional Oath" in 1932, a group of Harvard professors, led by Roscoe Pound, Dean of the Law School, protested the "coercion" of anti-Fascist students and teachers to the League of Nations' International Institute of Intellectual Cooperation. In the *Manchester Guardian* British intellectuals and dons also protested Mussolini's dismissal of professors. The fate of Italian educators under Fascism was a grim reality that, as indicated in the following letter from Harold Laski to Oliver Wendell Holmes, Jr., gave scholars in every country cause to reflect upon the historical meaning of Liberty.

> I had also a very interesting interview with a young Italian exile—a professor who had published a protest against being compelled to laud the "Corporate State" of Mussolini. He was first dismissed; then nearly beaten to death in his house by a gang of Fascist ruffians; and escaped by night over the Swiss frontier leaving everything he possessed to be confiscated. The problem is what to do with such men. I have got him a few lectures, but that merely keeps a transitory wolf from the door. I wish I could reproduce his description of that escape—the horror of sound, the dread of being caught by the beam of a passing car, the fear of frontier guards, the sense that every passer-by must know who you are and can hear the beating of your heart. I made the poor fellow divinely happy by getting a friend of mine to make arrangements to take his fiancée out of the place by engaging her as his wife's lady's maid, and we hope that this will be effected in the next ten days. Certainly his experience makes you feel that the simplicity of 19th century liberty has much to commend it.[32]

[32] *NYT*, Jan. 3, 1932; the text of the professors' letter was reprinted in *School and Society*, xxxv (Jan. 9, 1932), 47-48; see also C. H. Abad, "Fascist Italy's Repression of Intellectual Freedom," *Current History*, xxxiii (Jan. 1931), 535-39; for Left-wing views see *Italian Intellectuals under Fascism* (Student League for Industrial Democracy, New York, 1934), pamphlet; *Holmes-Laski Letters*, ed. Mark DeWolf Howe (Cambridge, 1953), pp. 1114-15.

11.

The View from
Washington

IN THE LONG RUN EVERY
GOVERNMENT IS THE EXACT
SYMBOL OF ITS PEOPLE, WITH
THEIR WISDOM AND UNWISDOM.
Thomas Carlyle, 1843

INNOCENCE AND IRONY: FROM WILSONIANISM TO FASCISM

Except for a vicious outbreak of anti-Italian vigilante atrocities
in New Orleans in 1891, diplomatic relations progressed smoothly
throughout the nineteenth and early twentieth centuries between
Italy and America. The rise of Fascism did little to alter friendly
relations. Like the rest of the public, American diplomats were
at first disturbed by the Blackshirts and the bands of *Squadristi*.
After the March on Rome, however, Fascism's image improved
considerably. Even while maneuvering into power Mussolini
found time to send Secretary of State Charles Evans Hughes a
message expressing desire to continue the "economic and spiritual collaboration" between the United States and Italy. Hughes
congratulated Mussolini on the confidence he had just received
from the King of Italy, while George Harvey, Ambassador to the
Court of St. James, wired a dispatch in which he described
Fascism as the death knell of Bolshevism and advised the State
Department to encourage Ambassador Child "to manifest spirit
of somewhat notable friendliness and hopefulness" toward Italy's
new regime. Scarcely in need of such encouragement, Child immediately proceeded to exchange telegrams of felicitation. Thus
began the official policy of the United States government toward
Mussolini and Fascism.[1]

[1] Mussolini to Hughes, Oct. 31, 1922, DS, 865.00/67; Embassy (London)
to Department, Oct. 31, 1922, DS, 865.00/1168; State Department, 865.00/
1108, cited in Carter, pp. 404-06; De Santi, pp. 36-40. According to De
Santi, Harvey's cable carried the notation: "See President's Message to
Mussolini of November 1, 1922." (p. 41) De Santi was unable to locate

Owing to the way Mussolini moved to power the issue of recognition was never raised.[2] King Victor Emmanuel had asked Mussolini to form a new ministry, and since Il Duce cautiously refrained from immediately moving against legitimate institutions of authority, his ascendancy took on the legal character of a ministerial crisis. Nevertheless we are confronted with an apparent paradox. The United States, a nation that had just fought a war "to make the world safe for democracy," tacitly acknowledged the rise of a leader who saw himself as the political mortician of democratic liberalism. How does one explain the disparity between theory and practice?

First of all, the rise of Fascism posed no immediate threat to America's vital interests. Neither diplomatic security nor economic trade were seriously jeopardized by the demise of Italian democracy. Ambassador Henry Fletcher may have been troubled by the crude militarism of the movement; yet Fletcher soon became convinced that Il Duce could be dissuaded by the realization that a reckless imperialism would drive away American loans.[3] As to the international spread of Fascism, Fletcher was assured by Italians that the rise of similar organizations in other countries by no means signified a "real international of the Russian model"; instead they demonstrated the desire of working toward the "internationalization of nationalism" through the

---

Harding's message in the State Department files and this writer had no better luck with the Harding Papers. The message was probably of a general congratulatory nature, but if it were anything more—assurance of moral or material support—it would obviously tell us something about Harding's initial response to Mussolini, assuming he had one.

[2] From the time Jefferson was Secretary of State, the policy of the United States had been generally to recognize any foreign government in actual control and able and willing to carry out international obligations. This "de facto" policy of regarding the origin and nature of the government as secondary usually worked to the advantage of rising republics in revolt against monarchist and imperialist regimes. In the case of twentieth-century Fascism, however, the "de facto" policy aided "constitutional dictators" who, unlike the Bolsheviks, paraded under a veneer of legitimacy.

[3] "It has been hinted to me by my colleagues that Italy looks to the U.S. for the financial support of Mussolini's so-called imperialistic policy," Fletcher wrote the Secretary of State. But, he added, "in private conversations I make no secret of my belief that our financial markets will not be open for borrowings for warlike or adventurous projects for any country." Fletcher to Secretary of State, May 13, 1926, Container 13, FP.

"moral rapprochement of the conservative parties of all countries."[4]

As with the popular press, Fascism also appeared in diplomatic circles as the bright dawn after the nightmare of the "Red Scare." Significantly, the fact that the Italian Left had shot its bolt in the sporadic strikes of 1921 did not seem to matter to the State Department. This consuming fear of radicalism of any stripe blinded American officials to the possibility of a non-Communist and non-Fascist alternative. Not that a viable anti-Fascist opposition existed in the early years. Far from it. The point is the Communist "menace" in Italy became such a paralyzing fixation that the State Department could scarcely discern the difference between a radical and a republican, a Togliatti and a Turati. Thus when former Premier Nitti tried to tell the State Department that Fascism, a frustrated form of "white bolshevism," should be regarded as an "international danger," Secretary of State Frank Kellogg and his assistant William Castle made a perfunctory acknowledgment of the letter and privately wrote Nitti off as a discontented Bolshevik "troublemaker" who was "very *persona grata*" in Moscow.[5]

Finally, the official approval of the Fascist take-over represents a repudiation of Wilsonian liberalism. The Fascist movement, coming to power after the bitter fruit of victory, made more rancid by the selfish pickings at the Versailles conference table, caught the American government in a profoundly anti-liberal mood. The diplomacy of the twenties, in comparison to that of the war years, was characterized by diplomatic disengagement and psychological disenchantment; by a desire to withdraw from European intervention as well as forsake the historic dream of universal democracy. Hence Ambassador Child could state publicly in 1924: "I haven't the slightest idea in these days what democracy means to any other man; but if you mean by it an effective expression of the will and willingness of the people, you may be sure there is more in Italy today than there has been since the days of Crispi. Democracy is not created by the label."[6]

In a crude sense Child was correct. For although the Wilsonian

[4] Fletcher to David Reed, Feb. 11, 1926; Fletcher to Secretary of State, Jan. 16, 1926, Container 12; Fletcher Diary, Jan. 5, 1926, FP.

[5] Quoted in De Santi, pp. 60-61.

[6] Child, "Mussolini in the Making," p. 156.

264

liberals had clear ideas about democracy, they showed little understanding of the difficulties in trying to export the "new diplomacy" of the Fourteen Points to a Europe unprepared for America's instant "packaged regeneration." Dubiously equating democracy with nationalism, American progressives believed that Wilson's ideal of self-determination would be entirely compatible with the political liberalization of Europe. Whatever the consequences of Wilson's diplomacy in the rest of Europe, in the Mediterranean where he stood unalterably opposed to territorial acquisition it served only to fester the wounds of Italian nationalism. Ultimately Wilson's evangelical diplomacy and Italy's "sacro egoismo" were incompatible. American liberalism did not beget Fascism; but the tragedy is that Wilson's lofty visions of a new Europe helped kindle in Italy an embittered super-patriotism which, born in humiliation, quickly flamed into a reactionary will to power and pride. Wilson's desperate attempt in Rome to speak over the heads of Italian statesmen directly "to the people" is a poignant chapter in American innocence. It was not that the Italians loved democracy less but that they loved nationalism more. Ironically, Wilson's hope of infusing Italy with the spirit of home-made American liberalism is only the first of many instances where the road to Fascism would be paved by good intentions.

RECEPTION AT THE WHITE HOUSE

The repudiation of Wilsonian internationalism by no means meant the State Department would pursue a "neutral" or "objective" policy toward Italy. At the ambassadorial level, several diplomats used the Embassy in Rome to promote the good name of Mussolini and Fascism, either by publicity work, negotiating loans, or by quietly ignoring the protests of anti-Fascists. We are familiar with Ambassador Child's propaganda activities, but his use—or abuse—of diplomatic office is even more astounding. Child fancied himself an adviser to Il Duce. Convinced that he had influenced Mussolini's decision to carry out the March on Rome, Child proudly boasted that immediately prior to the event he told the hesitating Mussolini that it was "easier to snatch the tiller than to steer the boat." Enthralled with his self-appointed role as Il Duce's confidant, the Ambassador took it upon himself to discuss with Mussolini the possibility of a formal diplomatic alliance with the United States. Apparently Child was oblivious to the fact that America had not entered such an alliance since 1778 and was in no mood to do so after having rejected the League of Nations. Showing poor judgment of history as well as protocol, Child was scolded for his "most shocking misuse of power" by a superior State Department official.[7]

Less exuberant were the views of Child's successor, Henry P. Fletcher. Although Fletcher continued to praise Mussolini as the only source of strong leadership in Italy, his opinions were tempered by Fascism's aggressive élan. Unlike Child, Fletcher often pointed out to the State Department the repugnant side of the Blackshirts: their explosive rowdiness, expansionist bravado, cult of violence. He was also concerned about the rise of Fascism in other countries and he discerned the dangerous link between internal tension and external aggression, the possible need for "a dramatic stroke of foreign policy to offset unsatisfactory political conditions." Yet Fletcher, a conservative champion of individualism, saw no alternative to Il Duce. On one occasion following an attempt on the Premier's life, Fletcher recoiled in horror. "If Mussolini should be assassinated, which God forbid," he informed the State Department, "there would be a reign of terror. Authorities would be powerless to preserve order for some time."[8]

More discriminating was the attitude of Secretary of State Charles Evans Hughes, one of the few urbane members of the Harding cabinet. Hughes tactfully nipped in the bud a proposal made by Child and Italian authorities for the King of Italy to visit the United States; similarly, he himself refused to pass through Rome while touring Europe in 1924. It was Hughes, moreover, who reprimanded the Chargé d'Affaires in Rome for allowing the American Embassy to become involved in the transactions of the Sinclair Company in Italy. Other than extending normal diplomatic pleasantries, Hughes refrained from evincing great faith in the statesmanship of Benito Mussolini.[9]

The same cannot be said of his two respective successors, Frank B. Kellogg and Henry L. Stimson. Mussolini won Kel-

[7] *Ibid.*, pp. 156-58; De Santi, p. 27.

[8] Fletcher to Secretary of State, Jan. 16, 1926, Container 12, FP; De Santi, p. 55; Embassy to Department, 865.00/1534, cited in Carter, p. 425; on Fletcher's political philosophy, see Fletcher "Press Release," May 30, 1932, HP.

[9] De Santi, pp. 74-78.

logg's respect because the Secretary had success in obtaining Il Duce's cooperation in peace, disarmament, and loan negotiations. More than once the Secretary complained to the Ambassador in Rome about the anti-Fascists in the United States ("communists, socialists, and anarchists") who insulted visiting Italian dignitaries. Stimson, Hoover's Secretary of State, was equally polite to Fascism's friends while disparaging its enemies. Compared to relations with other countries, Stimson found those with Italy "least difficult," and he termed Mussolini a "sound and useful leader."[10]

As to presidential opinion, Harding, Coolidge, and Hoover neither praised nor criticized Mussolini in public statements. Harding, of course, was at his wit's end trying to comprehend his own brief tragic years in the White House, much less the obscurantism of Italian Fascism. Coolidge, whose silence on the subject was deafening, was deluged by letters from Italian-Americans informing him of the patriotic virtues of the *fascisti* and the stern ideals of Il Duce. Relaying information about the new labor laws in Italy, Fletcher advised Coolidge in 1926: "With the establishment of this compulsory jurisdiction neither employers nor workers can take justice into their own hands," and, Fletcher stressed by underlining the last clause, *"both strikes and lockouts are declared illegal."* To Coolidge, the solemn strike-breaker, these last words must have brought an approving smile.[11]

On the topic of Fascism President Hoover neither smiled nor frowned. This reticence is revealing, for in the 1930s Hoover would maintain that Mussolini's government was as despotic as Stalin's Russia and Hitler's Germany, and, what is more, that the Corporate State inspired Roosevelt's NRA. Yet during Hoover's administration not a word of criticism issued from the White House. On the contrary, it was during his administration that Italian-American relations reached, according to Louis De Santi, "a zenith of cordiality." Moreover, as Secretary of Commerce, Hoover evinced not a little curiosity about Mussolini's economic programs. He was very interested in new Fascist legislation abolishing the inheritance tax, and he requested a copy of the law from Ambassador Caetani. Hoover also used the Commerce

[10] Kellogg to Fletcher, July 10, 1926, Container 13, FP; Henry L. Stimson and McGeorge Bundy, *On Active Service in Peace and War* (New York, 1948), p. 269.
[11] Fletcher to Coolidge, March 24, 1926, Box 82, CP.

Department to facilitate the lenient debt settlement with Italy, and Treasury Secretary Andrew Mellon, who believed Mussolini was "making a new nation out of Italy," worked closely with Ambassador Fletcher to help Mussolini secure the Morgan loan. All this activity could be regarded as quite normal by Hoover, who viewed Italy's new regime as merely a business proposition. Hence when Child resigned his post in 1924 Hoover was quick to advise Coolidge on the new appointment.

Dear Mr. President:

I am taking the liberty of saying a word on the question of the appointment of an Ambassador to Italy to fill the forthcoming vacancy. There are commercial and financial reasons why this office is of utmost interest to us at the present time.

Italy offers a special opportunity for American investment in reproductive enterprise as Italy is anxious to free herself from continental dependence. Furthermore, the Italians have a very large portion of the distributing trades through the eastern Mediterranean and the Balkan states. Italy does not possess raw materials and partly finished materials with which to manufacture for this distribution. Her natural source of these materials plus capital with which to increase her industry for the purpose is from the United States. England, Germany and France possess now or will possess their own capital for these purposes.

If the Ambassador could be a man of large industrial, financial and commercial vision, a relationship could be developed which would give us entry into those sections which we could not otherwise obtain, either directly or through any other source.

I have no one to suggest but I do have the feeling that a man of the above character would, for the present, be better adapted to this position than men of large literary or purely diplomatic qualities.[12]

With the appointment of Fletcher, Secretary Hoover obtained a man whose "vision" well suited American enterprise in Italy.

[12] *The Memoirs of Herbert Hoover, Vol. II: The Cabinet and the Presidency* (New York, 1952), p. 331; id., *Addresses Upon the American Road* (New York, 1938), p. 154; De Santi, p. 57; Hoover to Caetani, Nov. 15, 1923, Container 176, Hoover to the President, Feb. 7, 1924, Container 175, HP; Mellon is quoted in the *NYT*, Oct. 13, 1926.

Published Weekly

The Curtis Publishing Company

Cyrus H. K. Curtis, President

George H. Lorimer, First Vice-President
William Boyd, John D. Williams and
Walter D. Fuller, Second Vice-Presidents
Philip S. Collins, Treasurer

Independence Square, Philadelphia

London: 6, Henrietta Street
Covent Garden, W. C.

THE SATURDAY EVENING POST

Founded A°D¹ 1728 *by* Benj. Franklin

George Horace Lorimer
EDITOR

Frederick S. Bigelow, A. W. Neall,
Thomas B. Costain, Wesley W. Stout,
B. Y. Riddell, Thomas L. Masson,
Associate Editors

Entered as Second-Class Matter, November 18, 1879,
at the Post Office at Philadelphia. Under Act of
March 3, 1879. Additional Entry at Columbus, O.,
St. Louis, Mo., Chicago, Ill., Indianapolis, Ind.,
Saginaw, Mich., Des Moines, Ia., Portland, Ore.,
Milwaukee, Wis., St. Paul, Minn., San Francisco,
Cal., Kansas City, Mo., Savannah, Ga., Denver, Colo.,
Louisville, Ky., Houston, Tex., Omaha, Neb., Ogden,
Utah, Jacksonville, Fla., New Orleans, La., Portland,
Me., Los Angeles, Cal., Richmond, Va., Boston, Mass.

lume 200   5C. THE COPY   PHILADELPHIA, PA., MAY 5, 1928 $2.00 By Subscription (52 issues)   Number 45

YOUTH – By Benito Mussolini

Mussolini inaugurates his serialized autobiography in the *Saturday Evening Post* with a chapter on "Youth," May 5, 1928.

President Herbert Hoover, Secretary of State Henry Stimson, and
Foreign Minister Dino Grandi, White House, 1931. From Hoover
Library, West Branch, Iowa

Italian-American Blackshirt rally, Camp Nordland, New Jersey, 1938.
From *Fortune* Magazine

New York Italian-American anti-Fascist demonstration, Garibaldi Day, July 4, 1932.

Gaetano Salvemini.
The Italian anti-Fascist exile
and Harvard historian.

Carlo Tresca. Anarchist folk hero of
the Italian-American Left
and anti-Fascist resistance.

Peter Blume, "The Eternal City," 1937 (1934-37; date on painting, 1937.) Blume's painting expresses well the puppet image of Il Duce among Left-Wing intellectuals.

New York Times correspondent Herbert Matthews interviewing the esteemed Italian philosopher Benedetto Croce. In November 1943, *Life* called upon Croce to assume political responsibility and help Italy withdraw from the war and switch allegiance to the Allies. George Rodgers, from *Life* Magazine ©, Time, Inc.

Ezra Pound at 72. After his release from St. Elizabeth's hospital, where for ten years
he had been interned following a treason indictment. Pound returned to Italy.
David Lees, from *Life* Magazine ©, Time, Inc.

As President, moreover, Hoover likewise appeared quite satisfied with the government in Rome. Indeed with Fletcher as Ambassador, Mellon as Treasury Secretary, and Stimson as Secretary of State, the Hoover administration was untroubled by any doubting critics. The highly publicized meeting between Hoover and Foreign Minister Dino Grandi in 1931 symbolized the amity between Italy and the United States. To the anti-Fascists, it will be recalled, the Grandi visit was the ultimate insult to a nation dedicated to the principles of the open society. But while Secretary Stimson turned a deaf ear to anti-Fascist protests,[13] the State Department received a request from Grandi to "arrange" a favorable editorial in a major newspaper. Hoover himself was "delighted" (Stimson's expression) by the Grandi visit. In the three-hour interview Hoover and his guest talked about the economic crisis in Europe, Mussolini's speeches on revisionism (which Grandi assured the President posed no danger to peace), disarmament, and the threat of Communism in Germany. Not a word was mentioned about the suppression of liberty in Italy. In light of Hoover's silence on Mussolini's dictatorship while in office, one can only conclude that the ex-President's belated repudiation of Fascism in the thirties showed more concern about the rise of the welfare state than the fall of Italian democracy.[14]

Although the American government was doubtless sympathetic to Fascism, the amity between the United States and Italy

[13] The man directing the protest against Grandi's visit was the respectable anti-Fascist Dr. Charles Fama. With stiff formality Stimson informed Fama: "It would appear that you and your friends have misunderstood the attitude of the Secretary of State. He is the guardian of American hospitality to representatives of foreign governments and cannot be asked to hold public meetings, which will make him a vehicle for public criticism against foreign governments or their representatives." Stimson's position is understandable enough, but less defensible is the manner in which the State Department categorized anti-Fascists. Earlier Under-Secretary William Castle told the White House that Fama was a man of "exceedingly unsavory reputation. I think the government has a good deal on him. He is, whatever he calls himself, the leader of the militant anti-Fascist Italian group in this country and we have almost proof that he has been implicated in one or two bad riots in New York." Stimson to Hoover, March 4, 1931; Castle to George Akerson, May 25, 1929, Box 856, HP.

[14] De Santi, pp. 101-03; Stimson is quoted in Robert Ferrell, *American Diplomacy in The Great Depression* (New Haven, 1957), pp. 204-05; "Conversations Between President Hoover and Signor Grandi," Nov. 18, 1931, memo, Container 856, HP.

was probably more influenced by what American statesmen regarded as major diplomatic achievements. For example, the Dawes and Young plan for loans to Europe, the Pact of Paris and the Kellogg-Briand Treaty all won the support of Mussolini, which in turn won Mussolini the gratitude of the State Department. Relations between Italy and America were a matter for congratulations on both sides of the Atlantic.

Aware of the favor he enjoyed in American diplomatic circles, Mussolini did not hesitate to exploit it. Aside from trying to secure loans and having enemies prosecuted, Mussolini intervened in American affairs through the State Department when he tried unsuccessfully to have the Immigration Act of 1924 postponed. But another cause for intervention—the trial and execution of Sacco and Vanzetti—presented a dilemma. Mussolini could hardly come to the defense of the two anarchists, the *cause célèbre* of the American Left. Yet at the same time opinion in Italy, growing more hostile toward America as the day of execution approached, necessitated some gesture of concern. Thus a few days before the accused were strapped to the electric chair, Mussolini appealed to Fletcher as a personal friend, suggesting that the Ambassador and the State Department persuade Governor Fuller to commute the death sentence—not because Sacco and Vanzetti were innocent but because their execution would play into the hands of radicals everywhere by making them twin martyrs. Patiently the State Department explained to Mussolini that it had no jurisdiction in the case.[15]

CONGRESS AND THE WAR DEBT DEBATES

In Congress many representatives followed the line of least repercussion and remained silent on the issue of Fascism. Even Fiorello La Guardia refrained from publicly attacking Mussolini, though privately his sympathies went out to the anti-Fascists. Congressional criticism, if it sounded at all, generally came from rural representatives with sparse Italian constituencies. In the northeast, especially in metropolitan areas like Boston and New York, pro-Fascist sentiment was as thick as Catholic and Italian populations were dense. Few congressmen could ignore this political fact of life, and during the Ethiopian War even a radical like Vito Marcantonio would have to accommodate himself to it.

[15] De Santi, p. 69; Mussolini to Fletcher, July 24, 1927, Container 13, FP.

270

One southern congressman, Milford W. Howard, saw fit to write a book on the subject. Irked by the prestige of Soviet achievements in the eyes of American liberals, Howard traveled through Italy in the mid-twenties apparently in the hope of finding an answer to Stalin's regime. What Howard discovered was edifying in more ways than he expected. Not only did Fascism seem a possible response to the materialism of Russian Communism but to the spiritual emptiness of American democracy as well. A reproach to both the crass boosters of capitalism and the starry-eyed advocates of collectivism, Fascism also affirmatively answered the question which, Howard stressed, every good pragmatist must ask: "Does it work?"[16]

But Howard spoke neither for the South nor for Congress. Indeed it was a fellow Alabama politician, Democratic Senator Thomas Heflin, who led the move in Congress to undertake an investigation of Fascist activities in the United States. Along with Senator William Borah (Rep-Ida) and Representatives Henry Rainey (Rep-Ill) and Hamilton Fish (Rep-NY), Heflin lectured Americans on the dangers of Fascism. In his Congressional speeches Heflin often drew upon letters and documents supplied by Dr. Fama, Antonini, Valenti, and other anti-Fascists. And it was Heflin's speech demanding an investigation of the FLNA that finally forced Count di Revel to dissolve the organization. For his stand against an American *fascisti*, the Sons of Italy dubbed Heflin a "destructive parasite."[17]

Aside from the occasional tongue-lashings delivered by Heflin, Rainey, Fish, Borah, and the Socialist Victor Berger, Congress rarely made reference to Mussolini during the twenties. Yet there arose one issue that did generate relatively meaningful debates on the issue of Fascism—the debt settlement with Italy. Since the war debt debates of 1926 offer the nearest thing to a forum of Congressional attitudes on Mussolini's regime, they deserve close attention.

The debates show, for one thing, that Congress was not entirely in accord with the State Department and the White House on the issue of Italian Fascism. Senator Reed Smoot (Rep-Utah), Chairman of Congress's Debt Commission, was upset when Italian Finance Minister Volpi rushed to Washington in the hope of

[16] Milford W. Howard, *Fascism: A Challenge to Democracy* (New York, 1928).

[17] *Bulletin, Italian-American National Union* (Feb., 1929).

271

persuading the Commission to give special consideration to Italy. Yet Ambassador Fletcher was convinced that generous terms were in the best interests of Italy and the United States, and Treasury Secretary Mellon advised Coolidge that a lenient settlement was essential in order to keep open America's "money market" in Rome. At the same time Kellogg made clear to the Italian government that he could be of no help in facilitating the Morgan loan unless Italy cooperated in reaching a mutual solution to the debt. Eventually the Commission arrived at terms satisfactory to all parties.[8]

The negotiations could be regarded as a diplomatic victory for both governments. Mussolini, eager to mine Wall Street's bulging vaults, was now in a position to bargain for loans. American diplomats, convinced that the United States could exercise a moderating influence on Italy's militaristic foreign policy through economic pressure, were in a position to bargain for sobriety. Thus the administration solidly supported the Commission's terms. But while the administration professed to regard the whole affair as above ideological considerations, a group of liberal deputies in the Italian parliament informed Senator Robert L. Owen that the terms extended to Italy represented "an endorsement of Fascism by the United States." Did the settlement betoken official sanction of the Mussolini regime? This question went to the heart of the Congressional debates.[19]

In the House George Crisp (Dem-Ga) introduced the administration's bill and spelled out the rationale—the lenient settlement was based solely on Italy's low capacity to pay. Presented thus, the measure was defended by S. Wallace Dempsey (Rep-NY), William Green (Rep-Iowa), Jasper Tincher (Rep-Kan), Theodore Burton (Rep-Ohio), Ogden Mills (Rep-NY), and Sol Bloom (Dem-NY).[20] Vocally opposed were Henry Rathbone (Rep-Ill), Walter Lineberger (Rep-Calif), George Huddleston (Dem-Ala), Tom Connally (Dem-Tex), John McSwain (Dem-

[18] Fletcher Diary, Jan. 1, 1926, FP; Fletcher to Coolidge, Feb. 24, 1926, Box 82; Mellon to Coolidge, Feb. 10, 1926, Box 133, CP; De Santi, p. 87.

[19] De Santi, p. 100.

[20] A vigorous supporter of Mussolini during the debates, Bloom could think of no better reason to justify his position other than citing a courteous interview Il Duce and D'Annunzio kindly granted his daughter. Another instance when the dictator's highly personalized style of politics literally paid off in America. *The Autobiography of Sol Bloom* (New York, 1948), pp. 196-98.

272

SC), Charles Abernathy (Dem-NC), William Stevenson (Dem-SC), William Upshaw (Dem-Ga); the two Farmer-Laborites, Knud Wefald and Ole Kvale, both from Minnesota; the Socialist Victor Berger from Wisconsin, and House Speaker Henry Rainey (Dem-Ill). Leading the attack, Rainey argued in the simplest terms that the repugnant character of the Italian government rendered the easy debt terms intolerable. Proponents replied that Rainey's notions about Fascism were based on hearsay and anonymous letters, that the nature of the Italian government was immaterial, and that it was improper for American statesmen to criticize foreign regimes. This last point, which drew applause, was answered by Rathbone and Lineberger, who perused American history to cite numerous examples of statesmen speaking out against foreign tyranny (e.g., Daniel Webster's defense of Greek independence). The thinness of the impropriety issue became all the more transparent when Rathbone noted that the United States refused to recognize Soviet Russia because of the nature of her government. Then Connally, sensing more truth in poetry than in history, took up the propriety argument with a flourish: "You may say that it is none of our business, but I reply, in the words of our American poet:

He's true to God who's true to man; wherever wrong is done
To the humblest and the meanest 'neath the all-beholding sun
That wrong is also done to us, and we are slaves most base,
Whose love of right is for ourselves and not for all the race.[21]

The opposition raised other issues. Blackshirt activities in the United States, for example, were cited to show that Il Duce did not hesitate to interfere in the affairs of other nations. Opponents also made explicit what the proponents tried to keep implicit: the suggestion that a rejection of the bill might mean the end of Mussolini's government. If Mussolini falls, declared Rathbone, "There is room for liberty [applause]. There will be freedom for Italy once more. . . . Italy has been self-governing and every true American ought to want her to remain such. Through this loan[22] you give our investors a stake in the perpetuation of this

---

[21] *Congressional Record*, 69th Cong., 1st Sess., II, 1975-2017, 2055-2094; Connally's statement is on p. 2073.

[22] Rathbone was referring to the Morgan loan, which appeared to be tied in with the debt settlement. In the Senate debates opponents had more time to dwell on this dubious transaction.

obnoxious tyranny. 'Where your treasure is, there will your heart be also.' "[23]

When the role call was taken, on January 15, 1926, 253 voted for and 133 against the bill. The nay vote included 113 Democrats, 17 Republicans, the two Farmer-Laborites and the one Socialist. In mid-April the measure went to the Senate where it was introduced by Reed Smoot. In general the arguments heard in the lower house were echoed in the upper. The one new issue that emerged in the Senate dialogue was the Morgan loan of $100,000,000 to the Italian government, a delicately quiet transaction which infuriated staunch opponents like James R. Reed (Dem-Mo). The completion of the Morgan loan only a week after the Commission had fixed a favorable debt figure for Italy made it appear that American bankers pushed for an easy Italian settlement solely for investment reasons. When the details of the loan were fully (if erroneously) publicized, Reed excoriated American financiers and pointed out that the high interest rates on the Italian loan merely betrayed the shaky nature of the Fascist government. Smoot and several business spokesmen denied the high interest rate and continued to defend the Morgan loan as well as the debt terms. Yet the proponents were caught in a triple bind: by maintaining that Italy warranted generous treatment lest Mussolini be toppled, they were admitting that the Fascist government was financially unsound; by arguing that Italy deserved leniency because of her low capacity to pay, they were likewise arriving at the same conclusion; and most seriously, by approving the loan and failing to criticize the alleged high interest rates they were hard put to explain why an "impoverished" Italy would be able to pay large dividends to the Morgan Company but not to the American taxpayer.

While advocates of the administration's bill became enmeshed in a web of contradictions, critics struck out at the Fascist regime itself. Reed, who termed the bill "grand larceny," minced no words as he labeled Mussolini with the complete lexicon of tyranny. Kenneth D. McKellar (Dem-Tenn) itemized a fifteen-point indictment against Il Duce that was printed in full in the *New York Herald Tribune*. This unwelcome publicity caused Ambassador De Martino to be overcome with "zeal," reported Fletcher, and he pressured the State Department to do "all sorts

[23] *Congressional Record*, pp. 2072-73.

of foolish things" to try to smother the attacks on his government. Secretary Mellon issued a statement declaring that the expressions in the Senate did not reflect the sentiment of the American people. Several papers, including the *New York Times*, also criticized the southern senators.[24]

After a week of vituperation the issue came to a vote. The roll call saw nine Republicans joining southern Democrats in opposing the bill: William Borah and Frank Gooding, Idaho; Robert Howell, Nebraska; Hiram Johnson, California; Robert La Follette and Irving Lenroot, Wisconsin; William McMaster, South Dakota; Lynn Frazier and Gerald Nye, North Dakota. Henrik Shipstead, the Farmer-Laborite from Minnesota, also opposed. The vote was 54 for and 33 against, with 4 senators paired. The 54 affirming senators included 13 Democrats.[25]

Since the bill was an administrative measure, since the Republicans had a majority, and since Hoover, Mellon, and others quietly pulled strings to assure its passage, the issue was never in doubt. Still, it is significant that opposition came from southern and mid-western congressmen and that not one eastern senator opposed the bill or spoke against Mussolini. If the debates could be regarded solely as a mirror of Congressional attitudes on Fascism, some interesting inferences might be drawn. Unfortunately the debates comprised more of a kaleidoscope, reflecting not only sentiment for and against Fascism but also strong convictions regarding international debt obligations and the dangers of Wall Street economic diplomacy, convictions which in turn reflected deeper undercurrents of isolationalism. Moreover, if southern and mid-western senators displayed a certain ideological prescience in attacking Fascism, their position was facilitated by the rural nature of their constituencies, whose anti-Catholicism and anti-Italianism made the attack politically possible as well as morally honorable. As for the proponents of the bill, with few exceptions (e.g., Sol Bloom in the House, David Reed in the Senate) they refrained from defending Mussolini against his detractors, responding instead with the impropriety argument. Few proponents, it would seem, consciously looked upon passage of the bill as an explicit "endorsement" of Mussolini.[26]

[24] Fletcher Diary, Jan. 16, 1926, FP; "The Duce and the Debt," *LD*, LXXXIX (May 1, 1926), 10-11.

[25] *Congressional Record*, III, 7902, for the Senate vote.

[26] In the course of the debates Rathbone announced: "Is there any de-

Nevertheless, despite these qualifications it cannot be denied that in Congress in 1926 one finds some of the most eloquent criticisms of Mussolini during the twenties. Compared to what one finds in the White House and State Department, the Congressional debates seem like the body politic's one twitch of anti-Fascism.

"THAT ADMIRABLE ITALIAN GENTLEMAN":
ROOSEVELT AND MUSSOLINI

Franklin Roosevelt's administration brought to Washington everything but a new attitude toward Fascist Italy. Many State Department officials remained under the lingering spell of the Italian "genius" during the early thirties. Wilbur Carr, Under-Secretary of State, believed Mussolini to be Italy's "only one first-class mind." Charles H. Sherrill, Ambassador to Turkey and author of the euology *Bismarck and Mussolini* (1931), pointed out similarities among Ataturk, Mussolini, and Roosevelt. Norman Davis, Ambassador to Great Britain, happily reported that in Roosevelt's peace and disarmament proposals the President found a most cooperative Italian Premier. This satisfying state of affairs, however, was soon darkly clouded over by Hitler's appointment as Chancellor. After 1933 American diplomats could no longer consider Fascism apart from Nazism and the dread of

fendant of Mussolini in this House today? I pause for one to rise. There is none. The facts concerning his ruthless rule have been laid bare in this debate, and they will not be denied." In all likelihood no one bothered to accept Rathbone's challenge because for the most part they agreed with Ogden Mills that the settlement with Italy was strictly a "business question" (*Congressional Record*, 69th Cong., 1st Sess., II, 1915, 2071-72). By the same token opposition behavior cannot be interpreted simply as a censure of Fascism. Rathbone and Rainey in the House and James Reed and McKellar in the Senate showed a deep concern about the dangers of Fascism, calling attention to information supplied by exiles like Salvemini and reading verbatim to fellow congressmen articles like James Murphy's "Italian Tyranny," which appeared in the *Atlantic Monthly*. Still, the nay vote included a large number of representatives who made no comment on Fascism as such but did express concern for the American taxpayer. That considerations other than Fascism should be acknowledged becomes even more clear when we observe that, within the two major parties, the few politicians anti-Fascists could consistently count upon to attack Mussolini in Congress included a western isolationist (Borah), a southern racist (Heflin), and a northern witch-hunter (Fish).

war. Now more than ever diplomatic considerations took precedence over domestic.[27]

For the first three years of Roosevelt's administration Breckinridge Long was Ambassador to Italy. Like previous American ambassadors given to first impressions, Long was seduced by the "quiet dignity" and "determined energy" of Benito Mussolini. "The magnificence of my reception at this Royal Court," he informed Roosevelt, "has been like Alice in Wonderland for a simple little Democrat from the U.S.A." These extravagant impressions led Long to praise highly Italy's domestic programs. But unlike previous ambassadors, Long was less sanguine about Mussolini's diplomatic machinations. He saw the Nazi triumph in Germany and its rise in Austria as evidence of Mussolini's influence as a "political evangelist." Because he took seriously Fascism's undying bellicosity, he remained unimpressed with Mussolini's peace gesturing in the winter of 1934. Throughout the following spring he came to see the outbreak of the Ethiopian War as almost inevitable. Roosevelt was grateful to Long for his unsettling but perceptive dispatches. "You and Dodd[28] have been far more accurate in your pessimism in the past two years than any of my other friends in Europe," Roosevelt wrote to Long in 1935. Yet when the chips were down, Long's disdain for Fascist diplomacy was not strong enough to support the administration's embargo against Italy in the Abyssinian crisis. Possibly because of his neutralist inclinations, his fear of a communized Europe,[29] or his belief that an oil boycott would be ineffective, Long opposed taking such a step to halt Fascist aggression. Before resigning in 1936 he sent Roosevelt a final letter advising recognition of the Italian occupation of Ethiopia. The United States,

[27] Katherine Crane, *Mr. Carr of State* (New York, 1960), p. 338; *Franklin D. Roosevelt: His Personal Letters 1928-1945* (New York, 1950), p. 436; De Santi, p. 211.

[28] William Dodd, Ambassador to Germany.

[29] Observing that there would inevitably be a world war from which there could emerge only one victor, Long informed Roosevelt: "I doubt if Russian education and technique is sufficient to establish itself in a dominant position. . . . I believe the German technique, determination, and character is such that it can. I shudder to think of a Russian domination of Europe. While a German domination would be hard and cruel—at least in the beginning—it would be an intensification of a culture which is more akin to ours than would be that of Russia." Long to Roosevelt, April 19, 1935, Box 10, RP.

277

suggested Long, might as well take advantage of the mid-Eastern trade opportunities previously dominated by the British.[30]

Of a different frame of mind was Long's successor, William Phillips. Like Long, Phillips desired "de jure" recognition of the Italian conquest as a means of restoring amicable relations. But unlike his predecessor, Phillips assessed Italy's foreign policy with unwarranted optimism. Accepting on face value the perfunctory and impatient reassurances of Count Ciano, he continued throughout the late thirties to inform Roosevelt that Italy had no intention of going to war or aligning with Hitler. Fascist militarism Phillips dismissed as a vital "martial spirit" that reinvigorated the will of the Italian people. Perhaps more telling was Phillips' suggestion to Roosevelt in the spring of 1941: "Could we at the same time make it clear that we have nothing against any form of government which the Italians, in their judgment, desire for their country, but rather that it is the spirit of aggression against other states to which we are fundamentally opposed? I do not think it does any good to denounce Mussolini, as Churchill does from time to time." When Phillips submitted this advice he was, of course, trying to help the State Department detach Mussolini from the Axis. Yet when the Ambassador frankly conceded that America had no quarrel with Mussolini and Fascism but merely with Italy's "spirit of aggression" he described well the cold heart of the matter.[31]

Clearly New Deal diplomats suffered few qualms about domestic Fascism in Italy. What of Roosevelt himself? According to Arthur Schlesinger, Jr., Roosevelt saw Mussolini and Stalin not as "mere distant relatives" but as "blood brothers," phrases the President himself used in a letter to the editor of *Fortune*. In writing the letter Roosevelt was merely declaring his opposition to dictatorship as a political proposition. We can hardly expect less from an American politician. Yet to liken Mussolini to Stalin

[30] Long to Roosevelt, June 1, 1933, PPF 434; Long to Roosevelt, June 27, 1933, OF 447; see Long's "Highly Confidential" analysis of Fascism, Monarchism, Nazism, the Action Française, and the like, in Long to Roosevelt, Feb. 7, 1934, Box 10, Long Folder; Roosevelt to Long, Sept. 19, 1935; Long to Roosevelt, April 19, 1935, Box 10; Long to Roosevelt, Nov. 8, 29, 1935, June 23, 1936, PPF 434 RP.

[31] Phillips to Roosevelt July 30, 1937, April 14, July 14, 1939, PC Box 10, RP; *Ciano's Diary 1937-1938*, trans. Andreas Mayor (London, 1952), esp. pp. 93, 155; Phillips to Roosevelt, April 22, 1937, May 17, 1941, PSF, Italy, Box 10, RP.

in a guilt-by-association relationship not only gets us nowhere but obfuscates the genuine regard Roosevelt had for Mussolini in the early years. In June 1933, Roosevelt wrote to Long of Mussolini: "There seems no question that he is really interested in what we are doing and I am much interested and deeply impressed by what he has accomplished and by his evidenced honest purpose of restoring Italy and seeking to prevent general European trouble." In reply to John Lawrence, another correspondent who praised Mussolini, Roosevelt remarked: "I don't mind telling you in confidence that I am keeping in fairly close touch with that admirable Italian gentleman." Roosevelt himself wrote to Mussolini, "thrilled" at having received from the Premier "those two very wonderful volumes" of Virgil and Horace. Even as late as 1939, when Mussolini had embraced the Axis, Roosevelt could still look back on Il Duce's regime with some sympathy. Roosevelt's reflections were prompted by a request from the historian Douglass Southall Freeman, who asked the President's secretary, Steve Early, if it would be possible to have Roosevelt recall his early impressions of Mussolini and Fascism. In a memo Roosevelt noted that in the beginning and up through 1932 he analyzed Fascism as a "phenomenon somewhat parallel to the Communist experiment in Russia." But it should be remembered, he continued, "that during those years Mussolini still maintained a semblance of parliamentary government, and there were many, including myself, who hoped that having restored order and morale he would, of his own accord, work toward a restoration of democratic processes." Another question that must be considered, Roosevelt added, is whether Mussolini could have survived alone had not Hitler and Nazism emerged in 1933: ". . . could [he] have put through an increasingly great absolutism . . . or would [he] have been compelled to reestablish some form of popular representation." "Doubtless during that period the development of Fascism in Italy was of great importance to the world," concluded Roosevelt, "but it was still in the experimental stage."[32]

The tolerance of a liberal President for an illiberal Premier can

[32] Roosevelt, *Personal Letters*, p. 163; Schlesinger quotes the "blood brother" remark in *The Age of Roosevelt, Vol. III: The Politics of Upheaval* (Boston, 1960), p. 648; Roosevelt, *Personal Letters*, p. 352; Roosevelt to John Lawrence, July 27, 1933, PPF 101; Roosevelt to Mussolini, May 14, 1933, PSF, Box 10; Memo, Roosevelt to Early, Jan. 10, 1939, OFF 5763, RP.

be understood in view of the diplomatic and domestic background. After the rise of Hitler, Roosevelt desired more than ever a personal conference with Mussolini on problems of peace and disarmament, and the latter's verbal cooperation in such matters enhanced the President's opinion of the Premier. With the announcement of the Four Power Pact in 1933 the diplomatic picture brightened, and Mussolini won Roosevelt's hearty congratulations for bringing about an apparent rapprochement among France, Italy, Great Britain, and Germany. At the same time both leaders found themselves fighting the severest depression in modern history. Itching to innovate, the curious Roosevelt urged Harry Hopkins to ". . . make a trip abroad as soon as you can possibly get away and look over the housing and social insurance schemes in England, Germany, Austria and Italy, because I think you might pick up some ideas useful to us in developing our own American plan for security." Curiosity got the best of at least two other New Dealers: James Farley, who had traveled in Italy in 1933, wrote Roosevelt a brief but glowing estimate of Mussolini's reclamation projects; Hugh Johnson, head of the NRA, carried a copy of Raffaello Vigone's *The Corporate State*, spoke respectfully of Fascism, and upon resigning invoked in a farewell speech what he called the "shining name" of Mussolini.[33]

This is not to suggest that Roosevelt was in any way influenced by Mussolini or that the New Deal was a bastard of the Corporate State, a polemic hurled by both the Left and Right in the thirties.[34] What it does suggest is that the common do-

---

[33] De Santi, pp. 211-15; Roosevelt's advice to Hopkins is quoted in Daniel Boorstin, *America and the Image of Europe* (Cleveland, 1960), p. 33; Farley to Roosevelt, Dec. 8, 1933, OPF 309, RP; for Johnson's curiosity about corporatism, see Frances Perkins, *The Roosevelt I Knew* (New York, 1946), p. 206, and Schlesinger, *The Age of Roosevelt, Vol. II: The Coming of the New Deal* (Boston, 1959), pp. 153-54.

[34] Hugh Johnson notwithstanding, the published writings of the Brain Trusters reveal no evidence of the influence of Italian Fascism upon the New Deal. Even Rexford Tugwell, who more than any other adviser advocated disciplined national planning, never suggested that the Italian method be adopted in the United States—although a remark he made in a speech in Rome regarding the need for "an orderly mode of procedure" was wrenched out of context and misconstrued as an endorsement of Fascism. *International Problems of Agriculture* (International Institute of Agriculture, Rome, 1935), pp. 17-26.

The Roosevelt administration, moreover, was sensitive to the charge. Ambassador Long discovered in 1934 that Colonel Knox of the *Chicago Daily*

mestic challenges facing the two statesmen led the American President to regard the Premier as something of a comrade in crisis. Both governments, for example, used the analogue of war in the rhetoric of reconstruction: the Corporate State called for a "Battle of the Grain," the New Deal for a "War on Want." Moreover, Mussolini was as curious about the New Deal as Roosevelt was about the Corporate State. Il Duce had read Roosevelt's *Looking Forward* (1933) and was moved to write a critique. Convinced that Roosevelt had repudiated the liberalism of the Manchester School, Mussolini called the New Deal "boldly . . . interventionist in the field of economics." But he was not sure whether Roosevelt interpreted the crisis as "in" the system or "of" the system, whether the depression exposed a temporary malady or a malignant rot in the capitalist order. "Many persons in America and Europe have wondered how much 'fascism' there may be in the doctrines and practices of the American President," observed the Premier. Roosevelt's insistence that all factors of production collaborate toward a common good was a far-reaching ideological innovation "which might recall the bases of fascist Corporatism." Yet Roosevelt refused to go to the root of the problem and solve it by adopting such measures as "the juridicial recognition of associations of workers and employers, the prohibition of strikes and lockouts, the labor courts, and lastly, the national corporations." Thus only in the theoretical "atmosphere" of the two systems could one find parallels. Beyond that, concluded Mussolini, "It would be an exaggeration to say anything more."[35]

In the estimation of the Italian master, the improvising and reluctant Roosevelt scarcely qualified as a genuine corporatist. But more seriously, the two leaders never really understood one another. Mussolini, it will be recalled, believed Roosevelt a "dic-

---

News had come to Rome to collect "ammunition" on the "alleged failure" of Fascism to be used in syndicated newspapers as an argument against the NRA. Long believed that former Ambassador Child had been hired for the assignment. Informed of this tactic, Roosevelt asked Cordell Hull to arrange a personal conference with Knox. The meeting was scheduled, but whether it was held has not been recorded in Roosevelt's papers. Long to Roosevelt, May 23, 1934, Box 10; Memo, Secretary of State to Roosevelt, May 24, 1934, OF 447, RP.

[35] Benito Mussolini, "Roosevelt e il Sistema," *Bolletino del R. Ministero degli Affari Esteri*, XL (Luglio, 1933), 715-17, in PPF 432, RP.

tator" with infinite power; and just as Il Duce could not grasp the idea of limited authority, Roosevelt was baffled by the idea of unlimited despotism. According to Frances Perkins, Roosevelt "never could understand or comprehend the dictators. He used to laugh, as I did too, at the dire predictions that he would make himself a dictator. He was totally incapable of comprehending what a dictator is, how he operates, how he thinks, how he gets anything done. A man like Mussolini was a puzzle to him, Hitler worse than a puzzle."[36]

But aside from his vague impressions of Mussolini's "experiment," Roosevelt confronted a more immediate matter: the Italian-American community. The President and his party could never afford to forget that Italian dictricts wildly supported Mussolini and that the "Roosevelt coalition" drew heavily upon the urban Italian vote. In New York especially Roosevelt had the backing of the Italian press. Generoso Pope, the pro-Fascist publisher and Tammany politician who wielded influence in the administration, made this plain to the President. As Chairman of the Italian Division of the Democratic National Committee, Pope continually reminded Roosevelt of his power in the Italian community. "My newspaper will spare no effort to give their readers all the information in news and editorials in English and in Italian in your behalf," Pope informed Roosevelt. "*Il Progresso* and *Corriere d'America* will conduct an intensive campaign and they are at your disposal." Given the relationship between the administration and predominant Italian press, one can surmise that even if Roosevelt harbored private doubts about Mussolini he would not risk alienating Italian-Americans with a slip of conscience.[37]

Despite differences between the Harding-Coolidge-Hoover administrations on the one hand and the Roosevelt administration on the other, Italian diplomacy was characterized more by continuity than by change. In general, and with some variation in emphasis, both the Republican and the Democratic administrations accepted these assumptions: that Mussolini was generating economic and social progress; that although a dictator he enjoyed the overwhelming support of the people; that with the rise of Nazism he would prove a moderating foil to Hitler; and that despite his quixotic temperament he was good for Italy and

[36] Perkins, p. 156.

[37] Pope to Roosevelt, Sept. 1, 1936, OF 233A, RP.

good for the United States. Doubtless these assumptions contain a modicum of truth, but beginning with the Ethiopian War they collapsed one by one. The real rub, however, is not that history proved these attitudes wrong but that they were based on so shallow an understanding of Fascism in the first place. Roosevelt's hope that Mussolini would restore "democratic processes," for example, betrayed a complete ignorance of Il Duce's scorn for liberal democracy. Similarly, the general belief so prevalent in the State Department under Coolidge and Hoover that Mussolini had exterminated Bolshevism and was rapidly advancing Italy economically appears, in the light of Italy's subsequent economic troubles and the upsurge of Communist strength after the fall of Fascism, only to compound ignorance with illusion.

But dispelling the illusions of the past is the luxury of the historian, not the statesman. In fairness we must ask whether any real diplomatic options were possible in the conduct of America's Italian diplomacy. The reality is that the United States could have done little to affect the course of Fascism in Italy. To have denied recognition of Mussolini's regime (even if technically possible) or to have thrown up an economic boycott could hardly be considered, not only because of public opinion but simply because such policies most likely would have strengthened rather than weakened the dictatorship, as was the case during the Ethiopian War.

In the end, however, to acknowledge the limits of what could have been done does not dismiss the problem of what should have been thought. And here the irony is that the attitude of the American government was not so much "reactionary" as "progressive." Most public officials sincerely believed that an Italy under Mussolini would improve economically and that, once the pace of modernization increased, political liberalization would eventually follow. This concept of democracy through industrial progress has been one of America's most cherished assumptions; applied internationally, it has been one of America's most vulnerable illusions. For the doctrine of political salvation by economic growth evolves from America's own national experience, and therein lies its limitation. The lesson of Fascism for American diplomacy is basically this: If there is one historical experience rarer than a Right-wing dictatorship achieving genuine social progress, it is a Right-wing dictatorship transforming itself into a genuine democracy.

Part Three

FASCISM AT WAR

12.

The Ethiopian War

I NOT ONLY DO NOT BELIEVE
IN PERPETUAL PEACE, BUT
I CONSIDER IT DEPRESSING AND
A NEGATION OF THE FUNDA-
MENTAL VIRTUES OF MAN,
WHO ONLY IN THAT CRUEL
STRUGGLE REVEALS HIMSELF IN
THE FULL LIGHT OF THE SUN.

Mussolini, 1934

WAR IS THE HEALTH OF THE
STATE.

Randolph Bourne, 1918

ITALIAN EXPANSIONISM AND AMERICAN SANCTIONS

During 1934, perhaps the apogee of Mussolini's world fame, a Cole Porter hit tune featured the line, "You're the tops—— you're Musso——li——ni." By the following year, when the popular number was being sung by Americans young and old, all references to Mussolini had been deleted. The time for lyrical salutes was over; the Ethiopian War had begun.

The complex diplomatic background of the Ethiopian War need not detain us. What is relevant in ascertaining America's changing attitudes toward Fascism is the public's response to Italy's expansion into North Africa prior to the outbreak of war. We can begin with a simple question: Could Italian expansion be justified?

American attitudes had been slow to crystallize. The overt penetration of Ethiopia in 1934 had perhaps won more approval than criticism. Certainly no surge of anti-expansionist sentiment had materialized. The Right-wing press, spearheaded by the *Chicago Tribune*, actually defended Mussolini's African imperialism on the grounds of "commercial, evangelical, scientific, and humanitarian purposes." At the same time, some Americans believed, as a *Boston Evening Transcript* writer put it, that Western colonial nations could hardly say to Italy: "Yes, we did, but you musn't." Other writers, seeking to expiate their Wilsonian past, viewed Italian expansion as a legitimate reversal of the Versailles settlement. Then, too, many Americans saw Italian expansion as the result of sheer desperation, an interpretation shared by both pro and anti-Fascist writers. Carrying economic determinism to its logical conclusion, the *New Republic* argued that, since capitalist expansion is "the primary impulse toward conquest," and since Fascism is only "one of the latest disguises of capitalism," it would be "naive to place the blame on the personal wickedness of the fascist dictators in Germany and Italy."[1]

The point is that while the American Right justified Italian colonialism, while the liberal Center looked on with a troubled conscience, and while the Left saw the thrust into Africa as economically inevitable, neither constructive colonialism, Versailles revisionism, nor Leninist imperialism completely explain Italy's behavior. Ethiopia, with its unfertile soil and fertile boa constrictors, was neither the long-sought dream of colonial capitalism nor the culmination of the frustrations of 1919, a surrogate irredentism arising historically from Italy's rivalries in the Balkans and the Aegean. Yet while many Americans were willing to explain away Italy's peaceful economic penetration of Africa, they were also prepared to condemn Italy's aggressive military activities. As tension mounted through the spring and summer of 1935, American sympathy went out to Haile Selassie and his pathetic, ragged army. Selassie's appeals to Washington, although made when public attention seemed almost transfixed by the Lindbergh kidnapping trial, received widespread sympathy in the press. In contrast, many newspapers ascribed the basest motives to Il Duce, some even suggesting he manufac-

---

[1] *Chicago Daily Tribune*, Oct. 4, 1934; *Boston Evening Transcript*, Oct. 4, 1934; Chester P. Higby, "Aspiring Italy," American Academy of Political and Social Science, *Annals*, CLXXV (Sept. 1934), 44-50; *NYT*, Feb. 4, Oct. 13, 20, 1935; "Italy's Economic Crisis," *New Republic*, LXXXIII (Aug. 7, 1935), 347-49; "Ethiopia: Lesson in War," *ibid.* (July 17, 1935), pp. 264-66. Economic determinism dies hard among Left-wing intellectuals who witnessed the events of 1935. Almost thirty years after the Ethiopian War E. H. Carr felt it necessary to ridicule Arnold Toynbee, who in 1935 described Mussolini's invasion as a "deliberate personal sin." *What Is History?* (New York, 1961), p. 98.

tured the crisis to divert internal pressures. When war broke out, in October 1935, even the *Chicago Tribune*, which had defended Italy's imperialism in Africa, denounced outright war itself as a species of "scalp collecting" born of Mussolini's egotism.[2]

Angry demonstrations now erupted in American cities: in San Francisco police had to disperse crowds outside the Italian consulate; in Chicago three hundred demonstrators were arrested; and in Brooklyn the inevitable "Fair Play for Ethiopia" committee was organized. Although Italians were led to believe, thanks to Italy's controlled press, that Americans looked on sympathetically because of their own experience with the "semibarbarism" and "incurable immaturity" of American Negroes, Italian statesmen knew better. American public opinion, Count Ciano commented privately, "is dead against us in the Abyssinian question." "Our worst opposition comes not from the Harlem Negroes," Mussolini admitted, "but from many genuine white men in Europe and America." Acutely aware its stock had fallen in America, the Fascist government sought to create a new image.[3]

The plan called for sending a "Mission" to the United States headed by Commendatore Bernardo Bergamaschi of the Ministry of Press and Propaganda. Bergamaschi's report, among the documents captured during World War II, was an exercise in self-delusion. He maintained that the sources of America's unexpected hostility sprang from British propaganda, nativist Protestantism, the Communist-influenced Negro population, and the Jews and their "preconceived hostility" toward Fascism and Nazism. Yet even though Bergamaschi conceded that the great majority of newspapers and the British-dominated Roosevelt administration were against Italy, he believed it still possible to win over or at least neutralize American opinion. The major factor in Italy's favor, Bergamaschi reported, was the rising isolationism in Congress and in the press, particularly the Hearst

[2] "Current Opinion on the Italian-Ethiopian Imbroglio," *LD*, cxix (May 25, 1935), 13; "Ethiopia's Appeal to the United States," *LD*, cxx (July 13, 1935), 7; editorial excerpts of various dailies were carried in the *NYT*, June 30, July 7, Aug. 11, 18, Sept. 22, Oct. 13, 20, 29, 1935; *Chicago Daily Tribune*, Dec. 12, 1935.

[3] *NYT* Sept. 1, 21, Oct. 4, 5, 31, 1935; Ciano and Mussolini are quoted in Brice Harris, *The United States and the Italo-Ethiopian Crisis* (Stanford, 1964), pp. 44, 46, 51.

papers. Outlining in detail the tactics for a new propaganda offensive, Bergamaschi not only suggested radio stations, newsreel outlets, and the coordination of all Italian-American societies, but he also hired the services of the Wendell P. Colton Company, a New York public relations firm. In a prospectus, "A Plan for Promoting Favorable Opinion for Italy in America," the Colton Company recommended depicting the Ethiopian campaign as benign colonialism, playing up American tourism in Italy, making use of motion pictures, and unifying all publicity and propaganda agencies. The estimated expense of both Bergamaschi's and Colton's proposals came to $325,000.[4]

The elaborate plan was a fool's paradise based on absurd assumptions about the nature of American opinion during the war. Nevertheless, the Rome government probably thought the effort necessary since Italian-American diplomatic relations had become so strained during the crisis. Indeed despite the rising tide of isolationist sentiment and Congress's passage of the Neutrality Laws of 1935, within administration circles feelings against Italy grew increasingly partisan and bitter. "I have not met anyone whose sympathy in this situation is not with Ethiopia," Interior Secretary Ickes recorded in his diary after a cabinet meeting, "and I suspect that . . . the whole civilized world has the same point of view." Roosevelt himself, according to Harry Hopkins, "scanned the news dispatches and everything favorable to Ethiopia brought a loud 'good.' "[5]

The war sorely tried America's and Roosevelt's patience with the once "admirable" Italian Premier. When hostilities first broke out Secretary Cordell Hull issued a "moral embargo" which was directed mainly against Italy and which had the overwhelming support of the American public. And when the League moved to impose economic sanctions on Italy the administration, despite possible adverse isolationist sentiment in Congress, hoped to cooperate independently. Finally Roosevelt himself, realizing Il Duce's ego needed assuaging, appealed privately to the dictator to take the "magnificent position" of calling off military activity and submitting to arbitration. His plea ignored, Roosevelt went before Congress, in January 1936, and delivered

[4] "Report of the Bergamaschi Mission," 433, IR.
[5] De Santi, pp. 214-16; Ickes, *Secret Diary*, I, 446; Robert Sherwood, *Roosevelt and Hopkins* (New York, 1950), I, 97.

his first unequivocal indictment of Fascism's "twin spirits of autocracy and aggression."[6]

Since gasoline was the lifetime of the Italian army in Africa, oil was the key to effective sanctions. In an "authoritative definition" of the problem, *World Petroleum* revealed that Italy was counting on the United States, which had no obligations to the League, not to support sanctions. Ambassador Long also opposed sanctions, convinced that Italy's war spirit made Mussolini's decision to invade "irrevocable." But Roosevelt, aware that voluntary sanctions were crucial to the League's effort, ignored Long's advice and persuaded shippers to restrict their trade with Italy. Public opinion favored the policy of moral suasion, if not as a punitive measure against Italy at least as an effort to isolate the U.S. from the imbroglio.[7]

But the administration could offer the Abyssinians and the anti-Fascists only the sympathy of the spectator. Although large oil firms cooperated with Roosevelt, smaller companies seized the chance to expand operations in the Mediterranean. The strategy of sanctions was further complicated by the startling revelation, in December 1935, of the Hoare-Laval plan for the partial dismemberment of Ethiopia. This secret plan, whose appeasement rationale ominously foreshadowed the Munich mentality, caused an intense but mixed response in the United States: the liberal press denounced it as the return of the "old discredited spoils diplomacy," but isolationists like Senators Borah and Vandenberg believed it confirmed their suspicions about European statecraft, while scholarly journalists like Lippmann and Allen Nevins could even justify the plan as the only way to prevent war and to keep Mussolini out of Hitler's orbit. Thus public opinion in the United States, like that in the rest of Europe, was scarcely committed to a rigorous enforcement of

[6] Robert Divine, *The Illusion of Neutrality* (Chicago, 1962), pp. 124-30; Memo, Hull to Roosevelt, Aug. 19, 1935, PSF Box 10, RP; Harris, pp. 116-17.

[7] "Mediterranean Fleets and Italian Oil," *LD*, cxxi (Jan. 18, 1936), 13-14; William Lingelbach, "Italy in the Grips of Sanctions," *Current History*, xliii (Jan. 1936), 395-97; Long to Roosevelt, Nov. 29, 1935, PSF Box 10, RP. William Dodd, Ambassador to Berlin, also believed Mussolini could not turn back the invasion without risk of being overthrown. Dodd to Roosevelt, May 9, 1935, PSF Box 6, RP; Divine, pp. 122-30; Herbert Feis, *Seen from E.A.* (New York, 1947), pp. 304-07.

sanctions. Unfortunately Americans would never know how effective an oil boycott might have been. Later Mussolini told Hitler that "if the League of Nations had followed Eden's advice in the Italo-Ethiopian dispute and had extended economic sanctions to oil, I would have had to withdraw from Abyssinia in a week." At the time, however, Mussolini piously informed the *Chicago Daily News* that if war broke out as a result of sanctions it would be the youth of the world who would suffer. While the American liberal press was willing to call Mussolini's bluff, convinced that sanctions would not only curb aggression but undermine his regime, American correspondents in Rome were impressed by Il Duce's determination to hold out against world opinion. In the end the Ethiopian War caused American opinion of Italy to decline considerably, even to the point where Americans declared themselves in a poll to be "less friendly" to Italy than to the Soviet Union. Nevertheless, the isolationist and anti-war character of American opinion was such that America could easily remain on good terms with Mussolini and Fascism if only Italy could remain on good terms with the world.[8]

[8] "Peace Bombshell Over Europe," *LD*, cxx (Dec. 28, 1935), 9-10; "A World Opinion Exists," *Nation*, cxlii (Jan. 1, 1935), 7; *NYT*, Dec. 12, 1935; *St. Louis Post Dispatch*, Dec. 12, 1935; *San Francisco Chronicle*, Dec. 12, 1935; *Boston Evening Transcript*, Dec. 9, 11, 1935; Lippmann's column was carried in, among other papers, the *New Orleans Times-Picayune*, Dec. 17, 1935; Allan Nevins, "The Hoare-Laval Mystery," *Current History*, xliii (Feb. 1936), 502-07; Mussolini is quoted in Harris, p. 103; "Italy's Fight Against Sanctions," *LD*, cxxi (Feb. 15, 1936), 13-14; Maxwell Stewart, "Can Italy Avert Bankruptcy?" *Nation*, cxli (Oct. 23, 1935), 457-58; Sylvia Saunders, "What Sanctions Have Meant to Italy," *New Republic*, lxxxv (Jan. 22, 1936), 300-02; William Lingelbach, "Italy Defies Sanctions," *Current History*, xliii (Feb. 1936), 509-11; "The Meaning of Sanctions," *New Republic*, lxxxv (Nov. 27, 1935), 59-60; *NYT*, Dec. 8, 1935, May 17, July 12, 1936.

George Gallup stated that American sentiment was definitely with the underdog Ethiopia but that seven persons in every ten were opposed to the idea of joining with the League of Nations in imposing sanctions. *NYT*, April 30, 1939. Also revealing was a poll taken by Elmo Roper. The questions (asked in the fall of 1935) and the answers are as follows:

What foreign country do you feel least friendly toward?
What foreign country do you feel most friendly toward?

	Least Friendly	Most Friendly
Germany	17.3%	4.4%
Japan	11.2	.1

(*Continued*)

AMERICAN CORRESPONDENTS IN ETHIOPIA

The Ethiopian War was to be the showplace for Mussolini's military machine and the proving grounds for the Italian race. Exploiting his quick victories over the hapless Abyssinians, Mussolini announced to the world that the warrior qualities of the Italian character, resurrected by the discipline of Fascism, had surmounted the moment of truth (later he lamented that only 1,537 Italians had been killed, too easy a victory to stiffen his countrymen's mettle). At first even Western observers were impressed. Ambassador Long informed Roosevelt that "the efficiency of the army has been increased enormously till it is not recognizable as the same military organization, and the whole civil and military elements of the population are moving as pieces of a single organism, spurred on by the thought that failure means utter collapse and that they must succeed." Fortunately for public opinion, American correspondents took a dimmer view of the campaign.[9]

American journalists found the Ethiopian War a disappointment and a bore. Expecting Selassie to make short shrift of the Italian invaders, as his ancestors had done in 1896, correspondents like Laurence Stallings and Floyd Gibbons rushed to Africa in hope of covering a colorful desert campaign and perhaps even discovering another T. E. Lawrence. But when clashes between native tribesmen and armored half-tracks failed to materialize, some journalists "manufactured" battle stories mainly to "produce something" even though, as one writer confessed, "no fighting worthy of the name" had taken place nine weeks after the war began. As the more experienced correspondents soon realized, such "lurid stories of sanguinary encounters" did enormous damage to the Abyssinian cause by

(Continued)	Least Friendly	Most Friendly
Italy	6.7	1.2
Russia	5.8	.8
France	4.5	4.7
England	1.2	28.6
China	.7	.5
Finland	.1	2.3

Geographically, the southwestern United States had the highest dislike for Italy (13.4 percent). *Fortune*, XII (Oct. 1935), 170-73.

[9] Denis Mack Smith, *Italy*, p. 451; Long to Roosevelt, Sept. 6, 1935, PSF Box 10, RP.

leading world opinion to believe, until it was too late, that the natives were bravely holding off the enemy. "I believe that journalism, on the whole," Herbert Matthews later reflected, "failed its public in the African campaign." Yet if journalists sympathized too much with the underdog and thereby misled world opinion about the outcome of the war, the American public itself was eager to believe whatever enhanced Ethiopia's image. By the same inclination, Americans could not believe the "atrocity stories" the Italian government told about Ethiopia. When summoned to appear before the League of Nations, Italian officials brought many documents purporting to display to the world Ethiopia's treatment of prisoners, persecution of slaves, and other so-called crimes against civilization. A study of this affair showed that the alleged atrocities reported by Italy "created not the slightest ripple in a country where German atrocities had been so gullibly devoured two decades earlier."[10]

One writer America could count on to be in the thick of the action was Ernest Hemingway. Characteristically, he described the "ornithological aspects" of the war, how desert vultures devoured dead soldiers and how the wounded were advised to roll on their faces so the buzzards could not pluck their eyes. Hemingway's renewed attack on Fascism was both personal and philosophical; personal because Mussolini fell far short of Hemingway's stoical code; philosophical, because by the mid-thirties the novelist had come to see Fascism as a form of "mechanized doom." In *Green Hills of Africa* he had depicted the alien intrusion of the machine upon organic nature; in 1935 the technological symbolism shifts from the hunter's truck to the Italian tank and airplane. Thus almost instinctively Hemingway sided with the African natives who were close to the earth and to nature's animals; yet his instincts did not preclude sympathy for the misled Italian soldiers. The war itself, he wrote, was a result of Italy's bankruptcy, arranged behind the scenes by "criminals and swine" who exhaled the vapor of patriotism so that the

[10] " 'Birnam Wood' for Ethiopia," *LD*, cxxi (March 28, 1936), 13-14; Herbert Matthews, *Eyewitness in Abyssinia* (London, 1937), pp. 16, 61-62; P.L.B., "The War in Ethiopia," *Current History*, xliii (Jan. 1936), 398; " 'Birnam Wood,' " p. 13; Wayne D. Hubbard, "What Reporting in Ethiopia Has Been Like," *Harper's*, clxxii (May, 1936), 700-09; F. O. Wilcox, "Use of Atrocity Stories in the Ethiopian War," *American Political Science Review*, xxxiv (Dec. 1940), 1168-1178.

masses would be slaughtered while Il Duce made Ethiopia "fit for Fiats." "Mussolini's sons," Hemingway warned, "are in the air where there are no enemy planes to shoot them down. But poor men's sons all over Italy are foot soldiers, as poor men's sons all over the world are always foot soldiers. And me, I wish the foot soldiers luck; but I wish they could learn who is their enemy—and why."[11]

Hemingway's choice of the airplane as the symbol of impersonalized terror was more than a literary coincidence. For if there was one event that shocked the American conscience it was the sadistic dive bombing raids carried out by Vittorio Mussolini. This "magnificent sport" he practiced not only on the enemy but on a British Red Cross unit. His own ecstatic description was widely publicized by the international press: ". . . one group of horsemen gave me the impression of a budding rose unfolding as the bomb fell in their midst and blew them up." Horrified, Americans of that generation were never quite able to forget this aeronautical barbarism even though they might forget the mustard gas and dum-dum bullets.[12]

AMERICAN SOCIETY AND WAR FASCISM, I

Watching in dismay in 1936 as American opinion rose against Mussolini, the Italian Embassy in Washington noted that the "hostility" and "uncomprehension" in America was greater even after the Neutrality Laws assured that the United States would not be drawn into the war. Since isolationism could not account for America's turn of mind, Italian officials were frankly perplexed, and with good reason. For over a decade America had admired Fascism for its industrial virtues and patriotic pieties. But now that Italy pitted all the strength of its modernized

[11] Allen Guttmann, *The Wound in the Heart: America and the Spanish Civil War* (New York, 1962), pp. 167-75; Ernest Hemingway, "Wings Always Over Africa," *Esquire*, v (Jan. 1936), 31, 174-75; "Notes on the Next War," *ibid.*, IV (Sept. 1936), 19, 156.

[12] Thirty years later, when an American Naval pilot flying sorties over North Vietnam told reporters, "It's like playing golf, the more you bomb the better you become," the *San Francisco Chronicle* angrily responded (April 13, 1965): "We have problems enough in Vietnam without becoming identified with the Mussolini tradition."

Vittorio Mussolini is quoted in Fermi, p. 325; on Dec. 6, 1935, the *Boston Evening Transcript* headlined a story of the Fascist bombing of an American hospital in Ethiopia.

technology and fervent nationalism against the primitive tribes of Africa, America reacted with condemnation. How was America's "betrayal" of Fascism to be explained?[13]

For the ardent Blackshirts in Italy there was no contradiction between domestic Fascism and the conquest of Africa. Had not Mussolini himself said "Though words are beautiful things, rifles, machine guns, planes and cannon are still more beautiful," and that "War is to man as maternity is to women"? To Americans, however, the martial spirit of Fascism had usually been obscured by the glitter of its proclaimed economic achievements and by Mussolini's imposing presence. Thus when the ugly side of Fascism revealed itself in Ethiopia, America reacted with the outrage of innocence. Yet in many instances America's angry response was not provoked by Fascism as much as it was by War Fascism. The distinction is an important one, and perhaps it can best be illustrated by surveying briefly the response of certain sectors of American society.

We can begin with liberals—who in the 1930s embraced much of the Left as well as the Center. Briefly, the liberal press suggested everything short of intervention to oppose Fascist aggression. Even pacifist Oswald Villard demanded a boycott of Italy's economy and nonrecognition of her conquest. Other liberals called upon the State Department to halt loans, and John T. Flynn, with his characteristic conspiratorial view of politics, blew the whistle on American bankers and Italian financiers for allegedly instigating the imperialistic venture. But despite Flynn's shrill charges, the Ethiopian War complicated the liberals' progressive-Marxist interpretation of Fascism.[14] The *New Republic*'s readers were told, in a letter ("Mussolini's Megalomania") smuggled out of Rome, that the main reason for the war was neither land hunger nor internal unrest but the "unsettling effect that extreme nationalism and limitless power have upon the sanity and sense of balance of a dictator." Similarly Louis Fischer, after interviewing Edmondo Rossoni, informed the *Nation*'s readers that the *fascisti*'s idolization of war sprang from a messianic nationalism that would grow more insatiable with every conquest. Seemingly it followed that if economic motives alone failed to account for Italy's behavior, then economic pres-

[13] Harris, p. 139.

[14] For a fuller discussion of the liberal interpretation of Fascism in the thirties, see below, pp. 460-74.

296

sure itself would be insufficient to halt Fascist aggression. Not until the late thirties, however, did such an inference begin to appear in the liberal interpretation of Fascism.[15]

The leadership of organized labor, if not every rank-and-file worker, also condemned both Fascism and the war in Africa. Not only Leftist leaders like Antonini, Dubinsky, and Hillman, but even conservatives like Matthew Woll and William Green struck out angrily at the Italian invasion. What is more, labor supported Roosevelt's warning against trading with Italy, and throughout 1935 there were rumors of a seaman's and longshoreman's strike. Workers who refused to load cargoes or man ships carrying supplies to Italy had the full support of Labor Secretary Frances Perkins. Although no nationwide boycott materialized, in several ports workers picketed docks where cargo was being loaded for Italy.[16]

Whereas liberals, labor, and the Left equated Fascism with war and condemned both, American business criticized mainly the chaos of war itself. "Abyssinia for the Italians," declared a *Business Week* editorial in February 1935 (stating candidly that Italy should have the privilege of "exploiting" the last area of Africa unpossessed by Europe). "What Italy Wants," another editorial announced, is merely the raw materials essential for her economic growth. *Forbes*, unlike *Business Week*, did not endorse Italian expansion, but neither could it bring itself to believe that Mussolini would be so rash as to push beyond the brink. When hostilities did break out, *Forbes* remained convinced Il Duce would "come to his senses." *Nation's Business* chided a *New York Times'* headline ("Mussolini Faces Ruin if He Yields in African Dispute"), maintaining that not profits but overwhelming political ambition explained the dictator's invasion. *Barron's*, certain that Mussolini was nearing the end of his rope, believed he would be succeeded by another "strong man" who

[15] "Terrifyingly Unchartered Paths," *Nation*, CXLI (Sept. 25, 1935), 343; "Can America Remain Unentangled?" *ibid.*, CXLI (Oct. 16, 1935), 425; "Mussolini's Conquest Must Not Be Recognized," *ibid.*, CXLII (June 3, 1936), 698-99; "Little War or Big One?" *New Republic* LXXXIV (Oct. 16, 1935), 256-57; John T. Flynn, "What of Mussolini's Finances?" *ibid*, LXXXIII (Aug. 7, 1935), 362; "Mussolini's Megalomania," *ibid.*, LXXXV (Nov. 20, 1935), 41-43; Louis Fischer, "Why Mussolini Went to War," *Nation*, CXLII (Jan. 15, 1936), 67-69.

[16] *NYT*, Sept. 2, Nov. 19, 26, 27, Dec. 18, 19, 1935; Helen Hiett, *Public Opinion and the Italo-Ethiopian Dispute* (Geneva, 1936), pp. 18-19.

would withdraw Italy from the war on the condition of receiving a foreign loan. *Fortune*, offering its readers graphic illustrations of the North African terrain and maps on Ethiopia, remained curiously neutral on the war itself. On the other hand, the *Commercial and Financial Chronicle* declared that Italy had no "moral right to so much as a square foot of the present Ethiopian territory," and when the editors got word of the Hoare-Laval plan they disgustedly termed it "shocking to the moral sense." Yet the *Commercial and Financial Chronicle* was almost alone in its anti-Italian utterances. More typical of business opinion was the *Magazine of Wall Street*: "Madman or colossal bluffer, Mussolini brings the world to the edge of war." It was, in short, a nervous concern about international instability and world war rather than the moral issue of Italian aggression that characterized much of the business commentary.[17]

Similar apprehensions about War Fascism characterized the activities of Wall Street. American businessmen were approached by Italian officials for loans in the summer of 1935. To those Americans who recalled their country's alleged economic involvements in World War I and who were following in the press the Nye Committee investigations, the Italian overture had all the earmarks of a "merchants of death" plot. Hence the ever-watchful John T. Flynn demanded that the State Department make public any loans to Italy. When rumors spread through the press that the Italian government was making contacts up and down Wall Street, New York investors immediately denied they intended to negotiate with either the government of Italy or its representatives. The Roosevelt administration, moreover, expressed criticism of any loans for Italy, and the government-controlled Export-Import Bank announced that no credits would be extended to belligerents. The refusal of America to invest in Italy during the war incensed the Italian-American community. Dr. Bruno Rovere, President of the Bank of Sicily Trust Company, criticized American newspapers for undermining faith in Italy's economy, and the financier Luigi Criscuolo attacked the

[17] *Business Week* (Feb. 23, 1935), 24; (Aug. 10, 1935), 31; (Oct. 5, 1935), 7; (July 11, 1936), 52. *Forbes*, xxxvi (Oct. 1, 1935), 4; (Nov. 1, 1935), 4; (Nov. 15, 1935), 4. *Nation's Business*, xxiii (Sept. 1935), 35; *Fortune*, xii (Nov. 1935), 82-90; *Barron's* xvi (Jan. 20, 1936), 18; *Commercial and Financial Chronicle*, cxli (Oct. 1935), 2163-65, 3750-51; *Magazine of Wall Street*, lvi (Sept. 18, 1935), 573.

State Department for allowing itself to be "bulldozed" into economic neutrality by isolationists and pacifists. From North Africa General Graziani himself complained about Henry Ford the "private sanctionist," remarking that had not the American industrialist cancelled a prepaid order by the Italian government for 800 motor cars, the Italian army would have been well down the road to Addis Ababa.[18]

In the fall of 1936, Italian officials made another attempt to obtain a loan in the United States. The new Italian Ambassador, Fulvio Suvich, arrived in New York where he was welcomed by Myron C. Taylor, Chairman of United States Steel. At a Waldorf-Astoria dinner Taylor assured the Ambassador that the whole world admired Mussolini's success in "disciplining a nation" and in taking responsibility as the "guardian and administrator of an alien and backward nation of 10,000 souls." At the same time Italy proposed to renew payment on the twenty-year-old World War I debt, a step probably taken in order to circumvent the Johnson Debt Default Act, which prohibited private loans to countries having outstanding obligations to the United States government. Although Italy desperately needed American money to develop the newly acquired Ethiopia, and although Suvich would be introduced to influential financiers, it is doubtful that anything came of Italy's probes. Most likely Suvich's attempt to approach American capital was thwarted when Italy actively intervened in the Spanish Civil War a few months later, thereby becoming a "belligerent" and subject to the strictures of the Neutrality Laws. In any case, Mussolini no longer found the American businessman, as he had in the 1920s, a soft touch.[19]

With respect to religious groups, the position of the Vatican was crucial for American Catholics. During the summer of 1935 Pope Pius XI condemned, in obvious reference to the impending Italian invasion, a "war of conquest"; but the official Vatican newspaper, *Osservatore Romano,* vitiated any possibility of

[18] Flynn, "What of Mussolini's Finances?" p. 362; *NYT,* July 14, 17, 26, Aug. 23, Oct. 4, 1935; Divine, p. 129; *St. Louis Post Dispatch,* Dec. 16, 1935. Actually some American money was on the side of Ethiopia in the form of a petroleum concession granted to a subsidiary of the Standard Vacuum Oil Company. Shrewdly extended by the insecure Selassie in order to involve American interests in Ethiopia, the concession was cancelled at the request of the State Department. George W. Baer, *The Coming of the Italo-Ethiopian War* (Cambridge, 1967), pp. 295-98.

[19] *NYT,* Nov. 6, 1936.

meaningful opposition by publishing an article in favor of coloni-
zation. Meanwhile Italian bishops and lower clerics gave their
blessing to the crusade—newsreels showed priests waving benedictions and sprinkling tanks with holy water. Once the shooting
began, the Pope expressed deep concern that the conflict might
spread through Europe, yet he uttered no condemnation of the
war in Ethiopia itself. The Vatican's ambiguous position would
be, tragically enough, the first of several diplomatic instances
when Catholics looked to Rome for spiritual guidance and
found only silence.[20]

Left without counsel, Catholic opinion in America was divided on the war. In a few scattered editorial remarks, *Commonweal* decried the helpless League of Nations and called upon the
President to follow the spirit of Theodore Roosevelt and intervene. The same journal relied on the frequent analyses of Pierre
Crabites, an international jurist who defended Mussolini's adventure, arguing that Italy was not fomenting racial conquest
but merely extending her legitimate sphere of influence and
establishing a worthwhile "community of interest" in Africa.
Even more apologetic was *America*. Taking its cue from the
Papacy, the Jesuit weekly fretted over the consequences of
general war but nonetheless approved of Italy's presence in
Abyssinia. On the other hand, the *Pilot*, the Boston Archdio-
cese's weekly which reflected Irish-Catholic opinion, minced no
words in charging that "the alleged affront to Italian dignity is
little more than a pretext for attacking Ethiopia."[21]

The only major Catholic periodical, clerical or lay, to take an
uncompromisingly critical position during the war was the anti-
Fascist *Catholic World*. Addressing himself to Catholics and
non-Catholics alike, editor James Gillis cried shame upon journalists who, like Arthur Brisbane, condoned the war as the harbinger of a "higher civilization" in Africa. To those who would
justify Italy's expansion in light of British colonialism, Gillis

20 Hiett, pp. 14-15; Binchy, pp. 637-51.
21 "Face to Face with War," *Commonweal*, xxii (Aug. 30, 1935),
413-14; "Dictatorship Triumphant," *ibid.*, xxiii (March 27, 1936), 587-88;
Pierre Crabites, "Ethiopia and Africa," *ibid.*, xxii (Sept. 20, 1935), 485-86;
"National Sovereignty," *ibid.*, xxiii (Dec. 13, 1935), 173-74. "The Pope
and Ethiopia," *America*, liii (Sept. 7, 1935), 506; Laurence Patterson, S.J.,
"The Ethiopian Church," *ibid.*, liii (Aug. 24, 1935), 462-63; John Keating,
S.J., "The European Crisis," *ibid.* (Sept. 21, 1935), 501-503. The *Pilot* is
quoted in Harris, p. 40.

replied sharply: "England's cupidity is no excuse for Italy's rapacity." The editor chastised especially the lay and clerical Catholics in Italy and in America who supported a "Manifestly Unjust War." After receiving numerous letters criticizing his "anti-Italian" statements, Gillis tried to make clear that "a true Catholic is not opposed to German tyranny or Italian tyranny; a true Catholic is opposed to tyranny." When liberals demanded to know how Catholics could invoke the "universality of their ethics" and at the same time support specific dictators, the *Catholic World*, elaborating a set of "journalistic principles," maintained that the Church transcends the "caprice" of a narrow nationalism and the "prejudice" of "racial preference." "So you don't find," Gillis added in reference to the American press, "the Catholic editor blowing hot against Hitler and cold against Mussolini, excoriating Lenin and Stalin and tolerating Calles and Cardenas though guilty of the same crimes."[22]

Father Gillis, unfortunately, was only speaking for himself and perhaps a small number of *Catholic World* readers. Protestant groups were much more unanimous than Catholics in their criticism of both Italian aggression and Fascism. *Christian Century* believed that Italy's actions represented a "most disgraceful" imperialism and that the war itself, by dramatizing the bankruptcy of the Mussolini government, would be the undoing of his regime. Various Protestant organizations, working through the Federal Council of Churches, aroused sympathy for Ethiopia and instigated hopeful peace movements. Church officials, moreover, feared for the future of Protestant missionary programs in Ethiopia if the country fell to Catholic Italy. Yet the Protestant response, however morally encouraging, was politically inadequate. In an open letter to Haile Selassie, the Fellowship of Reconciliation lectured to the embattled warrior on the virtues of passive resistance; while *Christian Century*, believing the history of the Italian-Ethiopian controversy remote and obscure, insisted on America's "right to stay neutral at any cost." To the cause of anti-Fascism, American Protestantism could offer only an honest but troubled conscience.[23]

22 "The Ambition of Mussolini," *Catholic World*, cxlii (Oct. 1935), 1-9; *ibid.* (Nov. 1935), 129-39; V. White, "Manifestly Unjust War," *ibid.* (Dec. 1935), 358-59; *ibid.*, cxliii (April 1936), 1078; *ibid.* (May 1936), 129-31; "The Ethiopian Fiasco—And After," *ibid.* (June 1936), 247-64.

23 *Christian Century*, lii (July 17, Aug. 7, 14, 21, Sept. 4, 1935), 931-32, 1003, 1005-06, 1033-34, 1055, 1099. Harris, pp. 39-40.

The conscience of American Jewry, racked more by German anti-Semitism than liberal neutralism, tended to support Ethiopia as the victim of aggression. *Jewish Frontier*, representing the League for Labor Palestine and the more radical currents of Jewish social thought, advised minority peoples and mandated countries that their own security might turn on the fate of Ethiopia. The *American Hebrew and Jewish Tribune* took *Time* to task for describing Haile Selassie as the "acquisitive, Semitic Emperor," noting that "the acquisitive bent seems to us to be more evident in Mussolini's hankering for a chunk of Ethiopia or the subjection of that kingdom." For many Jewish leaders the war led to a rediscovery of religious and ethnic ties in Africa. *B'nai B'rith* remarked with pride that "Semitic kinship and influences seem to be very broad" among the Abyssinians, especially the Falashas, native "black Jews" whose culture bore traits of the Mosaic code. Still, despite its remote identity with black brethren in Africa, American Jewry as a whole did not denounce Italian Fascism during the Ethiopian War. In 1935 Jews throughout the world were sickened by the sight of Hitler's pogroms. Since many German-Jewish refugees were finding asylum in Italy, American Jews were in no position to attack the Mussolini government which thus far had scorned Hitler's anti-Semitic policies.[24]

ITALIAN-AMERICANS: HOME COUNTRY AT WAR

For Italian-Americans the Ethiopian War was a sustained catharsis. Tens of thousands of them turned out for rallies in New York, Chicago, Philadelphia, Boston, and elsewhere. Here women contributed their gold wedding rings, receiving in turn steel rings from Mussolini which were blessed by a parish priest. At a Brooklyn rally the Italian Red Cross passed trays to collect gold watches, cigarette lighters, crucifixes, and other metallic mementoes needed to finance the war effort—two hundred tons of copper postcards, it was estimated, were sent to the home country when the United States government halted copper shipments to Italy. At a Madison Square Garden meeting $14,000

[24] *Jewish Frontier* and the *American Hebrew and Jewish Tribune* are quoted in Harris, p. 40; *B'nai B'rith Magazine*, L (Oct. 1935), 6, 16; (Nov. 1935), 70; (Dec. 1935), 75-76. Many rabbis as well as ministers were involved with the Committee on American Aid for Ethiopia; see *Boston Evening Transcript*, Dec. 2, 1935.

was collected and presented to Clemente Giglio, emissary of the "Committee of One Thousand," who immediately sailed to Italy to offer the gift to Marshal Badoglio as a token of loyalty to a "greater Italy." At another Garden rally, Generoso Pope told an audience of 20,000 that he had sent a check for $100,000 to Rome, and his paper, *Il Progresso*, confidently announced that "5,000,000 Italian-Americans who live in the United States are ready to immolate themselves on the altar of the great motherland."[25]

Despite *Il Progresso*'s incendiary grandeur, only a few Italian-Americans returned to Italy to fight for the mother country. When in the fall of 1935 Mussolini issued a call for volunteers, rumor immediately circulated in the United States that consular agencies and Italian-American societies were being employed to round up recruits. Yet Italian officials denied that Italian-American war veterans had been approached, and the Italian Ambassador announced that no applications from American citizens would be accepted. Most likely officials had no desire to exacerbate the United States government, which had earlier warned that Americans who enlisted for service would be subject to fine and imprisonment and that naturalized citizens who took the Fascist oath could lose their citizenship. Despite all warnings, however, some Italian-Americans volunteered to serve. On October 20, 1935, 117 "reservists" embarked on the *S. S. Rex* for duty in Ethiopia, and on December 1, 75 more under the command of Captain Paul Sterbini set sail for Africa with a "war chest" of assorted precious metals and an ambulance unit of Italian-American doctors. After December the Italian government began ordering former World War I officers to return to Italy, and at one point Rome newspapers reported that 500 volunteers from the United States were training at Sabaudio, Italy.[26]

Meanwhile Rome sent to America lecturers like Daniele Vare, a prominent Italian novelist who was supposed to help the Italian Ambassador sell what Helen Lombard called "a little bit of inevitable aggression." New Italian-American organizations also sprang up during the war, like the American League for Italy and the Unione Italiana d'America—the latter, run by Ugo D'Annunzio, was probably started at Bergamaschi's suggestion.

25 *NYT*, June 14, Dec. 19, 1935, June 14, 1936; *Il Progresso*'s statement is quoted in Hugo V. Maile, *The Italian Vote in Philadelphia between 1928 and 1946* (Philadelphia, 1950), p. 95.

26 *NYT*, July 21, Sept. 16, Oct. 4, 5, 6, 20, 26, Dec. 1, 8, 1935.

While depicting Ethiopia as the truculent aggressors, such organizations singled out England as the imperialist Leviathan whose influence extended to the American State Department. Aware that American sentiment favored the underdog, propagandists described the Abyssinians as slave traders who had contempt for the Negro race, black barbarians who held back the march of civilization.[27]

Although Italian-Americans first welcomed America's declaration of neutrality, it soon became clear Roosevelt did not have in mind a Wilsonian neutralism of thought as well as deed. The President let it be known—despite the preponderance of Italian-American democrats—that he disapproved of Mussolini's adventure and was willing to attempt a "moral embargo" and cooperate independently with Britain and the League. Italian-Americans reacted angrily to the administration's meddling, and when in the spring of 1936 Roosevelt moved to revise the Neutrality Act, their propaganda agencies countered with maximum pressure. The chief tactic utilized was a letter-writing campaign. By inundating with envelopes urban and eastern congressmen, organizations like the Friends of Italy and the Unione Italiana d'America succeeded beyond all expectations: before the campaign started mail ran in favor of the administration's policy; afterwards it ran five to four against, with 90 percent of the opposition correspondence composed of form letters from Italian-Americans. Adding a personal touch, Generoso Pope went to the capital and spoke to Senator Robert Wagner, Secretary Ickes, and other important figures, including Roosevelt himself.[28]

[27] Lombard, pp. 160-61; *The Italo-Ethiopian Controversy* (Italian Historical Society, New York, 1935), pamphlet; Lee Meriwether, *Carrying Civilization to Ethiopia* (address to the Italian Club of St. Louis, May 7, 1938), pamphlet; *Italy, Great Britain, and the League* (Unione Italiana d'America, New York, 1935); regarding Italian papers, see Eleanor Clark, "The Press Goes to War: The Italian Press, New York," *New Republic*, LXXXIV (Nov. 6, 1935), 356-57.

[28] John Norman, "Influence of Pro-Fascist Propaganda on American Neutrality, 1935-1936," in Dwight Lee and George McReynolds, *Essays in History and International Relations* (Worcester, 1949), pp. 193-98; id., "Pro-Fascist Activities in Western Pennsylvania during the Ethiopian War," *The Western Pennsylvania History Magazine*, xxv (Sept.-Dec. 1942), 143-48; Thomas Novia to Roosevelt, Nov. 20, 1935, OF 233A, RP; *Chicago Italian Chamber of Commerce* (Nov. 1935), pamphlet; see also John Norman, "Italo-American Opinion in the Ethiopian Crisis: A Study in Fascist Propaganda" (Ph.D. Thesis, Clark University, 1942).

The Neutrality Act was not revised. Roosevelt, faced with the mounting opposition of Italian-Americans as well as isolationists, eliminated a crucial clause that would have given the President discretionary power to ban specific exports. In Congressional circles it was obvious that Italian-American pressure helped defeat revision, and Assistant Secretary of State Walton Moore could not doubt that the Italian Embassy was behind the entire letter campaign. The Embassy, of course, was more than pleased, and in its 1936 report it described "the brilliant job" carried out by the Italian-Americans. The ultimate compliment came from Il Duce himself, who thanked the Italians of America for standing loyally by during the ordeal of sanctions.[29]

Hostility toward Roosevelt continued to smoulder in Italian neighborhoods during the 1936 election. Even radical politicians like Vito Marcantonio, not to mention liberals like La Guardia and Cotillo, succumbed to the pressure. One desperate congressman asked the President for a copy of a reported friendly letter from Mussolini, which he planned to show to his Italian constituents. The letter did not exist. Publisher Criscuolo warned Roosevelt that the bitterness lingering in the Italian communities could only be mitigated if the government recognized Italy's annexation of Ethiopia. Tensions increased as Republicans urged Italians not to vote for a President who opposed Italy and supported the Negro. The day before the elections Philadelphia's Republican papers printed a speech of Mussolini's telling Italian-Americans to "remember the sanctions." But all along the administration refused, in face of diplomatic as well as domestic pressure, to recognize Fascism's conquest. Recognizing Italy's occupation of Ethiopia might have regained the Italian vote, but it would also have incurred the wrath of the many more Americans who reacted angrily to War Fascism if not to Fascism itself. As Ambassador Phillips remarked a few years later, the "American government and people had not forgiven Italy for its ruthless campaign against Ethiopia."[30]

[29] Harris, pp. 124-25; *Bulletin Italo-American National Union* (Sept. 1936).

[30] For Marcantonio's opposition to neutrality revision, see *Congressional Record*, 74th Cong., 2nd Sess., Vol. 80, Pt. 2, p. 2221. Although Cotillo and La Guardia opposed Fascist infiltration into the Sons of Italy ten years earlier, during the Ethiopian crisis political expediency forced both to go along with the Italian community. See Cotillo's "Memorandum and Open

If Americans could not forgive Italy, Italian-Americans could not forget her. The Italian-Americans' behavior during the war sprang from the same wounded sensitivities as their philofascism. The spectacle of an Italian army marching gloriously into Africa and of Mussolini's defying the League warmed the hearts of immigrants who were continually told that their old country was a second-rate nation and Il Duce a first-rate buffoon. "Whether you like it or not, Mr. Pegler," the Sons of Italy reminded Westbrook Pegler of the *Chicago Daily News*: "the truth is this: Since the coalition of fifty-two nations could not stop the triumphal march of Italy to Ethiopia, neither can all your lies, or somebody else's lies, harm Italy." Therein lay the confused state of the Italian-American mind.[31]

The "New Negro" and the Ethiopian War

On the sultry evening of June 26, 1935, 60,000 spectators poured into Yankee Stadium to see the heavyweight match between the young American Negro Joe Louis and the towering Italian Primo Carnera. Circulating through the tense crowd were 1,500 policemen, the largest detachment ever assigned to a prize fight. Outside the stadium emergency squads stood by with riot equipment.

Precautions taken by New York authorities reflected the growing animosity between the Negro and Italian populations in the United States. Throughout the summer of 1935 tension heightened as the Ethiopian dispute dragged on, and after Louis easily knocked Carnera to the canvas vengeful Italian-Americans taunted Negroes with threats of what Mussolini's army would do to the Abyssinians. When street brawls erupted in New York and in New Jersey, Representative Arthur W. Mitchell, the only Negro in Congress, vainly tried to ease tension by suggesting to his people that Italian-Americans were not to blame. But the clashes continued even though Mayor La Guardia assigned 1,200 extra police to patrol Italian neighborhoods in New York; and a few months later 400 Negroes, returning from a pro-Ethiopia rally, marched through Harlem smashing the windows of Italian

---

Letter to the President" (Italian Library of Information, New York, 1936), pamphlet, HIL; F. J. Sisson to McIntyre, Oct. 14, 1936, OF Box 1; Criscuolo to Roosevelt, Oct. 26, 1936, OFF 233A, RP; Maile, pp. 48-57, 95; Phillips is quoted in Harris, p. 144.

[31] *Bulletin, Order Sons of Italy* (Illinois, May 1937).

stores. "No black man could, in good conscience, go into most Italian bars in Harlem," recalled the Black Nationalist James R. Lawson twenty-two years later. "Mussolini's picture hung over almost every Italian cash register up there. At that time, black people owned only two bars in Harlem. When Mussolini's war was over, black people owned thirty-five."[32]

Moved by anger and compassion, Negro organizations rushed to the support of Ethiopia. The NAACP telegraphed the League of Nations on behalf of "12,000,000 American Negroes and many white Americans," urging the Council to restrain Italian aggression. Negro Methodist and Baptist church groups lent their support, and in Harlem a "Pan African Reconstruction Association" was formed, as well as a "Committee for Ethiopia," whose vice-chairman was the young and suave Adam Clayton Powell, Pastor of the Abyssinian Baptist Church. Of all the groups to emerge, the most important was the Friends of Ethiopia. Under the leadership of Dr. Willis Huggins, an eminent Negro educator and author, the Friends merged with the American Aid for Ethiopia Committee and both organizations appealed for funds to churches of all denominations, to liberal affiliations, and to Negro colleges and the Negro press.[33]

During the course of the war black Americans all but adopted Ethiopia as their home country. Some were even willing to fight for her. One Negro, Randolph Mitchell of Oklahoma, told the press that he had suggested, in a letter to Addis Ababa, that a move be undertaken to recruit black soldiers in the United States. Mitchell then claimed he had received authority from the Ethiopian government to enlist volunteers. It was reported that in Oklahoma alone one hundred Negroes signed up in the first week, prepared, if Italy attacked, to leave for Ethiopia on August 1, their transportation financed by Emperor Selassie. As in the case of Italian-Americans, however, the government issued a warning about possible loss of citizenship, and the Ethiopian Consul-General announced he was instructed to cease recruiting.[34]

The abortive attempt to enlist Negro volunteers did not discourage the formation of famous flying squads. One white group

[32] NYT, June 26, 27, Aug. 12, Oct. 4, 6, 1935, May 19, 1936; "The Corner," The New Yorker (Jan. 7, 1967), 20.
[33] Hiett, pp. 17-18; NYT, July 14, 15, 22, 25, Aug. 2, 4, 1935.
[34] NYT, July 13, 14, 18, 19, 21, 22, 1935.

consisted of a dozen stunt flyers, some of whom were former members of the Lafayette Escadrille of World War I fame. Another squad was made up of Negroes under the leadership of Colonel Hubert Julian. Julian, the "Black Eagle of Harlem" who trained his aviators at New York's Roosevelt Field, made a trip to Ethiopia to ask for the right to fly for Emperor Selassie. For a while his pleas were ignored, but in the summer of 1935 he was granted Ethiopian citizenship and allowed to join the Emperor's army. Shortly after he had a falling out when he insisted that America's alleged indifference to the plight of Ethiopia be publicly protested in a cablegram, a stand that resulted in his coming to blows with John C. Robinson, a Chicago Negro. Robinson, the "Brown Condor of Ethiopia" who reportedly was the first American volunteer, replaced the impetuous Julian as squadron head. This incident was the last newsmen heard of the celebrated American-Ethiopian air force. Most likely, for want of planes and materials, it never got off the ground.[35]

But the political spirits of a few black radicals did soar, however sporadically. Although the black community was unable to mount an effective movement on the Left to support Ethiopia and counter the Italian-American campaign, the war had ideological significance for the black intelligentsia. The Marxist historian W.E.B. DuBois, for example, saw the war as the second act of southern reconstruction, as final evidence of "the last great effort of white Europe to secure the subjection of black men." That racism was the handmaiden of imperialism was a conviction accepted by many educated Negroes. Indeed for black Americans in general the war in Africa represented the first encounter with Fascism, and many black activists had no reservations about cooperating with the Communist American League Against War and Fascism. Of all American Negroes, the one who made the most Marxist mileage out of the war was James W. Ford, vice-presidential candidate for the Communist Party in 1932 and in 1936. Addressing an audience at Madison Square Garden in 1936, Ford told his people that the conflict would lead to a common front based on class rather than color, a front that would combine not only the American Negroes who were "seething with indignation" but the "toiling masses" of Africa who were "groaning under the heavy yoke of imperialist domination." Con-

[35] *NYT*, July 13, Aug. 2, 9, 23, Nov. 17, 20, 1935.

vinced of the inevitable insurgency of the "black, white, yellow and brown" proletariat, Ford's anti-Fascism was innocently color-blind.[36]

The anti-Fascism of the Communist Party, however, was not. Following the lead of the Party Congress in Moscow, American Communists looked upon the Negro question in the United States as part of the international colonial question. At the Sixth Comintern in 1928, the Soviets formulated the "Black Belt" doctrine of racial self-determination, which for the Negroes implied segregated status within America. During the depression the CP made some inroads among Negroes, but it never came to grips with the human realities of the race problem. As a result the relationship between leading Negro voices like the NAACP's *Crisis* and the CP was strained, and during the Ethiopian War strain turned to suspicion as black spokesmen criticized the evasive and timid diplomacy of the Soviet Union. The NAACP asked Foreign Minister Maxim Litvinov to explain Russia's ambivalent position on the war. Moscow answered by ousting George Padmore, editor of *The Black Worker* and described by *Crisis* as "the leading Negro Communist in Europe." Padmore was expelled from the Soviet Union for protesting Russia's failure to rally to Ethiopia's cause. Finally in October 1935, *Crisis* issued a blistering editorial, "Soviet Union Aids Italy," excoriating the "pious flub-dub" of Russia for having succumbed to capitalist "opportunism" by selling wheat and coal to Italy for use in the war against Abyssinia.[37]

[36] W.E.B. DuBois, "Inter-Racial Implications of the Ethiopian Crisis: A Negro View," *Foreign Affairs*, XIV (Oct. 1935), 82-92; James W. Ford, *The Negro and the Democratic Front* (New York, 1938), pp. 159-60.

[37] Theodore Draper, *American Communism and Soviet Russia* (New York, 1960), p. 387; Lewis Coser and Irving Howe, *The American Communist Party: A Critical History* (Praeger paperback edn., New York, 1962), pp. 204-16; *NYT*, May 23, 1935; George Padmore, "Ethiopia and World Politics," *Crisis*, XLII (May 1935), 138-39, 156; see Padmore, "An Open Letter to Earl Browder," *ibid.* (Oct. 1935), p. 302, and editorial, p. 305. As with France and England, reasons of national security against Hitler dictated that the Soviet Union do nothing to alienate Italy. But Russian policy appeared all the more insidious in view of the Communist "popular front" against Fascism. Moreover, Russia increased its shipments of cereals, coal, timber, and petroleum, the last of which constituted almost one quarter of Italy's oil imports. Because of these actions Soviet Russia's anti-imperialist image was shattered for many black Africans. (Baer, p. 316.) Arthur Koestler has a moving, if fictionalized, account of the repercussions

However expedient the Communist position, the war aroused Negro emotions to a high pitch. There were at least two states of mind among black people. The militants, represented by columnist George Schuyler and Negro journals like *Opportunity*, believed the struggle in Africa could be the spark that would unite black men everywhere, even if this meant a cataclysmic war of races. But the moderates, represented by physician Reuben Young, the NAACP, and the Negro Methodist and Baptist churches, feared war would only increase racial tensions. Thus the latter group called for League action, requesting in addition that economists, engineers, and educators help reconstruct ravaged Abyssinia. But no matter what plan of action was advocated, militant and moderate blacks alike were among the first Americans to see in Fascism a clear and present threat to minority peoples throughout the world.[38]

Convinced of the total depravity of the *fascisti*, Negroes made the mistake of seeing total virtue in the Abyssinians. For the war caused black Americans to leap to a most unrealistic defense of what seemed to be their skin brothers. Hence Negroes ignored the racism and the slavery carried on by the Ethiopians themselves. Even the otherwise discerning Reuben Young could exclaim fervently: "Ethiopia Awakens!" Caught up in the illusion of a black renaissance in North Africa, American Negroes succumbed to what Margaret Halsey has called "the myth of the Wonderful Oppressed." White America only added to the confusion. For if the *Christian Science Monitor* pointed out the "Uncle Toms of Ethiopia," the *New York Times* lauded the high quality of the Abyssinian race. Similarly, nativist Americans could not understand why Negroes would sympathize with the plight of the Africans. Pointing out that the Abyssinians had ill-treated and enslaved black men for centuries, Carleton Coon patronizingly advised the Negro not to crusade in Ethiopia but to stay in New York where, instead of being shot down by Blackshirts or taken into captivity by tribesmen, he could at least toss bricks at Italian-Americans.[39]

---

of Russian policy on Communist dockworkers in Europe in *Darkness at Noon* (Signet edn., New York, 1961), pp. 67-72.

[38] George E. Haynes, "Negroes and the Ethiopian Crisis," *Christian Century*, LII (Nov. 20, 1935), 1485-86; David H. Pierce, "Fascism and the Negro," *Crisis*, XLII (April 1935), 107, 114.

[39] Reuben Young, "Ethiopia Awakens!" *Crisis*, XLII (Sept. 1935), 262-63;

While nativists like Coon and racists like Lothrop Stoddard
failed to appreciate the joyous pride swelling in the breast of
black men, Negroes failed to appreciate the extent of Abyssinian
hostility toward black Americans. Thus when war broke out
Marcus Garvey, heralded leader of the back-to-Africa "Black
Nationalism" movement of the 1920s, rose to the defense of his
beloved Ethiopia. He called upon all Negroes to unite behind
their ancestral fatherland, and he lashed out at Mussolini in
verse.

We'll march to crush the Italian dog
And at the points of gleaming, shining swords,
We'll lay quite low the violent, Roman hog.

Yet when Haile Selassie fled to London and let it be known he
wanted nothing to do with American Negroes, the astounded
Garvey turned on the arrogant Lion of Judah, the "great coward
who ran away from his country." He called upon the Ethiopians
to fight on without their leader. The Abyssinians could win, Garvey was convinced, if they drew upon the spirit and stamina of
their common race.

But to continue the fight there must be real patriotism. There
must be a real recognition of the Negro Abyssinian. He must
not be ashamed to be a member of the Negro race. If he does,
he will be left alone by all the Negroes of the world, who feel
proud of themselves. The new Negro doesn't give two pence
about the line of Solomon. Solomon has been long dead. Solomon was a Jew. The Negro is no Jew. The Negro has a racial
origin running from Sheba to the present, of which he is proud.
He is proud of Sheba but he is not proud of Solomon.[40]

Garvey's reference to "the new Negro" is the key to the psychic
impact of the war on black America. To the American Negro,
nurtured for centuries in a morass of self-hatred and shame at his

Halsey is quoted in Francis L. Broderick, *W. E. B. DuBois: Negro Leader
in a Time of Crisis* (Stanford, 1959), p. 135; *Christian Science Monitor*,
Sept. 11, 1935; *NYT*, Aug. 4, 1935; Carlton S. Coon, "A Realist Looks at
Ethiopia," *Atlantic Monthly*, CLVI (Sept. 1935), 310-15.

[40] Lothrop Stoddard, "Men of Color Aroused," *Review of Reviews*, XCII
(Nov. 1935), 35-36; E. David Cronon, *Black Moses: The Story of Marcus
Garvey and the Universal Negro Improvement Association* (Madison, 1962),
pp. 162-63.

African ancestry, the Ethiopian War signified the awakening of a viable political consciousness. Perhaps no other diplomatic event until the post-World War II movements of African independence inspired black men to a new sense of identity and commitment. Regardless of the Abyssinians' ethnocentricism, the American Negro's racial pride was profoundly stirred. Although few were able to strike back at Fascism in Ethiopia, the Spanish Civil War provided just such an opportunity. Black literati like Countee Cullen, Frank Marshall Davis, DuBois, Langston Hughes, James Weldon Johnson, Paul Robeson, Edward Strong, Richard Wright, and the young James Baldwin (age twelve) used their talents to attack Franco's rebellion and Il Duce's intervention, while almost one hundred other Negroes joined the Abraham Lincoln Brigade. In one short story by O. H. Hunter a wounded American Negro spoke for many of his people when he gave his reason for volunteering to fight for Loyalist Spain: "I wanted to go to Ethiopia and fight Mussolini. . . . This ain't Ethiopia, but it'll do."[41]

[41] The quote from Hunter's short story and reference to Negro writers and the Spanish Civil War is in Guttmann, pp. 100, 98-101. Because of the excessive claims made by Communist propagandists it is difficult to estimate precisely the number of black Americans who fought in Spain, as Harold Cruse notes in *The Crisis of the Negro Intellectual* (Apollo edn., New York, 1968), p. 168. But Robert Rosenstone, in a forthcoming study of the "Men of the Abraham Lincoln Brigade," states "cautiously" that "at most 100 Negroes" went to Spain (Rosenstone to author, Jan. 27, 1969).

13.

The Eclipse of Fascism: Nazi Germany, Mussolini, and the Coming of World War II

Thomas Wolfe, *You Can't Go Home Again*, 1939*

* Reprinted by permission of Harper & Row, Publishers, Inc. (See Acknowledgments)

I THINK THE ENEMY COMES TO US WITH THE FACE OF INNOCENCE AND SAYS TO US: "I AM YOUR FRIEND."

I THINK THE ENEMY DECEIVES US WITH FALSE WORDS AND LYING PHRASES, SAYING:

"SEE, I AM ONE OF YOU— I AM ONE OF YOUR CHILDREN, YOUR BROTHER, AND YOUR FRIEND. BEHOLD HOW SLEEK AND FAT I HAVE BECOME— AND ALL BECAUSE I AM JUST ONE OF YOU, AND YOUR FRIEND. BEHOLD HOW RICH AND POWERFUL I AM—AND ALL BECAUSE I AM ONE OF YOU—SHAPED IN YOUR WAY OF LIFE, OF THINKING, OF ACCOMPLISHMENT. WHAT I AM, I AM BECAUSE OF YOU, YOUR HUMBLE BROTHER AND YOUR FRIEND. BEHOLD," CRIES ENEMY, "THE MAN I AM, THE MAN I HAVE BECOME, THE THING I HAVE ACCOMPLISHED —AND REFLECT. WILL YOU DESTROY THIS THING? I ASSURE YOU THAT IT IS THE MOST PRECIOUS THING YOU HAVE. IT IS YOURSELVES, THE PROJECTION OF EACH OF YOU, THE TRIUMPH OF YOUR INDIVIDUAL LIVES, THE THING THAT IS ROOTED IN YOUR BLOOD, AND NATIVE TO YOUR STOCK, AND INHERENT IN THE TRADITIONS OF AMERICA. . . . WOULD YOU DESTROY THIS GLORIOUS INCARNATION OF YOUR OWN HEROIC SELF?"

NAZI GERMANY AND THE IRONY OF
AMERICAN NATIVISM

No discussion of American attitudes toward Italian Fascism in the thirties is meaningful without some reference to the rise of Nazi Germany. With the appearance of the German Brownshirts the whole Fascist question took on a chilling international connotation. Yet Mussolini's image as a sane and sober statesman was enhanced when contrasted with the shrieking outbursts of Adolf Hitler. Moreover many Americans were quick to stress the distinctions which set the Italian experiment apart from the German phenomenon, favorable distinctions which, as we saw earlier, Mussolini himself was forever pointing out to a candid world. Thus the exact impact of the Third Reich upon American opinion of Fascism in Italy is difficult to gauge. Nevertheless, when contrasted to the various responses to Mussolini's Italy, America's immediate reaction to Hitler's Germany illuminates further the curious values by which Americans judged and misjudged European dictatorships.

In general, American popular opinion expressed no great distress over Hitler's advent to power. During the formative period of the new German government the picture that emerged in the *Saturday Evening Post, Collier's*, and *American Magazine* was on the whole favorable. As with Mussolini's March on Rome, again the emphasis was on the need for order and stability. Although most journalists described harshly leaders like Goering and Streicher, a few depicted Hitler as a reasonable statesman who had abandoned his demagogic demonology; and even when editorials frequently rebuked Hitler, Nazi Germany itself came off rather well. Aside from the familiar anti-Communist mentality of the *Saturday Evening Post* and similar weeklies, the explanation of America's tolerance lies in two dominant themes pervading the middle-brow press.[1]

[1] For material on this subject I have drawn upon Roberta S. Sigel's "Opinion on Nazi Germany: A Study of Three Popular American Magazines, 1933-1941" (Ph.D. Thesis, Clark University, 1950). Focusing solely on the *SEP, Collier's,* and *American Magazine,* Miss Sigel's study is regrettably limited. But see also Neil R. McMillen's account of Right-wing groups, "Pro-Nazi Sentiment in the United States, March 1933-March 1934," *Southern Quarterly,* II (Oct. 1963), 48-70; and F. K. Wentz's more illuminating "American Catholic Periodicals React to Nazism," *Church History,* XXXI (Dec. 1962), 400-20.

First, many Americans viewed the rise of Hitler's Germany as the inevitable consequence of the Versailles treaty. Rejecting vehemently the whole experience of World War I and the supposedly anti-German peace settlement, magazine writers saw Hitler as a desperate but understandable answer to Wilson's "betrayal" of the Fourteen Points. Just as Americans interpreted Nazism as a righteous challenge to the impossible restrictions the West imposed on Germany's recovery, so could they view Hitler's dictatorship as a legitimate answer to the false, planetary illusions of Wilsonian democracy. In short, the tolerant indulgence of 1933 can be explained by the original sin of 1919.[2]

But if America's tolerance of early Nazism was founded on guilt, it was a guilt that could be unburdened by pride. Time and again writers expressed great admiration for the Germans as a people. By the thirties the anti-German hysteria of the war years had disappeared and many Americans, perhaps making amends, began to reassess the greatness of the Germans and their culture. The land of Goethe and Einstein emerged as a land of spiritual idealism and scientific achievement, a country that could be readily appreciated by a people whose cultural hero was Emerson and folk hero Henry Ford. The Germans were virile and honorable, clean and efficient, generous and hospitable, a fitting self-image for nativist America.[3] Because of this sympathetic identification many Americans felt that Hitler by no means represented the real Germans, the "good Germans" who would moderate the excesses of Nazism. These solid, middle-class citizens, so devoted

[2] Sigel, pp. 1-4, 28-42, 72-73, 105-106, passim.

[3] As late as 1938 one historian, though by no means an admirer of Hitler or Nazism, conveyed clearly these themes of pride and guilt: "Here is a brave and vigorous people, which in the last war stood off almost the whole world alone; a people that has probably done more for music than any other in modern history, and more for philosophy, and more for science, and more for scholarship; which [sic] of us can write history today without falling back upon the researches of Germans from Niebuhr to Edward Meyer? Now, with the wisdom of hindsight, we can see how magnificent in every cultural way, in all but its swashbuckling way, was the civilization of Germany under Wilhelm II, and how childish it was for us to force upon it a democracy that could not possibly find there the conditions that had supported self-government among ourselves—geographical location, military security, libertarian traditions and abounding natural resources. It seems unbelievable that a professor of history should have led us into this absurdity." Will Durant, "No Hymns of Hatred," *SEP*, ccx (June 4, 1938), 49.

to the fatherland and to the ideals of German civilization, were the surest guarantee that "normalcy" will prevail.[4]

America's popular response to Nazism should be contrasted with the attitudes expressed toward Italian Fascism a decade earlier. For while some of the same themes reappear—Versailles humiliation, Bolshevik threat, the need for order and authority, etc.—American opinion of Italians and Germans differed strikingly. Much of the apology for Fascism, it will be remembered, sprang from a nativist dislike for Italy and almost everything Italian. The Mussolini experiment appeared to be Americanizing Italy by imposing on an indolent people the virtues of discipline and hard work. The Germans, on the contrary, already possessed these uplifting Anglo-Saxon values. Highly cultured and ambitious, the dynamic German people needed Nazism less than Nazism needed them. Thus Hitler's regime, a temporary expedient at best, would be incapable of altering the decent German character. So perceived, many Americans tolerated Nazism because of their faith in the sobriety and prudence of the people themselves, while at the same time continuing to applaud Fascism because of their scorn for the hopelessly improvident Italians.[5]

History plays cruel tricks on the public mind. Strangely enough, the exact opposite of what Americans expected actually occurred. Whereas Mussolini was unable to basically transform the resilient

[4] Sigel, pp. 72-73, 169-71.

[5] It is more than coincidence that Kenneth Roberts and Edgar Ansel Mowrer were among the most frequent commentators on Nazism in 1933, as they had been on Fascism eleven years earlier. In 1922, as we have seen, Mowrer attacked Fascism as alien to the Italian national character, while Roberts championed it as a necessary medicine for the unwashed masses of Italy. In 1933, the two writers also stood opposed on the Nazi issue; and again, significantly enough, their differences derived more from ethnic than ideological considerations. Roberts, of course, never let an opportunity slip by to inject an anti-Bolshevik aside into his articles, but his defense of the Nazis was based on an unconcealed admiration for the tough German people, an admiration which led him to ridicule all stories about Nazi terrorism. Mowrer, on the other hand, was one of the few American journalists to see that the much celebrated German civilization was a fragile veneer laid over a desperately restless people, a "nation of natural extremists" given to "pathological exaggeration" and a "ghastly strengthening of the death urge (*Todestrieb*), already unnaturally strong in the unbalanced German soul." Kenneth Roberts, "Hitler Youth," *SEP*, ccvi (May 26, 1934), 8-9, 98-104; Edgar Ansel Mowrer, *Germany Puts the Clock Back* (New York, 1933), p. 322.

Italian character, the "respectable" Germans succumbed to
Nazism with hardly a pang of conscience or a gesture of resistance. There is a delicious irony in all this. After the outbreak
of World War II America would begin to call upon the Italians
to overthrow their government. No such appeal was extended to
the Germans who had, it seemed, so willingly and thoroughly
regimented themselves to the Nazi state. What is more, when the
Italians did rise up it was the *lazzaroni* of Naples who were
among the first to spur the insurrection. Perhaps it is a bit much
to expect the poor of the earth to inherit the respect of America.
A people nursed on "Poor Richard" and rocked to the rhythm of
the industrial machine can hardly be expected to see, even in the
face of totalitarianism, the beauty of idleness. Yet Americans
ought to have been thankful that Mussolini failed to do precisely
what they wanted him most to do—to make the Italians run on
time.

The Alienation of the Press

After the Ethiopian War American opinion grew increasingly
critical of Mussolini and Fascism. Seldom could anything unquali-
fiedly favorable be read in popular weeklies like *Time* and *Newsweek* or in literary monthlies like the *Atlantic* and *Harper's*. Even
the *Saturday Evening Post* no longer featured the blatant apologists who dominated the magazine in the twenties. In the *New
York Times* Arnaldo Cortesi continued to write approvingly of
his country and Anne O'Hare McCormick still carried on her
infatuation with Mussolini. But editorially America's leading daily
remained as skeptical as ever of Il Duce's celebrated charm, remarking on Fascism's Fifteenth Anniversary that a "tyrant remains
a tyrant no matter how benevolently he may philosophize and
smile." Moreover, while discerning correspondents like C. L.
Sulzberger and Herbert Matthews made up for Cortesi's self-
serving journalism and McCormick's fawning scenarios, the *Times*
carried a most penetrating series of articles by Harold Callendar.
The psychological basis of Fascism, Callendar informed Americans, was the Italians' "almost pathological" craving for self-
esteem which Mussolini exploited by trying to maintain "an
atmosphere of ideal tension." Although the dictator would be
unable to sustain this energizing mood, he was meanwhile, Callendar shrewdly noted, riding the proverbial tiger he dared not

317

dismount: if the tension subsided, domestic unrest would erupt; if it heightened, war would follow.[6]

A clearer indication of the decline of American sympathy for Fascist Italy may be seen in the deterioration of press relations between the two countries. In the late thirties the Italian government banned publications like the *New Republic, Esquire, Collier's*, and *Time*, and in response to such harassment the American Newspaper Guild passed a blistering anti-Fascist resolution. Perhaps the situation reached a breaking point in 1938 when Virginio Gayda, Mussolini's mouthpiece in the *Giornale d'Italia*, castigated the American press for its "target practice against Italy." Specifically, Gayda cited an espionage accusation by Congressman Byron Scott, a magazine article by Hemingway, Admiral William Leahy's statement about the possibility of an Italian-German invasion of the United States, a *New York Times* report of Italian intrigue in Brazil, a *Herald-Tribune* column on Italy's intention to align with Germany and Hungary against Czechoslovakia, and Harold Ickes' statement that Fascism was "the greatest danger" facing the world. The "defamatory, offensive, and threatening" anti-Fascist campaign Gayda blamed on American Jews, Protestants, and Negroes.[7]

Gayda's savage attack on the American press was followed by several other ominous developments. In the summer of 1939 the Italian government closed down the Rome office of the United Press. Fascist officials moved against UP because one of its newsmen reported that Mussolini had been taken ill. When the correspondent was expelled from the country, Maxwell Macartney of the *London Times* humorously reminded his colleagues of the "three sacrosanct rules" for reporters in Rome: "You never write anything that hints the lira isn't sound. You never write anything that might cast doubts upon the valor of the Italian army. And certainly, at no time, do you dare hint that the Duce is not a Gibraltar of good health." But these matters seemed almost minor compared to Italy's adoption of Germany's policies against the Jewish people. To American correspondents especially the sudden announcement of Italy's anti-Semitic laws made the state of

[6] *NYT*, Sept. 20, 1936, June 27, July 11, 18, 31, Dec. 12, 1937, Jan. 14, 23, 29, Feb. 5, 1939. For a brief survey of magazine opinion, see Diggins, "Mussolini's Italy," pp. 295-300.

[7] *NYT*, April 30, May 22, 1938, April 11, Aug. 11, 1939.

Mussolini's mental health not a matter of "hints" but of serious speculation.[8]

Officially the anti-Semitic campaign began on July 14, 1938, with the publication of the fabricated *Carta della Razza*. To most watchful Americans the publication came as a stunning shock. That the cancer of anti-Semitism could afflict the people of Italy seemed incredible to those who had always pointed to the absence of racism in Italy as the saving remnant of Italian Fascism. Thus the announcement of a "scientific" racial policy had an air of unreality. Moreover the decrees, which would involve the exportation of thousands of Italian Jews, confiscation of property, and exclusion from government and professional occupations, did not go into effect immediately (and when they did many measures were either ignored or sabotaged by the Italians themselves). Consequently America did not react as hostilely as in the case of the German pogrom. Nor did the Jews. The journalist Martin Agronsky reported from Rome that even Italian Jewish leaders assured him Mussolini's adopted racial policy amounted to nothing more than "diplomatic expediency." But Agronsky, perhaps with the Nazi experience in mind, was appalled when six months later world opinion still appeared indifferent: "One wonders at the capacity for understatement of the foreign press which even today writes about Mussolini's 'mild' anti-Semitic measures."[9]

Yet once it became clear what was in store for Italian Jewry, informed American publications reacted angrily. The conservative *Catholic World* condemned Il Duce's "Aryan madness" and the liberal *New Republic* denounced "Italy's Cold Pogrom," demanding the State Department protect American Jews in Italy by making Blackshirts "cringe before a show of firmness." While the Roosevelt administration registered its protests through diplomatic channels a bewildered public wanted an explanation for the gruesome turn of events. Ignazio Silone told Americans that Mussolini was attempting to nip in the bud solidarity between Catholics and Jews in Italy and thus thwart any sympathy for their brethren in Austria and Germany. American writers offered

[8] *NYT*, Aug. 10, 11, 1939; Macartney is quoted in Reynolds and Elenor Packard, *The Balcony Empire* (New York, 1942), pp. 98-99.

[9] Martin Agronsky, "Racism in Italy," *Foreign Affairs*, xvii (Jan. 1939), 391-401.

319

other interpretations: the racial legislation was either an outcome of Italy's "excessive nationalism," a means of providing opportunity for new Blackshirt recruits by depriving Jews of their property and positions, an attempt to divert dissatisfaction from the unfulfilled rewards of the Spanish intervention, an effort to appease Hitler and keep him from annexing the South Tyrol, or Mussolini's way of "playing Near-Eastern politics" by cementing ties between Italy and the Arab world in order to strengthen his hand against England. Yet no matter how the racial laws were interpreted, most writers were convinced the people would resist. Typical was Albert Viton's observation in the *Nation*: "Have the Italian masses all of a sudden become conscious of their exalted Aryan origin and begun to despise the lowly Jew? Nothing of the sort. . . . Italians have confessed to me that, coming on top of his other recent mistakes, the anti-Jewish laws have convinced them that Mussolini has lost his head."[10]

Mussolini may have lost his head but his few remaining American sympathizers kept their cool. Anne O'Hare McCormick, to cite one, played down the importance of the racial document released by Italian professors. She explained the laws as an unfortunate consequence of diplomatic pressures and argued that Mussolini, in contrast to Hitler, had all along ridiculed the idea of racism. Stressing the "universality" of Italy's Catholicism and the Augustan "Romanità" of its history, she also maintained that "Aryanism in Italy just doesn't make sense. What motive is strong enough to impel a regime basing its appeal on the imperial past ever to tolerate a movement undermining the strongest tradition of the Roman empire?"[11]

Miss McCormick's strange argument that Italy could not be "both racist and imperial" rang hollow. For no matter how much Il Duce's remaining supporters tried to explain away Italy's racial policies, the Blackshirts themselves made it clear anti-Semitism should be taken seriously. Indeed anti-Semitism was a major part of a vicious anti-American campaign formally launched in 1938. Directed by Gayda and Roberto Farinacci, Italy's new policy

[10] *Catholic World*, cxlvii (Sept. 1938), 644-47; *New Republic*, xcvi (Sept. 14, 1938), 142; (Nov. 2, 1938), 346; Ignazio Silone, "Italian Anti-Semitism," *ibid.*, xcvii (Nov. 23, 1938), 67-69; Agronsky, pp. 400-01; *Christian Science Monitor*, Nov. 23, 1938; Albert Viton, "Italy Under Hitler," *Nation*, cxlviii (Dec. 31, 1938), 7-11.

[11] *NYT*, July 18, Aug. 13, 1938.

served to release passions that had long been officially repressed among Fascist extremists.[12] In *La Difesa della Razza* malicious slurs were flung at American Jews, with the vilest directed at public figures like Bernard Baruch, Sol Bloom, John Lewis, and Billy Rose. The Fascist organ *Il Tevere* excommunicated the "mongrel" La Guardia, who had criticized Blackshirt activities in the United States, while Farinacci lauded Father Coughlin for standing up against "Jewish democratic propaganda." America itself came to be seen as a Babylon of decadance and frivolity, a playland of "alcool, afrodisiac e depravazione." And running the degenerate country were Jewish or Hebraized plutocrats like Felix Frankfurter and Cordell Hull. As for Roosevelt, a Rome paper claimed that the President's "physical infirmity" was the "mainspring" of his spasmodic foreign policy. Adding salaciousness to scurrility, the name "Franklin" was dropped and Roosevelt was referred to as "Delano," the sound of which translates in Italian as "of the anus" (Dell'Ano).[13]

[12] Among rabid Fascist ideologues anti-Semitism was not merely a German import, as most observers believed at the time. Instead Italian religious racism derived from traditional Catholic arguments against the Jew as the harbinger of, first, atheistic capitalism and, later, international Socialism. Conservative Catholic values, together with the metaphysical organicism of Hegel, furnished the ideological foundation for Fascism's indictment of American civilization. For this information I am indebted to Professor Gene Bernardini, whose paper, "Italian Fascist Uses of 'Decadent' American Democracy," was presented to the Pacific Coast Branch of the American Historical Association, Aug. 30, 1967.

[13] It is highly doubtful that the extremist attacks on America, and especially on Roosevelt, had any significant effect on the Italian masses. For most Italians the United States remained the chosen land of sons and daughters, a second Italy of the mind. The novelist Carlo Levi, whom the Fascists exiled to the province of Lucania, was often, as a medical doctor, called to the homes of peasants. His sensitive observation warrants full quotation:

> But what never failed to strike me most of all—and by now I had been in almost every house—were the eyes of the two inseparable guardian angels that looked at me from the wall over the bed. On one side was the black, scowling face, with its large, inhuman eyes, of the Madonna of Viggiano; on the other a colored print of the sparkling eyes, behind gleaming glasses, and the hearty grin of President Roosevelt. I never saw other pictures or images than these; not the King nor the Duce, nor even Garibaldi; no famous Italian or any king, nor any one of the appropriate saints; only Roosevelt and the Madonna of Viggiano never failed to be present. To see them there, one facing the other, in cheap prints, they seemed the two faces of the power that had divided the universe between

321

The malice of a few anally-fixated Fascists, however, was not what really troubled Americans. Ultimately it was Italy's heedless diplomacy that caused most serious concern. No sooner had Ethiopia been routed than Mussolini again unleashed the dogs of war, this time dispatching "volunteers" to support Franco's attack upon Spain's embattled republic. For many sensitive Americans the Spanish Civil War was a bitter trauma. Although American opinion was hopelessly complex and painfully divided, recent studies show that Americans on the whole tended to sympathize with the Loyalists, and as the brutalities of the war dragged on they turned against Franco. Mussolini's meddling thus won few friends in the United States. Moreover, Italy's army, which had been marching proudly as the conquerors of Africa, suffered a debacle at Guadalajara and its image fell, according to Hanson Baldwin, "unwarrantedly low." Losing honor, prestige, and credibility, Italy's intervention in Spain was plainly a bad show.[14]

Of more enduring significance was the formation of the Rome-Berlin Axis. Newsmen watched with concern as smiling diplomats shuttled between the two capitals; but when the announcement was made, on October 25, 1936, the new alignment appeared shrouded in a fog of diplomatic language. A few days later Mussolini made a speech in Milan brashly explaining the Axis as a form of "armed peace." The American press was critical of the rapport, but there was little consensus as to its significance. Conservative isolationists begrudgingly complimented Mussolini for exposing as a sham the League's collective security mentality; and while a few moderate papers believed he was exploiting the Axis merely to bargain with France and Great Britain, almost all observers dismissed Il Duce's bombast as his familiar "modicum

---

them. But here their roles were, quite rightly, reversed. The Madonna appeared to be a fierce, pitiless, mysterious, ancient earth goddess, the Saturnalia mistress of this world; the President a sort of all-powerful Zeus, the benevolent and smiling master of a higher sphere. Carlo Levi, *Christ Stopped at Eboli* (Pocket Cardinal edn., New York, 1965) pp. 102-03.

"Gli Ebrei d'America," *La Difesa della Razza*, iv, no. 13 (n.d.), 23-24; *NYT*, July 31, 1938, Feb. 4, 1939, Sept. 12, 1940, May 1, 1941; Luigi Olivero, *Babilonia Stellata: Gioventù Americana d'Oggi* (Milan, 1943); Virginio Gayda, *Roosevelt ha ingannato il suo popolo* (Rome, 1941); Giovanni Ortolani, *La Responsabilità di F. Delano Roosevelt* (Milan, 1943); "Mussolini's Slur on Roosevelt's Name," *Il Mondo*, June 15, 1941.

[14] Guttmann, p. 65, passim; *NYT*, May 16, 1937.

of sound and fury." As a result few commentators were inclined to render any permanent significance to the Axis. Not only Mussolini sympathizers but even some critics believed him too shrewd to ride the tail of the Third Reich. "Mussolini is no fool," observed the anti-Fascist *New Republic*. If forced to choose, "it is reasonably certain he will cast his lot with the democracies."[15]

Clearly Italy's association with Nazi Germany was the acid test of American opinion. To the disappointment of many Americans, the partnership began to seem more binding than expected. Mussolini's decision to "Prussianize" Italy, which first appeared as a cavalier but cruel parody, was soon regarded more alarming than amusing. But it was the *Anschluss* that did more than anything else to shatter Il Duce's image as the protector of southeastern Europe and a reliable antagonist to Hitler. Informed Americans were aware of how unpopular the *Anschluss* was in Italy, and they sensed how embarrassing the whole affair was for the stunned Mussolini. Yet just when it appeared that he had become "second fiddle" in the Axis duet, his dramatic moves during the Czechoslovakian crisis restored him to the podium. The manner in which Il Duce seemed to step forward to settle the Sudeten issue impressed Americans, who erroneously believed that he had done so at the prompting of President Roosevelt. Munich was Mussolini's finest hour.[16]

But the trend of events after Munich contributed to Mussolini's waning popularity. Italy's shameless invasion of Albania in April 1939 stirred much resentment in the United States; even Mussolini's warmest admirers regarded it as ill-conceived. The following month Germany and Italy announced the "Pact of Steel," a blatant offensive alliance allowing Hitler a free hand in eastern Europe. The American press, aware the Pact was unpopular with the Italian people, appeared bewildered. Some papers believed the Pact meant an end to all Allied attempts to divide the Axis

[15] *Chicago Daily Tribune*, Nov. 4, 1936; *Washington Post*, Nov. 3, 1936; *San Francisco Chronicle*, Nov. 3, 1936; *New Orleans Times Picayune*, Nov. 3, 1936; *Boston Evening Transcript*, Nov. 3, 1936; *NYT*, Nov. 3, 1936; "The Dictators Meet" (editorial), *New Republic*, xcv (May 18, 1938), 29; see also "Careers in Contrast," *LD*, cxxiv (Oct. 16, 1937), 25; *Time*, xxx (Oct. 11, 1937), 23-24; *ibid.*, xxxi (May 16, 1938), 22-24; *Newsweek*, xi (May 9, 1938), 17; *Foreign Policy Report*, xiii (June 1937), 66-76; *Christian Science Monitor*, June 3, 1939.

[16] *NYT*, March 24, 1937; Frank C. Hanighen, "Italy from the Inside," *Nation*, cxlv (June 11, 1938), 669-72; *Washington Post*, Sept. 20, 1938.

powers; others hoped, rather faintly, that Mussolini would never commit himself to "a scrap of paper." Then, when Germany invaded Poland the following month and Italy refrained from mobilizing, an anxious America expressed deep gratitude. Italy's neutrality at the outbreak of World War II seemed to rekindle hope that Mussolini had retained his saving sense of realism. Yet as some commentators suspected, this hope would prove a desperate illusion. As we shall see, when Italy attacked France in June 1940 American opinion rose to a crescendo of condemnation.[17]

Because Americans became more concerned about the diplomatic threat of Germany and Japan in the late thirties, Italy was all but ignored in the various opinion polls. Nevertheless a few indirect questions contained in these polls reveal the shifting nature of American opinion of Mussolini's Italy. In the summer of 1937, 73 percent of Americans believed there would be another world war, and 30 percent placed responsibility for starting it on Germany, 27 percent on Italy, 19 percent on Japan, 11 percent on Russia, and 13 percent on various other countries. In January 1939, a somewhat similar question was asked, but here the answers differed: 62 percent chose Germany alone, 12 percent Italy alone, 20 percent Italy and Germany together, and only 6 percent chose other major powers. A question regarding responsibility for the arms race, asked in January 1938, yielded the following responses: Germany 38 percent, Italy 23 percent, and Japan 10 percent. There was also a question on anti-Semitism which, though confined to Germany, revealed that 94 percent of Americans disapproved of Nazism's treatment of the Jews. As to the Axis and Allied powers, Americans unmistakably sympathized with England and France, even though isolationist qualms led many to withhold judgment. In April 1938, for example, 65 percent of Americans supported England and France, and while only 3 percent preferred Germany and Italy, 32 percent refused to choose, and even this neutralist sentiment shifted overwhelmingly to the Allies after the war began. Yet significantly enough, two months before Italy attacked France 96 percent of Americans expressed a desire to see Italy join the Allies. At the same time

[17] *Boston Evening Transcript*, May 23, Sept. 8, 1939; *NYT*, April 8, 10, May 23, 1939; *Washington Post*, May 23, Sept. 14, 1939; *New Orleans Times Picayune*, May 23, 1939; "Mussolini's Margin" (editorial), *Nation*, CL (May 4, 1940), 556.

Americans were asked to select the country they regarded as the "worst influence" in Europe. The replies: Germany, 53 percent; Russia, 34.2 percent; England, 1.8 percent; Italy, 1.2 percent; France, 0.3 percent; and "Don't Know," 12.9 percent.[18]

It is understandable that in 1937 Americans, grieved by Mussolini's actions in Ethiopia and in Spain, would regard Italy as much a menace as Germany. During the Ethiopian crisis 6.7 percent of Americans looked upon Italy as the country towards which they were "least friendly," making her more disliked than even the Soviet Union (5.8 percent). In 1940, however, only 1.2 percent thought Italy the "worst influence" in Europe, a more favorable ranking than that received even by England (1.8 percent).[19] Despite all the anti-American abuse of Fascist extremists and the obnoxious anti-Semitic policy, despite the Axis diplomacy and the Albanian invasion, after 1939 American attitudes became more lenient toward Italy. The reasons for this moderation are not difficult to discover. Public opinion is often shaped by comparisons, and if comparisons are odorous, Mussolini's dictatorship, when contrasted with Hitler's and Stalin's, enjoyed the fragrance of mildness. The comparative advantage worked in Italy's favor in diplomatic as well as domestic affairs. In the eyes of Americans, any villainy Italy may have perpetrated in Ethiopia was more than surpassed by the notorious Russo-German Neutrality and Nonaggression Pact.[20] But even more important, by the end of the decade Americans began to sense a growing estrangement of the Italian people from their government. They knew that Italians were reluctant belligerents who resented Germany and all it stood for. They knew, too, that for most Italians Fascism had lost its ideological thunder. Thus in 1940 all but 4 percent of Americans could easily accept Italy as an ally. And even when the United States and Italy were at war with one another, Americans could appeal to the people of Italy as freedom-loving compatriots.

[18] *Public Opinion Quarterly*, II (July 1938), 388; III (Oct. 1939), 598; IV (June 1940), 357; "American Opinion About the War," *Harper's*, CLXXXII (April 1941), 549-52; Francis Still Wickware, "What We Think about Foreign Affairs," *ibid.*, CLXXIX (Sept. 1939), 397-406.

[19] For the poll taken at the time of the Ethiopian affair, see pp. 292-93n.

[20] In the late thirties Russia had received favorably low ratings in terms of responsibility for war and the arms race, ranking behind Germany, Italy, and Japan. In 1940, however, the Soviet Union and Germany were emphatically singled out as the "worst influence" in Europe. No doubt the Nonaggression Pact accounted for the change in Russia's image.

As for Mussolini, he received the ultimate insult: Americans by and large had simply stopped paying attention to him. In the tense period between Germany's invasion of Poland and Italy's attack on France, he appeared a fading eminence who had lost all control of the situation. Worse still, he had let America down by failing to halt Nazi expansion and by insanely "Prussianizing" his own country, all of which only indicated that Hitler, once regarded as Mussolini's pupil, had clearly dethroned his master. Il Duce still had some spark left, but gone was the dazzling, iron-willed genius who had almost mesmerized America during the twenties. Above all, Americans were convinced that Italy had lost its freedom of action because of Mussolini's failure of nerve. And for Americans a dictator without power to influence events becomes an actor without an audience. Il Duce's demise affirms Emerson's adage: "Every hero becomes a bore at last."

AMERICAN SOCIETY AND WAR FASCISM, II

Moving from the general public to particular social groups one notices a similar pattern of opinion. As to economic categories, organized labor had posed a splendid but isolated opposition since 1924, and throughout the thirties union leaders denounced Mussolini, various locals occasionally boycotted Italian goods, and in 1937 several American unions joined the International Federation of Labor in an anti-Fascist pact. The Catholicism of the many rank-and-file Italian and Irish workers, however, made religious conviction as important a factor as class feeling—a matter we shall return to shortly in examining poll data. With respect to business opinion, Italy as a topic of editorial comment almost disappeared from the business press as it focused its attacks on Soviet Russia, Nazi Germany, and, inevitably, the Roosevelt administration. There were, of course, some exceptions. *Fortune*, which in 1934 had devoted an entire issue to the marvels of the Corporate State, came out in 1940 with a detailed exposé of Blackshirt activities in the United States. But, by and large, most business publications, seeing little reason to reexamine their belated repudiation of Fascism, ignored Italy. Moreover, in contrast to the Wall Street pilgrims of the twenties, the few businessmen who visited Italy in the late thirties returned with harsh accounts of the country's corruption and inefficiency. Finally, the image of the Corporate State, which had so impressed business-

326

men in the early depression years, became stale and odious. Convinced of its stigma, businessmen likened corporatism to the New Deal, while Roosevelt liberals, equally convinced that any label can beat a libel, equated it with the "economic royalism" of the Republican Right.[21]

Ultimately American business came around, albeit for different reasons, to a conviction that labor had preached for over a decade—corporatism was a snare and a delusion. Yet significantly, American liberal intellectuals, who also shared this conviction, felt it necessary to take up again the question of the Corporate State because of a growing rumor that Mussolini, true to his Socialist origins, was finally moving to the Left. Earlier John Strachey, citing a Hearst headline, "Mussolini Abolishes the Capitalist System," warned American liberals to dismiss the story as a conservative-inspired canard. But the rumor persisted, and in 1936 Paul Douglas had to inform the *New Republic* that the Corporate State, a clever, systematic "eye wash," had done nothing to increase welfare, alleviate unemployment, nationalize property, raise real wages, or revamp Italy's regressive taxation policy. Similarly a *Nation* editorial, "Is Mussolini Moving Toward Socialism?" advised readers that the Fascists merely exploited "egalitarian catchwords" and that nationalization under Mussolini would only increase state power. Thus American liberals, a few

[21] E.g., "Labor and Fascism," *LD* cxxiv (Dec. 4, 1937), 24-25; *NYT*, Nov. 28, 1937, May 15, 1938; "War of Nerves," *Fortune*, xxii (Nov. 1940), 85-93, 102-04; "Fascist Slump: Troubled Times Disturb Italy, U.S. Business Man Reports," *LD*, cxxiii (April 10, 1937), 15-16; "Mussolini Is in Trouble" (editorial), *New Republic*, cxi.vii (Aug. 24, 1938), 58. According to Ickes the Roosevelt administration intended to run its 1940 campaign against Willkie by identifying his platform with Italian corporatism. *Secret Diary*, iii, 221-23. As to business anti-Fascism, it should be noted that business attitudes did not necessarily affect business behavior. Certain major industries like General Motors continued to do business with Germany even though American management found Nazism repugnant. In respect to Italy, though trade fell off after Ethiopia it doubled after the outbreak of World War II. Indeed the State Department tried to purchase Italy's neutrality by offering new trade agreements. Gabriel Kolko, "American Business and Germany, 1930-1941," *Western Political Quarterly*, xv (Dec. 1962), 713-28; Roland N. Stromberg, "American Business and the Approach of War, 1935-1941," *Journal of Economic History*, xiii (Winter 1953), 58-78; "U.S. vs. Italy," *Time*, xxxv (June 10, 1940), 77; "Mussolini's Timing," *ibid.*, cl (May 11, 1940), 585-86.

of whom had once been taken in by Fascism's syndicalist, pragmatic rhetoric, were not deceived in the thirties by Italy's new "Socialist" image.[22]

Those who read the *New Republic* and *Nation* for knowledge about Fascism found an anthology of anathemas. They could also find the two leading liberal philosophers in Italy and America, Benedetto Croce and John Dewey, analyzing the "pathological conditions" which produced dictatorships. But what Americans could not find in the liberal weeklies was a political answer to War Fascism. Sensing the need for a program of action, a few liberal intellectuals turned to the European literary resistance, to Thomas Mann and André Malraux, and particularly to Ignazio Silone, whose reputation in America had been established with *Fontamara* and had flourished with *Bread and Wine*. By 1939 *Partisan Review* was publishing interviews with the Italian novelist as well as selections from his forthcoming book, *The School for Dictators*. Yet even though Silone's vogue in America reflected the intellectual's desire to translate conviction into action, the drama of Silone's isolated hero bravely struggling against Fascism seemed unrealistic. Hemingway's *For Whom the Bells Toll* and *To Have and Have Not* offered a different political lesson: refusing to organize collectively to fight Fascism only leads to lonely defeat.[23]

How to oppose Fascism was a question that immobilized many American intellectuals. The paralysis of liberalism mirrored a crisis of confidence in traditional democratic moral values. With the patriotic hysteria of World War I uppermost in their minds, noninterventionist liberals believed that another war would only lead to another diplomatic inferno resulting in unbridled militarism throughout the world and possibly even a native-born Fascism in the United States. Some isolationist liberals tended to dismiss the war against Fascism as a struggle of sordid national interests rather than high political principle. Referring to the antiwar liberals, Oswald Villard righteously proclaimed: "They will not be moved by the argument that wrong may triumph." That the struggle against Fascism was a struggle of right against wrong

[22] *New Republic*, LXXVIII (March 7, 1934), 26-28; LXXXVI (March 4, 1936), 103-05; *Nation*, CXLII (April 8, 1936), 438-39.

[23] *New Republic*, XC (April 7, 14, 21, 1937), 255-26, 287-89, 350-51; *Partisan Review*, VI (Fall 1939), 22-30.

could not be accepted by many liberals for whom the very terms ceased to have meaning.[24]

When we turn to Catholic thinkers we encounter one group of intellectuals who were not reluctant to think in ethical categories. Yet on the question of Fascism, Catholic writers were also devoid of a consistent moral vision. As a result, during the Spanish Civil War American Catholics found themselves profoundly divided. While much of the hierarchy gave its blessing to the Falange's "Cruzada," polls indicate that 39 percent of Catholics in general were pro-Franco, 30 percent pro-Loyalist, and the remaining 31 percent neutral. Significantly, the Jesuit *America*, having supported Italian Fascism from the very beginning, kept the faith by rushing fervently to Franco's side. At the same time *America* played down the unholy developments taking place in Italy. When Italy launched its anti-Semitic program there was some mention of the Pope's dissent, but for the most part the whole affair was dismissed as an ill-advised move instigated by Italian Naziphiles in search of scapegoats. One writer maintained that if Mussolini would only remain independent of Germany, the Fascist government could continue to command the respect of Catholics; another insisted that the racial laws were not in keeping with "the tenets of Fascism or the past record of the Duce." *America* asked its readers to pray for the misguided Mussolini.[25]

America eventually issued a plague-on-both-your-houses attack on Nazism and Communism. Even while doing so, however, it rationalized the case for Italian Fascism. Associate editor John La Farge argued that although both Fascism and Communism violated Christian and American principles, Fascism was the lesser of two evils. Communism was the greater menace because it was international and, what is more, only because of the threat of Communism did the need for Fascism arise. The following year an *America* writer held that the Church was justified in collaborating with Fascism and that one could be a practicing Fascist and a devoted Catholic.[26]

[24] Villard is quoted in Wreszin, p. 245.

[25] The polls are cited in J. David Valaik, "Catholics, Neutrality, and the Spanish Embargo, 1937-1939," *Journal of American History*, LLV (June 1967), 73-85; *America*, LIX (Aug. 13, 1938), 434; *ibid.* (Oct. 1, 1938), 604-06; *ibid.*, LX (March 4, 1939), 508-09; see also Wentz, "American Catholic Periodicals React to Nazism," pp. 400-20.

[26] *America*, LVI (Oct. 10, 1936), 4-5; *ibid.*, LVII (May 1, 1937), 77-78;

No such accommodation with Fascism could be found in *Catholic World*. Even before the outbreak of racism in Italy Father Gillis attacked the populistic reflex "praise of the people" as a false shibboleth that glossed over the reality of dictatorship in Italy as well as in Germany and Russia. When the racial policy was announced, Gillis assailed the Italian professors who "prostituted" themselves by writing the pseudo-scientific rubbish and the Catholic London *Tablet* which paid it lip service. To the Fascist assertion that "discrimination" against Jews did not necessarily constitute "persecution," Gillis enumerated the list of restrictions and asked: "If all the disabilities listed above constitute nothing more than discrimination, God save the Jews from real persecution." A few months later he struck at the "Hegelian" foundations of Fascism itself, maintaining that the "essential antagonism" between Catholicism and Communism was no less true for Catholicism and Fascism. Thus Father Gillis took sharp issue with the Jesuit argument:

As for those of my brethren of the Catholic press who see the viciousness and the danger of Communism so clearly and who attack it so persistently and with so much justifiable vigor, I cannot but wonder that they have little or no worry about Nazism and Fascism, which may in a hundred years do us more harm than Communism. The devil we know is less dangerous than the devil we don't know.[27]

When readers blasted the above editorial as anti-Italian, Father Gillis wondered how anyone could claim that Fascism was the true expression of the free spirit of Augustine, Dante, and St. Paul. Again and again he excoriated myopic Catholic apologists with increasingly impatient editorials ("Getting Wise to Fascism"). Particularly galling was the way in which the Encyclical *Non abbiamo bisogno* (We Have No Need) was "soft pedaled" in the United States and received scant attention in the clerical

---

ibid., LX (April 8, 1939), 627. It is understandable that Jesuits, given their dedication to the defense of the Holy See, would take a softer position on Italian Fascism. Nevertheless even some Catholic writers criticized *America* for failing to take a stand independent of the Papacy. See, for example, the view of the exiled German liberal Catholic, Prince Humbertus Lowenstein, "Catholicism at the Crossroads," *Atlantic*, CLXII (Sept. 1938), 325-30.

[27] *Catholic World*, CXLVII (May 1938), 136-37; *ibid.* (Sept. 1938), 644-47; *ibid.*, CXLVIII (Oct. 1938), 1-7.

press. According to Gillis, the Encyclical was smuggled out of Italy only to be "killed" by the American Catholic press which failed to give it the emphasis it deserved.[28] Then, recalling the Ethiopian slaughter, Gillis directed his most bitter salvos at priests who "thought themselves obligated to justify a war . . . that would have revolted St. Thomas Aquinas or St. Augustine, or for that matter any orthodox moralist"; pagan padres who "might better have been in Church praying that no unjust war should occur, or in their monastic cells applying the discipline to their backs rather than pinning war medals to their chests."[29]

In admonishing brothers under the cloth, *Catholic World* did not ignore the equally culpable Mussolini. The rationale for Italian diplomacy particularly affronted Father Gillis. After Mussolini invaded Albania, Gillis ridiculed all the slogans (e.g., the "inequalities of Versailles," the "Communist menace") used to justify Fascist aggression. A month before the invasion of France he criticized the Axis with Germany, asking how Italy could profess to be anti-Communist when she had entered into an alliance with a nation that had signed a pact with Russia. Summing up the diplomatic situation in May 1940, Gillis saw no way out for Italy. Mussolini would not side with France for fear of his imperial ambitions; he would not respond to the demands of his people for peace lest he acknowledge their sovereignty; and he would not listen to the Pope, for this would require humility. Hence the Italian dictator was the victim of his own delusions and "that's the kind of predicament a man gets himself into who, being a blacksmith's son, fancies himself a match for half a dozen Machiavellis."[30]

As did *Catholic World*, *Commonweal* featured anti-Fascist critics like Prince Lowenstein, Count Sforza, Gorham Munson, and C. G. Paulding. But as a progressive weekly appealing to lay readers, *Commonweal*, unlike *Catholic World*, felt it necessary to answer the *New Republic*'s series on "The Catholic Church in Politics," which appeared in winter 1938. Stirred by the widespread support for Franco in the Catholic community, the *New*

[28] Mgr. Francis Spellman had dispatched several hundred copies of the text from Vatican City to Paris. The Encyclical was a brisk attack on the Fascist party for interfering with Catholic Action.

[29] *Catholic World*, cxlviii (Jan. 1939), 389-94; *ibid.*, cxlix (April 1939), 1-9.

[30] *Ibid.*, cxlix (July 1939), 392-93; *ibid.*, cl (May 1940), 134-37.

Republic launched a free-wheeling attack on the "intrinsic authoritarian character" of the Church as well as the Vatican's unpardonable relations with Mussolini. Its liberal conscience deeply troubled, *Commonweal* left no charge unanswered in rising forth with rebuttals. What followed was a dialogue of accusations and denials in which *Commonweal* took on both the *New Republic* and the *Nation*, a tiresome debate which generated more temperature than theology. With James A. Magner and Michael Williams defending the Church, and with Leo Lehman and George Seldes prosecuting for liberalism, perhaps it was appropriate for novelist Hamilton Basso to step in and advise both sides to read Jacques Maritain's *True Humanism*. For this is what really appalled liberals: whereas European Catholics like Maritain, Sturzo, François Mauriac, and Georges Duhamel defiantly spoke out against Fascism, American Catholic intellectuals seemed strangely silent.[31]

The charge that Catholic thinkers remained mute witnesses to the destruction of European democracy is a bit harsh. For despite *Commonweal*'s defensive stance, despite managing editor Williams' unmitigated Francoism, the liberal weekly's apology for Fascism of the twenties ended in 1931 when Mussolini turned on Catholic Action. True, *Commonweal* was never as firm as *Catholic World* in rejecting Fascism, but neither was it as sanguine as *America* in espousing it. At worst *Commonweal* sympathized with the Vatican's support of Mussolini on the grounds of sheer survival; at best it realized, especially in the late thirties, that Fascism itself was a squalid fraud. In 1939 Williams, writing from Rome, described the "resigned bewilderment" among the Italian people, and the following year he asserted that Vatican City was the only sanctuary in Italy where "true liberty" still survived. Shortly afterwards *Commonweal* pronounced dead the original regenerating spirit of Fascism, while in its pages Sturzo went so far as to concede that even the anticlericalism of Italian liberals was preferable to that of the Blackshirts, whose political agnosticism was so dangerously "subtle" that it "infiltrates and corrodes the soul." Finally in May 1941, the Left-wing tabloid *PM* published a thirteen-page essay on "The Catholic Church and the

[31] *New Republic*, xcvii (Sept. 9, 21, 1938), 6-9, 202-03; *ibid.* (Nov. 16—Dec. 21, 1938), 34-36, 64-68, 94-96, 122-25, 165-68, 195-98; *Nation*, cxlviii (Jan. 21, 1939), 82-83; *Commonweal* xxviii (Sept. 2, 1938), 462-64.

Fascist Question," welcoming the shift of Catholic opinion in America. *Commonweal* expressed deep gratitude for this "straight talk" which at last cleared the air of acrimony and established liberal Catholicism as a respectable ally of anti-Fascism.[32]

From this brief survey of social groups it would be a gross mistake to conclude that on the eve of World War II America finally awoke from its political slumber and became consciously anti-Fascist. Not only did many Americans still harbor kind thoughts about Mussolini and the peculiar Italian "experiment," but more importantly, many perceived the approaching war in continental Europe as a death struggle between reactionary Fascism and revolutionary Bolshevism. Perhaps we can get a better understanding of the way in which this cruel alternative was seen by many Americans if we turn to a few relevant questions posed in public opinion surveys conducted in the late thirties.

PUBLIC OPINION ON EUROPEAN DICTATORSHIPS:
A STATISTICAL NOTE

During the height of the Cold War many Americans took an almost morbid delight in asking whether it would be better to be "red than dead." A quarter century ago an equally grotesque proposition was put to the American people. In April 1937, Americans were asked the unpleasant question: "If you HAD to choose between Fascism and Communism, which would you choose?" Of those answering, 61 percent chose Fascism and 39 percent Communism.[33]

[32] *Commonweal*, xxx (April 28, 1939), 16-17; *ibid.*, xxii (May 17, 1940), 80-81; *ibid.* (Nov. 18, 1940), 99-100; *ibid.*, xxxiii (April 4, 11, 1941), 587, 612-14; *ibid.*, xxxiv (May 16, 1941), 75-76. With respect to other religious groups, American Protestants were always more critical of Fascism than Catholics (as the following poll data show), and during the Spanish Civil War, Protestant opinion became hostile toward clerical dictatorships. As for Jewish opinion, Italy's anti-Semitic decrees in 1938 may be regarded as a turning point, but a gradual and belated one. For although American Jews at first were not unduly alarmed by the legislation, they could no longer consider Mussolini a courageous defender of the faith, as they had in 1933. Jewish leaders now pinned their hopes on the Papacy, on the Protestant churches, and on the good sense of the Italian people. See, for example, *The American Jewish Committee: Twenty-Second Annual Report* (1939), pp. 24-26.

[33] Computations on this and subsequent polls were made from IBM cards kindly supplied by the Roper Public Opinion Research Center, Wil-

Admittedly the question was permeated by an air of unreality, a nominal exercise that conveyed no sense of real choice, no "live option" (as William James might put it) to be acted upon and possibly even realized. That is to say, the great majority of those interviewed most likely, and quite rightly, viewed the question as a matter of abstract opinion rather than a responsible political decision between two plausible alternatives. Moreover the question would have had greater validity for the purposes of the present study had it been made clear that Americans were to choose not for themselves but for Europeans. Nonetheless a Hobson's Choice on European totalitarianism can tell us something about American attitudes, especially when we are able to analyze political preferences in terms of economic and religious categories. In this particular poll the results show the following breakdown along income lines:[34]

---

liams College. The particular polls used were AIPO 75-A (April 6, 1937), AIPO 134 (Oct. 8, 1939), AIPO 145-A (Jan. 20, 1939).

A word about the statistical limitations of these data is in order. The writer cannot stress too much that complete quantitative information on this topic is sorely wanting, rendering impossible any definitive analysis of all the nuances of opinion. For example, although in one of the above polls respondents totaled as high as 2,700, those answering the specific questions studied here numbered considerably less, occasionally only in the hundreds for minority subgroups (e.g., Jews). There are several reasons for this. First, many skipped the questions entirely, and even those who considered it often chose "No Opinion" despite the fact they theoretically "HAD" to choose. More seriously, some of the questions on totalitarianism were prefaced by a "filter question" which first asked if the person knew anything about, or had recently read anything on, the subject of Fascism and Communism. Only if the person answered affirmatively was he directed to the following question asking for his preference. While this procedure had the virtue of invoking answers only from the more well informed, it had the defect of eliminating the curbstone opinion of the "gut thinker" (most likely lower class), an important factor in mass opinion. However, as for the problem of representativeness, the "quota sampling" methodology used in these early AIPO Gallup polls has been judged reliable by authorities. See, for example, Harold L. Childs, *Public Opinion: Nature, Formation and Role* (Princeton, 1965), pp. 71-72.

[34] Compared to the sophisticated studies of later years, polling techniques in the thirties were a bit primitive. Consequently questions were seldom designed to elicit the quality or intensity of an opinion on a given subject. In the question above, and in those which follow, there was no opportunity for a respondent to indicate a preference for American democracy as op-

Income	Fascism	Communism
Average plus	66%	34%
Average	60	40
Poor plus	60	40
Poor	52	48

Although the breakdown indicates Fascism received substantially more support from all income groups except the "Poor," the distribution is not very revealing. Perhaps a more telling economic correlation can be derived from a question posed a year and a half later (October 1938): "If you absolutely HAD to decide which dictator you liked best—Mussolini, Stalin, or Hitler—which would you choose?" The answer: Mussolini 53 percent, Stalin 34 percent, and Hitler 13 percent. Of course this question, dealing with the dictators themselves, cannot be compared exactly with the previous one. Yet for most Americans a foreign ruler manifestly symbolizes the character and essence of his regime. Because of this identification, mass opinion, moved more by style than by substance, is usually more susceptible to the cult of personality than to those inscrutable "alien isms." Hence in the minds of many

---

posed to European dictatorship; nor were there any "scaled" questions to measure the degree of preference, or "depth" questions to ascertain why Americans would choose one form of totalitarianism over another. Fortunately, however, some of the very limitations of these questions yield certain advantages. For one thing, it is safe to assume that the overwhelming majority of Americans would have, if the option were offered, preferred their own government to any foreign totalitarian system. In this sense Americans were explicitly asked to form a judgment for their own country on the basis of their limited knowledge of two remote and vague European phenomena. But in choosing for themselves Americans were, it seems reasonable to believe, implicitly choosing for Europeans as well. Another advantage of these questions is that they were asked without reference to diplomatic policy. For example, the question above, posed during the ordeal of the Spanish Civil War, avoided all suggestions of American aid or intervention. Because these queries were asked apart from more touchy issues like neutrality and isolationism, they caught public opinion when it was relatively free from the stresses of diplomacy and the strains of domestic politics. What we have, then, is pure opinion as opposed to "responsible" opinion (or "real assent"). For a provocative discussion of the latter terms, as well as some cautionary advice regarding the historian's use of opinion polls, see Arthur Schlesinger, Jr., "The Humanist Looks at Empirical Social Research," *American Sociological Review*, xxvii (Dec. 1962), 768-71.

Americans Mussolini was, in fact, the personification of Fascism, just as Hitler was the expression of Nazism and Stalin of Communism. In forming an opinion on European dictators, then, many Americans were judging the nature of the respective governments as well. But even more important, this second poll contained a greater range of economic categories, with the result that income divisions become considerably more emphatic.

Income	Mussolini	Stalin	Hitler
Wealthy	62%	25%	13%
Average plus	58	28	14
Average	56	32	12
Poor plus	46	39	15
On Relief (WPA)	49	36	15
On Relief (home)	49	37	14
On Old-Age Assistance	52	41	7
Poor	48	41	11

In this poll the higher degree of Fascist sympathy among the wealthier classes is well illustrated. It is interesting to note that whereas preferences for Hitler remained constantly low in all groups (dropping especially, curiously enough, in the "Old-Age Assistance" class), support for Stalin increased significantly with the descent of income level. As for Mussolini, his support ranged widely, falling as much as 16 percent from the "Wealthy" to the "Poor plus" classes.

Clearly, economic status went far toward shaping one's attitude toward Fascism and Communism. But perhaps of equal importance was the influence of religion. In this connection we must turn to a survey taken in January 1939, when the public was again asked to choose between Fascism and Communism in a question worded exactly like the one composed in 1937. The overall results of the 1939 poll showed a marked shift, with Fascist support dropping from the previous 61 percent to 54 percent and, conversely, Communist backing advancing from 39 percent to 46 percent. I shall comment on this shift shortly; but first let us see how various religious persuasions influenced choices between the extreme Right and Left. In this 1939 poll respondents were asked to indicate their specific religious affiliation; and this classification, when broken down, yields a most interesting distribution:

336

Religion	Fascism	Communism
Roman Catholic	66%	34%
Protestant (all denominations)	50	50
Baptist	49	51
Methodist	43	57
Lutheran	63	37
Presbyterian	50	50
Episcopalian	63	37
Congregational	48	52
Reformed	50	50
Protestant (no church specified)	47	53
Jewish	33	67
No Religion*	40	60

* Answered "no" to the question: "Are you a member of a Church?"

Here evidence of the religious factor is abundant. Where Protestants were evenly divided, Catholics were decidedly for Fascism and Jews just as decidedly against. Together with the Jews, Fascism received its lowest rating from agnostics, atheists, and various other non-church-goers. Thus it would appear that religious conviction as well as economic position played an important role in shaping the American's opinion of Fascism and Communism. But the question that remains is whether class or creed was the decisive consideration affecting one's preference. The answer may be obtained from the following breakdown of both religious and income categories.

Religion and Economic Class*	Fascism	Communism
Catholic Upper Income	65%	35%
Catholic Average Income	67	33
Catholic Lower Income	66	34
Protestant Upper Income	63	37
Protestant Average Income	49	51
Protestant Lower Income	43	57
No Religion Upper Income	46	54
No Religion Average Income	44	56
No Religion Lower Income	34	66

* I have omitted a Jewish-income breakdown since the cases were so numerically small in the upper income category as to render it statistically unreliable.

These correlations clearly indicate that the religious factor was paramount for Catholics only. In all other religious (and non-

337

religious) groups opinion fluctuated with the change of income level, whereas for Catholics it remained steadily pro-Fascist. Revealing too is the fact that both upper-class Protestants and upper-class Catholics preferred Fascism, with only a shade of a percentage separating the two groups. In contrast, lower-class Catholics and lower-class non-religious Americans differed as much as 32 percent in their choice of opposing ideologies. For Catholics the issue of Communism versus Fascism transcended class lines.

What conclusions may be drawn? Perhaps a better way of stating the question is to ask what conclusions ought *not* be drawn from the data. It would be absurd to stretch a causal connection between the above findings and any "authoritarian" tendencies lurking in the American mind. The polls were too crude and incomplete, the questions too hypothetical, and the choices too limited to afford evidence of this nature. But the value of these polls is that they functioned as a kind of Rorschach test in reverse: if they tell us little about the nation's political psyche, they at least shed some light on the social and religious prisms through which Americans viewed Fascism and Communism in the late thirties. And it is these perceptions which warrant further comment.

If Americans are, as Louis Hartz has persuasively argued, incurably Lockean individualists, the usefulness of these polls is that they literally forced Americans to abandon that ideological lifesaver known as "liberal consensus" and plunge into the treacherous currents of totalitarianism. In this baptism by questionnaire, American society revealed, however reluctantly, some interesting divisions. Fascism was able to elicit the preferences of almost all wealthy groups save Jews and nonbelievers, while at the same time drawing just about half the Protestant middle class and roughly two-thirds of all Catholics. On the other side, Communism could attract, in addition to the emphatic majority of Jews and lower-class nonbelievers, a fraction more than half of the Protestant middle class, considerably more than half of its lower class, and slightly more than half of upper and middle-class nonreligious Americans. Having established this much, however, we are still left in a limbo of statistical abstractions. What we need to know is what Americans may have had in mind when choosing between these two unpleasant alternatives. On this the data are dead silent. But one thing seems obvious enough. In deciding between Fascism or Communism most Americans were thinking of Mussolini's Italy and Stalin's Russia, not Hitler's Germany. Observe, for example, that as a general concept Fascism won the preference of 61 percent of Americans in 1937; but the following year, in the question offering the three dictators as personal leaders, Hitler appealed to only 13 percent of the public. It is also significant that even "Wealthy" Americans chose Stalin over Hitler by a sizable margin of almost two to one. Yet neither dictator was a match for Mussolini, the dominant choice of all classes, the middle and upper especially. Hence it is clear that on the general question of Fascism or Communism almost all who chose the former—and most certainly the Jews—had Mussolini's regime in mind.

That Americans preferred their Fascism mild, with a touch of the gentle despot who could combine charisma with comedy, seems understandable to anyone familiar with the Mussolini vogue of the 1920s. But in terms of motivational insight, the opinion polls above are meaningless unless placed in proper context. The particular historical context of these surveys was the period from April 1937 to January 1939, a period of international tension which saw American opinion disposed to Fascism drop from 61 percent to 54 percent. In all probability foreign and domestic events in Italy account for Fascism's waning sympathy in America. By 1939 the Rome-Berlin Axis, which many Americans had dismissed so complacently in 1936, had now appeared as a real ideological bond that would soon seal Italy's fate. The effects of other developments on Mussolini's image, like the *Anschluss* and the dubious Munich settlement, we have already discussed. But what is significant is that 7 percent of Americans who previously chose Fascism now preferred Communism. Although it might be argued that they had no choice, Americans still could have registered a preference for "Fascism" with Hitler and German Nazism in mind; instead they chose Stalin and Communism. In this connection the shift of opinion with respect to the Soviet Union deserves a few words. Note, for instance, that all economic classes chose Stalin over Hitler. But note too that in the 1937 poll Communism was unable to attract even a majority of those who assigned themselves "Poor"; nor in the 1938 question on personal dictators could Stalin win the preference of any of the lower income groups. Yet by 1939, when Communism had advanced an overall 7 percent, it had gained significant support from all lower-class elements except Catholics. There can be little doubt that the image of Stalin and Communism would have continued to ascend had it not been for the Russo-German Neutrality and Nonaggression Pact, which aroused a furious denunciation in America and spoiled Stalin's chance to succeed in Mussolini's earlier role as Hitler's foil.

These scattered surveys, so incomplete and unimaginatively formulated, tell us little about American political values. They do suggest, however, that on the issue of European Fascism, American society displayed significant religious and class strains. To be sure, America was not emotionally torn over the question as were European countries like Léon Blum's France. Even that heart-rending trauma of the Spanish Civil War proved incapable of eroding America's "liberal consensus." Yet one cannot escape the conclusion that if Americans were less divisive than Europeans it was only because the great majority believed they would never really have to face the two dreadful alternatives. How Americans would have chosen, had history forced the agony of choice upon them, remains the unanswered question.[35]

ITALIAN-AMERICANS AND THE APPROACH OF WAR

In the mid-thirties Italian-Americans had good reason to be pleased with the old country. After almost a century of contemptible abuse, Italy at last had emerged as a power to be

---

[35] "One explanation for the faintness of pro-Franco sentiment among businessmen and professionals is that American conservatives are—as I have been arguing in this chapter—still more or less a part of the 'liberal consensus' and, as such, they found Franco's Spain ideologically repugnant. . . . Equally important as an explanation is the so-called 'religious issue.' In a sentence, differences in religion were more important than differences in income. Of Catholics polled, 39 per cent were for General Franco; of Protestants, 9 per cent; of Jews, 2 per cent. One scarcely need comment that the average income of American Catholics is lower than that of American Protestants and Jews" (Guttmann, p. 65). At first glance Guttmann's thesis may appear to conflict with the one presented here. We both found that on foreign politics the religious factor determined Catholic opinion; but while he argues that income status was a negligible influence, the data here suggest that economic class was as important as religion, indeed more important for non-Catholics. One explanation for this apparent disparity is, I believe, that many Americans simply refused to see the war in Spain as a struggle between Fascism and Communism. Even more important, for upper-class Americans Spain's *Nuevo Estado* was not Italy's *Stato Corporativo*, nor was El Caudillo Il Duce. While Franco appeared a dull Moloch standing in the way of industrialization, the dynamic Mussolini was, at least until Ethiopia, the darling of Wall Street.

reckoned with. Il Duce succeeded beyond all expectations not only in conquering Abyssinia but in overcoming sanctions and defying the League of Nations. What is more, amid the chaos and despair of world depression Mussolini's reaffirmation of corporatism in 1936 seemed to display once again the guiding genius of Italian civilization, a genius that had languished since the Renaissance. Thanks to Mussolini and Fascism, modern Italy had found her place in the sun.

In New York, on Columbus Day 1937, Italian-Americans could well count their blessings as they listened to flattering speeches by Governor Herbert Lehman and Thomas Dewey. During the ceremony, which had been arranged by publisher Generoso Pope, several spectators gave the Fascist salute while a number of agitators, led by Leftist Congressman Vito Marcantonio, heckled the speakers. Then the flamboyant Fiorello La Guardia stepped forward to make the major address. Like most political speeches, La Guardia's combined bustle with blandness to celebrate ritualistically the enduring ties between Italy and the United States. The appearance of La Guardia was a bitter disappointment to anti-Fascists who knew that the liberal mayor had no use for Mussolini. But official ceremonies of this sort served to remind anti-Fascists once again how isolated they remained from the Italian-American masses. This was true in press commentary as well as public rituals. The previous year a group of distinguished *fuorusciti* had written a letter, "After Mussolini, What?" which was published in several newspapers and periodicals. The manifesto declared that if and when Mussolini falls from power a Monarchist-Papal collaboration must be resisted, separation of church and state must be restored, and social and political reform must be undertaken at once. Yet the message, which represented the undying spirit of *Risorgimento* liberalism, was easily lost upon Italian-Americans. Indeed the financier Luigi Criscuolo spoke for most Italian-Americans when, in answering the letter, he maintained that if Mussolini should fall Italy would return to the "old spoils system," the Mafia would slink out of the shadows, beggars would reappear on the streets, and Italy would once again be relegated to a fourth-rate power. Against such arguments anti-Fascists could hardly hope to reach the Italian-American mind, which remained entranced in the afterglow of nostalgic nationalism.[36]

[36] *NYT*, Oct. 13, 1937, Nov. 14, 1937; Max Ascoli, et al., "After Musso-

Still, thoughtful philofascists knew that all was not well in Italy. After the conquest of Ethiopia the grandeur of that long-awaited victory gave way to the sober realities of both diplomatic and domestic problems. With the possible exception of the fanatic Domenico Trombetta, few Italian-Americans could look blithely on the formation of the Rome-Berlin Axis, the insidious Prussianization of Italy, and the insulting anti-American campaign of Gayda and Farinacci. Of course Italian-American publishers, as we shall see, tended to rationalize these events; but even while turning necessity into virtue they betrayed unmistakable misgivings over the recent trends in Italy. The anti-Semitism episode provides one illustration of the uncertain mood.

Not surprisingly, the racist Trombetta showed his true colors when the Fascist government announced the anti-Semitic decrees in 1938. Of all the foreign Italian journals, not only in the United States but in the Western world, his *Il Grido della Stirpe* was the most flagrantly bigoted. With warped glee Trombetta ardently defended Fascist racism in both his paper and on his evening radio broadcasts. On the West Coast Ettore Patrizi, though no racist, also defended the Italian measures. The publisher of *L'Italia* (San Francisco), Patrizi rationalized the decrees by claiming that the confiscation of Jewish property was necessary for economic development. Far more significant than the positions of Trombetta and Patrizi, however, was that of Generoso Pope. On the anti-Semitism issue Pope questioned the Fascist government for the first time in his career. All along Pope had opposed vigorously the Nazi pogrom, and when Mussolini aped Hitler's "solution" in 1938, the publisher did not hide his disgust. Mincing no words, he attacked the Italian decrees on constitutional and humanitarian grounds, and he warned the Fascist government against alienating the friendship of the six million Italians and four million Jews in the United States. He further pointed out that America was free of anti-Semitism, that he himself employed Jews in important positions, and that he engaged in business with peoples of all races. For Pope to stand up to Mussolini and the

lini, What?" *New Republic*, LXXXVI (Feb. 12, 1936), 20-21; Luigi Criscuolo, "After Mussolini, What? A Reply to Messrs. Ascoli, Borgese, Cantarella, Ferrando, Salvemini, and Venturi," *Publications of the American League for Italy* (Feb. 1936), p. 8; the reply also appeared in the *NYT*, Feb. 16, 1936.

Fascist government represented a most courageous act, even though on all other matters he continued his avid support of the regime, doubtless believing that there was still more in Mussolini to be praised than pardoned. Nonetheless, given the vast circulation of his newspapers, Pope's editorials opposing anti-Semitism at least served to inform Italian-Americans that some things in Italy were undeniably rotten.[37]

All was not going well in the United States either. In late 1937 there appeared a series of articles exposing Fascist activities in this country. It was at this time, one recalls, that Italian-American Blackshirts and German-American Bundists staged a joint rally at Camp Nordland, New Jersey, a ghoulish political vaudeville that could be dismissed at best only with nervous laughter. Shortly afterwards Frank C. Hanighen wrote a disquieting article in the respectable *Foreign Affairs* describing the defunct FLNA, its successor the Lictor Federation, the Fascist infiltrated Sons of Italy, and the indoctrination programs carried on in the Italian language schools. This exposé was followed up in the *Nation* by M. B. Schnapper's "Mussolini's American Agents," to be capped later by *Fortune*'s thorough investigation of "Hitler's Helpers" in the United States and *Harper's* detailed survey of American Fascist organizations. Before long several book-length studies had been started by undercover agents or pseudonymous authors. Fears of a Right-wing "Fifth Column" in America seemed real enough to those who read Sinclair Lewis' *It Can't Happen Here* and anxiously watched the death agonies of the European democracies. Perhaps it is helpful to remember that the controversial House Un-American Activities Committee was originally conceived as a means of halting the nascent Fascist movements in America as well as subversion by the radical Left. Moreover, several who investigated the foreign-inspired Right-wing movements concluded that, although Germany as a nation posed a greater international threat, Italian Fascist activities comprised a greater internal menace in the United States. Whereas the assimilated German-Americans and their sedate press stayed relatively clear of the home country's politics, the more alienated Italian-Americans, who maintained solidarity through their traditional

[37] For *Il Grido della Stirpe*'s response, see Renzo De Felice, *Storia degli ebrei italiani sotto il fascismo* (Turin, 1961), p. 389; De Medici, pp. 78-79; "Hitler e gli ebrei," *Il Progresso*, March 25, 1933; "For a Better Understanding," *ibid.*, Dec. 25, 1938; see also De Felice, pp. 388-89.

ethnic institutions and politically impassioned newspapers, took to Fascist propaganda with ravenous gusto.[38]

The exposés and investigations, which increased as the country drew closer to hostilities with the Axis powers, caused many Italian-Americans to begin to have second thoughts about their dual loyalties. Equally embarrassing was the arrival of greater numbers of *fuorusciti* in the late thirties. After the fall of France in 1940, the United States became a sanctuary for important Italian political leaders like Count Carlo Sforza, Don Luigi Sturzo, Alberto Tarchiani, Giuseppe Lupis, and Randolfo Pacciardi.[39] With the arrival of these prestigious figures Mussolini's American enemies now had the basis for a broad and more effective anti-Fascist movement. One of the *fuorusciti*'s first moves was to establish counterpublications in order to reach both the Italian-American community and the American public. In 1939 Lupis began printing the influential biweekly *Il Mondo* (New York); the following year G. A. Borgese collaborated with Robert Hutchins in bringing out *Common Cause*; soon other anti-Fascist journals appeared, like Pacciardi's *L'Italia Libera* (New York) and *Quaderni Italiani* (Boston). As for anti-Fascist organizations, the most important to emerge in these years was the Mazzini

[38] Hanighen, "Foreign Political Movements," p. 16; M. B. Schnapper, "Mussolini's American Agents," *Nation*, CXLVII (Oct. 15, 1938), 374-76; "The War of Nerves: Hitler's Helper," *Fortune*, XXII (Nov. 1940), 85-87; Dale Kramer, "Survey of Fascist Organizations in the United States," *Harper's*, CLXXX (Sept. 1940), 380-93; for alarmist exposés see also George Britt, *Fifth Column in America* (New York, 1940), John Ray Carlson, pseud., *Under Cover* (New York, 1943); George Seldes, *Facts and Fascism* (New York, 1943).

In the HUAC investigations considerably less attention was given to Italian-American Fascism than to the motley bevy of American Naziphiles. In view of the blatancy of the Italian propaganda effort this is surprising. One explanation held that some of the investigations, particularly those at the state level, were instigated by Jewish public officials disturbed by German anti-Semitism (e.g., the Dickstein-McCormick Committee of New York). More plausible was the suggestion that politicians from urban centers feared offending their Italian constituencies. Whatever the case, Italian Fascist activities escaped the close scrutiny they deserved. See, for example, Joseph S. Roucek, "Foreign Politics and Our Minority Groups," reprint of pamphlet, *Phylon* (Spring 1941).

[39] In the postwar era Carlo Sforza became minister of foreign affairs; Alberto Tarchiani, ambassador to the United States; Randolfo Pacciardi, minister of defense; Giuseppe Lupis, an under-secretary of state; while Luigi Sturzo became an influential leader of the Christian Democratic party.

Society, founded in 1940 by such exiles as Ascoli, Lupis, Tarchiani, Robert Bollafio, Umberto Gualtieri, and Dante Gnudi.
Dedicated to the principles of the *Risorgimento*, the Mazzinian
liberals published the weekly *Nazioni Unite* (New York) and
discussed the strategy of internal resistance in Italy and Allied
cooperation with the underground. Finally, Frances Keene, Salvemini's secretary, edited an anthology of anti-Fascist essays,
explaining to American readers that the exiles, however disparate
ideologically, were bound together by what she termed a Jeffersonian sense of morality and justice.[40]

Meanwhile the seemingly omnipresent Salvemini was writing
as prolifically as ever in English and Italian journals alike. In
1940 the American Council of Public Affairs issued his informative but unduly alarming pamphlet, *Italian Fascist Activities in
the United States*. Perhaps the most important publication was
Lupis' *Il Mondo*. An exiled parliamentarian, the Sicilian Lupis
had the tough features of an Al Capone and the humane instincts
of a Danilo Dolci. As editor, his main role was to expose the
Fascist infiltration of the Italian-American community, and, after
the United States entered the war, to promote the liberation in
terms compatible with the restoration of Italian social democracy.
But all along *Il Mondo* did not hesitate to attack prominent
American figures and institutions for allegedly misleading the
public. *New York Times'* journalists—C. L. Sulzberger, Herbert
Matthews, Cortesi, and McCormick—were continually lambasted
for their softheaded illusions about Mussolini and Italian Fascism.
Unlike many anti-Fascist publications, *Il Mondo* was not a voice
in a wilderness of indifference. Many of its articles found their
way into major publications, and often respectable periodicals
like *Fortune* drew upon *Il Mondo* for information and paid
tribute to editor Lupis as a prophetic anti-Fascist veteran to
whom America must awake and listen.[41]

But the great majority of Italian-Americans were not listening.
As war clouds darkened the skies of Europe the Italian-American
press made heroes out of isolationists like Ambassador Joseph
Kennedy, publisher William Randolph Hearst, Senators Burton
Wheeler and William Borah, and occasionally even Nazi sympa-

[40] Frances Keene, ed., *Neither Liberty Nor Bread: The Meaning and
Tragedy of Fascism* (New York, 1940).
[41] "The *New York Times* and Mussolini," *Il Mondo* (Oct. 15, 1939), pp.
29-31; "The Foreign Language Press," *Fortune*, xxii (Nov. 1940), 93, 112.

thizers like Charles Lindbergh. One outlet for Italian opinion was the American First Committee (an expedient alliance of liberal isolationists, Republican reactionaries, genuine patriots, and pro-Nazi supporters) whose officers made their appearance at rallies in Italian neighborhoods. Inevitably the Italian-American press was forced to explain away all Axis aggressions. During the Munich crisis *Il Progresso* maintained that the "Rights of Italy" were equally at stake, for Hitler was only trying to do what Mussolini had all along realized must be done: rectify the inequities of Versailles. After the whole of Czechoslovakia was swallowed up by the German army, *L'Italia* maintained that the Czech state was a "country without a soul" and thus "there is no need to weep." "To say that Germany and other nations want war is madness," added *L'Italia*. "What the DEFEATED nations like Germany and the ROBBED nations like Italy are looking for . . . [is] to find a place in the sun WITHOUT WAGING WAR." When Hitler invaded France in September 1939, *Il Progresso* stood firmly by the Axis: "This war . . . was begun by Germany for an indisputably just cause." By the spring of 1940, the pro-Fascist press was blaming the war on Churchill's "international gangsterism."[42]

In view of the disposition of the pro-Fascist press any attempt to support the cause of European democracy was bound to alienate the great mass of Italian-Americans. The Roosevelt administration discovered this in the election of 1940, when its grand ethnic coalition suffered one of its first casualties. More than anything else, what incensed Italian voters was Roosevelt's angry speech attacking Mussolini for "plunging the dagger" into France when Italy declared war on her neighbor (more on this later). Some Italian-American papers failed to mention the speech; others attempted to tone it down through skillful paraphrase. *L'Italia*, for example, transcribed the pertinent passage in these words: "Unfortunately the Chief of the Italian Government did not judge it convenient to accept the suggested procedures, and,

[42] *Il Progresso*, Dec. 4, 1938, Dec. 5, 1939; *La Voce del Popolo* (San Francisco), March 27, 1939; De Medici, pp. 86-88, 106, 184; on *Il Progresso's* reaction to Hitler's invasion of France, see *PM*, Aug. 20, 1943, and John Norman, "Repudiation of Fascism by the Italian-American Press," *Journalism Quarterly*, xxi (March 1944), 1-6; see also Max Ascoli, "On the Italian-Americans," *Common Ground*, iii (Autumn 1942), 45-49; and Constantine Panunzio, "Italian-Americans, Fascism, and the War," *Yale Review*, xxxi (Summer 1942), 771-82.

therefore, the war saber, which was held by a string, had fallen on the back of the neighbor." But no matter how much editors tried to blunt Roosevelt's slashing remarks, the damage had been done. In the fall election Italian voters in New York, San Francisco, Philadelphia, and elsewhere swung toward Wendell Willkie and the Republican party, which had been exploiting the President's speech for all it was worth.[43]

In the meantime the anti-Fascist press kept up its war of words against the major Italian-American papers. A weekly fusillade of invective issued from Felicani's *Controcorrente*, Clemente's *La Parola del Popolo*, Valenti's *La Parola*, Lupis' *Il Mondo*, and Zito's *Il Corriere del Popolo*. Some of these papers were bringing to a climax noisy ideological feuds that had been going on for almost a decade. Zito's *Il Corriere del Popolo*, for example, was finally in a position to put the finger on Mussolini's San Francisco fan club, whose loudest cheerleader was publisher Patrizi. Due to the efforts of Zito, Gino Neri, Giuseppe Facci, and others, sufficient publicity was generated to have the California state legislature undertake an investigation of the alleged propaganda activities of several *prominenti*—including San Francisco's Italian-American Police Chief.[44]

Watching developments in California closely, *Il Mondo* informed its New York readers that "Ettore Patrizi is no less shady and dangerous than our own Generoso Pope." The counterpart to Patrizi, Pope was the archenemy of East Coast anti-Fascists. In almost every bimonthly issue of *Il Mondo* appeared some exposé of Pope and his *Il Progresso* and *Corriere d'America*. Lupis' efforts, like those of Zito in San Francisco, soon paid off. In 1941, as government attention began to focus on Pope, major periodicals like *Time* brought the partisan quarrel into the public limelight. At the same time Count Sforza informed Roosevelt that the "poison" coming from Pope's "pseudo-patriotic" daily must not be allowed to deceive Italian-Americans any longer. To counter the great influence of Pope's papers, Sforza advised the President to use his position to help establish an anti-Fascist daily which would possibly be edited by the Mazzinian liberal, Tarchiani. With this information at hand, Roosevelt sent for Pope and, according to Secretary Ickes, promised he "would talk to him

[43] *Il Mondo*, Nov. 15, 1940; *L'Italia*, Sept. 11, 1940; De Medici, p. 156; Maile, pp. 95-96.

[44] *Il Corriere del Popolo*, March 24, 1942.

straight from the shoulder." Apparently Roosevelt's chat was enough to convince the Tammany publisher that Fascism, even Italian Fascism, was no longer respectable. Thereafter Pope ceased his pro-Fascist editorials and began to criticize mildly Il Duce himself. But *Il Mondo* kept up the pressure, claiming that, while Pope printed anti-Fascist editorials in English, the Italian section of his paper remained as unregenerate as ever. This direct challenge to the sincerity of Pope's conversion, in September 1941, finally caused him to print unadulterated denunciations of Mussolini in both languages.[45]

Generoso Pope emerged from the whole affair a much maligned man. It is understandable that anti-Fascists, who waged a lonely, uphill struggle against his powerful influence for almost twenty years, should have regarded him with disgust and suspicion. Yet Pope was not a hopeless reactionary, as his courageous stand against Italian anti-Semitism and continued support of Roosevelt attest. Moreover, as we shall see shortly, when Italy entered the war Pope made absolutely clear his undivided loyalty to the United States, though admittedly his position on Italy itself, like that of many Italian-Americans, was tortuously ambivalent.[46] Then in the summer of 1941, Pope turned over the editorship of his papers first to his son and later to a public relations firm. Undoubtedly all these belated decisions can be interpreted—as they were by anti-Fascists—as mere steps to avoid legal prosecution. But in this connection it is important to know what the Italian government itself thought about Pope during this critical period. In June 1941, Italian authorities discovered that the American government was about to investigate the Rome branch of *Il Progresso*. Moving quickly, the Ministry of Popular Culture advised Rome officials to suspend immediately all telegraph services to *Il Progresso* in order to prevent American officials from finding out that Pope "enjoyed special privileges from us." Meanwhile the Italian Ambassador in Washington wired the Ministry

45 "Is Mr. Pope a Fascist?" *Il Mondo*, July 15, 1941; *La Parola*, May 24, 1941; *Il Corriere del Popolo*, March 14, 1942; *Time*, xxxviii (Sept. 22, 1941), 57; Memo, Sforza to Roosevelt, April 5, 1941, Box OF 233A, RP; Ickes, *Secret Diary*, iii, 477; Samuel Dickstein to Valenti April 4, 1941, VP.

46 For anti-Fascists, of course, it was not so much a question of Pope's loyalty to America as his long dedication to Italian Fascism. Pope became a controversial figure again in 1943 when Italian-Americans started to form various liberation committees. See below, pp. 402-07, 412-13.

of Foreign Affairs to report on Pope's increasing criticism of Mussolini. Ambassador Colonna stressed that even though the attacks had not been printed in the Italian section of *Il Progresso*, Pope should be "classified among the anti-Italians and anti-Fascists." The Ambassador also added that Pope was basically a political opportunist and therefore unreliable. With Pope's defection, the Ministry of Popular Culture began to negotiate with Vincenzo and Filippo Giordano, *Il Progresso's* Rome correspondents, to establish a new Italian-language paper in New York. Of this move, suggested by the Giordano brothers and approved by high Fascist officials, Pope was unapprised.[47]

Thus while many of his subordinates went completely over to Fascism,[48] Pope remained unswervingly loyal to the United States. During the war Pope's enemies would claim that he was a "post-Pearl Harbor anti-Fascist" while his friends maintained that he broke with Mussolini as early as 1938 over the anti-Semitism issue. Both claims are inaccurate. Although Pope began to repudiate Fascism several months before Pearl Harbor, his earlier criticisms of Italy's racial policies failed to lead to any significant ideological reconsiderations. Like many other Italian-American publishers, Pope's conversion came gradually, beginning with Italy's attack on France in June 1940, and culminating in September 1941.[49]

Until the summer of 1940 there was no question that Italian-Americans in general were solidly behind Mussolini. But the attack on France, though anticipated in many quarters, came as a sobering shock. In the Little Italys, where residents gathered in small circles to listen to Roosevelt's broadcast, the mood was one of "stunned amazement." News of the invasion was extremely "painful" for Italian-Americans, La Guardia informed reporters. Eagerly interviewing residents, newsmen discovered a few Fascist sympathizers who boasted a quick victory for the Axis powers; but most Italian-Americans could only express concern for their relatives; and while others were willing to concede that Mussolini made "a great mistake," the anti-Fascist *La Parola* extended its

[47] Memo, Ministry of Popular Culture, Sept. 13, 1941; *ibid.*, Oct. 17, 1941; Ambassador Colonna to Ministry of Foreign Affairs, July 25, 1941, IR.

[48] In addition to the Giordano brothers, Angelo Guidi and Vincenzo Comito also left *Il Progresso* to write and broadcast for the Axis powers.

[49] For Pope's claim that he had repudiated Fascism in 1938, see, for example, *Il Progresso*, Aug. 1, 1943.

"heartfelt sympathy to the French people fighting in defense of Western civilization." Immediately spokesmen for Italian organizations, including the Sons of Italy, came forward with declarations of undivided allegiance to America. In New York alone representatives of 122 Italian groups assembled a few days later to approve of resolutions condemning the invasion and even Roosevelt's characterization of Mussolini as a "backstabber." As for Pope, he "regretted" Mussolini's decision to enter the war against the side "with which the American people are in sympathy." Politicians of Italian extraction were more emphatic. Congressman Thomas D'Alessandro told his colleagues in the House that Italian-Americans were willing to die for their adopted country.[50]

Meanwhile government men began to close in on various Italian propaganda agencies. When officials began investigating the "centri educativi" in New York City, Ambassador Colonna complained that such harassments were "unjustified efforts to foment anti-Italian feelings." A more serious development occurred when Consul Edoardo Bertolini brazenly announced that Italian-Americans were secretly supporting Mussolini but were forced into silence by social and business pressures. Bertolini's statement caused an uproar in the Italian communities. To demonstrate that his accusation was groundless, an "Italian Emergency Committee" was hurriedly organized, headed by New York Lieutenant Governor Charles Poletti, Mayor La Guardia, and labor leader Luigi Antonini. Demanding that the Italian government recall Bertolini at once, the Committee set out to publicize the propaganda activities of consulates throughout the country. When Ambassador Colonna protested the attacks on the consulates, which were now under heavy police guard, Secretary of State Cordell Hull warned the Rome government that any of its representatives in the United States engaged in "inappropriate activity" would be immediately expelled. Hull also invited Colonna to attend the HUAC hearings. The shaken Ambassador declined.[51]

For a year and a half, from June 10, 1940 to December 7, 1941, Italian-American sentiment hung suspended between hope and fear; hope that somehow the United States could remain out of the war; fear that once the country entered the war, Italians in

[50] NYT, June 11, 14, 1940; New York Herald Tribune, June 11, 1940.
[51] NYT, June 14, 15, 16, Aug. 4, Nov. 15 1940; L'Italia, June 18, 1940.

America would be compelled to fight against their own *parentela*. The Italian-American press, though upset by Mussolini's rash actions, stood behind Italy in her war with England. Hence most papers opposed revision of the neutrality laws and withdrew into a gloomy and desperate isolationism. Gradually *Il Progresso* and *L'Italia* swung around to supporting preparedness, conscription, and other measures short of aid to England or direct intervention. But all along Italian papers, while stressing again and again their American patriotism, played down Mussolini's role in the Axis war. Ultimately Pearl Harbor resolved the dilemma. Now that Italy and the United States were at war the question of undivided allegiance transcended all other considerations. (Three days after Pearl Harbor, Italy declared war on the United States.) *Il Progresso* declared that it was "The Supreme Duty" to defend the Allied cause, and *L'Italia* announced that "all people of Italian blood will stand loyally by America."[52]

Within days following Pearl Harbor *prominenti* began to return their medals and decorations to the Fascist government. At the same time the more avid champions of Il Duce burned their Fascist membership cards and severed all ties with suspected Italian-American clubs and lodges. Some of the notorious philofascists, as we shall see in a subsequent chapter, were rounded up by government agents and sent to internment camps. Consequently during the war the Italian-American became the object of a mild loyalty scare. But this episode was short-lived and one which, interestingly enough, produced the opposite effect. Instead of generating widespread suspicion, the war between Italy and the United States gave rise to a groundswell of sympathy for the Italians. In the press and in Congress nothing but praise was spoken on their behalf (except for the comments of Westbrook Pegler). America was indeed grateful; for when the moment of truth arrived the Italian-Americans did not hesitate. Nor did their reassertion of American loyalty necessarily involve the sacrifice of traditional Italian patriotism. For Italians and Americans alike could now maintain that the real betrayer of the Italian nation was Benito Mussolini. Moreover, the behavior of Italian-Americans flattered the nation's ego. At last it was clear that Italian-Americans were more American than Italian. The historic anxiety about ethnic divisiveness, in short, proved more fear than

[52] *Il Progresso*, March 19, 1939, June 19, 23, 1940, Dec. 8, 12, 1941; *L'Italia*, June 5, 1940, Dec. 12, 1941.

fact. Indeed in the super-patriotic spirit that began to catch hold in the 1940s it almost seemed that, for Italian-Americans, war was the fuel of the melting pot.[53]

WASHINGTON, ROME, AND THE OUTBREAK OF WAR

Diplomatic relations between Washington and Rome in the late thirties showed the same strains as public opinion. Beginning in late 1936, with the outcome of the Ethiopian War no longer in doubt, Mussolini resumed correspondence with Roosevelt, sending the most conciliatory letters and later even forwarding to the President a prized literary gift—the Premier's complete speeches. The picture of politeness, Il Duce was obviously trying to bury the hatchet of sanctions now that the Abyssinian crisis had been settled to his satisfaction. Italy had much to gain by reestablishing cordial relations with the United States: tariff and trade agreements, renewed prestige, and above all, recognition of her new "empire" in the Mediterranean. Not to be outcharmed, Roosevelt responded in kind ("My dear Duce"), particularly to Mussolini's suggestion that the President intervene to halt the arms race. But all along Roosevelt—who was aware Il Duce preached disarmament while dispatching troops and munitions to Spain—never made any substantive diplomatic concession to Italy. In fact when it appeared England was about to extend recognition to Italian Abyssinia, Roosevelt vigorously protested to Chamberlain. Almost alone among nations, the United States continued to refuse recognition of Italy's African conquest.[54]

The lenient attitudes of Roosevelt and his diplomats toward Mussolini and Fascism have already been discussed. Here it is only necessary to observe their views of Italian diplomacy in the post-Ethiopian period. In the main, administration officials seldom spoke harshly of the drift of Italian foreign policy. Two of Roosevelt's chief ambassadors, Joseph P. Kennedy in London and William C. Bullitt in Paris, were not going to raise their voices against Italy. The Irish-Catholic Kennedy not only feared the outbreak of war but was sensitive to the Vatican's precarious situation within the Mussolini regime, while Bullitt's fear of the

[53] For the House's reaction to Pegler's slurs on the Italian-Americans see the *Congressional Record*, 76th Cong., 3rd Sess., Vol. LXXXVI, 11689-90.

[54] Roosevelt to Mussolini, July 28, 1937, in *F.D.R., His Personal Letters, 1928-1941*, ed. Elliott Roosevelt (New York, 1950), I, 700-01; De Santi, pp. 261-80.

Soviet Union blinded him to the possibility, however remote, of any anti-Fascist alternatives in western Europe. Similarly Breckinridge Long, the ambassador in Rome who had earlier brooded over the prospect of Italian expansionism, soon came to take a soft line toward Italy. By 1938 Long was convinced that the main threat to European peace lay in Britain's unreasonable attitude toward Italy. Meanwhile William Phillips, Long's successor, remained as optimistic as ever. Time and again Phillips assured Roosevelt that Mussolini neither wanted nor could afford another war. "He is essentially interested in bettering the conditions of the masses and his accomplishments in this direction are astounding and are a source of constant amazement to me," Phillips informed Roosevelt in April 1937. "To inspire in the people a 'martial spirit' and intense patriotism are the methods which he has adopted to lift the people out of the 'slough of despond' into which they had sunk before he appeared on the stage." Phillips was also convinced that Mussolini had no further Mediterranean ambitions and that Italy was a "satisfied power."[55]

While overseas diplomats assumed a position varying somewhere between apology and appeasement, administration attitudes were divided. The President himself rejected Long's and Phillips' advice to extend "de jure" recognition to Italian Ethiopia, and later Roosevelt, to the chagrin of some of his advisers, would speak out against Fascist aggression in general. But two of the leading cabinet members—Secretary of State Cordell Hull and Interior Secretary Harold Ickes—rarely agreed on how to approach Italy. Hull saw the Italian question as a problem of quiet diplomacy, apparently believing that there may have been some chance to appeal to Mussolini's better instincts. "No Government ever made a more sincere effort to keep another Government from going to war than the United States in the case of Italy," he later recalled in his memoirs. Ickes, on the other hand, was intemperate in his attacks on Fascism. More resigned to the inevitability of Italy's entry, Ickes watched the capricious Premier "pulling the petals off the daisy" while Hitler's armies advanced, an invidious

[55] Sumner Welles to Roosevelt, Aug. 2, 1939, PSF "Vatican," RP; Kaufmann, "Two American Ambassadors: Bullitt and Kennedy," passim; Breckinridge Long's attitude is recorded in his unpublished diary, mentioned in William E. Leuchtenburg, *Franklin D. Roosevelt and The New Deal* (Torchback edn., New York, 1963), p. 288; Phillips to Roosevelt, April 22, 1937, PSF Italy, Box 10, RP.

sideshow which led him to the cynical conclusion: "To the victor belongs Mussolini." Although Ickes speculated on the possibility of Italy coming over to the Allies, he had little regard for her potential military contributions. He was more than amused by General Gamelin's remark that, in Ickes' words, "if Italy fought by the side of Germany, it would take six French divisions to check her; and that if Italy came in on the side of England and France, it would take six French divisions to keep the Italian troops from running away." Because he saw the Italian issue as one of ideological principle rather than diplomatic expediency Ickes was forever lashing out publicly at the regime, despite the repeated objections of Secretary Hull. "I cannot understand Hull's attitude," Ickes noted on one occasion when he was up-braided. "He seems to defer unduly to Hitler and Mussolini while he all but rattles the saber when it comes to Japan."[56]

On the issue of anti-Semitism, however, neither Hull nor any other administration official would defer to Mussolini. The plight of European Jewry deeply troubled Washington. The Italian Ambassador, Fulvio Suvich, expressed bewilderment to Under-Secretary Welles over the "hostile" American reaction to Italy's recent decrees. Ciano insisted to Phillips that the decrees should not be interpreted as a Nazi-inspired pogrom, for whereas the Germans practiced "persecution" against the Jews, Italians engaged only in "discrimination." Unimpressed, Phillips warned Ciano that America could not accept the spurious distinction. Meanwhile the State Department tried to persuade Mussolini to "prevail upon Hitler to ameliorate" the assault on Jews. Then Roosevelt, informed of the fate of Jewish refugees uprooted in central and southern Europe, proposed to Mussolini (in January 1939) an urgently conceived plan to resettle them in Ethiopia. But Mussolini replied that the plan was "impractical" since the locale Roosevelt specified was unsympathetic to the idea and since another area, which he himself had selected, proved unacceptable to the Jews. The only countries with the "material possibility" of handling "the Jewish question," wrote Mussolini, were Brazil, Russia, and the United States. Nonetheless Il Duce, agreeing that Jews should have their own independent state, promised he would ask Hitler to deal with the refugee problem in a "reasonable

[56] Long to Roosevelt, June 23, 1936, PPF, 434, RP; Phillips to Roosevelt, July 30, 1937, Box 10, RP; Cordell Hull, *The Memoirs of Cordell Hull* (New York, 1948), I, 777; Ickes, *Secret Diary*, II, 348, 711-12, III, 175, 203.

manner." At the same time Phillips informed Roosevelt he was doing everything possible to influence the Italian Foreign Office. The Ambassador reported that he succeeded in having postponed from four to six months the date when foreign Jews would have to leave Italy. Ciano also let him know, Phillips wrote in March 1939, "that there was to be soft-pedaling of the anti-Semitic program. So far, so good." Yet hopeful diplomats like Phillips were mistaken in their belief that the Italian government would do more than mouth verbal assurances about the fate of the Jews. This was clear as early as March 1938, when Phillips asked the Italian government for its help in forming an international committee to assist the emigration of political refugees from Germany and Austria. "I replied," Ciano recorded in his diary, "that such a request was in conflict not only with our line of action in international affairs, but with our political morality. Phillips was surprised at my reply. He sees the proposal in a humanitarian light, I only in a political. The abyss of incomprehension between us and the Americans is growing steadily deeper."[57]

It took some time before the "abyss of incomprehension" became apparent in Washington. Phillips would soon be refused further private meetings with Mussolini (after which all communications went through Ciano), but he remained convinced that Mussolini would not follow Hitler into war. Always skeptical of Long's and Phillips' pro-Mussolini sentiments, Roosevelt began to wonder, after hearing of the attacks on him in the Fascist press, if the word "gentleman" existed in Italian. Yet some administration officials still believed that Mussolini could be won over. Both Hull and Welles hoped that the United States might be able to drive a wedge between the Axis powers by dangling trade as a bait before the Rome government. Even though Mussolini proved indifferent to these belated overtures, it could not be forgotten that many of his earlier diplomatic gestures had been encouraging. During the Czech crisis, for example, Mussolini did nothing to correct the erroneous impression that Roosevelt's personal appeal prompted him to intervene and persuade Hitler to negotiate (actually Roosevelt's letter was delivered after Hitler had agreed to Mussolini's suggestion for a conference). Then, too,

[57] *FRUS, 1938*, II, 582-606; *FRUS, 1939*, II, 63-64; Ickes, *Secret Diary*, II, 548; De Santi, pp. 287-89; De Felice, pp. 391-92; Phillips to Roosevelt, Jan. 20, 1939, March 17, 1939, Box 10, RP; *Ciano's Hidden Diary, 1937-1938*, tr. Andreas Mayor (New York, 1953), p. 93.

Mussolini's decision to remain neutral at the outbreak of World War II was regarded as a most welcome act of responsible statesmanship. Shortly afterwards Roosevelt sent Myron C. Taylor as America's first ambassador to the Vatican. Behind this unprecedented move lay several motives: Roosevelt's aim of aligning his efforts with those of the Pope in containing the war and working for a just peace; the State Department's desire to have access to the Vatican's vast resources of diplomatic information; and the overarching concern of supporting the Pope's efforts to deter Mussolini from entering the war on Hitler's side. Then in December 1939, when Russia invaded Finland, the United States and Italy for the first time stood together in denouncing military aggression.[58]

It was during this period of glimmering expectation that Roosevelt sent Sumner Welles on his "mission" to several European capitals, a sojourn that began and ended in Rome. One major purpose of the trip—aside from seeking a general cessation of hostilities—was to explore the possibility of sustaining Italy's neutrality. To this end Welles talked at length with the fluent and impressionable Ciano. He was then presented to Mussolini, whom he found "elephantine" and overcome by "a leaden oppression." Wasting little time on diplomatic bienséance, both went straight to the issues: trade agreements, territorial settlements, disarmament, war and peace. Although Mussolini stressed the justness of both his and Hitler's geographical aspirations, he believed (or professed to believe) that peace was still possible if the Allies moved quickly with new proposals. After visiting Hitler and Chamberlain, Welles returned to Rome for further talks with Mussolini. On this occasion the Premier informed him he was about to confer with Hitler at the Brenner Pass. He also let it be known that he had knowledge of a new German offensive that could occur within hours, an offensive that might be averted if Welles could give him assurances of the Allies' willingness to negotiate. Having already repudiated publicly any intention of

[58] Roosevelt to Phillips, Feb. 4, 1939, Phillips to Roosevelt, Oct. 18, 1939, Memo, Secretary of State to Roosevelt, July 6, 1937, Box 10, RP; Hull, *Memoirs*, I, 777; Sumner Welles, *The Time for Decision* (New York, 1944), p. 79; De Santi, p. 315; on the Munich Conference, see Phillips to Roosevelt, Oct. 6, 1938, Box 10, RP; William L. Langer and S. Everett Gleason, *The Challenge to Isolation* (Torchback edn., New York, 1964), I, 32-35, esp. fn. 39, p. 34; De Santi, pp. 285-87, 302.

establishing the terms of negotiation, neither Welles nor Roosevelt was in a position to give such assurances—nor was the British government ready to accept what could only seem a Munich encore. Thus Welles left Italy as pessimistic as ever, believing all along that his mission was "a forlorn hope."[59]

Had Welles been aware of what transpired at the Brenner Pass even his dimmest hopes would have been shattered. For although Ciano assured him Italy had not departed from nonbelligerency as a result of Mussolini's meeting with Hitler, Il Duce had done just that. We now know that on March 17 Mussolini promised Hitler that Italy's entry into the war was "inevitable." Thus it was not a question of *whether* Italy would enter but simply *when*. Welles almost sensed this predicament, realizing that Italy's ultimate course of action would be decided solely by Mussolini, at heart a "vindictive" Italian peasant obsessed with power, egotism, and national pride. Upon leaving Rome Welles did observe the widespread opposition to intervention on the part of the Crown, the military, large business interests, high-ranking officials like Ciano and Grandi, and the anti-German Italian people. But Welles could not place much hope in these dissident groups, so convinced was he of Mussolini's complete control. After Italy entered the war, however, Phillips began describing to Roosevelt the dismal mood of silent desperation that had overtaken the country. Informing Roosevelt (on July 8, 1941) that "Mussolini's day is past and that, given the opportunity, the country would not be averse to discarding him," Phillips speculated on the possibility of a military coup. He also told Welles of the anti-Fascist underground and suggested steps be taken to try to make contact with it. But Phillips' refreshingly intelligent advice went unexplored.[60]

On May 29, 1940, Dorothy Thompson wrote a much discussed "Open Letter to Mussolini" in the *New York Herald Tribune*. Never one to bleach words, she warned Il Duce that the American people were ready to rush to the defense of the Allies and that he thus would do well to contain his vulturine instincts. Miss Thompson may have exaggerated America's commitment to intervention, but on other matters she spoke for the overwhelming majority of Americans. It will be recalled that 96 percent of the public ex-

[59] Welles, pp. 76-78, 135-47.

[60] *Ibid.*, pp. 145-47; De Santi, pp. 303-15; Phillips to Roosevelt, July 8, 1941, Phillips to Welles, March 21, 1941, Box 10, RP.

pressed a desire to see Italy join the Allies; and in May 1940, nearly half of the people polled believed that Mussolini would enter the war on France's side. The administration, however, was far more pessimistic during the period of the "phony war" (November 1939—April 1940). According to Ickes, by 1940 Roosevelt was convinced that Mussolini would bring Italy in on Hitler's side. Still, when the decision came (on June 10), both the President and the American people appeared stunned. Riding down to Charlottesville to give the commencement address at the University of Virginia, Roosevelt grew "hot" thinking and "grumbling" about the deed. When he delivered his address he angrily castigated the Italian government for disregarding "the rights and security of other nations" and for shunning all appeals to remain a nonbelligerent. Then Roosevelt added the famous sentence which was not in the final draft of the speech (possibly because Welles had advised its deletion): "On this tenth day of June, 1940, the hand that held the dagger has struck it into the back of its neighbor."[61]

The American press endorsed Roosevelt's speech, though a few papers feared its combative tone boded ill for America's isolation. In both Houses of Congress Roosevelt's speech also received wide acclaim. No one in America (except Italian-Americans), not even the most adamant isolationists, dared challenge Roosevelt's characterization of Mussolini as a "backstabber." Indeed if there was one dominant image that emerged in the public mind it was that of the "jackal":

> With the courage of a jackal at the heels of a bolder beast of prey, Mussolini has now left his ambush. His motives in taking Italy into the war against the Allies are as clear as day. He wants to share in the spoils which he believes will fall to Hitler, and he has chosen to enter the war at the precise moment when he thinks that he can accomplish this at the least cost and risk to himself. This is the end of all these weeks of hesitation, all the eager watching, all the cautious sniffing of the air, all the splendid courage held in the leash so carefully for some sign of the weakness of its victims. Fascismo marches when it thinks that it smells carrion.[62]

[61] *New York Herald Tribune*, May 29, 1940; *Il Progresso*, June 1, 1940; Thomas A. Bailey, *Man in the Street* (New York, 1948), p. 163; Ickes, *Secret Diary*, III, 175; Langer and Gleason, *Challenge to Isolation*, II, 514-17.
[62] *NYT*, June 11, 1940.

Virulent attacks like the above *New York Times* editorial deeply offended Italian-Americans. In Congress, for instance, some western and southern representatives indiscriminately passed censure on Italy as a nation, while those from eastern and urban areas were quick to make clear that the loyalty of Italian-Americans, who had been so tragically deceived by Mussolini, remained as uncontestable as ever. But there was no denying that the Italian population was deeply hurt by Roosevelt's stinging remarks. A few hours before the Charlottesville address Criscuolo somehow got wind of what Roosevelt was about to say. Desperately wiring the President, Criscuolo suggested that he appeal to Italian-Americans to cable Mussolini and their old-country relatives in order to press upon them the dire necessity of not going to war. Had Roosevelt seen Criscuolo's telegram before his address he might have been more sensitive to Italian-American feelings (even though Criscuolo's cable campaign would by then be moot). In any case, the President's "stab-in-the-back" speech returned to haunt him during the fall election, at which time he was more careful to distinguish Fascism from Italianism. Several newspapers had already drawn this crucial distinction between the unfortunate Italians and their unscrupulous Premier, a distinction that applied indirectly to Italian-Americans as well. The same *New York Times* editorial which excoriated Mussolini, for example, went on to exonerate with genuine sympathy the people themselves:

> It is questionable whether any statesman in our time has done a greater wrong to his own people. . . . If there was ever a decision made by one man, and not by the whole people, it is the decision that now takes Italy into the darkness of night and makes her a moral enemy of every democratic people. If that decision had to be made, if the Italian people had to be led upon this tragic course, it is at least fortunate, from our domestic point of view, that the decision was made by a dictator and not by his people. For there are great numbers of Americans of Italian ancestry—fine, loyal citizens of the nation which they or their forbears adopted as their own—who can in all justice lay the responsibility for the crime at the door of Hitler's accomplice, a traitor to the true interests of his country.[63]

[63] *Congressional Record*, 76th Cong., 3rd Sess., LXXXVI, Pt. 16, 3762; *ibid.*, 77th Cong., 1st Sess., LXXXVII, Pt. 12, Appendix, 4198; Criscuolo to

After Italy's entrance into the war American society engaged in a frantic disassociation from the Fascist regime. Actually it could be said that the defection began subtly years earlier. In 1937, for example, Roosevelt would no longer allow his news secretary to issue press releases on his correspondence with Mussolini; and the following year, when Italian anti-Semitism came to the fore, some of Il Duce's former admirers renounced him publicly. But it was after June 10, 1940, that America washed its soiled hands of the whole affair. Medals and decorations which the Italian government had bestowed upon prominent citizens were now returned with almost as much fanfare as when they were accepted. Then came the righteous civic rituals. In the town of Italy, Texas, anti-Italian demonstrations were held; in St. Louis Missouri, the Immaculate Heart Society set blaze to a Fascist emblem; in Union City, New Jersey, Mussolini was burned in effigy; and in Providence, Rhode Island, town leaders considered rededicating a street named after the once illustrious dictator.[64]

Of these rituals it might be said better never than later. One merely has to glance at the editorial statements above to see what really troubled Americans. The public rejected Mussolini not for what he was but for what he had done. And in rejecting the personal figure of Mussolini Americans focused the whole thrust of their denunciation on the moral failing of one man rather than on the ideological premises of his movement. In this sense Americans as a whole did not condemn Fascism; Fascism condemned itself. Had not Il Duce embarked upon his militaristic adventures beginning in 1935 he could have continued to enjoy the popularity he won during the early depression years. True, the Spanish intervention, the anti-Semitism and anti-Americanism of extremists like Gayda and Farinacci alienated substantial segments of American opinion. But ultimately it was Mussolini's irrevocable decision to go with the Axis powers that caused Americans to turn against him. Had he sat out the war he might have commanded the same support a thankful America extended to Franco; had he initially remained neutral and then swung over to the Allies he might even have shared some of the prestige showered upon

Stephen T. Early, June 10, 1940, OF, Box I, RP; Luigi Criscuolo, *The United States and Italy* (New York, 1943), pamphlet; *NYT*, June 11, 1940.

[64] Memo, Roosevelt to Secretary of State, Aug. 26, 1937, OF Box I, RP; *NYT*, June 12, July 15, 1940, Jan. 9, 11, Nov. 2, 1942.

360

Joseph Stalin—everyone's idol in World War II. This is just another way of saying that Americans liked and preferred pre-Ethiopian Italy. Of course, developments after 1935 may have been due to the inner logic of the Fascist state and the dynamic tensions of its restless ideology. Or perhaps they were due to the pressure of diplomatic events or to the undying romantic militarism of Il Duce himself. Whatever the case, a majority of people in this country would readily have tolerated a continuation of the "old" Fascist Italy. Thus in the end America did not repudiate Fascism; Mussolini rejected America. And his spurning of America only demonstrated that he had not learned well his Machiavelli: in aligning with the Third Reich, Benito Mussolini identified himself with a nation that could hardly be intimidated by him while abandoning the very country which would have continued to admire him. After 1940 he was neither loved nor feared; he was dismissed.

14.

Liberation:
American Ideals and
Italian Realities

CORRESPONDENTS IN ROME

Sitting around their customary table in the Associazione della Stampa Estera in Rome were Herbert Matthews and Camillo Cianfarra of the *New York Times*, Allan Raymond of the *Herald Tribune*, Mark Watson of the *Baltimore Sun*, John Whitaker of the *Chicago Daily News*, Richard G. Massock of the AP, and Reynolds and Eleanor Packard of the UP. Here, at 8:00 p.m. on December 10, 1941, America's Rome correspondents first heard the "official confirmation" that Mussolini was about to declare war on the United States. They were also informed their offices had been closed and they would not be allowed to send further cables. On that grim but inevitable note the group had a final round of drinks with fellow Spanish, Scandinavian, Swiss, and Italian newsmen. It was a hasty toast as the Americans quickly rushed off to pack their bags, since they were aware that they would have to get out of the country before the police seized them in reprisal for the arrest of Italian journalists in the United States. But few got out in time; most were detained for over a year before they were deported to various neutral countries whence they eventually made their way back to the United States. Though a personal misfortune, their confinement proved a blessing for American public opinion. Upon their return these journalists would publish some of the most informative accounts of life in wartime Italy.[1]

Meanwhile the American press had been describing vividly and bleakly Italy's spiraling inflation, desperate food rationing, lack of milk for infants, and, amid these human privations, the

[1] Reynolds and Eleanor Packard, *The Balcony Empire: Fascist Italy at War* (New York, 1942).

widespread blackmarket operations and Mussolini's trysts with Clara Petacci. By spring 1943, discussion turned to the bombing of Italian cities, the chances of an internal insurrection, the possible emergence of a reliable opposition leader ("Where Is Signor X?"), and the cruel dilemma of the Italians themselves. "If we lose the war, we'll simply be losers," one Italian told *Current History*'s Ann Lingelback; "if we win, that is, if Germany wins, we'll be lost."[2]

Beginning in 1942 several books appeared which conveyed Italian realities with even greater immediacy. Perhaps the most widely discussed was *Agent in Italy* by the anonymous "S.K." According to the book's preface, the author was a German who had, as an employee in an Italian silk firm, aided Jews escaping his country until he himself was forced to flee to Italy. Privy to underground activities, "S.K." described the sabotage tactics of the partisans, the composition of the anti-Fascist factions, and various other matters which helped Americans understand better the subterranean political currents in Mussolini's Italy. *Life* serialized chapters of *Agent in Italy* and *Time* enthusiastically reviewed it as a request that the Allies publicly offer the Italian people some alternative to Fascism.[3]

Writers interned in Italy also contributed to America's education. Richard Massock's *Italy from Within*, Reynolds and Eleanor Packard's *Balcony Empire: Fascist Italy at War*, John Whitaker's *We Cannot Escape History*, Herbert Matthews' *The Fruits of Fascism* and *Education of a Correspondent*, and the pseudonymous Jane Scrivener's *Inside Rome with the Germans* offered a miscellany of personal journalism and political information. Among the questions that concerned the authors, the possibility of a popular uprising seemed most urgent. All could agree that the Italians loathed the Germans, that Mussolini's prestige had declined "with sensational rapidity," and that the war against the United States was "distinctly unpopular." But whether this profound disaffection would culminate in mass rebellion was another matter. The Packards believed there was "little chance" of an uprising, even though Il Duce only commanded the "undivided loyalty" of less than 10 percent of the population. Dismissing the notion of the Italians as "hot-blooded" revolutionaries, the most they hoped for was something of a palace *coup d'état*. Much

[2] *Current History*, I (Dec. 1941), 343-36; IV (March 1943), 51-54.
[3] *Life*, XII (Feb. 9, 1943), 94-101; *Time*, XXXIX (April 13, 1942), 98-102.

more optimistic was "S.K." "Take away the German soldiers, whose bayonets are pinning Italy to the Axis," declared the anonymous German, "and the fabric of Fascism would vanish like morning mist in the sun." Whitaker, too, toyed with the idea that the Italians might rise as soon as the Germans withdrew; but whereas Whitaker noted that the "memories of Garibaldi [lie] deep in the Italian soil," he also sternly warned readers that Fascism had made the Italians a "debauched, cynical and wholly unheroic people." Similarly Massock believed an insurrection improbable until the Anglo-American forces drove out the German army. On the other hand, Matthews used Paretan sociology to demonstrate the possibility of internal revolution. Convinced that Fascism's monolithic, elitist party had alienated almost every class, that opportunity had been closed off to the young generation, and that the war shattered the regime's martial mystique, Matthews believed Mussolini would be toppled by the very "centrifugal forces" that paved the way for Fascism: "regionalism, anti-clericalism, municipal or communal strife."[4]

As Matthews' remarks suggest, how writers interpreted Mussolini's impending fall indirectly reflected their perception of the nature of Fascism itself. The same could be said when these writers speculated on the strength of the resistance and, even more importantly, on the composition of Italy's post-Fascist government. "S.K." believed that "the skeleton of future Italy" would be made up of the "almost half a million" Italians who belonged to the "united" underground. The monarchy, "blighted by Fascism," will be ignored as the new government forms around a small Left and Right and a "heavy democratic center" unified by liberal idealism and "middle way" reform. The Packards and Whitaker also dismissed the royal family as "bankrupt politically" and called for immediate Allied support to an "Anglo-American Fifth Column in Italy." But the Catholic Scrivener believed only the Papacy could see Italy through her time of troubles, while Massock, who acknowledged the Crown's Fascist past, reported he heard of "no talk of republicanism inside of Italy as I have heard of it outside." The monarchist-leaning Massock also doubted the *fuorusciti* could provide any leadership, claiming

[4] Packard, pp. 364-68; S.K., *Agent in Italy* (New York, 1942), p. 319; John Whitaker, *We Cannot Escape History* (New York, 1943), pp. 93-94; Richard Massock, *Italy from Within* (New York, 1943), pp. 378-92; Herbert Matthews, *Fruits of Fascism* (New York, 1943), pp. 325-27.

that the "pre-Fascist parties had been buried so profoundly that not even their ghosts were abroad in the land." Finally Matthews, who later would enjoy a rare interview with Victor Emmanuel III, believed that though the King would fight tenaciously and even move to the Left, the growing disenchantment with the monarchy and its traditional antiquated social base had sealed its fate. More and more Matthews, seeing disunity among the anti-Fascists, held out vague hope for a revival of Croce's genteel liberalism.[5]

As there had been no consensus on the nature of Fascism, so would there be little unanimity on the meaning of its collapse. Witnessing the overthrow of Mussolini and pondering the political future of Italy, America revealed again a society of conflicting perspectives. For after 1943 the United States was forced to deal with the very questions most Americans believed Mussolini had solved twenty years earlier. Without a unified politics of vision, the stage was set for confusion and suspicion.

"THE SAWDUST RUNS OUT"

It was Sunday afternoon, July 25, 1943, when the stadium address system interrupted the Yankee-Pirate game to announce that Benito Mussolini had been ousted from power. The game halted, jubilant men and women poured into the aisles leaping with joy while the band struck up the "Star Spangled Banner." Across town at Rockefeller Plaza Arturo Toscanini was conducting an all-Verdi program. He had just completed "Pace, Mio Dio" when the loudspeaker told of Mussolini's resignation. As the audience, composed largely of servicemen, rose and applauded wildly, the maestro rushed back to the platform, "clasped his hands to his head, and gazed heavenward, as if his prayers had been answered."[6]

Mussolini's sudden fall was the most encouraging news from Europe until the invasion of Normandy a year later. For the American press July 26 was a day for reflection as well as celebration. The *New York Times* used the occasion to reexamine Ambassador Child's introduction to Mussolini's autobiography.

[5] S.K., pp. 321-25; Packard, pp. 368-80; Jane Scrivener (pseud.), *Inside Rome with the Germans* (New York, 1945), passim; Massock, pp. 391-92; Matthews, *Fruits of Fascism*, pp. 327-32; id., *Education of a Correspondent* (New York, 1946), pp. 482-505.

[6] *NYT*, July 26, 1943.

According to the *Times*, it was not Mussolini who was, in Child's words, "humane and wise," but the Italian people who finally dumped him. Like the rest of the press, the *Times* later speculated on the relevance of the *Risorgimento* and Italian liberalism to post-Fascist institutions. The *Herald Tribune*, also complimenting the Italians for rejecting Mussolini's "Napoleonic egoism," believed his fall presaged the collapse of the Axis. On the other hand the *Christian Science Monitor*'s Rome correspondent, Saville Davis, was among the first to report that the coup may have been inspired either by the Germans to keep Italy in the war or by Italian reactionaries who wanted to leave the war in order to save their own skins. But no matter how uncertain the coup may have appeared in relation to the war effort, most writers welcomed the momentous event—with one exception. Anne O'Hare McCormick seemed almost regretful as she used the event not to reflect on her fallen hero but to indict the Italians themselves. "In an ironic but very literal sense," wrote McCormick, "it can be said that even the negative power of the people, the power of apathy, was sufficient in the end to render the dictator powerless."[7]

What is perhaps more telling is the imagery and anecdote with which the press summed up Mussolini's career. The *Christian Science Monitor* commented on his "balcony braggadocio" and on Fascism's "facade of force and fraud"; the *Washington Post* dubbed him a "Sawdust Caesar," and his "Humpty Dumpty" regime a "gingerbread empire" that "expanded until he exploded"; the *Herald Tribune* titled its editorial "The Sawdust Runs Out" and spoke of his "pasteboard empire," and, when Mussolini was rescued by the Germans, of the "sick and empty husk of a discredited dictator." Similarly, Homer Smith titled his *Saturday Review of Literature* piece the "Flight of the Jackal," and Malcolm Cowley, writing in the *New Republic*, articulated perceptively what was in everyone's mind: "Mussolini was like the heavily moustached villain of a Mack Sennett comedy, who tries to stab the hero in the back, but slips on a banana peel and falls with his face in custard pie."[8]

[7] *NYT*, July 26, 27, 31, 1943; *New York Herald Tribune*, July 27, 29, 1943; *Christian Science Monitor*, July 26, 28, 1943.

[8] *Christian Science Monitor*, July 27, 1943; *Washington Post*, July 26, 27, 1943; *New York Herald Tribune*, July 26, 1943; *Saturday Review of Literature*, xxvi (July 31, 1943), 12; *New Republic*, cix (Aug. 16, 1943), 226-27.

These "autopsies" are suggestive. For the editorials protested too much the hollow nature of Fascist Italy and the actor-like character of its leader. The *Christian Science Monitor*, for example, printed Shelley's "Ozymandias" to dramatize the decadent and cynical ruler who, in final self-judgment, bitterly cries out: "Look on my works, Ye mighty, and despair!" The poem is studded with references to the "colossal wreck" and the "boundless and bare" regime. What emerges here, as in many other editorials, is the distinct impression that Mussolini's Italy was nothing more than a house of cards whose rotting foundations had been perceived all along. Given the widespread sympathy for Fascism in its early years, this judgment is sheer hindsight. Perhaps psychological necessity compelled Americans to dismiss Fascism as a political bubble. How else could they explain their earlier support for a leader and an ideology against which they now found themselves fighting? To regard the entire Fascist experiment as a theatrical facade or a political wasteland implied that America's uncritical curiosity was merely a matter of deception. And to admit one has been taken in by staged propaganda is far more comforting than to admit one had consciously approved of a regime which America ultimately had to face on the field of battle. The symbol of "sawdust"—porous, baseless, invertebrate—was necessary if Americans were to emerge from the whole affair with their innocence intact.[9]

SALVEMINI VS. LIPPMANN

On the momentous Sunday in July, the liberal *New York Post* journalist Samuel Grafton announced over his OWI broadcast (relayed in 24 languages) that "the moronic little King, who has stood behind Mussolini's shoulder for twenty-one years, has moved forward one pace. This is a political minuet, and not the revolution we have been waiting for. It changes nothing; for nothing can change in Italy until democracy is restored." The OWI also relayed statements by public figures. La Guardia informed the king that he would be held "personally responsible" if Italian factories continued to supply Germany, while Senator Claude Pepper declared that the Italians must "cleanse themselves of Fascism." But the blast at the King produced an explosion in the press. Although several papers sympathized with Grafton's uncompromising anti-Fascism, editors believed the

[9] *Christian Science Monitor*, July 27, 1943.

367

statement unwarranted and tactless. The *Christian Science Monitor* even offered the advice that it was dangerous to discredit "the only authority now visible in Italy." Worse still, *New York Times'* Arthur Krock claimed that the OWI had always been "closer to Moscow than the Washington-London line," while the *Chicago Tribune*, noting that the broadcast had not been cleared by Washington, maintained that members of the OWI were trying to "foment a Communist revolution in Italy." Finally Roosevelt, whose first reaction to the coup was the public proclamation that "we will have no truck with Fascism in any way, in any shape or manner," was forced to disavow the broadcast.[10]

The administration, as we shall see, was reluctant to open up a Pandora's box in the midst of the Italian campaign. But while the government was willing to settle for a *modus vivendi* with Marshal Badoglio, opinion divided sharply over recognizing a regime tainted with Fascism.[11] The American Right voiced a familiar alarm when the *Chicago Tribune* demanded the silencing of the OWI's "fellow travelers" lest they "risk the sacrifice of hundreds of thousands of American soldiers" in their attempt to "throw Italy into anarchy and serve the end of Communism." For the Right it logically followed that the crown and the military, not the anti-Fascism underground, were the only elements in Italy strong enough to oust Mussolini. In these institutions, Anne O'Hare McCormick advised, were lodged "all the residual power there was left, and all the instruments of power." Hence America must heed the wisdom of Churchill's warning that "it would be a mistake to act so as to break down the whole structure and expression of the Italian State."[12]

More prevalent, however, was the view that the succession

[10] Grafton is quoted in Roger Burlingame, *Don't Let Them Scare You: The Life and Times of Elmer Davis* (New York, 1961), pp. 228-29; "OWI and the King," *New Republic*, CIX (Aug. 9, 1943), 80; *NYT*, July 26, 27, Aug. 1, 1943; *Christian Science Monitor*, July 30, 1943; *Chicago Daily Tribune*, July 28, 1943; "History Unrecognized," *Nation*, CLVII (Aug. 7, 1943), 144-45.

[11] General Pietro Badoglio served under Mussolini until he was dismissed from command during the Greek War in November 1940. Although he was no admirer of Il Duce the opposition claimed, perhaps with some exaggeration, that his cabinet was represented from top to bottom by the very elements that had welcomed Fascism twenty years earlier: the monarchy, the military, and the police.

[12] *Chicago Daily Tribune*, July 30, 1943; *NYT*, July 28, 31, 1943.

question must not be permitted to interfere with the war effort. The priority of military objectives over politics was so axiomatic that the *New Orleans Times-Picayune*, looking to Italy as a future ally, noted Badoglio was reputed to be "the greatest professional soldier in modern Italian history." And although the *New York Times* military analyst Hanson Baldwin described Badoglio as "a modern Italian Kerensky" who would most likely keep Italy in the war, most papers believed the overriding objective was to maneuver Italy out as soon as possible. Thus it was not "a question of 'trusting' Badoglio or the King, or of 'making a deal' with them," advised the *Herald Tribune*; it was simply a matter of facilitating surrender, safeguarding Allied prisoners, and maintaining crucial services. Similarly Ernest K. Lindley and Walter Fitzmaurice, answering the Left's attack on the King as a "triple turncoat" and on State Department officials as "blind reactionaries," maintained in the *Washington Post* that negotiations with Badoglio by no means violated the administration's democratic war aims. To the majority of writers Badoglio was only a transitional figure and his regime a liquidation government. The *New York Times* best expressed this moderate position when it suggested that for the purpose of surrender "it does not matter whether King Victor Emmanuel or Marshal Badoglio are to be considered as Fascist, semi-Fascist, or anti-Fascist, or as good or bad men, or as wise or foolish men. . . . The politics of the regime which turns over Italy's sword is of no immediate importance. It is the relinquished sword that matters."[13]

While this strategy seemed acceptable to most Americans, a few commentators looked to the monarchy itself as a source of cohesion in postwar Italy. One such writer was Walter Lippmann. As the war dragged on Lippmann came more and more to express a conservative appreciation for organic institutions and moral order. Although he had little regard for Victor Emmanuel himself, Lippmann believed monarchism among the first "vestiges of legitimate and historic authority," the only institution that could facilitate the transition to "the new Italy" once Fascism crumbled. Such sentiments incensed the watchful Salvemini, who grew angrier as he listened to Lippmann hold forth on the tactics of capitulation. Briefly, Lippmann insisted that the initial demand

[13] *New Orleans Times-Picayune*, July 26, 1943; *NYT*, July 27, 31, 1943; *New York Herald Tribune*, July 30, 1943; *Washington Post*, July 28, Sept. 13, 1943.

369

of unconditional surrender did not go far enough. The Italians must be made "so furiously insistent" on peace that they will force the King and Badoglio to wage war against the "German invaders." Anticipating a situation something similar to the Salò Republic—where one half of Italy fought with the Allies while the other remained under Nazi control—Lippmann was convinced that the Vichy precedent must be avoided at all costs since Italy could not cease to be Germany's ally without becoming her enemy.[14] Moreover, the surest way for the Italians to expiate their Fascist past was to rally to the Allied cause. Thus while it was physically impossible for Italy simply to withdraw from the war, it was, Lippmann contended in September 1943, morally imperative for the Italians to rise against the German army.[15]

Lippmann's argument—given official expression in General Eisenhower's address to the people of Italy—was criticized bitterly by the exasperated Salvemini. That Italians must take up arms to assist the invasion without any leadership, without any specific guarantees regarding Italy's political future, and, most seriously, without any fear of German reprisal, seemed pernicious. Even more galling was Lippmann's defense of the monarchy on the basis of "legitimacy." According to the *fuoruscito*, Lippmann's definition of legitimacy was narrowly Metternichian: a regime is legitimate by virtue of its historical tradition. In place of this doctrine of continuity Salvemini substituted the concept of "popular" legitimacy derived from Guglielmo Ferrero: a government is legitimate if it is freely elected and free of coercion. On the basis of Ferrero's definition, Lippmann's argument was patently false; but even in Metternichian terms, Salvemini maintained, Lippmann's case was still questionable. For the Crown under Mussolini was in no way connected with the pre-Fascist principle of monarchism, just as the "parliament" under Mussolini was in no way an extension of the truly liberal parliaments prior to 1922. Hence the advent of Fascism, openly endorsed by the King, meant that the "allegiance of the nation to the Mon-

[14] The Republic of Salò was set up in northern Italy after the Germans rescued Mussolini (September 12, 1943). Proclaimed a "social republic," in reality it was a rump Fascist government which Hitler established to conduct a rearguard action against the advancing Allies.

[15] *New York Herald Tribune*, Nov. 21, 1943; *New Orleans Times-Picayune*, July 29, 30, 1943; *Washington Post*, Sept. 11, 1943.

archy, based on a definite contract represented by the constitution, was severed. It cannot be renewed without any consent of the people."[16]

Whatever the merits of Salvemini's theory of popular sovereignty, his views had the sympathy of a great many Americans. Not only the liberal and Left journals but a sizable segment of the daily press supported the anti-Fascist attacks on Badoglio and the Crown. The *San Francisco Chronicle* virtually echoed Grafton's position in declaring that the "Italian hats on the hooks are changed. That's all." The *Washington Post*, although critical of the OWI, warned that any dealing with Mussolini's "henchmen" unrelated to unconditional surrender would be a "betrayal of our war aims." Even the two popular Luce publications, *Life* and *Time*, criticized the State Department's "chronic expediency." The former featured an anti-Fascist "manifesto" and guest editorials by Arturo Toscanini, while *Time* reprinted William Shirer's savage indictment:

> There is no use kidding ourselves any longer about a great American failure. Our propaganda . . . is not getting any place. The masses of Europe have become distrustful of us. Many hate or fear us. Not one American in ten thousand probably realizes it; but this youthful republic, where the common man is still the backbone of the nation, is coming to represent to the mass of the people of the outside world a sterile and black reaction. Frightened to death of the great popular forces which this war—like all other wars—has unleashed, insisting only that half starved, brutalized people of the continent maintain "law and order," and prepared to traffic with a miserable little Italian King or his reactionary henchman Badoglio or the Fascist Franco as it once trafficked with a Pétain, a Darlan, a Peyrouton, to avoid "revolt" or "trouble." . . . The frightened timid little men who make our foreign policies . . . move about in their Washington hothouse, engulfed in their petty feuds and silly prejudices, segregated from the robustness of plain American democracy, fearful of the common man in Europe.[17]

[16] Gaetano Salvemini and George La Piana, *What to Do with Italy* (New York, 1943), pp. 32-38.

[17] *San Francisco Chronicle*, July 28, 1943; *Washington Post*, July 28, 1943; *Time*, XLII (Sept. 13, 1943), 36; see also, Arturo Toscanini, "To the People of America," *Life*, XV (Sept. 13, 1943), 32.

To liberals like Shirer it seemed incredible that Roosevelt's New Deal could not be exported to Europe in the wake of the Allied army. To Left-wing writers like I. F. Stone, Washington's evasiveness only further proved that Allied policy was bent on restoring the old capitalist order. The attacks from the center and the Left aroused the equally vociferous Right. Journals like *Collier's* and the *Saturday Evening Post* rushed to the defense of the State Department, denouncing the "ideologists" and "fellow travelers" who hewed to the Moscow line and praising the "power politics" of Secretary of State Hull. Thus it seemed that Mussolini's ignominious fall, no less than his spectacular rise, profoundly divided America. But the Fascist question in the forties had graver implications. Whereas twenty years earlier America could only pass judgment on Italy, during World War II it was in a position to affect her political future. Not surprisingly, the charges and countercharges after July 1943 intensified almost to the point of paranoia. In view of the seriousness of these accusations, the administration's Italian diplomacy must be given careful consideration.[18]

WASHINGTON AND THE BADOGLIO AFFAIR

The administration began speculating on the nature of post-Fascist Italy well before the fall of Mussolini. As early as February 1943, Secretary Hull had written to the ambassador in London regarding the propaganda to be employed in Italy. Cautioning against making too many postwar commitments, Hull advised that the Italians should be guaranteed territorial integrity and that the House of Savoy could be useful as a "sovereign power at least during the interim period between the Fascist regime and its successor." Then on June 8, six weeks before Il Duce's deposal, Roosevelt received a statement from an anonymous anti-Fascist asking the President to broadcast that he "will assure the Italian people their freedom to choose the kind of democratic government they wish to establish." The request, which Roosevelt forwarded to Hull for comment, had been altered by either the President or one of his advisers. For the words "the kind of demo-

[18] I. F. Stone, "How Washington Reacted," *Nation*, CLVII (Aug. 7, 1943), 146-47; "Would They Rather Lick Hull Than the Axis?" (editorial), *SEP*, CCXVI (Oct. 9, 1943), 112; Demaree Bess, "Power Politics Succeeded in Italy," *ibid*. (Oct. 30, 1943), 20-21; George Creel, "The War on Cordell Hull," *Collier's* CXIII (March 11, 1944), 11, 78-80.

cratic government they wish to establish" had been penciled out and replaced with "non-Fascist or non-Nazi kind of..." government. Hence the administration was already beginning to hedge: the Italians would be assured the right to choose only a "non-Fascist" government, a choice that could range all the way from republicanism to royalism. Perhaps one can make too much of this substitution of an accordion-like phrase. Perhaps Roosevelt and the State Department wanted to avoid the constricting rhetoric of Wilsonian self-determinism. Nevertheless, to anti-Fascists such equivocation could only indicate that the administration would settle for "Fascismo senza Mussolini."[19]

When Roosevelt first heard of Mussolini's dismissal his immediate thoughts were on its military implications. Noting the importance of Italy as a passageway to the Balkans, he told Churchill that the Allies should hold out for "unconditional surrender followed by good treatment of the Italian populace. But I think also that the head devil should be surrendered together with his chief partners in crime." The more cautious Churchill, however, suggested that "we should not be too particular in dealing with any non-Fascist government even if it is not all we should like." Rather, the Allies should deal with any non-Fascist government that "can deliver the goods." Churchill also forwarded a lengthy memo which laid down the conditions for Italy's capitulation: Allied control of all Italian territory, surrender of the Navy, immediate liberation of all British prisoners of war. The Prime Minister further suggested that they "stimulate" the "fury of the Italian population [which] will now be turned against the German invaders. . . ." A few days later he reiterated the armistice terms and spelled out their urgent military importance, thanking the President for his "promise to put the screw on through the Pope or any other convenient channel."[20]

But the armistice was slow to materialize and during the delay different expectations emerged. The President saw Badoglio and the King merely as instrumental to the diplomacy of surrender; the Prime Minister regarded the monarchy as the buttress of political stability. For the purpose of surrender, Churchill wrote to Roosevelt on July 31, "I am not in the least afraid . . . of seeming to recognize the House of Savoy or Badoglio, provided they

[19] *FRUS, 1943,* ii, 321-24; Memo, Hull to Early, June 8, 1943, OF Italy, Box I, RP.
[20] *FRUS, 1943,* ii, 332-36.

373

are the ones who can make the Italians do what we need for our war purposes. Those purposes would certainly be hindered by chaos, bolshevisation or civil war." It may well be, continued Churchill, that after the armistice the King and Badoglio "will sink under the odium of surrender and that the Crown prince and a new Prime Minister may be chosen." What is significant is not merely that Churchill advised Roosevelt to avoid going "beyond what is implicit in the Atlantic Charter," but that he believed the King would suffer the stigma of surrender, not the shame of Fascism. Clearly for Churchill, the monarchy, whether personified by the unpopular Victor Emmanuel or the unknown Prince Humbert, was the one institution that would prevent "chaos, bolshevisation or civil war."[21]

The weird "forty-five days" between Mussolini's fall and the armistice (July 25 to September 8, 1943) were a period of confusion and illusion. Few Americans were aware of the enormous difficulties standing in the way of Italy's leaving the war. Like the Italians themselves, Americans believed that Italy had opted for peace and freedom. But the main obstacle was the presence of German troops, who were pouring into the southern peninsula in menacing numbers after July 25. Negotiations between Badoglio and Eisenhower hinged on timing the Allied landings on the mainland with the announcement of the armistice. Yet Badoglio originally hoped to obtain a reversal of alliances without surrendering. When this proved unrealistic, he tried to bargain for terms less than unconditional surrender. Even after Badoglio agreed to the Allied terms he still delayed announcing the armistice, until Eisenhower angrily threatened to do it for him. On the evening of September 8 Badoglio made the formal statement.[22]

The American press was jubilant. The *New York Times* believed that the act broke the "spell of Hitlerism" and that Badoglio's cryptic remark about the Italians opposing attacks from "any other quarter" amounted to a tacit declaration of war against Germany. The *Herald Tribune* and the *New Orleans Times-Picayune* also believed that Italy would now cooperate fully with the Allies, while the *Chicago Tribune* praised Badoglio for displaying "the honor of a soldier." But the perceptive *Christian Science Monitor* doubted that Italy could make a significant

[21] *Ibid.*, p. 339.

[22] Hughes, pp. 127-32; Norman Kogan, *Italy and the Allies* (Cambridge, 1956), pp. 26-41.

military contribution, and the *San Francisco Chronicle* rebuked Eisenhower for failing to give the Italians assurances that they would have the immediate help of the United Nations forces when they rose against the *Wehrmacht.* Within a matter of days all fond expectations evaporated. The Italians' failure to resist the Nazi entry into Rome, reported the *Washington Post,* "dashed to the ground" all hope of a military role for Italy. On September 12, the *Herald Tribune*'s editorial summed up in four words the widespread skepticism: "Second Thoughts on Italy."[23]

But far more clamor and confusion were generated by the "Badoglio Affair" and the monarchical question. Anti-Fascists believed that by negotiating with Badoglio the State Department recognized the unrepentant militarist and his cowering King. The whole transaction smacked of collaboration, and the names "Darlan" and "Quisling" hissed through the liberal and Left-wing press while in the Senate William Langer asked: "Shall the People of Italy Rule?" Yet an examination of government documents indicates that in 1943 Washington evinced little sympathy for the Crown. Two weeks after the armistice Victor Emmanuel III wrote personally to Roosevelt, and to the King of England, to ask that he be returned to Rome (from which he had infamously fled on September 9 as the Germans approached) and to request that "my government" be granted civil powers over the Nazi-held territories to the north. Such a move, implored Victor Emmanuel, would help "carry out the political reconstruction of the country, which would be completed with the return of the parliamentary regime which *I have always wished for*" [italics added]. The appeal received a cold shoulder, and a "brassy" one. For a few days earlier General Eisenhower warned the State Department that even the abdication of the King in favor of the Crown Prince would require "careful study as it might prove more popular abroad than with the Italian people." At this juncture—late 1943 and early 1944—the administration tried to remain aloof from the monarchical issue, believing that the problem should be left to a postwar plebiscite and insisting to Badoglio that he publicly spell out such a pledge.[24]

[23] *NYT,* Sept. 9, 1943; *New Orleans Times-Picayune,* Sept. 9, 1943; *Chicago Daily Tribune,* Sept. 9, 1943; *Christian Science Monitor,* Sept. 9, 1943; *San Francisco Chronicle,* Sept. 9, 1943; *Washington Post,* Sept. 11, 1943; *New York Herald Tribune,* Sept. 9, 12, 1943.

[24] *Congressional Record,* 78th Cong., 1st Sess., Pt. 11, Appendix, 4228-29; *FRUS, 1943,* II, 370, 374-75, 387; Kogan, p. 44.

But the situation was complicated by rightfully impatient resistance leaders who, once Mussolini fell, sniffed the sweet smell of political success for the first time in twenty years. Anti-Fascist groups composed roughly six major parties: Socialists, Communists, Christian Democrats, Actionists, Liberals, and Democracy of Labor. For the most part exiles in the United States represented Socialist and Action party factions. The State Department cooperated with these *fuorusciti*, and the Allied intelligence agencies helped transport some back to Italy, while General William Donovan of the OSS proposed an Italian volunteer corps headed by Action party leadership. The status of Count Sforza, however, was a matter of bitter contention between the United States and Great Britain. Originally Churchill approved of the State Department's allowing Sforza to return to Italy, informing Roosevelt that "Badoglio would be very foolish not to embrace him after his generous letter. A shotgun marriage will have to be arranged if necessary." But Churchill would later annul the marriage as Sforza proceeded to flay the Crown and to advise Americans (in a letter to La Guardia) that "Italians will fight only for a democratic Italy, and not for an Italy where there are still old tools of the Fascists who speak of democracy only to fool us and to fool you." Ultimately it was only over the opposition of the British that the State Department arranged Sforza's return.[25]

During the crucial "forty-five days" and for almost a year afterwards the administration by no means expressed much sympathy for either the monarchy or the military. Basically the State Department's Italian diplomacy was determined by the policy of strategic surrender. And even this opportunistic policy plagued the conscience of New Dealers. Convinced that both the King and Badoglio could not "be considered to represent a democratic government," Harry Hopkins remarked: "I surely don't like the idea that these former enemies can change their minds when they know that they are going to get licked and come over to our side and get help in maintaining political power." But Badoglio was a bitter pill the administration had to swallow, and the capitulation of Italy, together with the surrender of her fleet to the Allies, eased their discomfort. In the fall of 1943 there was simply no alternative to the only Italian in a position to proffer

[25] *FRUS, 1943*, II, 378; Sforza to La Guardia, Feb. 27, 1944, OF Italy, Box I, RP.

376

the "relinquished sword." Ideologically, Badoglio warranted a complaint, not a moral convulsion. The true test of the administration's democratic sensibilities would come at the close of the war, to which we now turn.[26]

ROOSEVELT AND CHURCHILL

In early 1944 Italian monarchism and militarism remained unacceptable to many New Deal diplomats. Adlai Stevenson, upon returning from an official tour of Italy in January, reported to the State Department that the King and Badoglio "commanded little respect or support among the people." The chargé in Algiers, after relaying the resolutions of the Bari Congress's six anti-Fascist parties,[27] informed Hull that there "is no doubt the King must go"—it was only a question of when. Further, when Badoglio complained that the Psychological Warfare Branch of the OWI had, by broadcasting the Bari declarations, undermined Italy's present military and political leaders, the State Department and the Allied Commission ignored his request for censorship. Administration instincts, then, were clearly toward the restoration of an Italian democracy that would include the underground and exiled Left. Yet such instincts were continually thwarted by the omnipresence of Winston Churchill.[28]

In March 1944, Roosevelt informed the Prime Minister that, in view of the growing unrest in Italy, he favored the program put forth by the six opposition parties: the abdication of Victor Emmanuel, and the delegation of power to a Lieutenant-General of the Realm, with Croce mentioned as the possible choice.

[26] Quoted in Robert E. Sherwood, *Roosevelt and Hopkins* (Universal Library edn., New York, 1950), p. 744.

[27] The Bari Congress (January 28-29, 1944) was the first democratic assembly to meet openly in Italy for almost two decades. The Congress established an Executive Junta composed of one representative from each of the six resistance parties in the Committee of National Liberation. Although factionally divided, the Congress issued a compromise resolution calling for abdication of the King and settlement of the institutional question by popular referendum after the war.

[28] Stevenson is quoted in Kogan, p. 56; see also, John Norman, "Adlai Stevenson's Report on AMG in Italy: A Review Article," *The Bridgeport Sunday Herald Magazine*, Sept. 9, 1956 (Norman's article was written in response to the 1956 campaign charge that Presidential candidate Stevenson "connived" to bring the PCI into the Italian government and to bring Togliatti back from Moscow. An offprint is in the library of the Istituto Italiano di Cultura, New York); *FRUS, 1944*, III, 1007, 1029-30.

Churchill, who continually warned the President that "no agitation calculated to disrupt the military situation will be tolerated," was furious. Reminding Roosevelt that he had given him his complete support in the Darlan affair, Churchill warned that the Bari program might be temporarily popular but only a "transitory success." He also dismissed Italy's liberal leaders as political cripples: "I understand from Macmillan that Croce is a dwarf professor about 75 years old who wrote good books about aesthetics and philosophy. I have no confidence in either Sforza or Croce." Roosevelt replied sharply, maintaining that the Bari proposal would not hamper the military effort. "I cannot for the life of me understand why we should hesitate any longer in supporting a policy so admirably suited to our common military and political aims. American public opinion would never understand our continued tolerance and apparent support of Victor Emmanuel." Roosevelt was right in fearing the exasperation of American opinion, but his remark about "our common . . . political aims" indicates he did not gauge the ideological gap between his own democratic idealism and Churchill's tory conservatism. For Churchill, the war in Italy was being waged solely against Mussolini ("one man, and one man alone") and not necessarily against the reactionary forces that had propped up his regime. Publicly, Churchill could endorse the Atlantic Charter; privately, he never lost sight of the rivalry between England and Italy in the Mediterranean. Thus the Prime Minister tried to prevent the provisional governments of Badoglio and his successor, Ivanoe Bonomi, from gaining co-belligerent status and exercising greater military and political authority in Italy's liberated areas. While Roosevelt offered verbal encouragement to the anti-Fascists and while the State Department thwarted the King's attempt to re-establish himself in Rome, the administration bowed again and again to the will of the Prime Minister.[29]

Churchill's prudent conservatism is not the whole explanation of America's cautious Italian policy. Although the last thing American officials wanted to see erupting in Italy was political chaos, the logic of the situation called for chaos. From the beginning of the war Americans had urged the Italians to overthrow Mussolini—even though many regarded such an event as improbable. Once Mussolini fell, Italy succumbed to complete

[29] *FRUS, 1944*, III, 1054-55; Kogan, pp. 42-75, passim.

378

turmoil. One close observer described Italy in the fall of 1943 as "nearer to a state of literal anarchy than she has been at any time in the past four centuries." But in some respects it was a most admired disorder, directed mainly against German occupation. Thus Americans applauded the heroic efforts of the Italians who rose up sporadically against the *Wehrmacht*. The "four days of Naples" (September 27-30, 1943), a spontaneous insurrection of the *lazzaroni*, bourgeoisie, and courageous youths, was described in all its glory and gore by Hal Boyle of the *New York Times*: "An 8-year-old boy lay with a rosary gripped in his hand, which almost covered the hole in his abdomen, ripped open by a German bullet." The amazing feat of the Neapolitans led many Americans to a newly found respect for the Italians' courage. But Americans failed to see that the very passions which moved Italians to rise bravely against the German army would also be vindictively unleashed against Blackshirts and collaborators. Thus the public drew back in horror a year later when newspapers reported outbreaks of violence and terror throughout Italy. The most publicized incident was the Carretta affair.[30]

A few months after Rome was liberated a mob stormed the Palace of Justice in search of Pietro Caruso, Rome's chief of police during the Nazi occupation who allegedly was instrumental in the German massacre of Italians in the Ardeatine Cave atrocity. Failing to get Caruso, the mob turned on Donato Carretta, an innocent prosecution witness.[31] While police stood helplessly by, Carretta was savagely battered, his half-conscious body thrown into the Tiber and clubbed to death; his mutilated corpse then hung from a window. The vigilantism outraged many Americans who saw the gory photographs in the press. The British and American governments reacted sharply; in a joint statement Churchill and Roosevelt declared: "The American and British people are of course horrified by the recent mob action in Rome, but feel that a greater responsibility placed in the Italian people and in their government will most readily prevent a recurrence

[30] Christopher Buckley, *Road to Rome* (London, 1945), p. 209; *NYT*, Oct. 3, 1943.

[31] Carretta, vice-director of the Regina Coeli prison during the Nazi occupation, had actually helped many political prisoners escape, including the future President of the Italian Republic, Giuseppe Saragat. See Herbert Matthews, *The Education of a Correspondent*, pp. 473-77; Delzell, p. 398. On the Ardeatine atrocity see the recent study by Robert Katz, *Death in Rome* (New York, 1967).

of such acts." The statement seemed reassuring enough, and had the Carretta affair been an isolated incident it might not have stirred so much alarm. But behind the spectacle of violence lurked another factor: the specter of Communism. More than anything else it was this factor that began to determine American diplomacy in Italy beginning in the spring of 1944.[32]

On March 13, 1944, Italy's royal government declared it was resuming diplomatic relations with the Soviet Union; on April 1, Palmiro Togliatti, the sagacious Communist leader who had just returned from Russia, announced his party was not opposed to Victor Emmanuel's remaining on the throne. The world looked on incredulously as the Soviet Union and the PCI seemed to extend the Left hand of comradeship to the Right hand of royalism and clericalism. A restrained but unmistakable consternation seized the conservative press in the United States. Ironically the fiercest critics of the Soviet Union now found themselves espousing the Stalinist line. Arthur Krock and Anne O'Hare McCormick, for example, cautiously approved of the actions of the Soviet and Italian governments. And the CP quickly fell into line. The *Daily Worker*, which had been thundering against the King, praised Moscow's move. The acrobatics caused the *Saturday Evening Post* to quip: "The policy which had been decried when attempted by Mr. Hull became an evidence of masterly diplomatic realism when carried out by Russia." The non-Communist Left and the *fuorusciti*, of course, bitterly attacked Stalin's maneuver. Sforza informed Robert Murphy of the State Department that Russia's recognition and Togliatti's return were the first steps in the "diplomatic Sovietization of Europe." Churchill's pro-monarchism, Sforza warned, was the very thing the PCI would exploit to the hilt.[33]

Recognition of the King also shocked the administration. Hull immediately asked the Soviets for an explanation. In reply, Moscow claimed that the act, rather than violating the terms of the Allied Control Commission, amounted to nothing more than the *de facto* recognition already extended by the United States and England. The explanation failed to convince the State Department, which began to speculate apprehensively on Soviet motives. Was the move primarily military, designed to obtain

[32] *NYT*, Oct. 3, 1943.

[33] "The Somersault of the Left Wing" (editorial), *SEP*, ccxvi (June 10, 1944), 108; *NYT*, April 4, 1944; *FRUS, 1944*, iii, 1090-91.

air bases to aid Tito? Was it a diplomatic power play agreed upon covertly by the Big Three? Or was the tactic political, aimed at keeping in power a reactionary regime whose unpopularity would provide the Stalinists with the best conditions under which to promote the PCI and social revolution? Whatever the answer, Roosevelt was handicapped further by the Soviet action. For the Russian announcement came precisely when the President was pressuring Churchill to accept the Bari Congress program. Thus Churchill, while characteristically dismissing the Bari leaders as "ambitious windbags," could now maintain that his pro-monarchist position had been adopted by the "realistic" Russians. But Churchill's prophetic guffaw could not conceal his own dismay at the sudden turn of events. Nervously he warned Roosevelt that "it may suit them to use the King and Badoglio till everything is ready for an extreme solution. This danger is also in my mind I can assure you." From the moment of Soviet recognition the thought of a Communist take-over in Italy haunted the State Department. A month after recognition the Allied Control Commission forwarded a portentous memo to Washington. Describing the growing strength of Togliatti and the PCI, the Commission concluded with a cryptic warning: "More than twenty years ago a similar situation provoked the March on Rome and gave birth to Fascism. We must make up our minds—and that quickly—whether or not we wish to see this second march developing into another 'ism.' "[34]

FROM BONOMI TO PARRI

Shortly after the liberation of Rome in June 1944 a new cabinet was formed, headed by Ivanoe Bonomi, moderate leader of the Rome Committee of National Liberation. Roosevelt was pleased with the new cabinet (which included Sforza); Churchill was enraged. The replacement of Badoglio for "this group of aged and hungry politicians," the Prime Minister informed the President, was a "great disaster." Maintaining that the six anti-Fascist parties presented an "absolutely unrepresentative crew," Churchill all but accused Roosevelt of betrayal for not supporting the Badoglio regime until the north was liberated. But the administration began to take Churchill's gruff lectures rather lightly, realizing that his views were incorrigibly at variance with

[34] *FRUS, 1944*, III, 1039-41, 1043-44, 1051, 1062-64, 1112-14.

American opinion. In the fall the British exerted pressure on the moderates in the Bonomi government to reorganize the ministry to the Right in order to bolster the monarchy. At the same time the administration stood firm with the six-party coalition. Then in November a new cabinet was formed and in the reshuffling Sforza was assigned the important position of Foreign Minister. On hearing the news, the British government immediately vetoed the appointment. When word of the veto leaked out the following month the administration publicly criticized Churchill and Eden for their intervention, and in the Senate angry protests were voiced by liberals like Claude Pepper (Dem-Fla), Joseph Guffey (Dem-Pa), James Murray (Dem-Mont), and Robert La Follette, Jr. (Rep-Wis). But the British veto was sufficient to throw the Bonomi government into a crisis, and when his second ministry was formed in November the two major parties of the moderate Left, PSI and Action, boycotted the new government. Thus Bonomi now found himself working precariously with elements of the Communist Left and the monarchist Right.[35]

The political situation in Italy continued to deteriorate. Shortly after the war ended Bonomi was succeeded by Ferruccio Parri, the courageous and respected underground leader who years earlier had been associated with Carlo Rosselli's *Giustizia e Libertà*. More than any other, Parri's ministry expressed the Action party's unrelenting demand to purge the country of Fascists and settle the institutional question. Militant idealism, however, proved insufficient to cope with more pressing matters such as relief and unemployment, Communist violence in the rural areas, the black market, separtist agitation in Sicily, and (inevitably) lack of party consensus. But when the Parri government fell, in December 1945, it was more than the predictable "rite of ministerial chairs." In many respects the Parri government was the spiritual heir of the anti-Fascist resistance; its collapse meant the end of the

[35] General Mason-MacFarlane, Chief of the Allied Military Mission, took it upon himself to advise Bonomi that Sforza would not be a good choice as foreign minister. When Robert Murphy angrily informed Hull of Mason-MacFarlane's unauthorized counsel, the Secretary of State immediately countermanded Mason-MacFarlane's advice, stating that the appointment of Sforza "would be entirely agreeable." *FRUS, 1944*, iii, 1126, 1129, 1130-31. In part, the Congressional attack appeared directed at the Anglo-Soviet understanding regarding the political fate of liberated southeastern Europe. *NYT*, Dec. 19, 1944.

resisters' hope for a new Italy based on purified liberal democracy and thoroughgoing social justice. The gloomy implications of the event were dramatized in Parri's last official act. Calling into his office reporters from the world press, the shaken Prime Minister proceeded in a gentle, *sotto voce* to pinpoint responsibility for the demise of his government. It was, he alleged, the Rightist Fifth Column within the government, the Liberals and Christian Democrats, that had deliberately undermined his administration in order to restore to power the very elements which had formed the social basis of Mussolini's regime. Thus the new government represented a "retrogression to Fascism." At this point Alcide De Gasperi, the incoming Christian Democratic Prime Minister, jumped to his feet and bitterly denied the accusations. De Gasperi also pleaded with journalists to disregard Parri's remarks. But most correspondents reported the whole scene, for they too sensed that the awakening dreams of the militant anti-Fascists had been entombed by the base realities of Italian political life. Milton Bracker, who covered Parri's conference for the *New York Times,* quoted an "official American observer" as saying that "the highest American authorities had been 'very happy' with Signor Parri." Yet Parri went under, deserted not only by the opposition in Italy—Communists bent on thwarting democratic reformism, liberal anti-republicans out to salvage the monarchy, Christian Democrats seeking the premiership—but also by the "highest American authorities" who, while respecting Parri, allowed him to perish.[36]

"SHADOWS OF 1919"

In June 1944, Allan Raymond wrote an article for the *Saturday Evening Post* that reflected America's growing apprehension about developments in Italy. The author provided Americans a thumbnail description of the political parties: Christian Democrats represented nonrevolutionary reform guided by the "coaching of the clergy"; Democratic Labor stood for the Norman Thomas brand of "mild socialism"; Action, like the *New Republic* circle, was composed of a liberal intelligentsia dedicated to democracy but at the same time quite ready to join forces with the "extreme left"; and the Communists, organized, disciplined, and subservient to Moscow, enjoyed the largest following among

[36] Kogan, pp. 122-24; Hughes, pp. 150-51; *NYT,* Nov. 25, 1945.

the masses. "On thousands of walls of southern Italy," wrote Raymond, "where the little white patches of white-wash have hidden the old slogans of long live Il Duce, one now finds long live the Red Army or viva Stalin or viva proletarian unity, and the crossed hammer and sickle of Communism is becoming a common roadside sign." Once again loomed the sinister specter of Bolshevism; 1944 was the second act of the "Red Scare." Widespread discontent, economic paralysis, sporadic strikes, rural violence, political bankruptcy, wounded pride—all the ingredients were there, so it seemed. In three words *Newsweek* showed America's sober mood: "Shadows of 1919."[37]

To many Americans it seemed history was repeating itself with a vengeance, the red peril was rising from the ashes of Fascism. As a result sentiment began to veer to the Right (slightly so with the general public, more so within government circles). Myron C. Taylor, Roosevelt's representative at the Vatican, advised the President, after warning of the growing Communist strength, that the Italian people were "accustomed to the monarchical form of government," and that "in an honest test of strength the nation would rally around the House of Savoy as being traditional, definite, and more dependable than any vague or untried group or system." Eventually the administration tacitly swung behind the monarchy in the summer elections of 1946, giving what Norman Kogan has called "covert" support on all procedural questions to forces of the Right, which had induced Victor Emmanuel to hand over the throne to Prince Humbert. But despite the indirect influence of the United States government and the Catholic hierarchy, on June 2 Italian voters chose to reject the monarchy by a majority of over two million, roughly 54 percent of the vote. As for the election of the constituent assembly, De Gasperi's Christian Democrats emerged first with 207 deputies, the Socialists second with 115, and the Communists third with 104.[38]

Insofar as newspaper editorials indicate, American opinion accepted the Crown's defeat. Administration apprehensions not-

[37] Allan Raymond, "We Run Third in Italy," *SEP*, ccxvi (June 17, 1944), 16-17, 88-90; see also Raymond's "Bankrupt Italy Is Capable of Anything," *ibid.*, ccxvii (Sept. 23, 1944), 9-11, 42; *Newsweek*, xxiv (July 24, 1944), 57; *ibid.*, xxviii (July 29, 1946), 37.

[38] Memo, Taylor to Roosevelt, Jan. 22, 1945, Box 17, RP; Kogan, pp. 129-31; Hughes, pp. 154-55.

384

withstanding, the public all along believed the institutional question must ultimately be decided by the Italians themselves. But what rendered palatable the House of Savoy's demise was, of course, the victory of Christian Democracy. The *Christian Science Monitor* welcomed the victory as indicating the "ebbing" of the "Communist tide." The *New York Times* viewed the election as demonstrating sound political maturity, and the *Herald Tribune* expressed relief that Italy's "difficult and dangerous" future would be entrusted to parties reflecting a "mood of conservatism and moderation." Similarly, although the Hearst *San Francisco Examiner* and the conservative *Chicago Tribune* kept editorial tongues between their teeth, the anti-monarchist *San Francisco Chronicle* hailed the wisdom of the Italians, while the *Washington Post* interpreted the simultaneous monarchical defeat and Christian Democratic victory as signifying the end of the old alliance between clericalism and royalism.[39]

To many Americans the triumph of Christian Democracy reaffirmed American democracy. As such De Gasperi's election could be looked upon as American liberalism *redivivus*. But Americans were blinded to the seamy realities of post-Fascist political life. As H. Stuart Hughes noted, Americans only saw "the upper part of the Christian Democratic iceberg"—the part that symbolized Western democratic values. "They could not see the lower part—larger and more ramifying, where actions and entrenched practices belied the lofty aims of the official leadership." Americans failed to see that the ascension of Christian Democracy was a sullied victory, signifying not just the restoration of representative government but the return to power of social forces that had supported Mussolini for twenty years.[40]

Less than two years later Americans again watched the Italian scene anxiously. By the spring of 1948 the political situation had polarized—due to the weakness of the Action party, the splintering of the PSI, and the shrewd parliamentary tactics of De Gasperi—into an apparent choice between Communism and Christian Democracy. At least this is how it appeared to many Italians and most Americans. This time the Truman administration, to-

[39] *Christian Science Monitor*, June 6, 1946; *NYT*, June 6, 1946; *New York Herald Tribune*, June 6, 1946; *San Francisco Examiner*, June 6, 1946; *Chicago Tribune*, June 6, 1946; *Washington Post*, June 8, 1946; see also "American Press Hails Infant Republic," *Il Mondo*, June 1946.

[40] Hughes, p. 144.

gether with Italian-Americans, Catholics, business, and other influential groups, made an all-out effort to persuade and even pressure the Italians into rejecting Communism—and Communism meant a vote for any party other than the Christian Democrats. The election results surpassed all expectations. The Christian Democrats won 307 seats, thereby becoming the first continental party in recent history to win an absolute parliamentary majority; the People's Bloc trailed far behind with 135 Communists and 51 Left-wing Socialists.[41]

American diplomacy left anti-Fascists weary and disillusioned. As they viewed it, the administration's support of Christian Democracy indirectly enabled many of those who had been *fiancheggiatori* of Fascism to reemerge in influential positions and thereby restore the *immobilismo* of the old order. The diplomatic and ideological inhibitions which frustrated a scrupulous American policy must be explained. Yet before doing so it is necessary first to discuss the attitudes of the three most concerned American social groups: intellectuals, businessmen, and Catholics.

CONFLICT WITHIN CONSENSUS

In the *New Republic* and *Nation* America's non-Communist Left intellectuals found a salmagundi of well-informed writers on Italian affairs: J. Alvarez del Vayo, the former Spanish Loyalist foreign minister; the anonymous "Argus" and his "Behind the Enemy Lines Column"; *fuorusciti* like Pacciardi, Salvemini, and Tarchiani; and *literati* such as George De Santillana and Nicola Chiaromonte. The Italian resistance also aired its aspirations in new publications like James Wechsler's and Ralph Ingersol's *PM*, in Robert Hutchins' and Borgese's *Common Cause*, and in the short-lived but lively *Politics*, where Chiaromonte explained to Americans the inflexibility of Croce's haughty liberalism while publisher Dwight Macdonald anatomized Badoglio's "proper flexibility of the spine."[42] Since America's liberal and Socialist in-

---

[41] *Ibid.*, pp. 158-59.

[42] After inverviewing Croce in Naples, Herbert Matthews noted that the philosopher was being attacked by "the eccentric Salvemini-Borgese group, and he was bitter about that, also." (*Education of a Correspondent*, p. 485.) But Croce had a number of American admirers, among them the notable journalist Vincent Sheean, who translated and wrote a laudatory introduction

tellectuals shared with Italy's exiles a democratic vision of liberated Europe, both groups regarded Stalin's recognition of Badoglio as lustful as Churchill's reassertion of colonialism. Thus when the Soviets tried to sweeten the pill with calls for unity, J. Alvarez del Vayo declared that "unity built through appeasing the right at the cost of the left is not the kind of unity needed at the moment." The attack brought scores of letters to the *Nation*, one from Earl Browder who lectured liberals on sabotaging the war against Hitler by criticizing the Soviet Union. The editors, however, dismissed the spurious imperative of solidarity and informed Browder that the tactics used by Stalin could not be condoned by democratic statesmen like Roosevelt. Similarly, the *New Republic* blasted the fellow-traveling Hollywood Writers Congress when it demanded that Salvemini, who was to speak at its conference at Los Angeles, refrain from criticizing the Italian policies of both Russia and the United States. "Quite properly," the *New Republic* reported, "he told the Hollywood Congress to go to hell."[43]

While the rest of the nation rejoiced in Russia's valiant victories on the eastern front, anti-Fascists were once again isolated from the mainstream of American opinion. On foreign policy they had only the support of the lonely anti-Stalinist publications like *Labor Action, Socialist Call,* and the *New Leader.* Throughout the summer and fall of 1943 the *New Leader* ran a symposium, "What to Do with Italy?" that included Antonini, Borgese, Mario Einaudi, Dr. Charles Fama, Frances Keene, Salvemini, Sturzo, and even the ex-Fascist sympathizer, Generoso Pope. The questions put to the participants indicate the hopes and fears of liberal anti-Fascism:

1. Are the Allies at war with "one man," Mussolini—or against the entire hierarchy of Fascism—its roots and development?

2. How shall the leaders of post-war Italy be chosen?

3. Shall the U.S. Government take steps to render immediate help to the underground groups of Italy?

---

to Croce's *Germany and Europe: A Spiritual Dissension* (New York, 1944). For the debate over Croce's book, see *Saturday Review of Literature,* xxxvii (Aug. 18, Sept. 2, Oct. 14, 1944), 12-13, 11-12, 13-16.

[43] *Nation,* clviii (June 3, 24, 1944), 651-52, 746-47; *New Republic,* cx (May 1, 1944), 588.

4. What effective steps can Italo-American institutions and organizations take to speed American victory and help the common people of Italy in the peace settlement?

5. What steps can we take for the "reeducation" of Italian youth after the defeat of Fascism?[44]

Although there were minor points of disagreement, the participants felt that, while England may be at war only with Mussolini, America's aims were less clear and thus more hopeful; that aid must be rushed to the underground and democratic elections held as soon as feasible; and that, above all, the Italians did not have to be "reeducated" to the virtues of democracy. The behavior of the Italians after liberation, they warned, will depend on the Allies' conduct in Italy. A symposium carried in the *New Republic* ("What Free Italians Think"), featuring Chiaromonte, De Santillana, Milano, Salvemini, and Sforza, echoed similar conclusions.[45]

Although an echo in the wilderness, the various symposia served to draw closer together American liberals and the Italian Left. In September 1943, a conference on "After Fascism What?" was held in Carnegie Hall. Serving as panelists were Sforza; Leon Henderson, former head of the Office of Price Administration; Reinhold Niebuhr, Chairman of the Union for Democratic Action (later the Americans for Democratic Action); and James Battistoni, President of the Mazzini Society. But such conferences failed to elicit any reassurance from Roosevelt or the State Department. Thus the following spring the Committee for a Democratic Foreign Policy took out in several publications a full-page advertisement, declaring boldly: "MR. PRESIDENT—ARE WE FIGHTING FOR THE ITALIAN KING?" The statement was signed by Louis Adamic, Antonini, Ascoli, Baldanzi, Roger Baldwin, Louis Bromfield, Van Wyck Brooks, Carrie Chapman Catt, Emmanuel Celler, Lewis Corey, George S. Counts, John Dewey, Dixon Ryan Fox, Waldo Frank, Dorothy Kenyon, Freda Kirchway, Paul Klapper, Max Lerner, James Loeb, Jr., Reinhold Niebuhr, E. George Payne, John H. Randall, Elmer Rice, Lionello Venturi, and Louis Wirth.[46]

[44] *New Leader*, xxvi (April 24—Sept. 4, 1943); the questions were posed in the April 24 issue (p. 5) and the symposium was continued erratically during the next four months.

[45] *New Republic*, cix (Aug. 9, 1943), 189-91.

[46] *Ibid.*, cix (Sept. 20, 1943), 374; cx (April 3, 1944), 480.

Roosevelt's reluctance to commit himself publicly to militant anti-Fascism generated the worst of fears. Yet Roosevelt's expedient reticence was not the only grounds for suspicion. By 1944 the very American social groups which had formerly praised Mussolini as the redeemer of capitalism and Christianity had begun to reassert themselves.

"Imagine Huey Long's having marched on Washington in the midst of Mr. Hoover's troubles, somewhat multiplied," *Business Week* remarked in response to Mussolini's fall. "Then imagine the average American businessman accepting the Kingfish's protection for the status quo and his propaganda for discontent as an easy shortcut to salvation. This may be a strain, but it is not too fantastic a comparison with what happened in Italy." Coming from a leading business journal, this "Parable for Conquerors" editorial was remarkable. With complete candor *Business Week* placed the responsibility for Fascism on the panic-stricken Italian businessmen who betrayed their country at the moment of truth. Admonishments of this sort were all too rare in business circles. In the *Nation's Business*, editor Merle Thorpe asserted that the "Moral of Italy" clearly pointed up the danger of subordinating individualism to an "arbitrarily created social-economic order"; while in the *Commercial and Financial Chronicle* Roger Babson welcomed the collapse of all dictatorships—"whether governments of Fascists, Nazis, Revolutionists, Socialists, or New Dealers"—as a healthy "return to religion and democracy." And writing in the *Wall Street Journal*, ex-New Dealer Raymond Moley noted that the OWI broadcasts "seem to aim" at a "communist revolution" in Italy. Given such sentiments, it is not surprising that the *Journal of Commerce* found the Badoglio regime "a constituted government, ready and able to govern the country," and thus acceptable to the Allies.[47]

In contrast to the twenties, during World War II Wall Street had no significant influence on the State Department's Italian policies. True, Ambassador Myron C. Taylor, former United States Steel executive, advised Roosevelt to back the monarchy in 1945. Until that time, however, Taylor's dispatches to the

[47] *Business Week* (July 31, 1943), 108, (May 20, 1944), 120; *Journal of Commerce*, July 28, 1943; *Nation's Business*, XXXI (Oct. 1943), 21; *Commercial and Financial Chronicle*, July 29, 1943, June 8, 1944; *Wall Street Journal*, July 30, 1943, Dec. 11, 1944; see also *Magazine of Wall Street*, LXXII (Aug. 7, 1943), 445, 496.

President described judiciously and impartially the Italian liberal and Socialist parties. Moreover, Henry F. Grady, a San Francisco businessman and deputy vice president of the economic section of the Allied Control Commission, vigorously opposed Badoglio and the King. Doubtless the business press sided with the Italian Right; yet there is no reason to believe that Roosevelt, the scourge of Wall Street, played fast and loose with men of money. Where business made its pressure felt was outside of government channels, specifically in the person of Amedeo Pietro Giannini, head of the mammoth Bank of America. In the fall of 1945 Giannini went to Rome to explore the prospects of extending private loans to the Italian government—a trip that brings to mind Thomas Lamont's sojourn in 1926. In an interview Giannini made it clear that credits would not be possible as long as partisans continued to control the factories and until a stronger government, headed by old-time conservatives Orlando and Nitti, was established. The publication of Giannini's stringent stipulations inflicted the *coup de grâce* upon the Parri government, causing an immediate collapse of the liberal center and moderate Socialist coalition. Although this form of bankers' blackmail was carried on independently of the administration, it went far toward furthering the anti-Fascist suspicion that the State Department defined the liberation of Italy as the resuscitation of capitalism.[48]

The resurrection of Catholic power created similar suspicion. Anti-Fascists watched with bewilderment as a Protestant America began to pay court to the Papacy, first dramatized in Roosevelt's appointment of Myron Taylor as his personal representative to the Vatican. Observing the "secrecy which envelops" Taylor's "shuttling back and forth between Washington and Rome," even the acute Salvemini, a Roosevelt admirer who always held the President above suspicion, could not help but be reminded of Mussolini's negotiating the Concordat fourteen years earlier. Then in 1943 Salvemini's and La Piana's *What to Do with Italy* rocked the Catholic intellectual community in America. Perhaps it was fitting that a fellow exile, Don Luigi Sturzo, should write a lengthy five-point critique in *Commonweal*. What disturbed the

[48] E.g., Taylor to Roosevelt, May 14, 1943, PPF 423, RP; Grady's opposition to Badoglio and the Crown was reported in *L'Italia* (San Francisco), April 7, 1944, and in the *NYT*, April 1, 1944; on Giannini's activities, see Kogan, pp. 124-25.

Sicilian priest was not that Salvemini cited unverifiable statements by the Pope; but rather that he ignored the Pope's strictures against anti-Semitism, totalitarianism, and "exaggerated
nationalism," and that he slighted *Commonweal*'s and *Catholic
World*'s long-standing opposition to Fascism. Moreover, because
His Holiness had remained politically neutral while morally engaged in issuing peace appeals and in aiding war victims and
prisoners, Sturzo agreed with Roosevelt that the liberation of
Rome and the Vatican was a most noble "crusade."[49]

Salvemini could hardly regard America's liberation of the
Vatican as a crusade; nor could he regard himself as he described
his caricature in the Catholic press: a fanatical anticleric "who
eats a priest for breakfast and a bishop for dinner." Salvemini was
indeed anticlerical, but not without good reason, as he made
clear in recounting the extent of philofascism among the American
Catholic hierarchy. Thus Salvemini responded with a point-by-
point rebuttal of Sturzo. Significantly, out of this exchange the
two esteemed exiles reestablished their respect for one another.
Sturzo, admitting in his rejoinder that the anti-Fascism of the
Catholic World and *Commonweal* may have been "exceptions,"
reminded Salvemini that "it is often the exceptions who ferment"
a renewal of moral idealism. He then concluded with a plea to
men like Salvemini and La Piana ("reasonable men, honest, sincere lovers of truth"), to work together to rebuild their beloved
Italy. Even *Commonweal* editors were caught up in the ecumenical spirit, admitting that Salvemini and La Piana were not
attacking religion as such but only advocating for the Church
in Italy "the enjoyment of all liberties and rights to which religion
is entitled in a truly democratic regime."[50]

But the quarrel, ironed out in *Commonweal*, had earlier erupted
in the *New Republic*. Here Father John A. Ryan responded
to Salvemini's piece on "Catholicism and Liberalism," reminding
the *fuoruscito* that totalitarianism and Catholicism were incom-

[49] Salvemini and La Piana, *What to Do with Italy*, p. 100; Luigi Sturzo,
"Vatican and Fascism: As Seen by Salvemini and La Piana," *Commonweal*,
xxxix (Dec. 17, 1943), 228-31.

[50] Gaetano Salvemini and George La Piana, "Don Sturzo, the Vatican,
Fascism: A Reply to Sturzo," *Commonweal*, xxxix (Jan. 28, 1944), 369-71;
Luigi Sturzo, "Beyond Salvemini-La Piana: Rejoinder," *ibid.*, xxxix (Feb.
25, 1944), 467-69; for Sturzo's reflections on his polemical wars during
these years, including his rejection of Lippmann's definition of monarchism,
see *La mia battaglia da New York* (Milan, 1949).

patible because of the Church's belief in the "supernatural dignity of the soul." This position, it is necessary to recall, Father Ryan had all along maintained. But Salvemini—who unfortunately was ignorant of the Monsignor's valiant anti-Fascist career —replied that liberalism and Catholicism, though potentially reconcilable, failed to "coincide" because the Church would not abide the principles of pluralism. In one respect Father Ryan and Salvemini were both correct: the former in stressing the anti-étatisme of pure Catholic theory, the latter in citing the compromising corporatism of Catholic practice. Catholic intellectuals found themselves answering to Salvemini in 1943 only because they refused to answer to Father Ryan in 1926.[51]

One writer who needed to answer to no one was Father James Gillis. To Gillis, Mussolini's fall vindicated completely the *Catholic World*'s lonely, twenty-year vigilance against Fascism. Thus in good faith the tenacious editor could maintain it was not "logical or just to punish Catholicism for the crimes of Fascism" since no one "can be a good Catholic and a Fascist at the same time." The career of *America* would belie Gillis's argument. Yet if *America* had no anti-Fascist heritage to claim, it did have a sermon to preach. Il Duce fell, the Jesuit weekly announced, because of his difficulties with the Church. Fascism could only succeed by establishing harmonious relations with the Vatican; once the Concordat had been violated by the regime Fascism itself was doomed. Reasoning thus, *America* emerged from the whole affair with a clear conscience. Then in 1945, upon hearing of Mussolini's execution, *America* proceeded to lecture to the dead dictator for violating the sacred tradition of Roman law, while at the same time attacking Fascism as "the poison that might have corroded civilization." Surely this is a curious judgment coming from a journal that once regarded Italian Fascism as refreshing as holy water.[52]

Searching for an alternative to the totalitarianism of both Right and Left, the liberal *Commonweal* made overtures to militant anti-Fascists like Salvemini and La Piana and published articles by moderates like Ascoli and Chiaromonte, as well as uncompromising State Department critics like G. C. Paulding. Perhaps what is most significant is that all three journals remained re-

[51] *New Republic*, CIX (Sept. 20, 1943), 395-97.
[52] *Catholic World*, CLVII (June 1943), 224-34; (Sept. 1943), 561-65. *America*, LX (Aug. 7, 1944), 491; LXXIII (May 12, 1945), 114.

markably objective during the Italian elections. The welfare of the Roman Church, of course, would inevitably be the touchstone of Catholic periodicals, of *America* especially. Yet even the conservative *America* featured anti-monarchist Sturzo. More significantly, during the crucial elections of 1946 *America, Catholic World,* and *Commonweal* remained strangely quiet. Obviously Catholic writers prayed for a Christian Democratic victory; but it was a silent prayer, with hardly a "Hail Mary" for the monarchy.[53]

Still, the moderation of these journals was cold comfort to anti-Fascists who for years had fought the good fight against clerical-Fascism. Salvemini did not have to read Bishop Sheen's *Philosophies at War* (1942) to discover that Catholicism and liberalism remained irreconcilable; nor did Borgese have to read *Commonweal* to find its former editor, George N. Shuster, attacking him for maintaining that Italy would be resurrected on the basis of a new secular faith. Similarly, the American public could find in books like Thomas Morgan's *The Listening Post* (1944) and Camillo Cianfarra's *The Vatican and the War* (1944) a rationale for sustaining Catholic authority in postwar Italy—a rationale designed not to offend a Protestant America imbued with the principle of separation of church and state. That Italy must avoid a "Godless government" was an axiom put forth in *Collier's* by Archbishop Spellman, and it reached messianic heights in William Christian Bullitt's notorious article in *Life*. Bullitt, former Ambassador to Moscow and Paris, informed Americans that the only hope for tempestuous Italy was the Holy See, whose "authority over the hearts of the Italian people has never been greater." Calling forth like a medieval Pontiff, Bullitt exclaimed: "If the Communists come close to power there will arise . . . a wind in Italy, a gale of the spirit, and the Italians, who have no longer much to live for but much faith to die for, will begin to march in defense of the Holy Father, as the Crusaders marched to the old battle cry: 'Christians are right!' "[54]

Perhaps Bullitt's hosanna signified little more than his own

[53] Luigi Sturzo, "Italy, What of the Night?" *America,* LXIX (Sept. 18, 1943), 655-56; *Commonweal,* XLIV (June 7, 1946), 180; *America,* LXXV (June 15, 1946), 205.

[54] George N. Shuster, "No Abiding Place," *Commonweal,* XXXIX (Dec. 24, 1943), 248-50; Francis J. Spellman, "Report from Italy," *Collier's,* CXV (Jan. 20, 1945), 11, 58-59; William C. Bullitt, "The World from Rome," *Life,* XVII (Sept. 4, 1944), 94-109.

zealous Russophobia. As an advocate of Soviet recognition in 1919 and ostracism in 1940, he was, after all, something of a *Childe Harold* of lost causes. Nevertheless, as a leading diplomatic official writing in a mass secular weekly, his views could not be dismissed lightly by anti-Fascists like Salvemini. Moreover, that a Protestant like Bullitt would cry holy havoc to defend the Papacy raises again the question of who speaks for American Catholicism. It was a question that caused not a little confusion and much misapprehension.[55]

One example of this misapprehension occurred in late 1943. During the invasion of Sicily *The Tablet*, the Right-wing organ of the Brooklyn diocese, demanded that all American officials assuming administrative positions in liberated Italy be of Catholic religion. The proposal that Catholic Italy be governed only by American Catholics was then endorsed at the annual convention of the Knights of Columbus. To Protestants such a demand conjured up visions of a tyranny of faith. Thus when the Italian Protestant Ministers Association heard of the proposal, it immediately "jumped into the jihad." Not only was *The Tablet's* demand a violation of the principle of separation, declared the Association, it smacked "brimful of that intolerance so often demonstrated by various agencies acting under the name of the Catholic Church." Although *Time* described the clash as a minor religious "Battle for Italy," significantly no major Catholic spokesman took up the proposal and the incident went unnoticed by most Protestant writers. Despite the exhortations of Bullitt, *The Tablet*, and the Knights of Columbus, the Italian question in the forties did not revive the anti-Romanism surrounding the Spanish question several years earlier.[56]

MÉSALLIANCE: AMERICAN LIBERALISM AND ITALIAN ANTI-FASCISM

To sum up, American intellectuals looked to a new Italy reconstructed on the basis of social democracy; business to a more familiar Italy rehabilitated by the curative power of free capital; Catholics to a God-fearing Italy regenerated by the divine wisdom of the Holy See. Despite these conflicting views there remained something of a consensus in the broader sweep of public

[55] Gaetano Salvemini, "Mr. Bullitt's 'Romans,'" *Italia Libera*, Oct. 1, 1944.
[56] *Time*, XLII (Nov. 1, 1943), 79.

opinion. The general press shed few tears over the ousting of the monarchy while welcoming wholeheartedly the advent of Christian Democracy. Save for the business press and a few fearful Catholic writers, most Americans would have accepted Italy's moderate socialists and Mazzini liberals, had these elements been able to present a viable Center. And had the PSI and Bari Congress republicans emerged victorious, America's liberation of Italy would have enjoyed a certain ideological purity.

Whether intervention in the expression of moral and material support could have sustained Parri's CLN and the parties of the moderate Left is questionable. For the Action party proved to be an intellectual elite with few ties to the masses, and the inexperienced Parri could hardly have survived the wily opposition of De Gasperi on the Right and Togliatti on the Left. American diplomatic officials soon came to see that the non-Communist Left parties were numerically weak and poorly organized. Yet even though there may have been no alternative to Christian Democracy by 1945, it does not follow that in the election of 1946 the administration had to shun earlier advice regarding the monarchy's unpopularity. As Sforza and Sturzo warned State Department officials, it is foolish to perpetuate an anachronism to prevent radicalism. But the advice went unheeded, and when the monarchy went under America had now to turn to Christian Democracy as the last bulwark of order. In the crucial elections of 1948, when Communist strength appeared to surge alarmingly, even Protestant America embraced Christian Democracy, seemingly oblivious to the deep-rooted anticlericalism among many Italians. Though committed to the principle of separation in their own country, Americans felt no great compunction in encouraging the Roman Church to interfere in politics with threats of Communist damnation and promises of Christian salvation.[57]

The election of 1948, of course, took place amid the tremors of the Communist coup in Czechoslovakia. Yet the ominous realities of the Cold War ought not allow us to overlook the limited possibilities in Italy prior to the Russo-American confrontation. For it cannot be denied that in 1945 the administration drew back from supporting elements of the Center and moderate Left, particularly Parri's CLN. And in so doing it forsook the one faction whose leadership and social programs came closest to

[57] For the advice of Italian exiles, see *FRUS, 1944,* III, 1090-91, 1149-51.

395

New Deal liberalism. This is not to suggest America's support for Christian Democracy betrayed the cause of Italian freedom. Despite what many partisans claimed at the time, Christian Democracy stood for more than the doffing of the Blackshirt for the black cassock. Committed to constitutional democracy and electoral government, cautious reform and piecemeal planning, De Gasperi's remarkable reign was a vast improvement over Mussolini's farcical adventure. Nor should it be forgotten that the Roosevelt administration clearly sympathized with the Mazzinian liberals and Socialists in 1943 and early 1944. Time and again government officials advised against committing Allied policy to either the Crown or Badoglio, and the State Department eventually prevailed over Churchill in winning military status for Italy, in recognizing Sforza and in pushing the Bari Congress platform. With the rapid rise of Communist strength, however, the weakness of the democratic Left was exposed. And as the administration covertly backed monarchism in 1946 and openly embraced clericalism in 1948, Italian social democracy was expediently left in the lurch.

It is all too easy to make the ideologically embarrassing diplomatically expedient. In truth, the administration's Italian policies after 1944 did amount to an abandonment of America's war aims established in the early years by President Roosevelt. The support of Christian Democracy and clericalism did less than justice to Roosevelt's vision of a postwar "world founded upon four essential freedoms." True, Christian Democrats were committed impeccably to constitutionalism, yet their limited social programs offered a far cry from the principle of freedom from want, and their reluctance to "defascistize" betrayed little concern for purging those who would jeopardize freedom of speech and expression. Similarly, the Vatican might speak eloquently of the dignity of the soul, but its history of convenient concordats spoke poorly of its fitness to assure freedom of religion, a precious freedom defined by Jefferson and extended abroad by Roosevelt only to be sabotaged by an unholy alliance of clerics and Communists.[58]

[58] When incorporated into the Atlantic Charter, Roosevelt had to persuade the Soviets to accept the principle of freedom of religion. He did so by explaining to Foreign Minister Litvinov that in the traditional Jeffersonian sense the term religious freedom was, in the words of Robert Sherwood, "so broadly democratic that it included the right to have no religion

Moreover, while many elements of the moderate Left had been committed to ferreting out all Fascists and quasi-Fascists in Italian society, the State Department was searching for order and stability. Thus the priorities of American diplomacy and the undying vendetta of the anti-Fascists invested the meaning of liberation with a dual vision whose implications became more acute as the war drew to a close. This latent discord may be further illustrated by drawing a parallel between the New Deal liberals[59] and the Italian *fuorusciti*. When the Roosevelt liberals came to office they, like the anti-Fascists, were returning to power after a long period of "exile." Both American liberals and Italian partisans, moreover, were out to purge their countries of the creatures responsible for the depression on the one hand and for Fascism on the other. If 1933 was a rendezvous with destiny, 1945 was a rendezvous with a new *Risorgimento* that would carry on the historic mission of Italian democracy. Yet here the parallel abruptly ends. For the New Dealers were determined to save America's economic system; Italian radicals were bent on revamping theirs. After a decade of watchful wonderment in the twenties, American progressives finally rejected rampant free enterprise; the Italian Left hardly had to repudiate what it never considered. In order to reform America, liberals called for a balance between the dynamic energies of business and the enlightened discipline of government; in order to reform Italy, the exiles demanded a complete *trasformazione* of the social order. Thus the liberal imagination proved sorely limited when it came to sympathizing with the various structural reformations the dis-

---

at all—it gave to the individual the right to worship any God he chose or no God." (Sherwood, p. 449.) Ironically, it was Togliatti's PCI that sided with the Christian Democrats in approving Article 7 of the 1948 constitution, which reaffirmed Mussolini's Concordat with the Vatican. The opposing Italian liberals and Socialists apparently took Cavour's dictum of "a free church in a free state" as seriously as Jefferson took the principle of separation. For American Catholics, on the contrary, the perpetuation of Il Duce's 1929 Concordat was an unquestioned article of faith. See, for example, John La Farge, "The Lateran Treaty Is Outside Power Politics," *America* LXX (Feb. 26, 1944), 568-70.

[59] By New Deal liberals I mean those officials who stayed with the Roosevelt administration, as contrasted to the independent liberals who showed, insofar as the *Nation* and *New Republic* reveal, greater sensitivity to the needs and aspirations of Italian social democracy.

parate Italian Left envisioned. The restoration of formal political democracy in Italy was a genuine fulfillment of the Wilsonian mission, but between the boundless dreams of Italian anti-Fascism and the provincial ideals of American liberalism inhered an inevitable *mésalliance*.

15.

Italian-Americans
and the *Fuorusciti*
in World War II

PURGATORY: 1940-1942

In August 1940, *Collier's* made a plea to Americans to "Lay Off The Italians." The popular magazine felt it necessary to offer brotherly exhortations because some Americans had begun to look askance at their Italian neighbors. The uneasiness became more widespread after December 7, 1941, when a veritable loyalty scare gripped the nation. Many Americans felt they had good reason to suspect Italian-Americans of subversive intent: the propaganda broadcasts beamed directly from Rome to New York and Boston Italian neighborhoods; the Italian-American press which, unlike that of the German-Americans, remained faithful to Italy almost until Pearl Harbor;[1] and the various state and federal investigations of "un-American" activities which gave anti-Fascists their day in court but gave Americans an unduly alarming picture of Italian-American Fascism.[2]

Fears of a Fascist Fifth Column, however unrealistic, caused the government to take action against the Italian community. The first move, in January 1942, called for the reclassification of the non-citizen Italian-American as an "enemy alien." Italians, whose 600,000 aliens comprised the largest number in the country, were thoroughly shaken by the sudden announcement. Although only

---

[1] Except for Fritz Kuhn's *Deutscher Weckruf und Beobachter*, most major German-American papers remained either noncommittal regarding Hitler, like the staid *Staats-Zeitung*, or emphatically anti-Fascist, like the social democratic weekly *Neue Volkszeitung*. Out of 178 German language papers, *Fortune's* study concluded that only about a dozen could be categorized as "outright pro-Fascist." But this same survey concluded that out of 129 Italian language papers "about eighty are more or less Fascist." See "The Foreign Language Press," *Fortune*, XXII (Nov. 1940), 90-93, 102-04.

[2] *Collier's*, CVL (Aug. 3, 1940), 54.

228 of the Italian aliens eventually were interned for the duration of the war (compared to 1,891 German-Americans and 2,020 Japanese), the "alien enemy" was kept under close surveillance and many were relocated in the Western Defense Command areas. The resettlement orders caused some Italian-American home owners living within prohibited zones to succumb to a panic of coerced selling; others had their personal assets confiscated. Some workers, like the fishermen of San Francisco, were dispossessed of their boats; others, like the restaurant employees, lost their very livelihood because of curfew restrictions.[3]

For all Italian-Americans, both alien and citizen, the year 1942 was almost like a purgatory where the sons of Italy would have to suffer and expiate the sins of Fascism. Unfortunate as the hardships and insults were, however, Italian-Americans fared reasonably well when compared to the deplorable plight of the Japanese Nisei. Within months alien Italians learned that, unlike the Japanese, they would not be interned, and before the year was out the classification had been rescinded. On Columbus Day Attorney General Francis Biddle announced the lifting of what Antonini rightly termed the "intolerable stigma." No doubt the administration's quick decision to rescind the classification was prompted by many motives—pressure from Italian-American politicians and trade union leaders, the desire to boost the morale of Italian-American soldiers and to spur relatives in Italy into resisting the war effort—but it was largely due to the awareness of the abiding loyalty of the great majority of Italian-Americans.[4]

[3] U.S. Congress, House, 77th Cong., 2nd Sess., *Hearings Before the Select Committee Investigating National Defense Migration* (Washington, 1942), esp. Pt. 29.

[4] Though Italian-Americans were doubtlessly loyal, the determination of loyalty was often less a matter of evidence than influence. In light of the tragic fate of the Nisei, the following repartee between Congressman John Tolan and attorney Chauncey Tramultolo suggests something about the social logic of law:

Chairman: Tell us about the Di Maggios. Tell us about Di Maggio's father.

Tramultolo: Neither of the Di Maggio seniors is a citizen. They have reared nine children, five boys and four girls, eight of whom were born in the United States, and the other one is a naturalized citizen. Three of the boys are outstanding persons in the sports world. Joe, who is with the Yanks, was leading hitter for both the American and National Leagues during the years 1939 and 1940. His younger brother, Dominic, is with the Boston Red Sox, and his older brother, Vincent, is with the Pittsburgh team

400

If government authorities had any doubts about the complete loyalty of Italian-Americans, they had only to observe the passionate outburst of patriotism after Pearl Harbor. From Boston's north end to San Francisco's North Beach, Italians staged rallies to declare their opposition to Fascism and reaffirm their devotion to democracy. Matching words with deeds, many *prominenti* started a massive propaganda campaign aimed at undermining Mussolini's government. *Il Progresso*, recommending a closing of anti-Fascist ranks, endorsed the Italian-American Labor Council's proposal for a national conference to unite all organizations into "one hard-hitting body dedicated to supporting the democratic program in Italy." Working closely with the OWI, numerous New York Italian-American officials broadcast shortwave programs to the old country. For the bewildered people of Italy these broadcasts offered a ray of hope as they defiantly listened behind closed doors and drawn shutters. Indeed the garrulous La Guardia, combining human compassion with dramatic gusto, became as popular on the *marciapiedi* of Italy as he was on the sidewalks of New York; one town, Torre Annunziata, adopted him as a patron hero.[5]

The propaganda offensive in Italy had its historical analogue in Wilson's appeal in 1918 to the German people to throw over the Kaiser and accept an armistice. The Roosevelt administration, however, believed a democratic revolution unrealistic and premature. The OWI merely wanted to prepare the Italians psychologically so that when the invasion came they would wholeheartedly support the Allies and not just opt for neutrality. Thus when Antonini tried to prevail upon the OWI to stimulate an all-out insurrection, Elmer Davis, head of the OWI, reminded him that his office was subservient to the Executive, who had final say on the nature of propaganda used in Italy. The *fuorusciti*, moreover,

---

of the National League. . . . To evacuate the senior Di Maggios would, in view of the splendid family they have reared and their unquestioned loyalty, present, I am sure you will agree with me, a serious situation. *Ibid.*, p. 11128.

Regarding the "political pressure" imposed on the military in behalf of the Italian-Americans, see also Stetson Conn, et al., *Guarding the United States and Its Outposts* (Washington, D.C., Office of the Chief of Military History, Department of Army, 1964).

NYT, Jan. 11, 1942; "Italy: Loss of Morale," *Current History*, iii (Dec. 1942), 327-28; Cordell Hull, *Memoirs* (New York, 1948), ii, 1548.

[5] *Il Progresso*, July 25, 1943; *Christian Science Monitor*, July 26, 1943; *NYT*, Oct. 3, 1943.

could not understand why propaganda relayed to their homeland should be tailored to the needs of American foreign policy, while Italian-Americans, who fancied themselves "experts" on Italy, impatiently scorned "ignorant" Americans for having no comprehension of the Italian character. On one occasion the OWI broadcast Henry Wallace's "Common Man" address in which the Vice President spoke of a healthy new world where every person would be entitled to a quart of milk daily. Wine-loving *paesani*, scoffed one Italian-American, would "puke" at the thought.[6]

"Muzzo Got His"

The electrifying news of Mussolini's fall buzzed through Italian-American neighborhoods, leaving the inhabitants emotionally exhausted. The joy they felt could not overcome the anguish they experienced as their thoughts immediately turned to the fate of relatives in Italy who might now be the victims of German reprisals. Thus the ordeal of Fascism was over, but the future of Italy still hung in doubt. Eyes misty with emotion, Italian-Americans expressed both deep satisfaction and weary resignation, perhaps best summed up in the often-heard remark, "Muzzo got his."[7]

But the Italian-American press, crowing with profundity, hailed July 25 as a day of vindication. "*Il Progresso* consistently and vigorously denounced Mussolini and his cohorts for the misery they inflicted upon and the bloodshed they caused the Italian people and for the aid and comfort that he rendered to Hitler and Nazi Germany," declared Generoso Pope in what generously might be termed a lapse of memory. Publishers like Pope and Patrizi spent the next two years preaching sobriety and moderation. They wanted Italy out of the war as soon as possible and they counted on Badoglio and the King to bring off the maneuver. "If the House of Savoy will err in the next immediate decision," *L'Italia* warned on July 28, "it will write its own condemnation and disappear from the political scene and from the age old history of Italy and from the world." As disenchanted as they were with Victor Emmanuel, Pope and Patrizi feared more the threat of social upheaval. Welcoming Badoglio as a "sincere monarchist" who was never a Mussolini disciple, Pope praised heaven that Fascism had been defeated without an "internal revolution which

[6] Burlingame, pp. 221-27.

[7] *NYT*, July 26, 1943; *Chicago Daily Tribune*, July 26, 28, 1943.

would have brought suffering to the Italian people." During the crucial "forty-five days" *Il Progresso* and *L'Italia* were appalled at the disturbances taking place in Milan and Turin and at the ineptitude of Victor Emmanuel. By fall both editors had shifted their support to Prince Humbert, but both also maintained that the national government must eventually be reformed on a "broad democratic basis." In October *Il Progresso*, now under the influence of Antonini and the IALC, began featuring Count Sforza on its front page. Sforza publicly refused to write for Pope unless his paper "repudiated in good faith with a courageous gesture" its Fascist record. *Il Progresso* complied gladly. *L'Italia* also made overtures to the *fuoruscito* while defending Badoglio as the tough "rude military man" Italy needed to survive the war, at which time he could be replaced by the esteemed Sforza. Throughout 1944 and 1945 the Italian-American press called for Italy's co-belligerent status and membership in the United Nations, for economic relief and the use of underground partisans, and for a just treaty that would assure the nation's territorial integrity. With Russia's recognition of the Badoglio-Victor Emmanuel diumvirate, *Il Progresso* warned against the "totalitarian elements" bent on "boring from within" the monarchy "in the manner of Il Duce's slide into power." For both *Il Progresso* and *L'Italia* the monarchical question must be decided by a popular vote rather than by the *realpolitik* of the Big Three. Publishers like Pope and Patrizi thus sympathized contritely with Sforza and the moderate liberals while continuing to criticize the militant Left.[8]

Emerging from the Fascist era as sadder but wiser men, Italian-American *prominenti* organized the American Committee for Italian Democracy. In order to influence the administration, the ACID adopted a platform summoning the complete support of six million Italian-Americans to the Allied cause and calling for Italy's immediate withdrawal from the war followed by a just peace settlement, cooperation with relief agencies, and a "democratic solution" to Italy's political future. ACID also made unmistakable its opposition to both "Communist and Darlanist influences." Although the *New York Times* hailed the ACID as "Another Risorgimento," some Italian-Americans had good reason

[8] *Il Progresso*, July 26, Aug. 28, Oct. 24, Nov. 21, 1943, April 30, 1944. *New York Herald Tribune*, July 26, 1943; *L'Italia*, July 28, Sept. 10, 30, 1943; Norman, "Repudiation of Fascism by the Italian-American Press," pp. 4-5.

to question this venerable image. Not only did excluded Communists attack the organization but even some moderates refused to join because it had indiscriminately accepted members with dubious political backgrounds. Actually, ACID represented an expedient fusion of ex-Fascist sympathizers and anti-Fascist fighters; the former seeking new democratic respectability, the latter trying to organize for a coming showdown with the Stalinists. For what had developed during the 1940s was a veritable war within a war among the anti-Fascist Left.[9]

The Anti-Fascist Inner War

World War II vindicated the anti-Fascist opposition in America. No longer regarded as bellicose revolutionaries bent on overthrowing Il Duce's orderly government, the resisters now enjoyed the image of respectable freedom fighters out to redeem Italy's democratic heritage. The preeminence of the newly discovered prophets, however, was short-lived; for America's involvement in the war raised three questions that profoundly divided the opposition: should former Mussolini propagandists be prosecuted by the government and isolated from the Italian community; should anti-Fascists collaborate with the Communist opposition; and must all anti-Fascists support the State Department's Mediterranean policies?

Anti-Fascists wanted everyone to remember what Mussolini's former sympathizers wanted everyone to forget. Dismissing their breast-beating declarations of loyalty as a spurious gallows confession, anti-Fascists thus demanded the government purge Il Duce's former admirers. Yet only a handful were apprehended and either prosecuted, relocated, or interned. In New York, for example, Trombetta received a ten-year prison term (later paroled) for secretly accepting money from a foreign government; and in California several Italian-American civic leaders and about forty *ex-combattenti* (World War I veterans) were "evacuated" from the state by the attorney general. The hit-or-miss roundup however, seemed a half-hearted effort, and when the government issued the "enemy alien" classification anti-Fascists believed it only punished Mussolini's enemies who had just arrived in America while allowing his former champions to go undisturbed.[10]

[9] *Il Progresso*, July 27, 1943; *NYT*, July 26, 27, Aug. 2, 1943.
[10] *TCR*, pp. 282-321; *Il Mondo*, Jan., July, Nov. 1942; see also the re-

Even more dismaying to many anti-Fascists was the sight of their comrades accepting former philofascists into the newly formed Italian-American committees. When Antonini assumed office in the ACID and accepted Pope as treasurer he was attacked by both friend and foe, by non-Communist labor leaders as well as Stalinists. Antonini's maneuver may be justified on tactical grounds, for Communists as well as Socialists realized the importance of the repentant recruits to anti-Fascism in view of reaching the Italian-American masses. Thus Antonini's success in persuading Pope to place *Il Progresso* at the disposal of the non-Communist Left was a master stroke. Yet Antonini's defense of Pope as a conscience-stricken convert who had repudiated Fascism as early as 1938 was a bit too much, and the ILGWU's expedient tactics splintered the labor opposition as many anti-Fascists, Socialists and Communists alike, continued to denounce the *prominenti's* conspicuous rituals of recantation.[11]

The issue of collaborating with Communists was equally divisive. Failure to establish a united front in 1926 could not be forgotten by early anti-Fascists. Several events in the thirties—the Soviet Union's compromising of their boycott against Italy during the Ethiopian crisis, the Stalinist-Trotskyite split, and the Popular Front experience of the Spanish Civil War—also fostered suspicion among the non-Communist Left. But more than any other event it was the Molotov-Ribbentrop pact of 1939 that shattered once and for all the Popular Front mystique. *L'Unità del Popolo*, the New York Communist daily edited by Gino Bardi and Mary Testa, now discarded its anti-Fascist suit of armor and, donning the garb of noninterventionism, argued that war would mean domestic reaction and that liberalism, as the fall of France demonstrated, could not be saved anyway. Congressman Marcantonio turned his coat inside out and found a pacifist lining. "When I voted against the war program in Congress," he announced, ". . . I voted to keep everyone of you boys from dying on the battlefields in Europe." Attempting to slander anti-Fascist interventionists, *L'Unità* maintained the Free Italy movement,

---

marks of Salvemini and Sforza in "Biddle's Orders: Two Views," *Nation*, CLV (Nov. 7, 1942), 476-78.

[11] Minutes, Local 89, ILGWU, Oct. 10, Nov. 9, 16, 1944, IA; *NYT*, Aug. 12, 1943; *Il Progresso*, Aug. 29, 1943; *Il Mondo*, April 1943; see also the letters from Antonini and Joseph Salerno to the *New Leader*, XXVII (Jan. 22, 1944), 14.

like that of the Free French, was composed of "unemployed generals," "hungry aristocrats," and "unprincipled social democrats," and the Mazzini Society was "a group of discredited liberals [who] made public application to Messrs. Churchill and Roosevelt for the job of stabbing the Italian people in the back."[12]

Hitler's invasion of Russia on June 22, 1941, again caught the Stalinists ideologically naked; once more a quick change of uniform was required. L'Unità now summoned all anti-Fascists to take up arms against Fascism. Past differences must be buried, exclaimed editors Bardi and Testa, for the new political situation has just been clarified beyond all doubt. "He who does not see it, he who remains in the old circles of his own petty, sectarian preoccupations, is obstructing the anti-Hitler front." L'Unità then hailed Antonini's IALC and welcomed to the ranks the Mazzini Society, "a group of highly respectable Italian intellectual émigrés." In keeping with the ecumenical spirit, the editors supported the election of liberals like La Guardia and even embraced the misguided Generoso Pope, declaring that, like Antonini, they "sincerely want to help him fight Hitlerism." Shortly afterwards L'Unità believed it "unfortunate" that some anti-Fascists questioned Pope's conversion, which signaled the rebirth of political consciousness in the Italian community. In the war against Hitler Italian-American Stalinists turned Leninism on its head: no enemies on the Right. Celebrating July 4, 1941, L'Unità devoted a full page of sketches and photos to the American Declaration of Independence and the Constitutional Convention. Thus within two years the Stalinist Left had gone from interventionism to isolationism to maudlin nationalism without so much as a blush.[13]

These startling twists and turns only confirmed the skepticism of the non-Communist Left on the question of cooperation. No one was more opposed to collaboration than Antonini. The head of ILGWU's Local 89 believed that another Popular Front must be avoided at all costs. Military aid to the Soviet Union he conceded; a common cause with Communists he condemned outright. Antonini's opposition brought down the wrath of the Stalinist Left. Then, when the ACID organized, a number of fellow traveling anti-Fascists declared their "secession" from Antonini's IALC

[12] L'Unità del Popolo, July 13, 20, 1940, March 15, 1941.
[13] Ibid., July 5, Aug. 11, Sept. 20, 1941; Jan. 3, 1942.

and announced a new Free Italy Labor Council. This faction was headed by Joseph Catalanotti, Vice President of the ACWU; Jay Rubin of the Hotel Trades Council of New York; and August Bellanca, a leading ACWU official. Serving as political spokesmen were Marcantonio and Peter Cacchione, a Brooklyn Communist councilman. The bolt, a direct challenge to Antonini's leadership, was answered at the New York state AFL convention the following month. Here delegates voted by an overwhelming majority to reject Rubin's motion to withdraw support from Antonini and the IALC.[14]

While Antonini charged the secessionists were Communist conspirators trying to bore from within, Catalanotti and the *Daily Worker* accused him of creating a red "smoke screen" in order to cover his recent association with Pope. Like most dialogues of acrimony, there is an element of truth on both sides. Doubtless the break represented an attempt on the part of the small Stalinist minority to exploit Mussolini's demise in order to foment social revolution in Italy; but doubtless too a good number of embattled anti-Fascists, especially those in the ACWU, bolted because they could not countenance Antonini's tolerating the *volte-face* of former enemies like Pope. By the same token, if Antonini was merely crying the Communist "wolf," the Stalinist complaint about Pope plainly seemed like sour grapes.[15]

In any case, Antonini continued his vigilance against Communist penetration in Italy as well as in the United States. After

[14] Luigi Antonini, "Contro i Fronti Popolariste," *Dynamic Democracy* (New York, 1941), pp. 141-45; *L'Unità del Popolo*, July 24, 1943; *NYT*, Aug. 12, 26, 27, 1943; Luigi Antonini, *Vito Marcantonio: The Man on the Flying Trapeze* (New York, n.d.), pamphlet (microfilm, NYPL); *New Leader*, xxvi (Dec. 4, 1943), 4.

[15] As indicated above, the Stalinists had no compunctions about working with Pope; only when he rejected their overtures did he become a class enemy. The *fuorusciti* were also aware of the importance of Pope and his paper. After Ascoli, as President of the Mazzini Society, denounced the publisher in a letter to the Attorney General, Pope asked him for a meeting. As one condition for an "entente" Ascoli demanded that the ex-Fascist turn over editorship of his paper to Tarchiani and Cianca. When Ascoli consulted Sforza and Salvemini the latter insisted that this "very secret" transaction be submitted to a general assembly of the Mazzini. In the meantime *Il Progresso* attached itself to Antonini and the IALC. See Max Ascoli, "Salvemini negli Stati Uniti," *La Voce Repubblicana*, Dec. 20-21, 1967.

NYT, Aug. 12, 1943; *Daily Worker*, July 26, 1943; *L'Unità del Popolo*, July 31, 1943.

the Soviets recognized Badoglio, Antonini and Montana warned the State Department that any support of an Italian coalition government that included Togliatti Communists "and their neo-Fascist followers" would be a "calamity." Antonini's opposition to the PCI had the support of the anti-Stalinist *New Leader*, the *Socialist Call*, and the liberal *New Republic* and *Nation*. Interestingly enough, Antonini's conversations in Italy with Socialists like Pietro Nenni and Giuseppe Saragat convinced him to shift ground. Informed of the increasing popularity of the PCI and of the "imperative necessity of unity," he now realized that the PSI could not afford to blackball Communists and be left by itself outside the coalition government. Upon his return, Antonini therefore wrote an article in the *New Leader* calling for a "United Front in Italy." Although his shift disturbed the anti-Stalinist Left, Antonini made it clear the strategy required in Italy did not necessarily apply to the United States. Here the common-front tactic would still be held up to execration.[16]

The *fuorusciti* also felt the strain of the collaboration question. In June 1943, Pacciardi went before a national convention of the Mazzini Society and made the stunning proposal to organize a liberation brigade which would include Communists. To some members the suggestion smacked, whether correctly or not, of another Stalinist-controlled "Alleanza Garibaldi" of Spanish Civil War vintage. The idea that Pacciardi had been duped by Communists must have occurred to some members in the audience. But when Edoardo Vergara, a young engineer and a recent exile from Italy, rose and stated loud and clear the accusation, the staunchly anti-Communist Pacciardi rushed over to Vergara and angrily slapped him across the face. The ugly incident dramatized the depth of anti-Communist sentiment among all the Mazzinians, who quickly and unanimously agreed to avoid a repetition of the Popular Front and the "Alleanza Garibaldi." This decision was made despite the OWI, whose directors had been encouraging the exiles to come to terms with the PCI and the American CP

16 *NYT*, April 15, 1944; *New Leader*, xxvii (Dec. 16, 1944), 7; *L'Unità del Popolo*, July 29, 1944. In August 1943, the *Daily Worker* reported that Socialists Ignazio Silone and Giuseppe Modigliani, both refugees in Switzerland, were engaged in international underground activities with the OSS. Angry anti-Fascists regarded publication of the story as a vicious Stalinist attempt to expose Socialist resisters to the prosecution of the Swiss government. *New Leader*, xxvi (Aug. 14, 1943), 1.

408

in order to form a more effective and united liberation vanguard. But Italian liberal Socialists desired to maintain a "democratic front," a unique position that distinguished the Mazzinians from other resistance groups in Europe.[17]

Like the IALC, the *fuorusciti* felt the sting of the Stalinist Left. Claiming "The End of the Mazzini Society," *L'Unità* accused the exiles of doing Antonini's dirty work. Then in 1944 when the exiles refused to support Bonomi's government, *L'Unità* spoke hopefully of "The Anti-Salvemini Coalition." To form such a coalition Communists counted on Valenti of *La Parola* and Bellanca of the ACWU, both having broken with Antonini. But the support of these two non-Communists failed to materialize. By the end of 1944 *L'Unità* and the *Daily Worker* were completely isolated from both the Italian-American Left and the *fuorusciti*.[18]

The Murder of Tresca

Actually the isolation began on January 11, 1943. On that evening Carlo Tresca left his office together with Giuseppe Calabi to attend a Mazzini Society meeting. While waiting for a traffic signal on the dark and deserted corner of New York's Fifteenth Street and Fifth Avenue, Tresca was shot from behind, one bullet piercing his back, another lodged in his skull. Before his companion grasped what had happened, the gunman jumped into a dark sedan that disappeared under the dim lights of Fifteenth Street. Tresca died instantly.[19]

As with Trotsky's assassination, there was a fatalism about Tresca's which made his death all the more tragic.[20] His funeral

[17] Interview with Carmelo Zito, Sept. 26, 1967; with Vanni Montana, Aug. 10, 1967; Randolph Pacciardi, "A Free Italian Legion," *Nation*, CLV (Oct. 3, 1942), 299-300; *L'Unità del Popolo*, Feb. 6, 1943; Press Release, Italian American Labor Council, Jan. 23, 1943, Box 233A, RP; Delzell, pp. 201-02; Valenti to James Battistoni, May 10, 1943, VP.

[18] *L'Unità del Popolo*, July 24, Dec. 4, 1943; April 22, 29, 1944.

[19] *Who Killed Carlo Tresca?* Forewords by Arturo Giovannitti and John Dos Passos (Tresca Memorial Committee pamphlet, New York, 1945); for a detailed account of the murder, with a map of the scene of the crime, see *PM*, Jan. 14, 1943.

[20] "For poetry's sake," Max Eastman wrote at the time, "for the sake of his name and memory, Carlo had to die a violent death. He had to die at the hand of the tyrant's assassin. He had lived a violent life. He had loved danger. He had loved the fight. His last motion was to swing and confront the long-expected enemy. So let us say farewell to Carlo as we hear him say—as surely he would if his breath came back—'Well, they got me at

was jammed with writers and labor leaders who shared, as Suzanne La Follette put it, "a common grief and a common awareness that with Carlo a vital warmth had gone out of their lives that could never be rekindled." "The passing away of Carlo Tresca," Arthur Garfield Hays lamented, "leaves a void in about as great variety of hearts as could be affected by any man's death." But the void could be "rekindled" with the afterglow of memory. "Can you name any man," Lewis S. Gannett asked, "who lived in the midst of so many quarrels of every scale and dimension, who loved so many different kinds of people, and was so universally loved in return?" John Dewey, whose optimism had little room for tragedy, could also see a brighter lesson in the death of a warrior who always fought the right causes: "We have all lost a wonderful lover of all mankind. But the world is much richer because of his life." Even the *New York Times* deigned to editorialize affectionately about the anarchist who had inveighed against the paper for twenty years: "The murder of Carlo Tresca removes a man who was capable of expressing and inspiring violent disagreement, but whom only an embittered fanatic could have hated."[21]

---

last!' " (quoted in *Omaggio alla memoria imperitura di Carlo Tresca* [New York, 1943], p. 43.)

Perhaps Mary McCarthy best expressed (a few years later) that deep revulsion which swells up after a political assassination and leads one to the fatalistic conclusion that only the good die young: "The Crucifixion, the murder of Thomas à Becket, and other historical precedents notwithstanding, many of us still believe that there are limits to man's capacity for evil. . . . Even the Nazis, after all, did not kill their great opponents, and were they really deterred, as some people think, by practical considerations alone? On the left, however, a new set of values seem to have appeared. On the left, it is Gandhi who can be killed or Trotsky or Tresca, men *integri vitae scelerisque puri*, while Stalin remains invulnerable to the assassin's bullet. . . . In Gandhi's death, as in Tresca's and Trotsky's, the very amiability and harmlessness of the victim appears to have formed part of the motive: Gandhi on his way to a prayer-meeting, the Old Man in his study, Tresca stepping out from a spaghetti dinner—the homely and domestic attitudes in which these sages were caught emphasize the horror of the crimes and suggest the reason for them; to the murderer, the serenity of the victim comes as the last straw." A protest against such deaths, observed Miss McCarthy, "can only be made to God. It is God, metaphorically speaking, that is, some ideal assumption of an unwritten law governing human conduct, that we call to account for such an outrage; it is this assumption, indeed, which is injured." *Politics*, v (Winter 1948), 1-2.

[21] La Follette is quoted in Russell, "The Last of the Anarchists," pp.

Although the murder remains unsolved, the killing climaxed years of vicious vituperation between Tresca and the Stalinists. The battle began as early as 1934 when Tresca accompanied Dewey and other writers to Mexico City to conduct a "counter-trial" for Leon Trotsky. The American tribunal cleared Trotsky of his alleged "crimes" against the Soviet Union and later published a book that exposed much of the Kremlin's purge atrocities. The grateful Trotsky later wrote to Tresca: "I hope you will permit me to express the deepest esteem for you, as for a man who is every inch a fighter." But the Stalinists too realized that Tresca had the guts of a gladiator. In 1938 the fearless anarchist was the first American courageous enough to come straight out and indict the Russian OGPU in the kidnapping of Juliet Poyntz. Despite Emma Goldman's warning that he was endangering his life,[22] Tresca pressed the attack, assailing the New York Police Department for relegating the Poyntz case to the Bureau of Missing Persons. By the outbreak of war in Europe, Tresca had declared his own all-out war on Stalinism.[23]

Tresca's *bête noire* was Enea Sormenti (alias Vittorio Vidali and Carlos Contreras).[24] Ironically the two were friends in the

---

63-64; Hays, Gannett, Dewey, and the *NYT* are in *Omaggio alla memoria imperitura di Carlo Tresca*, pp. 23, 44, 48.

[22] In February 1938, Goldman wrote to Tresca from London: "I said that we are both busy people. I see that you have added a new job to the many, that is to show up the long arm of Stalin. Well, I do not envy you! In the first place it will prove a difficult task because Russia has poisoned all the wells of decent public opinion and one cannot hope to get a hearing even in the so called liberal press. In the second place you will become a target for the rotten Communist gang not only to besmirch your character but also to endanger your life. For they are capable of murder open and under-hand as they have proven for a very considerable number of years. Then too it's rather a disagreeable job to have to apply to a Capitalist Court to expose the Stalin gangsters. All in all I do not envy your job though I think you should go ahead to expose the disappearance of Miss Poyntz." Quoted in *Omaggio alla memoria imperitura di Carlo Tresca*, p. 10.

[23] M. S. Venkataramani, "Leon Trotsky's Adventure in American Radical Politics, 1935-37," *International Review of Social History*, IX (1964), Pt. I, 1-46, esp. 18-19; see also Isaac Deutscher, *The Prophet Outcast: Trotsky, 1929-1940* (Vintage edn., New York, 1963), III, 371-82; 393; Trotsky is quoted in *The Militant*, Jan. 23, 1943; "Dove si trova Giulia Poyntz?" *Il Martello*, July 25, 1938.

[24] Sormenti took the *nom de guerre* of Colonel Contreras during the Spanish Civil War; in the twenties he used the name Vidali. After World War

twenties, when Tresca sided with Sormenti in the AFANA and assisted him in his fight against deportation. But Tresca's discovery of Sormenti's butchery of the anarchist Andrés Nin during the Spanish Civil War, as well as his possible connection with the assassination of Trotsky, made him an impassioned antagonist. In 1940 the feud grew dangerously tense as Tresca accused the Stalinists of trying to capture the Mazzini Society; and in 1942 he railed at Pacciardi for allegedly trying to revive "Il Fronte Unico" with Sormenti's backing. He also made clear his determination to keep Stalinists out of the Italian-American Victory Council (IAVC), a committee organized by the OWI and a potentially key instrument in the shaping of American policy toward Italy's future.[25]

Stalinists were not slow to respond to his barbed drafts. According to the Tresca Memorial Committee, headed by Norman Thomas, the Communist press began its attack in 1938 as a result of the Poyntz exposé. The Italian National Commission of the CP, in a statement printed in the Stalinist *L'Unità Operaia* (New York), maintained that "Tresca's isolation is a measure of elementary defense for all anti-Fascism." In his pamphlet, *The Moral Suicide of Carlo Tresca*, the Communist Pietro Allegra described Tresca as "politically dead," spoke of his "elimination from society," and advised that "it is a duty to put a stop to his deleterious, disgusting work." Moreover, a few hours after the killing, Antonini informed the district attorney's office that two weeks earlier Tresca told him he had seen Sormenti in town. "Where he is, I smell murder," Tresca remarked to Antonini. "I wonder who will be his next victim." All these thinly veiled threats led Antonini to advise Thomas that the Stalinists were "95 percent" responsible for the murder.[26]

But no one could be completely sure. For the Fascists as well as the Stalinists had good reason to liquidate the undaunted anarchist. All along Tresca had opposed allowing Pope on the IAVC, and he repeatedly criticized Antonini for accepting Pope

---

II he became a senator in the Italian parliament, representing the Trieste Communists.

[25] On Sormenti (Contreras) in Spain, see Hugh Thomas, *The Spanish Civil War* (Colophon edn., New York, 1963), p. 454; "I pretoriani di Stalin all'assalto della Mazzini Society," *Il Martello*, May 14, 1942.

[26] Quoted in *Who Killed Carlo Tresca?* pp. 10, 12; Antonini to Thomas, May 4, 1945, TMC.

as treasurer of the ACID. To illustrate the long-standing hostility, *Controcorrente* reprinted a 1934 *Il Martello* statement in which Tresca told of several threats on his life allegedly made by Pope's henchmen. The Memorial Committee also compiled evidence to show how Tresca incessantly beleaguered the millionaire publisher, even challenging Pope's midnight conversion to anti-Fascism.[27]

Suspicion thus surrounded both Right and Left. Nevertheless the greater weight of guilt fell on the Stalinists.[28] When the popular press hinted as much the *Daily Worker* immediately denied the "slanderous" insinuations. Robert Minor, the CP's assistant general secretary, admitted that his party was at odds with Tresca; but since the anarchist had no following, Communists did not bother to oppose his views; and besides, murder was "alien to everything the Communist Party stands for." Interestingly enough,

[27] *Controcorrente*, May 1943; *Who Killed Carlo Tresca?* pp. 14-15.

[28] Scrupulously, the Memorial Committee was less interested in casting guilt than in establishing facts and seeing justice done. Chaired by Thomas, the Committee consisted of Angelica Balabanoff, William Henry Chamberlin, Frank Grosswaith, John Dewey, Varian Fry, Aron S. Gilmartin, America Gonzales, Sidney Hertzberg, John Haynes Holmes, Sidney Hook, Harry Kelly, Liston M. Oak, A. Philip Randolph, Sheba Strunsky, Oswald Garrison Villard, M. R. Werner, Edmund Wilson, and Bertram D. Wolfe. The Committee remained active over a dozen years, compiling information, tracing new leads, and demanding that the district attorney's office reopen the case. The demands often were occasioned by the publication of an ex-Communist confession—like Ben Gitlow's *The Whole of Their Lives* or Louis F. Budenz's *This Is My Story*—which recounted the murder and placed blame at the door of the Stalinists. But renewed interest was also stirred by Walter Cronkite's CBS television program, "Death of an Editor," which showed the killing as the work of the Mafia in the pay of Mussolini. In light of Il Duce's antagonism to the Mafia, the CBS version, which displayed America's typical paranoia about organized crime, seemed ludicrous to most anti-Fascists. The anarchist Felicani, for example, was convinced that the investigation languished either because of domestic politics or Soviet-American relations. In an open letter to La Guardia entitled, "Are Dark Forces Shielding the Guilty?" Felicani asked in May 1944: "Is there some political reason why the Tresca mystery has not been solved? Would it complicate our international relations or embarrass any one in the coming election campaign, if the forces which inspired the murder were revealed at this time?" Roger Baldwin, it should be noted, disagreed with Felicani, pointing out that the district attorney had done everything in his power and that too many anti-Fascists were simply ignorant of the difficulties involved in murder investigations. *Controcorrente*, May 1944; Baldwin to Felicani, Dec. 5, 1949, TMC.

the OWI went further than the CP. Alan Cranston and Lee Falk of the OWI's foreign language division asserted that Tresca was *not* opposed to Communists in the IAVC because he realized that "all anti-Fascists should unite until Fascism is defeated." The non-Communist Left, astonished by the OWI's version, suspected the administration of squelching the Tresca case lest its revelations destroy any hope for a united front.[29]

Meanwhile the Stalinists fumed. *L'Unità* called for a full investigation and lashed out at Socialists and liberals for putting the finger on Sormenti. "The sole aim of this insidious canard," stated *L'Unità*, "is to fan another Reichstag-fire fiction for the vile purpose of creating anti-Soviet sentiment." Maintaining that the anti-Hitler front was at stake, *L'Unità* warned that the Mazzini Society would soon claim that the Soviet Union is the "nemico di domani" (tomorrow's enemy). As for Tresca's murderer, Minor announced in the *Daily Worker* that he could be found among the "anti-social dregs in our society."[30]

The body of Carlo Tresca rendered a death sentence on all prospects for collaboration. Perhaps more important, "America's Matteotti Case" (as the *New Republic* aptly termed it) gave the non-Communist Left an even greater sense of urgency as it re-dedicated itself to the restoration of democratic Italy. "The greatest tribute we can pay to Carlo," Norman Thomas eulogized, "is to carry on."[31]

ANTI-FASCISTS AND THE ADMINISTRATION

To carry on anti-Fascists still had to face the third question of whether or not to support the State Department. At the outset of the war a promising rapport developed between the *fuorusciti* and the administration. Thanks to Nicholas Murray Butler's introduction, Sforza gained entrée to Roosevelt's confidence and made a fine impression, while Sturzo, on his own, commanded the respect of Assistant Secretary of State Berle. Several other anti-Fascists worked for the OWI and used the OSS to channel funds to the underground, and some asked Roosevelt's assistance in organizing an Italian liberation brigade. Before long, however, it seemed Roosevelt was hardly aware of the ideological war that

[29] *Daily Worker*, Jan. 14, 1943; *Who Killed Carlo Tresca?* p. 14; IALC Press Release, Jan. 23, 1943, RP; *Socialist Call*, Jan. 22, 29, 1943.
[30] *L'Unità del Popolo*, Jan. 23, Feb. 6, 1943; *Daily Worker*, Jan. 14, 1943.
[31] *Omaggio alla . . . Tresca*, p. 46.

414

had embittered the Italian community for decades.[32] Anti-Fascists also had misgivings when Roosevelt failed to renounce King Victor Emmanuel in his appeal to the Italian people. And they became increasingly alarmed when Roosevelt seemingly allowed Churchill to dictate policy in the Mediterranean. Paraphrasing H. G. Wells, *Il Corriere del Popolo* declared: "Either we finish Churchill or Churchill will finish us.[33]

The revival of the Italian-American Right also created apprehension. After Mussolini's demise several former philofascists overcame their deathbed contrition and once again began to assert their influence in the Italian communities. Gene Rea, a former *Il Progresso* columnist who became a foreign correspondent during the war, wrote dispatches from Rome warning Americans that Italy was on the verge of a Communist take-over. Even more inflammatory was Luigi Criscuolo, the Wall Street banker and publisher of *Rubicon*. A tireless polemicist, Criscuolo published in 1942 the pamphlet, *Il Mondo and the Mercenaries of Karl Marx*, distributing copies to Italian-Americans and even sending one to Attorney General Biddle. Writing directly to Roosevelt himself, Criscuolo informed the President that Grafton and the anti-Fascists were Fifth Columnists, that England was better suited than America to appreciate Italy's political needs, and that the King was "a heroic figure" and a "man of high principle."[34]

[32] Roosevelt, it appears from Ickes' account, knew little about the Italian factions and scarcely seemed to recognize that not all Italian-Americans felt the same way about Mussolini. Thus when the Interior Secretary asked him to help Sforza establish a liberal Italian paper in New York, Roosevelt replied that he would try to seek the help of A. P. Giannini. Ickes, perhaps more aware the banking magnate was a former admirer of Il Duce, advised the President "to put the screws on Giannini and make him finance it." Ickes, *Secret Diary*, III, 465, 474, 477.

[33] Butler to Roosevelt, July 8, 1940, PPF 6741, RP. Ickes assured Roosevelt that Count Sforza, despite his noble lineage, was "an honest-to-God democrat." Ickes to Roosevelt, Aug. 3, 1942, PSF, Box 19, RP; Ickes, *Secret Diary*, III, 462; Berle, "Memo of Conversation with Sturzo," *FRUS, 1944*, III, 1149-51; *NYT*, June 8, 1943; "Minutes" of Local 89, ILGWU, Jan. 1944, IA; *Il Corrier del Popolo*, Dec. 21, 1944.

[34] Gene Rea, "Revolution Threatens Italy," *American Mercury*, LIX (Dec. 1944), 647-53; id., "The Communist Threat to Italy," *ibid.*, LXI (Sept. 1945), 263-70; Luigi Criscuolo, *Il Mondo and the Mercenaries of Karl Marx* (New York, 1942), HIL; Criscuolo to Roosevelt, July 27, 1943, OF 233A, June 19, 1944, OF Italy, Box I, RP. Significantly, Criscuolo had a

With over twenty years of exasperating protest behind them, anti-Fascists had good reason to fear the resurgence of the Italian-American Right; with the newly-won respectability of Communism facing them, they had equally good reason to fear the rehabilitation of the Stalinist Left. In reality, however, the very anti-Fascists who opposed the State Department had more influence in the administration than those who supported it. On the Right, former Mussolini crusaders like Pope were only too ready to do Roosevelt's bidding in order to avoid prosecution. On the Left, Stalinists rallied to the Big Three's recognition of Badoglio and the Monarchy only to find themselves impotent in Washington. In 1944, for example, *L'Unità* criticized the State Department's issuing exit permits to Sforza, Garosci, Tarchiani, and other Liberal-Socialists while denying them to Communist Giuseppe Berti and Dr. Ambrogio Donini. Similarly, *L'Unità* challenged the OSS's airmail privileges for Valenti's *La Parola*, Lupis' *Il Mondo*, Clemente's *La Parola del Popolo*, Pacciardi's *L'Italia Libera*, and the Mazzini Society's *Nazioni Unite*. These papers, complained Bardi and Testa, did not even endorse the Allied-sponsored coalition government in Italy, whereas *L'Unità*, which faithfully supported the State Department, was denied such services. Nevertheless Italian-American Communists continued to back the administration. Although they opposed Roosevelt in 1940 as a "warmonger," in the election of 1944 the Communists campaigned vigorously for the President. At one mass rally in New York, Marcantonio's ideological croaking was sweetened by the melodic crooning of the young Frank Sinatra. But despite all the support, the Roosevelt administration proved tone deaf to the Stalinist serenades.[35]

The non-Communist Left fared better in Washington but even its limited influence diminished once the invasion of Italy was under way. Whereas the administration believed the war against Hitler had to take precedence over events in Italy, anti-Fascists could not ignore the many pressing issues in their homeland. One

---

checkered political career: he supported Mussolini until 1926, at which time he began to attack the dictator for muzzling the press and exporting Fascism into the United States; then in the thirties he turned his attack upon the anti-Fascists and returned his support to Mussolini. See Criscuolo, *Italy's Grim Determination* (New York, 1934), pamphlet, Paterno Library, Columbia University.

[35] *L'Unità del Popolo*, Jan. 8, June 3, Aug. 12, Nov. 4, 1944.

such issue was economic relief. With the Allied invasion Italy's economy collapsed. As the American Army's exchange rates threw the whole monetary system into chaos, economic life virtually came to a standstill and near-starvation swept the land. Diplomats like Adlai Stevenson advised the State Department that economic assistance must be extended as soon as possible. But throughout the liberation no effective action was taken. By fall 1945 the situation grew desperate, and Myron C. Taylor ominously warned Washington: "To delay is catastrophic."[36]

The warnings of diplomats sounded like whispers compared to the pressures building up at home. With foods and clothes packed and ready to be shipped, Italian-Americans could not understand why the administration refused to cut through the red tape of the State Department and the Relief Control Board. "Why this discrimination?" asked Judge Pecora. "Why are Americans of Italian extraction the only ones who are not permitted to transmit relief to the suffering in the land of their origin?" Responding to the mounting protests, the administration issued several statements. On September 26, 1945, it was announced from Hyde Park that the United Nations Relief and Rehabilitation Administration would ship medical supplies and that general aid would soon arrive. Then on October 10, the administration announced an extension of dollar credit to the Italian government as reimbursement for the lire spent by the GI's in Italy. But since the Allies lacked transportation facilities to carry out such promises (due to the great shipping crisis of 1944-45), the administration's announcements amounted to nothing more than barren gestures.[37]

To account for these gestures one need only keep in mind that this was an election year which saw Republican Thomas Dewey vying with Roosevelt for the Italian vote. Dewey exploited the issue effectively, and in a Columbus Day speech he called for immediate Allied status for Italy. In Congress Vito Marcantonio succeeded in getting the House Foreign Affairs Committee to open hearings on Italy's plight, and while La Guardia threatened to suspend his propaganda broadcasts to Italy the Catholic hierarchy, spurred on by the Pope's plea for immediate aid, resorted to both pressure and prayer. Finally, Roosevelt's own advisers reminded him of the political implications of further delay: "One

[36] Kogan, p. 82; Taylor to Roosevelt, June 5, Oct. 4, 1944, Box 17, RP.
[37] Pecora is quoted in John Rich, "A Labor Leader Goes to Italy," *New Leader*, xxvii (Sept. 9, 1944), 7; *NYT*, Oct. 11, 1944; Kogan, pp. 80-89.

reason for the disaffection of the Italians is they are getting letters from Italy describing the misery there. The Italians here feel helpless because they cannot send packages as the Army will not distribute them. . . . If it could be arranged for the Army to accept only a few of these, you making the announcement to that effect, Baldanzi believes it would help you more than any other thing that could be done at this time." Four days after receiving this memo Roosevelt issued his statement regarding extension of credits. And to counter the Republican charge that food and clothing headed for Italy was being allowed to rot on the docks, that Roosevelt gave Italy, in Dewey's words, only "a batch of alphabetical agencies," the administration made sure pictures of food distribution to skinny but smiling Italian children were given full publicity.[38]

To many anti-Fascists the failure to realize a substantial aid program—as well as to affect political changes in Italy—indicated their waning influence in Washington. Thus as the war in Europe drew to a close much of the non-Communist Left—anarchists like Felicani and Socialists like Zito—castigated the "Tory" character of American diplomacy and its "intrighe capitalistici." Inevitably the anti-Fascists split on the question of supporting the State Department. Always on close terms with Roosevelt, Antonini and the IALC went along with the administration. Antonini's position, which displayed more anxiety about Togliatti than Churchill, angered some Italian-American labor leaders. But it was the Mazzini Society that completely parted company in the face of the administration's diplomacy. As refugees with suitcases packed to return to their homeland, the *fuorusciti* were less committed than Italian-American labor to the Roosevelt administration. Thus when Assistant Secretary Berle appealed to the Mazzini Society for support in November 1943, the Society broke sharply into two factions. One group, including Sforza and Ascoli, sided with the administration on the ground that Salvemini's fears were exaggerated and that, in any case, it would be better to oppose from within rather than protest from without. But many others, including Bollaffio and Cantarella, attacked the government's "appeasement" policy which tolerated Badoglio and allowed "pre-Pearl Harbor Fascists" to assume important positions on

[38] Memo, Biddle to Roosevelt, Oct. 6, 1944; Roosevelt to Stimson, Oct. 31, 1944; Memo, Lt. Colonel D. W. Davenport to Mrs. Rumelt, Nov. 4, 1944, Box 1, RP.

various liberation committees. In June 1944, the latter group declared its opposition in an eloquent four-page "An Italian Manifesto" in *Life*, signed by Borgese, La Piana, Pacciardi, Salvemini, Toscanini, and Venturi.[39]

Whether to purge ex-Fascists, collaborate with Communists, or support the State Department were agonizing questions that eroded much of the élan of the resistance. Add to the turmoil of this inner war the objective situation in Italy—especially the Allies' equivocal "defascistization" of the government and the State Department's vacillation on the monarchical question—and one can readily understand the mood of disenchantment that overcame the anti-Fascists. Then, the election of Christian Democracy after the war made the disillusionment complete. The dreams of the great majority of original anti-Fascists looked to a democratic republic based on Socialist reforms, but their dreams receded before the realities of a war based on military and political imperatives.

In assessing the twenty-year career of the active anti-Fascists in the United States several things must be kept in mind. First, Mussolini's enemies had little popular support in this country. From the very beginning their efforts to expose Fascist propaganda were handicapped not only by an unsympathetic government but also by a mass public fascinated by the charismatic Il

[39] The six notables believed that Allied policy aimed at ridding Italy only of Mussolini's pro-German regime, thereby preserving the "fascist monarchy" and creating a "demofascist government to be supported by a coalition of reactionary forces." To awaken America, the signers warned of Churchill's cynical attitude toward Italy, related the history of Italy's republican heritage in order to discredit the monarchy, and called for the fulfillment of the Atlantic Charter. The following month Ascoli wrote to *Life*, challenging the Manifesto's implication that figures like Sforza and Croce, who were willing to assume political responsibility with the throne intact, were "quislings or rags in the hands of allied leaders." *Life*, xvii (July 10, 1944), 4-5.

Il Corriere del Popolo, July 22, Aug. 5, 26, 1943, Dec. 7, 1944; "About the Mazzini Society," *Free Italy* (Feb. 1945), 13; Enzo Tagliacozzo, "Gaetano Salvemini: Nota biografica," in Ernesto Sestan and others, *Gaetano Salvemini* (Bari, 1959), 270-73; see also "Gaetano Salvemini: Numero Speciale," *La Voce Repubblicana* (Dec. 20, 21, 1967), esp. Max Ascoli, "Salvemini negli Stati Uniti," pp. 16, 24. *Life*'s "An Italian Manifesto" is something of a collector's item; for the magazine stopped its presses after 900,000 copies had been printed, remade its pages to announce the invasion of France, and dropped the "Manifesto." *Life*, xvi (June 19, 1944), 38.

Duce. Even during the 1940s when the United States and Italy were at war, the goals of the anti-Fascists and those of the government were at cross-purposes. After failing to detach Mussolini from Hitler, America found herself at war with Italy, and Roosevelt expressed an encouraging outburst of anti-Fascist rhetoric. But while most of the opposition had been fighting Mussolini for two decades, the government was forced into the fight because of diplomatic events rather than ideological commitments. Thus whereas anti-Fascists looked forward to a postwar rebirth of liberty and social justice in Italy, the State Department settled for a restoration of stability and constitutional respectability. Against the general public's isolationism and indifference, the Italian community's confused hostility, and the government's quixotic foreign policies, the resisters fought on. But their struggle, beginning in solitary isolation, ended in lonely frustration.

A second question to be kept in mind is whether there were real alternatives open to the anti-Fascists. Had they succeeded in affecting popular opinion in this country, there was still little chance of spurring an uprising in Italy. Had they been able to persuade the government to take a strong stand against the dictatorship, there was still no certainty that this move would not have caused the Italian masses to rally all the more to Mussolini, as was the case during the Ethiopian crisis. The peculiar nature of their predicament dictated that their role be a limited one of engaging in counterpropaganda, raising funds for the scattered underground, facilitating the escape of *fuorusciti*, and providing media of expression for the exiles. In these activities they succeeded admirably, as indicated by the worried correspondence of the Italian ambassadors in Washington. Their very presence, in short, was a foil to Fascism's claim to legitimacy and a thorn in Mussolini's inflated imagery.

All this is not to suggest that the history of anti-Fascism in America is a spotless success story. The internal doctrinal disputes, to be sure, made it impossible for the anti-Fascists to act as a coherent political force, and the extreme radicalism of some elements caused them to be out of touch with American political life. But an even more serious criticism is that the opposition was never capable of reaching the Italian-American masses. Salvemini believed that the Italian-Americans were beyond approach because the *fuorusciti* had no roots among the working class. While probably true of the exiles, this explanation cannot

420

account for the failure of Italian-American labor unions to reach the workers. Perhaps Sforza came closer to the truth in pointing out that the opposition gravely erred in allowing Fascists to exploit the rhetoric of patriotism and thus appear to immigrants as the only genuine Italophiles.[40]

If anti-Fascists can be criticized for failing to attract Italian-Americans, they cannot be so judged for failing to reach Americans themselves. Here the blame lies with a myopic public opinion. Indeed one can only wish that the public had paid some attention to the anti-Fascists both here and abroad. For the very existence of the non-Communist opposition, which comprised the bulk of the resistance in this country, at least served to explode the myth of the false alternative: Italy must remain Fascist or go Communist. In the end it was the bugbear of Bolshevism that prevented the anti-Fascists from winning an audience. Convinced that Mussolini was the *only* answer to Communism, America ignored the anti-Fascists, only to discover in 1945 that Il Duce's twenty-year rule, rather than stamping out radicalism, had produced the largest Communist Party in all of western Europe.

[40] "Gli Italo-Americani e L'Italia: Un Intervista di Salvemini," *Controcorrente*, Dec. 1945; Aurelio Natoli, "Il Problema dell'organizzazione degli Italiani in America," *Il Mondo*, Sept.-Oct. 1941; *Il Progresso*, Oct. 17, 1943.

16.

The Rediscovery
of Italy

. . . WITHOUT A FASCISM TO
FIGHT, WITHOUT, THAT IS,
INCARNATING HISTORICALLY
PROGRESSIVE THOUGHT,
AMERICA, HOWEVER MANY
SKYSCRAPERS, MOTORCARS
AND SOLDIERS SHE TURNS OUT,
WILL NOT STAND AT THE
FOREFRONT OF ANY CULTURE.
WITHOUT A LEADING THOUGHT,
WITHOUT THE STRUGGLE FOR
PROGRESS, IT RATHER RISKS
RUNNING INTO A FORM OF
FASCISM ITSELF, EVEN IN THE
NAME OF ITS OWN GREATEST
TRADITIONS.

Cesare Pavese, *Yesterday and
Today*, 1947

YANKS AND PAESANI

Outside the town of Anzio stands a statue of two soldiers. Both
figures are stripped to the waist and, with the arm of one around
the other's shoulder, leaning forward with unconquerable determination. Surrounding the statue are sprinklers which dart play-
fully into the air, spreading precious water into the dark soil, a
small, rich breast of earth amid the barrenness of the Anzio
countryside. This is the American military cemetery. Its thousands of rows of simple, marble crosses bear silent testimony to
America's contribution to the liberation of Italy.

The primary concern of this chapter is the encounter between
Americans and Italians during the war years, a brief coexistence
shedding further light on America's comprehension of the Fascist experience. America's first direct contact with the people of

Italy involved the propaganda effort of the Psychological Warfare Branch (PWB) of OWI. Naples, the first major European city captured by American soldiers, offered a test case for the PWB. The city was showered with leaflets ("paper bullets"); loudspeakers were set up in the piazzas; flags of Italy and the United States raised; U.S. Information Service libraries trucked into town; and even a special film prepared, *Hymn of Nations*, a musical derived from a Verdi composition and the French, English, American, and Italian national anthems and conducted by the Italians' beloved Toscanini.[1]

When the American Army marched into the city, skeptical and frightened Italians at first remained out of sight. But slowly they appeared on balconies and doorsteps. Soon they crowded onto the streets, then with a burst of passion they rushed to embrace the American GI's. The Neapolitans hailed the "conquerors" with precious scraps of affection: a bunch of grapes, a handful of flowers, a bottle of red wine. Elderly Italian men hugged and planted wet kisses on the cheeks of American soldiers who, blushing awkwardly, shuffled on to the roar of applause. For Yanks and *paesani* alike, October 1, 1943 was a day of wine and roses.[2]

The genuine outpouring of emotion in Naples and elsewhere led many to believe American propaganda had deeply touched the hearts of Italians. Journalists wrote excitedly of "Fighting with Confetti," of how "Propaganda Wins Battles," and how the Allies were "Talking Them Out of It." Yet it is doubtful that propaganda had much impact on the Italian military, and even the flush of friendship with which civilians hailed American troops petered out once the thrill of liberation subsided and the dreariness of occupation set in.[3]

The occupation was presided over by the Allied Military Government, a *pasticcio* of agencies hampered by red tape, jurisdic-

[1] Robert W. van de Velde, "The Role of U.S. Propaganda in Italy's Return to Democracy, 1943-1948" (Ph.D. Thesis, Princeton University, 1954), pp. 167-87.

[2] See John Steinbeck, *Once There Was a War* (New York, 1958), a collection of his war correspondence from the *New York Herald Tribune*, June–December, 1943.

[3] *American Legion Magazine*, xxxv (Dec. 1943), 24; *Nation*, clviii (Feb. 12, 1944), 184-86; *Collier's*, cxiv (Aug. 19, 1944), 23, 72-73; Martin Merz, "Some Psychological Lessons from Leaflet Propaganda in World War II," *Public Opinion Quarterly*, xiii (Fall 1949), 471-86.

tional conflict, and brass-hat bureaucracy. In addition to the enormous difficulties of relief, unemployment, and the black market, the most trying problem facing AMG was the status of the Italian ex-Fascist. Although AMG often replaced local Blackshirt prefects, it was not in a position to carry out a full-scale purge. Under orders to avoid "political implications of any kind," and unable to find civil servants in a country where the best men had gone underground or into exile, AMG frequently had to work with unsavory elements. Yet despite what some critical journalists claimed, AMG was not honeycombed with ex-Fascists, whom writers and cartoonists took delight in depicting as obsequious creatures, fat and sleek with shifting eyes and quivering lips. Sensitive to the stigma, AMG issued orders to employ only those who were not active party members. Moreover, on one occasion when AMG did intervene politically it obtained the release of four anti-Fascists jailed by Badoglio for publishing a newspaper, and it then brought pressure on Badoglio and the King to repeal Fascist press regulations.[4]

An OSS investigation later disclosed that the occupation made some progress in "defascistization" but was almost helpless when it came to the question of the purge (*epurazione*). "Defascistization"—the abrogation of all laws and civil measures associated with the Mussolini government—was hindered by technical matters but still could be termed "a moderate success." On the other hand, *epurazione*—the removal of Fascists from government positions—proved considerably more difficult because of Badoglio's refusal to cooperate and because of the priorities of the war effort. As a result the occupation appeared to many Italians as a continuation of Italy's tradition of government by dissimulation and deception.[5]

Yet one AMG administrator who won the respect of the Italians was Colonel Charles Poletti, the honest and industrious ex-Governor and Lieutenant Governor of New York. Regional commissioner for the Naples area, Poletti left no stone unturned in his relentless effort to plant the seeds of grass-roots democracy. Immediately he had the bomb debris cleared from the streets, then had the power and plumbing facilities repaired, installed

[4] van de Velde, pp. 189-205; *NYT*, Oct. 23, 30, 1943.

[5] U.S. Office of Strategic Service: Research and Analysis Branch; *Treatment of Former Fascists by the Italian Government* (Washington, March 17, 1945).

424

veteran anti-Fascist administrators, granted trade unions bargaining rights and encouraged business associations, and started a $250,000 public works project. The affable and handsome Poletti also made himself available to the Naples populace. Slouched behind his desk in a wrinkled uniform, the ex-Governor listened patiently to the people's complaints. He helped when he could, but he also reminded them of their own responsibilities and opportunities in rehabilitating Naples, all the while sharing their wine and cracking jokes in fluent Italian. A rare find in any war, Poletti had the right personal touch and the knowing heart.[6]

As a hastily organized body of government the AMG itself seemed to Italians to have neither a heart nor a head. Its shunning of *fuorusciti* and native labor leaders, its willingness to work with ingratiating, Janus-faced bureaucrats, if not actual Fascists, and its distrust of radical partisans, who had emerged as heroes in the eyes of many Italians, all contributed to its waning popularity. Perhaps this was inevitable. For military priorities dictated that economic and political problems be kept in abeyance, and these very problems, after all, would continue to frustrate even postwar Italian governments. But to many Italians, liberation meant a surging expectation of dramatic political and social changes; and thus America's military rule seemed more and more to be the familiar spectacle of betrayed promises.[7]

THE INNOCENCE OF ITALIANS

In the early years of the war British and American intelligence produced anti-Fascist films like *Blood on the Balcony* and *Yellow Caesar*. These documentaries were amateur efforts at best, and they must have appeared all the more crude with the revival of Italy's own cinematography, a revival that began, amazingly enough, during the last months of German occupation. In *Open City* and *Paisà*, and later in *Bicycle Thief*, *Shoe Shine*, and *La Trema Terra*, Americans not only saw political passion translated into artistic expression, they also had their first glimpse of Italian

[6] Charles Poletti, "Bread, Spaghetti, But No Fascisti," *NYT Magazine*, July 16, 1944; *Time*, XLIII (May 1, 1944), 36.

[7] U.S. Office of Strategic Services: Research and Analysis Branch, *Italian Propaganda Organization* (Washington, D.C., 1943); U.S. Army: Seventh Army, *The Sicilian Campaign: Report of Psychological Warfare* (July 10—Aug. 17, 1943); Joseph Albert Hearst, "The Evaluation of Allied Military Government Policy in Italy" (Ph.D. Thesis, Columbia University, 1959), esp. pp. 265-68.

life under siege, occupation, and postwar reconstruction. The neo-realism of directors like Roberto Rossellini, Luchino Visconti, and Vittorio De Sica had as its purpose the exposure of the Mussolini regime and the social conditions which made it possible. In order to unveil the cruel lies of Fascism, as well as the sunny illusions foreigners entertained about romantic Italy, the camera was the best possible instrument, the montage of misery the best possible vehicle.

Italian cinema stunned America with its intense and yet restrained power of social realism and political idealism. The characters in *Open City* led Edmund Wilson to think of Carlo Tresca and the "antique virtue" of the Italians, the heroic quality of individuals who are willing to die for ideas. "You can see it coming to life in this film," observed Wilson. Yet by concentrating upon the German occupation, films such as *Open City* conveyed the impression that Fascism was basically an unpopular and alien ideology imposed upon an unwilling Italian populace. However questionable, this impression emerged among the American public in general as the press began to absolve the Italian people of responsibility for Fascism. The *Wall Street Journal* best summed up the reasoning:

> Putting on one side the debate over the German and Japanese peoples, it should be clear to anyone with any acquaintance with the history of the Italian people that to hold it, as a people, guilty of the crimes of Fascismo is totally to misunderstand that history. If there is one thing which is definitely not an element in the Italian character or genius or whatever one chooses to call it, it is fanaticism of any kind.
>
> The political unity of Italy under the House of Savoy never reached the stage attained by the Germanies after 1870, nor did the Italians ever dally with the "blood and soil" nonsense of Gabineau [sic], Chamberlain and their followers, much less adopt it as a national slogan. Fascismo in Italy was at bottom alien to Italy's traditions.[8]

This rationale represents an embarrassing reorientation of American attitudes. Years earlier many Americans believed Fascism a natural expression of Italian "traditions" and praised Mussolini as the new Machiavelli who would whip into shape an improvi-

[8] *Wall Street Journal*, Dec. 20, 1944; Edmund Wilson, *Europe Without Baedeker* (New York, rev. edn., 1966), pp. 78-79.

dent national character. Now Americans seem to be waxing sentimental about the essential goodness of the tragically misled Italians. "We like the Italians," declared *Fortune*, "and want to be
their big brothers and give them a chance in the world." A con-
descending note is still present, but a faint note of guilt is here
too. Sensing a twitch of conscience, Americans could excuse the
Italians and thereby exonerate themselves for having been similarly misled.[9] In the summer of 1942, Americans were asked:
"When the war is over how do you think we should treat the
Italian people?" Fifty percent chose to "treat them kindly, hu-
manely, fairly, as we would like to be treated," and while smaller
numbers of others preferred a slightly different leniency, only a
fraction of a percentage expressed a desire to impose harsh punishment. Significantly, in a poll on Germany's future (worded
differently), roughly three-fourths of Americans felt that Germany should be demobilized and occupied; one third wanted
to see the nation broken up into small states and de-industrial-
ized; and, even more telling, almost half of the respondents believed that German labor should be forced to rebuild other devas-
tated countries, and over 80 percent desired to see Germany
saddled with a harsher peace than that imposed at Versailles.[10]

[9] It may have been a bit awkward for the *Wall Street Journal* to mention
its own support for Fascism, but it did the next best thing: "Of course, this
people should not have tolerated the Fascist regime for even a moment.
But before we hold it to a strict account for this we might remember the
Huey Long phenomenon of a few years ago and its political consequences
in the state of Louisiana in this democratic land of ours." *Ibid.*

[10] As Edmund Burke first pointed out and Hannah Arendt has reminded
us, the problem of collective guilt is an enormously difficult proposition.
By the same reasoning, it is also difficult to understand why Americans
believed Germans so much more responsible, and hence deserving of punishment, than Italians. True, the crimes of Nazism were much greater than
those of Fascism, but then the totalitarian nature of Hitler's oppressive
regime was far greater than Mussolini's creaking dictatorship. True, Hitler
was voted into power by the German people, but Mussolini was sustained
in power by the Italian people. The excessive punishment Americans wanted
to impose upon the Germans is understandable in light of the suffering
Germany inflicted upon other peoples and in view of the fear of a resurgence of German power after the war. But the leniency with which Americans viewed Italians may also be due to the fact that, whereas few
Americans admired Hitler's Germany after 1934, many Americans admired
and continued to admire Mussolini's Italy until the Axis became a permanent reality. Among other things, the claim for the innocence of Italians
may also be seen as America's claim for innocence; a claim, however, that

Since the Italians were innocent and thus not to be treated punitively, America could in good conscience assume some responsibility in redeeming Italy from the curse of Fascism. The *fuorusciti* had long given thought as to how Italy would be "remade" after the war. But America had its own peculiar prescription: to export the one commodity that had always been the cure-all aspirin for social headaches—education. Thus after Mussolini's fall a flurry of articles appeared on the "Re-Education of Fascist Italy." Following Italy's surrender United Nations officials met at Harper's Ferry, West Virginia, to determine how best to restructure the school systems in various liberated countries. Here American educators, focusing on Italy, voiced some displeasure at Washington's indifference and the Roman Catholic Church's interference. Subsequently a special study by the OSS revealed that the "role of the Catholic Church in education presents a highly delicate problem." Nevertheless, the study suggested that Fascist educational laws be revised and new principles based on human values replace "narrowly nationalistic concepts"; that provision be made for minorities and private schools; that the profession be purged of Fascist sympathizers and new recruits be drawn from the ranks of "liberals and intellectuals"; and that the new Minister of Education be a man "of universally recognized liberalism." If it seems strange that an army document should be so pregnant with democratic sensibilities, it might not be irrelevant to note the study was directed by the young historian, Captain H. Stuart Hughes. This may also explain why the document was so sensitive to psychological realities. As the report warned, a meaningful reorientation to democratic values would require as much therapy as pedagogy:

> Most difficult of all, however, is the intellectual and emotional somersault inevitably involved in the transition from education for Fascism to education for democracy. How can children be told to execrate the man, symbols, and ideas which they have always been taught to reverence with quasi-religious fervor, and to admire nations and ideals which they have been encouraged

---

must stop short of its logical conclusion: if everyone is innocent, no one is innocent.

Fortune, xxiv (Aug. 1940), 158; *Public Opinion Quarterly*, viii (Spring 1944), 151, (Winter 1944), 587; *Public Opinion, 1935-1946*, ed. Hadley Cantril (Princeton, 1951), p. 208.

to despise? May not such an effort result in undermining their faith, not only in the schools but in the whole political, social, and moral order? What are they to be told about Fascism and the much-publicized exploits of the Mussolini regime, domestic and foreign? Obviously they cannot be persuaded that everything which had happened in Fascist Italy is bad. Where is the line to be drawn? How are the events of the past twenty years to be rationalized?[11]

Although the OSS's Research and Analysis Division made specific suggestions, its awareness of the complexity of the problem led to a recommendation that America intervene as little as possible in Italy's educational affairs. Others also began to see that the psychology of the situation required that Italians themselves undertake the transformation of their schools. One writer went so far as to claim that America's obsession with "re-educating" Italians sprang from a deplorable ignorance of Italy's own democratic heritage, a deceptive ignorance born of America's overweening political piety.[12]

The more Americans became aware of the human dimensions latent in Italy's social problems the more they sensed the limitations of America's influence—and the presumptuousness of that influence. The United States had provided the munitions and muscle to drive out the *Wehrmacht*; but the moral reconstruction of Italy was another matter entirely. The realization that Italy's redemption was beyond the reach of American values and traditions must have been a quiet disappointment to the well-meaning liberals stirred by Roosevelt's "Four Freedoms" and Wendell Willkie's vision of a "One World" moral community. Yet there were other Americans who began to realize that the New World had little to bring to the Old World; that historic Italy, for all her foibles, must reject the platitudes of American culture. America rescued Italy from Fascism; who would save Italy from America? Since the question was first posed by poets and novelists, it is to them we turn for the answer.

11 *Christian Science Monitor*, Sept. 10, 1943; Randel Elliott, "Re-Education of Fascist Italy," *News Bulletin: Institute of International Education*, xix (Jan. 1, 1944); U.S. Office of Strategic Services: Research and Analysis Branch, *The Reform of Italian Education* (Washington, D.C., 1943), pp. 4-5.

12 Stephen Naft, "Re-Education in Italy," *Saturday Review of Literature*, xxvi (Oct. 23, 1943), 9-10.

AMERICAN WRITERS IN ITALY

Mussolini's sudden fall from power was an act of poetic as well as political justice. The first nation to succumb to Fascism, Italy would soon be the first liberated by the democracies. To many Americans, the Allied advance up the Italian boot seemed a cleansing "wind of the south" which, matched by the partisans' "vento del nord," would soon expurgate Italy of her Fascist past, redeem her liberal heritage, and ultimately destroy the Thousand Year Reich beyond the Alps. Yet there were at least two American writers in Italy who saw things quite differently: Ezra Pound and John Horne Burns. Pound, of course, had long been a champion of Mussolini, and during the war he became a familiar voice on Radio Rome's propaganda broadcasts. Burns, on the other hand, "discovered" Italy during the invasion, and, having "conquered" it, proceeded to question the whole moral meaning of liberation. That both a pro-Fascist poet and an anti-Fascist novelist could fear the intrusion of American civilization into the Old World suggests a central question: how did American writers interpret Italy's liberation, especially those writers who participated in the event?

American literary intellectuals had been keenly interested in Italy, particularly in the plight of anti-Fascist writers. Silone's novels, as we saw, gave compelling artistic expression to the politics of heroic endurance. Later the more politically engaged American writers became disenchanted when Silone turned to an "ethical" Socialism based upon the "inner life," a primitive Christianity which seemed as mystical as it was ineffectual. But aside from Silone other writers like Giuseppe Berti and Alberto Moravia drew American acclaim, as did Lauro de Bosis, who earlier had lost his life when his plane, pursued by Il Duce's aircraft, plunged into the Tyrrhenian Sea. Thornton Wilder dedicated his *The Ides of March* to the valiant anti-Fascist poet.[13]

With the invasion of Italy American writers no longer had to rely upon Italian *literati* to learn about the realities of Fascism. Numerous writers were present when the country was liberated. John Steinbeck was sending dispatches to the *New York Herald Tribune* from "Somewhere in the Mediterranean Theater," John Hersey reported on the invasion, and Edmund Wilson covered

[13] See the dialogue between Silone and Malcolm Cowley, *New Republic*, CVII (Aug. 24, 1942), 234-35; (Nov. 2, 1942), 582-83.

occupied Italy for *The New Yorker*. Then, too, the liberation provided the setting for several novels, many by authors who took part in the historic event. Not all American writers, of course, viewed the experience as somber political moralists. Some wrote only of the battles themselves (Harry Brown, *A Walk in the Sun*, 1944) or of the regimentation of army life (Robert Lowry, *Casualty*, 1946). Others, a few years later, used the Italian campaign as a springboard to discuss the war's effects on American domestic life (Sloan Wilson, *The Man in the Grey Flannel Suit*, 1955) or as a backdrop to explore the postwar readjustments of an army officer (Hemingway, *Across the River and into the Trees*, 1950). More recently, a particular infantry assault could be recalled by one who took part in it (now a Dartmouth professor) to contemplate the meaning of war and victory (Harold L. Bond, *Return to Cassino*, 1964). And, inevitably, after almost two decades, the horrors of the Italian campaign could so fade from memory that the war against Fascism becomes the setting for a compassionate comedy (Robert Crichton, *The Secret of Santa Vittoria*, 1966), or, even more significantly, a Rabelaisian satire (Joseph Heller, *Catch-22*, 1961). Yet three American authors wrote of the liberation of Fascist Italy in deeper personal and broader social terms. Because their novels are prose statements of a particular historical experience, and because they reveal unquestioned assumptions in America's native values, these literary documents deserve closest attention.

The book making the most favorable impact on Americans during the war was John Hersey's *A Bell for Adano* (1944), a novel that won Hersey the Pulitzer Award and was soon after made into a popular Hollywood film. Hersey, who spent three months with the Allied invading forces, wrote of a Sicilian village occupied by the American Army under Major Victor Joppolo, an Italian-American from the Bronx. A man of patience and integrity with a concern for honesty and justice, Joppolo feels that only simple good works reaching those at the bottom will reconstruct ravaged Italy. After winning the respect of the villagers by his grass-roots activism, Joppolo becomes convinced that he must replace the town's historic bell, which the Fascists had melted down for munitions. The parallel with America's Liberty Bell is clear (as is Joppolo's resemblance to Colonel Poletti). To find a bell and sustain the support of the people, Joppolo must circumvent or defy the bureaucratic red tape of the AMG and the arbitrary dictates of his irascible superior, General Marvin, who embodies all that is Prussian and authoritarian in the American military. Ultimately Joppolo's quest succeeds; the restoration of the bell symbolizes the town's rebirth—but Joppolo himself is relieved of his command for disobeying General Marvin's orders.

Hersey was chiefly concerned with making Americans think beyond the military aspects of war and victory and to consider "what kind of politics the war itself represented." Clearly he believed America's only chance for permanent recovery of Europe depended not on abstract slogans but on simple deeds, not on governments but on those who govern. "I beg you to get to know this Joppolo well," Hersey wrote (in a foreword to the Modern Library Edition published a year later). "We have need of him. He is our future in the world. Neither the eloquence of Churchill, nor the humaneness of Roosevelt, no Charter, no four freedoms or fourteen points, no dreamer's diagram so symmetrical and so faultless on paper, no plan, no hope, no treaty—none of these things can guarantee anything. Only men can guarantee, only the behavior of men under pressure, only our Joppolos."

As a study of American democracy exported, Hersey's novel projected Wilsonian visions of traditional liberal humanitarianism. Like many Progressives who could never recognize the despair of a Diogenes, he believed there were enough men of goodwill and hope to make democracy work both here and abroad. No doubt this theme explains the book's popular reception; in many respects the humane appeal of "Adano" struck the same moral response as the Peace Corps ethic did for the generation of the 1960s. But with all its idealism for participatory democracy, *A Bell for Adano* falls short of presenting the "real" Italy of 1944, the Italy that Americans needed to know if they were to understand the problems of postwar reconstruction. Writing as a sincere but anxious reformer, Hersey's narrow American point of view failed to convey the heavy effects of Fascism and war on the Italian people, their desperation and bewilderment during the liberation, and the tensions that occasionally existed between Italians and American soldiers. As a result, the Italian characters are pale caricatures who, although rich in humor, appear devoid of any deeper emotion or passion (save in one scene describing the return of the prisoners). Hersey observed his Italians keenly, and he understood them sympathetically, but always on his own

432

terms—as a paternalistic, liberal humanitarian. Because the folk idealism and progressive assumptions of his native political values governed his observations, Hersey's polite novel slighted the stark reality of Italy and the *blasé* Italian attitude toward American political ideals. *A Bell for Adano*, in a word, rings more willed than true.

An entirely different view of the experience of liberation can be found in Alfred Hayes's *All Thy Conquests* (1946) and *A Girl on the Via Flaminia* (1949). Here is no morality tale with oversimplified characters like Hersey's Joppolo and Marvin personifying good versus evil, nor any sentimentally quaint Italian characters waiting to be shown the American way of political life. Instead, Hayes paints an authentic picture of war-weary Italians who are either cynically indifferent or consumed with revenge, envy, and hatred for each other as well as for Americans. Hersey tended to interpret Fascism as a temporary aberration in Italian history, Hayes regarded it as a far more subtle phenomenon with roots deep in the corruption and opportunism that characterized much of Italian political and social life. Thus *All Thy Conquests* gives an incisive sociological sketch of the career of a bureaucrat whose "very defects as a human being contributed to his success as a Fascist." Hayes believed that two decades of Fascist totalitarianism had spiritually maimed the Italian people. The lawyer in the book speaks for the author: "Our understandings have been crippled by twenty years of tyranny and six years of war, our sympathies debased, natural instincts of the heart distorted. And he who would today put together his broken world must mend more than his house and repair more than his garden." Where Hersey implied that a mere "mending" of material conditions would suffice, Hayes felt that nothing short of a regeneration of the hearts of the Italians themselves would do, for Fascism had wrenched human nature and perverted natural morality. "Who knows what terrible surgery may be needed before we are healed?"

The theme of the "liberatori" turned "conquistatori" runs through Hayes's two novels. *A Girl on the Via Flaminia* is a delicate account of an indelicate relationship between a GI and a Roman girl which points up the degradation Italian youth suffered at the hands of their liberators. When the threat of starvation forces the young Lisa to become an American soldier's mistress, she is excoriated by an embittered Italian youth: "Shall I tell you what I see, Signorina, when I look at you? Italy's shame, my shame." In *All Thy Conquests* a mother, who discovers her daughter has been violated by an American officer, exclaims: "Dio mio, one thing I pray: send them away! Send them back where they came from! Let the ocean take them and their feed and their money! Let them ruin and disgrace their own country!" Had Hayes pushed this theme of exploitation too far, had he focused solely on the responsibility of Americans, he would have committed an error opposite to that of Hersey, who depicted the American Army (save General Marvin) as benign emancipators. Yet Hayes rightly avoided an idealized view of the Italians as helpless victims. For him, the problem of evil was too diffuse, the problem of ideology too ambiguous. Thus he balanced his descriptions of the cynical indifference among American soldiers with a bleak picture of the moral decadence and despair among all social classes in Italy, almost rendering indistinguishable the Fascists from the anti-Fascists. Significantly, Hayes's political didacticism never interferes with his artistic intent—to study the characters' reactions to events and their interactions with each other; to penetrate the collective surface and probe the psychological wounds suffered by individual Italians as a result of Fascism, war, and foreign occupation.

What adds to the historical verisimilitude of Hayes's work is not only the realistic description of the personal vices of Italians and Americans alike. It is, rather, an actual incident of mob violence—the Carretta affair. The details of this brutal gang slaying have already been mentioned; it is enough to note here that the incident is the focal point of *All Thy Conquests* and that the author, with a Jamesian respect for the preeminence of private experience, could not allow its moral significance to go unanalyzed. "They wanted, I think, some unimaginable death for him, some terrible form of it. Yes: one feels, now, after it is over, a little sick; kill him, one thinks, but not so, not with such bestiality. Well, and have you and I had to lift the lid on those coffins, to go there into the caves to look at what bones are left, and to identify, by a ring or a gold tooth, what one has once loved? Have we had their tears, you and I?" Hayes was addressing himself to Americans; yet he was uncertain that Americans would be able to comprehend this orgiastic vendetta. His fears were well founded. *New York Times* correspondent Herbert Matthews, for example, used his firsthand account of the killing to lecture

434

Americans on the barbarism of Italians who had lost "all sense of civic virtue." Matthews' article prompted an angry reply from Lewis Mumford, who accused Americans like Matthews of being blinded by "self-righteousness and unctiousness." According to Mumford, the violence must be understood in light of Italy's recent experience, not only the long-endured oppression of Fascism but the brutalizing terror of Nazi occupation. For the sake of law and order Americans cannot "obliterate" the "bestial" crimes of Fascism, nor can they reproach "those truly humane men and women who are goaded into actions of violence by the law's delays and the law's leniency." Americans cannot afford to overlook the horrendous evil of totalitarianism and its unnatural effects on normal human behavior. "This attack of many Americans," he warned, "is a greater betrayal of morality than the most summary acts of retaliation by an inflamed mob; our superficial sensitiveness covers a deeper indifference to moral evil. Nothing could bring down upon us more deservedly or more surely the hatred of the people we are helping to liberate than such a perversion of moral judgments as Mr. Matthews has exhibited." Mumford's references to "a deeper indifference to moral evil" sums up well America's sententious grasp of the meaning of totalitarianism. In truth, most Americans failed to understand the spiritual and psychic consequences of war and Fascism for the Italian people, as the popular reception of Hersey's novel indicates. In this respect Hayes came much closer than Hersey in sensitively recording Fascism's impact on the moral character of the Italians. Yet both Hersey and Hayes were surpassed by John Horne Burns, whose *The Gallery* (1947) recorded with epigrammatic brilliance not only the moral implications of Fascism, but the baneful consequences of the American occupation itself.[14]

Hersey was concerned with what Americans could do *for* the Italians, Burns with what Americans did *to* them. *The Gallery* captured the Naples of 1944 and the Italian idiom in a prose that recalls Thomas Wolfe's ability to evoke reactions in our sensations of sight, sound, and smell. And employing a device similar to Dos Passos' "Camera Eye," Burns used "Portrait" and "Promenade" sections to provide impressionistic sketches of both Italian and American figures as well as his own poetic reflections. The locus of the novel, which has no conventional plot, is the Galleria

[14] *NYT*, Sept. 19, 28, 1944.

435

Umberto Primo, the "unofficial heart" of Naples. All the characters pass through the gallery: Louella, an American Red Cross
worker whose provincial, outdated standards wall her off from
social reality; Momma, the Italian proprietress of a homosexual
hangout; Father Donovan and Chaplain Bascom, the latter dis-
dainful of the Neapolitans, the former defending them and calling
for a "gradual return to the simplicities and felicities of Our
Lord's life"; Captain Motes, an American businessman turned
military officer who is applying his bureaucratic talents to the
"serious" business of censorship; Moe, a Jewish taxi driver from
Brooklyn who writes a poor man's version of Herzog's letters on
the futility of war and of life itself; Hal, a handsome, neurotic
young officer who suffers from cosmic pessimism when he realizes
man's inability for natural love; and Giulia, a young Italian girl
who observes the younger brother she worships taking to crime
in the streets as "a symbol of the scabrous destiny which was
debasing them all." These portraits blend into a sordid montage;
the characters are either killed meaninglessly, go insane, or, perhaps just as painfully, sense their realization of moral inadequacy.
"Guess I'm out of time," says Motes. "I'm a gentleman from
Virginia. Such must suffer in Naples of August, 1944."

Burns's haunting scenes of decadent officer life, lucrative blackmarket operations, camps for those with venereal disease, and
other scatological realities underlying the liberation, offer a
needed corrective to the genteel *kitsch* of *A Bell for Adano*. But
the brilliant achievement of *The Gallery* is its sensitive portrayal
of the drama of mutual misunderstanding between Italians and
Americans. To make this cultural conflict emphatic, Burns juxta-
posed the two national characters: on the one hand, the Italians
with their genuine spontaneity, their passion for the present life,
their aesthetic sensibility, their ebullience and sensuousness; on
the other, the Americans with their strident acquisitiveness, their
coarse moral numbness ("I decided Americans cried less because
they lived mostly in a vacuum. They weren't close enough to
birth or close enough to death"), their inability to distinguish
between "love and having sex" (the latter "an ejaculation without
tenderness as the orgasm of a frigidaire"), their cultural barrenness and brooding Protestant conscience. The contrast, of course,
is exaggerated, and Burns's treatment of Italians approaches
idolatry. Yet his central purpose was to show that America was
not so much liberating the Italians as imposing a new way of life

upon them, a gross existence that tears the delicate web of their community, disrupting the natural rhythm of their culture, leaving them without, in Giulia's words, "the old quiet delight she once took from life." Even more emphatically, Burns tried to expose a cruel contradiction between the rhetoric of American idealism and the reality of the American performance. "I remember the crimes we committed against the Italians," he recalled, citing the collaboration with ex-Fascists, the exploitation of women, the "making of money out of human misery," and other symptoms of "a deficient moral and humane sense in Americans as a people." The Americans' moral indifference stemmed in part from the GI's contempt for the Italians, whose opposition in the war "was taken as a license for Americans to defecate all over them." "They figured it this way: These Ginsoes have made war on us; so it doesn't matter what we do to them, boost their prices, shatter their economy, and shack up with their women." Burns's realization of the emptiness of American values was all the more agonizing because of the "tragic spectacle" of Italians initially putting so much faith and trust in their American "emancipators." Seeing no "collective and social decency" in Naples, he could find solace only in occasional acts of "individual goodness and loveliness" on the part of a few Americans. But Burns's hope in an "individuality consecrated and unselfish" could not sustain his vision. The "vulturism" of most Americans' behavior in Italy was too grotesque: "I saw that we could mouth democratic catchwords and yet give the Neapolitans a huge black market. I saw that we could prate of the evils of Fascism, yet be just as ruthless as Fascists with people who'd already been pushed into the ground. That was why my heart broke in Naples in August, 1944."

THE ARCADIAN POLITICAL VISION:
EZRA POUND AND JOHN HORNE BURNS

What caused Burns's heart to break in 1944 had been bothering Ezra Pound's for two decades. To Pound, World War II was less a crisis of conscience than a confirmation of conviction ("This is my war all right, I've been in it for twenty years"). Thus the expatriate poured into his propaganda broadcasts all the passionate labor of a poet who, at last, "had" the Western world over a wire. Prefacing his broadcasts, "Ezra Pound speakin'," he spewed forth his attack on Jews, on Roosevelt, on all aspects of

437

an America governed by the curse of filthy lucre. By the same token, Pound informed Americans that they have been "fed on lies," that they should not be fighting against Italy and her allies, and that "every sane act you commit is committed in homage to Mussolini and Hitler." As propaganda, Pound's broadcasts were a flat failure. Unintelligible (Pound would abruptly digress to explicate certain *Cantos*), the messages had no influence on Allied morale. Short-wave monitors had difficulty telling where the static ended and the stanzas began. Nevertheless, Pound's activities could not be ignored. In 1943 the United States government declared him a traitor, and in May 1945 he was arrested and imprisoned in the Discipline Training Center outside Pisa. Here, crouched inside a wire-built cage, Pound wrote his famous *The Pisan Cantos*, indicating he had by no means compromised his early pro-Fascism. For the wizened poet Il Duce would always remain the true martyr of World War II.[15]

After the war Pound's relationship with Italian Fascism would become a matter of bitter protracted controversy.[16] What con-

[15] PT; see especially Pound's broadcasts on April 16, May 26, and July 20, 1942. Some of these broadcasts have been printed in Ezra Pound, *America, Roosevelt and the Causes of the Present War: Selected Radio Speeches*, trans. Carmine Amore (London, 1950); see also Bruno Foa, "The Structure of Rome Short-Wave Broadcasts to North America," in *Propaganda by Short Wave*, eds. Harold L. Childs and John B. Whitton (Princeton, 1951), pp. 153-80.

[16] There are at least two separate chapters to the Pound controversy. In the first phase, he was brought back to the United States in 1945 to face trial for thirteen counts of treason. His attorney argued—and many sympathizers agreed—that Pound did not knowingly commit treason (defined by the Constitution as "adhering" to the enemy's cause and giving him "aid and comfort"), that he did nothing to discourage American soldiers, and that conscientiously he was merely "exercising the good old American prerogative of criticizing his government including even President Roosevelt," Julien Cornell, *The Trial of Ezra Pound* (New York, 1966), pp. 1-2. Anyone who reads the wearisome broadcast transcripts, however, could just as easily arrive at the opposite conclusion. After all, Pound did advise Americans to give up the war: "Every hour that you go on with this war is an hour lost to you and your children"; "You are not going to win this war. None of our best minds ever thought you could win it. You never had a chance in this war." (May 26, June 28, 1942, PT.) Whether such advice constitutes treason only the courts could say, and Pound was denied his day in court. A medical report submitted by four psychiatrists found him "insane and mentally unfit for trial." In 1946 he was confined to St. Elizabeth's mental hospital in Washington. Twelve years later, after numer-

438

cerns us is not the "literary scandal" but the perspective which both Pound and Burns shared, a perspective that brings our discussion of literary relations between Italy and America full circle. For Burns's contrast between a meretricious America and an Arcadian Italy recalls Pound's contrast between a defiled America, "an old bitch gone in the teeth," and a medieval Italy where "Beauty alone" prevails. Whatever their ideological differences, both the Fascist poet and the liberal novelist were measuring the seamy vices of the New World against the supposedly noble virtues of the Old World. If Pound reflected personal alienation from a mendacious America, his *Cantos* refracted an exalted vision of Fascist idealism; if Burns revealed an anguished disillusionment with the vacuity of American ideals, his *Gallery* refracted an Italophilic conception of the experience of liberation. What we have, in effect, is a dramatic reversal of the "Edenic" motif of American literature. The depraved Old World was not to be judged against the sinless spirit of the New.

---

ous legal motions and expressions of support from fellow literary peers, Pound was released in the custody of his daughter, with whom he returned to Italy.

The second chapter of the Pound affair involves the selection of *The Pisan Cantos* as the first Bollingen Prize for Poetry in 1948. The committee which recommended the award to Pound was made up of the Fellows of the Library of Congress, then consisting of Conrad Aiken, W. H. Auden, Louise Brogan, T. S. Eliot, Paul Green, Robert Lowell, Katherine Anne Porter, Karl Shapiro, Theodore Spencer, Allen Tate, Willard Thorp, and Robert Penn Warren. The selection of Pound was first challenged by the *Saturday Review of Literature* ("Treason's Strange Fruit"); soon other voices joined the attack, such as the Left-wing *Partisan Review* and the Jewish *Commentary*. See also the useful anthology, *A Casebook on Ezra Pound*, eds., William Van O'Connor and Edward Stone (New York, 1959).

The storm over the Pound affair stirred up many old debates regarding the poet and society. In view of the fact that Pound's Fascism escaped the criticism of his peers before World War II, it is important to note the aesthetic apology used in 1948. The most frequent defense of the Bollingen Prize was the "New Criticism" thesis that form and technique can be appreciated apart from content and meaning. This argument might be regarded, in the context of our study, as the counterpart to the pragmatist's conviction that method is the master. Since technique is a subjective act of creativity and method an adaption of intelligence to changing social problems, both literary art and social theory result in a value-free relativism. In the face of totalitarianism, this form of ideological innocence makes the poet not the "antenna" but the eunuch of the human race.

On the contrary, the Old World—and particularly Italy—stood as a cultural citadel holding off the invasion of the new barbarians. Viewed in this light, Burns's novel brings us back not only to Pound's "botched" America of the twenties or Van Wyck Brooks' bifurcated America of the teens, but to the America of the "passionate pilgrims" of the *fin de siècle*—to the literary Italophiles like Henry James. For all these travelers had come to the realization that American culture had failed them. And it was this conclusion that John Horne Burns arrives at a half century later. By depicting his own culture as devoid of moral order and by projecting an idyllic portrait of Italy, Burns' *Gallery* gave to the generation of the forties the intellectual rite of passage that has been so curiously celebrated by American novelists and poets: the loss of innocence.

The dichotomy of the two worlds has been a persistent obsession in the American mind. As Melvin Lasky has noted, formulations have been pushed to the point of triteness: the Jamesian vision of America's primitive innocence and Europe's profound experience; the Jeffersonian view of a young and healthy America and an old and decadent Europe; and the modern liberal's version of an experimental and buoyant America and a stagnant and reactionary Europe. These transatlantic images have allowed Americans to hold up Europe as a vast mirror to gaze on their own self-image. But Italy has always remained the particular looking glass. Years after the liberation, writers would still be traveling to Italy in order to find themselves, in order to discover what it means to be an American. As the following confession indicates, Leslie Fiedler carries on a tradition of self-discovery that began with Hawthorne, fructified in James, and burned itself out in despair in John Horne Burns (who killed himself in Naples in 1953).

No, Italy is hell enough for us still; what is disconcerting, however, is the realization that for many Italians we do not seem the gingerly visitors from an upper world that we appear to ourselves, but refugees from our own authentic and ultimate inferno. America has become the hell of its own favorite hell! This is the most disturbing and diverting thing I have learned thus far in Italy. I have had the unexpected sense of Italy as a mirror, a distorting mirror to be sure, one of those diabolical things from a Coney Island Fun House, that gives you for the

440

laughs a brutal caricature, at once a nightmare and a joke, a travesty and a disturbing criticism of yourself.[17]

The enduring presence of Italy in America's literary mind, a theme which returns us to our first chapter, makes it tempting to use *The Gallery* as a coda upon which to close our study on the same note it opened. Yet the artful embroidery of Burns's prose, the inner consistency of his convictions, and the delicate sensitivity of his vision must not tempt us into accepting imaginative literature as historical reality. Burns's novel, to be sure, caught vividly many aspects of the liberation which the press and propaganda may have played down. There can be little doubt, for example, that the American military had little respect for the Italian fighting man. In Harry Brown's *A Walk in the Sun* one character uttered a judgment echoed throughout *The Gallery*: "Tyne did not hate Italy, nor did he hate the Italians. He merely ignored them. Some of the men, he knew, hated them—not necessarily because they had killed their share of Americans, but because they were cowards. They ran. They always ran. A soldier could hate the Germans, but he could respect them at the same time. He would respect the stubborn bravery and their cunning and their battle wisdom. But the Italians had none of these negative virtues. The Italians had nothing."[18] Yet Burns overdrew his collective portrait of American soldiers as irresponsible, corrupt, and callous. The Italians themselves, though demoralized by and impatient with the occupation, were not nearly so negative in their estimate of the conduct of American forces.[19] The

[17] Melvin J. Lasky, "Literature and the Arts," in *America and the Mind of Europe*, ed. Lewis Galantière (New York, 1952), p. 89; Leslie Fiedler, "Italian Pilgrimage: The Discovery of America," *An End to Innocence: Essays on Culture and Politics* (Boston, 1955), p. 93.

[18] Surveys conducted at the end of the war indicated that the American soldier showed slightly more admiration for the Russian military effort than that of the British. But more revealing, although the American soldier expressed greater respect for Englishmen than for the Russians, the same soldier expressed greater admiration for the German people over the Frenchmen. Unfortunately, although no questions were asked of the Italians, it seems clear enough that ideology counted less than military prowess. See the statistics in Samuel A. Stouffer, et al., *Studies in Social Psychology in World War II* (Princeton, 1949), II, 564-78, esp. 576.

[19] In 1947 Italians were asked: "Of all the Allied soldiers whom you have seen in Italy, which made the best impression on you?" Sixty-two percent chose the Americans while only 14 percent chose the British, which

441

behavior of American soldiers was neither as benign as Hersey implied nor as brutal as Burns described.

Burns's perceptions become more convincing when we turn to the political implications of *The Gallery*. D. H. Lawrence recognized that "you have got to pull the democratic and idealistic clothes off American utterance, and see what you can of the dusky body of it underneath." Such an exposure was the major achievement of *The Gallery*. Of all the American novelists who wrote of America's wartime involvement in foreign countries, Burns must be regarded as among the most important, not merely because of his poetic descriptions of the suspended emotions of the Neapolitans, but because of his profound, if exaggerated, ability to see the liberation from the Italian point of view, thereby peeling rhetoric away from reality and offering an incisive critique of American "ideals" in action. Louis Hartz has suggested that America's inescapable relation with the outside world provides the best hope for a fresh perspective on our own unquestioned political values; that therefore "America must look to its contact with other nations to provide that spark of philosophy, that grain of relative insight that its own history has denied it." World War II provided the first massive contact between Americans and Europeans, but the experience suggests the shortcomings of Hartz's essentially correct advice. "Can a people 'born equal' ever understand peoples elsewhere that have to become so? Can it ever understand itself?" asks Professor Hartz. Another way to pose the question is to ask whether Americans who have never experienced totalitarianism can understand those they are liberating from totalitarianism; whether Americans ignorant of their own parochial history can act as missionaries to those victimized by an entirely different history; whether Americans can come to understand others while performing as conquering soldiers; and whether Americans can achieve that precious "grain of relative insight" without trying to transcend the constricting uniqueness of their own political and cultural values. What gives Burns's novel such tragic vision is that the author answered these ques-

---

included Scottish, Irish, New Zealander, and South African troops. A close student of this subject concluded that the more favorable impression of Americans was due to their general behavior as well as the presence of Italian-American soldiers and the influence of economic assistance (van de Velde, p. 213).

tions before he asked them. Indeed he sensed, even though he may not have been fully aware of America's earlier admiration for Mussolini's Italy, that American soldiers had liberated Italy from Fascism while bringing to Italy the very individualistic values with which American citizens had formerly praised Fascism. This is why *The Gallery*, perhaps the one literary document of World War II that succeeds in rising above a narcissistic nationalism, remains a sobering reminder of America's limitation for political and cultural transcendence.[20]

Burns's heart broke in Naples because he demanded from America what America could not give. His plea for a heightened self-awareness and a deeper self-knowledge was nothing less than a call for Americans to liberate themselves if they are truly to liberate others. Americans failed this awesomely heroic challenge. Whether American intellectuals failed to rise above their own political values and assumptions enough to understand the meaning of Fascism is the subject of our concluding chapter.

[20] D. H. Lawrence, *Studies in Classic American Literature* (Anchor edn., New York, 1959), p. 18; Louis Hartz, *The Liberal Tradition in America* (New York, 1955), pp. 287, 309.

17.

American Intellectuals and Fascism: The Ambiguous Legacy

IF WE MUST TAKE A STAND . . . WE CANNOT WAIT FOR THE UNCERTAIN CONCLUSIONS OF HISTORIOSOPHICAL DISCUSSION, WHICH MAY REMAIN UNRESOLVED FOR A HUNDRED YEARS. OUR CHOICE WILL THEREFORE BE BEST IF IT IS DETERMINED BY WHAT SMALL PARTICLES OF CERTAINTY WE POSSESS. ENDURING MORAL VALUES, DEVELOPED THROUGHOUT THE HISTORY OF MAN UP TO THIS MOMENT, ARE THE SUREST SUPPORTS WE HAVE IF REALITY REQUIRES OF US A CHOICE WHICH ULTIMATELY IS OF A MORAL NATURE. IN ANY EVENT, THESE VALUES ARE MORE WORTHY OF CONFIDENCE THAN ANY HISTORIOSOPHICAL EXPLANATION. AND ULTIMATELY THIS IS WHY I MAINTAIN MY POSITION.

WHATEVER HAPPENS? WHATEVER HAPPENS.

Leszek Kolakowski, "The Escapist Conspiracy," in *Toward a Marxist Humanism: Essays on the Left Today,* 1968*

* Reprinted by permission of Grove Press, Inc. (See Acknowledgments)

AMERICANS have always known their enemies better than themselves, what they stand against better than what they stand for. Thus in World War II many Americans, even American intellectuals, believed they understood why it was necessary for the United States to wage a world war against Fascism. Yet though America could defeat Mussolini's Italy and Hitler's Germany, few American thinkers could define adequately the nature of Fascism. This continues to be true even among contemporary scholars, and due to the absence of agreement I feel all the more reluctant to try to impose a precise definition upon a polymorphous reality. By no means, however, does this impasse prevent us from examining the various interpretations of the phenomenon during the war years. As Henry James observed, if one cannot penetrate to the essence of reality there is still considerable satisfaction in viewing it from all perspectives. And if the meaning of Fascism continues to elude historians there is still something to be gained by studying the meanings Americans gave it; indeed there is much more to be gained by comparing American interpretations with those of European émigrés. Only then can the values and assumptions inherent in the American mind be analyzed and the implications of the Fascist experience understood.

THE HUMANIST THESIS

In May 1940, a long essay appeared in the *New Republic* provocatively entitled "Our Guilt in Fascism." Waldo Frank, its author, admitted at once that his argument—a reassertion of his earlier rhapsody, *The Rediscovery of America* (1929)—derived from "a statement of a vision which . . . all my books embody." Fascism, according to Frank, was a "symptom" of the postmedieval revolution of "empirical rationalism," a false "modern religion" which, reacting from such concepts as "tragedy, sin, [and] God," led man away from the eternal "mystery of human freedom." Thus to answer Fascism, Americans must return to "The Great Tradition," to the "pre-rational" world where man sensed the spirit of God within, where man's yearning for the infinite was commensurate with his capacity for self-realization, and where his "primordial intuitions" were at one with nature and society. Merging a Whitmanesque pantheism with a Whiteheadian fusion of nature and life, Frank sought to achieve an "awareness of the organism as a whole" through the "process of experience," even though in the modern western world man's

445

"emotional conduits" were clogged by natural philosophy and unnatural technology. As long as western liberals continued to ignore the redemptive qualities of pastoral intuitionalism they will continue to share "the same fundamental values as their foes." Having foisted a "modern solipsist religion of things and words" upon western society, American liberals, like European Fascists, have thus helped to dam up man's deepest, most vital emotions of organic wholeness.[1]

Waldo Frank was not alone in perceiving Fascism as a crisis of a deformed spirit. His close friend Lewis Mumford had recently written an equally provocative essay entitled "The Corruption of Liberalism." Challenging the *New Republic*'s political philosophy, Mumford distinguished two traditions of liberalism —first, an "ideal liberalism" founded in classical humanism and sustained by absolute "moralizing" values, a liberalism based on the concepts of "universality" and "historic continuity" which stressed, above all, personal responsibility and political freedom; and second, a "pragmatic liberalism" which emphasized utilitarian ethics and quantitative valuation, thereby shutting its eyes to "an understanding of constant human phenomena—sin, corruption, evil." The latter tradition of liberalism, Mumford insisted, paved the way for Fascism by undermining moral values and blinding man to the limitations of human nature. With myopic faith in progress and reason, pragmatic liberals could not acknowledge the need for force in human affairs; committed to a vulgar economic determinism, they refused to see that "it is not in Ricardo or Marx or Lenin, but in Dante and Shakespeare and Dostoevski, that an understanding of the true sources of Fascism are [sic] to be found."[2]

In his highly publicized *Nation* article, "The Irresponsibles," poet Archibald MacLeish agreed with the humanist argument. He criticized "scientific, neuter, skeptical, detached" scholars as well as writers who think "without responsibility to anything but truth of feeling." Since both refused to become engaged in the world of political action they would never be able to come to grips with Fascism. Drained of all sense of values in his "laboratory insulation," the American intellectual had become "a refugee

[1] *New Republic*, cii (May 6, 1940), 603-08; see also Frank's *Charter for Rough Waters* (New York, 1940).

[2] *New Republic*, cii (April 29, 1940), 568-73; see also Mumford's *Faith for Living* (New York, 1940).

from consequences, an exile from the responsibilities of moral choice."[3]

In one respect the humanists were right. The disillusionment after World War I combined with the delusions of naturalistic thought to produce among many liberals an atrophy of will and vision. Dismissing moral ideas and values as mere shadows of the mind, pragmatic liberals especially believed the technique of intelligence and social control could provide all the answers modern political man needed to know. This faith in the ethical sufficiency of empirical method, which led several liberals to withhold judgment on Italian Fascism in the twenties, enabled countless liberals a decade later to see the Soviet Union as a profound social "experiment" which only a philistine would hold up to moral scruple. By the end of the thirties, however, some liberals became as disenchanted with the methods of science as with the "methods" of Stalin. Sensing that man could not live by empirical facts alone, they now unblushingly re-embraced what Carl Becker would later call "the generalities that still glitter." Even so, and even at the edge of a world cataclysm, many liberals could still not bring themselves to oppose Fascism with military force. It was this prospect of all-out war with Germany and Italy that plunged liberals into an abyss of indecision in which all remaining appeals to "reason" and "intelligence" sounded like echoes in Forster's Marabar caves.[4]

In this respect the writings of Frank, Mumford, and MacLeish helped to point up the political hazards in the liberalism of pragmatic rationalism. Yet they probably helped further to confuse the Americans' understanding of Fascism. Sharing a common bias against modern industry and science, all three writers assumed that Fascism arose from the cultural malaise of materialism; all spoke of the need to replace the contemporary man of doubt and division with the historic man of faith and wholeness, of the society of drift with the community of purpose, of "arid pragmatism" with powerful beliefs. But what must be stressed is that the three pro-interventionist writers confused what they believed was a pragmatic acquiescence to Fascism with the nature of Fascism itself. Whether America's pragmatic temperament was responsible for Fascism's diplomatic triumphs

[3] *Nation*, CL (May 18, 1940), 618-23.

[4] Frank A. Warren, *Liberals and Communism: The "Red Decade" Revisited* (Bloomington and London, 1966), esp. Chap. IV.

was one thing; whether that philosophic temperament explained the historical significance of Fascism was altogether a different proposition. Indeed what is so ironic in this anti-liberal *meâ culpâ* ("Our Guilt in Fascism") is that in railing against American pragmatism the authors came close to reiterating the arguments of Fascist intellectuals themselves. Whatever the diverse origins of Fascist doctrine, many Fascist ideologues in Europe had proudly declared their opposition to the amorphous and mechanical quality of bourgeois society. Biological vitalism, the mystical idea of transcendence, the purity of the soil and its elemental union with nature, the theory of the organic state and the quest for community, the power of intuition and emotion, and the ultimate realization of authentic consciousness—such were the metaphysical tenets of the European Right. Fascism, it is true, practiced a vulgar pragmatic opportunism and cloaked its doctrine in technocratic syndicalism; but both the Italian and the German varieties of Fascism had little in common with the "empirical rationalism" which the three American writers identified as the bitch-goddess of twentieth century totalitarianism. Indeed Waldo Frank and European reactionaries had one thing in common: they were both at war with liberalism, rationalism, and modernity.[5]

RELUCTANT REVISIONISTS: THE MARXISTS

Where humanist writers saw Fascism as a disease of the spirit born of the sin of scientific naturalism, Marxists saw it as the sickness of society born of the curse of monopoly capitalism. We have already discussed the American Left's blithe response to Mussolini in 1922 and the subsequent theory of "social fascism." In the thirties it was only the small Lovestonite "opposition" and a few independent Marxists like Sidney Hook who dared question Moscow's disastrous position on Fascism. Instead, most of the Left fully accepted the thesis of John Strachey's *The Menace of Fascism* (1933) and R. Palme Dutt's *Fascism and Social Revolution* (1934). The two British writers hammered out the standard Marxist interpretation of Fascism as the death spasm of the old order. Dutt, whose works were widely quoted in Left-wing

[5] The anti-modernity motif is stressed in Wolfgang Sauer's "National Socialism: Totalitarianism or Fascism?" *American Historical Review*, LXXIII (Dec. 1967), 404-24; for its cultural ramifications, see Raymond Williams, *Culture and Society, 1780-1950* (New York, 1958).

circles, was profoundly disturbed by the rise of Hitler. Yet he was certain that Fascism would only intensify the tensions within capitalism and thereby escalate the social revolution. Moreover, Dutt believed that since Fascism had at last exposed the betrayal of the working class by reformist leaders, the "brutal" experience "may yet prove a salutary shock."[6]

The only way to comprehend Fascism, Marxists insisted, was by analyzing its "class content." Starting from this premise, American Communists were certain that Fascism represented a diabolical plot of the industrial capitalists alone. Unlike many non-Marxists thinkers, Communists played down the role of the middle class, maintaining that the bourgeoisie's mass support was merely a matter of manipulation on the part of the ruling capitalists. In fact, the very idea that the middle class—the dupes of the social democrats—could be a decisive force in the later stages of capitalism was alien to Marxist theory. Convinced that only men of enormous capital held dominant power in all western countries, it was almost heresy for a Marxist to see Fascism arising from any other class.[7]

No less an article of Marxist faith was Fascism's imminent collapse. But whereas in the twenties Communists were more inclined to see Mussolini's regime crumbling from within, in the thirties they claimed that Fascism—still based on capitalism's inexorable "contradictions"—could only lead to a heightened imperialism, which in turn would bring on international war. Watching intently for every sign of this prophecy, Communists believed (as did many liberals) that the Ethiopian War was the beginning of the end of Mussolini's rule. Yet the Abyssinian adventure produced just the opposite effect: instead of bringing down Il Duce, the war served only to strengthen his grip over the nation; and instead of expediting the collapse of German capitalism, the war in Africa allowed Hitler to move into the Rhineland, a calculated gamble which also enabled him to extend

[6] *Workers Age*, Feb. 6, 1932; Jay Lovestone, *The People's Front Illusion* (New York, 1937, pamphlet); Sidney Hook, "The Fallacy of the Theory of Social Fascism," *Modern Monthly*, VIII (July 1934), 342-53; Theodore Draper, "The Ghost of Social Fascism," *Commentary*, XLVII (Feb. 1969), 29-42; R. Palme Dutt, *Fascism and the Social Revolution* (New York, 1934), p. vii.

[7] Dutt, pp. 72-90; John Strachey, *The Menace of Fascism* (New York, 1933).

personal power over all phases of German life. By 1936 a reappraisal of Fascism was clearly overdue.[8]

Actually the reappraisal had been underway since mid-1934, and the following year the Seventh Comintern Congress tacitly acknowledged some second thoughts on Fascism with the formation of the Popular Front. The strategy of the "peoples's front," calling for the collaboration of all enemies of reaction, was a belated admission that Mussolini and Hitler would be around for some time. Although the new Soviet position represented a tactical shift, and though the American Left responded enthusiastically to the siren call of solidarity, the Popular Front led to no significant reevaluation of Fascism. True, social democrats and liberals would no longer be regarded as the midwives of Mussolini and Hitler; nonetheless, Fascism continued to be identified with monopoly capitalism. And it was this identification which would be used four years later to justify the Russo-German Nonaggression Pact—since monopoly power dominated not only in Italy and Germany but in France and England as well, it was ideological nonsense to defend the democratic West.[9]

By the outbreak of World War II the official Communist definition of Fascism remained little more than a Pavlovian reflex. Fortunately many American Marxists had now broken with the Communist Party. Shocked by the horrors of Stalinism and by the betrayed promises of Communism itself, a number of Left-wing writers began to formulate their own theories of Fascism. At least two lines of thought developed to account for what now appeared as Fascism's fatal illusion of impermanence. One approach was to admit the passing of capitalism's irrational competitive drive and emphasize instead its unchanging acquisitive spirit. Taking this view, some writers conceded that capitalism had matured far beyond its anarchic stage of open competition. Yet the same writers maintained that, although free enterprise was now restricted and the economic crisis thereby forestalled, labor exploitation still remained the basis of Fascism; and although competition may have declined in the realm of distribution, it continued in the area of production, an area that would lead inevitably to foreign rivalry and war. Thus, no matter how

[8] E.g., "The Crisis in Italy," *New Masses*, xvi (July 16, 1935), 19-20; S. Herman, "When War Comes," *Class Struggle*, v (May 1935), 17-32.

[9] "Keep America Out of the Imperialist War!" *The Communist*, xviii (Oct. 1939), 899-904; Laqueur, *Russia and Germany*, pp. 232-33.

the various economic institutions had been revamped in Italy and Germany, the power of capital still reigned supreme.[10]

Reasoning along these lines, Left-wing thinkers could still maintain that Fascism by no means rendered orthodox Marxism obsolete, a position held by the more tenacious European ideologues. In the United States, however, some of the most trenchant reinterpretations of Fascism came from the followers of Trotsky. This was only fitting, for Trotsky had all along criticized the doctrine of social fascism and, drawing upon the experience of Italian Communist leaders, he offered an analysis of Fascism that rose above the frozen categories of Stalinist Marxism. Painfully aware that Soviet policy on Fascism had been an unmitigated disaster, Trotsky's disciples soon came to doubt whether Marxism could any longer be relied upon for its vaunted predictive value. This was the second approach: to go beyond Marxism to grasp Fascism.[11]

The views of Dwight Macdonald serve to illustrate the shifting positions of the Trotskyists. In 1937 Macdonald wrote the introduction to the American edition of the French Communist Daniel Guerin's *Fascism and Big Business*. Here he fully endorsed the Marxist argument that any discussion of Fascism must be brought "down from the cloudy realms of abnormal psychology and moral categories to the solid ground of economic and social analysis." Likening Guerin's book to Ferdinand Lundberg's *America's Sixty Families*, Macdonald saw Fascism as capitalist domination pure and simple. By 1941, however, Macdonald could no longer maintain this view. He now interpreted Fascism as "bureaucratic collectivism," a completely novel form of economic organization which arose as an answer to the old Marxist contradictions between private property and the socialized nature of advanced industrialization. A product of mature capitalism, Fascist totalitarianism had effectively reduced the classical tensions within private enterprise, and thus the unexpected staying power of postcapitalism made *Das Kapital* a poor guide to *il corporativismo*.[12]

[10] Marceau Pivert, "Fascism and Capitalism," *Partisan Review*, VIII (Sept.-Oct. 1941), 425; Paul Mattick, "How New Is the 'New Order' of Fascism?" *ibid.*, (July-Aug., 1941), 289-310; "What Is Fascism: The Discussion Continued," *ibid.* (Sept.-Oct. 1941), 418-30.

[11] "Democracy and Fascism" (1932), *The Basic Writings of Trotsky*, ed. Irving Howe (New York, 1965), pp. 234-44.

[12] Macdonald's introduction to Guerin's book was also published as a pamphlet, *Fascism and the American Scene* (New York, 1938); for his

Sociologist C. Wright Mills offered a variation on this theme. Like Macdonald, Mills admitted that orthodox Marxism could not satisfactorily account for the Fascist state. But Mills believed he could update Marx by drawing upon Max Weber's insights regarding the unanticipated structural shifts in modern industrial society. Advanced capitalism is not, as Marx believed, an orgy of ruinous production; instead it is planned, rationalized, and cartelized; a process, Mills pointed out, which enabled capitalists to continue to wield power in the Fascist state along with the party, the bureaucracy, and the military. Far more startling was James Burnham's highly publicized thesis on the "Managerial Revolution." Maintaining that capitalism was a dead reality and Socialism an impossible dream, Burnham challenged the familiar Left-wing assumption that Socialism stood as the only alternative to capitalism. In reality, the modern industrial system was run by "managers"—technicians, administrators, and bureaucrats who had recently emerged to achieve control over the instruments of production and thereby mitigate the familiar crises of capitalism. And it was this new ruling class, Burnham contended, that explained the three major dictatorships in Europe.[13]

Whether Trotskyists consulted Weber, Pareto, or even the recently discovered writings of the Polish anarchist Waclaw Machajski, they interpreted Fascism as a novel form of organized power that arose from the technical imperatives of post-capitalist society. Yet no matter how unprepared classical Marxism was for the advent of Fascism, Left-wing writers were reluctant to abandon most of the basic assumptions of Marxian analysis. Hence in interpreting Fascism they continued to stress the primacy of economic power over political institutions, social structure over national character, scientific materialism over human emotion.

---

reinterpretation, see "The End of Capitalism in Germany," *Partisan Review*, VIII (May-June, 1941), 198-200.

[13] C. Wright Mills, "Locating the Enemy," *ibid.*, IX (Sept.-Oct., 1942), 432-37; James Burnham, *The Managerial Revolution* (New York, 1941).

In redefining Fascism, Trotskyists like Burnham were, of course, also trying to account for the repugnant spectacle of Stalinism. But Burnham had little doubt that his theory of managerial oligarchy applied to Italy and Germany as well. Indeed he would soon turn to Italy to absorb the "scientific" wisdom of Machiavelli, Mosca, and Pareto, "enlightened" realists who were the first to demonstrate that the story of history is the story of ruling elites. See James Burnham, *The Machiavellians* (New York, 1943).

Dismissing man's spiritual and psychic nature as mere epiphe-
nomena, Marxists could also dismiss the role of ideas and ideologies in Fascism as nothing more than "political cloaks" (Mills).
Even those who turned to Pareto and Weber did not forsake
Marxian economic determinism. As a result philosopher Burnham
merely substituted one form of determinism (economic) for another (technological), while sociologist Mills employed Weber's
theory of bureaucracy to demonstrate that monopoly capitalism
would lead inevitably to Fascism and war. Unfortunately both
these approaches proved insufficient. In Italy and in Germany
power was no longer completely in the hands of either technological elites or industrial capitalists. In fact, if we accept Weber's
model of the bureaucratic capitalist as one who desires above all
to rationalize the economy by making it stable, predictable, and
secure, then it is rather hard to conceive of this cautious creature
embracing a system as wanton as "full fascism" and an adventure
as incalculable as world war. Weber's description of the rationalization and bureaucratization of modern economic life was a
necessary advance beyond Marxism, but Weberian sociology
could scarcely account for the irrational activism of Fascism, the
personal atavism of Mussolini and Hitler, and what Sigmund
Neumann called the "boundless dynamics" of the totalitarian
state.[14]

[14] Mills, p 436. Arthur Schweitzer has shown that in Germany up to
1936 big business was, along with the Nazi party, the SS, and the army,
a powerful influence. But this experiment in "partial fascism" broke down
in 1936 when Hitler established complete control over all phases of German
life. It was only in the period of "full fascism" that Hitler was free to
embark on wholesale war. Schweitzer also contends that the shift to total
Fascism and war was not inevitable had the army and big business resisted:
"The major lesson of the earlier Nazi experience is that partial fascism and
organized capitalism do not necessarily constitute a transitional phase to full
fascism, which in turn need not necessarily become the victim of a war
of its own making." *Big Business in the Third Reich* (Bloomington and
London, 1964), p. 556. See also, Henry A. Turner, "Big Business and the
Rise of Hitler," *American Historical Review*, LXXV (Oct. 1962), 56-70.

As for Italy, Fascism may have been a formless oligarchy of shifting elites;
yet in contrast to Burnham's thesis, elitist rule in Mussolini's Italy had
little to do with technological developments. The precise connection between Italian capital and Fascism is also more complex than most American Marxists were aware. In the beginning Italian industrialists were suspicious of Mussolini and his volatile followers, and although they acquiesced
to the March on Rome they were not active participants in the event. Thereafter the relationship between Italy's Confederation of Industry and the

Both the devoted and the doubting Marxists contributed a great deal to America's understanding of the social realities of Fascism. But their tendency to think of Fascism in terms of the iron laws of economics explains in part why they were so consistently wrong in evaluating it in all its complexity. Having dismissed Fascism in 1922 as a passing curiosity, they welcomed it in 1933 as the "labor pain" of Communism's triumphant birth. Then having shifted to the Popular Front in 1935, many American Marxists came to assume, especially after the Nonaggression Pact of 1939, that industrial capitalism would everywhere lead to Fascism once the dogs of war were unleashed. Still under the spell of inevitability, a number of intelligent Socialists and Trotskyists were thus unable to bring themselves to support the war against Mussolini and Hitler, so convinced were they that democratic America and Fascist Europe were diseases caused by the same virus. In effect, the brilliant insights of *Das Kapital* afforded little guide to political action against Fascism, which is one way of suggesting that a major nineteenth-century social theory could not fully account for a major twentieth-century political reality. Fascism may have been the "iron heel" of capitalism; it was also the Achilles' heel of Marxism.[15]

Fascist regime wavered between enthusiasm and antagonism, and after 1935 the divergence between the two became more pronounced. See Roland Sarti, "Fascism and the Industrial Leadership in Italy before the March on Rome," *Industrial and Labor Relations Review*, xxi (April 1968), 400-17; Felice Guarneri, *Battaglie Economiche tra le due grandi guerre*, 2 vols. (Milan, 1953); Luigi Salvatorelli and Giovanni Mira, *Storia d'Italia nel periodo fascista* (Turin, 1961). As indicated in Sarti's footnotes, however, the extent and nature of Fascism's financial support is still an open question in Italian scholarship. Significantly, a few non-Communist Marxists in America approached Fascism with a high level of sophistication, particularly when they focused on a single country and avoided the pitfall of simple economic determinism. See, for example, Carl T. Schmidt, *The Corporate State in Action* (New York, 1939). Finally, many Italian Marxists seemed much more sensitive to the complexity of the problem. See, for example, Renzo De Felice, "Il Problema storiografica del fascismo: Interpretazioni e richerche," *Cultura e Scuola*, no. 17 (1966), 92-97; and *Il Fascismo: Antologia di scritti critici*, ed. Costanzo Casucci (Bologna, 1961). Sigmund Neumann, *Permanent Revolution: Totalitarianism in the Age of International Civil War* (second edn., New York, 1965), p. 230.

[15] Communists, of course, supported the war the moment Germany marched on Russia. But many independent Marxists—the only ones who did any original thinking on the Fascist question—were too jaded by the

THE CATHOLIC INTERPRETATION

Curiously, the Catholic interpretation shared some of the same deterministic assumptions as the Marxist. Catholic thinkers also saw Fascist dictators as pawns of history, of underlying forces whose poison was bringing Western civilization to a climax. "Far from being prime movers," asserted the Thomist scholar Mortimer Adler, Hitler and Mussolini "are but paranoiac puppets, dancing for a moment on the crest of the wave—the wave that is the historic motion of modern culture of its own destruction." Like Marxists, moreover, Catholics believed that if the democratic West were to win the war against Fascism it would have to undergo a fundamental transformation—the Marxists, of course, believing it must occur in the social structure, the Catholics in the realm of spiritual conscience. Finally, both Marxists and Catholics saw Fascism as a dangerous but not altogether unexpected challenge that would serve to open America's eyes to the rottenness of her economic order or to the flabbiness of her moral fibre. Fascism thus emerges as a mirror-image of the decadent West, a clear warning of the perils of property on the one hand and of impiety on the other. This eschatology of spiritual brinksmanship and redemption reached its most morbid heights in Adler's admonition:

> If I dared to raise my voice as did the prophets in ancient Israel, I would ask whether the tyrants of today are not like the Babylonian and Assyrian kings—instruments of Divine

experience of Stalinism to believe that the war had any ideological significance. Their reasoning was based on at least four assumptions: (a) that the war was "imperialist" through and through; (b) that capitalist America was economically weaker than either collectivist Russia or corporatist Germany; (c) that for America to enter the war would mean a Fascist garrison state; (d) that only a truly socialized America could defeat the Fascist powers. Dwight Macdonald, who shared all these assumptions, expressed the cynicism of the disenchanted Marxists in spring 1941. Ridiculing the popular notion of the "mad Germans," Macdonald bluntly stated: "Actually, the lunacy lies deep in the economic and social system of modern monopoly capitalism, and the Germans are guilty merely of doing consciously and systematically what other imperialist nations do under cover of a smoke screen of hypocrisy. But, of course, everyone is shocked when the fig leaf is dropped." A few months later he declared: "The truth is that the democracies cannot defeat Hitler by force." Macdonald, "Reading from Left to Right," *Partisan Review*, VIII (Jan.-Feb. 1941), 31; id. and Clement Greenberg, "10 Propositions on War," *ibid.* (July-Aug. 1941), 278.

justice, chastening a people who had departed from the way of truth. In the inscrutable Providence of God, and according to the nature of man, a civilization may sometimes reach a rottenness which only fire can expunge and cleanse. If the Babylonians and Assyrians were destroyers, they were also deliverers. Through them, the prophets realized, God purified His people. Seeing the hopelessness of working peaceful reforms among a people who had shut their eyes and hardened their hearts, the prophets almost prayed for such deliverance, through the darkness of destruction, to the light of a better day. So, perhaps, the Hitlers in the world today are preparing the agony through which our culture shall be reborn.[16]

Adler spoke these words before the "Conference on Science, Philosophy, and Religion in Their Relation to the Democratic Way of Life," which met in New York in September 1940. Gathered here were intellectuals and scholars of all varieties, brought together by the urgent conviction that, as Van Wyck Brooks put it, "the totalitarian way of life is rapidly spreading through the world, to the imminent peril of civilization." Many participants believed that Fascism arose because of the breakdown of the intellectual unity of the West, an imperiled culture whose Christian roots had withered away. This message was driven home by Fordham professors like Anton Pegis and by European Catholics like Jacques Maritain; and later, at a second symposium, even by eight Protestant Princeton professors who issued a manifesto on "The Spiritual Basis of Democracy." Although Catholic and Protestant thinkers avoided an explicit definition of Fascism, they agreed that totalitarianism had come about because of the demise of the Judaic-Christian heritage and the advent of scientific positivism and naturalism. Adler even went so far as to claim that "the most serious threat to democracy" was not Hitler but the "positivism of the professors," the "nihilistic" liberal educators whose naturalism paved the way for Fascism by corrupting modern culture. In the eyes of Catholics, then, Fascism was the political paganism that came from modern science; and since religion was supposedly the source of democracy, it followed that irreligion must be the basis of Fascism. This interpretation, which was widely echoed in the Catholic press, served to make

[16] Mortimer Adler, "God and the Professors," in Science, Philosophy and Religion: A Symposium (New York, 1941), pp. 37-38, 121.

the war against Hitler and Mussolini into a moral crusade. Whether it served to help Americans better understand the nature of Fascism is questionable.[17]

In the first place, the notion that Fascism sprang from positivism and naturalism is historically unfounded. It is true that positivism pervaded western European culture around the turn of the century; but it is equally true that Fascism arose in the very countries where its influence was least felt—in Italy and Germany where neo-idealism and romanticism proved immune to positivism's wan appeal to dispassion. To be more exact, one might even argue that Fascism was actually a revolt against positivism. Wherever Fascism's roots are to be found—in Italy's synthesis of syndicalism and nationalism, in the messianic quest for "the Third Rome," in the primitive Christianity of Sorel's *ricorso* (recurrence); or, in the case of the other classic example, in Germany's characteristic, restless *Sehnsucht* (longing), in its intoxicating life-worship, or its passionate *Völkisch* ideology—Fascism's central ethos invoked an idealistic vitalism completely at odds with the mechanistic temper of science. We need only go to the official "Doctrine of Fascism," published in 1932 in the *Enciclopedia Italiana*, a frequently quoted essay signed by Mussolini but actually written by Gentile. Here we are told that the Fascist State is "the result of the general reaction of modern times against the flabby materialistic positivism of the nineteenth century."[18]

[17] Van Wyck Brooks, *Symposium*, p. 1; *Second Symposium*, II, 256; Adler, p. 128; significantly, a few months before Adler's attack a respected Catholic academic journal asked William Y. Elliott to comment on his earlier thesis (1927) regarding the relationship of pragmatism to Fascism; see Elliott, "The Pragmatic Revolt in Politics: Twenty Years in Retrospect," *Review of Politics*, II (Jan. 1940), 1-11; see also Thomas P. Neill, "Democracy's Intellectual Fifth Column," *Catholic World*, CLV (May 1942), 150-55.

[18] Mussolini, "The Doctrine of Fascism," in *Communism, Fascism, and Democracy: The Theoretical Foundations*, ed. Carl Cohen (New York, 1962), p. 350; for an incisive discussion of the "anti-positivist revolt" in Europe, see H. Stuart Hughes, *Consciousness and Society: The Reconstruction of European Social Thought, 1890-1930* (Vintage edn., New York, 1961), pp. 33-66; for the intellectual background of Nazism, see George L. Mosse, *The Crisis of German Ideology: Intellectual Origins of the Third Reich* (New York, 1964); Fritz Stern, *The Politics of Cultural Despair* (Berkeley, 1961); for Italy, see Dante Germino, "Italian Fascism in the History of Political Thought," *Midwest Journal of Political Science*, VIII (May 1964), 109-26; Jack J. Roth, "The Roots of Italian Fascism: Sorel and Sorelismo," *Journal of Modern History*, XXXIX (March 1967), 30-45.

In describing Fascism as the product of nineteenth-century positivism, American Catholics either overlooked or deliberately slighted the anti-materialist and anti-rational bias of its ideology. And in doing so they ignored the spiritual content of the phenomenon. This is not to say Fascism should be seen as a "secular religion"—the epithet so often applied to Communism—for Italian Fascism scorned all teleological chiliasms and stressed instead the sufficiency of endless "movement." Yet there is much in the emotional side of Fascism to indicate that it appealed to a genuine spiritual hunger. In theory at least, Fascism attempted to offer a reunifying faith to mold together what modern science had torn asunder. Science, by bringing about a sharp division between feeling and thought, between faith and reason, left man with "a heap of broken images" (T. S. Eliot). Fascism would provide an answer to this paralysis of rational doubt by restoring the will to believe. In this sense, Fascism was anything but an expression of the scientific mind, with its cautious skepticism, its systematic technique and cult of objectivity. On the contrary, Fascism was profoundly subjective, with a deep faith in will, instinct, and the illusion of destiny. In theory it was closer to political mysticism than to pragmatic methodology, though in practice it attempted to avoid both these extremes. Ernst Nolte, in terming Fascism a "metaphysical phenomenon," catches its essential ambivalence in the succinct assertion that "Fascism is at the same time resistance to practical transcendence and struggle against theoretical transcendence." Fascism is the simultaneous striving against social transcendence which, if realized, would dissipate the dialectic of conflict; and against individual transcendence which, if fulfilled, would destroy the organic coherence of man, nature, and society. Of course such a grasp of Fascism treats it as the highest refinement of intellectual ideas, with small allowance for the way in which a dictator like Mussolini could manipulate and pervert the craving for religiosity. Nevertheless, since Catholic thinkers in America viewed Fascism basically as a philosophical movement, it is legitimate to question on this ground their narrow interpretation of it as the triumph of scientific materialism over spiritual consciousness. The obverse seems closer to the truth when we read in the official Italian statement that "Fascism believes, now and always, in holiness and heroism," and that it represents a "negation of historical materialism" and a rejection of the "materialistic conception of 'happiness.'" Mussolini's ideological opportunism notwithstanding, there is little reason to doubt the sincerity of the classic definition of Fascism put forth by Gentile:

> Fascism is a religious conception in which man is seen in his immanent relationship with a supreme law and with an objective Will that transcends the particular individual and raises him to conscious membership of a spiritual society. Whoever has seen in the religious politics of the Fascist regime nothing but mere opportunism has not understood that Fascism besides being a system of government is also, and above all, a system of thought.[19]

It should not surprise us that during the war Catholics would refer to the governments in Italy and Germany with the same disdain reserved for the Soviet Union. But what is interesting is that this belated condemnation amounted to almost a redefinition of Fascism. During the earlier period Catholic thinkers took pains to distinguish Fascism from Communism; in the war years Fascism emerges in the Catholic mind as the heretical twin of Communism, the first curse of the misbegotten mind of naturalism. In a previous chapter I discussed how much of the earlier Catholic apology represented an unholy marriage of piety and *realpolitik* which tolerated Fascism because allegedly it did not lay claim to the human soul. Significantly this secular rationale prevailed in some Catholic circles even after the attack on Ethiopia and the Italian anti-Semitic decrees. As late as 1938, for example, editor James Magner felt compelled to instruct *Commonweal*'s readers on the controversial question of "The Church and Fascism." Maintaining that Fascism "as a cultural system" was "not predicated on atheism," Magner argued that the Church's policy toward any regime must be one of "realism," a policy that did not necessarily imply approval of "the political or ethical claims of individual rulers and states." But, he added, "ample justification" for the Church's relations with Fascist governments could readily be "found in the example of Christ 'who consorted with sinners' . . . ." Then, summing up in one sentence the attitude that characterized the Catholic position all along, Magner boldly declared: "The Church is far larger than any

[19] Ernst Nolte, *Three Faces of Fascism* (New York, 1965), p. 453; Mussolini, "Doctrine of Fascism," p. 351.

political system, and it learned from experience that consistency is not the chief of its virtues."[20]

Since a faithful consistency did not trouble the Church even during the war, few American Catholics evinced great concern over the lingering clerical Fascism in Europe or even over the Pope's conspicuous silence (up to 1945) on the outcome of the conflict. Again, as in the twenties and thirties, it was European Catholics who were the first to speak out. The French Catholic Georges Bernanos stated the predicament with unflinching courage in *Commonweal*: "Nothing is more difficult to speak about than fascism, and particularly about fascist Catholics, without appearing unjust toward brothers from whom we are separated, people say, only by differing political ideas." In his three *Commonweal* essays, Bernanos intimated a painful truth about the levity of political Catholicism: when a religious dogma can embrace incompatible or even neutral positions with respect to the defeat of Mussolini and Hitler, one can only wonder whether the dogma offers any insight into the meaning of Fascism.[21]

But in the end it is not an inconsistency of position which vitiates the Catholic thesis but an inconsistency in language. Indeed if one compares the Catholic apology in the twenties and early thirties with the criticisms of Fascism during the war, it almost seems Catholic writers were using two different vocabularies. When approving Mussolini's government they used the language of pragmatism; when condemning it they resorted to the language of metaphysics. Such linguistic manipulation suggests that for most Catholics Fascism was not a matter of truth but of consequences. Thus few Catholic writers in America made an attempt to understand the doctrinal essence of Fascism—strange behavior for those who believe in the doctrine of "revealed" truth.

LIBERAL PERSPECTIVES: BETWEEN MARXISM AND PROGRESSIVISM

In many respects the liberal and Marxist interpretations of Fascism were similar. This should not surprise us, since much of

---

[20] *Commonweal*, XXVIII (Sept. 2, 1938), 462-64.

[21] Guenther Levy, *The Catholic Church and Nazi Germany* (New York, 1964), p. 329; Georges Bernanos, "Notes on Fascism, I," *Commonweal*, XXXVII (March 19, 1943), 534-36; for parts II and III, see *ibid.* (March 26, 1943), 560-62 (April 2, 1943), 587-88.

modern American liberalism evolved from a philosophy of history which, deriving from Darwinism and pragmatism, presupposed a naturalistic theory of man, an environmental theory of progress, and a philosophical theory of relativism. Because of their materialist premises, most liberals could not subscribe to the religious and humanist interpretations of Fascism as the bankruptcy of the spirit rather than of the system. Yet if liberals could not view Fascism as moral degeneration, neither could they accept the deterministic implications in the Marxist point of view. The traditional values of progressivism prevented liberals from either reaching for supernatural solutions or calling for revolutionary conclusions.

The liberal writer who came closest to the Marxist analysis was Max Lerner, a prolific scholar whose radical mentors were Veblen and Beard. Lerner rejected the Frank-Mumford-MacLeish thesis and he brushed aside Dorothy Thompson's and Walter Lippmann's argument that Fascism represented the tyranny of the majority spurred on by the expansion of the "providential state." Doubtful that Fascism signified a deranged moral upheaval, he was also skeptical of Hermann Rauschning's highly popular *The Revolution in Nihilism*. Lerner conceded that Fascism appeared to manifest a variety of tendencies, and he acknowledged that the road to dictatorship in Italy and Germany had been prepared by economic crisis, political stagnation, and psychological panic, all of which allowed Fascists to drum up middle-class support and win over the military. But the driving force behind it all, Lerner insisted, was the desperate power of capital. Admitting that Marxism had been blind to the forces of nationalism and human irrationality, and conceding that it had ignored the role of the middle class, on whom the immense psychic burden of capitalism fell, Lerner nonetheless refused to see Fascism as either a middle-class movement or an authentic intellectual revolt. His commitment to the Marxian analysis basically unshaken,[22] Lerner arrived at the obvious but useless definition of Fascism as "the bastard successor of Trotsky's dream of 'permanent revolution!' "[23]

[22] "Its [Marxism's] great strength lies in its theory of history, its method of class analysis, its well-knit interrelation of the aspects of society, its sense of direction, its insistence on the unbroken web of theory and practice. It is still, for all its shortcomings, the most useful and illuminating body of social thought in our world." Max Lerner, "Marxism: Six Errors," in *It Is Later Than You Think* (New York, 1943 edn.), p. 72

[23] Max Lerner, "The Pattern of Dictatorship," in *Dictatorship in the*

In contrast to Lerner, Alfred Bingham, John Chamberlain, and Stuart Chase believed that Fascism sprang from middle-class anxieties rather than capitalist power; that it represented not so much a historic reaction as a genuine social revolution gone sour; that it was, in Chase's words, "an *alternative* for an abdicated capitalism, not a *prop*"; and that, because Fascism posed a "third way" out of the depression crisis, its future was by no means predictable. In the early thirties the *New Republic* and *Nation* also subscribed to the non-Marxist position, maintaining that Fascism was anti-capitalist in origin and that the Fascists themselves actually seized power and were not placed there by men of marks and lire. Yet after 1935 the *New Republic* and *Nation* came around to the Communist position, now admitting that, regardless of the origins of Fascism, the German and Italian dictatorships were sustaining by violence the capitalist order.[24]

By the outbreak of World War II many writers converged on big business as the malignant handmaiden of Fascism. In fact, after Pearl Harbor liberals believed the war against European Fascism must be matched by a domestic war against monopoly power. "I don't like to over-use the word 'fascist,'" wrote the young New Dealer and head of the Office of Price Administration, Chester Bowles, "but it does seem to me the only phrase that can be applied to the kind of thinking which I ran into among some groups in business." That corporate power should be equated with Fascism was the thesis of Kemper Simpson's *Big Business, Efficiency and Fascism* (1941), and Robert Brady's *Business as a System of Power* (1943). In both works the reader is told he need look no further than the oligopolistic structure of the Italian and German economies to find the causes of Fascism. Simpson's book is especially significant since it reflects a New Deal attitude toward Fascism. His research derived from his own investigations while a member of the Federal Trade Commission and Roosevelt's Temporary National Economic Committee. In brief, Simpson attempted to demonstrate that in all countries large business associations restricted competition, lusted after wasteful specula-

---

Modern World, ed. Guy Stanton Ford (Minneapolis, 1935), pp. 3-20; id., *It Is Later Than You Think* (New York, 1943), pp. 31-43; id., *Ideas for the Ice Age* (New York, 1941), pp. 161-79, 407-11.

[24] Warren, *Liberals and Communism*, pp. 91-102; id., "Alfred Bingham and the Paradox of Liberalism," *Historian*, xxviii (Feb. 1966), 252-67.

tive profits, cut back production and increased unemployment, thereby paving the way for a Fascist *coup d'état*. This was as true of Italy as of Germany, Simpson argued, for it was Mussolini who first proclaimed "the end of free competition" and first perceived that a "trustified capitalism turns to the State."[25]

To a certain extent liberals and Marxists shared a common perspective. Accepting a materialist conception of history, both dug beneath the surface to uncover the sordid economic basis of Fascism and both studied Fascism in terms of historical development rather than moral predicament. When they went from diagnosis to prognosis, however, irreconcilable differences emerged. Believing Fascism arose inexorably from the original sin of property, Marxists were convinced that nothing short of proletarian revolution could arrest its development; believing Fascism represented only a perverted form of consolidated property, liberals were certain that institutional reform would be sufficient. Lerner, for example, maintained that rational economic planning could cleanse capitalism, while Simpson settled for nothing less than a restoration of *laissez-faire*. What this suggests is that American liberals drew not upon Marx but upon the American progressive tradition in order to assess the meaning of Fascism. Indeed in the case of Simpson it is the Wilsonian suspicion of big business that emerges: if Fascism signified the tyranny of the trusts, the spirit of Brandeis would suffice to break up the empires of Olivetti and Krupp along with Standard Oil. To make the world safe from Fascism was to make it safe for competitive capitalism.

Certainly not all liberals focused only on the economic foundations of Fascism. Several writers, particularly scholars in the fields of history and political science, attempted to ascertain the meaning of Fascism without recourse to either Marxist or Progressive categories of understanding. One example of this scholarship was the anthology, *Dictatorship in the Modern World* (1935, 1939), edited by the historian Guy Stanton Ford. With the exception of Lerner, most contributors viewed Fascism in light of historical tradition and parallel. Professor Ford believed that only the techniques and expressions of historic despotism had

[25] Bowles is quoted in Alonzo L. Hanby, "Sixty Million Jobs and the People's Revolution: Liberals, the New Deal, and World War II," *Historian*, xxx (Aug. 1968), 581-82; Kemper Simpson, *Big Business, Efficiency and Fascism* (New York, 1941), pp. 12, 16.

changed and that therefore modern dictatorships were based on the "old forces" of propaganda and myth. Writing on Mussolini's Italy, Henry B. Spencer referred to Caesar and the deterioration of the Roman Republic, while Harold Deutsch, writing on Hitler's regime, spoke of Germany's national character, her political immaturity, and other "precedents" which were "in conformity with the general pattern of dictatorship." None of the authors was prepared to define Fascism in terms of the classical concept of dictatorship, nor did they try to demonstrate that Mussolini and Hitler were lineal descendants of the despots of the past. Nevertheless their essays suggested a deterministic interpretation of Italian and German history which tended to stress the forces of continuity rather than the factors of change.[26]

By the end of the thirties few liberal writers could continue to see Fascism solely in light of historical analogy. In 1939, the American Philosophical Society sponsored a symposium on "The Totalitarian State." The substitution of the word "totalitarian" for "dictatorship" indicated that a new vocabulary would have to be formulated to analyze satisfactorily an unprecedented phenomenon. In an address revealingly entitled "The Novelty of Totalitarianism in the History of Western Civilization," historian Carlton J. H. Hayes observed that, even though the pattern of dictatorship remained a "constant" in history, the twentieth-century variety differed in kind as well as degree. The main difference, Hayes noted, was that modern dictators came from plebeian social backgrounds, their movements inspired mass enthusiasm, and their ideologies filled spuriously the void left by the decline of traditional religion and Western values.[27]

Most of the above writers tended to see Fascism as either a variant of historical dictatorship or as a species of modern totalitarianism. This over-schematic approach resulted in blurring the distinctive features of different expressions of Fascism within different countries. In this connection it is interesting that fourteen years later, when the American Academy of Arts and Science sponsored another conference on "Totalitarianism," references to Mussolini's Italy were few and far between. This is not surprising, for in light of the ghastly realities of Nazi Germany and Soviet Russia, Fascist Italy seemed to be a peculiar kind of incomplete

[26] *Dictatorship in the Modern World*, pp. vii, 21-78.
[27] "Symposium on the Totalitarian State," *Proceedings of the American Philosophical Society*, LXXXII (Feb. 23, 1940), 91-102.

totalitarianism lacking those very morbid traits that intrigue intellectuals: brutality, terror, and an incredibly credible "mystical imperative" (Alex Inkeles). Italy had no Buchenwalds, and instead of gas ovens and firing squads it could only offer castor oil and the spectacle of prisoners being forced to swallow live toads. But Fascist Italy, which had attracted so much attention in America in the twenties and early thirties, was slighted not only because it was now regarded as a nontotalitarian dictatorship. The real difference between the 1939 and 1953 symposia can be summed up in one word: Stalinism.[28]

Be that as it may, several liberal writers in the thirties and early forties addressed themselves specifically to the problem of Fascism apart from the question of totalitarianism. One such study was Stephen Raushenbush's *The March of Fascism* (1939). Raushenbush felt moved to write an account of Fascism because he feared that an oblivious America was far from immune to its symptoms and because he believed it arose from common problems shared by all western nations. He discussed all the familiar background factors that gave rise to Mussolini's *coup d'état*—frustrated nationalism, economic crisis, political instability—but when it came to defining Fascism precisely, Raushenbush could only say that it resulted from the breakdown of the fragile liberal Italian state: "Fascism was and is a substitute for a non-operating democracy." While Raushenbush provided a helpful survey of events in Italy and Germany, his suggestion that Fascism arose as an answer to the failure of political institutions merely confused the effect with the cause.[29]

THREE AUTHORS IN SEARCH OF A REALITY: LIPPMANN, NIEBUHR, AND DEWEY

In order to achieve a better understanding of the liberal interpretation of Fascism we must turn to the three leading liberal intellectuals of the period: Walter Lippmann, Reinhold Niebuhr, and John Dewey. As noted earlier, in the twenties Lippmann re-

[28] *Totalitarianism*, ed. Carl J. Friedrich (Universal Library edn., New York, 1964). Whereas many American scholars used the term "Stalinism" to describe Russia after World War II, few used "Hitlerism" or "Mussolinianism" to describe Germany or Italy before the war. This is ironic in light of the fact that while the Soviet Union continued long after Stalin, no Fascist regime ever survived its leader.

[29] Stephen Raushenbush, *The March of Fascism* (New Haven, 1939), p. 164.

buked Mussolini's government as a violation of moral philosophy and political civility. Not until the rise of Hitler, however, did Lippmann devote much attention to European Fascism. Observing Hitler maneuver to power in 1933, Lippmann, whose major concern was the implications of Nazi revisionism for world peace, believed that in both Rome and in Berlin the advent to power was facilitated by "impotent and demoralized" parliamentarians, and that while Italy's Fascism had become "increasingly realistic and conservative," Germany's was "still highly romantic, nervous, and confused." Then the following year, when Hitler's power seemed secured, Lippmann optimistically announced: "The doctrine preached by the Fascists that a nation can think and feel with one mind and one heart . . . is contrary to all human experience. For a short time, in a mood of exaltation or under the crushing power of terrorism, a nation may appear to be of one mind. But that cannot possibly last, and among highly civilized people it has neither been expected nor desired. . . . The idea that these armies of Black Shirts and Brown Shirts represent some great new twentieth-century invention can be entertained only by those who have never read any history." The idea of Fascism as a stubborn attempt to go against the grain of human history would be an article of faith for Lippmann until the outbreak of World War II.[30]

It was in *The Good Society* (1937) that Lippmann first addressed himself to the problem of European totalitarianism. It is here that he defines Fascism as a form of collectivism resulting from the disorders and deficiencies of nineteenth-century liberalism. According to Lippmann, economic planning was the central principle of totalitarianism, both Left and Right. Focusing on the dangers of the omnipotent state, he showed little patience with the intellectual background of Fascism. Its ideology of social reconstruction and its semi-mystical doctrines of transcendence did not concern him. To Lippmann the reality of Fascism was its power to mobilize people for the sole purpose of war and conquest: "Fascism is nothing less, and probably nothing more, than the latest and completest development of the nation in arms. It

[30] Walter Lippmann, *Interpretations, 1933-1935* (New York, 1936), p. 322; "Vindication of Democracy," (July 5, 1934), in *The Essential Lippmann*, eds. James Lare and Clinton Rossiter (Vintage edn., New York, 1965), pp. 229-30.

is militarism without qualification preparing for a totalitarian war."[31]

Lippmann also believed Fascism doomed to a short life. His conviction stemmed from what he believed to be the illusions of collectivism in general and of Fascism in particular. As Lippmann read history, collectivism was more in accord with primitive societies which had no need of economic specialization. Modern industrialism, on the other hand, required a division of labor and a market economy, neither of which could be realized in a society of total regimentation. Moreover Fascist regimes, claiming to last a thousand years, required a continual supply of fresh, talented leadership. But the emergence of such resourceful men, Lippmann pointed out, will be impossible in a Fascist state that preaches the sterile principle of absolute obedience. Thus the coerced uniformity of collectivism would prove incompatible with modern economic diversity, while the absolute conformity of Fascism would serve only to stifle curiosity, imagination, and intellect. How a government of servile people could produce a cadre of great leaders was for Lippmann the central "paradox of Fascism."[32]

Strangely enough, Lippmann's interpretation of Fascism suggested a kind of inverted Marxism. For his analysis rested on the following assumptions: that the economic mode of collectivist production determined the totalitarian state; that Fascism was keyed to inevitable expansion and war; and that Mussolini's and Hitler's regimes carried within them their own contradictions or "paradoxes." Yet Lippmann's ultimate conviction of Fascism's inner deterioration rested on an ethical rather than an economic determinism. More precisely, Lippmann could not accept the Fascist conception of man as a docile object who could be molded into uniformity. With dismay he quoted Mussolini as saying that Fascism "demands remaking not the forms of human life, but the contents: man, character, faith. And to this end it demands a discipline and authority which descends within the spirit and then dominates unchallenged." Believing instead in the inviolability of the human person, in the spiritual and natural rights of man, and in man's indomitable will to be free, Lippmann was

[31] Walter Lippmann, *The Good Society* (Universal Library edn., New York, 1965), 229-30.
[32] *Ibid.*, pp. 57-63.

convinced that Fascism "must fail, because it rests upon a radically false conception of the economy, of law, of government, and of human nature."[33]

Lippmann was sadly mistaken in his belief that the wonderful contrariety of the human spirit would suffice to undermine Fascism, and it was not long before he turned from mankind in general to the "people of light and leading" who would save the world from totalitarianism because of their respect for the "self-evident truths" of natural law—the elitist theme that later emerges in *The Public Philosophy* (1955).[34] As for the problem of Fascism, Lippmann's definition was based on questionable moral and economic assumptions. His ethical interpretation of Fascism as a pagan attempt to ground out the moral character of man offered an admirable indictment; but such a view prevented him from appreciating Fascism's own spiritual appeal, an appeal which might in part account for its mass emotional élan and which might, in any case, explain why Fascism was not to collapse from within, as Lippmann predicted. Even more questionable is Lippmann's assumption that Fascism could be explained by subsuming it under the general category of "collectivism." Reading Lippmann's interpretation, one comes away with the impression that economic collectivism gave rise to Fascism. In reality the opposite is true: Fascism antedated collectivism; corporatism was the result of the Fascist seizure of power, not the cause of it. It can be said, of course, that without the prerequisite of economic centralization neither Mussolini nor Hitler could have succeeded in consolidating power. But since nearly all major western countries experienced such centralization, including the United States, this tendency fails to explain why Fascism emerged in some countries and not in others.

Where Lippmann believed that Fascism would fail because it was based on a false conception of human nature, Niebuhr believed it would succeed because it revealed human nature in its truest light. A tough-minded pessimist with a deep sense of sin, Niebuhr was certain that liberals would be unable to comprehend Fascism because of their refusal to look evil straight in the eye. In *Moral Man and Immoral Society* (1932), he severely criticized

[33] *Ibid.*, pp. 99, 388.

[34] Although *The Public Philosophy* was not published until 1955, Lippmann began writing it after the Munich Conference ("that fateful summer of 1938") and then shelved it for the duration of the war.

Italian Socialists for allegedly taking a naive pacifist stand against early Fascism. For Niebuhr, the spectacle of Fascism dramatized the need to accept coercion in human affairs, the need to recognize the inescapability of conflict. Only when liberals and Socialists disabuse themselves of their rational ideals can a true anti-Fascist resistance begin.[35]

Niebuhr's definition of Fascism combined Christian realism with radical Marxism. In the early thirties he perceived it as an example of the collective egoism of the rapacious privileged classes, whose actions demonstrated the religious reality of evil as well as the social reality of exploitation. In these years Niebuhr was full of cataclysmic forebodings, as indicated in his chilling *Reflections on the End of an Era* (1934). His message spelled doom: "Next to the futility of liberalism we may set down the inevitability of Fascism as a practical certainty in every western nation." Fascism was a lesson, Niebuhr warned, not only in the class realities of industrial society but in the sentimental illusions of progressive history. As events in Germany demonstrated, the development of higher civilization only cloaks the savage tribal passions within the soul of every man. Fascism has stripped away the veneer, laying bare the Hebraic laws of Moses as well as the historical laws of Marx.[36]

But Niebuhr's commitment to Marxism was always tempered by his suspicion of redemptive ideologies and by his awareness of the aggressive character of all social classes, even the proletariat. Possibly the events in Stalin's Russia caused him to reassess his early conviction that Fascism was the death agony of the old order and that social evil could be ascribed to a single class of capitalist predators. Whatever the case, by 1936 he repudiated the Marxist viewpoint, stating that the "radical interpretation of fascism as essentially a contrivance for the preservation of a dying capitalistic civilization is inaccurate. . . . The real source of fascism lies in the social resentments and the political confusion of lower middle-class life." By shifting the focus to the *petite bourgeoisie*, Niebuhr

[35] Reinhold Niebuhr, *Moral Man and Immoral Society* (New York, 1932), pp. 268-69.

[36] Id., *Reflections on the End of an Era* (New York, 1934); Niebuhr's reference to "the inevitability of Fascism" is quoted in Arthur Schlesinger, Jr., "Reinhold Niebuhr's Role in Political Thought," in *Reinhold Niebuhr: His Religious, Social, and Political Thought*, eds. Charles Kegley and Robert Bretall (New York, 1961), p. 137; for Niebuhr on Nazi Germany, see Daniel D. Williams, "Niebuhr and Liberalism," *ibid.*, pp. 199-200.

was moving away from the catastrophic forebodings that marked his earlier writings on Fascism. Niebuhr also began to equate Fascism with Communism. The cult of the state and the cult of the proletariat, he maintained, were but two expressions of the same illusion of perfectionism. In addition, the "spiritual kinship" of the two movements was "illustrated by the fact that many of the best nazis were formerly communists." It was for this reason that Niebuhr could not accept the Pope's appeal to all religions to oppose Communism while remaining indifferent to Fascism. Referring to Pius XI, Niebuhr asserted that the "axe and rods that he blesses are as red with blood as the flag and hammer and sickle that he curses."[37]

In the late thirties Niebuhr shifted from the vocabulary of Socialism to that of Protestantism to describe reactionary dictatorships in Europe. Fascism was "a pagan religion of tribal self-glorification" that "defies all the universal standards of justice which ages of a Christian and humanistic culture have woven into the fabric of our civilization"; a "maniacal fury" that "threatens the Jewish race with annihilation" and subjects other people of Europe to the slavery of "the 'master race' "; an imperial venture based "upon the very negation of justice rather than upon that minimal justice which even ancient empires achieved." Obviously Niebuhr's descriptions suffered from a lack of precision and an excess of passion. Nevertheless he came closer than most liberal intellectuals in assessing accurately the dangers of Fascism. When World War II erupted he had no illusions. Adopting the existential ethic, he set about the "tragic business of resisting tyranny and establishing justice by coercion."[38]

John Dewey could accept neither the dim moral verities of Lippmann nor the dark tragic visions of Niebuhr. Among American liberals Dewey was one of the few who seemed unshaken by Fascism. One finds in Dewey no crisis of values, no change of vocabulary, no shift in philosophical position. Instead of fear and trembling, Dewey reasserted his faith in human intelligence and scientific control, an exercise in methodological exhortation, if not ideological direction.

[37] Reinhold Niebuhr, "Pawns for Fascism—Our Lower Middle Class," *American Scholar*, VI (Spring 1937), 147; id., "Shall Protestants Accept Pope's Invitation?" *Christian Century*, LIII (Nov. 25, 1936), 1550-52.

[38] Id., "If America Enters The War . . ." *Christian Century*, LVII (Dec. 18, 1940), 1578-80.

Perhaps Dewey's unwavering faith can be partly explained by the fact that he paid so little attention to the problem. As we have seen, Dewey never had much regard for Mussolini's "experiment"; yet even in the thirties when Fascism seemed to be overrunning Europe he devoted no more than a paragraph or two on the subject. In his prodigious writings he spent considerable time exposing the fallacies in Marxism's "monistic block-universe theory of social causation," but when he addressed himself to the ideology of Fascism it was only in the manner of an occasional aside.[39]

Despite his scant treatment of the subject, Dewey's scattered remarks deserve attention. First of all, Dewey observed that Fascism fed upon a herd-like instinct for hate and intolerance, and he noted disturbingly that it held great attraction for European youth. Several explanations accounted for this behavior: the manipulation of national pride and fear, the desire to avoid political responsibility, the cultural tendencies to submission and obedience. But Dewey believed there also existed "love for novelty" in some new "idealistic faith" which gives people "a sense of sharing in creative activities." To the extent that Fascism combined nationalism and Socialism, it represented an "emotional fusion" which allowed people to enjoy "a sense of union with others." Something of a collectivist himself, Dewey was forced to admit Fascism reflected a yearning for community. Yet this communalistic appeal must not be mistaken for genuine fraternity, Dewey warned, for Fascism was really a perverted solidarity promoted merely by exorcising scapegoats within and phantom enemies without. In short, Fascism was founded on fear and hate rather than reason and love.[40]

But Fascism was far more than a politically manufactured paranoia. To account for its collectivist mystique Dewey did not resort to a Marxian analysis of class tensions or a sociopsychological investigation of mass neuroses. Instead he turned to the educational culture of Europe, and particularly to German idealism. Accordingly, just as Hegel's organic idealism emerged as a response to the nineteenth-century theory of atomistic human nature, so did Hitler's *Weltanschauung* arise as an answer to the "spiritual" craving of the German mind. Though Hitler was a pseudo-Hegelian, his message appealed to the characteristic Ger-

[39] John Dewey, *Freedom and Culture* (New York, 1939), p. 88.
[40] *Ibid.*, pp. 36-38.

man attempt to break down the dualism of the real and ideal in order to achieve unity of mind and spirit. The German hunger for the "absolute spirit," Dewey observed, explains Nazism's return to primitive Teutonic mythology and nature worship. Hitler was forever reminding Germany that the weakness which produced its defeat was, in Dewey's words, " 'spiritual' (*geistige*) and that therefore its redemption must also first be spiritual." It was this turning to the inner world of instinct, of blood and race, passion and impulse, which provided the link between German idealism and Nazi irrationalism; and the transition from Hegel's exalted State to Hitler's mythical folk community constituted the political expression of that imprisoned mentality.[41]

In ascertaining the meaning of Fascism it is obvious Dewey was carrying on his life-long war against Kantian Idealism. Twenty-five years after he wrote his major critique of Kant he maintained that his original dictum—"The chief mark of distinctively German civilization is its combination of self-conscious idealism with unsurpassed technical efficiency and organization"—applied to National Socialism as well. For Dewey, Fascism was a product of the German mind whose passionate intensity had descended from the intellectual to the emotional level, from the divine to the demonic, from Hegel to Hitler.[42]

Now all this suggests an interesting philosophical digression, but it also suggests how little attention Dewey gave to the problem. When Dewey addressed himself to Fascism he merely projected his own earlier philosophical preoccupations. Thus we find the most tenacious naturalist looking not to social reality

[41] Id., *German Philosophy and Politics* (rev. edn., New York, 1942), pp. 13-49.

[42] *Ibid.*, p. 37. Like Herbert Marcuse, however, Dewey saw clearly that Nazism was actually a misapplication of Hegel's ideas: "It will be recalled that Hegel attacked the Kantian separation of what is and what ought to be, of the actual and the ideal. He declared that what is actual is the rational and what is rational becomes in virtue of its own activity the actual. But in his dialectic scheme, knowledge of their identity exists only in philosophy as the ultimate manifestation of Absolute Spirit. Any outward manifestation of the identity has to be left to the majestic onward procession of that spirit. Hitler's philosophy, or world-outlook, is that the identity of the ideal with hard fact may be effected here and now, by means of combining faith in the ideal to which destiny has called the German people with force which is thoroughly organized to control every aspect of life, economic, cultural, artistic, educational, as well as military and political." *Ibid.*, p. 26.

472

but to the loftiest, most abstract ideas to account for a political phenomenon. Indeed, when Dewey spoke of the dangers of Fascism in America it was the economic structure he saw as crucial; but when he discussed National Socialism he ascended to the rarefied peak of German consciousness—with hardly a side glance at the reactionary movements in other countries, especially Italy where "classical" Fascism was first conceived. Whether Fascism should be interpreted as the abnormality of a single country or as a universal tendency, whether it should be regarded as the culmination of philosophical ideas or as a product of the social environment—whether, in short, it was a disease of the head or of the stomach—Dewey did not say.[43]

Nor did Dewey suggest what course of action Americans must take to resist Fascism in Europe. Unlike Lippmann and Niebuhr, he did not believe Americans had to fall back upon moral philosophy or move forward to existential theology in order to find the ethical will to oppose Mussolini and Hitler. A staunch anti-interventionist, he simply reiterated his faith in human nature and rational intelligence. As war approached he had six clear words of advice: "No Matter What Happens—Stay Out." A few months after the outbreak of hostilities he could only say: "I hesitate to predict anything whatsoever about the outcome of the present war." Thereafter he lapsed into silence.[44]

Dewey's reluctance to predict the outcome of the war suggests a great deal about the political helplessness of pragmatic liberals when confronted with a movement like Fascism. It was not so much that the pragmatic comprehension of Fascism lacked moral vision—even the most value-boasting moralist could be found in the camp of reaction or isolationism. The real fault with pragmatism is the *ex post facto* nature of its epistemology. Those liberals in the twenties who were willing to regard Fascism as an "experiment"—and who did the same for Communism in the thirties—were awaiting the certainty of hindsight when what was needed was the wisdom of foresight. Surely this is the most ironic flow in the political philosophy of James and Dewey.

[43] See, for example, Dewey's review of Alfred Bingham's *Insurgent America* in *Common Sense*, IV (Dec. 1935), 23.

[44] *Common Sense*, VII (March 1939), 11; *ibid.*, VIII (Dec. 1939), 9-11. Actually Dewey did modify his anti-individualism in response to totalitarianism and war in 1939. See the recent study by A. H. Somjee, *The Political Theory of John Dewey* (New York, 1968), pp. 40-41.

Pragmatism prides itself in making knowledge useful; yet when confronted with totalitarianism it offers the most useless knowledge imaginable. What one needs to know, in evaluating a movement like Fascism where there are no self-correcting democratic mechanisms, is not retrospective knowledge but some sense beforehand of what the consequences will be. Because the *New Republic* could not predict the results of Fascism in 1927, it suspended judgment; because Dewey could not predict the outcome of war against Fascism in 1939, he suspended commitment. When applied to the question of Fascism, America's pragmatic philosophy becomes painfully reminiscent of Hobbes' remark about truth—hell seen too late.[45]

FASCISM: A PROBLEM IN INTELLECTUAL HISTORY AND BEHAVIORAL SCIENCE

It is ironic that Dewey, who believed fervently that ideas were only instrumental expressions of a given social matrix, perceived Fascism not in the light of its social context but solely as a legacy of intellectual history. In 1942, when he added the new introduction to his *German Philosophy and Politics* (1915), he entitled the chapter "The One World of Hitler's National Socialism" in order to contrast it with the "Two Worlds" of German Kantian and Hegelian philosophy. Here Fascism is described within the interior structure of German ideas, not, as we might expect of a pragmatist, through an environmental analysis of the origins of ideas. Once the internal affinity between German philosophy and National Socialism had been established, Fascism emerged as an affair of the mind, a paradigm of human thought, the vertiginous climax of Germany's cultural heritage.[46]

That Fascism represented the tyranny of mind over the limits of reason was the conclusion reached by several other outstanding American writers. George Santayana, for example, also reissued his earlier *Egotism in German Philosophy* (1916) with a new preface and postscript written in 1939. Egotism—"subjectivity in thought and willfulness in morals"—Santayana regarded as the

[45] In fairness, Dewey's position in the early months of World War II was much more than a simple pragmatic reflex. In order to fully appreciate his dilemma one cannot ignore the enthusiastic support he had given years earlier to America's entry into World War I, a wayward adventure he never got over.

[46] Dewey, *German Philosophy*, pp. 13-49.

474

mirage of German philosophy. A misty delusion, egotism led man to the consuming conviction that will controls reality ("Je suis, donc, tu n'es pas"), thereby causing him to revolt insanely against the finitude of his existence. But it was Peter Viereck who went on to demonstrate that the romantic "madness" of German philosophy actually culminated in Nazism. In *Metapolitics: From the Romantics to Hitler* (1941), Viereck maintained that it was the "Wagnerian idea-heritage" of German romanticism that unleashed the intellectual forces of the Nazi mind, namely the elemental Faustian hunger for the fullness of life. All these writers obviously treated Fascism as a study in the history of ideas. But it is equally obvious they saw the phenomenon as peculiar to Germany and to the demonically defiant German mind. In this sense, Fascism was treated as a national expression characteristic of Germany alone. For a broader discussion of European Fascism, one that devotes full attention to Italy as well as to Germany, and one that treats Fascism as a cultural crisis of western civilization itself, we must turn to another book written on the eve of World War II.[47]

Melvin Rader's *No Compromise: The Conflict between Two Worlds* (1939) was the first American book solely devoted to a systematic analysis of the intellectual origins of Fascism. A professor of philosophy, the author stated at the outset that Fascism cannot be studied in isolation, that one cannot neglect "the constant interplay between spirit and matter, man and nature, thought and things." But after this cursory acknowledgment of environmental forces, and even after suggesting that Fascist ideology may only be an "afterthought" or "window dressing," he treats the philosophical foundations of Fascism with utmost seriousness and with no reference to social milieu. Uncertain of the role of ideas in history, Rader was nonetheless certain that ideas are consequential.[48]

Rader's basic thesis is Fascism as a "flight from reason." Accordingly, Sorel's "myths," Nietzsche's "vital lies," and Wagner's "ethical intuition" supposedly presaged the doctrine of Fascism,

[47] George Santayana, *Egotism in German Philosophy* (New York, 1940), pp. ix, 153; Peter Viereck, *Metapolitics: The Roots of the Nazi Mind* (New York, 1965). This latest paperback edition, published with a new subtitle, contains an appendix with responses to Viereck's thesis, both favorable (Thomas Mann) and unfavorable (Jacques Barzun).

[48] Melvin Rader, *No Compromise: The Conflict between Two Worlds* (New York, 1939), pp. 4, 19.

as did the "timocratic" ideas of Michels and Mosca. But it was Vilfredo Pareto who stood out as the chief prophet. Pareto's divorce of scientific thought from ethical behavior, his belief that moral ideas were "derivations" or rationalizations of deeper human drives, and his theory of the "circulation of elites" planted the intellectual seed for the rise of European Fascism. In Italy this was especially true, for Rader had no doubt about Mussolini's indebtedness to Paretan relativism and elitism. And what Pareto and other "Machiavellians" presented was nothing less than *the denial of universality*," the repudiation of eternal truths for the technique of force and fraud, the rejection of humanistic norms for the doctrine of myth and violence.[49]

In a study like Rader's, which approaches Fascism from the point of view of philosophical ideas, at least three implications emerge. First of all, after spending over three hundred pages tracing the origins and development of Fascism, Rader is forced to conclude that Fascism is a fraudulent ideology. It is false not only because its premises were wrong but because its political purposes were basically deceitful. The Fascists, wrote Rader, "employ the mask of idealism to conceal the bitter truth. Much of the appeal of Fascism depends upon its supposed opposition to materialism, but its idealism is like the esprit of a military corps: it reenforces aggressive intent and overweening chauvinism, and diverts attention from misery and predatory interests." While there is certainly much truth in Rader's argument, it scarcely considers the idea that Fascism may have been, at least intellectually, an honest moral revolt against the decadence and hypocrisy of bourgeois society—an idea which is presently receiving recognition among scholars. At one point Rader did admit: "I do not mean to suggest that there is nothing fine about Fascist idealism," yet the very chapter's title—"The Idealistic Mask and the Real Face"—belied any effort to accord much sincerity to Fascist ideology. A false idealism, Fascism must be unmasked.[50]

[49] *Ibid.*, pp. 20-87, 185-215, 334-38, passim.
[50] *Ibid.*, pp. 292, 337. It is worth noting that both Dewey and Santayana, in their respective studies of German philosophy, also believed that German idealism was exploited as an apology for the state. For a view of Fascism as an anti-bourgeois intellectual movement see, for example, "International Fascism, 1920-1945," *Journal of Contemporary History*, 1 (1966), esp. the essays by Adrian Lyttelton and Eugen Weber.

A second implication in the intellectual interpretation was the tendency to see Fascism as completely alien to "western civilization." Rader quotes Mussolini as stating: "The struggle between the two worlds [Democracy and Fascism] can permit no compromise." Using Spenglerian metaphors of atrophy and aberration, Rader goes on to describe the sharp contrast between the primordial impulses of the Fascist *Weltanschauung* and the healthy and sane heritage of the West. What emerges is the imagery of ancient "barbarism" pitted against the "rationalism" of modern culture. Such sermonizing is probably understandable on the eve of World War II. But to assert that Fascism threatened an assault on western civilization is to imply that its origins lay outside the West. The truth is that Fascism was every bit a part of western culture: it first arose solely in western countries; it had its intellectual roots in western sources; it made use of western technology; and, in the case of both Italy and Germany, it harked back to a Romanic grandeur or a Teutonic mythos.[51]

Finally, to approach Fascism from the viewpoint of intellectual history could lead inadvertently to conservative conclusions. Not only did such an approach divert attention from the social and economic bases of Fascism, but more importantly, the suggestion that Fascism signified a cultural crisis implied that responsibility for it lay in the realm of human consciousness. If Fascism dramatized a failure of nerve on the part of western culture, the cause of that failure was the individual—his ethics, intelligence, and spiritual fiber. Hence all the moral exhortations by natural-law advocates like John Hallowell, normative theorists like William McGovern, conservative humanists like Viereck, and even pragmatic rationalists like Rader. Fascism as an intellectual proposition posed an urgent problem of values, and for the problem of value the root is man.[52]

The interpretation offered by social scientists differed in several respects from that of intellectual historians and political philosophers. For one thing, behaviorists were less inclined to see Fascism as alien to western culture. There was no philosophical clash of "two worlds," for Fascism was potentially inherent in all societies given the right combination of circumstances. And

[51] Rader, p. 297.

[52] John Hallowell, *The Decline of Liberalism as an Ideology: With Particular Reference to German Politico-Legal Thought* (Berkeley, 1943); William M. McGovern, *From Luther to Hitler* (Boston, 1941).

477

since its roots were to be found not in the realm of ideas but in the nature of industrial society, man was regarded less the creator of Fascism than its helpless victim. Aside from this deterministic outlook, social scientists tended to see Fascism as a unique contemporary movement for which there were few historical analogues. Fascism may have exposed the bestial side of man, and thereby revealed again the constancy of human aggression; but it was the peculiar anxieties of modern man that gave rise to the mass movements of the twentieth century.

In the thirties some political scientists were concerned with enumerating the typological manifestations of Fascism and determining whether it was an ideological movement or a political technique designed to gain and hold power under the pretext of ideology. Most behaviorists agreed with Harold D. Lasswell that the real sources of Fascism go deeper than ideology and that "muscle movements must occur in a context of verbal legitimacy." Lasswell himself approached Fascism from the point of view of personality research, interest politics, symbol analysis, and Freudian psychology. It was a wide-ranging approach and one which allowed him to explain behavior as due to the unconscious forces of fear or the conscious drives to power. When he interpreted Nazism, for example, he saw it as precipitated by lower middle-class "emotional insecurities" brought on by the depression; but when he interpreted Italian Fascism he saw it in terms of shifting power relationships and elitist rule. Lasswell's socio-psychological analysis was a step in the right direction, illuminating, as it did, the stresses of personality disorder as well as the strains of class dislocation. Yet his positivistic desire to reduce all behavior to the almost cynical drives of interests and power subsumed even the most irrational aspects of Fascism under the most rational categories. In short, Lasswell's interpretation was impatient with Fascism's most intriguing characteristic—its ambiguity.[53]

Sociologists also brought their conceptual tools to bear on the

[53] H. Arthur Steiner, "Fascism for America?" *American Political Science Review*, xxix (Oct. 1935), 821-30; id., *Government in Fascist Italy* (New York, 1938); Harold D. Lasswell, *World Politics and Personal Insecurity* (New York, 1935), pp. 23-24; id., "The Psychology of Hitlerism," *Political Quarterly*, iv (June-Sept. 1933), 373-84; id. and Renzo Sereno, "The Fascists: The Changing Italian Elite," *American Political Science Review*, xxxi (Oct. 1937), 914-29.

problem. Some, like David Riesman, concentrated on the pathology of anti-Semitism; others, like Daniel Bell, on the economic basis of Fascism. Among the various sociological explanations perhaps that of Talcott Parsons was the most theoretical. Applying the relatively new method of functional analysis, Parsons tried to show that Fascism could be an expression of radical as well as reactionary tendencies. He was critical of the Marxist interpretation, noting that the relationship between business and Fascism was tenuous and that much of the emotional drive behind Fascism was anti-capitalist. Drawing upon Durkheim, Weber, and Pareto, he explained Fascism as a product of the subtle pressures of "anomie" that result from the "rationalization of society" under industrial capitalism and technology. The rationalizing drift of modern society devaluated the "non-logical" aspects of human behavior while at the same time "debunking" many of the older values and institutions, thereby leaving the mass of mankind in a state of utter normlessness and disorientation. "The reaction against the 'ideology' of the rationalization of society," Parsons observed in 1941, "is the principal aspect at least of the ideology of fascism." A consequence of "an imperfect structural integration," Fascism was a desperate answer to the social disintegration of contemporary industrial society.[54]

Fascism was also a research concern of the psychologist. In the area of psychology, however, much of the work has been preempted by political behaviorists like Lasswell or by European analysts like Carl Jung, who saw Fascist movements as manifestations of "tribal instincts" and dictators as akin to "medicine men" and "Gods of old." The few Americans who addressed themselves to the problem tended to use questionnaires in order to establish common Fascist attitudes among their subjects by correlating such items as nationalism, imperialism, militarism, racial antagonism, anti-radicalism, middle-class consciousness, and preference for strong-man government. All this, of course, anticipates T. W. Adorno's later study of the "authoritarian personality" with its famous "F scale" (discussed below). But what should be noted is that psychologists believed Fascism could be

[54] David Riesman, "Politics of Persecution," *Public Opinion Quarterly*, VI (March 1942), 41-56; Daniel Bell, "Monopoly Can Lead to Fascism," *Common Sense*, X (Sept. 1941), 267-69, 280; Talcott Parsons, "Some Sociological Aspects of Fascist Movements," *Social Forces*, XXI (Dec. 1942), 138-47.

479

studied as characterology, as deviant behavior and personality maladjustment. And since the psychic pressures which generate a reactionary mentality inhere in every society, Fascism's "latent content" could be studied in America as well as in Italy and Germany.[55]

Yet it is curious that no American undertook a thorough examination of Fascism from the point of view of social-psychology. Such a study would have to await the arrival of anti-Fascist *émigrés*. Perhaps the reluctance on the part of American social scientists was due to the methodological issues they faced. Should Fascism be approached from the familiar categories of interest politics, or should it be regarded as a novel development in status politics? Should the primary focus be the objective conditions of a sick society or the subjective illusions of neurotic personalities? Did Fascism spring from conscious economic oppression or unconscious instinctual repression, from external pressure or from inner experience, from social reality or psychic reality? To answer these endless questions it was obvious that scholars had to come to grips with Marx and Freud. Formerly regarded as mutually exclusive social theories, both Marxism and Freudianism could shed some light on the phantasmagoric world of Fascism. It is far from coincidence that the Fascist problem led many thinkers to try to reconcile the two schools of thought, and it is no accident that European exiles were the first to do so.[56]

[55] "The Psychology of Dictatorship: Interview with C. G. Jung," *Living Age*, CCLI (Dec. 1936), 340-41; Ross Stagner, "Fascist Attitudes: An Exploratory Study," *Journal of Social Psychology*, VII (Aug. 1936), 309-19; id., "Fascist Attitudes: Their Determining Conditions," *ibid.* (Nov. 1936), 438-54; Evelyn Raskin and Stuart Cook, "A Further Investigation of the Measure of an Attitude Toward Fascism," *ibid.*, IX (May 1938), 201-06; Ross Stagner and E. T. Katzoff, "Fascist Attitudes: Factor Analysis of Item Correlations," *ibid.*, XVI (Aug. 1942), 3-9.

[56] Hadley Cantril, in *The Psychology of Social Movements* (New York, 1941), touched upon the problem; see also Daniel Katz and Hadley Cantril, "Analysis of Attitudes Toward Fascism and Communism," *Journal of Abnormal Psychology*, XXXV (July 1940), 356-66. Eric Hoffer's *The True Believer* (New York, 1951), though more a product of the Cold War than of World War II, is an important essay that might be regarded as an unintended social-psychological analysis of Fascism. Yet his thesis regarding the interchangeable nature of all "mass movements" and the universal character of all "fanatics" is much too sweeping. To my knowledge, one of the first

Émigré Scholars and the Power of Darkness

European intellectuals were well acquainted with the psychological interpretation of Fascism. As early as 1929, Thomas Mann, in "Mario and the Magician," used the character Cipolla to portray brilliantly the Freudian principle that the instinct to submission was merely an unconscious will to domination. A few years later the Italian anarchist Camillo Berneri wrote *Mussolini: psicologia di un dittatore* (1932), depicting Il Duce's militant "exhibitionism" as a guise to divert social unrest and as "compensation" for his own personality problems. In England the Left Book Club published R. Osborne's *The Psychology of Reaction* (1938), and during the war there appeared Peter Nathan's *The Psychology of Fascism* (1943). But in regards to Marxism and Freudianism, perhaps the most interesting of all the psychological studies was Wilhelm Reich's pamphlet, *Benito Mussolini: Corporativer Staat* (1934), and particularly his book, *Die Massenpsychologie des Faschismus* (1933). An Austrian psychoanalyst who fled Hitler and eventually settled in the United States, Reich attempted to rescue Marxism from its one-dimensional determinism by offering a new "sex-economic sociology" of Fascism. According to Reich, Marxism could account for the political power wielded by capitalists under Fascism, but it could not account for the feverish enthusiasm of the masses. To explain these "irrational contradictions," Reich went "to the root of things" by arguing that "fascist mysticism is orgiastic longing under the conditions of mystification and inhibition of natural sexuality." In disclaiming that mass neuroses were due to man's fixed biological nature, Reich departed from the stoicism of Freud; but by asserting it was due to the mechanistic culture of capitalism he was able to salvage Marx. Whatever the merits of this fanciful thesis, Fascism as the tyranny of sensual repression and the unconscious explosion of "orgone" (sexual energy) was too shocking for horrified Communists and too weird for American behaviorists. In the United States the writings of this eccentric exile went virtually unnoticed until after the war, when his book

---

American Marxists to attempt an assimilation of Freudianism was Harry Slochower in *No Voice Is Wholly Lost* . . . (New York, 1945), which was later published as *Literature and Philosophy between Two World Wars: The Problem of Alienation in a War Culture* (New York, 1964).

481

was published by the Orgone Press Institute as *The Mass Psychology of Fascism* (1946).[57]

It was a fellow German exile, Erich Fromm, who offered Americans a far more agreeable interpretation. Fromm's *Escape from Freedom* (1941) was an urgent attempt to explain why a people would flee freedom into the arms of totalitarianism. Like the Marxists, Fromm believed that Fascism was related to monopoly capitalism; but unlike Marxists, he refused to see Fascism as the creature of monopoly power alone. For what industrial capitalism did was not so much to forge the march of Fascism as to render the masses powerless to resist its attractions. Stripped of pre-capitalist communal ties, the modern citizen found himself isolated, lonely, afraid, an uprooted automaton deprived of his basic need of "belongingness." To overcome the agonizing "burden of freedom," man succumbs to the "mechanisms of escape": he identifies sadistically with authority figures and he surrenders masochistically his authentic self to the power of the aggressive state. Presented in these terms, Fascism emerged as a product of almost all the ills of modern society: depersonalization, bureaucracy, alienation, conformity, and anxiety. Fascism, then, was the psychology of every man, or at least of every man laboring under the false consciousness of bourgeois liberalism.[58]

It can be argued that, in trying to fuse Marx and Freud, Fromm made a mishmash of both, and, as later research reveals, he exaggerated the relationship between Fascism and the rootlessness of urban industrial society. Nevertheless, *Escape from Freedom* was widely acclaimed in America as a discerningly fresh approach to understanding Fascism, and the reasons for its appeal are as significant as the accuracy of the interpretation itself. First of all, in describing Fascism in terms of the interaction of society on character development, Fromm was attempting to balance the economic collectivism of Marx with the psychoanalytic individualism of Freud, while avoiding the determinism of both. But

[57] Thomas Mann, "Mario and the Magician," in *Death in Venice and Seven Other Stories* (Vintage edn., New York, 1958), esp. p. 164; Camillo Berneri, *Mussolini: psicologia di un dittatore* (Richiedetele a Edizioni Azione Commune, Milan, 1966); no original date is cited for this work but the editor, Pier Carlo Masini, states that Berneri wrote it "around 1932" (p. 14); Wilhelm Reich, *The Mass Psychology of Fascism*, trans. Theodore P. Wolfe (New York, 1946), pp. xvii-xxiii, passim.

[58] Erich Fromm, *Escape from Freedom* (Avon edn., New York, 1965), pp. 17-38, 157-64, passim.

even more importantly, Fromm's thesis enjoyed popularity among intellectuals because the prescriptions he offered for the ills of modern alienation blended in nicely with the winning creed of American progressivism. As a solution to the supposed anxieties of freedom which led to Fascism, Fromm spoke of the need for "relatedness," "spontaneity," and "self-realization" in a "productive" society of abundance. Implicit here is the suggestion that Fascism sprang neither from the rigors of class war nor the dread of spiritual alienation but merely from the familiar malady of poor social institutions and personal relationships. Like so many other scholars of the time, Fromm was obviously more interested in expounding a cure for Fascism than in examining with precision all its complex causes. But his message of humane social engineering was one which American liberals could readily understand. Whatever may be the ultimate validity of his highly impressionistic *Escape from Freedom*, Fromm managed the remarkable, if unconvincing, feat of translating Dostoevski's anxieties into Dewey's aspirations.[59]

While Fromm combined European existentialism with American progressivism, another German exile, Theodor W. Adorno, combined Freud's qualitative depth-analysis with quantitative research in social psychology. *The Authoritarian Personality* (1949) was originally undertaken in 1944 to devise a way to measure anti-Semitism, but it was soon extended to include an "F-scale" to measure "implicit fascist tendencies." Briefly, Adorno and his associates drew up questionnaire and interview items which attempted to correlate ethnocentrism, anti-Semitism, and "reactionary politico-economic views." Like most pioneering works in methodology, *The Authoritarian Personality* proved only as valid as its assumptions, and when it was eventually published the book provoked considerable controversy. For our purposes what should be stressed is that Adorno and his collaborators believed that they knew, without investigating actual Fascist character profiles or movements, what the reality of Fascism was. And

---

[59] Seymour Martin Lipset noted, after studying election data in Weimar Germany, that the Nazis were more successful in small communities and that *"the larger the city, the smaller the Nazi vote."* Lipset concludes: "These facts sharply challenge the various interpretations of Nazism as the product of the growth of anomie and the general rootlessness of modern urban industrial society." *Political Man: The Social Bases of Politics* (New York, 1960), p. 144; Fromm, pp. 265-303, passim.

483

implicit in their assumption that political opinions are an index of personality traits was their conviction that they could uncover "fascistic potential" by dealing solely with the opinions of their subjects. This assumption led to some interesting contradictions, not the least of which was the fact that the authors believed that political opinions should be rational and that opinions function not to interpret reality psychically but to reflect the world as it really is. Thus while the authors purported to be testing psychoanalytic insights with empirical methods they, like Fromm, were forced to depart from Freud's central dictum that wish is father to thought, that human imagination is more important than rational perception. If one accepts the dictum that "primal emotions" determine political opinion, then the idea of Fascism as a measurable external behavior becomes almost meaningless while the "authoritarian personality" evaporates into an immeasurable entity. Hence the authors were in the paradoxical position of believing in irrationality and yet demanding the most rational responses to their questions, assuming, of course, that any normal (i.e., non-authoritarian) person could see the self-evident reality of Fascism. It was an awkward position, and one which suggests that, when confronted with Fascism, the political implications of orthodox Freudianism lead only to despair.[60]

The psychological interpretation was not the only contribution of *émigré* scholarship on Fascism. Many Italian exiles in the United States, for example, approached the problem from more traditional disciplines. In *Fascism for Whom* (1938), Max Ascoli referred to Fascism as "the product of democratic decay" and went on to discuss ways in which liberalism could be revitalized in America as well as in Italy. In *Goliath: The March of Fascism* (1937), G. A. Borgese spent considerable time explaining the intellectual background of Fascism only to conclude that Musso-

[60] T. W. Adorno, et al., *The Authoritarian Personality* (New York, 1950); id., "Scientific Experiences of a European Scholar in America," in *The Intellectual Migration: Europe and America, 1930-1960*, Vol. II, *Perspectives in American History*, eds. Donald Fleming and Bernard Bailyn (Charles Warren Center, Harvard University, Cambridge, 1968), 338-69; for a critique of Adorno, see Richard Christie and Marie Johoda, eds., *Studies in the Scope and Method of "The Authoritarian Personality"* (Glencoe, Ill., 1954); for a discussion of the epistemological premises of the work, see Gene Wise, "Political 'Reality' in Recent American Scholarship: Progressives versus Symbolists," *American Quarterly*, XIX (Summer Supplement, 1967), 313-28.

lini's movement amounted to "an outburst of emotionalism and pseudo-intellectualism" born of Italy's moral deterioration. In *Under the Axe of Fascism* (1936), Salvemini dismissed much of Fascist ideology as "usually fabrication of the whole cloth" and Il Duce's regime he termed an "elephantine bureaucratic machine" that had no connection whatsoever to Sorel's Socialism. And Sturzo, in his essay "The Totalitarian State" (1936), maintained the roots of Fascism could be traced to Machiavelli and Luther, whose legacy allowed the State to be revered as a divine institution. Perhaps Silone's *The School for Dictators* (1939) came closest to a psychological interpretation in its suggestion, addressed explicitly to Americans, that demagogy and mass politics lie at the root of populistic Fascism.[61]

The achievement of German *émigré* scholarship was equally notable, and perhaps more influential with the American public. Some of this research, like William Ebenstein's *Fascist Italy* (1939), has already been mentioned in connection with the exiles' work in American universities. But German scholarship answered a need that went beyond academic circles. In *Communism, Fascism or Democracy* (1938), Eduard Heimann defined Fascism as "anti-humanism" and went on to advise how the West could cure the defects of liberal democracy and individualism. In his comparative analysis, *Permanent Revolution* (1942), Sigmund Neumann turned Trotsky's phrase on its head to demonstrate that all totalitarian governments attempt to "institutionalize revolution" and make the citizen's daily life into a natural state of constant war. Hermann Rauschning, another exile who eventually came to America, wrote the highly popular *The Revolution of Nihilism* (1939), a sensitive if impassioned work in which the disillusioned aristocrat described Nazism as a "directionless revolution" manipulated by an elite and propelled by the cult of action. Equally popular was Franz Neumann's *Behemoth* (1942). A former German labor lawyer steeped in Veblen as well as Marx, Neumann tried to anatomize the imperialistic nature of Germany's corporate oligarchy and its alliance with National Socialism, pointing out to Americans that in Germany there had never been anything resembling an extensive

---

[61] Sturzo's essay on "The Totalitarian State" appeared in *Social Research*, III (May 1934), 225-35; although Silone did not emigrate to America his writings were greatly admired in this country.

anti-trust movement such as that which occurred in the Theodore Roosevelt and Wilson administrations.[62]

It is no mere literary coincidence that *émigrés* resorted to biblical terms to depict the new political state under Mussolini and Hitler. Neumann's "Behemoth," Borgese's "Goliath," and Sturzo's "Leviathan" all intimated that Fascism foreshadowed a new epoch, that history had turned a corner from which there was no return. One of the more interesting intellectual harvests of World War II was this desperate philosophical reappraisal of the political destiny of western man. Such was the effort of Pitirim Sorokin's *The Crisis of Our Age* (1941), a cyclical interpretation of history reminiscent of Henry Adams, which regarded Fascism as further manifestation of the disintegration of the "sensate culture" that arose at the end of the twelfth century. Other *engagés* singled out great thinkers of the past as forerunners of modern totalitarianism, as Karl Popper did in his attack on "historicists" in *The Open Society and Its Enemies* (1945). Occasionally the record had to be set straight, as in Herbert Marcuse's *Reason and Revolution* (1941), where the German exile explained that since Gentile's "actualism" deviated from Hegel's dialectical idealism, and since Alfred Rosenberg falsely substituted the German *volk* for Hegel's *staat*, "Fascist Hegelianism" was a contradiction in terms. But of all the philosophical reflections by *émigrés*, perhaps the most seminal was Peter Drucker's provocative thesis in *The End of Economic Man* (1939). Here the Austrian refugee offered the astounding idea that not only was Fascism devoid of doctrinal significance but that even those who embraced it refused to believe in its promises. According to Drucker the prime symptom of Fascism was mass despair. No longer able to believe that either capitalism or Socialism could fulfill the historic dream of freedom and equality, the masses could no longer accept the economic values and rationalist ideals on which both bourgeois liberalism and Marxism had been founded. As a result they turned to the "new sorcerers," Mussolini and Hitler, the only leaders who could work miracles, defy reason and reality and thus allay its desperate fears. The "new demons," Drucker observed, "are far more unbearable than the old ones ever were. A Kierkegaard, a Dostoevski, an isolated,

[62] On Neumann's career in America, see H. Stuart Hughes, "Franz Neumann: Between Marxism and Liberal Democracy," in *The Intellectual Migration*, pp. 446-62.

consciously lonely poet or philosopher, might be able to look at them unflinchingly and yet remain sane. The average individual cannot bear the utter atomization, the unreality and senselessness, the destruction of all order, of all society, of all rational individual existence through blind, incalculable, senseless forces created as a result of rationalization and mechanization."[63]

One writer who would have agreed with much of Drucker's argument was Hannah Arendt, the German exile and author of the monumental work on Fascism, *The Origins of Totalitarianism* (1951). Although Arendt's book was not published until several years after the war, many of her germinal ideas appeared in periodicals in the early forties, and thus her interpretation of Fascism, like most of the works discussed above, can be regarded as a product of World War II. Moreover, although Arendt saw Fascism as a genre of totalitarianism from which Italy was all but excluded as a "one party dictatorship," her treatment of Fascist totalitarianism deserves our attention not only because it brought to fruition much of the *émigré* scholarship but because it came to be esteemed almost as gospel by a whole generation of American intellectuals.

Like Drucker, Arendt maintained that modern society had become so atomized that traditional economic interests no longer completely bound human behavior. "The loss of interests," she noted, "is identical with the loss of 'self,' and modern masses are distinguished in my view by their self-lessness, that is, by their lack of 'selfish interests.'" But Arendt went further than Drucker in arguing that under totalitarianism there occurred a transvaluation of values wherein all sense of traditional order and legality is shattered; where the omnipresence of death becomes a way of life; where criminal behavior is praised and Christian behavior punished. Totalitarianism represented "a permanent state of lawlessness" in which "everything is possible," a blind revolt against the imperfections of human nature itself. To trace the background of this twentieth-century nightmare, Arendt discussed the history of anti-Semitism, a subterranean stream she took much more seriously than did exiles like Neumann and American scholars like Riesman; imperialism and the nineteenth-

[63] Herbert Marcuse, *Reason and Revolution: Hegel and the Rise of Social Theory* (Beacon edn., Boston, 1960), pp. 402-19; Peter Drucker, *The End of Economic Man: A Study of the New Totalitarianism* (New York, 1939), p. 67.

century pan-movements, which were likewise tinged with racism; and the rise of nationalism and the simultaneous breakdown of the nation-state and breakup of the social structure, which issued in the phenomena of "statelessness" and "classlessness." Insofar as Arendt perceived Fascism as a repudiation of man's natural rights and legal personality, she displayed a Burkean scorn for abstract egalitarianism. Yet the most interesting feature of Arendt's interpretation of Fascism was her ability to capture the irrational flavor of the movement. Fascist totalitarianism, she maintained, was more than a study in Marxian class struggle or even in Machiavellian power politics. Like Rauschning, she saw that Fascism was driven not by utilitarian logic but by an inner dynamism of its own, which had as its aim the complete suppression of individuality and conscience. Once the individual became part of an amorphous mass, and once the masses were subjected to systematic terror, then the traditional categories of political understanding and personal responsibility passed beyond the pale of reason and logic. What resulted was a delirium of Christian sensibility chillingly summed up in Arendt's Yeatsian epigram: "Nothing perhaps distinguishes modern masses as radically from those of previous centuries as the loss of faith in the Last Judgment: the worst have lost their fear and the best have lost their hope."[64]

Although more a comment on modern man's fate than a historical analysis of Fascism, the value of Arendt's interpretation for Americans lies in its unique European orientation. Indeed, some of the very tendencies of mass society which she perceived as leading to Fascist totalitarianism Americans have generally regarded as the mainstay of democracy. For example, Arendt focused on the phenomenon of "classlessness" as a prime factor in the rise of Fascism. Clearly this interpretation would be discomforting to most Americans. For whatever the reality may be, Americans have always imagined their society as free of class antagonisms. Of course, there are important distinctions between

[64] Hannah Arendt, "Race Thinking before Racism," *Review of Politics*, VI (Jan. 1941), 36-73; id., "Imperialism, Nationalism, Chauvinism," *ibid.*, VII (Oct. 1945), 441-63; id., "Stateless People," *Contemporary Jewish Record*, VIII (April 1945), 137-53; id., "Parties, Movements, and Classes," *Partisan Review*, XII (Fall 1945), 504-13; id., "Organized Guilt and Universal Responsibility," *Jewish Frontier*, XII (Jan. 1945), 19-23; some of the quotes used are from Arendt's reply to Eric Voegelin's "The Origins of Totalitarianism," *Review of Politics*, XV (Jan. 1953), 68-85.

what Arendt saw as the debility of "classlessness" and what Americans highly regard as the characteristics of an open class society. But the point is that whereas Americans have prided themselves on the absence of class consciousness, for Arendt the very absence of class identity can lead to rootlessness, insecurity, and other social anxieties that combine to produce the mental germs of Fascism.

Moreover, Arendt's interpretation of Fascism was peculiarly European in its conservative critique of the Enlightenment. As she surveyed history from the eighteenth to the twentieth century, the idea of progress seemed to turn back on itself. The heralded Rights of Man, the cornerstone of liberty, not only proved unenforceable outside a national context but culminated in tyranny at the moment of their realization. That is, modern man lost his human rights when he became a complete human being by liberating himself from the state, nation, class, and other associations which previously enabled him to assert those rights. Believing political rights inalienable, man fled the fixed restraints of established institutions only to discover the diffuse tyranny of the "homeless" masses. In short, undifferentiated mass man was most vulnerable to Fascist totalitarianism precisely when he was most free of historical institutions. A densely pessimistic interpretation of Fascism, Arendt's ironic thesis scarcely rhymed with the optimistic temper of Americans. A people whose political assumptions are rooted in the Enlightenment; a people who believe that liberty is not the story of historic continuity but instead is born of a brave denial of the Old World;[65] a people who traditionally have been suspicious of institutions and who have regarded political rights as inalienably given; a people who believe that the defects of democracy are solved by more democracy —such a people could only be bewildered by Arendt's apocalyptical proposition that freedom may very well be a fundamental paradox of human existence.

Finally, the picture of Fascism Arendt leaves us with is a nihilistic grotesquerie whose moral implications are almost be-

[65] "Democracy . . . is revolutionary, not formative. It is born of denial. It comes into existence in the way of denying established institutions. Its office is rather to destroy the old world, than fully to reveal the new." Henry James, Sr., "Democracy and Its Issues" (1853), quoted in R. W. B. Lewis, *The American Adam: Innocence, Tragedy, and Tradition in the Nineteenth Century* (Chicago, 1955), p. 13.

489

yond good and evil. After completing her book Arendt later recalled that the most frightening thing in writing it was Montesquieu's statement: "Man, this flexible being, who submits himself in society to the thoughts and impressions of his fellow men, is equally capable of knowing his own nature when it is shown to him as it is and of losing it to the point where he has no realization that he is robbed of it." That man may lose his identity without knowing it, that Fascism may be the loss of one's sense of self and hence the loss of all sense of limitations, is for Arendt the psychological terror of Fascism. And conversely, to refuse to accept man's finite condition, to succumb to the seductive totality of ideology in the face of the dizzy chaos of history, to strive for essence in defiance of the enigma of existence, is the metaphysical dread of Fascism. Thus we shall never be able to understand Fascist totalitarianism until we are prepared to accept the ambiguity of the human condition. There can be no wisdom, Arendt insists, until we comprehend "radical evil." In the end the precious crust of civility has disintegrated and modern totalitarianism has brought to the surface the moral nausea that plagues all western culture. With this existential glimpse of political reality, American intellectual history felt the power of darkness and sensed the shadow of Melville.[66]

"IT CAN'T HAPPEN HERE"?

At first, during World War II, the experience of Fascism deeply troubled and perplexed many American intellectuals. Unlike Stalinism, the frightening paradox of Fascism was its combination of repression and enthusiasm, its tyranny and its popularity. A new form of "democratic totalitarianism," Fascism made political theorists sensitive to the tragic ironies inherent in western democracy. A mass movement arising in large part from the *déclassé* anxieties of the bourgeoisie, it gave historians cause to wonder whether America's middle-class populism and liberalism could

[66] In the last page of *The Origins of Totalitarianism*, Arendt glumly concludes: "It is inherent in our entire philosophical tradition that we cannot conceive of a 'radical evil' . . . . Therefore, we actually have nothing to fall back on in order to understand a phenomenon that nevertheless confronts us with its overpowering reality and breaks down all standards that we know" (p. 459). Significantly, years later Arendt turned to Melville, and particularly to *Billy Budd*, to explore the radical ambiguity of good and evil. See *On Revolution* (Compass Viking edn., New York, 1965), pp. 74-83. See also Arendt on Voegelin's "Origins of Totalitarianism," p. 84.

any longer be regarded as simple progressive forces. An eclectic ideology that transcended both capitalism and Socialism, it suggested to economists and sociologists that a mixed economy may be a mixed blessing and that political power may have a cunning of its own. A theory that made a virtue of irrationality and immorality, it challenged assumptions cherished by Jefferson and carried forward by Dewey, and it made philosophers and psychologists aware of the perilous ambiguities in modern political behavior. In the face of Fascism almost every truth became questionable, every old idea took on a new double meaning.

Yet the legacy of Fascism in American thought is itself curiously ambiguous, resulting in both a cheerful reaffirmation of American history and a somber reappraisal of American society. Before and during World War II intellectuals seemed gripped by catastrophism, overwhelmed by a crisis of confidence in their country and in themselves. With the dreadful terrors of the twentieth century dramatized in European totalitarianism, several writers doubted whether America could escape Europe's fate. But when America survived the ordeal without resorting to the extremism of the Right or Left the idea again arose, as it had so often in American history, that America led a charmed political life. Historians, sociologists, and literary critics, many of whom had been Marxists of one persuasion or another, now began to search the American past in order to discover why the United States could survive the greatest depression and the most ghastly war with its democratic institutions basically intact. Perhaps even more than Communism, Fascism forced intellectuals to reconsider the values of western culture and to reexamine what now appeared to be the basic healthiness of the ridiculed middle class and the basic soundness of America's abused liberal institutions. The result was something of an intellectual counterrevolution. Reacting against European ideology, many scholars reacted against ideology and theory in general and sought security in the raw facts of empiricism and behaviorism. Chastened by the moral fever of European metapolitics, some advocated the complete divorce of ethics from politics. Repelled by mass movements and centralized power, others embraced liberal pluralism, praised the institutional foundations of freedom, and, having rediscovered de Tocqueville, preached the virtues of "consensus." Recoiling from the relativism and nihilism of Fascism, a few even began the long climb toward a new transcendent faith. But above all,

491

as the de-radicalized American scholar turned inward and abandoned European categories of thought, America emerged as a distinct entity, a separate and special nation almost completely outside history itself. Out of the crisis-ridden and cataclysmic mood of the thirties and forties appeared a new America, a "unique" America that supposedly evolved from a prudent people blessed by common values and beliefs, a placid history unburdened by feudalism and class warfare, and an even-tempered American mind untroubled by a restless *Weltanschauung*. Among other things, the heralded "end of ideology" meant that Americans no longer had to regard the harsh problems of the Old World as the problems of the New. Thus Americans could learn little from Italy and Germany. Like Communism, Fascism was alien to the American experience. Despite the pleas of John Horne Burns and the pessimism of Hannah Arendt, the conclusion seemed to be that a European catastrophe was not an American tragedy.

Others were not so sure. Several literary intellectuals contemplated with horror the perpetuation in America of the same dreck culture and mass society that had produced European Fascism. And since they had always regarded Fascism as a human condition rather than a political phenomenon, the end of World War II proved to them almost nothing about the future of America and its numbing "civilization" of things and machines. At the same time scholars in various academic disciplines, drawing upon the analytical tools brought over by *émigrés*, discovered in the American people previously unknown sources of social and psychological strain: middle-class status anxieties, racist and authoritarian personalities, conspiratorial phobias; mingled fits of repression, frustration, and aggression; chronic outbursts of anti-Communism; and a general, vague feeling of anomie and alienation. Dissecting the uglier side of the American character, these scholars seemed less certain that when the full depths of the bourgeois psyche were plumbed a Fascist impulse would not be found. The rise of McCarthyism, of course, seemed to bring to the surface what many social scientists suspected, and several writers began to explore the American past to discover its deeper sources. An enormously complex phenomenon, and far from a prototype of European Fascism, McCarthyism nonetheless made Americans of the fifties suddenly aware of the meaning of "the Right." Then the following decade, when the Cold War hardened into a permanent quagmire in Asia, some of the metaphors European anti-Fascists had used to describe the Italian and German state returned to haunt America as anti-war dissenters discovered America's own "Behemoth" and "Leviathan" in the "power structure" and the "military-industrial complex." Even the New Left's contemporary revolt against technology had its earlier expression in the Old Left's conviction that managerial elites are the brain merchants of Fascism's permanent war economy. Finally, on a more subtle but nonetheless more profound level, America's encounter with Fascism called up from the depths a darker moral vision as Americans began to rediscover the strange deceits of human depravity. Those who learned well the lesson of innocence realized that evil lurks in every man's banal existence, from the soldiers who liberated Italy to the soldiers who "liberated" My Lai.

America may have emerged from the experience of European Fascism with its innocence assured. But two decades later American intellectuals would find cold consolation in the easy explanations and hopeful analysis of the more simple interpretations of Fascism that characterized their writings in the forties. Indeed, after World War II the militarism, racism, and violence that had been the horror of European Fascism now seemed to emerge as the darker reality of American democracy. Stunned by the polarization of the sixties, some Americans began to sense that their experience with Fascism had been more intense than they knew and perhaps more lasting than they wished. And for the sensitive American who watched his government destroy Asian villages in order to "save" them, perhaps the moral significance of Fascism became as painfully meaningful to him as it had been unbearable to John Horne Burns. The sin of pride and the fear of humiliation, the fetish of military victory and technological power, and the insensitivity to the "normality" of evil were now the burden of American history. With its conscience plagued by self-doubt, with the encounter between innocence and guilt a daily nightmare, America no longer needed Italy to raise the question of Fascism.

But only for a few Americans did the meaning of Fascism remain in the deeper recesses of conscience. The great majority of robust citizens came out of World War II with little or no understanding of its history or ideology. Lacking an informed collective memory, the American public had a vivid image of

493

Mussolini and Hitler but a fuzzy impression of the background and nature of Fascism. Thus in the postwar period it was tempting for writers to begin to equate Fascism with Communism in order to propagandize the urgency of the Cold War and to transfer America's hatred of Nazi Germany to Soviet Russia; and it was even more tempting for an older generation of Americans to see the presumed Ethiopian and Munich parallel in subsequent events occurring in Southeast Asia. If it is ironic that Stalin's own system of terror made the analogy between Fascism and Communism possible, it is even more ironic that America's struggle for the "free world" began to take on the crude power politics and anti-Communist hysteria that went far toward making Fascism possible. Indeed, to the extent to which America has allowed anti-Communism to become an end in itself, America runs the risk of unconsciously inheriting the legacy of European Fascism. Thus it is distressing to find, a half century after Mussolini came to power, American political leaders reiterating the very arguments which Italians and Americans alike had used to justify the March on Rome:

> *Fulbright*: Does the Senator think there is a free government in Greece now?
> *Dirksen*: Yes, I do. Just because they have a military junta for a specified purpose for a little while to shove back the Communist influence—
> *Fulbright*: Communist influence?
> *Dirksen*: Surely, and it has been trying to move into Greece.
> *Fulbright*: Is the Senator saying that the previous government was a Communist government?
> *Dirksen*: I did not say anything about the previous government. You can have a new government move in without there being a Communist government. We have Communists in this country, do we not?[67]

[67] "Dirksen vs. Fulbright," *New Leader*, L (Oct. 23, 1967), 18; for the development of the Fascist-Communist analogy in postwar American thought, see Les K. Adler and Thomas G. Patterson, "Red Fascism: The Merger of Nazi Germany and Soviet Russia in the American Image of Totalitarianism, 1930s—1950s," *American Historical Review*, LXXV (April 1970), 1046-64; for a severe critique of the presumed diplomatic parallel between Munich and America's justification for intervention in Southeast Asia, see Arthur Schlesinger, Jr., "On the Inscrutability of History," *Encounter*, XXVII (Nov. 1966), 10-17.

From their experience with Italian Fascism most Americans learned nothing and forgot nothing. Americans tended to externalize the problem, to regard Fascism as Europe's peculiar institution and thereby deny what many *émigrés* believed was its universal significance. Yet if we regard Fascism as a state of mind and not merely as an authoritarian state, as an attitude and mentality as well as an institution and ideology, the problem remains as much America's as Europe's. That "it can't happen here" may seem a reassuring historical judgment. But it is a political truth that can easily become a moral lie. Politically man is what he does, morally he is what he thinks. Between the idea and the deed lurks the condition of mind and heart. Perhaps this study of America's admiration for Mussolini's Italy may help us analyze the fascism within ourselves.

495

Bibliographical Note

SINCE an enumeration of all materials used in this study would be redundant, the following statement aims merely to offer some direction to anyone wishing to pursue further the subjects taken up in various chapters. Briefly, the intent is to cite the basic scholarship, indicate the location of various unpublished materials, comment upon the usefulness and reliability of other sources, occasionally suggest the value of certain materials for further research, either on this subject or related topics; and lastly, describe the growing interest in Fascist studies on the part of contemporary American scholars.

IMAGES OF ITALY

The best place to begin is Luigi Barzini's *The Italians* (New York, 1964), an insightful national character study whose opening chapters describe sensitively the romantic longing for Italy on the part of non-Italians. For the American impulse see Van Wyck Brooks, *The Dream of Arcadia* (New York, 1958), and Paul Baker, *The Fortunate Pilgrims: Americans in Italy, 1800-1860* (Cambridge, 1964). More specific treatments are found in the anthology, *Testimonianze americane sull'Italia del Risorgimento*, ed. Elizabeth Mann Borgese (Milan, 1961), and in A. William Salomone's perceptive article, "The Nineteenth Century Discovery of Italy: An Essay in American Cultural History," *American Historical Review*, LXXIII (June 1968), 1359-91. Broader studies of American perspectives are dealt with in *Discovery of Europe: The Story of American Experiences in the Old World*, ed. Philip Rahv (Boston, 1947); Cushing Strout, *The American Image of the Old World* (New York, 1963); and Melvin J. Lasky,

497

"America and Europe: Transatlantic Images," in *Paths of American Thought*, eds. Arthur Schlesinger, Jr. and Morton White (Boston, 1963), pp. 465-91. The outstanding work on the nativist response to immigration is John Higham's *Strangers in the Land: Patterns of America* (New Brunswick, 1955). Thus far no extensive study has been published on the American response to the Italian immigrant in particular, but a start has been made in Salvatore Mondello's "Italian Migration to the U.S. as Reported in American Magazines, 1880-1920," *Social Science*, XXXIX (June 1964), 131-42. For the post-World War II studies see *America and the Mind of Europe*, ed. Lewis Galantière (London, 1951); Edmund Wilson, *Europe without Baedeker: Sketches Among the Ruins of Italy, France and England* (New York, 1947); and Leslie Fiedler, "Italian Pilgrimage: The Discovery of America" and "Roman Holiday," in *An End to Innocence: Essays on Culture and Politics* (Boston, 1955), pp. 91-108, 115-23.

THE PRESS AND PUBLIC OPINION

For the period of the thirties and forties I examined a half dozen major city newspapers in order to ascertain editorial responses to particular events in Italy. A good deal of the coverage for the twenties had already been accomplished in John Booth Carter's "American Reactions to Italian Fascism, 1919-1933" (Ph.D. Thesis, Columbia University, 1953). Roughly a dozen popular magazines were studied for the entire Fascist period. Fortunately there were occasional press surveys printed in the *Literary Digest*; and, even more valuable, a detailed survey by the Italian government itself, which can be found among the captured Italian Records in the National Archives. The memoirs of journalists offer a mixed bag. Most useful were Herbert Matthews' *Eyewitness in Abyssinia* (London, 1937); *Fruits of Fascism* (New York, 1943); and *Education of a Correspondent* (New York, 1946). George Seldes' *Lords of the Press* (New York, 1938) and *Facts and Fascism* (New York, 1942) are heavy with polemics; and Anne O'Hare McCormick's *Vatican Journal, 1921-1954* (New York, 1957) is a narrowly selected anthology of her writings for the *New York Times*. While these works suffer from a lack of detachment, Edgar Ansel Mowrer suffers from too much detachment in his recent *Triumph and Turmoil: A Personal History of Our Times* (New York, 1968), in which the author appears to have forgotten his own vacillating judgments on

498

Mussolini. In this respect the most reliable reflections can be found in Lincoln Steffens, *Autobiography* (New York, 1931), Vol. ii; Ida Tarbell, *All in the Day's Work* (New York, 1939); and Isaac F. Marcosson, *Before I Forget* (New York, 1959).

ITALIAN-AMERICANS AND ANTI-FASCISTS

By and large these chapters were based on the Italian-American press. Some of the main sources were *Il Progresso Italo-Americano* (New York), *Il Nuovo Mondo* (New York), *Controcorrente* (Boston), *L'Italia* (San Francisco), and *Il Corriere del Popolo* (San Francisco). Also helpful were the following secondary works: John Norman, "Repudiation of Fascism by the Italian-American Press," *Journalism Quarterly*, xxi (March 1944), 1-6; "The Foreign Language Press," *Fortune*, xxii (Nov. 1940), 90-93, 102-04; Marino de Medici, "The Italian Language Press in the San Francisco Bay Area from 1930-1940" (Master of Journalism Thesis, University of California, Berkeley, 1963); and "A Survey of the Italian Language Press in the United States" (mimeographed paper prepared at the Institute for Advanced Study, Princeton, 1942). Some Fascist propaganda activities are described in the following government reports: House Special Committee on Un-American Activities, *Investigations of Un-American Propaganda Activities in the United States*, 75 Cong., 3 Sess., ii (Washington, D.C., 1938); Senate (California), 55 Sess., 1943, *Report of the Joint Fact-Finding Commission of Un-American Activities in California*, Vol. i, Part v, "Fascist Activities," 282-321. Though most of the Italian-American papers are now defunct, a number of complete sets have been collected recently by the University of Minnesota's Director of Immigrant Archives, Professor Rudolph Vecoli.

Some of the anti-Fascist literature may be found in the pamphlet collections of Stanford University's Hoover Library. The Panunzio Papers, also in the Hoover Library, contain a useful compilation of press clippings and a report on American films in Italy. The Tresca Files, in the New York Public Library, are important for the late thirties and early forties. His own unpublished autobiography stops at 1925; but Max Nomad's unpublished biography of Tresca, "Rebel without a Uniform," also covers the later period. The Valenti Papers, in the Taminent Library, New York, include information on the various state and federal government investigating committees. As for the *fuoru-*

sciti, Armando Borghi, *Mezzo secolo di anarchia, 1895-1945* (Naples, 1945); Massimo Salvadori, *Resistenza ed azione: Ricordi di un liberale* (Bari, 1961); Luigi Sturzo, *La mia battaglia da New York* (Milan, 1949); and Giuseppe Lupis' biweekly *Il Mondo* (New York) offer valuable impressions on the American and Italian-American encounters with Fascism. Of all the exiles, Salvemini was the most informed observer of the American scene. See especially his *What to Do with Italy?* (New York, 1943) and *Memorie di un fuoruscito* (Milan, 1960). Most of Salvemini's unpublished papers have been returned to Italy, but his scrapbooks remain in the Houghton Library, Harvard University. Professor Michele Cantarella is presently compiling an anthology of Salvemini's writings from 1939 to 1945, *L'Italia vista dall'America*. Two especially worthwhile pieces are Norman Kogan, "Salvemini in America," *Il Mondo* (Rome), October 8, 1957, pp. 9-10, and Max Ascoli, "Salvemini negli Stati Uniti," *La Voce Repubblicana* (Rome), December 20-21, 1967, pp. 16, 24.

AMERICAN SOCIETY AND FASCISM

In this catch-all category I can do no more than suggest some of the main sources which convey the views of various economic, religious, and intellectual groups. For business attitudes I surveyed *Barron's, Business Week, Commercial and Financial Chronicle, Forbes, Fortune, Journal of Commerce, Magazine of Wall Street*, and the *Wall Street Journal*. Particularly helpful for the early period was Dante L. Posella, "The American Business Press and the Rise of Fascism in Italy, 1919-1926" (M.A. Thesis, Columbia University, 1949), and the Thomas L. Lamont correspondence with Oswald G. Villard, in the Villard Papers, Houghton Library. In regard to American-Italian economic relations an important statistical source is "Sale of Foreign Bonds or Securities in the United States," *Hearings before the Committee on Finance*, U.S. Senate, 72 Cong., 1 Sess. (Washington, D.C., 1932). As for labor attitudes, much of my survey concentrated on such publications as *Advance, American Federationist, Justice, Labor*, and the reports of the ACWA, AFL, and ILGWU. The minutes of Local 89 of the ILGWU, on microfilm in the Immigrant Archives, are a valuable source for Italian-American labor history in general.

Of the three major religious groups, Catholic attitudes were relatively easy to ascertain since *America, Catholic World*, and

Commonweal continually and forcefully announced their positions. More difficult to isolate was Protestant opinion since journals like *Christian Century, Missionary Review,* and *The Protestant* seldom spoke out on the subject. But most difficult of all was Jewish opinion, for when publications like *The Menorah Journal, Jewish Quarterly Review,* and *B'nai Brith Magazine* eventually turned to the problem of Fascism in the thirties, Hitler's anti-Semitism became the overriding issue.

To gauge Fascism's cultural and educational impact in America one must peruse all the *avant-garde* reviews, the personal letters, memoirs, autobiographies, and the academic journals. Perhaps the one major document is the symposium "An American Looks at Fascism," *Survey,* LVII (March 1, 1927), though unfortunately the sections on literature, drama, music, and art were written by Italians. Donald Heiney's *America in Modern Italian Literature* (New Brunswick, 1964) is concerned with the opposite impact, as is the special number, "Italian Criticism of American Literature: An Anthology," ed. Agostino Lombardo, *The Sewanee Review,* LXVIII (Summer, 1960); but neither of these two pioneering works, nor the contemporary journal, *Studi Americani* (Rome), can be ignored in studying Italian-American literary relations. An intimate recollection of one American writer's response to Ignazio Silone may be seen in Alfred Kazin, *Starting Out in the Thirties* (New York, 1965). Malcolm Cowley's "War Novels: After Two Wars," in *The Literary Situation* (New York, 1958), pp. 23-48, contains a brief but illuminating discussion of John Horne Burns. A good place to begin unraveling the complex Ezra Pound affair is *A Casebook on Ezra Pound,* eds. William Van O'Connor and Edward Stone (New York, 1959). The history of the cultural migration from Fascist Europe to the United States is just beginning to receive the attention it deserves. The story is well told in Laura Fermi's *Illustrious Immigrants: The Intellectual Migration from Europe, 1930-1941* (Chicago, 1964); but priceless are the personal memoirs and analytical essays in *The Intellectual Migration: Europe and America, 1930-1960,* eds. Donald Fleming and Bernard Bailyn (Charles Warren Center, Harvard University, Cambridge, 1968).

To delineate the intellectual spectrum of political opinion one must also scan a wide range of other publications. During the twenties the American Right had no single journal around which it could rally; but in the early thirties there was Seward Collins'

American Review, which Clinton Rossiter has aptly described as "a rich depository of conservative musings of every possible variety: distributism, agrarianism, monarchism, neo-scholasticism, guildism, crypto-fascism, the New Humanism, traditionalism, antique republicanism, feudalism, and, unfortunately, Francoism." (*Conservatism in America: The Thankless Persuasion* [Vintage edn., New York, 1962], p. 275.) For the Left's belated response to Fascism the best sources are the independent Marxist *Modern Monthly*, the official party organ *The Communist*, and the Lovestonite opposition's *Workers Age*. Liberal attitudes are, of course, best recorded in the *Nation* and *New Republic*; but among the many related writings not to be ignored are William Y. Elliott, *The Pragmatic Revolt in Politics: Syndicalism, Fascism, and the Constitutional State* (New York, 1928); Horace Kallen, "Mussolini, William James, and the Rationalists," *Social Frontier*, IV (May 1938), 253-56; *The Fascist Dictatorship* (New York, 1926), eds. William Y. Elliott and Gaetano Salvemini, a pamphlet published by the ICPP which contains statements by a number of liberal intellectuals. On the alleged "pragmatism" in Mussolini's ideology, see the running debate between philosophers Brand Blanshard and Sidney Hook, "Metaphysics and Social Attitudes," in *Social Frontier*, IV (December 1937), 80-81; (February 1938), 154-55; (April 1938), 221-26. On the ambiguity between political and philosophical ideas, see John P. Diggins, "Pragmatism and Ideology: Philosophy or Passion?" *American Political Science Review*, LXIV (September 1970), 899-906.

GOVERNMENT ATTITUDES AND FOREIGN POLICY

Aside from the occasional comments appearing in the daily press, the politicians' attitudes were culled from the *Congressional Record*. The political implications of the Fascist question are touched upon in Hugo V. Maile, *The Italian Vote in Philadelphia between 1928 and 1946* (Philadelphia, 1950). Although no complete study of diplomatic relations between the U.S. and Italy has been published, Allen Cassels' *Mussolini's Early Diplomacy* (Princeton, 1970) covers the years 1922 to 1927 from the view of Italian foreign affairs. A useful study of American State Department documents can be found in Louis De Santi, "U.S. Relations with Italy Under Mussolini, 1922-1942" (Ph.D. Thesis, Columbia University, 1951). For the mid-thirties there is the solid monograph by Brice Harris, Jr., *The United States and the*

Italo-Ethiopian Crisis (Stanford, 1964); and John Norman's "Italo-American Opinion in the Ethiopian Crisis: A Study in Fascist Propaganda" (Ph.D. Thesis, Clark University, 1942); two of Norman's articles have been published: "Influence of Pro-Fascist Propaganda on American Neutrality, 1935-1936," in Dwight Lee and George McReynolds, *Essays in History and International Relations* (Worcester, 1949), pp. 193-99; and "Pro-Fascist Activities in Western Pennsylvania During the Ethiopian War," *Western Pennsylvania History Magazine*, xxv (September-December 1942), 143-48. The World War II period has been well investigated: see the comprehensive studies by William L. Langer and S. Everett Gleason, *The Challenge of Isolation, 1937-1940* (New York, 1952), and *The Undeclared War, 1940-1941* (New York, 1953); the closely researched treatment by Norman Kogan, *Italy and the Allies* (Cambridge, 1956); the discerning appraisal by H. Stuart Hughes, *The United States and Italy* (Cambridge, 1953); the scholarly military evaluation by Lt. Colonel Albert N. Garland and Howard McGaw Smyth, *United States Army in World War II: The Mediterranean Theater of Operations, Sicily and the Surrender of Italy* (Washington, D.C., 1965); and, from the Italian side, the archival research by Mario Toscano, *Del 25 luglio all'8 settembre* (*Nuove rivelazioni sugli armistizi fra l'Italia e le Nazione Unite*) (Florence, 1966), and the vast day-by-day chronicle by F. W. Deakin, *The Brutal Friendship: Mussolini, Hitler, and the Fall of Fascism* (New York, 1962).

The Warren G. Harding and Calvin Coolidge Papers reveal little on Mussolini's Italy. The Herbert Hoover Papers are significant primarily for economic relations between Italy and the United States. Ambassador Henry P. Fletcher's Papers, which include an unpublished diary and scrapbooks, are highly useful; but those of Ambassador Richard Washburn Child have little value for the diplomatic historian. By far the most important source is the Franklin D. Roosevelt Papers, which contain a substantial correspondence with Italian-Americans and with Ambassadors Breckinridge Long and William Phillips (for the location of the above materials, see p. 3-4). Two worthwhile diplomatic memoirs are William Phillips, *Ventures in Diplomacy* (Boston, 1952), and Sumner Welles, *A Time For Decision* (New York, 1944). Considerable information on relations between the U.S. and Italy can also be gleaned from the Italian Records; and for an amusing account of the machinations of the Italian Embassy in Washington, see Helen Lombard, *Washington Waltz: Diplomatic People and Policies* (London, 1944).

THE STUDY OF FASCISM

Among the many surprising intellectual developments of the 1960s the revival of interest in Fascism is most curious. One senses that historians are beginning to feel that the real nature of Fascism had not been sufficiently explained by a previous generation of writers caught up in the ideological passions of their age. Significantly, the officers of the newly established Institute of Contemporary History in London chose to devote the first issue of their publication to "International Fascism, 1920-1945," *Journal of Contemporary History*, I (1966). But the renewed interest is also related to the way in which "Fascism" has become almost a metaphorical category—a term of abuse used to indict all that is ugly in modern society and to attack those on the other side of the barricades. The misuse of the term troubled S. J. Woolf who, in his introduction to a series of recent essays on *European Fascism* (London, 1968), began with the apt remark: "Perhaps the word fascism should be banned, at least temporarily, from our political vocabulary" (p. 1). Clearly Theodore Draper was deeply concerned about the problem in his brilliant historical analysis of "The Ghost of Social Fascism," *Commentary*, XLVII (February 1969), 29-42. And no doubt the misconceptions surrounding the meaning of "Fascism" and the threat of its political revival account for the abundance of books that have appeared in the last several years: F. L. Carsten, *The Rise of Fascism* (Berkeley and Los Angeles, 1967); John Weiss, *The Fascist Tradition* (New York, 1967); Allen Cassels, *Fascist Italy* (New York, 1968); Nathanael Greene, *Fascism: An Anthology* (New York, 1968); Renzo DeFelice, *Le interpretazioni del fascismo* (Bari, 1969); Angelo Del Boca and Mario Giovana, *Fascism Today: A World Survey* (New York, 1969); Charles F. Delzell, *Mediterranean Fascism, 1919-1945* (New York, 1971).

With respect to Italy, in addition to the previously discussed *émigré* scholarship, one of the best works for the early period is by the Marxist A. Rossi (Angelo Tasca), *The Rise of Italian Fascism, 1918-1922* (London, 1938), which has been reprinted (Howard Fertig, New York, 1966). A brief but lucid survey of the whole period is found in Federico Chabod, *History of Italian*

504

Fascism (London, 1963). Many shrewd observations regarding propaganda and public opinion are made in relevant chapters of Denis Mack Smith's *Italy: A Modern History* (Ann Arbor, 1959). As for American scholarship, Herman Finer's *Mussolini's Italy* (New York, 1935) is still the best institutional study; it has been reissued in paperback by Universal Library (New York, 1965); Charles F. Delzell's *Mussolini's Enemies: The Italian Anti-Fascist Resistance* (Princeton, 1961; reprinted by Howard Fertig, New York, 1971) is a masterly account of the opposition both inside Italy and abroad. See also Delzell's "Studi americani sul fascismo," *Il Nuovo Osservatore*, Nos. 56 and 57 (November-December 1966), 952-62.

If Italian Fascism can be equated with "Mussolinianism," as S. William Halperin argues in *Mussolini and Italian Fascism* (Princeton, 1964), one cannot ignore the numerous biographies of Il Duce. Doubtless the most definitive work will be Renzo De Felice projective five-volume study, three of which have already been published: *Mussolini il rivoluzionario, 1883-1920* (Turin, 1965); *Mussolini il fascista: La conquista del potere, 1921-1925* (Turin, 1966); *Mussolini il fascista: L'organizzazione dello Stato fascista, 1925-1929* (Turin, 1968). The best American study of Mussolini's early years is still Gaudens Megaro, *Mussolini in the Making* (New York, 1938), which for many years has been the standard work. Sir Ivone Kirkpatrick's *Mussolini: A Study in Power* (New York, 1964) is a well-written narrative that should be balanced by Laura Fermi's judicious biography, *Mussolini* (Chicago, 1961). See also Charles F. Delzell, "Benito Mussolini: A Guide to the Biographical Literature," *Journal of Modern History*, xxxv (December 1963), 339-53.

For the philosophical bases of European Fascism in general the epochal work is Ernst Nolte, *Three Faces of Fascism: Action Française, Italian Fascism, National Socialism* (New York, 1966). Relevant chapters in *The European Right: A Historical Profile*, eds. Hans Rogger and Eugen Weber (Berkeley and Los Angeles, 1966), also touch upon this theme. Eugen Weber's *Varieties of Fascism* (Princeton, 1961) is a splendid anthology and commentary which, though succinct, actually speaks volumes on the ideological problem of Fascism as an intellectual proposition. A. James Gregor's *The Ideology of Fascism* (New York, 1969) is a valuable survey from the point of view of political theory.

One final note. American attitudes toward Fascism will never be fully explained unless some method of comparative analysis is used. Only then will we be able to judge how peculiar was America's response to the rise of Mussolini's Italy, to say nothing of Hitler's Germany. Until we have some knowledge of, for example, how the French and English responded to the same events, we simply cannot know whether America's sympathy for early Fascism was distinctly American; nor can we be sure whether such social, political, and intellectual forces as nativism, anti-Communism, and faith in industrial progress are characteristic of America alone. Indeed, in his recent essay, "Between Taylorism and Technocracy: European Ideologies and the Vision of Industrial Productivity in the 1920s," *Journal of Contemporary History*, v (1970), 27-61, Charles S. Maier has shown how intellectuals in Germany, Italy, and France made use of what Gramsci called "Americanism"—the techniques and values of scientific management—to bolster the strategy of bourgeois defense. Thus until the full spectrum of European attitudes is studied one must not assume that the American mind is unique. With respect to public attitudes, I am unaware of any extensive research on mass opinion of Italian Fascism undertaken in other European countries. Pierre Milza's *L'Italie Fasciste devant l'opinion française, 1920-1940* (Paris, 1967) is a beginning, but as a thin anthology it throws only a glimmer of light on a topic still dimly understood.

Index

Abernathy, Rep. Charles, 273
Abyssinian Baptist Church, 307
Abyssinians: and Fascist
  propaganda, 304; and Afro-
  Americans, 310-11; and white
  Americans, 288-90, 310. *See also*
  Ethiopian War
academic freedom: protest restriction
  of in Italy, 260-61. *See also*
  Columbia University
Acerbo electoral reform, 32
ACID, 404, 405, 406, 413
ACLU, 104, 118, 119, 132
Action Party, 376, 382, 383, 395
Action Française, 246
Acton, Lord, 236
ACWU, 112, 114, 117, 130, 138,
  169, 174, 202, 407
Adamic, Louis, 389
Adams, Brooks, 205
Adams, Henry, 7, 8, 63, 486
Adams, John, 226
Addis Ababa, 299, 307
Adler, Mortimer, 455-56
Adorno, Theodor W., 479, 483-84
Adunata dei Refrattari (New York),
  139
AFANA, 112-14, 119-20
AFL, 116, 136, 175, 180. *See also*
  Gompers and Green
Agronsky, Martin, 319
Albania, 323, 331
"Alleanza Garibaldi," 408
Allegra, Pietro, 114, 127, 412
Allied Control Commission, 380,
  381, 390
Altrochi, Rudolph, 260

America, 182, 185-86, 188, 190,
  196, 300, 329, 393
American Aid for Ethiopia
  Committee, 307
American Federationist, 171-72, 175
American League Against War and
  Fascism, 308
American League for Italy, 303
American Legion, 29, 205-206
American Newspaper Guild, 318
American Review, 211, 213
American soldiers in Italy, 441-42n
AMG, 423-25
anarchists, 111, 112, 133, 135. *See
  also* Borghi and Tresca
Anderson, Maxwell, 247
Angel, Sir Norman, 23
Anschluss, 40, 323
anti-Fascists, Italian-American:
  assessment of, 419-20; clashes
  with Blackshirts, 127-34;
  difficulties with government,
  117-19, 120-21, 209n; estimated
  number of, 117n; and *fuorusciti*,
  142-43, 403-404, 407-409, 418-19;
  ideological background, 111-13;
  internal disunity, 113-14; and
  Italian-American community,
  116-17, 420; and working class,
  116-17; in World War II, 403-419
anti-Semitism (Italian decrees):
  and American Catholics, 186, 329;
  and American Jews, 202-203n,
  302; and American journalists,
  318-20; and *fuorusciti*, 140; and
  Italian-Americans, 342-43; and
  Roosevelt administration, 354-55;

507

511

519